A MANUAL OF STYLE

A
MANUAL
OF
STYLE

A GUIDE TO THE BASICS
OF GOOD WRITING

Prepared by the U.S. Government Printing Office

PORTLAND HOUSE

This 1998 edition is published by Portland House,
a division of Random House Value Publishing, Inc.,
201 East 50th Street, New York, New York 10022

Printed and Bound in the United States of America

ISBN 0-517-18976-3

8 7 6 5 4 3 2 1

CONTENTS

FOREWORD

If you have bought, or are considering buying, *A Manual of Style*, presumably you already know how to write and probably how to write well. So why do you need a style manual?

For starters, you are probably interested in publishing something in a book or periodical that requires your work to be written to a specific format. This book will facilitate publication and also reduce the expense associated with having to make late changes in manuscript.

The more general question of why anyone who writes well needs a style manual, though, is best answered by considering something you yourself have read that needed styling. All of us have had the experience of reading an article or essay in which the point of view seemed inconsistent, or the tone of the piece was not appropriate for the context, or it was written in a disorganized fashion, or it just needed better proofreading. Invariably, we walked away from it aware that it had somehow failed to convey information or did not have the impact the author originally intended. This is the basic shortcoming of an unstyled piece of writing: it fails to make its subject as clear to the reader as it is to the writer.

When we refer to the "style" of a fiction writer, we generally mean something unique to that person's writing that distinguishes it from everyone else's. The "style" for which you have come to this book, on the other hand, refers to a set of formal rules imposed on manuscripts of varying content and composition to give them a common shape and format. The bond between these two definitions is that they both consider style as a consistency of exposition that enhances our understanding of what is being said.

Without consistency, we could still get the meaning from writing, but perhaps not the same meaning as every other reader gets, or worse, the meaning intended by the author. Imagine someone writing one chapter of a novel in twentieth-century vernacular and the next in high Victorian style; or writing one section of a science article as if for a textbook and the other in conversational prose. Any of these styles are valid for transmitting ideas, yet when put together for no reason other than authorial whim, they raise questions in the mind of a reader regarding the author's intentions. The discord leaves a reader justified in questioning things in the text that should otherwise be taken for granted.

But we don't have to create such a hypothetical situation to show why styling is an essential tool of communication. Think of how confusing it would be to read an article in which the author constantly shifts back and forth from degrees Celsius to degrees Fahrenheit or from measurements given in inches to measurements in centimeters. Or imagine references to a court case or the *Congressional Record* alternating between description and formal name or number throughout a text. The essential meanings of these things are not altered, but the way in which they are presented distances the reader from a point of reference he or she should be sharing with the writer.

Style is an organizing principle for the writer and a template that the reader can use to "decode" the text. It is the basis of the unwritten agreement between the reader and writer that what is being read has been written by recognized, comprehensible rules common to any writing, such as grammar and syntax. By styling a manuscript, a writer avoids fashionable and trendy breaches of these rules—such as slang and neologisms—for the sake of clarity. Since style is based on rules designed to be recognized by everyone, it is the means by which a writer sees his or her manuscript through the reader's eyes.

The usefulness of *A Manual of Style* is by no means limited to the preparation of documents for publication. The reader looking through its pages will find rules for organizing and proofreading a manuscript that should be used for all types of writing. Although the dictionary is still the authority on the spelling, pronunciation, and meaning of words, this style manual tells when it is appropriate to use certain words, whether they must be capitalized, how to compound them, what their abbreviations are—in other words, their proper usage. In a more formal vein, it gives information on how foreign terms are incorporated into a standard English text and which mathematical designations should be used. Even if you never have the need to write footnotes, indexes, and datelines, or to refer to courtwork or the *Congressional Record*, this book can be used to decipher the meaning of those you may run across in casual reading—assuming, of course, that they have been styled properly.

A style manual, like any reference book, is meant to be used for the occasional times a question of style arises. To make the task of finding the right answer less difficult, *A Manual of Style* is equipped with a comprehensive table of contents, index, chapter headings, and paragraphs designated by both chapter and section number that will take a lot of work out of the search. Following the best rules of style, this manual has been styled to benefit the reader.

New York,   RICHARD MICHAELS
1986

PREFACE

By act of Congress the Public Printer is authorized to determine the form and style of Government printing. *A Manual of Style* is the product of many years of public printing experience, and its rules are based on principles of good usage and custom in the printing trade. In addition, the *Manual* attempts to keep abreast of and sometimes anticipate changes in orthography, grammar, and type production. It has grown with Government and the ever-expanding body of language with new terms and expressions.

Essentially, it is a standardization device designed to achieve uniform word and type treatment, and aiming for economy of word use. Such rules as are laid down for the submission of copy to the Government Printing Office point to the most economical manner for the preparation and typesetting of manuscript. Following such rules eliminates the need of additional chargeable processing by the GPO.

It should be remembered that the *Manual* is primarily a GPO printer's stylebook. Easy rules of grammar cannot be prescribed, for it is assumed that editors are versed in correct expression. As a printer's book, it necessarily uses terms that are obvious to those skilled in the graphic arts. A glossary of such printing terms to be complete would unnecessarily burden the *Manual*. (See bibliography on pp. 2-4.)

Its rules cannot be regarded as rigid, for the printed word assumes many shapes and variations in type presentation. An effort has been made to provide complete coverage of those elements that enter into the translation of manuscript into type.

A
MANUAL
OF
STYLE

1. SUGGESTIONS TO AUTHORS AND EDITORS

1.1. This STYLE MANUAL is intended to facilitate Government printing. Careful observance of the following suggestions will aid in expediting publication and in reducing printing expenditures.

1.2. Changes on proofs add greatly to the expense and delay the work, therefore copy must be carefully edited before being submitted to the Government Printing Office.

1.3. Legible copy, not faint carbon copies, must be furnished. This is essential in foreign-language copy and in copy containing figures.

1.4. Copy should be sent flat, with the sheets numbered consecutively, and typewritten on one side of the paper only. If both sides of reprint copy are to be used, a duplicate must be furnished.

1.5. To avoid unnecessary expense, mutilation of copy, and to expedite GPO production, each page should begin with a paragraph.

1.6. Tabular matter and illustrations should be on separate sheets, as each is handled separately during typesetting.

1.7. Proper names, signatures, figures, foreign words, and technical terms should be written plainly.

1.8. The chemical symbols Al, Cl, Tl are sometimes mistaken for A1, C1, T1 in typewritten matter. Editors must indicate whether the second character is a letter or a figure. (See rule 2.37.)

1.9. Copy in a foreign language should be marked accurately as to capitalization, punctuation, accents, etc.

1.10. Footnote reference marks in text and tables should be arranged consecutively from left to right across each page of copy.

1.11. A requisition for work containing illustrations must be accompanied by a letter certifying that the illustrations are necessary and relate entirely to the transaction of public business (44 U.S.C. 118). The total number of illustrations and the processes of reproduction desired should also be indicated. Instructions should be given on the margin of each illustration if enlargement or reduction is necessary.

1.12. Photographs, drawings, legends, etc., for illustrations should appear in the manuscript in proper sequence.

1.13. If a publication is composed of several parts, a scheme of the desired arrangement must accompany the first installment of copy.

1.14. To reduce the possibility of costly blank pages, avoid use of new odd pages and halftitles whenever possible. Generally these refinements should be limited to quality bookwork. (See rule 2.3.)

1.15. Samples should be furnished if possible. They should be plainly marked, showing the desired type, size of type page, illustrations if any, paper, trim, lettering, or binding; but they will not be considered as style for typesetting if they conflict with the rules in this STYLE MANUAL.

1.16. In looseleaf or perforated-on-fold work, indicate folio sequence, including blank pages, by circling in blue. Begin with first text page (title). Do not folio separate covers or dividers.

1.17. Indicate on copy if separate or self cover. When reverse printing in whole or in part is required, indicate if solid or in tone.

1.18. Avoid use of oversize fold-ins wherever possible. This can be done by splitting a would-be fold-in and arranging the material to appear as facing pages in the text. Where fold-ins are numerous and cannot be split, consideration should be given to folding and inserting these into an envelope pasted to inside back cover.

1.19. Every effort should be made to keep complete jobs of over 4 pages to signatures (folded units) of 8, 12, 16, 24, or 32 pages. Over two blank pages at end should be avoided where possible.

1.20. Indicate alternative choice of paper on requisition. Wherever possible, confine choice of paper to general use items carried in inventory as shown in GPO Paper Catalog.

1.21. When nonstandard trim sizes and/or type areas are used, indicate head and back margins desired. Otherwise, GPO will determine margins.

1.22. On return of galley proofs for page makeup, departments should submit copy for running heads and numbering sequence of folios, including preliminary pages.

1.23. All corrections should be made on first proofs submitted, as later proofs are intended for verification only. All corrections must be indicated on the "R" set of proofs, and only that set should be returned to the Government Printing Office.

1.24. Corrections should be marked on the margins of a proof opposite the indicated errors, not by writing over the print or between the lines. All queries on proofs must be answered.

1.25. The following Government Printing Office and departmental publications relate to material included in the STYLE MANUAL. Most may be purchased from the Superintendent of Documents, Government Printing Office, Washington, DC 20402. For free lists of these and other such publications, request SB–077, Printing and the Graphic Arts, and SB–087, Stenography, Typing and Writing.

Word Division, a supplement to Government Printing Office Style Manual, 190 pages. 1982. GP 1.23/4:St 9/supp.976. S/N 021–000–00006–0.

Basic rules for division of words; division into syllables of about 20,000 words.

Photocomposition Type Faces, 320 pages. Illustrated. GP 1.2:T 98/14. S/N 021–000–00106–6.

Government Paper Specification Standards No. 9. December 1981. Y 4.P 93/1:7/9. S/N 052–070–81002–5.

Basic manual in looseleaf form. Should be of value and interest to paper manufacturers, printing establishments, and others concerned with paper standards. Contains standards to be used in testing and definitive color standards for all mimeograph, duplicator, writing, manifold, bond ledger, and index papers.

Technical and scientific guides

American National Standard Guidelines for Format and Production of Scientific and Technical Reports, 16 pages. American National Standards Institute, Inc. ANSI Z39.18–1974. (To order, see note (3), p. 8.)

Prescribes the order and specifications of the elements of a report. Takes into account the growing use of microform and electronic storage and abstract services. Contains guidelines that will help the researcher in locating, referencing, and comparing source information. Covers type and page size, tables, formulas, paper stock, and binding.

Clarity in Technical Reporting, 25 pages. 1964, reprinted 1977. NAS 1.21:7010. S/N 033-000-00513-0.

Levels of Edit, 26 pages. 1980. NAS 1.12/7:80-1. S/N 033-000-00785-0.

Prepared by the Jet Propulsion Laboratory, this booklet outlines a methodology for editing technical manuscripts.

Patents and Trademarks Style Manual. Supplement to United States Government Printing Office Style Manual.

Data base publishing

Publishing From a Full Text Data Base. Graphic Systems Development Division, Government Printing Office, 184 pages. Illustrated. 1983, 2d edition. S/N 021-000-00116-3.

Describes GPO's concept of full text data base development and discusses such factors as design, application, and job control.

Microfiche specifications

National Standard Microfiche of Documents, 15 pages. National Micrographics Association. ANSI PH5.9-1975 (NMA MS5-1975). (To order, see note (3), p. 8.)

Specifications provided for microfiche intended for direct use by the customer: "distribution fiche." Offers definitions of some terms.

Guide for Selecting Microfiche Requirements and Quality Attributes for Microfiche Contract. Available from GPO, Manager of Quality Control and Technical Department.

Writing aids

Effective Revenue Writing: Number 1, 268 pages. Illustrated. 1969, reprinted 1980. T 22.19/2:W 93/no.1/969. S/N 048-004-00036-9.

Basic course designed to give a brief, practical review of writing principles, grammar, and punctuation.

Effective Revenue Writing: Number 2, 198 pages. Illustrated. Rev. 1978. T 22.19/2:W 93/no.2/978. S/N 048-004-00037-7.

Advanced course to help experienced writers diagnose weaknesses.

Effective Writing: Manager's Role, Writing Seminar for Managers, 46 pages. 1975, reprinted 1977. T 22.19/2:W 93/2. S/N 048-004-01295-2.

Effective Writing: Workshop Course, 106 pages. Rev. 1975. T 22.19/2:W 93/3. S/N 048-004-01288-0.

A self-teaching text emphasizing effective communication for writers.

Gobbledygook Has Gotta Go, 112 pages. Illustrated. 1966, reprinted 1980. I 53.2:G 53. S/N 024-011-00002-0.

Concerned with improvement of Government communication.

Be a Better Writer, 38 pages. Illustrated. Environmental Protection Agency. 1980. EP 1.8:W 93. S/N 055-000-00188-0.

United States Air Force Effective Writing Course, 71 pages. Illustrated. 1980. D 301.35:13-5. S/N 008-070-00444-5.

Although written for Air Force personnel to coincide with three films (which are unavailable to the public), most of the principles are applicable to civilian use.

Correspondence style

U.S. Government Correspondence Manual, 66 pages. Illustrated. GS 4.6/2:C 81/2. S/N 022-000-00129-9.

Designed to standardize Government correspondence for uniform format styles: addresses, salutations, and closings. Government Interdepartmental Committee.

Plain Letters, 53 pages. National Archives and Records Service, General Services Administration. Illustrated. S/N 022-002-00041-4.

Directed at those who write and sign letters. Offers writing shortcuts and how to avoid cliches in writing.

Form and Guide Letters, 44 pages. National Archives and Records Service, General Services Administration. Illustrated. S/N 022-003-00903-5.

Basic elements of form-letter design. Describes use of form letters to replace formal correspondence.

Bibliographical style (See also rule 2.147.)

Bibliographical Procedures & Style: A Manual for Bibliographers in the Library of Congress. U.S. Library of Congress. By Blanche Prichard McCrum and Helen Dudenbostel Jones. Washington, 1954. Reprinted 1966 with list of abbreviations.

Outdated in places and will eventually be revised but not in the immediate future.

Legal writing aids

NLRB Style Manual, 119 pages. National Labor Relations Board. Washington, DC. 1983. S/N 031-000-00237-1. L/R 1.6/2:ST9.

The manual encourages use of plain English. Designed to simplify legal writing, it offers useful guidelines to all writers.

Document Drafting Handbook, 66 pages. Illustrated. 1980. GS 4.107/a:D 659. S/N 022-001-00088-4.

Designed to help Federal agencies prepare documents for publication in the Federal Register.

Title leaves of books

American National Standard for Title Leaves of a Book, 8 pages. American National Standards Institute, Inc. ANSI Z39.25-1980. (To order, see note (3), p. 8.)

Guidelines for determining the location and types of information that should appear on title leaves and in the contents of a book. Information includes: Title, author(s), contributors, publisher and place of publication, dates and details of edition, numbering of volume, copyright notice, cataloguing in publication data, international standard book number, Library of Congress catalog card number, abstract, and printer. Section on definitions included.

American National Standard for Periodicals: Format and Arrangement, American National Standards Institute, Inc., 16 pages. ANSI Z39.1-1977. (To order, see note (3), p. 8.)

Details of format and arrangement of periodicals to enable scholars, librarians, documentalists, and subscription agencies to identify periodicals and their component parts. Terms in standard defined. Includes specifications for cover and spine, table of contents and masthead, pagination, page format including margin width, errata, instructions to authors, volume specifications, etc.

Journalism

Journalist 1 and C, 363 pages. Illustrated. Rev. 1978. D 207.208/2:J 82/2/978. S/N 008-047-00242-4.

Navy training manual. Forms a self-study package designed for individual, rather than classroom, study.

Journalist 3 and 2, 518 pages. Illustrated. 1973, reprinted 1975. D 207.208/2:J 82/973. S/N 008-047-00177-1.

Although written for Navy trainees, subjects applicable for civilian journalism. Basic newswriting, advance stories, rewrites, and followups, libel, photo journalism, headlines and outlines, printing and layout, etc.

Newspaper Production Techniques: An Aid in Preparing and Designing a Modern Publication, 71 pages. Illustrated. 1981. D 101.2:N 47. S/N 008-020-00891-5.

Nine lessons on newspaper graphics, sample pages for use of typefaces, layouts, headline designs, and illustrations.

Also helpful to writers and editors are such publications as:

The Chicago Manual of Style, University of Chicago Press. 13th ed., revised and expanded. Chicago: University of Chicago Press, 1982.

Anglo-American Cataloguing Rules. 2d ed. Prepared by the American Library Association, the British Library, the Canadian Committee on Cataloguing, the Library Association, and the Library of Congress. Edited by Michael Gorman and Paul W. Winkler. Chicago: American Library Association. Ottawa: Canadian Library Association. 1978.

A Uniform System of Citation, 237 pages. 13th ed. Cambridge: Harvard Law Review Association. 1981.

1.26. Corrections in proofs read by authors or department readers must be indicated as follows:

⊙	Insert period	*rom.*	Roman type
⋏	Insert comma	*caps.*	Caps—used in margin
:	Insert colon	☰	Caps—used in text
;	Insert semicolon	*c+sc*	Caps & small caps—used in margin
?	Insert question mark	☰	Caps & small caps—used in text
!	Insert exclamation mark	*l.c.*	Lowercase—used in margin
=/	Insert hyphen	/	Used in text to show deletion or substitution
⋁	Insert apostrophe		
⋎⋎	Insert quotation marks	ℰ	Delete
⊣	Insert 1-en dash	ℨ	Delete and close up
⊣	Insert 1-em dash	*w.f.*	Wrong font
#	Insert space	⌒	Close up
ld>	Insert ( ) points of space	⊐	Move right
shill	Insert shilling	⊏	Move left
⋁	Superior	⊓	Move up
⋀	Inferior	⊔	Move down
(/)	Parentheses	‖	Align vertically
[/]	Brackets	=	Align horizontally
□	Indent 1 em	⊐⊏	Center horizontally
▭	Indent 2 ems	⊔⊓	Center vertically
¶	Paragraph	*eq.#*	Equalize space—used in margin
no ¶	No paragraph	⋁⋁⋁	Equalize space—used in text
tr	Transpose[1]—used in margin	....	Let it stand—used in text
∿	Transpose[2]—used in text	*stet.*	Let it stand—used in margin
sp	Spell out	⊗	Letter(s) not clear
ital	Italic—used in margin	*run over*	Carry over to next line
___	Italic—used in text	*run back*	Carry back to preceding line
b.f.	Boldface—used in margin	*out, see copy*	Something omitted—see copy
∿∿∿	Boldface—used in text	*?/?*	Question to author to delete[3]
s.c.	Small caps—used in margin	⋀	Caret—General indicator used to mark position of error.
☰	Small caps—used in text		

[1] In lieu of the traditional mark "tr" used to indicate letter or number transpositions, the striking out of the incorrect letters or numbers and the placement of the correct matter in the margin of the proof is the preferred method of indicating transposition corrections. (See rule 2.88.)

[2] Corrections involving more than two characters should be marked by striking out the entire word or number and placing the correct form in the margin. This mark should be reserved to show transposition of words.

[3] The form of any query carried should be such that an answer may be given simply by crossing out the complete query if a negative decision is made or the right-hand (question mark) portion to indicate an affirmative answer. (See example, p. 6.) (See rule 2.84.)

TYPOGRAPHICAL ERRORS

reset 8pt. C & SC

It does not appear that the earliest printers had any method of correcting errors before the form was on the press. The learned The learned correctors of the first two centuries of printing were not proofreaders in our sense, they were rather what we should term office editors. Their labors were chiefly to see that the proof corresponded to the copy, but that the printed page was correct in its latinity—that the words were there, and that the sense was right. They cared but little about orthography, bad letters, or purely printers errors, and when the text seemed to them wrong they consulted fresh authorities or altered it on their own responsibility. Good proofs, in the modern sense, were impossible until professional readers were employed, men who had first a printer's education, and then spent many years in the correction of proof. The orthography of English, which for the past century has undergone little change, was very fluctuating until after the publication of Johnson's Dictionary, and capitals, which have been used with considerable regularity for the past 80 years, were previously used on the miss or hit plan. The approach to regularity, so far as we have, may be attributed to the growth of a class of professional proofreaders, and it is to them that we owe the correctness of modern printing. More errors have been found in the Bible than in any other one work. For many generations it was frequently the case that Bibles were brought out stealthily, from fear of governmental interference. They were frequently printed from imperfect texts, and were often modified to meet the views of those who publised them. The story is related that a certain woman in Germany, who was the wife of a printer, and had become disgusted with the continual assertions of the superiority of man over woman which she had heard, hurried into the composing room while her husband was at supper and altered a sentence in the Bible, which he was printing, so that it read Narr instead of Herr, thus making the verse read "And he shall be thy fool" instead of "and he shall be thy lord." The word not was omitted by Barker, the king's printer in England in 1632, in printing the seventh commandment. He was fined £3,000 on this account.

NOTE.—The system of marking proofs can be made easier by the use of an imaginary vertical line through the center of the type area. The placement of corrections in the left-hand margin for those errors found in the left-hand portion of the proof and in the right-hand margin for right-side errors prevents overcrowding of marks and facilitates corrections. (See also rule 2.87.)

2. GENERAL INSTRUCTIONS

(FOR EDITORS, COPY PREPARERS, TYPESETTERS, AND COMPOSITORS)

JOB PLANNING

2.1. Before actual production begins, a job scheduled for printing is reviewed by a planner who designs a program by which the needs of the publication are met. The format selected by the planner establishes such things as the typefaces to be used in the job, the breakdown of headings, running heads and folios, page length, and spacing. The format determines the codes used by the preparer, who readies the manuscript for the keyboard stage of production. Following instructions of the submitting agency, the planner, in effect, lays out the job in advance. Thus, completely unlike procedures followed in the past, today's computer-oriented product is literally made up before it is put into type. Consequently, it is necessary for the customer agencies to communicate precise details of their needs before production begins.

2.2. Changes in recent years in the needs of the library community have led to a move toward uniform treatment of the component parts of publications. In developing standards to guide publishers of Government books, consideration has been given to the changing needs of those who seek to produce, reference, index, abstract, store, and retrieve data. Certain identifying elements shall be printed on all publications in accordance with this MANUAL and with standards developed by the American National Standards Institute, Inc. (ANSI).

Publications such as books and pamphlets should contain:

(a) Title and other title information;
(b) Name of department issuing or creating publication;
(c) Name of author(s) and editor(s) (department or individual);
(d) Date of issuance;
(e) Availability (publisher or printer and address);
(f) Superintendent of Documents classification and stock numbers; and
(g) The International Standard Book number (if assigned).
(See ANSI Standard Z39.15, Title Leaves of a Book.)

Reports of a scientific or technical nature should contain:

(a) Title and other title information;
(b) Report number;
(c) Author(s);
(d) Performing organization;
(e) Sponsoring department;
(f) Date of issuance;
(g) Type of report and period covered;
(h) Availability (publisher or printer and address); and
(i) Superintendent of Documents classification and stock numbers.
(See ANSI Standard Z39.18, Guidelines for Format and Production of Scientific and Technical Reports.)

358-807 O — 84 — 2

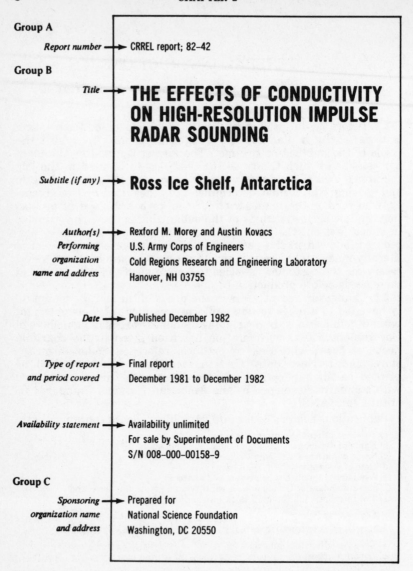

Group A

Report number ➤ CRREL report; 82–42

Group B

Title ➤ **THE EFFECTS OF CONDUCTIVITY ON HIGH-RESOLUTION IMPULSE RADAR SOUNDING**

Subtitle (if any) ➤ **Ross Ice Shelf, Antarctica**

Author(s) ➤ Rexford M. Morey and Austin Kovacs
Performing U.S. Army Corps of Engineers
organization Cold Regions Research and Engineering Laboratory
name and address Hanover, NH 03755

Date ➤ Published December 1982

Type of report ➤ Final report
and period covered December 1981 to December 1982

Availability statement ➤ Availability unlimited
For sale by Superintendent of Documents
S/N 008–000–00158–9

Group C

Sponsoring ➤ Prepared for
organization name National Science Foundation
and address Washington, DC 20550

NOTES:
(1) This sample report cover is reduced in size.
(2) In this sample items are justified left. Other cover designs and typefaces are acceptable.
(3) This sample page was prepared according to the guidelines of the American National Standards Institute, 1430 Broadway, New York, NY 10018. Users of ANSI standards are cautioned that all standards are reviewed and subject to revision periodically.

Journals, magazines, periodicals, and similar publications should contain:

(a) Title and other title information;
(b) Volume and issue numbers;
(c) Date of issue;
(d) Publishing or sponsoring department;
(e) Availability (publisher or printer and address);
(f) International Standard Serial Number; and
(g) Superintendent of Documents classification and stock numbers.
(See ANSI Standard Z39.1, Periodicals: Format and Arrangement.)

2.3. Government publications will be made up in the following order. The "new odd page" designations refer, generally, to book-work and are not required in most pamphlet- and magazine-type publications. (See rules 1.14 and 2.5.)

a. *Frontispiece,* faces title page.

b. *False title* (frontispiece, if any, on back).

c. *Title page.*

d. *Back of title,* blank, but frequently carries such useful bibliographic information as list of board members, congressional resolution authorizing publication, note of editions and printings, GPO imprint if departmental imprint appears on title page, price notice, etc.

e. *Letter of transmittal* (new odd page).

f. *Foreword,* differs from preface in that it is an introductory note written as an endorsement by a person other than the author (new odd page). An *introduction* differs from a foreword or a preface in that it is the initial part of the text; if the book is divided into chapters, it should be the first chapter.

g. *Preface,* by author (new odd page).

h. *Acknowledgments* (if not part of preface) (new odd page).

i. *Contents* (new odd page), immediately followed by list of illustrations and list of tables, as parts of contents.

j. *Text,* begins with page 1 (if halftitle is used, begins with p. 3).

k. *Glossary.*

l. *Bibliography* (new odd page).

m. *Appendix* (new odd page).

n. *Index* (new odd page).

2.4. To number preliminary pages, use small-cap numerals.

2.5. Booklets of 32 pages or less can be printed more economically with a self-cover. A table of contents, title page, foreword, preface, etc., is not usually necessary with so few pages. If some of this preliminary matter is necessary, it is more practical to combine this material; i.e., contents on cover; combine contents, title, foreword on cover 2, etc.

2.6. Before makeup can be started the length of type page and style of folios to be used must be ascertained.

2.7. Widow lines at top of pages are to be avoided, if possible, but are permitted if necessary to maintain uniform makeup and page length. Paragraphs may start on the last line of a page, whenever necessary. If it is found necessary to make a short page, the facing page should be of approximately equal length, if the text permits.

2.8. A blank or sink of 6 picas should be placed at the head of each new odd or even page of 46-pica or greater depth; pages with a

depth of from 36 to 45 picas, inclusive, will carry a 5-pica sink; pages less than 36 picas, 4 picas.

2.9. If top center folio is used, the folio on a new page must be placed at the bottom, centered, and enclosed in parentheses.

2.10. Where running heads with folios are used, heads are included in overall page depth. However, first pages of chapters and pages with bottom folios are made up with folios in margin. Bottom folios on short preliminary pages will be made up with page numbers 4 points from last line.

2.11. Jobs made up with bottom folios will have all page numbers, including preliminary pages, aligning on the bottom in the margin.

2.12. Avoid use of running heads in conjunction with bottom folios.

2.13. Contents, list of illustrations, preface, or any other matter that makes a page in itself should be placed 12 points or more nearer top than bottom, the difference depending upon the length of page.

2.14. Footnote references are repeated in boxheads or in continued lines over tables, unless special orders are given not to do so.

2.15. Six-point headnotes above tables are enclosed in brackets and are repeated with continued heads.

2.16. A broadside (lengthwise) table beginning on even (left) page and which carries over to facing right page will be made up flush right for left page (if left page is less than full width) and flush left for right page.

2.17. A broadside table of less than page width will center on the page.

2.18. Centerheads, whether in boldface, caps, caps and small caps, small caps, or italic, should have more space above than below. Uniform spacing should be maintained throughout the page.

2.19. In making up a page of two or more columns, text will be doubled up over illustrations.

2.20. Two or more short footnotes coming together may be combined into one line, with 2 ems of space between footnotes.

[1] Preliminary.   [2] Including imported cases.   [3] Imported.

2.21. Backstrips should run down (from top to bottom) on all publications.

COPY PREPARATION

2.22. The first duty of copy preparers is to mark those things that are not readily understood and to indicate headings, indentions, dashes, new pages, and other matters of style necessary to give the completed book a good typographic appearance.

2.23. If a preparer considers a customer's request for new odd pages and/or half titles unwarranted or excessive, he or she must bring this to the attention of the supervisor who will question these pages to the ordering agency.

2.24. Preparers must indicate point size and type series on copy, and whether matter is to be leaded or double leaded, etc.; verify folio numbers; and plainly indicate references, footnotes, cut-ins, etc. Unless otherwise marked, text matter will be set in 10-point

solid and tables in 7 point. Where down rules are requested in tables, hairline rules will be used. (See rule 13.3.)

2.25. Quoted, or extract matter, and lists should be set 2 points smaller than text, and quotation marks at beginning and end of paragraphs should be omitted. If the same type size is used, quoted matter should be cut in 1 to 3 ems, depending on measure, and initial and closing quotes should be omitted.

Capitalization

2.26. Unusual capital and lowercase letters must be indicated.

Datelines, addresses, and signatures

2.27. Copy preparers must mark caps, small caps, italic, abbreviations, and indentions; also indicate line breaks where necessary.

Decimals and common fractions

2.28. In figure columns containing decimals or common fractions, such decimals and/or fractions will not be aligned.

"Et cetera," "etc.," and "and so forth"

2.29. In printing a speaker's language, the words *and so forth* or *et cetera* are used—not the abbreviation *etc.* If a quoted extract is set in type smaller than that of the preceding text and the speaker has summed up the remainder of the quotation with the words *and so forth* or *et cetera,* these words should be placed at the beginning of the next line, flush and lowercase, and an em dash should be used at the end of the extract.

Folioing and stamping copy

2.30. Folio numbers should be placed in the upper right-hand corner, preferably half an inch from the top.

2.31. All other stamping—type size, measure, etc.—should be placed in the upper left-hand corner. On cards, any available space may be used.

2.32. If it is necessary to cut copy for parallel tables, portions will be folioed down the left-hand side first, then down the right-hand side.

Footnotes and reference marks

(For text, see rules 15.1–15.20; for tables, see rules 13.75–13.96.)

Headings

2.33. The locators to be used for all headings must be marked. Caps, caps and small caps, small caps, caps and lowercase, lowercase first up (first words and proper nouns capitalized), or italic must be prepared. (See rule 3.51.)

Pickup

2.34. The jacket number of a job from which matter is to be picked up must be indicated. New matter should conform in style to that of the pickup.

Sidenotes and cut-in notes

2.35. Sidenotes and cut-in notes should be avoided.

Signs, symbols, etc.

2.36. All signs, symbols, dashes, superiors, etc., must be plainly marked. Names of Greek letters must be indicated, as they are frequently mistaken for italic or symbols.

2.37. In the event typewriters use the same characters for figure 1 and lowercase l and cipher and capital O, all such characters will be printed as figures unless otherwise marked.

Letters illustrating shape and form

2.38. Capital letters of the text face will be used to illustrate shape and form, as U-shape(d), A-frame, T-bone, and T-rail.

2.39. Plurals are formed by adding the apostrophe and *s*, as T's, Y's, etc. *Golf tee(s)* should be spelled, as it does not indicate shape.

2.40. A capital is used in *U-boat, V–8,* and other expressions which have no reference to shape or form.

"Follow literally" and "FIC and punc."

2.41. After submittal to the GPO, manuscript copy is rubber-stamped "Fol. lit." or "FIC and punc." The difference between these two typesetting instructions is explained thus:

In "Fol. lit." (follow literally) copy we do not make any changes. Copy authorized to be marked "Fol. lit." must be thoroughly prepared by the requisitioning agency as to capitalization, punctuation (including compounding), abbreviations, signs, symbols, figures, and italic, and such copy, including even manifest errors, will be followed. The lack of preparation on copy so designated shall, in itself, constitute preparation. "Fol. lit." does not include size and style of type or spacing.

In "FIC & punc." (follow, including capitalization and punctuation) copy, we correct obvious errors.

2.42. Excerpts for congressional hearings (8 point) and the Congressional Record (7 point) will be stamped and set "FIC & punc." unless otherwise instructed. Datelines, address lines, signature lines, tables, and leaderwork are to be prepared according to STYLE MANUAL rules.

In all quoted amendments and excerpts of bills and in reprinting bills, bill style is to be followed at all times.

2.43. In congressional hearings, the name of interrogator or witness who continues speaking is repeated following a head set in Century bold, a paragraph enclosed in parentheses, and a paragraph enclosed in brackets.

In a head set in Century bold, the title "Mr." is not used, and "the Honorable" preceding name is shortened to "Hon." Street addresses are also deleted. Example: "Statement of Hon. John P. Blank, Member of American Bar Association, Washington, DC."

2.44. To prevent confusion and delay and to ensure economy in printing, all copy will be set in accordance with the rules laid down in this STYLE MANUAL, with which editors and compilers are expected to become familiar, except that in some classes of printing of a legal, technical, or historical nature it may be necessary to adhere strictly to the original text, and the requisitioning office may then properly mark such copy "Fol. lit."

2.45. Follow the position of quotation marks in relation to other punctuation marks in matter marked "Fol. lit." and "FIC & punc." Abbreviations with points (as in U.S.C., U.S.) close up. Abbreviations also close up in "Fol. lit." matter, unless prepared with spaces. (See rule 9.7.)

2.46. Paragraph or section numbers (or letters) followed by figures or letters in parentheses will close up, as "section 7(B)(1)(a)," "paragraph 23(a)," "paragraph b(7)," "paragraph (a)(2)"; but section 9(1) (a) and (b); section 7 a and b. In case of an unavoidable break, division will be made after elements in parentheses, and no hyphen is used. However, if spaces are prepared in "Fol. lit." matter, copy will be followed.

2.47. "Bill style" copy will follow the style of the Government Printing Office Bill Style Manual, which conforms to this STYLE MANUAL in many particulars, such as the use of figures in dates; sums of money; percentages; the numbers of articles, chapters, lines, pages, paragraphs, parts, sections, and volumes; the classification of vessels (A 1); and all other instances where *numbered* is used or implied. Punctuation, as prepared, must be followed.

2.48. Copy preparer's instructions, which accompany each job, are written to cover the general style and certain peculiarities or deviations from style. These instructions must be followed. The copy preparer must not deviate from the style laid down in this STYLE MANUAL unless authorized to do so by the supervisor in the markup section.

Abbreviations

2.49. In marking abbreviations to be spelled, preparers must show what the spelled form should be, unless the abbreviations are common and not susceptible of more than one construction. An unfamiliar abbreviation, with spelled-out form unavailable, is not changed.

TYPE COMPOSITION

2.50. Compositors and operators must study carefully the rules governing composition. Failure to do this will show plainly on proofs.

2.51. In correcting pickup matter, the operator must indicate plainly on the proof what portion was actually reset.

2.52. Every precaution must be taken to prevent the soiling of proofs, as it is necessary for the reviser to see clearly every mark on the margin of a proof after it has been corrected.

2.53. Corrections of queries intended for the author should not be made. Such queries, however, are not to be carried on jobs going directly to press.

Leading and spacing

2.54. Spacing of text is governed by the leading, narrow spacing being more desirable in solid than in leaded matter.

2.55. A single justification space (close spacing) will be used between sentences. This applies to all types of composition.

2.56. Center or flush heads set in caps, caps and small caps, small caps, or boldface are spaced with regular justification spaces between words.

2.57. Centerheads are separated from the text by slugs, the space below the head being at least 2 points less than the space above: 10 points above and 8 points below in 10-point text; 8 points above and 6 points below in 8- and 6-point text.

2.58. Heads set in caps are leaded, even in solid matter.

2.59. In solid matter, "2 leads," "3 leads," and similar space designations marked on copy mean "2 leads" (4 points), "3 leads" (6 points), etc.

In leaded matter (machine-leaded linotype, or monotype with shoulder), "2 leads," "3 leads," etc., will include space on type; e.g., "2 leads" means a 2-point lead plus space on type.

2.60. Unless otherwise marked, flush heads are separated from text by 2 leads above and 1 lead below in solid matter, and by 3 leads above and 2 leads below in leaded matter.

2.61. Full-measure numbered or lettered paragraphs and quoted extracts are not separated by space from adjoining matter.

2.62. Extracts which are set off from the text by smaller type or are indented on both sides or indented 3 ems on the left side (courtwork only) are separated by 6 points in leaded matter and by 4 points in solid matter.

2.63. Extracts set solid in leaded matter are separated from the text by 6 points.

2.64. Flush lines following extracts are separated by 6 points of space in leaded matter and by 4 points in solid matter.

2.65. Footnotes are leaded if the text is leaded, and are set solid if the text is solid.

2.66. Legends are leaded if text is leaded, and solid if text is solid. Leaderwork is separated from text by 4 points above and 4 points below.

Indentions

2.67. In measures less than 30 picas, the paragraph indention is 1 em. Paragraph indentions in cut-in matter are 3 ems, overs 2 ems. Overruns, datelines, and signatures are indented in multiples of 2 ems. Addresses are set flush left. (See examples, beginning p. 206.)

2.68. In matter set 30 picas or wider, the paragraph indention is 2 ems. Paragraph indentions in cut-in matter are 6 ems, overs 4 ems. Overruns, datelines, and signatures are indented in multiples of 2 ems. Addresses are set flush left. (See examples, beginning p. 206.)

2.69. In measures less than 30 picas, overruns in hanging indentions are 1 em more than the first line, except that to avoid conflict with a following indention (for example, of a subentry or paragraph), the overrun indention is made 1 em more than the following line.

2.70. In matter set 30 picas or wider, overruns in hanging indentions are 2 ems more than the first line, except that to avoid conflict with a following indention (for example, of a subentry or paragraph), the overrun indention is made 2 ems more than the following line.

2.71. Indention of matter set in smaller type should be the same, in points, as that of adjoining main-text indented matter.

2.72. Two-line centerheads are centered, but heads of three or more lines are set with hanging indention.

2.73. Overs in flush heads are indented 2 ems in measures less than 30 picas, and 3 ems in wider measures.

Legends for illustrations

2.74. Legends and explanatory matter of one or two lines are centered; if more than two lines, they are set with hanging indention. If an illustration is narrower than full measure and text is run at the side of it, the legend is set the width of the illustration; if text is not to be run at the side of the illustration, the legend is set full measure regardless of the width of the illustration, unless copy is otherwise marked.

2.75. Legend lines of illustrations which run the broad way should be printed to read up; that is, an even-page legend should be on the inside margin and an odd-page legend on the outside margin.

2.76. Unless other type is indicated, legends for illustrations are set in 8-point roman, lowercase.

2.77. Periods are used after legends and explanatory matter beneath illustrations. However, legends without descriptive language do not use a period. (See rule 8.115.)

2.78. At beginning of legend or standing alone, *Figure* preceding the identifying number or letter is set in caps and small caps and is not abbreviated.

FIGURE 5, *not* FIG. 5   FIGURE A, *not* FIG. A

2.79. If a chart carries both a legend and footnotes, the legend is placed above the chart.

2.80. Letter symbols used in legends for illustrations are set in lowercase italic without periods.

PROOFREADING AND COPYHOLDING

2.81. All special instructions, layouts, and style sheets must be sent to the Proof Section with the first installment of each job.

2.82. The proofreader should see that the rules governing spacing, division of words, and good printing generally have been observed.

2.83. If the proofreader detects inconsistent and erroneous statements, it is his or her duty to query them.

2.84. If the grammatical construction of a sentence or clause is questioned by a reader and it seems desirable to change the form, he must indicate the proposed correction, add a query mark, and enclose all in a ring.

2.85. A query appearing on copy must be carried to the author.

2.86. Proofs that are illegible or are in any manner defective must be called to the attention of the deskperson.

2.87. The manner in which correction marks are made on a proof is of considerable importance. Straggling, unsymmetrical characters, disconnected marks placed in the margin above or below the lines to which they relate, irregular lines leading from an incorrect letter or word to a correction, large marks, marks made with a blunt pencil, indistinct marks, and frequent use of the eraser to obliterate marks hastily or incorrectly made are all faults to be avoided.

2.88. In reading proof of wide tables, the reader should place the correction in white space as near as possible to the error, thus aiding all who handle the proof afterward. The reader should obliterate entirely a defective figure and rewrite it in a ring and should not use the transposition mark in little-known words or in figures. It is better to cancel the letters or figures and write them in the margin in the order in which they are to appear.

2.89. Proofreaders and revisers must draw a ring around footnote references on proofs.

2.90. Readers must not make important changes in indentions or tables without consulting the Referee.

2.91. The marks of the copy preparer will be followed, as he or she is in a position to know more about the peculiarities of a job than one who reads but a small portion of it.

2.92. Any mark which will change the proof from the copy as prepared must be enclosed in a ring.

2.93. All instructions on copy must be carried on proof by readers.

2.94. Folios of copy must be run by the copyholder and checked against those marked on the proof.

2.95. In reading copy an unnecessarily loud tone of voice must be avoided. Short words are as important as long ones, and should be pronounced distinctly. Plurals should be sounded clearly, and names of persons or places pronounced distinctly or read by letters.

IMPOSITION

2.96. Imposition is the general term applied to the task of laying out pages of plates or negatives for press. Imposing refers specifically to laying or arranging pages so that a press sheet, when printed and folded, will produce a signature with pages in proper sequence. A page is considered the unit of a signature; the two companion pages, the unit in imposition. Whether the imposition is from the outside or inside, a long or a broad form, work and turn, or sheetwise, these companion pages are never separated; their position in the printed pamphlet is determined by the fold.

2.97. In the layout of pages, each page must be in its proper sequence, determined by the type of fold desired. Margins are governed by the trim size of finished book or pamphlet. After trim size has been established, the sheet size of stock is selected. For example, GPO standard octavo is type width, 26½ picas; type depth, 45 picas; trim size of finished book or pamphlet, 5⅞ by 9⅛ inches. The number of pages to be printed is broken down into signatures of 16 pages each and the most practical layout is chosen. In this case, four rows of four pages each. Thus stock size is four times 5⅞ inches for width and four times 9⅛ inches for depth. As it is necessary to allow a minimum of ⅛-inch trim after signatures are folded, the sheet size will be 24 by 38 inches, standard stock size. The margins, which are the back, or binding edge, head or top, outside, and foot or bottom, are then determined by allowing enough white space from the type area to give a proper balance to the finished book. It is generally agreed that a 4-pica back and a 3-pica head, after trim, are standard margins for this particular trim size on saddle stitch or sewed jobs. Other standards have been incorpo-

rated in the GPO Layout Book. These margins are followed unless requisition specified nonstandard margins.

2.98. To illustrate further that these companion pages are the unit of imposition, it will be found when determining margins that these two pages are always printed in the center of the untrimmed sheet. The other two companion pages that make up the quarter of the 16 are likewise printed in the center of the quarter sheet, which is 19 inches, one-half of the 38-inch way. It will thus be observed that two pages were used to get the outside margins, and another multiple of two (four) to get the bottom margins.

2.99. Margins should be governed by the trimmed book and not by the untrimmed sheet. The back margin or gutter should be such that it will bring the pages nearly in the center of the open printed book, putting any excess space in the outer margins, except in books that are to be side stitched, in which additional space must be allowed for the stitching. The margins should be so planned that when the book is delivered from the binder the back margin is less than the outside. The top margin of the trimmed book should be at least 3 picas and the bottom margin at least 4 picas. The outside margin should be at least 1 pica greater than the back but not as wide as the bottom margin.

2.100. If a running head is used, the head margin should be the same as the back margin; but if a bottom folio is used, that line and the slug above it should be counted as part of the margin. (See also rules 2.10–2.11.)

REVISING

Galley revising

2.101. The importance of revising proofs cannot be overemphasized. Although a reviser is not expected to read proof, it is not enough to follow the marks found on the proof. He or she should be alert to detect errors and inconsistencies and must see that all corrections have been properly made and that words or lines have not been transposed or eliminated in making the corrections.

2.102. A reviser must not remodel the punctuation of the readers or make any important changes. If an important change should be made, the reviser must submit the proposed change to the supervisor for decision.

2.103. In the body of the work, new pages must be properly indicated on the proof. (For new page information, see under "Makeup".)

2.104. All instructions and queries on proofs must be transferred to the revises.

2.105. Extension numbers must be carried on revise proofs.

Page revising

2.106. Page revising requires great diligence and care. The reviser must see that the rules governing the instructions of previous workers have been followed.

2.107. The reviser is responsible for marking off all bleed and off-center pages.

2.108. A blank page must be indicated at the bottom of the preceding page.

2.109. Special care must be exercised in revising corrected matter. If it appears that a correction has not been made, the reviser should carefully examine each line on the page to see if the correction was inserted in the wrong place.

2.110. The following rules must be carefully observed:

a. See that proof is clean and clear; send for another if necessary.

b. Before beginning page revising, see that galley proofs run consecutively and that in continuous makeup the matter on the galleys connects.

c. Make sure that different sets of proofs of the same job are correctly marked in series ("R," "2R," "3R," etc.); where a sheet is stamped "Another proof," carry the same designating "R" on the corresponding clean proof. Advance the "R," "2R," "3R," etc., on each set of page proofs returned from the originating office.

d. See that page folios are consecutive. Make sure running heads are correct. Observe connection pages. Verify proper sequence of footnote references and footnotes, and check that footnotes appear or begin on the same page as the corresponding reference.

e. Watch for dropouts, doublets, and transpositions.

f. Legend lines of full-page illustrations that run broad should be printed to read up—that is, the even-page legend on the binding or inside margin and the odd-page legend on the outside margin.

g. If a footnote is eliminated, do not renumber the footnotes; just change footnote to read "Footnote eliminated."

2.111. If a footnote is added in proof, use the preceding number with a superior letter added, as [15a]

2.112. Where a table with footnotes falls at the bottom of a page containing footnotes to text, print the table footnotes above the text footnotes, separated by a rule 50 points long, flush left, with spacing on each side of the rule. (See also rule 13.88.)

Press revising

2.113. Press revising calls for the exercise of utmost care. The press reviser must be thoroughly familiar with the style and makeup of Government publications. He or she is required to OK all forms that go to press—bookwork, covers, jobwork, etc., and must see that all queries are answered. A knowledge of the bindery operations required to complete a book or job and familiarity with all types of imposition, folds, etc., is helpful. The reviser must be capable of ascertaining the proper head, back, and side margins for all work, to ensure proper trimming of the completed job.

2.114. Although speed is essential when forms reach the pressroom, accuracy must not be sacrificed.

SIGNATURE MARKS, ETC.

2.115. Unless otherwise indicated, signature marks are set 6-point lowercase and indented 3 ems.

2.116. Figures indicating the year should follow the jacket number in signature marks:

125-327—72——4	116-529—72—pt. 5——3	116-529—72—vol. 1——3
	92-694*—72——2	
92-694 O—72——2	92-694 OF—72——2 92-694 F—72——2	92-694ᵐ 72——2
	92-694ᵛ—72——2	

2.117. When allmark (O) and signature or imprint and signature appear on same page, the signature line is placed below the allmark but above the imprint.

2.118. The allmark is placed below the page, bulletin, or circular number but above the signature line, if both appear on the same page.

2.119. Imprints and signature lines appearing on short pages of text are placed at the bottom of the page.

2.120. All plated jobs take a degree mark (°) immediately after the jacket number in the signature line.

2.121. All offset jobs take a capital O immediately after the jacket number in the signature line. Offset-Fotosetter jobs are indicated by OF; Fotosetter by F.

2.122. When matrix is to be made of job, a superior m (^{m}) is placed immediately after jacket number in the signature line.

2.123. On a job reprinted on account of change, a black star (★) precedes the jacket number in the signature line and precedes the date on the title page:

★17–234—72——2   ★12–15–72

2.124. The following forms are used for signature marks in House and Senate documents and reports printed on session jackets:

H. Doc. 73, 92-1——2	S. Doc. 57, 92-1——2
S. Doc. 57, 92-2, pt. 1——2	S. Doc. 57, 92-2, vol. 1——2
H. Rept. 120, 92-2——8	S. Rept. 100, 92-2——9

2.125. In a document or report printed on other than a session jacket, use the jacket number, year, and signature number only, omitting the document or report number.

2.126. For pasters, the jacket number, the year, and the page to be faced by the paster are used as follows (note punctuation):

12–344——72 (Face p. 10)

2.127. On a paster facing an even page, the marks go at the lower right-hand side; on a paster facing an odd page, at the lower left side.

2.128. If more than one paster faces the same page, each is numbered as follows:

12–344——72 (Face p. 19) No. 1
12–344——72 (Face p. 19) No. 2

2.129. When a paster follows the text, the allmark is placed on the last page of the text and never on the paster.

REPRINTS, IMPRINTS, AND PRICE NOTICES

Reprints

2.130. To aid bibliographic identification of reprints or revisions, the dates of the original edition and of reprint or revision should be supplied by the author on the title page or in some other suitable place. Thus:

First edition July 1960	First printed June 1960
Reprinted July 1965	Revised June 1965

Original edition May 1955
Reprinted May 1958
Revised July 1960

2.131. The year in the imprint on cover, title page, or elsewhere is not changed from that in the original print, nor are the signatures changed, unless other mends are necessary.

Imprints

2.132. Unless otherwise stipulated, the Government Printing Office imprint must appear on all printed matter, except certain classified work.

2.133. Use full imprint on the title page of a congressional speech.

2.134. The imprint and allmark are not used together on any page; if one is used, the other is omitted.

2.135. The imprint is not used on a halftitle or (except on congressional hearings) on any page of a cover.

2.136. If there is a title page, the imprint is placed on the title page; but if there is no title page, or if the title page is entirely an illustration, the imprint is placed on the last page of the text 4 ems from flush right and below the bottom folio.

2.137. The Government Printing Office crest is used only on Government Printing Office publications. If it is printed on page II, the full imprint is used on the title page; if it is printed on the title page, use the half imprint only, thus—Washington : 1984.

Price notices

2.138. The use of price notices is discouraged. Where such notice is needed, see rule 2.139.

2.139. If there is a cover but no title page, the price notice is printed on page 1 of the cover. Unless otherwise indicated, if there is a title page, with or without a cover, the price notice is printed at the bottom of the title page below a cross rule; if there is no cover or title page, the price notice is printed at the end of the text, below the imprint, and the two are separated by a cross rule.

Samples of imprints, price notices, and stock numbers

2.140. On title page:

U.S. GOVERNMENT PRINTING OFFICE

WASHINGTON : 1984

For sale by the Superintendent of Documents, U.S. Government Printing Office
Washington, DC 20402 - Price 00 cents

S/N 000–000–12345–6

2.141. On last page of text:

U.S. GOVERNMENT PRINTING OFFICE : 1984
(16 points)

For sale by the Superintendent of Documents, U.S. Government Printing Office
Washington, DC 20402 - Price 00 cents

S/N 000–000–12345–6

U.S. GOVERNMENT PRINTING OFFICE: 1984

2.142. On last page of text (usually 4 ems from right), open star (☆) indicates outside purchase.

U.S. GOVERNMENT PRINTING OFFICE: 1984—455–995

2.143. Outside-purchase jobs which are reprinted by this Office use an em dash in lieu of open star.

—U.S. GOVERNMENT PRINTING OFFICE: 1984—455–995

2.144. Jobs which are set on outside purchase, but which are printed by this Office, use an asterisk in lieu of open star.

*U.S. GOVERNMENT PRINTING OFFICE: 1984—455–995

2.145. Jobs which are printed offset, take an O after the date.

U.S. GOVERNMENT PRINTING OFFICE: 1984 O—207–379

FRANKING

2.146. The franking (mailing) privilege on covers for Government publications should be at least 1⅛ inches from the trim.

Bibliographies or references

2.147. There are many styles available to bibliographers, for there are many classes of documents. A Government bulletin citation, according to one authority, would be treated as follows:

Author's name (if the article is signed); title of article (in quotation marks); the publication (usually in italic), with correct references to volume, number, series, pages, date, and publisher (U.S. Govt. Print. Off.).

Therefore the example would read:

U.S. Department of the Interior, "Highlights in history of forest and related natural source conservation," *Conservation Bulletin*, No. 41 (serial number not italic), Washington, U.S. Dept. of the Interior (*or* U.S. Govt. Print. Off.), 1966. 1 p. (*or* p. 1).

Another Government periodical citation would read as follows:

Reese, Herbert Harshman, "How To Select a Sound Horse," *Farmers' Bulletin*, No. 779, pp. 1–26 (1917), U.S. Dept. of Agriculture.

Clarity may be maintained by capitalizing each word in book titles, but only the first word in the title of articles.

Other examples are:

Preston W. Slosson, The Great Crusade and After: 1914–1928 (New York: Macmillan, 1930)
Edward B. Rosa, "The economic importance of the scientific work of the government," J. Wash. Acad. Sci. 10, 342 (1920)

Or:

Preston W. Slosson, *The Great Crusade and After: 1914–1928* (New York: Macmillan, 1930)
Edward B. Rosa, "The Economic Importance of the Scientific Work of the Government," *J. Wash. Acad. Sci.* 10, 342 (1920)
Note that the principal words in both book titles and titles of articles are capitalized. Consistency is more important in bibliographic style than the style itself.

The science of bibliography is covered in many texts, and the following references are available for study:

Bibliographic Procedures and Style: A Manual for Bibliographers in the Library of Congress. Superintendent of Documents, Washington, DC 20402.
Better Report Writing, by Willis H. Waldo. Reinhold Publishing Corp., New York, 1965.
Macmillan Handbook of English, by Robert F. Wilson. Macmillan Co., New York, 1982.
A Manual of Style, University of Chicago Press, Chicago, 1983.
Suggestions to Authors of the Reports of the U.S. Geological Survey. Superintendent of Documents, Washington, DC 20402.
Words Into Type, Prentice-Hall, New York, 1974.

3. CAPITALIZATION

(See also Abbreviations; Guide to Capitalization)

3.1. It is impossible to give rules that will cover every conceivable problem in capitalization; but by considering the purpose to be served and the underlying principles, it is possible to attain a considerable degree of uniformity. The list of approved forms given on pages 35 to 61 will serve as a guide. Manifestly such a list cannot be complete. The correct usage with respect to any term not included can be determined by analogy or by application of the rules.

Proper names

3.2. Proper names are capitalized.

Rome	John Macadam	Italy
Brussels	Macadam family	Anglo-Saxon

Derivatives of proper names

3.3. Derivatives of proper names used with a proper meaning are capitalized.

Roman (of Rome)	Johannean	Italian

3.4. Derivatives of proper names used with acquired independent common meaning, or no longer identified with such names, are lowercased. Since this depends upon general and long-continued usage, a more definite and all-inclusive rule cannot be formulated in advance. A list of derivatives is given on pages 43–44.

roman (type)	macadam (crushed rock)	italicize
brussels sprouts	watt (electric unit)	anglicize
venetian blinds	plaster of paris	pasteurize

Common nouns and adjectives in proper names

3.5. A common noun or adjective forming an essential part of a proper name is capitalized; the common noun used alone as a substitute for the name of a place or thing is not capitalized.

Massachusetts Avenue; the avenue	Crow Reservation; the reservation
Washington Monument; the monument	Federal Express; the express
Statue of Liberty; the statue	Cape of Good Hope; the cape
Hoover Dam; the dam	Jersey City; *also* Washington City; *but*
Boston Light; the light	city of Washington; the city
Modoc National Forest; the national forest	Cook County; the county
	Great Lakes; the lakes
Panama Canal; the canal	Lake of the Woods; the lake
Soldiers' Home of Ohio; the soldiers' home	North Platte River; the river
	Lower California; *but* lower Mississippi
Johnson House (hotel); Johnson house (residence)	Charles the First; Charles I
	Seventeenth Census; the 1960 census

3.6. If a common noun or adjective forming an essential part of a name becomes separated from the rest of the name by an interven-

ing common noun or adjective, the entire expression is no longer a proper noun and is therefore not capitalized.

> Union Station: union passenger station
> Eastern States: eastern farming States
> Western States: western farming States

3.7. A common noun used alone as a well-known short form of a specific proper name is capitalized.

> the Capitol (at Washington); *but* State capitol (building)
> the Channel (English Channel)
> the District (District of Columbia)
> the Soldiers' Home (District of Columbia only)

3.8. The plural form of a common noun capitalized as part of a proper name is also capitalized.

Seventh and I Streets	State and Treasury Departments
Lakes Erie and Ontario	British and French Governments
Potomac and James Rivers	Presidents Washington and Adams

3.9. A common noun used with a date, number, or letter, merely to denote time or sequence, or for the purpose of reference, record, or temporary convenience, does not form a proper name and is therefore not capitalized. (See also rule 3.39.)

abstract B	first district (not	rule 8
act of 1928	congressional)	schedule K
amendment 5	form 4	section 3
apartment 2	graph 8	signature 4
appendix C	group 7	spring 1926
article 1	history 3	State route 236
book II	interstate 95	station 27
chapter III	mile 7.5	table 4
chart B	page 2	title IV
class I	paragraph 4	treaty of 1919
collection 6	part I	volume X
column 2	phase 3	war of 1914
drawing 6	plate IV	ward 2
exhibit D	region 3	
figure 7	room A722	

3.10. The following terms are lowercased, even with a name or number. (For capitalized forms, see geographic terms, pp. 47–48.)

aqueduct	drydock	shipway
breakwater	irrigation project	slip
buoy	jetty	spillway
chute	levee	tunnel (*but* capitalize with
dam (*but* capitalize with	lock	proper name)
proper name)	pier	watershed
dike	reclamation project	weir
dock	ship canal	wharf

Definite article in proper place names

3.11. To achieve greater distinction or to adhere to the authorized form, the word *the* (or its equivalent in a foreign language) used as a part of an official name or title is capitalized. When such name or title is used adjectively, *the* is not capitalized, nor is it supplied at any time when not in copy.

> *British Consul* v. *The Mermaid* (title of legal case)
> The Dalles (OR); The Weirs (NH); *but* the Dalles region; the Weirs streets
> The Hague; *but* the Hague Court; the Second Hague Conference
> El Salvador; Las Cruces; L'Esterel

The Mall (Washington, DC)
The Gambia
The Netherlands
but the Congo, the Sudan

3.12. In common practice, rule 3.11 is disregarded in references to newspapers, periodicals, vessels, airships, trains, firm names, etc.

the Times	the *Mermaid*	the Federal Express
the Atlantic Monthly	the *Los Angeles*	the National Photo Co.
the Washington Post	the *U-3*	

Particles in names of persons

3.13. In foreign names such particles as *d', da, de, della, den, du, van,* and *von* are capitalized unless preceded by a forename or title. Individual usage, if ascertainable, should be followed.

> Da Ponte; Cardinal da Ponte
> Den Uyl; Johannes den Uyl; Prime Minister den Uyl
> Du Pont; E.I. du Pont de Nemours & Co.
> Van Rensselaer; Stephen van Rensselaer
> Von Braun; Wernher von Braun
> *but* d'Orbigny; Alcide d'Orbigny; de la Madrid; Miguel de la Madrid

3.14. In anglicized names such particles are usually capitalized, even if preceded by a forename or title, but individual usage, if ascertainable, should be followed.

> Justice Van Devanter; Reginald De Koven
> Thomas De Quincey; William De Morgan
> Henry van Dyke (his usage)
> Samuel F. Du Pont (his usage); Irénée du Pont
> (for firm names, see p. 46)

3.15. If copy is not clear as to the form of such a name (for example, *La Forge* or *Laforge*), the two-word form should be used.

De Kalb County (AL, GA, IL, IN); *but* DeKalb County (TN)

3.16. In names set in capitals, *de, von,* etc., are also capitalized.

Names of organized bodies

3.17. The full names of existing or proposed organized bodies and their shortened names are capitalized; other substitutes, which are most often regarded as common nouns, are capitalized only in certain specified instances to indicate preeminence or distinction. (See list on pp. 35-61.)

National governmental units:
　U.S. Congress: 98th Congress; the Congress; Congress; the Senate; the House; Committee of the Whole, the Committee; *but* committee (all other congressional committees)
　Department of Agriculture: the Department; Division of Publications, the Division; *similarly* all departmental units; *but* legislative, executive, and judicial departments
　Bureau of the Census: the Census Bureau, the Bureau; *but* the agency
　Geological Survey: the Survey
　Interstate Commerce Commission: the Commission
　Government Printing Office: the Printing Office, the Office
　American Embassy, British Embassy: the Embassy; *but* the consulate; the consulate general
　Treasury of the United States: General Treasury; National Treasury; Public Treasury; the Treasury; Treasury notes; New York Subtreasury, the subtreasury
　Department of Defense:
　　Military Establishment; Armed Forces; All-Volunteer Forces; *but* armed services

U.S. Army: the Army; All-Volunteer Army; the Infantry; 81st Regiment; Army
Establishment: the Army Band; Army officer; Regular Army officer; Reserve
officer; Volunteer officer; *but* army shoe; Grant's army; Robinson's brigade;
the brigade; the corps; the regiment; infantryman

U.S. Navy: the Navy; the Marine Corps; Navy (Naval) Establishment; Navy officer; *but* naval shipyard; naval officer; naval station

U.S. Air Force: the Air Force

U.S. Coast Guard: the Coast Guard

French Ministry of Foreign Affairs; the Ministry; French Army; British Navy

International organizations:

United Nations: the Council; the Assembly; the Secretariat

Permanent Court of Arbitration: the Court; the Tribunal (only in the proceedings
of a specific arbitration tribunal)

Hague Peace Conference of 1907: the Hague Conference; the Peace Conference;
the Conference

Common-noun substitutes:

Virginia Assembly: the assembly; the senate; the house of delegates

California State Highway Commission: Highway Commission of California; the
highway commission; the commission

Montgomery County Board of Health: the Board of Health, Montgomery County;
the board of health; the board

Common Council of the City of Pittsburgh: the common council; the council

Buffalo Consumers' League: the consumers' league; the league

Republican Party: the party

Southern Railroad Co.: the Southern Railroad; Southern Co.; Southern Road; the
railroad company; the company

Riggs National Bank: the Riggs Bank; the bank

Metropolitan Club: the club

Yale School of Law: Yale University School of Law; School of Law, Yale University; school of law

**3.18. The names of members and adherents of organized bodies
are capitalized to distinguish them from the same words used
merely in a descriptive sense.**

a Representative (U.S. Congress)	a Socialist
a Republican	an Odd Fellow
an Elk	a Communist
a Liberal	a Boy Scout
a Shriner	a Knight (K.C., K.P., etc.)

Names of countries, domains, and administrative divisions

3.19. The official designations of countries, national domains, and
their principal administrative divisions are capitalized only if used
as part of proper names, as proper names, or as proper adjectives.
(See table on p. 230.)

United States: the Republic; the Nation; the Union; the Government; *also* Federal,
Federal Government; *but* republic (when not referring specifically to one such
entity); republican (in general sense); a nation devoted to peace

New York State: the State, a State (a definite political subdivision of first rank);
State of Veracruz; Balkan States; six States of Australia; State rights; *but* state
(referring to a federal government, the body politic); foreign states; church and
state; statehood; state's evidence

Territory (Canada): Yukon, Northwest Territories; the Territory(ies), Territorial; *but*
territory of American Samoa, Guam, Virgin Islands

Dominion of Canada: the Dominion; *but* dominion (in general sense)

Ontario Province, Province of Ontario: the Province, Provincial; *but* province, provincial (in general sense)

Crown Colony of Hong Kong, Cyprus: the colony, crown colony

3.20. The similar designations *commonwealth, confederation (federal), government, nation (national), powers, republic,* etc., are cap-

italized only if used as part of proper names, as proper names, or as proper adjectives.

British Commonwealth, Commonwealth of Virginia: the Commonwealth: *but* a commonwealth government (general sense)

Swiss Confederation: the Confederation; the Federal Council; the Federal Government; *but* confederation, federal (in general sense)

French Government: the Government; French and Italian Governments; Soviet Government; the Governments; *but* government (in general sense); the Churchill government; European governments

Cherokee Nation: the nation; *but* Greek nation; American nations

National Government (of any specific nation); *but* national customs

Allied Powers, Allies (in World Wars I and II); *but* our allies, weaker allies; Central Powers (in World War I); *but* the powers; European powers

Republic of South Africa: the Republic; *but* republic (in general sense)

Names of regions, localities, and geographic features

3.21. A descriptive term used to denote a definite region, locality, or geographic feature is a proper name and is therefore capitalized; also for temporary distinction a coined name of a region is capitalized.

the North Atlantic States; the Gulf States; the Central States; the Pacific Coast States; the Lake States; East North Central States; Eastern North Central States; Far Western States; Eastern United States

the West; the Midwest; the Middle West; Far West

the Eastern Shore (Chesapeake Bay)

the Badlands (SD and NE)

the Continental Divide (Rocky Mountains)

Deep South; Midsouth

the Occident; the Orient

the Far East

Far Eastern; the East

Middle East, Middle Eastern, Mideast, Mideastern (Asia)

Near East (Balkans, etc.)

the Promised Land

the Continent (continental Europe)

the Western Hemisphere

the North Pole; the North and South Poles

the Temperate Zone; the Torrid Zone

the East Side, Lower East Side (sections of a city)

Western Germany; Western Europe (political entities)

but lower 48 (States); the Northeast corridor

3.22. A descriptive term used to denote mere direction or position is not a proper name and is therefore not capitalized.

north; south; east; west

northerly; northern; northward

eastern; oriental; occidental

east Pennsylvania; southern California

northern Virginia

west Florida; *but* West Florida (1763–1819)

eastern region; western region

north-central region

east coast; eastern seaboard

central Europe; south Germany; southern France

but East Germany; West Germany (political entities)

Names of calendar divisions

3.23. The names of divisions are capitalized.

January; February; March; etc.
Monday; Tuesday; Wednesday; etc.
but spring; summer; autumn (fall); winter

Names of historic events, etc.

3.24. The names of holidays, ecclesiastic feast and fast days, and historic events are capitalized.

Battle of Bunker Hill

Christian Era; Middle Ages; *but* 20th century

Feast of the Passover; the Passover

Fourth of July; the Fourth

Reformation

Renaissance

Veterans Day

War of 1812; World War II; *but* war of 1914; Korean war

Trade names

3.25. Trade names, variety names, and names of market grades and brands are capitalized. Common nouns following such names are not capitalized. (See market grades, p. 50; trade names, pp. 58–59.)

Foamite (trade name)
Plexiglas (trade name)
Snow Crop (trade name)

Choice lamb (market grade)
Yellow Stained cotton (market grade)
Red Radiance rose (variety)

Scientific names

3.26. The names of a phylum, class, order, family, or genus is capitalized; the name of a species is not capitalized, even though derived from a proper name. (See rule 11.9.)

Arthropoda (phylum), Crustacea (class), Hypoparia (order), Agnostidae (family), *Agnostus* (genus)
Agnostus canadensis; Aconitum wilsoni; Epigaea repens (genus and species)

3.27. In scientific descriptions coined terms derived from proper names are not capitalized.

aviculoid   menodontine

3.28. A plural formed by adding *s* to a Latin generic name is capitalized.

Rhynchonellas   Spirifers

3.29. In soil science the 24 soil classifications are capitalized. (For complete list, see p. 56.)

Alpine Meadow   Bog   Brown

3.30. Capitalize the names of the celestial bodies Sun and Moon, as well as the planets Earth, Mercury, Venus, Mars, Jupiter, Saturn, Uranus, Neptune, and Pluto. Lowercase the word *moon* in such expressions as "the moons of Jupiter."

3.31. For lists of geologic and physiographic terms, see page 227.

Fanciful appellations

3.32. A fanciful appellation used with or for a proper name is capitalized.

Big Four
Dust Bowl
Great Society
Holocaust

Hub (Boston)
Keystone State
New Deal
New Federalism

New Frontier
Prohibition
Great Depression
Third World

Personification

3.33. A vivid personification is capitalized.

The Chair recognized the gentleman from New York.
For Nature wields her scepter mercilessly.
All are architects of Fate,
Working in these walls of Time.

Religious terms

3.34. Words denoting the Deity except *who, whose,* and *whom;* names for the Bible and other sacred writings and their parts; and names of confessions of faith and of religious bodies and their adherents and words specifically denoting Satan are all capitalized.

Heavenly Father; the Almighty; Lord; Thee; Thou; He; Him; *but* himself; [God's] fatherhood

Mass; red Mass; Communion
Divine Father; *but* divine providence; divine guidance; divine service
Son of Man; Jesus' sonship; the Messiah; *but* a messiah; messiahship; messianic; messianize; christology; christological
Bible, Holy Scriptures, Scriptures, Word; Koran; *also* Biblical; Scriptural; Koranic
New Testament; Ten Commandments
Gospel (memoir of Christ); *but* gospel truth
Apostles' Creed; Augsburg Confession; Thirty-nine Articles
Episcopal Church; an Episcopalian; Catholicism; a Protestant
Christian; *also* Christendom; Christianity; Christianize
Black Friars; Brother(s); King's Daughters; Daughter(s); Ursuline Sisters; Sister(s)
Satan; His Satanic Majesty; Father of Lies; the Devil; *but* a devil; the devils; devil's advocate

Titles of persons

3.35. Civil, religious, military, and professional titles, as well as those of nobility, immediately preceding a name are capitalized.

President Reagan	Dr. Bellinger	Vice-Presidential
King George	Nurse Cavell	candidate White
Ambassador Gibson	Professor Leverett	*but* baseball player Jones
Lieutenant Fowler	Examiner Jones (law)	maintenance man Smith
Chairman Smith		

3.36. To indicate preeminence or distinction in certain specified instances, a common-noun title immediately following the name of a person or used alone as a substitute for it is capitalized.

Title of a head or assistant head of state:
   Ronald W. Reagan, President of the United States: the President; the President-elect; the Executive; the Chief Magistrate; the Commander in Chief; ex-President Carter: former President Truman; *similarly* the Vice President; the Vice-President-elect; ex-Vice-President Mondale
   Charles Robb, Governor of Virginia: the Governor of Virginia; the Governor; *similarly* the Lieutenant Governor; *but* secretary of state of Idaho; attorney general of Maine
Title of a head or assistant head of an existing or proposed National governmental unit:
   George P. Shultz, Secretary of State: the Secretary; *similarly* the Acting Secretary; the Under Secretary; the Assistant Secretary; the Director; the Chief or Assistant Chief; the Chief Clerk; etc.; *but* Secretaries of the military departments; secretaryship
Titles of the military:
   General of the Army(ies): United States only; Supreme Allied Commander; Gen. John W. Vessey, Chairman, Joint Chiefs of Staff; Joint Chiefs of Staff; Chief of Staff, U.S. Air Force; the Chief of Staff; *but* the commanding general; general (military title standing alone not capitalized)
Titles of members of diplomatic corps:
   Walter S. Gifford, Ambassador Extraordinary and Plenipotentiary: the American Ambassador; the British Ambassador; the Ambassador; the Senior Ambassador; His Excellency; *similarly* the Envoy Extraordinary and Minister Plenipotentiary; the Envoy; the Minister; the Chargé d'Affaires; the Chargé; Ambassador at Large; Minister Without Portfolio; *but* the consul general; the consul; the attaché; etc.
Title of a ruler or prince:
   Elizabeth II, Queen of England: the Queen; the Crown; Her Most Gracious Majesty; Her Majesty; *similarly* the Emperor; the Sultan; etc.
   Charles, Prince of Wales: the Prince; His Royal Highness
Titles not capitalized:
   Charles F. Hughes, rear admiral, U.S. Navy: the rear admiral
   Lloyd H. Elliott, president of George Washington University: the president
   C.H. Eckles, professor of dairy husbandry: the professor
   Patricia Rowles, chairwoman of the committee; the chairman; the chairperson; the chair

3.37. In formal lists of delegates and representatives of governments, all titles and descriptive designations immediately following the names should be capitalized if any one is capitalized.

3.38. A title in the second person is capitalized.

Your Excellency	Mr. Chairman	Not salutation:
Your Highness	Madam Chairman	my dear General
Your Honor	Mr. Secretary	my dear sir

Titles of publications, papers, documents, acts, laws, etc.

3.39. In the full or short English titles of periodicals, series of publications, annual reports, historic documents, and works of art, the first word and all important words are capitalized.

Statutes at Large; Revised Statutes; District Code; Bancroft's History; Journal (House or Senate) (short titles); *but* the code; the statutes

Atlantic Charter; Balfour Declaration; *but* British white paper

Chicago's American; *but* Chicago American Publishing Co.

Reader's Digest; *but* New York Times Magazine; Newsweek magazine

Monograph 55; Research Paper 123; Bulletin 420; Circular A; Article 15: Uniform Code of Military Justice; Senate Document 70; House Resolution 45; Presidential Proclamation No. 24; Executive Order No. 24; Royal Decree No. 24; Public Law 89–1; Private and Union Calendars; Calendar No. 80; Calendar Wednesday; Committee Print No. 32, committee print; *but* Senate bill 416; House bill 61

Annual Report of the Public Printer, 1966; *but* seventh annual report, 19th annual report (see rule 12.10)

Declaration of Independence; the Declaration

Constitution (United States or with name of country); constitutional; *but* New York State constitution: first amendment, 12th amendment (see rule 12.10).

Kellogg Pact; North Atlantic Pact; Atlantic Pact; Treaty of Versailles; Jay Treaty; *but* treaty of peace, the treaty (descriptive designations); treaty of 1919

United States v. *Four Hundred Twenty-two Casks of Wine* (law) (see also rule 17.12).

The Blue Boy, Excalibur, Whistler's Mother (paintings)

3.40. All principal words are capitalized in titles of addresses, articles, books, captions, chapter and part headings, editorials, essays, headings, headlines, motion pictures and plays (including television and radio programs), papers, short poems, reports, songs, subheadings, subjects, and themes. The foregoing are also quoted. (See rule 8.132, for examples of capitalization and use of quotation marks.)

3.41. In the short or popular titles of acts (Federal, State, or foreign) the first word and all important words are capitalized.

Revenue Act; Walsh-Healey Act; Freedom of Information Act; Classification Act; *but* the act; Harrison narcotic law; Harrison narcotic bill; interstate commerce law; sunset law

3.42. The capitalization of the titles of books, etc., written in a foreign language is to conform to national practice in that language.

First words

3.43. The first word of a sentence, of an independent clause or phrase, of a direct quotation, of a formally introduced series of items or phrases following a comma or colon, or of a line of poetry, is capitalized. (See rule 8.25.)

The question is, Shall the bill pass?

He asked, "And where are you going?"

The vote was as follows: In the affirmative, 23; in the negative, 11; not voting, 3.

Lives of great men all remind us

We can make our lives sublime.

3.44. The first word of a fragmentary quotation is not capitalized.

He objected "to the phraseology, not to the ideas."

3.45. The first word following a colon, an exclamation point, or a question mark is not capitalized if the matter following is merely a supplementary remark making the meaning clearer.

Revolutions are not made: they come.
Intelligence is not replaced by mechanism: even the televox must be guided by its master's voice.
But two months dead! nay, not so much; not two.
What is this?
Your knees to me? to your corrected son?

3.46. The first word following *Whereas* in resolutions, contracts, etc., is not capitalized; the first word following an enacting or resolving clause is capitalized.

Whereas the Constitution provides * * *; and
Whereas Congress has passed a law * * *;
Whereas, moreover, * * *: Therefore be it
Whereas the Senate provided for the * * *: Now, therefore, be it
Resolved, That * * *; and be it further
Resolved (jointly), That * * *
Resolved by the House of Representatives (the Senate concurring), That * * *. (Concurrent resolution, Federal Government.)
Resolved by the Senate of Oklahoma (the House of Representatives concurring therein), That * * *. (Concurrent resolution, using name of State.)
Resolved by the senate (the house of representatives concurring therein), That * * *. (Concurrent resolution, not using name of State.)
Resolved by the Assembly and Senate of the State of California (jointly), That * * * (Joint resolution, using name of State.)
Resolved by the Washington Board of Trade, That * * *
Provided, That * * *
Provided further, That * * *
Provided, however, That * * *
And provided further, That * * *
Ordered, That * * *
Be it enacted, That * * *

Center and side heads

3.47. Unless otherwise marked, (1) centerheads are set in capitals, and (2) sideheads are set in lowercase and only the first word and proper names are capitalized, In centerheads making two lines, wordbreaks should be avoided. The first line should be centered and set as full as possible.

3.48. Except as indicated elsewhere, everything in a cap heading is set in caps; in a cap and small-cap heading, in caps and small caps; and in a small-cap heading, in small caps, including, if available, parentheses, brackets, and figures.

3.49. In heads set in caps, a small-cap *c* or *ac,* if available, is used in such names as *McLean* or *MacLeod;* otherwise a lowercase *c* or *ac* is used. In heads set in small caps, a space is used after the *c* or the *ac.*

3.50. In such names as *LeRoy, DeHostis, LaFollette,* etc. (oneword forms only), set in caps, the second letter of the particle is made a small cap, if available; otherwise lowercase is used. In heads set in small caps, a space is used. (See rule 3.15.)

3.51. In matter set in caps and small caps or caps and lowercase, capitalize all principal words, including parts of compounds which would be capitalized standing alone. The articles *a, an,* and *the;* the

prepositions *at, by, for, in, of, on, to,* and *up;* the conjunctions *and, as, but, if, or,* and *nor;* and the second element of a compound numeral are not capitalized. (See also rule 8.132.)

World en Route to All-Out War
Curfew To Be Set at 10 o'Clock
Man Hit With 2-Inch Pipe
No-Par-Value Stock for Sale
Yankees May Be Winners in Zig-Zag Race
Ex-Senator Is To Be Admitted
Notice of Filing and Order on Exemption From Requirements
but Building on Twenty-first Street (if spelled)
One Hundred and Twenty-three Years (if spelled)
Only One-tenth of Shipping Was Idle
Many 35-Millimeter Films in Production
Built-Up Stockpiles Are Necessary (*Up* is an adverb here)
His Per Diem Was Increased (*Per Diem* is used as a noun here); Lower Taxes per Person (*per* is a preposition here)

3.52. If a normally lowercased short word is used in juxtaposition with a capitalized word of like significance, it should also be capitalized.

Buildings In and Near Minneapolis

3.53. In a heading set in caps and lowercase or in caps and small caps, a normally lowercased last word, if it is the only lowercased word in the heading, should also be capitalized.

All Returns Are In

3.54. The first element of an infinitive is capitalized.

Controls To Be Applied; *but* Aid Sent to Disaster Area

3.55. In matter set in caps and small caps, such abbreviations as *etc., et al.,* and *p.m.* are set in small caps; in matter set in caps and lowercase, these abbreviations are set in lowercase.

PLANES, GUNS, SHIPS, ETC.	Planes, Guns, Ships, etc.
JAMES BROS. ET AL. (no comma)	James Bros. et al.
IN RE THE 8 P.M. MEETING	In re the 8 p.m. Meeting

3.56. Accents in cap lines should be omitted even if the same words carry accents in text.

3.57. Paragraph series letters in parentheses appearing in heads set in caps, caps and small caps, small caps, or in caps and lowercase are to be set as in copy.

SECTION 1.580 (f)(1)

Addresses, salutations, and signatures

3.58. The first word and all principal words in addresses, salutations, and signatures are capitalized. (See "Datelines, Addresses, and Signatures," p. 205.)

Interjections

3.59. The interjection *O* is always capitalized; within a sentence other interjections are not capitalized.

Sail on, O Ship of State!
For lo! the days are hastening on.
But, oh, how fortunate!

Historic or documentary accuracy

3.60. Where historic, documentary, technical, or scientific accuracy is required, capitalization and other features of style of the original text should be followed.

3.61. Where strict adherence to a rule on capitalization in headings detracts from an intended meaning or effect, the supervisor in the markup section must be consulted.

NOTES

4. GUIDE TO CAPITALIZATION

(Based on the preceding rules for capitalization)

A-bomb
abstract B, 1, etc.
Academy:
  Air Force; the Academy
  Andover; the academy
  Coast Guard; the Academy
  Merchant Marine; the Academy
  Military; the Academy
  National Academy of Sciences; the
    Academy of Sciences; the academy
  Naval; the Academy
  but service academies
accord, Paris peace (see Agreement)
accords, Helsinki
Act (Federal, State, or foreign) , short or
    popular title or with number; the
    act:
  Appropriation
  Classification
  Economy
  Flood Control
  Lend-Lease Act; *but* lend-lease materi-
    als, etc.
  National Teacher Corps
  Organic Act of Virgin Islands
  Panama Canal
  Pay
  Public Act 145 (see also Public Act)
  Revenue
  River and Harbor
  Selective Training and Service
  Stock Piling
  Tariff
  Trademark
  Walsh-Healey Act; *but* Walsh-Healey
    law (or bill)
act, Labor-Management Relations
Acting, if part of capitalized title
ACTION (independent Federal agency)[1]
Adjutant General, the (see The)
Administration, with name; capitalized
    standing alone if Federal unit:
  Farmers Home
  Food and Drug
  Maritime
  Veterans' (follow apostrophe)
  but Reagan administration; adminis-
    tration bill, policy, etc.
Administrative Law Judge Davis; Judge
    Davis; an administrative law judge
Administrator of Veterans' Affairs; the
    Administrator

---

[1] Not an acronym. Capitalization represents
agency's preference.

Admiralty, British, etc.
Admiralty, Lord of the
Adviser, Legal (Department of State)
Africa:
  east
  East Coast
  north
  South
  South-West (Territory of)
  West Coast
Agency, if part of name; capitalized
    standing alone if referring to Feder-
    al unit:
  Chippewa (Indian); the agency
  Central Intelligence; the Agency
Ages:
  Age of Discovery
  Dark Ages
  Elizabethan Age
  Golden Age (of Pericles only)
  Middle Ages
  but atomic age; Cambrian age; copper
    age; ice age; missile age; rocket age;
    space age; stone age; etc.
Agreement, with name; the agreement:
  General Agreement on Tariffs and
    Trade (GATT); the general agree-
    ment
  International Wheat Agreement; the
    wheat agreement; the coffee agree-
    ment
  Status of Forces; *but* status-of-forces
    agreements
  but the Geneva agreement; the Pots-
    dam agreement; Paris peace agree-
    ment
Air Force:
  Air National Guard (see National)
  Base (see Base; Station)
  Civil Air Patrol; Civil Patrol; the
    patrol
  Command (see Command)
  One (Presidential plane)
  Reserve
  Reserve Officers' Training Corps
  WAF (see Women in the Air Force)
Airport: La Guardia; National; the air-
    port
Alaska Native (collective term for
    Aleuts, Eskimos, and Indians of
    Alaska); the Native; *but others* a
    native of Alaska, Ohio, etc.
Alliance, Farmers', etc.; the alliance
Alliance for Progress; the Alliance

Alliance for Progress program
alliances and coalitions (see also
 powers):
 Allied Powers; the powers (World
  Wars)
 Atlantic alliance
  Axis, the; Axis Powers; the powers
  Benelux (Belgium, Netherlands, Lux-
   embourg)
  Big Four (European); of the Pacific
  Big Three
  Central Powers; the powers (World
   War I)
  European Economic Community (see
   also Common Market)
  Fritalux (France, Italy, Benelux coun-
   tries)
  North Atlantic Treaty Organization
   (see Organization)
  Western Powers
  Western Union (powers); the union
Allied (World Wars I and II):
 armies
 Governments
 Nations
 peoples
 Powers; the powers; *but* European
  powers
 Supreme Allied Commander
Allies, the (World Wars I and II); also
 members of Western bloc (political
 entity); *but* our allies; weaker allies,
 etc.
Ambassador:
 British, etc.; the Ambassador; the
  Senior Ambassador; His Excellency
  Extraordinary and Plenipotentiary;
  the Ambassador; Ambassador at
  Large; an ambassador
amendment:
 Social Security Amendments of 1954;
  1954 amendments; the social secu-
  rity amendments; the amendments
 Baker amendment
 to the Constitution (U.S.); first amend-
  ment, 14th amendment, etc. (see
  rule)
American:
 Federation of Labor and Congress of
  Industrial Organizations (AFL–CIO);
  the federation
 Gold Star Mothers, Inc.; Gold Star
  Mothers; a Mother
 Legion (see Legion)
 National Red Cross; the Red Cross
 Veterans of World War II (AMVETS)
 War Mothers; War Mothers; a Mother
Amtrak (National Railroad Passenger
 Corporation)
Ancient Free and Accepted Masons; a
 Mason; a Freemason
Annex, if part of name of building; the
 annex
Antarctic Ocean (see Arctic; Ocean)
anti-Reaganomics

appendix 1, A, II, etc.; the appendix; *but*
 Appendix II, when part of title: Ap-
 pendix II: [2] Education Directory
appropriation bill (see also bill):
 deficiency
 Department of Agriculture
 for any governmental unit
 independent offices
Arab States
Arabic numerals
Arboretum, National; the Arboretum
Archipelago, Philippine, etc.; the archi-
 pelago
Architect of the Capitol; the Architect
Archives, National; the Archives
Archivist of the United States; the Ar-
 chivist
Arctic:
 Circle
 Current (see Current)
 Ocean
 zone
 but subarctic
arctic (descriptive adjective):
 clothing
 conditions
 fox
 grass
 night
 seas
Arctics, the
Area, if part of name; the area:
 Cape Hatteras Recreational
 White Pass Recreation; etc.
 but area 2; free trade area; Metropoli-
  tan Washington area; bay area
Arlington:
 Memorial Amphitheater; the Memori-
  al Amphitheater; the amphitheater
 Memorial Bridge (see Bridge)
 National Cemetery (see Cemetery)
Arm, Cavalry, Infantry, etc. (military);
 the arm
Armed Forces (synonym for overall Mili-
 tary Establishment); British Armed
 Forces; the armed forces of the
 United States
armed services
armistice
Armory, Springfield, etc.; the armory
Army, American or foreign, if part of
 name; capitalized standing alone
 only if referring to U.S. Army:
 Active
 Adjutant General, the
 All-Volunteer
 Band (see Band)
 branches; Gordon Highlanders; Royal
  Guards; etc.
 Brigade, 1st, etc.; the brigade; Robin-
  son's brigade
 Command (see Command)
 Command and General Staff College
  (see College)

---

[2] The colon is preferred; a dash is permissible; but a comma is too weak.

Army—Continued

Company A; A Company; the company

Confederate (referring to Southern Confederacy); the Confederates

Continental; Continentals

Corps (see Corps)

District of Washington (military); the district

Division, 1st, etc.; the division

Engineers (the Corps of Engineers); the Engineers; *but* Army engineer

Establishment

Field Establishment

Field Forces (see Forces)

Finance Department; the Department 1st, etc.

General of the Army; *but* the general

General Staff; the Staff

Headquarters, 1st Regiment

Headquarters of the; the headquarters

Hospital Corps (see Corps)

Medical Museum (see Museum)

Organized Reserves; the Reserves

Regiment, 1st, etc.; the regiment

Regular Army officer; a Regular

Revolutionary (American, British, French, etc.)

service

Surgeon General, the (see Surgeon General)

Volunteer; the Volunteers; a Volunteer

army:

Lee's army; *but* Clark's 5th Army

mobile

mule, shoe, etc.

of occupation; occupation army

Red

Arsenal, Rock Island, etc.; the arsenal

article 15; *but* Article 15, when part of title: Article 15:[3] Uniform Code of Military Justice

Articles of Confederation (U.S.)

Assembly of New York; the assembly (see also Legislative Assembly)

Assembly (see United Nations)

Assistant, if part of capitalized title; the assistant

assistant, Presidential (see Presidential)

Assistant Secretary (see Secretary)

Associate Justice (see Supreme Court)

Association, if part of name; capitalized standing alone if referring to Federal unit:

American Association for the Advancement of Science; the association

Federal National Mortgage (Fannie Mae); the Association

Young Women's Christian; the association

Astrophysical Observatory (see Observatory)

Atlantic:

Charter (see Charter)

Atlantic—Continued

coast

community

Coast States

Destroyer Flotilla; the destroyer flotilla; the flotilla

Fleet (see Fleet)

mid-Atlantic

North

Pact (see Pact)

seaboard

slope

South

time, standard time (see time)

but cisatlantic; transatlantic

Attorney General (U.S.); *but* attorney general of Maine, etc.

attorney, U.S.

Authority, capitalized standing alone if referring to Federal unit:

National Shipping; the Authority

Port of New York; the port authority; the authority

St. Lawrence Seaway Authority of Canada; the authority

Tennessee Valley; the Authority

autumn

Avenue, Constitution, etc.; the avenue

Award: Academy, Distinguished Service, Merit, Mother of the Year, etc.; the award (see also decorations, etc.)

Axis, the (see alliances)

Ayatollah

Badlands (SD and NE)

Balkan States (see States)

Baltic States (see States)

Band, if part of name; the band:

Army, Marine, Navy

Eastern, etc. (of Cherokee Indians)

Bank, if part of name; the bank; capitalized standing alone if referring to international bank:

Export-Import Bank of Washington (Eximbank or Exim); Export-Import Bank; the Bank

Farm Loan Bank of Dallas; Dallas Farm Loan Bank; farm loan bank; farm loan bank at Dallas

Farmers & Mechanics, etc.

Federal home loan bank at Cumberland

Federal Land Bank of Louisville; Louisville Federal Land Bank; land bank at Louisville; Federal land bank

Federal Reserve Bank of New York; Richmond Federal Reserve Bank; *but* Reserve bank at Richmond; Federal Reserve bank; Reserve bank; Reserve city

First National, etc.

German Central; the Bank

International Bank for Reconstruction and Development; the Bank

International Monetary; the Bank

International World; the Bank

---

[3] See footnote 2, p. 36.

Bank—Continued
  but blood bank, central reserve, soil
    bank
Barracks, if part of name; the barracks:
  Carlisle
  Disciplinary (Leavenworth)
  Marine (District of Columbia)
  but A barracks; barracks A; etc.
Base, Andrews Air Force; Air Force
  base; the base (see also Naval Base);
  but Sandia Base
Basin (see geographic terms)
Battery, the (New York City)
Battle, if part of name; the battle:
  of Gettysburg; *but* battle at Gettys-
    burg; etc.
  of the Bulge; of the Marne; of the Wil-
    derness; of Waterloo; etc.
battlefield, Bull Run, etc.
battleground, Manassas, etc.
Bay, San Francisco Bay area; the bay
  area
Belt, if part of name; the belt:
  Bible
  Corn
  Cotton
  Dairy
  Ice
  Sun
  Wheat
  but money belt
Beltway, capitalized with name; the
  beltway
Bench (see Supreme Bench)
Benelux (see alliances)
Bible; Biblical; Scriptures; etc. (see also
  book)
bill, Kiess; Senate bill 217; House bill 31
  (see also appropriation bill)
Bill of Rights (historic document); *but* GI
  bill of rights
Bizonia; bizonal; bizone
black (synonym for Negro)
Black Caucus (see Congressional)
Black Panther; Panther
bloc (see Western)
block (grants)
Bluegrass region, etc.
B'nai B'rith
Board, if part of name; capitalized
  standing alone only if referring to
  Federal, interdepartmental, or in-
  ternational board:
  Civil Aeronautics
  Employees' Compensation Appeals
  Federal Maritime
  Federal Reserve (see Federal)
  General (Navy)
  Loyalty Review
  Macy Board, etc. (Federal board with
    name of person)
  Military Production and Supply
    (NATO)
  of Directors (Federal unit); *but* board
    of directors (nongovernmental)
  of Health of Montgomery County;
    Montgomery County Board of

Board—Continued
  Health; the board of health; the
    board
  of Managers (of the Soldiers' Home)
  of Regents (Smithsonian)
  of Visitors (Military and Naval Acade-
    mies)
  on Geographic Names
Bolshevik; Bolsheviki (collective plural);
  Bolshevist; bolshevism
bond:
  Government
  savings
  series EE
  Treasury
book:
  books of the Bible
  First Book of Samuel; etc.
  Good Book (synonym for Bible)
  Ten Commandments
book 1, I, etc.; *but* Book 1, when part of
  title: Book 1:[4] The Golden Legend
border, United States-Mexican
Borough, if part of name: Borough of
  the Bronx; the borough
Botanic Garden (National); the garden
  (*not* Botanical Gardens)
Bowl, Dust, Ice, Rose, etc.; the bowl
Boxer Rebellion (see Rebellion)
Boy Scouts (the organization); a Boy
  Scout; a Scout; Scouting
Branch, if part of name; capitalized
  standing alone only if referring to a
  Federal unit:
  Accounts Branch
  Public Buildings Branch
  but executive, judicial, or legislative
    branch
Bridge, if part of name; the bridge:
  Arlington Memorial; Memorial
  Francis Scott Key; Key
  M Street
  but Baltimore & Ohio Railroad bridge
Brother(s) (adherent of religious order)
Budget of the United States (publica-
  tion); the Budget (Office implied);
  the budget
budget:
  department
  estimate
  Federal
  message
  performance-type
  President's
Building, if part of name; the building:
  Capitol (see Capitol Building)
  Colorado
  House (or Senate) Office
  Investment
  New House (or Senate) Office
  Old House Office
  Pentagon
  the National Archives; the Archives
  Treasury; Treasury Annex
Bulletin 420; Farmers' Bulletin No. 420

---

[4] See footnote 2, p. 36.

Bureau, if part of name; capitalized standing alone if referring to Federal or international unit:
  of Customs (name changed to U.S. Customs Service)
  of Engraving and Printing
  of Indian Affairs
  of Mines; Mines Bureau
  of Social Hygiene, New York; the bureau; etc.

Cabinet, American or foreign, if part of name or standing alone (see also foreign cabinets):
  British Cabinet; the Cabinet
  the President's Cabinet; the Cabinet; Cabinet officer, member
Calendar, if part of name; the calendar:
  Consent; etc.
  House
  No. 99; Calendars Nos. 1 and 2
  of Bills and Resolutions
  Private
  Senate
  Unanimous Consent
  Union
  Wednesday (legislative)
Cambrian age (see Ages)
Camp Lejeune; David, etc.; the camp
Canal, with name; the canal:
  Cross-Florida Barge
  Isthmian
  Panama
  Zone (Isthmian); the zone (see also Government)
Cape (see geographic terms)
Capital, Capital City, National Capital (Washington, DC); *but* the capital (State)
Capitol Building (with State name); the capitol
Capitol, the (Washington, DC):
  Architect of
  Building
  caucus room
  Chamber
  Cloakroom
  dome
  Grounds
  Hall of Fame; the Hall
  Halls (House and Senate)
  Halls of Congress
  Hill; the Hill
  Police (see Police)
  Power Plant
  Prayer Room
  Press Gallery, etc.
  rotunda
  Senate wing
  stationery room
  Statuary Hall
  the well (House or Senate)
  west front
caucus: Republican; *but* Black Caucus (incorporated name)
Cemetery, if part of name: Arlington National; the cemetery

Census:
  Nineteenth Decennial (title); Nineteenth Census (title); the census
  1980 census
  1980 Census of Agriculture; the census of agriculture; the census
  the 14th and subsequent decennial censuses
Center, if part of name; the Center (Federal); the center (non-Federal):
  Agricultural Research, etc.; the Center (Federal)
  Kennedy Center for the Performing Arts; the Kennedy Center; the Center (Federal)
  the Lincoln Center; the center (non-Federal)
central Asia, central Europe, etc.
Central America
Central States
central time (see time)
century, first, 20th, etc. (see rule 12.10)
Chair, the, if personified
Chairman:
  of the Board of Directors; the Chairman (Federal); *but* chairman of the board of directors (non-Federal)
  of the Committee of the Whole House; the Chairman
  of the Federal Trade Commission; the Chairman
  of the Loyalty Board; the Chairman
chairman (congressional):
  of the Appropriations Committee
  of the Subcommittee on Banking
  but Chairman Davis
Chamber of Commerce; the chamber:
  of Ada; Ada Chamber of Commerce; the chamber of commerce
  of the United States; U.S. Chamber of Commerce; the chamber of commerce; national chamber
Chamber, the (Senate or House)
channel 3 (TV); the channel (see also geographic terms)
Chaplain (House or Senate); *but* Navy chaplain
chapter 5, II, etc.; *but* Chapter 5, when part of title: Chapter 5:[5] Research and Development; Washington chapter, Red Cross
Chargé d'Affaires, British, etc.; the Chargé d'Affaires; the Chargé
chart 2, A, II, etc.; *but* Chart 2, when part of legend: Chart 2.—Army strength
Charter, capitalized with name; the charter:
  Atlantic
  United Nations
cheese: Camembert, Cheddar, Parmesan, Provolone, Roquefort, etc.
Chicano (see Hispanic)

---

[5] See footnote 2, p. 36.

Chief, if referring to head of Federal unit; the Chief:
Forester (see Forester)
Intelligence Office
Justice (U.S. Supreme Court); *but* chief justice (of a State)
Magistrate (the President)
of Division of Publications
of Engineers (Army)
of Naval Operations
of Staff
of the Bureau of Indian Affairs
Chief Clerk, if referring to head of Federal unit
Chief Judge, if referring to Federal unit
Christian; Christian name, etc.; Christendom; Christianity; Christianize; *but* christen
church and state
church calendar:
Christmas
Easter
Lent
Whitsuntide (Pentecost)
Church, if part of name of organization or building
Circle, if part of name; the circle:
Arctic
Logan
but great circle
Circular 420
cities, sections of, official or popular names:
East Side
French Quarter (New Orleans)
Latin Quarter (Paris)
North End
Northwest Washington, etc. (District of Columbia); the Northwest; *but* northwest (directional)
the Loop (Chicago)
City, if part of corporate or popular name; the city:
Hub (Boston)
Kansas City; the two Kansas Citys
Mexico City
New York City; *but* city of New York
Twin Cities
Washington City; *but* city of Washington
Windy City (Chicago)
but Reserve city (see Bank)
civil action No. 46
civil defense
Civil Air Patrol (see Air Force)
Civil Service Commission (obsolete) (see Office of Personnel Management)
Civil War (see War)
Clan, if part of tribal name; Clan MacArthur; the clan
class 2, A, II, etc.; *but* Class 2 when part of title: Class:[6] Leather Products
Clerk, the, of the House of Representatives; of the Supreme Court of the United States
clerk, the, of the Senate

─────────
[6] See footnote 2, p. 36.

coal sizes: pea, barley, buckwheat, stove, etc.
coast: Atlantic, east, gulf, west, etc.
Coast Guard, U.S.; the Coast Guard; Coastguardsman Smith; *but* a coastguardsman; a guardsman
Coastal Plain (Altantic and Gulf)
Code (in shortened title of a publication); the code:
District
Federal Criminal
Internal Revenue (also Tax Code)
International (signal)
of Federal Regulations
Penal; Criminal; etc.
Pennsylvania State
Radio
Television
Uniform Code of Military Justice
United States (see rule 9.10)
ZIP Code (copyrighted),
but civil code; flag code; Morse code
collection, Brady, etc.; the collection
collector of customs
College, if part of name; the college:
Armed Forces Staff
Command and General Staff
Gettysburg
National War
of Bishops
but electoral college
college degrees: bachelor of arts, master's, etc.
Colonials (American Colonial Army); *but* colonial times, etc.
Colonies, the:
Thirteen
Thirteen American
Thirteen Original
but 13 separate Colonies
colonists, the
Colony: Cyprus, Crown Colony of Hong Kong; the colony, crown colony
Cominform (see U.S.S.R.)
Command, capitalize with name; the command:
Air Materiel
GHQ Far East
Joint Far Eastern
Potomac River Naval
Zone of Interior
Commandant, the (Coast Guard or Marine Corps only)
Commandos, the; Commando raid; a commando
Commission (if part of name; capitalized standing alone if referring to Federal or international commission):
Alaska Road
International Boundary, United States, Alaska, and Canada
of Fine Arts
on Civil Rights
Public Buildings

Commissioner, if referring to Federal or international commission; the Commissioner:
Land Bank; *but* land bank commissioner loans
of Customs
of Immigration and Naturalization
of Patents
of the Five Civilized Tribes, etc.
U.S. (International Boundary Commission, etc.)
but a U.S. commissioner
Committee (or Subcommittee) (if part of name; the Committee, if referring to international or noncongressional Federal committee or to the Committee of the Whole, the Committee of the Whole House, or the Committe of the Whole House on the State of the Union):
American Medical Association Committee on Education; the committee on education; the committee
Appropriations, etc.; the committee; Subcommittee on Appropriations; the subcommittee; subcommittee of the Appropriations Committee
Democratic National; the national committee; the committee; Democratic national committeeman
Democratic policy committee; the committee
Interagency Advisory Committee on Domestic Transport and Storage and Post Utilization; the Committee
Joint Committee on Atomic Energy; the Joint Committee; the committee; *but* a joint committee
of Defense Ministers (NATO); the Committee (see also Organization, North Atlantic Treaty)
of One Hundred, etc.; the committee on Finance; the committee
on Post Office and Civil Service; the committee
on Public Safety; the committee
President's Advisory Committee on Management; the Committee
Republican National; the national committee; the committee; Republican national committeeman
Republican policy committee; the committee
Select Committee on Astronautics and Space Exploration; the select committee
Senate policy committee
Subcommittee No. 5, etc.; the subcommittee
Subcommittee on Immigration; the subcommittee
but Baker committee
ad hoc committee
Committee Print No. 32; Committee Prints Nos. 8 and 9; committee print
Common Cause

Common Market; the market (European Economic Community); *also* Common Market Treaty; Inner Six; Outer Seven
Commonwealth of Australia, Virginia, etc.; British Commonwealth; the Commonwealth
Commune (of Paris)
Communist; communism; communistic
Communist government, etc. (see U.S.S.R.)
Community, European Coal and Steel; European Economic; the Community; *but* the Atlantic community
compact, U.S. marine fisheries, etc.; the compact
Company, if part of name; capitalized standing alone if referring to unit of Federal Government:
Alaska Railroad Company; the Company
Panama Railroad Company; the Company
Procter & Gamble Co.; the company
Comptroller of the Currency; the Comptroller
Comptroller General (U.S.); the Comptroller
Comsat
conelrad
Confederacy (of the South)
Confederate:
Army
Government
soldier
States
Confederation, Swiss; the Confederation
Conference, if referring to governmental (U.S.) or international conference:
Bretton Woods; the Conference
Judicial Conference of the United States; U.S. Judicial Conference; Judicial Conference; the Conference
Tenth Annual Conference of the United Methodist Churches; the conference
Congress (convention), if part of name; capitalized standing alone if referring to international congress:
International Good Roads; Good Roads; the Congress
of Parents and Teachers, National; the congress
Congress (legislature), if referring to national congress:
of Bolivia, etc.; the Congress
of the United States; First, Second, 11th, 82d, etc. (see rule 12.10); the Congress
Congressional:
Black Caucus; the Black Caucus; the caucus
Directory, the directory
District, First, 11th, etc.; the First District, (see rule 12.10); the congressional district; the district
Library; the Library

Congressional—Continued
  Medal of Honor (see decorations)
  but congressional action, committee, etc.
Congressman; Congresswoman; Congressman at Large; Member of Congress; Member; membership
Constitution, with name of country; capitalized standing alone when referring to a specific national constitution; *but* New York State Constitution; the constitution
constitutional
consul, British, etc.
consul general, British, etc.
consulate, British, etc.
Consumer Price Index (official title); the price index; the index; *but* a consumers' price index (descriptive)
Continent, only if following name; American Continent; the continent; *but* the Continent (continental Europe)
Continental:
  Army; the Army
  Congress; the Congress
  Divide (see Divide)
  Outer Continental Shelf
  Shelf; the shelf; a continental shelf
continental:
  care not a continental, etc.
  Europe, United States, etc.
Continentals (Revolutionary soldiers)
Convention, governmental (U.S.), international, or national political; the convention:
  Constitutional (United States, 1787); the Convention
  Democratic National; Democratic
  Genocide (international)
  19th Annual Convention of the American Legion
  on International Civil Aviation
  Universal Postal Union; Postal Union *also* International Postal; Warsaw
copper age (see Ages)
Corn Belt (see Belt)
Corporation, if part of name; the Corporation, if referring to unit of Federal Government:
  Commodity Credit
  Federal Deposit Insurance
  Federal Savings and Loan Insurance
  National Railroad Passenger (Amtrak)
  Petroleum Reserves
  Rand Corp.; the corporation (see also abbreviations)
  St. Lawrence Seaway Development Corporation
  Union Carbide Corp.; the corporation
  Virgin Islands
Corps, if part of name; the corps, all other uses:
  Adjutant General's
  Army Hospital
  Artillery
  Chemical
  Counterintelligence

Corps—Continued
  Enlisted Reserve
  Finance
  Foreign Service Officer (see Foreign Service)
  Job
  Judge Advocate General's
  Marine (see Marine Corps)
  Medical
  Military Police
  Nurse
  of Cadets (West Point)
  of Engineers; Army Engineers; the Engineers; *but* Army engineer; the corps
  Officers' Reserve
  Ordnance
  Peace; Peace Corpsman; the corpsman
  Quartermaster
  Reserve Officers' Training (ROTC)
  VII Corps, etc. (see rule 12.10)
  Signal
  Teachers; *but* Teacher Corps Act
  Transportation
  Women's Army (WAC); a Wac; the Wacs
  Youth
  but diplomatic corps
  corpsman; hospital corpsman
corridor, Northeast
Cotton Belt (see Belt)
Council, if part of name; capitalized standing alone if referring to Federal or international unit (see also United Nations):
  Boston City; the council
  Choctaw, etc.; the council
  Federal Personnel; the Council
  Her Majesty's Privy Council; the Privy Council; the Council
  National Security; the Council
  of Foreign Ministers (NATO); the Council
  of the Organization of American States; the Council
  Philadelphia Common; the council
counsel; general counsel
County, Prince Georges; county of Prince Georges; County Kilkenny, etc.; Loudoun and Fauquier Counties; the county
Court (of law) (see also Courtwork, pp. 215–226); capitalized if part of name; capitalized standing alone if referring to the Supreme Court of the United States, to Court of Impeachment (U.S. Senate), or to international court):
  Circuit Court of the United States for the Tenth Circuit; Circuit Court for the Tenth Circuit; the circuit court; the court; the tenth circuit
  Court of Appeals for the State of North Carolina, etc.; the court of appeals; the court
  Court of Claims; the court

Court (of law)—Continued
 Court of Customs and Patent Appeals;
  the court
 Court of Impeachment, the Senate;
  the Court
 District Court of the United States for
  the Eastern District of Missouri; the
  district court; the court
 Emergency Court of Appeals; United
  States; the court
 International Court of Justice; the
  Court
 Permanent Court of Arbitration; the
  Court
 Superior Court of the District of Co-
  lumbia; the superior court; the
  court
 Supreme Court of the United States
  (see Supreme Court)
 Supreme Court of Virginia, etc.; the
  supreme court; the court
 Tax Court; the court
 U.S. Court of Appeals for the District
  of Columbia; the court
Covenant, League of Nations; the cov-
 enant
Creed, Apostles'; the Creed
Croix de Guerre (see decorations)
Crown, if referring to a ruler; *but* crown
 colony, lands, etc. (rule 3.19)
cruise missile
Current, if part of name; the current:
 Arctic
 Humboldt
 Japan
 North Equatorial
customhouse; customs official
czar; czarist

Dairy Belt (see Belt)
Dalles, The; *but* the Dalles region
Dam (see geographic terms)
Dark Ages (see Ages)
Daughters of the American Revolution;
 a Real Daughter; King's Daughters;
 a Daughter
daylight saving time
days (see holidays)
Declaration, capitalized with name:
 of Independence; the Declaration
 of Panama; the declaration
decorations, medals, etc., awarded by
  United States or any foreign nation-
  al government; the medal, the cross,
  the ribbon (see also awards):
 Air Medal
 Bronze Star Medal
 Commendation Ribbon
 Congressional Medal of Honor
 Croix de Guerre
 Distinguished Flying Cross
 Distinguished Service Cross
 Distinguished Service Medal
 Good Conduct Medal
 Iron Cross
 Legion of Merit
 Medal for Merit
 Medal of Freedom

decorations, medals, etc.—Continued
 Medal of Honor
 Purple Heart
 Silver Star Medal
 Soldier's Medal
 Victoria Cross
 Victory Medal
 also Carnegie Medal; Olympic Gold
  Medal; *but* gold medal
Decree (see Executive; Royal Decree)
Deep South
Defense Establishment (see Establish-
 ment)
De Gaulle Free French; Free French;
 but General de Gaulle; de Gaullist
Deity, words denoting, capitalized
Delegate (U.S. Congress)
delegate (to a conference); the delegate;
 the delegation
Delta, Mississippi River; the delta
Department, if part of name; capitalized
 standing alone if referring to Federal or international unit:
 of Agriculture
 of the Treasury
 Yale University Department of Economics; the department of economics; the department
Department of New York, American
 Legion
department:
 executive
 judicial
 legislative
Depot, if part of name; the depot (see
 also Station)
Depression, Great
Deputy, if part of capitalized title; *but*
 the deputy
derivatives of proper names:

alaska seal (fur)	castile soap
angora wool	cesarean operation
angstrom unit	chantilly lace
apache (Paris)	chesterfield coat
argyle wool	china clay
artesian well	chinese blue
astrakhan fabric	climax basket
axminster rug	collins (drink)
babbitt metal	congo red
benday process	cordovan leather
bohemian set	coulomb
bologna sausage	curie
bordeaux mixture	decauville rail
bourbon whiskey	degaussing appara-
bowie knife	tus
braille	delftware
brazil nut	derby hat
brazilwood	diesel engine, diesel-
brewer's yeast	ize
bristolboard	dotted swiss
britannia metal	epsom salt
britanniaware	fedora hat
brussels carpet	fletcherize
brussels sprouts	frankfurt sausage
bunsen burner	frankfurter
burley tobacco	french chalk
canada balsam (mi-	french dressing
croscopy)	french-fried potatoes
carlsbad twins (pe-	fuller's earth
trography)	gargantuan
cashmere shawl	gauss

derivatives of proper names—Continued

georgette crepe
german silver
gilbert
glauber salt
gothic type
graham bread
harderian gland
harveyized steel
herculean task
hessian fly
holland cloth
hoolamite detector
hudson seal (fur)
india ink
india rubber
intertype slug, *but*
　Intertype machine
italic type
jamaica ginger
japan varnish
jersey fabric
johnin test
joule
kafircorn
knickerbocker
kraft paper
lambert
leghorn hat
levant leather
levantine silk
lilliputian
linotype slug, *but*
　Linotype machine
logan tent
london purple
ludlow type, *but*
　Ludlow machine
lufbery circle
lynch law
lyonnaise potatoes
macadamized road
mach (no period)
　number
madras cloth
maginot line(nonlit.)
manila paper
maraschino cherry
mason jar
maxwell
melba toast
mercerized fabric
merino sheep
molotov cocktail
monotype matter,
　but Monotype machine
morocco leather
morris chair
murphy bed
navy blue
nelson, half nelson,
　etc.

neon light
newmarket cloak
newton
nissen hut
norfolk jacket
oriental rug
osnaburg cloth
oxford shoe
panama hat
parianware
paris green
parkerhouse roll
pasteurized milk
persian lamb
petri dish
pharisaic
philistine
pitman arm
pitot tube
plaster of paris
prussian blue
quisling
quixotic idea
quonset hut
rembert wheel
roentgen
roman candle
roman cement
roman type
russia leather
russian bath
rutherford
sanforize
saratoga chips
scotch plaid, *but*
　Scotch tape
shanghai
siamese twins
simon pure
spanish omelet
stillson wrench
stubs wire
surah silk
swiss cheese, *but*
　Swiss watch
taintor gate
timothy grass
turkey red
turkish towel
utopia, utopian
vandyke collar
vaseline
venetian blind
venturi tube
victoria (carriage)
vienna bread
virginia reel
wedgwoodware
wheatstone bridge
wilton rug
woodruff key
zeppelin

deutsche mark
Diet, Japanese (legislative body)
diplomatic corps (see also Corps; service)
Director, if referring to head of Federal
　or international unit; the Director:
District Director of Internal Revenue
of Coast and Geodetic Survey
of Fish and Wildlife Service
of the Budget
of the Mint
but director, board of directors (non-
　governmental)

Director General of Foreign Service; the
　Director General; the Director
disease:
　acquired immune deficiency syndrome
　　(AIDS)
　German measles
　Hodgkin's
　Parkinson's
Distinguished Service Medal, etc. (see
　decorations)
District, if part of name; the district:
　Alexandria School District No. 4;
　　school district No. 4
　Chicago Sanitary; the sanitary district
　Congressional (with number)
　Federal (see Federal)
　1st Naval; naval district
　Los Angeles Water; the water district
　Manhattan Engineer (atomic)
　but customs district No. 2; first assem-
　　bly district
District of Columbia; the District:
　Anacostia Flats; the flats
　Arlington Memorial Bridge; the Me-
　　morial Bridge; the bridge
　District jail; the jail; *not* D.C. Jail
　Ellipse, the
　General Hospital; the hospital
　Highway Bridge; 14th Street Bridge;
　　the bridge
　Mall, The
　Mayor (when pertaining to the Dis-
　　trict of Columbia only)
　Metropolitan Police; Metropolitan po-
　　liceman; the police
　Monument Grounds; the grounds
　Monument, Washington; the monu-
　　ment
　police court
　Public Library; the library
　Reflecting Pool; the pool
　Tidal Basin; the basin
　Washington Channel; the channel
Divide, Continental (Rocky Mountains);
　the divide
Divine Father; *but* divine guidance,
　divine providence, divine service
Division, Army, if part of name: 1st Cav-
　alry Division; 1st Cavalry; the divi-
　sion
Division, if referring to Federal govern-
　mental unit; the Division:
　Buick Division; the division; a division
　　of General Motors
　Passport; the Division
　but Trinity River division (reclama-
　　tion); the division
Dixie; Dixiecrat
docket No. 66; dockets Nos. 76 and 77
Doctrine, Monroe; the doctrine; *but*
　Truman, Eisenhower doctrine
doctrine, fairness
Document, if part of name; the docu-
　ment:
　Document No. 130
　Document Numbered One Hundred
　　and Thirty

Dominion of Canada, of New Zealand, etc.; the Dominion; *but* British dominions; a dominion; dominion status

drawing II, A, 3, etc.; *but* Drawing 2 when part of title: Drawing 2.—Hydroelectric Power Development

Dust Bowl (see Bowl)

Earth (planet); (see rule 3.30)

East:
  Coast (Africa)
  Europe (political entity)
  Germany (political entity)
  Middle, Mideast (Asia)
  Near (Balkans)
  South Central States
  the East (section of United States); *also* Communist political entity

east:
  Africa
  coast (U.S.)
  Pennsylvania

Eastern:
  Europe (political entity)
  Far (Orient) (see Far East)
  Germany (political entity)
  Gulf States
  Hemisphere (see Hemisphere)
  Middle, Mideastern (Asia)
  North Central States
  Shore (Chesapeake Bay)
  States
  United States

eastern:
  France
  seaboard
  time, eastern standard time (see time)
  Wisconsin

easterner

EE-bond

electoral college; the electors

Elizabethan Age (see Ages)

Emancipation Proclamation (see Proclamation)

Embassy, British, etc.; the Embassy

Emperor, Japanese, etc.; the Emperor

Engine Company, Bethesda; engine company No. 6; No. 6 engine company; the company

Engineer officer, etc. (of Engineer Corps); the Engineers

Engineers, Chief of (Army)

Engineers, Corps of (see Corps)

Envoy Extraordinary and Minister Plenipotentiary; the Envoy; the Minister

Equator, the; equatorial

Establishment, if part of name; the establishment:
  Army
  Army Field
  Defense
  Federal
  Military
  Naval; *but* naval establishments
  Navy
  Postal

Establishment—Continued
  Regular
  Reserve
  Shore
  but civil establishment; legislative establishment

Estate, Girard (a foundation); the estate

estate, third (the commons); fourth (the press); etc.

Eurodollar

European theater of operations; the European theater; the theater

Excellency, His; Their Excellencies

Exchange, New York Stock; the stock exchange; the exchange

Executive (President of United States):
  Chief
  Decree No. 100; Decree 100; *but* Executive decree; direction
  Document No. 95
  Mansion; the mansion; the White House
  Office; the Office
  Order No. 34; Order 34; *but* Executive order
  power

executive:
  agreement   document
  branch   paper
  communication   privilege
  department

exhibit 2, A, II, etc.; *but* Exhibit 2, when part of title: Exhibit 2:[7] Capital Expenditures, 1935–49

Expedition, Byrd; Lewis and Clark; the expedition

Experiment Station (see Station)

Explorer I, etc.

Exposition, California-Pacific International, etc.; the exposition

Express, if part of name: Federal Express, the

Fair Deal

Fair, World's, etc.; the fair; Texas State Fair

fall (season)

Falls, Niagara; the falls

fanciful appellations capitalized:
  Bay State (Massachusetts)
  Big Four (powers, railroad, etc.)
  City of Churches (Brooklyn)
  Fair Deal
  Great Depression
  Great Father (the President)
  Great Society
  Holocaust
  Keystone State (Pennsylvania)
  New Deal
  New Federalism
  New Frontier
  the Hub (Boston)
  Third World

Far East, Far Eastern (the Orient); Far West (U.S.); *but* far western

---

[7] See footnote 2, p. 36.

Farm, if part of name; the farm:
  Johnson Farm; *but* Johnson's farm
  San Diego Farm
  Wild Tiger Farm
Fascist; Fascisti; fascistic; fascism
Father of his Country (Washington)
Fed, the (no period)
Federal (synonym for United States or other sovereign power):
  District (Mexico)
  Establishment
  Government (of any national government)
  grand jury; the grand jury
  land bank (see Bank)
  Register (publication); the Register
  Reserve bank (see Bank)
  Reserve Board, the Board; *also* Federal Reserve System, the System; Federal Reserve Board Regulation W, *but* regulation W
  but a federal form of government
federally
fellow, fellowship (academic); (lowercase with name)
Field, Byrd, Stewart, etc.; the field
fifth column; fifth columnist
figure 2, A, II, etc. (illustration); *but* Figure 2, when part of legend: Figure 2.—Market scenes
firm names:
  A-C Spark Plug Co.
  Allen-A Co.
  Allen B. Du Mont Laboratories
  Allis-Chalmers Manufacturing Co.
  Aluminium, Ltd.
  American Bank Note Co.
  American Telephone & Telegraph Co.
  Appleton-Century-Crofts, Inc.
  Bausch & Lomb Optical Co.
  Beech-Nut Life Savers, Inc.
  Bristol-Myers
  Carson, Pirie, Scott & Co.
  Champion Paper & Fibre Co.
  Chance Vought Aircraft, Inc.
  Chicago & North Western Railway Co.
  Colgate-Palmolive Co.
  Colt's Patent Fire Arms Manufacturing Co.
  Curtiss-Wright Corp.
  Deepfreeze Appliance Division
  De Laval Steam Turbine Co.
  DeVilbiss Co.
  Dillon, Read & Co.
  Dow Jones & Co.
  Dun & Bradstreet
  E.I. du Pont de Nemours & Co.
  Francis I. du Pont & Co.
  Eagle-Picher Co., Inc.
  Electric Auto-Lite Co.
  Fibreboard Paper Products Corp.
  Great Atlantic & Pacific Tea Co. (A&P)
  Grumman Aircraft Engineering Corp.
  Gulf & Western Industries, Inc. (legal)
  Gulf+Western Industries, Inc. (popular)
  Haloid Xerox Inc.

firm names—Continued
  Halsey, Stuart & Co.
  Harris-Intertype Corp.
  Hart Schaffner & Marx
  Houghton Mifflin Co.
  Ingersoll-Rand Co.
  Johns-Manville Corp.
  Kennecott Copper Co.
  R.G. LeTourneau, Inc.
  LeTourneau-Westinghouse Co.
  Libbey-Owens-Ford Glass Co.
  Libby, McNeill & Libby
  Macmillan Co.
  McDonnell Douglas
  Merck Sharp & Dohme Division
  Merrill Lynch, Pierce, Fenner & Smith
  Montgomery Ward & Co.
  Moore-McCormack Lines, Inc.
  Olin Mathieson Chemical Corp.
  Owens-Corning Fiberglas Corp.
  Parke, Davis & Co. *or* Parke-Davis
  Penn Central
  J.C. Penney Co.
  Phelps Dodge Corp.
  Pfizer Inc.
  Price Waterhouse & Co.
  Procter & Gamble Co.
  Proctor-Silex
  Rand McNally & Co.
  Rolls-Royce
  R.R. Donnelley & Sons Co.
  Sears, Roebuck & Co.
  Smith Kline & French Laboratories
  Sperry Rand Corp.
  Sunray-DX Oil Co.
  3M Co.
  Trans World Airlines
  Underwriters' Laboratories
  Weyerhaeuser
First Family (Presidential)
First Lady (wife of President)
First World War (see War)
flag code
flag, U.S.:
  Old Flag, Old Glory
  Stars and Stripes
  Star-Spangled Banner
flags, foreign:
  Tricolor (French)
  Union Jack (British)
  United Nations
Fleet, if part of name; the fleet:
  Atlantic
  Channel
  Grand
  High Seas
  Marine Force
  Naval Reserve
  Pacific, etc. (naval)
  6th Fleet, etc.
  U.S.
floor (House or Senate)
flyway; Canadian flyway, etc.
Force(s), if part of name; the force(s):
  Active Forces
  Air (see also Air Force)

Force(s)—Continued
  All Volunteer
  Armed Forces (synonym for overall U.S. Military Establishment)
  Army Field Forces; the Field Forces
  Fleet Marine
  Navy Battle (see Navy)
  Navy Scouting (see Navy); Reserve Force
  Rapid Deployment
  7th Task; the task force; *but* task force report (Hoover Commission)
  United Nations Emergency; the Emergency Force; the Force; *but* United Nations police force
foreign cabinets:
  Foreign Office; the Office
  Minister of Foreign Affairs; the Minister
  Ministry of Foreign Affairs; the Ministry
  Premier
  Prime Minister
Foreign Legion (French); the legion
Foreign Service; the Service:
  officer
  Officer Corps; the corps
  Reserve officer; the Reserve officer
  Reserve Officer Corps; the Reserve Corps; the corps
  Staff officer; the Staff officer
  Staff Officer Corps; the Staff Corps; the corps
Forest, if part of name; the national forest; the forest:
  Angeles National
  Black
  Coconino and Prescott National Forests
  but State and National forests (see System)
Forester (Chief of Forest Service); the Chief; *also* Chief Forester
form 2, A, II, etc.; *but* Form 2, when part of title: Form 1040:[8] Individual Income Tax Return; *but* withholding tax form
Fort McHenry, etc.; the fort
Foundation, if part of name; capitalized standing alone if referring to Federal unit:
  Chemical; the foundation
  Ford; the foundation
  Infantile Paralysis; the foundation
  National Science; the foundation
  Russell Sage; the foundation
Founding Fathers (colonial)
four freedoms
free world
Frisco (for San Francisco; no apostrophe)
Fritalux (see alliances)
Fund, if part of name; capitalized standing alone if referring to international or United Nations fund:
  Common Market

Fund—Continued
  Development Loan Fund; the Fund (U.S. Government corporation)
  International Monetary
  Rockefeller Endowment; the fund
  Special Projects (United Nations)
  but civil service retirement fund; mutual security fund; national service life insurance fund; revolving fund

Gadsden Purchase
Gallery of Art, National (see National)
Gallup Poll; the poll
Geiger counter
General Board (of Navy) (see Board)
General Order No. 14; General Orders No. 14; a general order
General Schedule
gentile
Geographer, the (State Department)
geographic terms (terms, such as those listed below,[9] are capitalized if part of name; lowercased are in general sense (rivers of Virginia and Maryland) (see also Geologic Terms, p. 227):

Archipelago	Crater
Area	Creek
Arroyo	Crossroads
Atoll	Current (ocean feature)
Bank	
Bar	Cut
Basin, Upper	Cutoff
(Lower) Colorado River, etc. (legal entity); *but* Hansen flood-control basin; Missouri River basin (drainage); upper Colorado River storage project	Dam
	Delta
	Desert
	Divide
	Dome (not geologic)
	Draw (stream)
	Dune
	Escarpment
Bay	Estuary
Bayou	Falls
Beach	Fault
Bench	Flat(s)
Bend	Floodway
Bight	Ford
Bluff	Forest
Bog	Fork (stream)
Borough (boro)	Gap
Bottom	Geyser
Branch (stream)	Glacier
Brook	Glen
Butte	Gorge
Canal; the canal (Panama)	Gulch
	Gulf
Canyon	Gut
Cape	Harbor
Cascade	Head
Cave	Hill
Cavern	Hogback
Channel; *but* Mississippi River channel(s)	Hollow
	Hook
	Hot Spring
Cirque	Icefield
Coulee	Ice Shelf
Cove	Inlet
Crag	Island
	Isle

9 List compiled with cooperation of the U.S. Board on Geographic Names.

geographic terms—Continued

Islet	Port (water body)
Keys (Florida only)	Prairie
Knob	Range (mountain)
Lagoon	Rapids
Lake	Ravine
Landing	Reef
Ledge	Reservoir
Lowland	Ridge
Marsh	River
Massif	Roads (anchorage)
Mesa	Rock
Monument	Run (stream)
Moraine	Sea
Mound	Seaway
Mount	Shoal
Mountain	Sink
Narrows	Slough
Neck	Sound
Needle	Spit
Notch	Spring
Oasis	Spur
Ocean	Strait
Oxbow	Stream
Palisades	Summit
Park	Swamp
Pass	Terrace
Passage	Thoroughfare
Peak	Trench
Peninsula	Trough
Plain	Valley
Plateau	Volcano
Point	Wash
Pond	Waterway
Pool	Woods

Geological Survey (see Survey)
GI bill of rights
Girl Scouts (organization); a Girl Scout; a Scout; Scouting
G-man
Gold Star Mothers (see American)
Golden Age (see Ages)
Golden Rule
Gospel, if referring to the first four books of the New Testament; *but* gospel truth
Government:
    British, Soviet, etc.; the Government
    Canal Zone; the government
    department, officials, -owned, publications, etc. (U.S. Government)
    National and State Governments
    Printing Office (see Office)
    U.S.; National; Federal
government:
    Churchill
    Communist
    District (of Columbia)
    European governments
    Federal, State, and municipal governments
    insular; island
    military
    seat of
    State
    State and Provincial governments
    Territorial
governmental

Governor:
    of Louisiana, etc.; the Governor; a Governor; State Governor(s); Governors' conference
    of Puerto Rico; the Governor
    of the Federal Reserve Board; the Governor
Governor General of Canada; the Governor General
grade, market (see market grades)
grand jury (see Federal)
Grange, the (National)
graph 2, A, II, etc.; *but* Graph 2, when part of title: Graph 2.—Production levels
Great:
    Basin
    Beyond
    Depression
    Divide
    Father (see fanciful appellations)
    Lakes; the lakes; lake(s) traffic
    Plains; *but* southern Great Plains
    Rebellion (see Rebellion)
    Seal
    Society
    War (see War)
    White Way (New York City)
great circle (navigation)
Greater Los Angeles, Greater New York
gross national product (GNP)
Group:
    Military Advisory Group; the group
    Standing (see Organization)
group 2, II, A, etc.; *but* Group 2, when part of title: Group II:[10] List of Counties by States
guaranteed annual wage (GAW)
Guard, National (see National)
guardsman (see Coast Guard; National Guard)
Gulf:
    Coast States; *but* gulf coast of Mexico; the gulf
    States
    Stream; the stream

Hall (U.S. Senate or House)
Halls of Congress
H-bomb; H-hour
Headquarters:
    Alaska Command; the command headquarters
    4th Regiment Headquarters; regimental headquarters
    32d Division Headquarters; the division headquarters
hearing examiner (now administrative law judge)
Heaven (Deity); heaven (place)
Hells (no apostrophe) Canyon
Hemisphere, Eastern; Western; etc.; the hemisphere
High Church
High Commissioner

---

[10] See footnote 2, p. 36.

High Court (see Supreme Court)
High School, if part of name: Western; the high school
Highway Bridge (Washington, DC); the bridge
Highway No. 40; Route 40; State Route 9; the highway
Hill (the Capitol)
His Excellency the Duke of Argyll, etc.; His Excellency; Their Excellencies
His Majesty; Her Majesty; Their Majesties
Hispanic
historic events and epochs:
  Reformation, the
  Renaissance, the
  Restoration, the (English)
  Revolution of July (French)
  Revolution, the (American, 1775; French, 1789; English, 1688)
holidays and some special days:
  Admission Day
  All Fools' (April Fools') Day
  Arbor Day
  Armed Forces Day
  Christmas Day, Eve
  Columbus Day
  D-day; D-plus-4-day
  Father's Day
  Flag Day
  Founders' Day
  Fourth of July
  Halloween
  Hanukkah
  Hogmanay
  Inauguration Day (Federal)
  Independence Day (Fourth of July)
  Labor Day
  Lincoln's Birthday
  Lord's day
  M-day (mobilization day)
  Memorial Day (also Decoration Day)
  Mother's Day
  New Year's Day, Eve
  Rosh Hashanah
  Thanksgiving Day
  V–E Day; V–J Day
  Veterans (no apostrophe) Day
  Washington's Birthday
  Yom Kippur
  but election day; primary day
Holy Scriptures; Holy Writ (Bible)
Home (see Naval; Soldiers')
Hospital, if part of name; the hospital:
  District of Columbia General
  5th Regiment
  Freedmen's
  St. Elizabeths (no apostrophe)
  but naval (marine or Army) hospital
hospital corpsman (see corpsman)
House, if part of name:
  Johnson house (private residence)
  Lee (hotel); the house
  of Representatives; the House (U.S.)
  of the Woods (palace); the house
  Office Building (see Building)
  Ohio (State); the house

House—Continued
  but both Houses; lower (or upper) House (Congress)
House of Representatives (U.S.), titles of officers standing alone capitalized:
  Chairman (Committee of the Whole)
  Chaplain
  Clerk; but legislative clerk, etc.
  Doorkeeper
  Official Reporter(s) of Debates
  Parliamentarian
  Postmaster
  Sergeant at Arms
  Speaker pro tempore
  Speaker; speakership
HUD (Department of Housing and Urban Development)
Hudson's Bay Co.
Hurricane Alexander, Brenda, Curtis, etc.

ice age (see Ages)
Indians:
  Absentee Shawnee
  Alaska (see Native)
  Eastern (or Lower) Band of Cherokee; the band
  Five Civilized Tribes; the tribes
  Shawnee Tribe; the tribe
  Six Nations (Iroquois Confederacy)
Inquisition, Spanish; the Inquisition
inspector general
Institute, if part of name; capitalized standing alone if referring to Federal or international organization:
  National Cancer; the Cancer Institute; the Institute
  National Institutes of Health; the Institutes
  of International Law; the Institute
  Woman's Institute; the institute
Institution, if part of name; capitalized standing alone if referring to Federal unit:
  Brookings; the institution
  Carnegie; the institution
  Smithsonian; the Institution
insular government; island government
intercoastal waterway (see waterway)
interdepartmental
International Court of Justice; the Court
international:
  banks (see Bank)
  dateline
  boundary
  law
  Morse code (see Code)
Interstate 95; I–95; the interstate
Intracoastal Waterway; the waterway (see also waterway)
intrastate
Irish potato
Iron Cross (see decorations)
Iron Curtain; the curtain
Isthmian Canal (see Canal)
Isthmus of Panama; the isthmus
Ivory Coast

Japan Current (see Current)
Jersey cattle
Jim Crow law, car, etc.
Job Corps
Joint Chiefs of Staff; Chiefs of Staff
Joint Committee on Printing (see Committee)
Journal clerk; the clerk
Journal (House or Senate)
Judge Advocate General, the
judge; chief judge; circuit judge; district judge; *but* Judge Bryan
Justice; Justice O'Connor
judiciary, the

Kennedy round
King of England, etc.; the King
Koran, the; Koranic
K-ration
Ku Klux Klan; the Klan

Laboratory, if part of name; capitalized standing alone if referring to Federal unit: Forest Products; the Laboratory; *but* laboratory (non-Federal)
Lake: Erie, of the Woods, Salt; the lake
Lane, if part of name: Maiden; the lane
Latter-day Saints
law, Walsh-Healey, etc.; law 176; law No. 176; copyright law; Ohm's, etc.
League, Urban; the league
Legation, Finnish, etc.; the Legation
Legion:
    American; the Legion; a Legionnaire; French Foreign; the legion
Legislative Assembly, if part of name: of New York; of Puerto Rico, etc.; the legislative assembly; the assembly
legislative branch, clerk, session, etc.
Legislature:
    National Legislature (U.S. Congress); the Legislature
    Ohio Legislature; Legislature of Ohio; the State legislature; the legislature
Letters Patent No. 378,964; *but* patent No. 378,964; letters patent
Liberty Bell; Liberty ship
Librarian of Congress; the Librarian
Library:
    Army; the library
    Harry S. Truman; the library
    of Congress; the Library
    Hillsborough Public; the library
Lieutenant Governor of Idaho, etc.; the Lieutenant Governor
Light, if part of name; the light:
    Boston
    Buffalo South Pier Light 2; *but* light No. 2; light 2
    but Massachusetts Bay lights
Lighthouse (see Light Station)
Lightship, if part of name; the lightship:
    Grays Reef Lightship
    North Manitou Shoal Lightship
Light Station, if part of name; the light station; the station:
    Minots Ledge Light Station
    Watch Hill Light Station

Line(s), if part of name; the line(s):
    Burlington Lines (railroad)
    Greyhound Line (bus)
    Holland-America Line (steamship)
    Maginot (fortification)
line:
    DEW (Distant Early Warning)
    Mason-Dixon line *or* Mason and Dixon's line
    Pinetree
    State
Little Inch; Big Inch (pipelines)
Local: Teamsters Local Union No. 15; *but* local No. 15
local time, local standard time (see time)
Loop, the (see cities)
Louisiana Purchase
Low Church
Lower, if part of name:
    California (Mexico)
    Colorado River Basin
    Egypt
    Peninsula (of Michigan)
lower:
    48 (States)
    House of Congress
    Mississippi

Mafia
Magna Carta
Majesty, His, Her (see His Majesty)
Majority Leader Baker; *but* the majority leader (U.S. Congress)
Mall, The (District of Columbia)
Mansion, Executive (see Executive)
map 3, A, II, etc.; *but* Map 2, when part of title: Map 2.—Railroads of Middle Atlantic States
mariculture
Marine Corps; the corps:
    Marines (the corps); *but* marines (individuals)
    Organized Reserve; the Reserve
    also a marine; a woman marine; the women marines (individuals); soldiers, sailors, coastguardsmen, and marines
Maritime Provinces (Canada) (see Province)
market grades and classes:
    U.S. grade A
    barley: Western, Mixed, Malting Two-rowed
    beans: Red Kidney, U.S. No. 2 Pea
    cattle: Prime, Choice, Good
    corn: Yellow, White, Mixed, Dent
    cotton: Middling, Strict Good Ordinary, Strict Low Middling, Good Ordinary, etc.
    hay: Timothy Light Clover Mixed, Upland Prairie
    oats: White, Red, Mixed
    soybeans: Yellow, Black, Mixed
    tobacco: Flue-cured, Fire-cured, Cigar-wrapper

market grades and classes—Continued
wheat: Hard Red Spring, Red Durum, Durum, Hard Red Winter, White, Mixed, etc.
wool: Grade 60's or one-half blood
Marshal (see Supreme Court)
marshall (U.S.)
medals (see decorations)
medicaid
Medicare Act; medicare plan
Member, if referring to Senator, Representative, Delegate, or Resident Commissioner of U.S. Congress; *also* Member at Large; Member of Parliament, etc.; *but* membership; member of U.S. congressional committee
Merchant Marine Reserve; the Reserve; *but* U.S. merchant marine; the merchant marine
Metroliner
Metropolitan Washington, etc.; *but* Washington metropolitan area
midcontinent region
Middle Ages (see Ages)
Middle Atlantic States
Middle East; Mideast; Mideastern; Middle Eastern (Asia)
middle Europe
Middle West, Midwest (section of United States)
Middle Western States; Midwestern States; *but* midwestern farmers, etc.
Midsouth (section of United States)
milepost N452, etc.
Military Academy (see Academy)
Military Establishment (see Establishment)
Militia, if part of name; the militia:
1st Regiment Ohio
Indiana
Naval
of Ohio
Organized
milkshed, Ohio, etc. (region)
Minister Plenipotentiary; the Minister; Minister Without Portfolio (see also foreign cabinets)
Ministry (see foreign cabinets)
Minority Leader Byrd; *but* the minority leader (U.S. Congress)
Mint, Philadelphia, etc.; the mint
minutemen (colonial)
missiles: capitalize such missile names as Hawk, Hound Dog, Redeye, etc.; *but* cruise missile, surface-to-air missile, air-to-air missile, etc.
Mission, if part of name; the mission:
Gospel Mission
Mission 66
but diplomatic mission; military mission; Jones mission
Monument:
Bunker Hill; the monument
Grounds; the grounds (Washington Monument)
National (see National)

Monument—Continued
Washington; the monument (District of Columbia)
Moon (see rule 3.30)
Mountain States
mountain time, mountain standard time (see time)
Mr. Chairman; Mr. Secretary; etc.
Museum, capitalize with name; the museum:
Army Medical; the Medical Museum
Field
National
National Air; the Air Museum

Nation (synonym for United States); *but* a nation; nationwide; *also* French nation, Balkan nations
Nation, Creek; Osage; etc.; the nation
nation, in general, standing alone
National, in conjunction with capitalized name:
Academy of Sciences (see Academy)
and State institutions, etc.
Archives, the (see The)
Capital (Washington); the Capital
Endowment for the Arts; the Endowment
Forest (see Forest)
Gallery of Art; the National Gallery; the gallery
Grange; the Grange
Guard, Ohio, etc.; Air National; the National Guard; the Guard; a guardsman; *but* a National Guard man; National Guardsman
Institute (see Institute)
Legislature (see Legislature)
Monument, Muir, etc.; the national monument; the monument
Museum (see Museum)
Naval Medical Center (Bethesda, MD)
Park, Yellowstone, etc.; Yellowstone Park; the national park; the park
Treasury; the Treasury
War College
Woman's Party; the party
Zoological Park (see Zoological)
national:
agency check (NAC)
anthem, customs, spirit, etc.
British, Mexican, etc.
defense agencies
stockpile
water policy
Native, Alaska; *but* Ohio native, etc. (see Alaska)
Naval, if part of name:
Academy (see Academy)
Base, Guam Naval; the naval base
District, 1st Naval (see District)
Establishment (see Establishment)
Home (Philadelphia); the home
Militia; the militia
Observatory (see Observatory)
Potomac River Naval Command (see Command)

Naval—Continued
  Reserve; the Reserve; a reservist
  Reserve Force; the force
  Reserve officer; a Reserve officer
  Shipyard (if preceding or following
    name): Brooklyn Naval Shipyard;
    Naval Shipyard, Brooklyn; *but* the
    naval shipyard
  Station (if preceding or following
    name): Key West Naval Station;
    Naval Station, Key West; the sta-
    tion
  Volunteer Naval Reserve
  War College; the War College; the col-
    lege
naval, in general sense:
  command (see Command)
  district (see District)
  expenditures, maneuvers, officer, serv-
    ice, stores, etc.
  petroleum reserves; *but* Naval Petro-
    leum Reserve No. 2 (Buena Vista
    Hills Naval Reserve); reserve No. 2
navel orange
Navy, American or foreign, if part of
    name; capitalized standing alone
    only if referring to U.S. Navy:
  Admiral of the; the admiral
  Battle Force; the Battle Force; the
    force
  Establishment; the establishment
  Hospital Corps; hospital corpsman;
    the corps
  Regular
  regulation 56
  Scouting Force; the scouting force; the
    force
  Seabees (construction battalion); a
    Seabee
  7th Task Force (see Force)
navy yard
Nazi; nazism
Near East (Balkans, etc.)
Negro; Negress (see black)
New Deal; anti-New Deal
New, if part of name: New Willard
New England States
New World
Nine Power Treaty; the treaty
North:
  Atlantic
  Atlantic Pact (see Pact)
  Atlantic States
  Atlantic Treaty (see Treaty)
  Atlantic Treaty Organization (NATO)
    (see Organization)
  Equatorial Current (see Current)
  Korea
  Pole
  Slope (Alaska)
  Star (Polaris)
  the North (section of United States)
north:
  Africa
  Ohio, Virginia, etc.
north-central region, etc.
Northeast corridor
northern Ohio

Northern States
northerner
Northwest Pacific
Northwest Territory (1799)
Northwest, the (section of United States)
Northwest Washington (see cities)
Northwestern:
  States
  United States
numbers capitalized if spelled out as
    part of a name:
  Air Force One (Presidential plane)
  Charles the First
  Committee of One Hundred
  Nineteenth Census (see Census)

Observatory, capitalized with name:
  Astrophysical; the Observatory
  Lick; the observatory (nongovernmen-
    tal)
  Naval; the Observatory
Occident, the; occidental
Ocean, if part of name; the ocean:
  Antarctic
  Arctic
  Atlantic
  North Atlantic, etc.
  Pacific
  South Pacific, etc.
  Southwest Pacific, etc.
Oceanographer (the Hydrographer),
    Navy
Office, if referring to unit of Federal
    Government; the Office:
  Executive
  Foreign (see foreign cabinets)
  General Accounting; the Accounting
    Office; the Office
  Government Printing; the Printing
    Office; the Office
  Naval Oceanographic
  of Alien Property
  of Chief of Naval Operations
  of General Counsel
  of Management and Budget
  of the Secretary (Defense); Secretary's
    Office
  Patent
  but New York regional office (includ-
    ing branch, division, or section
    therein); the regional office; the
    office
officer:
  Army
  Marine; *but* naval and marine officers
  Navy; Navy and Marine officers
  Regular Army; Regular; a Regular
  Reserve
  WAC, WAVE
Old Dominion (Virginia)
Old South
Old World
Olympic games; Olympiad; XXIII Olym-
    pic games
Operation Deep Freeze, Snowdrop, etc.;
    but Deep Freeze operation

Order of Business No. 56 (congressional calendar)

Ordnance:
  Corps (see Corps)
  Department; the Department
  Depot (see Depot)

Organization, if part of name; capitalized standing alone if referring to international unit:
  International Labor
  North Atlantic Treaty (NATO):
    Chiefs of Staff
    Committee of Defense Ministers
    Council
    Council of Foreign Ministers
    Defense Committee
    Military Committee
    Military Production and Supply Board
    Mutual Defense Assistance Program
    Pact (see Pact)
    Regional Planning Group; the Group
    Standing Group; the Group
  of American States (formerly Pan American Union)
  United Nations Educational, Scientific, and Cultural Organization (Unesco©) (formerly UNESCO)

Organized:
  Marine Corps Reserve; Marine Reserve; the Reserve
  Militia; the militia
  Naval Militia; the Naval Militia; the militia
  Reserve Corps; the Reserve

Orient, the; oriental

Outer Continental Shelf (see Continental)

Pacific (see also Atlantic):
  coast
  Coast (or slope) States
  Northwest
  seaboard
  slope
  South
  States
  time, Pacific standard time (see time) but cispacific; transpacific

Pact, capitalized with name; lowercased standing alone:
  Atlantic; Atlantic Defense
  Baghdad
  Four Power
  Kellogg
  North Atlantic; North Atlantic Defense

pan-American games; but Pan American Day

Pan American Union (see Organization of American States)

Panel, the Federal Service Impasses (Federal), etc.; the Panel

Panhandle of Texas; Texas Panhandle; the panhandle; etc.

papers, Woodrow Wilson, etc.; the papers; but white paper

Parish, Caddo, etc.; but parish of Caddo (Louisiana civil division); the parish

Park, Fairmount, etc.; the park (see also National)

Park Police, U.S.; park policeman

Park, Zoological (see Zoological)

Parkway, George Washington Memorial; the memorial parkway; the parkway

Parliament, Houses of; the Parliament

Parliamentarian (U.S. Senate or House)

part 2, A, II, etc.; but Part 2, when part of title: Part 2: [11] Iron and Steel Industry

Pass, Brenner, capitalized if part of name; the pass

patent (see Letters Patent)

Patrol, U.S. Border

Peninsula Upper (Lower) (Michigan); the peninsula

Penitentiary, Albany, etc.; the penitentiary

petrodollar

phase 2; phase I

Philippine Republic (see Republic)

Pilgrim Fathers (1620); the Pilgrims; a Pilgrim

Place, if part of name: Jefferson Place; the place

Plains (Great Plains), the

plan:
  Colombo
  controlled materials
  5-year
  Marshall (European Recovery Program)
  Reorganization Plan No. 6 (Hoover Commission); plan No. 1

Planetarium, Fels, Hayden; the planetarium

Plant, Rockford Arsenal; the plant; but United States Steel plant

plate 2, A, II, etc.; but Plate 2, when part of title: Plate 2.—Rural Structures

Plaza, Union Station (Washington, DC); the plaza

Pledge of Allegiance

Point 4 Program; point 4

Pole: North, South; the pole; subpolar

Pole Star (Polaris); polar star

Police, if part of name; the police:
  Capitol
  Park, U.S.
  White House

political action committee (PAC)

political parties and adherents (Party, if part of name; the party):
  Communist; a Communist; a Commie
  Conservative; a Conservative
  Democratic; a Democrat
  Independent; an Independent
  Liberal; a Liberal
  Libertarian; a Libertarian
  National Woman's; Woman's Party

---

[11] See footnote 2, p. 36.

political parties—Continued
  Progressive; a Progressive
  Republican; Grand Old Party; *but*
    grand old Republican Party; a Re-
    publican
  Socialist; a Socialist
Pool, Northwest Power, etc.; the pool
Pope; *but* papal, patriarch, pontiff, pri-
  mate
Port, if part of name; Port of Norfolk;
  Norfolk Port; the port (see Authori-
  ty)
Post Office, Chicago, etc.
P.O. Box (with number); *but* post office
  box (in general sense)
Postal Union (see Union)
Postmaster General
Powers, if part of name; the powers (see
  also alliances):
  Allied (World Wars I and II)
  Axis (World War I)
  Big Four
  Western
  but European powers
precinct; first, 11th precinct
Premier (see foreign cabinets)
Preserve, Wichita National Forest
  Game, etc.; Wichita Game Preserve;
  Wichita preserve
Presidency (office of head of Govern-
  ment)
President:
  of the United States; the Executive;
  the Chief Magistrate; the Commander
    in Chief; the President-elect; ex-
    President; former President; also
    preceding name
  of any other country; the President
    of Federal or international unit
  but president of the Erie Railroad;
    president of the Federal Reserve
    Bank of New York
Presidential assistant, authority, order,
  proclamation, candidate, election,
  timber, year, etc.
Prime Minister (see foreign cabinets)
Prison, Auburn, etc.; the prison
Privy Council, Her Majesty's (see Coun-
  cil)
Prize, Nobel, Pulitzer, etc.; the prize
Proclamation, Emancipation; Presiden-
  tial Proclamation No. 24; Proclama-
  tion No. 24; the proclamation; *but*
  Presidential proclamation
Program, if part of name. Examples:
  European Recovery
  Food-for-Peace
  Mutual Assistance
  Mutual Defense Assistance
  Point 4
  Social Security
  Universal Military Training
project:
  Central Valley
  Manhattan
  McNary Dam
  Rochester atomic energy
  University of California atomic energy

Project Farside, Sidewinder, Vanguard,
  etc.; *but* Vanguard project
Project Head Start
proposition 13
Prosecutor; Special Prosecutor (Federal)
Province, Provincial, if referring to an
  administrative subdivision: Ontario
  Province; Province of Ontario; Mari-
  time Provinces (Canada); the Prov-
  ince
Proving Ground, Aberdeen, etc.; the
  proving ground
Public Act 26; Public Law 9; Public 37;
  Public Resolution 3; *but* public
  enemy No. 1
Public Printer; the Government Printer;
  the Printer
public utility district (see District)
Pueblo, Santa Clara; the pueblo
Puerto Rico:
  government
  Governor of; the Governor
  Legislative Assembly of: the legisla-
    tive assembly
  Provisional Regiment; *but* Puerto Rico
    regiment
  Resident Comissioner
Purchase, Gadsden, Louisiana, etc.
Puritan; puritanical

Quad Cities (Davenport, Rock Island,
  Moline, and East Moline)

Radio Free Europe
Railroad, Alaska; the Railroad
Ranch, King, etc.; the ranch
Range Cascade, etc. (mountains); the
  range
Rebellion, if part of name; the rebellion:
  Boxer
  Great (Civil War)
  War of the
  Whisky
Reconstruction period (post-Civil War)
Red army
Red Cross, American (see American)
Reds, the; a Red (political)
Reformation, the
Reformatory, Elmira, etc.; the reforma-
  tory
Refuge, Blackwater Migratory Bird, etc.;
  Blackwater Bird Refuge; Black-
  water refuge
region, north-central, etc.; first region,
  10th region; region 7 (see rule
  12.10); midcontinent
Register of the Treasury; the Register
Regular Army, Navy; a Regular (see
  also officer)
regulation:
  ceiling price regulation 8
  56 (Navy)
  supplementary regulation 22
  Veterans Regulation 8; *but* veterans
    regulations
  W (see also Federal Reserve Board)
Reign of Terror (France, 1792)

religious terms:
  Bahai
  Baptist
  Brahman
  Buddhist
  Catholic; Catholicism; *but* catholic (universal)
  Christian
  Christian Science
  Evangelical United Brethren
  Hebrew
  Latter-day Saints
  Mohammedan
  New Thought
  Protestant; Protestantism
  Seventh-day Adventists
  Seventh-Day Baptists
  Zoroastrian
Renaissance, the (era)
reorganization plan (see plan)
Report, if part of name (with date or number); the annual report; the report:
  Annual Report of the Secretary of Defense for the year ended September 30, 1981
  1981 Report of the Chief of the Forest Service
  President's Economic Report; the Economic Report
  Report No. 31
  Railroad Retirement Board Annual Report, 1981; *but* annual report of the Railroad Retirement Board
  17th Annual Report of the Public Printer; *but* 17th annual report
  United States Reports (publication)
Reporter, the (U.S. Supreme Court)
Representative; Representative at Large (U.S. Congress); U.N.
Republic, capitalized if part of name; capitalized standing alone if referring to a specific government:
  French
  Irish
  of Panama
  of the Philippines; Philippine Republic
  United States
  also the American Republics; South American Republics; the Latin American Republics; the Republics
Reservation (forest, military, or Indian), if part of name; the reservation:
  Great Sioux
  Hill Military
Reserve, if part of name; the Reserve (see also Air Force; Army Corps; Foreign Service; Marine Corps; Merchant Marine; Naval):
  Active
  Air Force
  Army
  bank (see Bank)
  Board, Federal (see Federal)
  city (see Bank)
  Civil Air Patrol
  components

Reserve—Continued
  Enlisted
  Establishment
  Inactive
  Naval
  officer
  Officers' Training Corps
  Ready
  Retired
  Strategic
  Standby
  Volunteer Naval
  Women's (see Women's Reserve)
Reserves, the; reservist
Resident Commissioner (see Member; Puerto Rico)
Resolution, with number; the resolution:
  House Joint Resolution 3
  Public Resolution 6
  Resolution 42
  Senate Concurrent Resolution 18
  but Tonkin resolution
Revised Statutes (U.S.); Supplement to the Revised Statutes; the statutes
Revolution, Revolutionary (if referring to the American, French, or English Revolution) (see also War)
Road, if part of name: Benning; the road
Roman numerals, common nouns used with, not capitalized:
  book II; chapter II; part II; etc.
  but Book II:[12] Modern Types (complete heading); Part XI:[12] Early Thought (complete heading)
route No. 12466; mail route 1742; railway mail route 1144; *but* Route 40, State Route 9 (highways)
Royal Decree No. 24; Decree 24; the royal decree
rule 21; rule XXI; *but* Rule 21, when part of title: Rule 21:[12] Renewal of Motion
Ruler of the Universe (Deity)
Rules:
  of the House of Representatives; *but* rules of the House
  Standing Rules of the Senate (publication); *but* rules of the Senate
  also Commission rules

Sabbath; Sabbath Day
sanitary district (see District)
savings bond (see bond)
schedule 2, A, II, etc.; *but* Schedule 2, when part of title; Schedule 2:[12] Open and Prepay Stations
School, if part of name; the school:
  any school of U.S. Armed Forces
  Hayes
  Pawnee Indian
  Public School 13; P.S. 13
school district (see District)
Scriptures; Holy Scriptures (the Bible)
Seabees (see Navy)
seaboard, Atlantic, eastern, etc.

---

[12] See footnote 2, p. 36.

seasons:
  autumn (fall)
  spring
  summer
  winter
seaway (see geographic terms; Authority; Corporation)
Second World War (see War)
Secretariat (see United Nations)
Secretaries of the Army and the Navy;
  but Secretaries of the military departments; secretaryship
Secretary, head of national governmental unit:
  of Defense; of State; etc.; the Secre-
    tary
  of State for Foreign Affairs (British);
    for the Colonies; etc.; the Secretary
    of the Smithsonian Institution; the
    Secretary
  also the Assistant Secretary; the Ex-
    ecutive Secretary
  but secretary of the Interstate Com-
    merce Commission; secretary of
    state of Iowa
Secretary General: the Secretary Gener-
  al:
  Organization of American States
  South Pacific Commission
  United Nations
section 2, A, II, etc.; *but* Section 2, when
  part of title: Section 2:[13] Test Con-
  struction Theory
Selective Service (see Service; System)
Senate (U.S.), title of officers standing
  alone capitalized:
  Chaplain
  Chief Clerk
  Doorkeeper
  Official Reporter(s)
  Parliamentarian
  Postmaster
  President of the
  President pro tempore
  Presiding Officer
  Secretary
  Sergeant at Arms
Senate, Ohio (State); the senate
Senator (U.S. Congress); *but* lowercased
  if referring to a State senator,
  unless preceding a name
senatorial
Sergeant at Arms (U.S. Senate or
  House)
Sermon on the Mount
Service, if referring to Federal unit; the
  Service:
  Customs (formerly Customs Bureau)
  Employment
  Extension
  Fish and Wildlife
  Foreign (see Foreign Service)
  Forest
  Immigration and Naturalization
  Internal Revenue
  Mediation and Conciliation

Service—Continued
  National Park
  Postal
  Secret (Treasury)
  Selective (see also System); *but* selec-
    tive service, in general sense; selec-
    tive service classification 1–A, 4–F,
    etc.
  Soil Conservation
service:
  airmail
  Army
  city delivery
  consular
  customs (see Service)
  diplomatic
  employment (State)
  extension (State)
  general delivery
  naval
  Navy
  parcel post
  postal field
  railway mail (see Division)
  rural free delivery; rural delivery;
    free delivery
  special delivery
  star route
Shelf, Continental (see Continental)
ship of state (unless personified)
Sister(s) (adherent of religious order)
Six Nations (see Indians)
Smithsonian Institution (see Institution)
Social Security Administration, application, check, pension, etc.
Socialist; socialism; socialistic (see also
  political parties)
Society, if part of name; the society:
  American Cancer Society, Inc.
  Boston Medical
  of the Cincinnati
soil bank
soil classifications:

Alpine Meadow	Prairie
Bog	Ramann's Brown
Brown	Red
Chernozem (Black)	Rendzina
Chestnut	Sierozem (Gray)
Desert	Solonchak
Gray-Brown Podzo-	Solonetz
lic	Soloth
Half Bog	Terra Rossa
Laterite	Tundra
Pedalfer	Wiesenboden
Pedocal	Yellow
Podzol	

Soldiers' Home, if part of name: Ohio
  Soldiers' Home; the soldiers' home;
  etc.
Solicitor for the Department of Com-
  merce, etc.; the Solicitor
Solicitor General (Department of Jus-
  tice)
Son of Man (Christ)
Sons of the American Revolution (orga-
  nization); a Son; a Real Son
South:
  American Republics (see Republic)

---

[13] See footnote 2, p. 36.

South—Continued
  American States
  Atlantic
  Atlantic States
  Deep South (U.S.)
  Korea
  Midsouth (U.S.)
  Pacific
  Pole
  the South (section of United States);
    Southland
Southeast Asia
southern California, southeastern Cali-
  fornia, etc.
Southern States
Southern United States
southerner
Southwest, the (section of United States)
Soviet (see U.S.S.R.)
space shuttle; the shuttle
Spanish-American War (see War)
Special Order No. 12; Special Orders,
  No. 12; a special order
Spirit of '76 (painting); *but* spirit of '76
  (in general sense)
sputnik; *but* Sputnik I, etc.
Square, Lafayette, etc.; the square
Staff, Foreign Service (see Foreign Service); Air
Staked Plain
standard time (see time)
Star of Bethlehem
Star-Spangled Banner (see flag)
State:
  government
  legislature (see Legislature)
  line, Iowa, Ohio-Indiana, etc.
  New York
  of Israel
  of Pennsylvania
  of Veracruz
  of the Union Message/Address
  out-of-State (adjective); *but* out-of-
    stater
  prison
  rights; States rights
  Vatican City
state:
  and church
  of the art: state-of-the-art technology
  statehood, statehouse, stateside,
    statewide
  downstate, tristate, upstate, instate,
    substate, multistate
  welfare
State's attorney
state's evidence
States:
  Arab
  Balkan
  Baltic
  communistic
  Eastern; *but* eastern industrial States
  East North Central
  East South Central
  Eastern Gulf
  Eastern North Central, etc.
  Far Western

States—Continued
  Gulf; Gulf Coast
  Lake
  Latin American
  lower 48
  Middle
  Middle Atlantic
  Middle Western
  Midwestern
  Mountain
  New England
  North Atlantic
  Northwestern, etc.
  Organization of American
  Pacific
  Pacific Coast
  rights
  South American
  South Atlantic
  Southern
  the six States of Australia; a foreign
    state
  Thirteen Original; original 13 States
  Western; *but* western Gulf; western
    farming States
Station, if part of name; the station; not
  capitalized if referring to surveying
  or similar work:
  Grand Central
  Key West Naval (see Naval)
  Nebraska Experiment Station; Experi-
    ment Station, Nebraska; Nebraska
    station
  Syracuse Air Force
  television station WSYR–TV
  Union; Union Depot; the depot
  WRC station; station WRC; radio sta-
    tion WRC; broadcasting station
    WRC
station 9; substation A
Statue of Liberty; the statue
Statutes at Large (U.S.) (see also Re-
  vised Statutes)
stockpile, national
stone age (see Ages)
Stream, Gulf (see Gulf; Geographic
  terms)
Street, if part of name; the street:
  I Street (not Eye)
  Fifteen-and-a-Half
  110th Street
subcommittee (see Committee)
Subtreasury, New York, etc.; subtreas-
  ury at New York; the subtreasury
subtropical, subtropic(s) (see tropical)
summit meeting
Sun (see rule 3.30)
Superintendent, if referring to head of
  Federal unit; the Superintendent:
  of Documents (Government Printing
    Office)
  of the Naval (or Military) Academy
Supplement to the Revised Statutes (see
  Revised Statutes)
Supreme Bench; the Bench; *also* High
  Bench; High Tribunal

Supreme Court (U.S.); (the Court; *also* High Court; titles of officers standing alone capitalized:)
Associate Justice; Justice
Chief Justice
Clerk
Marshal
Reporter
Surgeon General, the (Air Force, Army, Navy, and Public Health Service)
Survey, if part of name of Federal unit; the Survey: Coast and Geodetic; Geological; National Wilderness Preservation
System, if referring to Federal unit; the System:
Alaska Communication; the system
Bell; the system
Federal Credit
Federal Home Loan Bank
Federal Reserve
National Forest; the System
National Highway; the System
National Park; the System
National System of Interstate and Defense Highways; National System of Interstate Highways; Interstate System of Highways; Interstate Highway System; the Interstate System; the National System; the system; *but* highway system; Federal road system
National Trails
National Wild and Scenic Rivers
New York Central System
Regional Metro System; Metro system
Selective Service (see also Service)
but Amtrak railway system; Amtrak system; the system
also Federal land bank system

table 2, II, A, etc.; *but* Table 2, when part of title: Table 2: [14] Degrees of Land Deterioration
task force (see Force; Report)
Team, USAREUR Field Assistance, etc.; the team
television station (see Station)
Territorial, if referring to a political subdivision
Territory:
Northwest (1799); the territory
Trust Territory of the Pacific Islands; Pacific Islands Trust Territory; the trust territory; the territory
Yukon, Northwest Territories; the Territory(ies), Territorial (Canada)
but territory of: American Samoa, Guam, Virgin Islands
The, part of name, capitalized:
The Dalles; The Gambia; The Hague; The Weirs; *but* the Dalles Dam; the Dalles region; the Hague Conference; the Weirs streets
but the Adjutant General; the National Archives; the Archives; the

The, part of name—Continued
Times; the *Mermaid;* the Federal Express
Third World
Thirteen American Colonies, etc. (see Colonies)
Thirteen Original States
Thruway, New York; the thruway
time:
Atlantic, Atlantic standard
central, central standard
eastern, eastern daylight, eastern daylight saving (no *s*), eastern standard
Greenwich civil, etc.
local, local standard
mountain, mountain standard
Pacific, Pacific standard
universal
title 2, II, A, etc.; *but* Title 2, when part of title: Title 2:[14] General Provisions
Tomb:
Grant's; the tomb
of the Unknown Soldier; Unknown Soldier's Tomb; Tomb of the Unknowns; the tomb (see also Unknown Soldier)
Tower, Eiffel, etc.; the tower
Township, Union; township of Union
trade names and trademarks:

Acrilan	CinemaScope
Airwick	Coca-Cola
Alemite	Coke
Alpha (protein)	Conelrad
Al Si Mag	Corex
Alumel	Crawlers
Alundum	Cyclone (fence)
Ameripol	
Anchor (fence)	Dacron
Areskap	Danforth (anchor)
Aresket	Decalin
Aresklene	Deepfreeze (home
Artgum	freezer)
	De-Ion
Bactratycin	Ditto
Bakelite	Dulux
Band-Aid	Duraloy
Belleekware	Duraplex
Benzedrine	
Bessemer (steel)	Electro-Silicon
Black Leaf 40	Elektron
Blendor (Waring)	Emulphor
Blue Rock (clay	
target)	Fairprene
	Formica
Calgon	Fathometer
Calrod	Fiberglas
Carbitol	(fiberglass in
Carbofrax	general sense)
Carborundum	Fig Newtons
Catalin	Filtrol
Caterpillar (tread)	Foamite
Celanese	Freon
Celastic	Frigidaire
Cellosolve	
Cellucotton (surgical	Geon
dressing)	Glyptal
Celluloid (plastics)	Go Kart
Celotex	Gyropilot
Chevron (machinery	Gyrosyn
packing)	
Chlorex	Halon (gas)
Chromel (alloy)	Hercolyn

trade names—Continued

Hush Puppies (shoes)
Hydroseal
Hyex

Igepon
Inconel
Intertype (typesetting)
Invar
Iron-Clad (batteries)
Jeep
Kepone (chlordecone)
Kiddie Kar
Klaxon
Kleenex
Klieglight
Kodak
Kodapak
Koroseal
Kovar

Lastex
Laundromat
Lavite
Leatherette
Lexide
Library (paste)
Lift Gate
Linotype
Lollypop
Lucite
Lux

Masonite
Methocel
Micarta
Mimeograph
Modutrol
Monel (metal)
Monotype
Mycalex

Nekal
Nichrome
Nicofume
Nitralloy
Nonex

Orlon

Paraplex
Peg Board
Perbunan
Permutit
Phosphor bronze
Photostat
Photronic
Phytin (pharmaceutical product)
Ping-Pong
Plastacele
Plexiglas
Pliofilm
Pliolite
Pliowax
Polane
Polaroid
Polymerin
Porocel
Portland cement
Primacord
Pullman car

Push-Back (theater chairs)
Pyralin
Pyrex glass

Quonset hut

Refinite
Resinox
Revertex
Rocklath (plasterboard)
Rockwell (tester)
Royal typewriter

Sanforized
Santomerse
Scotch (pressure-sensitive tape, etc.)
Shakeproof
Sheetrock
Slim Jims
Snow Crop
Solid Circuit
Solvesso
Speed-Nut (fastener)
Steel-Flex
Stellite
Steri-Pad (surgical dressing)
Stiflex
Styrofoam
Sylphon
Sylphrap
Synpor
Syntron

Tabasco sauce
Talon (fastener)
Technicolor
Teflon
TelePrompter
Teletype
Terramycin
Textolite
Thermit
Thermofax
Thermos (vacuum bottle)
Thiokol
Transite

Uformite
Univac
Urotropin

Vacumatic
Varsol
Vaseline
Verichrome
Victrola
Vinylite
Viscoloid
Vistac
Vistanex (-Medium)
Vu-Graph
Vultex

Windbreaker

Xerox
ZIP Code (Postal)
Zipper (heels)

transatlantic; transpacific; trans-Siberian, etc.; *but* Transjordan; Trans-Alaska
Treasurer, Assistant, of the United States; the Assistant Treasurer; *but* assistant treasurer at New York, etc.
Treasurer of the United States; the Treasurer
Treasury notes; Treasurys
Treasury, of the United States; General; National; Public; Register of the
Treaty, if part of name; the treaty:
  Jay Treaty
  North Atlantic; North Atlantic Defense
  of Versailles
  but treaty of 1919
triad
tribe (see Indians)
Tribunal, standing alone capitalized only in minutes and official reports of a specific arbitration; *also* High Tribunal; the Tribunal (Supreme Court); Copyright Royalty Tribunal, the tribunal
Tris (chemical)
Tropic of Cancer, of Capricorn; the Tropics
tropical; neotropic, neotropical, subtropic(s), subtropical
Trust, Power, etc.
trust territory (see Territory)
Tunnel, Lincoln, etc.; the tunnel; *but* irrigation, railroad, etc., tunnel
Turnpike, Pennsylvania, etc.; the turnpike
Twin Cities (Minneapolis and St. Paul)

U-boat
Under Secretary, if referring to officer of Federal Government; the Under Secretary:
  of Agriculture
  of State
  of the Treasury
Uniform Code of Military Justice (see Code)
Union (if part of proper name; capitalized standing alone if synonym for United States or if referring to international unit):
  International Typographical; the Typographical Union; the union
  Pan American (see Organization of American States)
  Station; *but* union passenger station; union freight station
  Teamsters Union; the Teamsters; the union; *also* the Auto Workers, etc.
  Universal Postal; the Postal Union; the Union
  Western (see alliances)
  Woman's Christian Temperance
  but a painters union; printers union
Union of Soviet Socialist Republics (see U.S.S.R.)

Unit, if referring to Federal branch; the
Unit:
  Alcohol Tax
  Income Tax
United Nations:
  Charter; the charter
  Conference on International Organiza-
    tion; the Conference
  Economic and Social Council; the
    Council
  Educational, Scientific, and Cultural
    Organization (Unesco©) (see Organi-
    zation)
  Food and Agriculture Organization
    (FAO); the Organization
  General Assembly; the Assembly
  International Children's Emergency
    Fund (UNICEF); the Fund
  International Court of Justice; the
    Court
  International Labor Organization (see
    Organization)
  Little Assembly; the Assembly
  Permanent Court of Arbitration (see
    Court)
  Secretariat, the
  Secretary General
  Security Council; the Council
  Special United Nations Fund for Eco-
    nomic Development (SUNFED)
  Trusteeship Council; the Council
  University
  World Employment Conference
  World Health Organization (WHO);
    the Organization
universal:
  military training (see Program)
  time (see time)
Universal Postal Union (see Union)
University, if part of name: Stanford;
  the university
Unknown Soldier; Unknown of World
  War II; World War II Unknown;
  Unknown of Korea; Korea Un-
  known; the Unknowns (see also
  Tomb)
Upper, if part of name:
  Colorado River Basin
  Egypt
  Peninsula (of Michigan)
  but upper House of Congress
U.S.S.R. (Union of Soviet Socialist Re-
  publics):
  Cominform (Communist Information
    Bureau)
  Communist International
  Communist States
  Politburo
  Red army
  Reds, the; a Red
  Soviet, if part of name; capitalized
    standing alone if referring to cen-
    tral governmental unit:
    Government; but Communist gov-
      ernment
    Moscow
    National
    of Labor and Defense

U.S.S.R. (Union of Soviet Socialist Republics)—Continued
  S.S.S.R. (Siberian Soviet Socialist
    Republics)
  but a soviet; sovietic; sovietism; so-
    vietize

Valley, Shenandoah, etc.; the valley; but
  the valleys of Virginia and Mary-
  land
V-E Day; V-J Day (see holidays)
veteran, World War
Veterans' Administration (see Adminis-
  tration)
Veterans Day (see holidays)
vice consul, British, etc.
Vice President (same as President)
Victoria Cross (see decorations)
Vietcong
Voice of America; the Voice
volume 2, A, II, etc.; but Volume 2,
  when part of title: Volume 2: [15]
  Five Rivers in America's Future
Volunteer Naval Reserve (see Reserve)

WAC (see Corps)
War, if part of name:
  Between the States
  Civil
  First World War; World War I; World
    War; Great War; Second World
    War; World War II; but world war
    III
  for Independence (1776)
  French and Indian (1754–63)
  Mexican
  of the Nations
  of the Rebellion; the rebellion
  of the Revolution; the Revolution
  of 1812; but war of 1914
  Philippine Insurrection
  Revolutionary
  Seven Years'
  Six-Day (Arab-Israeli)
  Spanish
  Spanish-American
  the two World Wars
  also post-World War II
war:
  cold, hot
  European
  French and Indian wars
  Indian
  Korean
  third world; world war III
  with Mexico
  with Spain
War College, National (see College)
War Mothers (see American)
ward 1, 2, etc.; first, 11th, etc. (see rule
  12.10)
Washington's Farewell Address
water district (see District)
waterway, inland, intercoastal, etc.; but
  Intracoastal Waterway

[15] See footnote 2, p. 36.

Week, Fire Prevention; etc.
welfare state
West:
  Bank (Jordan)
  Coast (Africa); *but* west coast (U.S.)
  End, etc. (section of city)
  Europe (political entity)
  Far West; Far Western States
  Florida (1763–1819)
  Germany (political entity)
  Middle (United States); Midwest
  South Central States, etc.
  the West (section of United States; *also* world political entity)
west, western Pennsylvania
Western:
  bloc
  civilization
  countries
  Europe(an) (political entity)
  Germany (political entity)
  Hemisphere; the hemisphere
  ideas
  North Central States
  Powers
  States
  Union (see alliances)
  United States
  World
  but far western; western farming States (U.S.)
westerner
Wheat Belt (see Belt)
whip, the (of political party in Congress)
Whisky Rebellion (see Rebellion)
White House:
  Blue Room
  East Room
  Oval Office
  Police (see Police)
  Red Room
  State Dining Room
white paper, British, etc.
Wilderness, capitalized with name; San Joaquin Wilderness, CA; the wilderness; *but* the Wilderness (Virginia battlefield)
woman marine, etc. (see Marine Corps)
Women's Army Corps (see Corps)

Women in the Air Force (WAF); a Waf, Wafs (individuals)
women's lib
Women's Reserve of the Coast Guard Reserve; Women's Reserve; the Reserve; SPAR, popular name, made up of initial letters of motto *semper paratus—always ready;* a Spar
Women's Reserve of the Naval Reserve; Women's Reserve; the Reserve; WAVES (*women accepted for volunteer emergency service*); a Wave
Wood, if part of name:
  Belleau Wood
  House of the Woods (palace)
World: New, Old, Third; *but* Free world
World Series
World War (see War)
World War II veteran

x ray (note: no hyphen)

Year, International Geophysical; the Geophysical Year; the Year
year:
  calendar
  fiscal
Young Men's Christian Association (see Association)
Your Excellency; Your Honor; Your Majesty; etc.
Youth Corps; the Corps

ZIP Code number; ZIP+4
Zone, if part of name; the zone:
  Bizonia; bizonal
  British (in Germany)
  Canal (Panama)
  Eastern, Western (Germany)
  Frigid
  New York Foreign Trade; Foreign Trade Zone No. 1; *but* the foreign trade zone
  of Interior (see Command)
  Temperate, Torrid; the zone
  Trizonia; trizonal
  but Arctic, eastern standard time, polar, tropical zone, etc.
Zoological Park (National); the zoo; the park

NOTES

5. SPELLING

(See also Compound Words; Abbreviations)

5.1. To avoid the confusion and uncertainty of various authorities on spelling, the Government Printing Office must of necessity adopt a single guide for the spelling of words the preferred forms of which are not otherwise listed or provided for in this MANUAL. The guide is Webster's Third New International Dictionary. Unless herein otherwise authorized, the Government Printing Office will continue to follow Webster's spelling. Colloquial and dialect spellings are not to be used unless required by the subject matter or specially requested.

Preferred and difficult spellings

5.2. In addition to indicating the preferred forms of words with variant spellings, the list also contains other words frequently misspelled or causing uncertainty. (See also Word Division, a supplement to the STYLE MANUAL; for brief description, see p. 2.)

A
abattoir
aberration
abetter
  abettor (law)
abridgment
absorb (take in)
  adsorb (adhesion)
abysmal
a cappella
accede (yield)
  exceed (surpass)
accepter
  acceptor (law)
accessory
accommodate
accordion
accouter
accursed
acetic (acid)
  ascetic (austere)
acknowledgment

acoustic
adapter
adjurer
adjuster
ad nauseam
adviser
  advisor (law)
adz
aegis
affect (influence, v.)
  effect (result, n., v.)
aging
aid (n., v.)
aide
aide-de-camp
albumen (egg)
  albumin (chemistry)
align
allottee
all ready (prepared)
  already (previous)

all right
altogether (completely)
all together (collectively)
aluminum
ambidextrous
ameba
ampoule
analog
analogous
anemia
anesthetic
aneurysm
anomalous
anonymous
antediluvian
antibiotics (n.)
  antibiotic (adj.)
anyway (adv.)
anywise (adv.)
appall, -ed, -ing

appareled, -ing
aquatic
aqueduct
archeology
arrester
artifact
artisan
ascendance, -ant
ascent (rise)
  assent (consent)
assassinate
atheneum
attester
autogiro
awhile (for some time)
  a while (a short time)
ax
aye

B
backward
baloney (nonsense)
  bologna (sausage)
bandanna
bargainer
  bargainor (law)
baritone
bark (boat)
barreled, -ing
bastille
bathyscaph
battalion

bazaar
behoove
beneficent
benefited, -ing
bettor (wagerer)
beveled, -ing
biased, -ing
bimetallism
blessed
bloc (group)
  block (grants)
blond (masc., fem.)
bluing

bombazine
born (birth)
  borne (carried)
bouillon (soup)
  bullion (metal)
boulder
bourgeoisie
breach (gap)
  breech (lower part)
brier
briquet, -ted, -ting
Britannia
broadax

bronco
brunet (masc., fem.)
buccaneer
buncombe
bunion
bur
burned
bus, bused, buses, busing
butadiene

C
caffeine
calcareous

calcimine
caldron
calender (paper finish)

caliber
caliper
calk

calligraphy
callus (n.)
  callous (adj.)

calorie
canceled, -ing
canceler
cancellation
candor
canister
cannot
canoeing
cantaloup
canvas (cloth)
  canvass (solicit)
capital (city)
  capitol (building)
carabao (sing., pl.)
carat (gem weight)
  caret (omission
    mark)
  karat (gold weight)
carbureted, -ing
carburetor
Caribbean
caroled, -ing
carotene
cartilage
caster (roller)
  castor (oil)

casual (unimportant)
  causal (cause)
catalog, -ed, -ing
cataloger
catsup
caviar
caviled, -er, -ing
center
centipede
cesarean
chairmaned
chaise longue
chancellor
channeled, -ing
chaperon
chautauqua
chauvinism
check
chiffonier
chili (pepper)
  chile con carne
chiseled, -ing
chlorophyll
cigarette
citable
clamor

clew (nautical)
  clue (other)
climactic (climax)
  climatic (climate)
cocaine
coconut
cocoon
coleslaw
colloquy
colossal
combated, -ing
commenter
  commentor (law)
commingle
commiserate
complement (complete)
  compliment (praise)
confectionery
confidant (masc., fem.)
  confident (sure)
confirmer
  confirmor (law)
conjurer
connecter
connoisseur
consecrator

consensus
consignor
consulter
consummate
contradicter
control, -lable, -ling
converter
conveyor
cookie
coolie
cornetist
corollary
corvette
councilor (of council)
  counselor (adviser)
counseled, -ing
cozy
crawfish
creneled, -ing
crystaled, -ing
crystalline
crystallize
cudgeled, -ing
cyclopedia
czar

D
debarkation
decalog
defense
deliverer
  deliveror (law)
demagog
demarcation
dependent
descendant (n., adj.)
desecrater
desiccate
desuetude
detractor
develop, -ment

device (contrivance)
  devise (convey)
dextrous
diagramed, -ing
diagrammatic
dialed, -ing
dialog
diaphragm
diarrhea
dickey
dieresis
dieretic
dietitian
diffuser
dike

dilettante
dinghy (boat)
diphtheria
discreet (prudent)
  discrete (distinct)
disheveled, -ing
disk
dispatch
dissension
distention
distill, -ed, -ing, -ment
distributor
diverter
divorcee
doctoral

doctrinaire
doggerel
dossier
doweled, -ing
downward
dreadnought
dreamed
drought
dueled, -ing
duffelbag
dullness
dumfound
dwelt
dyeing (coloring)
  dying (death)

E
eastward
ecstasy
edema
edgewise
electronics (n.)
  electronic (adj.)
eleemosynary
elicit (to draw)
  illicit (illegal)
embarrass
embed
embellish
emboweled, -ing
emboweler
emigrant (go from)
  immigrant (go into)
emigree

employee
enameled, -ing
encage
encase
encave
enclasp
enclose
enclosure
encumber
encumbrance
encyclopedia
endorse, -ment
endwise
enfeeble
enforce, -ment
engraft
enroll, -ed, -ing, -ment
enshade

ensheathe
ensnare
entrench
entrepreneur
entrust
entwine
envelop (v.)
  envelope (n.)
enwrap
eon
epaulet, -ed, -ing
epiglottis
epilog
equaled, -ing
erysipelas
escaloped, -ing
escapable
esophagus

esthetic
etiology
evacuee
evanescent
exhibitor
exhilarate
exonerate
exorbitant
expellent
exposé (n., exposure)
  expose (v., to lay
    open)
exsiccate
extant (in existence)
  extent (range)
extoll, -ed, -ing
eying
eyrie

F
falderal
fantasy
farther (distance)
  further (degree)
favor
fecal
feces
fetal
fetish
fetus
fiber
fiche (microfiche)

filigree
finable
finagle
fiord
flammable (*not*
    inflammable)
flection
fledgling
flexitime
flier
flotage
flotation
fluorescent

focused, -ing
forbade
forbear (endurance,
  etc.)
forebear (ancestor)
foresee
forgettable
forgo (relinquish)
  forego (precede)
format, formatted,
  formatting
forswear
fortissimo

forward (ahead)
  foreword (preface)
fricassee
fuchsia
fueler
fulfill, -ed, -ing, -ment
fulsome
fungus (n., adj.)
funneled, -ing
furor
fuse (all meanings)
fuselage
fusillade

G

gaiety
gaily
galosh
gamboled, -ing
garrote
gauge
gazetteer

gelatin
generalissimo
germane
glamorous
glamour
glycerin
gobbledygook
goodbye

gram
graveled, -ing
gray
grievous
groveled, -ing
gruesome
guarantee (n., v.)
  guaranty (n., law)

guerrilla (warfare)
  gorilla (ape)
guesstimate
guttural
gypsy

H

hallelujah
Halloween
kara-kiri
harass
harebrained
harken

healthful (producing
  health)
  healthy (with health)
heinous
hemoglobin
hemorrhage
heterogeneous

hiccup
highfalutin
hijack
Hindu
homeopath
homeward
homogeneity

homolog
hors d'oeuvre
hypocrisy
hypotenuse

I

idiosyncrasy
idyl
impaneled, -ing
impasse
imperiled, -ing
impostor
impresario
imprimatur

indict (to accuse)
  indite (to compose)
inequity (unfairness)
  iniquity (sin)
inferable
infold
ingenious (skillful)
  ingenuous (simple)
innocuous

innuendo
inoculate
inquire, inquiry
install, -ed, -ing, -ment
installation
instill, -ed, -ing
insure (protect)
  ensure (guarantee)
intelligentsia

interceptor
interment (burial)
  internment (jail)
intern
intervener
  intervenor (law)
intransigent (n., adj.)
iridescent
italic

J

jalopy

jeweled, -ing, -er
judgment

judgeship
jujitsu

K

kerneled, -ing

kerosene
kidnaped, -ing

kidnaper
kilogram

kopek

L

labeled, -ing
lacquer
landward
lath (wood)
  lathe (machine)
laureled
leukemia
leveled, -ing
leveler

liaison
libber
libelant
libeled, -ing
libelee
libeler
license
licenser (issuer)
  licensor (grantor)
licorice

likable
lilliputian
linage (lines)
  lineage (descent)
liquefy
liquor
  liqueur
liter
livable

loath (reluctant)
  loathe (detest)
lodestar
lodestone
lodgment
logistics (n.)
  logistic (adj.)
louver
luster

M

madam
Mafia
maize (corn)
  maze (labyrinth)
maneuver
manifold
manikin
mantel (shelf)
  mantle (cloak)
manywise (adv.)
marbleize
margarin (chemistry)
  margarine (butter
  substitute)
marijuana

marshaled, -ing
marshaler
marveled, -ing
marvelous
meager
medaled, -ing
medalist
medieval
metaled, -ing
metalize
material (goods)
  materiel (military
  stores)
meteorology (weather)
  metrology (weights
  and measures)

meter
mil (1/1000 inch)
  mill (1/1000 dollar)
mileage
miliary (tuberculosis)
milieu
milk cow
millenary (1,000)
  millinery (hats)
millennium
minable
missilry
misspell
miter
moccasin
modeled, -ing

modeler
mold
mollusk
molt
moneys
monogramed, -ing
monolog
mortise
Moslem
movable
mucilage
mucus (n.)
  mucous (adj.)
mustache

N

naphtha
Navajo

nazism
niacin
nickel

Nisei
niter
nonplused

northward
numskull

O

obbligato
obloquy
ocher
octet

offal
offense
omelet
oneself
onward

ophthalmology
opossum
orangutan
orbited, -ing

ordinance (law)
  ordnance (military)
organdie
overseas or oversea

P
pajamas
paleontology
paneled, -ing
paraffin
paralleled, -ing
parallelepiped
parceled, -ing
partisan
pastime
patrol, -led, -ling
peccadillo
peddler
Peking
penciled, -ing
pendant (n.)
  pendent (u.m.)
percent
peremptory (decisive)
  preemptory
    (preference)

perennial
periled, -ing
permittee
perquisite (privilege)
  prerequisite
    (requirement)
personal (individual)
  personnel (staff)
perspective (view)
  prospective
    (expected)
petaled, -ing
Pharaoh
pharmacopeia
phenix
phlegm
phony
phosphorus (n.)
  phosphorous (adj.)
photostated
pickax

picnicking
pipet
plaque
plastics (n.)
  plastic (adj.)
pledger
  pledgor (law)
plenitude
plow
poleax
pollination
pommeled, -ing
pontoon
  ponton (military)
porcelaneous
practice (n., v.)
precedence (priority)
  precedents (usage)
pretense
preventive

principal (chief)
  principle
    (proposition)
privilege
proffer
programmed, -mer,
    -ming
programmatic
prolog
promissory
pronunciation
propel, -led, -ling
propellant (n.)
  propellent (adj.)
prophecy (n.)
  prophesy (v.)
ptomaine
pubic (anatomy)
pulmotor
pusillanimous

Q
quarreled, -ing

quartet
quaternary

questionnaire
queue

R
raccoon
racket (all meanings)
rapprochement
rarefy
rarity
ratable
rattan
raveled, -ing

reconnaissance
reconnoiter
recyclable
referable
refusenik
registrar
reinforce
relater
  relator (law)

remodeler
renaissance
reparable
repellant (n.)
  repellent (adj.)
requester
  requestor (law)
rescission
responder (electronics)

responser (electronics)
reveled, -er, -ing
rhyme, rhythmic
RIF"ing, RIF"d, RIF"s
rivaled, -ing
roweled, -ing
ruble

S
saccharin (n.)
  saccharine (adj.)
sacrilegious
salable
sandaled, -ing
satellite
satinet
savable
savanna
savior
  Saviour (Christ)
scalloped, -ing
schizophrenia
scion (horticulture)
scurrilous
seismology
selvage (edging)
  salvage (save)
sentineled, -ing
separate

sepulcher
seriatim
settler
  settlor (law)
sewage (waste)
  sewerage (drain
    system)
sextet
Shakespearean
shellacking
shoveled, -ing
shriveled, -ing
sideward
signaled, -ing
siphon
sizable
skeptic
skillful
skulduggery
smolder
sniveled, -ing

snorkel
soliloquy
sometime (formerly)
  some time (some
    time ago)
  sometimes (at times)
southward
spacious (space)
  specious (plausible)
specter
spirituous (liquor)
  (not spiritous)
spirochete
spoliation
staunch
stationary (fixed)
  stationery (paper)
statue (sculpture)
  stature (height)
  statute (law)
stenciled, -ing

stenciler
stifling
stratagem
stubbornness
stupefy
subpoena, -ed
subtlety
succor
sulfur (also derivatives
  sulfanilamide
  sulfureted, -ing
supererogation
surreptitious
surveillance
swiveled, -ing
sylvan
synonymous
syrup

T
taboo
tactician
tasseled, -ing
tattoo
taxied, -ing
technique
teetotaler
tercentenary
theater
therefor (for it)
  therefore (for that
    reason)
thiamine
thralldom

thrash (beat)
  thresh (grain)
threshold
tie, tied, tying
timber (wood)
  timbre (tone)
tinseled, -ing
titer
tonsillitis
tormenter
totaled, -ing
toward
toweled, -ing
toxemia
trafficking

trammeled, -ing
tranquilize(r)
tranquillity
transcendent
transferable
transferor
transferred
transonic
transponder
  (electronics)
transshipment
traveled, -ing
traveler
travelog
triptych

trolley
troop (soldiers)
  troupe (actors)
troweled, -ing
tryptophan
tularemia
tunneled, -ing
tunneler
turquoise
typify
tyrannical
tyro

U	unwieldy	uremia	
unctuous	upward		

V	veranda	vilify	volcanism
vacillate	vermilion	villain	voluntarism
valance (drape)	vicissitude	visa, -ed, -ing	votable
valence (chemistry)	victualed, -ing	vitamin	vying
veld	victualer	vitrify	

W	warranty	whimsey	woeful
wainscoting	weeviled, -ing	whiskey, -s	woolen
warranter	welder	willful	woolly
warrantor (law)	westward	withe	worshiped, -er, -ing

Anglicized and foreign words

5.3. Diacritical marks are not used with completely anglicized words.

abaca	cortege	fete	porte lumiere
aide memoire	coulee	fiance (masc., fem.)	portiere
a la carte	coup de grace	frappe	pousse cafe
a la king	coup d'etat	garcon	premiere
a la mode	coupe	glace	protege (masc., fem.)
angstrom	creme	grille	puree
aperitif	crepe	gruyere	rale
applique	crepe de chine	habitue	recherche
apropos	critique	ingenue	regime
auto(s)-da-fe	critiquing	jardiniere	risque (masc., fem.)
blase	debacle	litterateur	role
boutonniere	debris	materiel	rotisserie
brassiere	debut	matinee	roue
cabana	debutante	melange	saute
cafe	decollete	melee	seance
cafeteria	dejeuner	menage	senor
caique	denouement	mesalliance	smorgasbord
canape	depot	metier	soiree
cause celebre	dos-a-dos	moire	souffle
chateau	eclair	naive	suede
cliche	eclat	naivete	table d'hote
cloisonne	ecru	nee	tete-a-tete
comedienne	elan	opera bouffe	tragedienne
comme ci	elite	opera comique	vicuna
comme ca	entree	papier mache	vis-a-vis
communique	etude	piece de resistance	
confrere	facade	pleiade	
consomme	faience	porte cochere	

5.4. Foreign words carry the diacritical marks as an essential part of their spelling.

à l'américaine	chargé d'affaires	exposé	pâté
attaché	congé	longéron	père
béton	crédit foncier	mañana	piña
blessé	crédit mobilier	maté	précis
calèche	curé	mère	raisonné
cañada	détente	nacré	résumé
cañon	doña	outré	touché
chargé	entrepôt	passé (masc., fem.)	

Plural forms

5.5. Nouns ending in *o* preceded by a vowel add *s* to form the plural; nouns ending in *o* preceded by a consonant add *es* to form the plural, except as indicated in the following list.

albinos	centos	falsettos	infernos
armadillos	didos	gauchos	juntos
avocados	duodecimos	ghettos	kimonos
banjos	dynamos	gringos	lassos
cantos	escudos	halos	magnetos
cascos	Eskimos	indigos	mementos

merinos	piccolos	sextodecimos	tobaccos
mestizos	pomelos	sextos	twos
octavos	provisos	siroccos	tyros
octodecimos	quartos	solos	virtuosos
pianos	salvos	tangelos	zeros

5.6. In forming the plurals of compound terms, the significant word takes the plural form.

Significant word first:

- adjutants general
- aides-de-camp
- ambassadors at large
- attorneys at law
- attorneys general
- billets-doux
- bills of fare
- brothers-in-law
- chargés d'affaires
- chiefs of staff
- commanders in chief
- comptrollers general
- consuls general
- courts-martial
- crepes suzette
- daughters-in-law
- governors general
- grants-in-aid
- heirs at law
- inspectors general
- men-of-war
- ministers-designate
- mothers-in-law
- notaries public
- pilots-in-command
- postmasters general
- presidents-elect
- prisoners of war
- reductions in force
- rights-of-way
- secretaries general
- sergeants at arms
- sergeants major
- solicitors general
- surgeons general

Significant word in middle:

- assistant attorneys general
- assistant chiefs of staff
- assistant comptrollers general
- assistant surgeons general
- deputy chiefs of staff

Significant word last:

- assistant attorneys
- assistant commissioners
- assistant corporation counsels
- assistant directors
- assistant general counsels
- assistant secretaries
- brigadier generals
- deputy judges
- deputy sheriffs
- general counsels
- judge advocates
- judge advocate generals
- lieutenant colonels
- major generals
- provost marshals
- provost marshal generals
- quartermaster generals
- trade unions
- under secretaries
- vice chairmen

Both words of equal significance:

- Bulletins Nos. 27 and 28; *but* Bulletin No. 27 or 28
- coats of arms
- masters at arms
- men buyers
- men employees
- secretaries-treasurers
- women aviators
- women students
- women writers

No word significant in itself:

- forget-me-nots
- hand-me-downs
- jack-in-the-pulpits
- man-of-the-earths
- pick-me-ups
- will-o'-the-wisps

5.7. When a noun is hyphenated with an adverb or preposition, the plural is formed on the noun.

comings-in	goings-on	listeners-in	makers-up
fillers-in	hangers-on	lookers-on	passers-by

5.8. When neither word is a noun, the plural is formed on the last word.

also-rans	go-betweens	run-ins
come-ons	higher-ups	tie-ins

5.9. Nouns ending with *ful* form the plural by adding *s* at the end; if it is necessary to express the idea that more than one container was filled, the two elements of the solid compound are print-

ed as separate words and the plural is formed by adding *s* to the noun.

> five bucketfuls of the mixture (one bucket filled five times)
> five buckets full of earth (separate buckets)
> three cupfuls of flour (one cup filled three times)
> three cups full of coffee (separate cups)

5.10. The following list comprises other words the plurals of which may cause difficulty.

addendum, addenda
adieu, adieus
agendum, agenda
alga, algae
alumnus, alumni (masc.); alumna, alumnae (fem.)
antenna, antennas (antennae, zoology)
appendix, appendixes
aquarium, aquariums
automaton, automatons
axis, axes
bandeau, bandeaux
basis, bases
bateau, bateaux
beau, beaus
cactus, cactuses
calix, calices
chassis (singular and plural)
cherub, cherubs
cicatrix, cicatrices
Co., Cos.
coccus, cocci
consortium, consortia
corrigendum, corrigenda
crisis, crises
criterion, criteria
curriculum, curriculums
datum, data
desideratum, desiderata
dilettante, dilettanti
dogma, dogmas
ellipsis, ellipses
equilibrium, equilibriums (equilibria, scientific)
erratum, errata
executrix, executrices
flambeau, flambeaus
focus, focuses
folium, folia
forum, forums
formula, formulas
fungus, fungi
genius, geniuses
genus, genera
gladiolus (singular and plural)
helix, helices
hypothesis, hypotheses
index, indexes (indices, scientific)
insigne, insignia
italic, italic
Kansas Citys
lacuna, lacunae

larva, larvae
larynx, larynxes
lens, lenses
lira, lire
locus, loci
madam, mesdames
Marys
matrix, matrices
maximum, maximums
medium, mediums *or* media
memorandum, memorandums
minimum, minimums
minutia, minutiae
monsieur, messieurs
nucleus, nuclei
oasis, oases
octopus, octopuses
opus, opera
parenthesis, parentheses
phenomenon, phenomena
phylum, phyla
plateau, plateaus
podium, podiums
procès-verbal, procès-verbaux
radius, radii
radix, radixes
referendum, referendums
sanatorium, sanatoriums
sanitarium, sanitariums
septum, septa
sequela, sequelae
seraph, seraphs
seta, setae
ski, skis
stadium, stadiums
stimulus, stimuli
stratum, strata
stylus, styluses
syllabus, syllabuses
symposium, symposia
synopsis, synopses
tableau, tableaus
taxi, taxis
terminus, termini
testatrix, testatrices
thesaurus, thesauri
thesis, theses
thorax, thoraxes
vertebra, vertebras (vertebrae, zoology)
virtuoso, virtuosos
vortex, vortexes

Endings "ible" and "able"

5.11. The following words end in *ible;* other words in this class end in *able.* Words with both endings indicated differ in meaning.

abhorrible
accendible
accessible
addible
adducible
admissible
appetible
apprehensible
audible
avertible
bipartible
circumscriptible
coctible
coercible
cognoscible
cohesible
collapsible
collectible(s)
combustible
comestible
commonsensible
compactible
compatible
competible
compossible
comprehensible
compressible
conducible
conductible
confluxible
congestible
contemptible
controvertible
conversible
   (convertible)
conversable (oral)
convertible
convincible
corrigible
corrodible
corrosible
corruptible
credible
crucible
cullible
decoctible
deducible
deductible
defeasible
defectible
defensible
delible
deprehensible
depressible
descendible
destructible
diffrangible
diffusible
digestible
dimensible
discernible
discerpible
discerptible
discussible
dispersible
dissectible

distensible
distractible
divertible
divestible
divisible
docible
edible
educible
effectible
effervescible
eligible
eludible
erodible
evasible
eversible
evincible
exemptible
exhaustible
exigible
expansible
explosible
expressible
extensible
fallible
feasible
fencible
flexible
fluxible
forcible
frangible
fungible
fusible
gullible
horrible
ignitible
illegible
immersible
immiscible
impartible
impatible
impedible
imperceptible
impermissible
imperscriptible
impersuasible
implausible
impossible
imprescriptible
imputrescible
inaccessible
inadmissible
inapprehensible
inaudible
incircumscriptible
incoercible
incognoscible
incombustible
incommiscible
incompatible
incomprehensible
incompressible
inconcussible
incontrovertible
inconvertible
inconvincible
incorrigible

incorrodible
incorruptible
incredible
indefeasible
indefectible
indefensible
indelible
indeprehensible
indestructible
indigestible
indiscernible
indivertible
indivisible
indocible
inducible
ineffervescible
ineligible
ineludible
inevasible
inexhaustible
inexpansible
inexpressible
infallible
infeasible
inflexible
infractible
infrangible
infusible
innascible
inscriptible
insensible
instructible
insubmergible
insuppressible
insusceptible
intactible
intangible
intelligible
interconvertible
interruptible
intervisible
invendible
invertible
invincible
invisible
irascible
irreducible
irrefrangible
irremissible
irreprehensible
irrepressible
irresistible
irresponsible
irreversible
legible
mandible
marcescible
misicible
negligible
nexible
omissible
ostensible
partible
passible (feeling)
   passable (open)
perceptible

perfectible
permissible
persuasible
pervertible
plausible
possible
prehensible
prescriptible
producible
productible
protrusible
putrescible
receptible
redemptible
reducible
reflectible
reflexible
refrangible
remissible
renascible
rendible
reprehensible
repressible
reproducible
resistible
responsible
reversible
revertible
risible
runcible
sconcible
seducible
sensible
sponsible
suasible
subdivisible
submergible
submersible
subvertible
suggestible
supersensible
suppressible
susceptible
suspensible
tangible
tensible
terrible
thurible
traducible
transmissible
transvertible
tripartible
unadmissible
uncorruptible
unexhaustible
unexpressible
unintelligible
unresponsible
unsusceptible
vendible
vincible
visible
vitrescible

Endings "ise," "ize," and "yze"

5.12. A large number of words have the termination *ise, ize,* or *yze.* The letter *l* is followed by *yze* if the word expresses an idea of loosening or separating, as *analyze;* all other words of this class, except those ending with the suffix *wise* and those in the following list, end in *ize.*

advertise	demise	exercise	prise (to force)
advise	despise	exorcise	prize (to value)
affranchise	devise	franchise	reprise
apprise (to inform)	disenfranchise	improvise	revise
apprize (to appraise)	disfranchise	incise	rise
arise	disguise	merchandise	supervise
chastise	emprise	misadvise	surmise
circumcise	enfranchise	mortise	surprise
comprise	enterprise	premise	televise
compromise	excise		

Endings "cede," "ceed," and "sede"

5.13. Only one word ends in *sede* (supersede); only three end in *ceed* (exceed, proceed, succeed); all other words of this class end in *cede* (precede, secede, etc.).

Doubled consonants

5.14. A single consonant following a single vowel and ending a monosyllable or a final accented syllable is doubled before a suffix beginning with a vowel.

bag, bagging	corral, corralled	*but* total, totaled
get, getting	input, inputting	travel, traveled
red, reddish	format, formatting	
rob, robbing	transfer, transferred	

5.15. If the accent in a derivative falls upon an earlier syllable than it does in the primitive, the consonant is not doubled.

refer, reference	prefer, preference	infer, inference

Indefinite articles

5.16. The indefinite article *a* is used before a consonant and an aspirated *h; an* is used before silent *h* and all vowels except *u* pronounced as in *visual* and *o* pronounced as in *one.*

a historical review	a union	an onion
a hotel	an herbseller	an oyster
a human being	an hour	*but* an H-U-D directive
a humble man	an honor	a HUD directive

5.17. When a group of initials begins with *b, c, d, g, j, k, p, q, t, u, v, w, y,* or *z,* each having a consonant sound, the indefinite article *a* is used.

a BLS compilation	a GAO limitation
a CIO finding	a PHS project

5.18. When a group of initials begins with *a, e, f, h, i, l, m, n, o, r, s,* or *x,* each having a vowel sound, the indefinite article *an* is used.

an AEC report	an NSC (en) proclamation
an FCC (ef) ruling	an RFC (ahr) loan

5.19. Use of the indefinite article *a* or *an* before a numerical expression is determined by the consonant or vowel sound of the beginning syllable.

an 11-year-old
a onetime winner
a III (three) group

an VIII (eight) classification
a IV–F (four) category (military draft)
a 4–H Club

Geographic names

5.20. The spelling of geographic names must conform to the decisions of the U.S. Board on Geographic Names (BGN). In the absence of such a decision, the U.S. Directory of Post Offices is to be used for names of post offices in the United States and its possessions.

5.21. If the decisions or the rules of the BGN permit the use of either the local official form or the conventional English form, it is the prerogative of the originating office to select the form which is most suitable for the matter in hand; therefore, in marking copy or reading proof, it is required only to verify the spelling of the particular form used. The Government Printing Office preference is for the conventional English form. Copy will be followed as to accents, but these should be uniform throughout each job.

Nationalities, etc.

5.22. The table on page 235 shows forms to be used for nouns and adjectives denoting nationality.

5.23. In designating the natives of the several States, the following forms will be used.

Alabamian	Indianian	Nebraskan	South Carolinian
Alaskan	Iowan	Nevadan	South Dakotan
Arizonan	Kansan	New Hampshirite	Tennessean
Arkansan	Kentuckian	New Jerseyite	Texan
Californian	Louisianian	New Mexican	Utahn [1]
Coloradan	Mainer	New Yorker	Vermonter
Connecticuter	Marylander	North Carolinian	Virginian
Delawarean	Massachusettsan	North Dakotan	Washingtonian
Floridian	Michiganite	Ohioan	West Virginian
Georgian	Minnesotan	Oklahoman	Wisconsinite
Hawaiian	Mississippian	Oregonian	Wyomingite
Idahoan	Missourian	Pennsylvanian	[1] Utahan (adjective)
Illinoisan	Montanan	Rhode Islander	

5.24. Observe the following forms:

Guamanian
Puerto Rican

Part-Hawaiian (applies to Hawaii only)
but part-Japanese

Indian words

5.25. In Indian words, including tribal and other proper names, copy is to be followed literally as to spelling and the use of spaces, hyphens, etc.

Ligatures

5.26. Ligatures are not used.

Transliteration

5.27. In the spelling of nongeographic words transliterated from Chinese, Japanese, or any other language that does not have a Latin alphabet, copy is to be followed literally.

6. COMPOUND WORDS

(See also Guide to Compounding; Word Division (supplement to STYLE MANUAL), description on p. 2)

6.1. A compound word is a union of two or more words, either with or without a hyphen. It conveys a unit idea that is not as clearly or quickly conveyed by the component words in unconnected succession. The hyphen in a compound is a mark of punctuation that not only unites but separates the component words, and thus facilitates understanding, aids readability, and ensures correct pronunciation.

6.2. In applying the following rules and in using the Guide to Compounding, the living fluidity of our language should be kept in mind. Word forms constantly undergo modification. Two-word forms often acquire the hyphen first, are printed as one word later, and not infrequently the transition is from the two- to the one-word form, bypassing the hyphen stage.

6.3. The rules as laid down cannot be applied inflexibly. Exceptions must necessarily be allowed, so that general good form will not be offended. However, current language trends point definitely to closing up words which, through frequent use, have become associated in the reader's mind as units of thought. The tendency to amalgamate words, particularly two short words, assures easier continuity, and is a natural progression from the older and less flexible treatment of words.

General rules

6.4. In general, omit the hyphen when words appear in regular order and the omission causes no ambiguity in sense or sound. (See also rule 6.16.)

banking hours	eye opener	real estate
blood pressure	fellow citizen	rock candy
book value	living costs	training ship
census taker	palm oil	violin teacher
day laborer	patent right	

6.5. Words are usually combined to express a literal or nonliteral (figurative) unit idea that would not be as clearly expressed in unconnected succession.

afterglow	forget-me-not	right-of-way
bookkeeping	gentleman	whitewash
cupboard	newsprint	

6.6. Unless otherwise indicated, a derivative of a compound retains the solid or hyphenated form of the original compound.

coldbloodedness	ill-advisedly	praiseworthiness	Y-shaped
footnoting	outlawry	railroader	

6.7. Except after the short prefixes *co, de, pre, pro,* and *re,* which are generally printed solid, a hyphen is used to avoid doubling a vowel or tripling a consonant. (See also rules 6.29 and 6.32.)

cooperation	semi-independent	shell-like
deemphasis	brass-smith	hull-less
preexisting	Inverness-shire	*but* co-occupant
anti-inflation	thimble-eye	
micro-organism	ultra-atomic	

Solid compounds

6.8. Print solid two nouns that form a third when the compound has only one primary accent, especially when the prefixed noun consists of only one syllable or when one of the elements loses its original accent.

airship	cupboard	footnote
bathroom	dressmaker	locksmith
bookseller	fishmonger	workman

6.9 Print solid a noun consisting of a short verb and an adverb as its second element, except when the use of the solid form would interfere with comprehension.

blowout	holdup	setup	*but* cut-in
breakdown	makeready	showdown	run-in
flareback	markoff	throwaway	tie-in
giveaway	pickup	tradeoff	
hangover	runoff		

6.10. Compounds beginning with the following nouns are usually printed solid.

book	house	school	way
eye	mill	shop	wood
horse	play	snow	work

6.11. Compounds ending in the following are usually printed solid, especially when prefixed word consists of one syllable. (See also rules 6.29 and 6.30.)

berry	headed	monger	tight
bird	hearted	over	time (not clock)
blossom	holder	owner	ward
board	hopper	*but* #ownership	ware
boat	house	person	water
book	keeper	picker	way
borne	keeping	picking	wear
bound	land	piece	weed
box	light	plane	wide
boy	like	power	wise
brained	line	proof	woman
bug	load	roach	wood
bush	maid	room	work
craft	maker	shop	worker
field	making	site	working
fish	man	skin	worm
flower	master	smith	worthy
fly	mate	stone	writer
girl	mill	store	writing
grower	mistress	tail	yard

6.12. Print solid *any, every, no,* and *some* when combined with *body, thing,* and *where;* when *one* is the second element, print as two words if meaning a single or particular person or thing; to avoid mispronunciation, print *no one* as two words at all times.

anybody	everybody	nobody	somebody
anything	everything	nothing	something
anywhere	everywhere	nowhere	somewhere
anyone	everyone	no one	someone

but any one of us may stay; every one of the pilots is responsible.

6.13. Print compound personal pronouns as one word.

herself	oneself	thyself
himself	ourselves	yourself
itself	themselves	yourselves
myself		

6.14. Print as one word compass directions consisting of two points, but use a hyphen after the first point when three points are combined.

northeast	north-northeast
southwest	south-southwest

Unit modifiers. (See also rules 7.14 and 8.73.)

6.15. Print a hyphen between words, or abbreviations and words, combined to form a unit modifier immediately preceding the word modified, except as indicated in rule 6.16 and elsewhere throughout this chapter. This applies particularly to combinations in which one element is a present or past participle.

agreed-upon standards	long-term-payment loan
Baltimore-Washington road	lump-sum payment
collective-bargaining talks	most-favored-nation clause
contested-election case	multiple-purpose uses
contract-bar rule	no-par-value stock
cost-of-living increase	part-time personnel
drought-stricken area	rust-resistant covering
English-speaking nation	service-connected disability
fire-tested material	state-of-the-art technology
Federal-State-local cooperation	tool-and-die maker
German-English descent	up-or-down vote
guided-missile program	U.S.-owned property; U.S.-flag ship
hard-of-hearing class	1-inch diameter; 2-inch-diameter pipe
high-speed line	10-word telegram
large-scale project	a 4-percent increase, the 10-percent rise
law-abiding citizen	*but* 4 percent citric acid, 4 percent interest [1]
long-term loan	

6.16. Where meaning is clear and readability is not aided, it is not necessary to use a hyphen to form a temporary or made compound. Restraint should be exercised in forming unnecessary combinations of words used in normal sequence.

atomic energy power	interstate commerce law	real estate tax
bituminous coal industry	land bank loan	small businessman
child welfare plan	land use program	social security pension
civil rights case	life insurance company	soil conservation measures
civil service examination	mutual security funds	special delivery mail;
durable goods industry	national defense appropriation	parcel post delivery
flood control study	natural gas company	speech correction class
free enterprise system	per capita expenditure	*but* no-hyphen rule (readability
high school student; elementary school grade	Portland cement plant	aided); *not* no hyphen rule
income tax form	production credit loan	
	public utilty plant	

6.17. Print without a hyphen a compound predicate adjective or predicate noun the second element of which is a present participle.

The duties were price fixing.	The shale was oil bearing.
The effects were far reaching.	The area was used for beet raising.

6.18. Print without a hyphen a compound predicate adjective the second element of which is a past participle; also, omit the hyphen in a predicate modifier of comparative or superlative degree.

The area is drought stricken.	This material is fire tested.
The paper is fine grained.	The cars are higher priced.
Moderately fine grained wood.	The reporters are best informed.
The boy is freckle faced.	

---

[1] Note the absence of an article: *a, an,* or *the.* The word *of* is understood here.

6.19. Print without a hyphen a two-word modifier the first element of which is a comparative or superlative.

better drained soil	*but* uppercrust society
best liked books	lowercase, uppercase type (printing)
higher level decision	undercoverman
highest priced apartment	upperclassman
larger sized dress	bestseller (noun).
better paying job	lighter-than-air craft
lower income group	higher-than-market price

6.20. Do not use a hyphen in a two-word unit modifier the first element of which is an adverb ending in *ly,* nor use hyphens in a three-word unit modifier the first two elements of which are adverbs.

eagerly awaited moment	often heard phrase
wholly owned subsidiary	*but* ever-normal granary
unusually well preserved specimen	ever-rising flood
very well defined usage	still-new car
longer than usual lunch period	still-lingering doubt
very well worth reading	well-known lawyer
not too distant future	well-kept farm

6.21. Proper nouns used as unit modifiers, either in their basic or derived form, retain their original form; but the hyphen is printed when combining forms.

Latin American countries	Anglo-Saxon period
North Carolina roads	Franco-Prussian War
a Mexican-American	*but* Minneapolis-St. Paul region
South American trade	North American-South American sphere
Spanish-American pride	French-English descent
Winston-Salem festival	Washington–Wilkes-Barre route
Afro-American program	

6.22. Do not confuse a modifier with the word it modifies. In some instances clarity can be achieved by the writer by using such terms as businessperson, shoe repairer, worker, etc.

elderly clothesman	old-clothes man
competent shoemaker	wooden-shoe maker
field canning factory	tomato-canning factory
gallant serviceman	service men and women
light blue hat (weight)	light-blue hat (color)
average taxpayer	income-tax payer
American flagship	American-flag ship
well-trained schoolteacher	elementary school teacher
preschool children (kindergarten)	pre-school children (before school)
but common stockholder	
stock ownership	
small businessman	
working men and women	
steam powerplant site	
meat packinghouse owner	

6.23. Where two or more hyphenated compounds have a common basic element and this element is omitted in all but the last term, the hyphens are retained.

2- or 3-em quads, *not* 2 or 3-em quads; 2- to 3- and 4- to 5-ton trucks
2- by 4-inch boards, *but* 2 to 6 inches wide
8-, 10-, and 16-foot boards
6.4-, 3.1-, and 2-percent pay raises
moss- and ivy-covered walls, *not* moss and ivy-covered walls
long- and short-term money rates, *not* long and short-term money rates
but twofold or threefold, *not* two or threefold
goat, sheep, and calf skins, *not* goat, sheep, and calfskins
intrastate and intracity, *not* intra-state and -city
American owned and managed companies
preoperative and postoperative examination

6.24. Do not use a hyphen in a unit modifier consisting of a foreign phrase.

ante bellum days	ex officio member	per diem employee
bona fide transaction	per capita tax	prima facie evidence

6.25. Do not print a hyphen in a unit modifier containing a letter or a numeral as its second element.

abstract B pages	class II railroad	point 4 program
article 3 provisions	grade A milk	ward D beds

6.26. Do not use a hyphen in a unit modifier enclosed in quotation marks unless it is normally a hyphenated term, but quotation marks are not to be used in lieu of a hyphen. (See also rule 8.136.)

"blue sky" law   "good neighbor" policy   "tie-in" sale   *but* right-to-work law

6.27. Print combination color terms as separate words, but use a hyphen when such color terms are unit modifiers.

bluish green	orange red	iron-gray sink
dark green	bluish-green feathers	silver-gray body

6.28. Do not use a hyphen between independent adjectives preceding a noun.

big gray cat   a fine old southern gentleman

Prefixes, suffixes, and combining forms

6.29. Print solid combining forms and prefixes, except as indicated elsewhere.

*after*birth	*fore*tell	*mono*gram	*pro*consul
*Anglo*mania	*hero*icomic	*multi*color	*pseudo*scholastic
*ante*date	*hyper*sensitive	*neo*phyte	*re*enact
*anti*slavery	*hypo*acid	*non*neutral	*retro*spect
*bi*weekly	*in*bound	*off*set	*semi*official
*by*law	*infra*red	*out*bake	*step*father
*circum*navigation	*inter*view	*over*active	*sub*secretary
*cis*alpine	*intra*spinal	*pan*cosmic	*super*market
*co*operate	*intro*vert	*para*centric	*thermo*couple
*contra*position	*iso*metric	*parti*coated	*trans*onic
*counter*case	*macro*analysis	*peri*patetic	*trans*ship
*de*energize	*meso*thorax	*plano*convex	*tri*color
*demi*tasse	*meta*genesis	*poly*nodal	*ultra*violet
*ex*communicate	*micro*phone	*post*script	*un*necessary
*extra*curricular	*mis*state	*pre*exist	*under*flow

6.30. Print solid combining forms and suffixes, except as indicated elsewhere.

port*able*	kilo*gram*	out*let*	home*stead*
cover*age*	geo*graphy*	wave*like*	north*ward*
oper*ate*	man*hood*	procure*ment*	clock*wise*
plebis*cite*	self*ish*	inner*most*	
twenty*fold*	pump*kin*	partner*ship*	
spoon*ful*	meat*less*	lone*some*	

6.31. Print solid words ending in *like*, but use a hyphen to avoid tripling a consonant or when the first element is a proper name.

lifelike	bell-like	Scotland-like
lilylike	girllike	MacArthur-like

6.32. Use a hyphen or hyphens to prevent mispronunciation, to insure a definite accent on each element of the compound, or to avoid ambiguity.

anti-hog-cholera serum	re-cover (cover again)
co-op	re-sorting (sort again)
multi-ply (several plies)	re-treat (treat again)
non-civil-service position	un-ionized
non-tumor-bearing tissue	un-uniformity
pre-position (before)	*but* rereferred

6.33. Use a hyphen to join duplicated prefixes.

re-redirect   sub-subcommittee   super-superlative

6.34. Print with a hyphen the prefixes *ex, self,* and *quasi.*

ex-governor	self-control	quasi-academic
ex-serviceman	self-educated	quasi-argument
ex-trader	*but* selfhood	quasi-corporation
ex-vice-president [2]	selfsame	quasi-young

6.35. Unless usage demands otherwise, use a hyphen to join a prefix or combining form to a capitalized word. (The hyphen is retained in words of this class set in caps.)

anti-Arab	post-World War II *or* post-	overanglicize
pro-British	Second World War	prezeppelin
un-American	non-Federal	transatlantic
non-Government	*but* nongovernmental	

Numerical compounds

6.36. Print a hyphen between the elements of compound numbers from twenty-one to ninety-nine and in adjective compounds with a numerical first element. (See also rule 12.22.)

twenty-one	5-to-4 vote	second grade children
twenty-first	.22-caliber cartridge	*but* one hundred and twenty-
6-footer	2-cent-per-pound tax	one
24-in ruler	four-in-hand tie	100-odd
3-week vacation	three-and-twenty	foursome
8-hour day	two-sided question	threescore
10-minute delay	multimillion-dollar fund	foursquare
20th-century progress	10-dollar-per-car tax	$20 million airfield
3-to-1 ratio	thirty- (30-) day period	

6.37. Print without a hyphen a modifier consisting of a possessive noun preceded by a numeral. (See also rule 8.14.)

1 month's layoff	2 hours' work
1 week's pay	3 weeks' vacation

6.38. Print a hyphen between the elements of a fraction, but omit it between the numerator and the denominator when the hyphen appears in either or in both.

one-thousandth	two one-thousandths	twenty-one thirty-seconds
two-thirds	twenty-three thirtieths	three-fourths of an inch

6.39. A unit modifier following and reading back to the word or words modified takes a hyphen and is always printed in the singular.

    motor, alternating-current, 3-phase, 60-cycle, 115-volt
    glass jars: 5-gallon, 2-gallon, 1-quart
    belts: 2-inch, 1¼-inch, ½-inch, ¼-inch

Civil and military titles

6.40. Do not hyphenate a civil or military title denoting a single office, but print a double title with a hyphen. (See also rule 5.6.)

ambassador at large	notary public
assistant attorney general	secretary general
commander in chief	under secretary; *but* under-secretaryship
comptroller general	vice president,[2] *but* vice-presidency
Congressman at Large	secretary-treasurer
major general	treasurer-manager
sergeant at arms	

---

[2] In official usage, the title of Vice President of the United States is written without a hyphen; the hyphen is also omitted in all like titles, such as vice admiral, vice consul, etc.

6.41. The adjectives *elect* and *designate,* as the last element of a title, require a hyphen.

President-elect
Vice-President-elect

ambassador-designate
minister-designate

Scientific and technical terms

6.42. Do not print a hyphen in scientific terms (names of chemicals, diseases, animals, insects, plants) used as unit modifiers if no hyphen appears in their original form. (See list of plant names, p. 257, and insect names, p. 266.)

carbon monoxide poisoning
guinea pig raising
hog cholera serum
methyl bromide solution
stem rust control

equivalent uranium content
whooping cough remedy
but Russian-olive plantings
Douglas-fir tree

6.43. Chemical elements used in combination with figures use a hyphen, except with superior figures.

polonium-210   uranium-235; *but* U^{235}; Sr^{90}; $_{92}U^{234}$ Freon-12

6.44. Note use of hyphens and closeup punctuation in chemical formulas.

9-nitroanthra (1,9,4,10)bis(1)oxathiazone-2,7-bisdioxide
Cr-Ni-Mo
2,4-D

6.45. Print a hyphen between the elements of technical compound units of measurement.

candela-hour
crop-year
horsepower-hour

light-year
passenger-mile
staff-hour
but kilowatthour

Improvised compounds

6.46. Print with a hyphen the elements of an improvised compound.

blue-pencil (v.)
18-year-old (n., u.m.)
know-it-all (n.)
know-how (n.)
lick-the-finger-and-test-the-wind economics
make-believe (n.)
one-man-one-vote principle
roll-on/roll-off ship

stick-in-the-mud (n.)
let-George-do-it attitude
how-to-be-beautiful course
hard-and-fast rule
penny-wise and pound-foolish policy
first-come-first-served basis
but a basis of first come, first served
easy come, easy go

6.47. Use hyphens in a prepositional-phrase compound noun consisting of three or more words.

cat-o'-nine-tails
government-in-exile
grant-in-aid
jack-in-the-box

man-of-war
mother-in-law
mother-of-pearl
patent-in-fee

but coat of arms
heir at law
next of kin
officer in charge

6.48. When the corresponding noun form is printed as separate words, the verb form is always hyphenated.

cold-shoulder   blue-pencil   cross-brace

6.49. Print a hyphen in a compound formed of repetitive or conflicting terms and in a compound naming the same thing under two aspects.

boogie-woogie	murder-suicide	young-old
comedy-ballet	nitty-gritty	*but* bowwow
dead-alive	pitter-patter	dillydally
devil-devil	razzle-dazzle	riffraff
even-stephen	walkie-talkie	
farce-melodrama	willy-nilly	

6.50. Use a hyphen in a nonliteral compound expression containing an apostrophe in its first element.

asses'-eyes	cat's-paw	*but* The cat's paw is soft.
ass's-foot	crow's-nest	There is the crow's nest.
bull's-eye		

6.51. Use a hyphen to join a single capital letter to a noun or a participle.

H-bomb	V-necked	*but* x ray
I-beam	S-iron	x raying
T-shaped	T-square	
U-boat	X-ed out	

6.52. Print idiomatic phrases without hyphens.

come by	insofar as	nowadays
inasmuch as	Monday week	

7. GUIDE TO COMPOUNDING

7.1. The following list is based on the rules for compounding given on pages 73 to 80. Manifestly, such a list cannot be complete. However, by analogy with listed words of like prefixes or suffixes, with consideration given to length and readability, and the application of the rules, fuller treatment of unlisted compounds will be achieved. Nevertheless, the list is reasonably complete for meeting the needs of printers, editors, and writers.

7.2. In order to keep the list from becoming cumbersome, certain restrictions had to be adopted.

7.3. The listing of hyphenated compounds ending in *ed* was kept to a minimum, it being thought adequate to give one or two examples under a keyword rather than to admit needless repetition.

7.4. Similarly, many two-word forms which create no difficulty were omitted.

7.5. On the other hand, care was exercised to achieve fuller coverage of solid compounds, particularly when the adopted form is at variance with that laid down in Webster's Third New International Dictionary. It should be added that while Webster's, with indicated exceptions (pp. 63–67), is our guide to the spelling of words, it is not our guide for the compounding of words. The rules and the guide prescribe and limit our practice.

7.6. Distinction should be made between words used in a nonliteral sense—e.g., *highlight* (prominent detail), *sideline* (added activity), where the one-word form differentiates from literal use—e.g., *high light* (elevation of a light), *side line* (physical line), where the two-word form frequently assures proper emphasis in pronouncing more distinctly each word in the group.

7.7. Distinction should also be made in the compounding of two words to form an adjective modifier and the use of the same words as a predicate adjective; e.g., "crystal-clear water," *but* "the water is crystal clear"; "fire-tested material," *but* "the material is fire tested."

7.8. Caution should be used in distinguishing when a succession of words is intended as a compound and when it is merely a collocation; e.g., "we know someone who will do it," *but* "we ought to master some one thing well."

7.9. For better appearance, it may sometimes be necessary to treat alike words which would have different forms when they appear separately; e.g., *bumblebee* and *queen bee, farmhand* and *ranch hand*. In juxtaposition, these and similar words should be made uniform by being printed as two words. This is only a temporary expedient and does not supersede the list.

7.10. Combining forms and prefixes are usually printed solid. For greater readability, the hyphen is sometimes required to avoid doubling a vowel *(anti-inflation, naso-orbital)*, except as indicated in

rule 6.7; or not to change a normally capitalized word *(mid-April, non-European)*; or to assure distinct pronunciation of each element of a compound or ready comprehension of intended meaning *(contra-ion, un-ionized)*; or to join a combining form or prefix to an already hyphenated compound *(equi-gram-molar, pro-mother-in-law)*.

7.11. As nouns and adjectives, *holdup, calldown, layout, makeup,* and similar words should be printed solid. Their *er* derivatives *(holder-up, caller-down, layer-out,* and *maker-up)* require hyphens. On the other hand, such compounds as *run-in, run-on,* and *tie-in* resist quick comprehension when solid. They are therefore hyphenated.

7.12. Words spelled alike but pronounced differently, such as *tear-dimmed* and *tearsheet, wind tunnel* and *windup,* are listed under the same keyword.

7.13. This list does not include the large group of plant and insect names which are covered in separate lists, pages 257 to 274.

7.14. The abbreviations *adv.* (adverb), *n.* (noun), *v.* (verb), *u.m.* (unit modifier), *pref.* (prefix), *c.f.* (combining form), and *conj.* (conjunction) indicate function.

[Words printed flush are combined with the words which follow to form solid or hyphenated compounds; a spacemark (#) indicates a two-word form (note that two-word forms in the adjective position use a hyphen, except as laid down in rules 6.16, 6.21, and 6.24.)]

A

A	**actino** (c.f.)	coach	port (all	**along**
BC('s) (n.)	*all one word*	-condition (all	meanings)	ship
–B–C (u.m.)	**addle**	forms)	scoop	shore
-bomb	brain	-cool (v.)	show	side
-day	head	-cooled (u.m.)	sleeve	**alpen**
-flat	pate	course	ship	glow
-frame	**add-on** (u.m.)	crew	sick	stock
-pole	**adeno** (c.f.)	-dried (u.m.)	-slaked (u.m.)	**alpha**
-sharp	*all one word*	-driven (u.m.)	space	-cellulose
a	**aero** (c.f.)	drome	speed	-iron
borning, etc.	-otitis	drop	stream	-naphthol
foot	*rest one word*	-dry (u.m., v.)	strike	also-ran (n., u.m.)
while (adv.)	**afore**	fare	strip	**alto**
abdomino (c.f.)	*all one word*	-floated (u.m.)	#time (radio and	cumulus
all one word	Afro-American	flow	TV)	relievo
able	**after** (c.f.)	foil	wave	stratus
-bodied (u.m.)	*all one word*	-formed (u.m.)	alder-leaved	**amber**
-minded (u.m.)	agar-agar	frame	(u.m.)	-clear (u.m.)
about-face	**age**	freight	**ale**	-colored (u.m.)
above	less	gap	cup	-tipped (u.m.)
-cited (u.m.)	long	glow	-fed (u.m.)	**ambi** (c.f.)
deck	-old (u.m.)	hammer	glass	*all one word*
-found (u.m.)	-stricken (u.m.)	head	alkali#land	amidships
-given (u.m.)	-weary (u.m.)	hole	**all**	**amino**
ground (u.m.)	**ague**	hose	-absorbing (u.m.)	#acid
-mentioned	-faced (u.m.)	lane	-aged (u.m.)	*as prefix, all*
(u.m.)	-plagued (u.m.)	lift	-American	*one word*
-named (u.m.)	-sore (u.m.)	#line (line for	-clear (n., u.m.)	**ampere**
-said (u.m.)	aide-de-camp	air)	-fired (u.m.)	-foot
-water (u.m.)	**air**	line (aviation)	-flotation	-hour
-written (u.m.)	bag	liner	(mining)	meter
absentminded	base	link	-inclusive (u.m.)	-minute
ace-high (u.m.)	bill	locked	mark (printing)	-second
acid	blast	mail	-out (u.m.)	**amphi** (pref.)
fast	-blasted (u.m.)	mark (v.)	-possessed (u.m.)	*all one word*
-treat (v.)	blown	marker	-round (u.m.)	**amylo** (c.f.)
works	brake	mass	spice	*all one word*
ack-ack	brush	minded	-star (u.m.)	**anchor**
acre	burst	park	**allo** (c.f.)	hold
-foot	cargo	path	*all one word*	#light
-inch	-clear (u.m.)	photo	almsgiver	plate

angel
  cake
  -eyed (u.m.)
  -faced (u.m.)
  food
angio (c.f.)
  all one word
angle
  hook
  meter
  wing
Anglo (c.f.)
  -American, etc.
  rest one word
anhydr(o) (c.f.)
  all one word
ankle
  bone
  -deep (u.m.)
  jack
ant
  eater
  hill
ante (pref.)
  #bellum, etc.
  -Christian, etc.
  #mortem
  mortem
    (nonliteral)
  rest one word
antero (c.f.)
  all one word
anthra (c.f.)
  all one word
anthropo (c.f.)
  all one word
anti (pref.)
  -American, etc.
  christ

god
  -hog-cholera
    (u.m.)
  -icer, -imperial,
    -inflation, etc.
  -missile-missile
    (u.m.)
  missile,
    personnel,
    trust, etc.
  -New#Deal, etc.
  rest one word
antro (c.f.)
  all one word
anvil
  -faced (u.m.)
  -headed (u.m.)
any
  how
  one
  #one (one thing
    or one of a
    group)
  place (adv.)
aorto (c.f.)
  all one word
apo (pref.)
  all one word
apple
  cart
  jack
  juice
  sauce
  -scented (u.m.)
April-fool (v.)
aqua
  culture
  lung
  marine

  meter
  puncture
  tint
  tone
aquo (c.f.)
  -ion
  rest one word
arc
  -over (n., u.m.)
  -weld (v.)
arch (pref.)
  band
  bishop
  duke
  enemy
  -Protestant
archeo (c.f.)
  all one word
archi (pref.)
  all one word
archo (c.f.)
  all one word
areo (c.f.)
  all one word
aristo (c.f.)
  all one word
arithmo (c.f.)
  all one word
arm
  band
  bone
  chair
  hole
  lift
  pit
  plate
  rack
  rest
  -shaped (u.m.)

armor
  -clad (u.m.)
  -piercing (u.m.)
  plate
  -plated (u.m.)
arm's-length
  (u.m.)
arrow
  head
  -leaved (u.m.)
  plate
  -shaped (u.m.)
  shot
  -toothed (u.m.)
arseno (c.f.)
  all one word
art-colored (u.m.)
arterio (c.f.)
  all one word
arthro (c.f.)
  all one word
asbestos
  -covered (u.m.)
  -packed (u.m.)
ash
  bin
  can
  -colored (u.m.)
  -free (u.m.)
  -gray (u.m.)
  pan
  pile
  pit
  tray
assembly
  #line
  #room
astro (c.f.)
  all one word

attorney#at#law
audio
  frequency
  gram
  meter
  tape
  visual
auri (c.f.)
  -iodide
  rest one word
authorship
auto (c.f.)
  -objective
  -observation
  -omnibus
  -ophthalmoscope
  rest one word
awe
  -bound (u.m.)
  -filled (u.m.)
  -inspired (u.m.)
  some
ax
  -adz
  -grinding (u.m.)
  hammer
  head
  -shaped (u.m.)
axletree
axo (c.f.)
  all one word
azo (c.f.)
  -orange
  -orchil
  -orseilline
  rest one word

B

B-flat
baby
  face (n.)
  sit (v.)
back
  ache
  band
  bite (v.)
  bone
  breaker
  cap
  chain
  charge
  -country (u.m.)
  cross
  date
  down (n., u.m.)
  drop
  face
  feed
  fill
  fire
  flap
  flash
  flow
  -focus (v.)
  furrow
  ground
  hand
  haul
  -in (n., u.m.)
  lash
  list (v.)
  log
  lotter

  packer (n.)
  paddle (v.)
  pay
  payment
  pedal (v.)
  plate
  rest
  road
  run
  saw
  scatter
  set
  shift
  slide
  space
  spin
  spread
  staff
  stage
  stairs
  stamp
  stay
  stitch
  stop
  strap
  -streeter
  stretch (n.)
  string
  strip (book)
  stroke
  -swath (v.)
  swept
  swing
  tack
  talk

  tender
  tenter
  -titrate (v.)
  track (v.)
  trail
  up (n., u.m.)
  wall
  wash
backer
  -down
  -off
  -up
bag
  -cheeked
    (u.m.)
  pipe
  -shaped (u.m.)
baggage#room
bailout (n., u.m.)
bake
  pan
  stove
bald
  faced
  head (n.)
  pate
ball
  -like
  park
    (nonliteral)
  #park (literal)
  player
  point (n., u.m.)
  stock
ballot#box

band
  cutter
  saw
  stand
  string
  -tailed (u.m.)
  wagon
  width
bandy
  ball
  -legged (u.m.)
bangup (n., u.m.)
bank
  note
  side (stream)
bantamweight
bar
  post
  tender
  -wound (u.m.)
bare
  -armed (u.m.)
  back
  bone
  faced
  foot
  handed
  legged
  necked
  worn
barge-laden (u.m.)
bark
  cutter
  peel
  -tanned (u.m.)

barley
  corn
  mow
  #water
barnstormer
barrel
  head
  -roll (v.)
  -shaped (u.m.)
base
  ball
  ball#bat
  line
  #line (surveying)
  -minded (u.m.)
basi (c.f.)
  all one word
basketball
bas-relief
bat
  blind
  -eyed (u.m.)
  fowl
  wing
bath
  mat
  robe
  tub
batswing (cloth)
battercake
battle
  ax
  dore
  -fallen (u.m.)
  front

ground
-scarred (u.m.)
ship
stead
wagon
baybolt
beach
comber
head
wagon
bead
flush
roll
beak
head
iron
-shaped (u.m.)
beam
filling
-making (u.m.)
bean
bag
cod
-fed (u.m.)
pole
pot
setter
-shaped (u.m.)
stalk
bear
baiting
herd
hide
hound
off (n., u.m.)
trap
beater
-out
-up
beauty
-blind (u.m.)
-clad (u.m.)
#shop
beaverpelt
bed
chair
chamber
clothes
cord
cover
-fallen (u.m.)
fast
fellow
frame
pad
pan
plate
post
quilt
rail
ridden
rock
sheet
sick
side
sore
space
spread
spring
stand
stead
straw
bee
bread
-eater
herd
hive

beechnut
beef
eater
-faced (u.m.)
head
steak
tongue
bees
wax
wing
beetle
-browed (u.m.)
head
stock
before
-cited (u.m.)
hand
-mentioned
(u.m.)
-named (u.m.)
behindhand
bell
-bottomed (u.m.)
crank
-crowned (u.m.)
hanger
hop
mouthed
ringer
wether
belly
ache
band
buster
button
fed (u.m.)
pinch
belowstairs
belt
-driven (u.m.)
saw
bench
fellow
-hardened (u.m.)
made (u.m.)
mark
(nonliteral)
#mark
(surveying)
warmer
bentwing (n.,
u.m.)
benzo (c.f.)
all one word
berry-brown (u.m.)
best
#man
seller (n.)
beta
-glucose
tron
between
decks
whiles
bi (pref.)
-iliac
rest one word
big
-eared (u.m.)
-eyed (u.m.)
head (ego)
horn (sheep)
-horned (u.m.)
-leaguer
mouthed
name (top rank)
(n., u.m.)

bill
back
beetle
broker
fold
head
hook
poster
sticker
billet
-doux
head
billingsgate
bio (c.f.)
-aeration
-osmosis
rest one word
birchbark
bird
bath
bander
cage
call
catcher
-eyed (u.m.)
-faced (u.m.)
life
lime
lore
mouthed
seed
shot
watcher
bird's
-eye
#nest (literal) (n.)
-nest (n., u.m.,
v.)
birth
bed
day
mark
place
right
biscuit-shaped
(u.m.)
bismuto (c.f.)
all one word
bitstock
bitter
-ender
head
sweet
-tongued (u.m.)
black
ball (nonliteral)
-bordered (u.m.)
damp
-eyed (u.m.)
face
fire
guard
jack
leg
list
mail
mark
-market (u.m.,
v.)
-marketeer
-marketer
mouthed
out (n., u.m.)
plate (printing)
print
-robed (u.m.)
shirted

snake
strap (n.)
top
blast
hole
plate
blasto (c.f.)
all one word
bleach
ground
works
blear
eye
-eyed (u.m.)
-witted (u.m.)
blepharo (c.f.)
all one word
blight-resistant
(u.m.)
blind
-bomb (v.)
-flying (u.m.)
fold
-loaded (u.m.)
#man
spot
stitch
story
blink-eyed (u.m.)
blithe-looking
(u.m.)
blitz
buggy
krieg
block
buster
head
hole (v.)
ship
blood
-alcohol (u.m.)
bath
beat
curdling
-drenched (u.m.)
-giving (u.m.)
guilty
-hot (u.m.)
hound
letting
mobile
-red (u.m.)
ripe
shed
shot
spiller
spot
stain
stock
stream
sucker
thirsty
-warm (u.m.)
bloody
-nosed (u.m.)
-red (u.m.)
blossom
-bordered (u.m.)
-laden (u.m.)
blow
back
by (n., u.m.)
cock
down (n., u.m.)
gun
hard (n.)
hole

iron
lamp
off (n., u.m.)
out (n., u.m.)
pipe
spray
through (u.m.)
torch
tube
up (n., u.m.)
blue
-annealed (u.m.)
beard (n.)
blood
bonnet
bottle
coat (n.)
-eyed (u.m.)
grass
-gray (u.m.)
-green (u.m.)
-hot (u.m.)
jack
jacket
nose
-pencil (v.)
point (oyster)
print
stocking
streak
(nonliteral)
tongue (n.)
blunder
buss
head
blunt
-edged (u.m.)
-spoken (u.m.)
boar
spear
staff
board
rack
walk
boat
builder
crew
hook
head
loader
setter
side
swain
wright
bob
cat
sled
stay
bobby
pin
-soxer
body
bearer
bending
builder
-centered
(u.m.)
guard
-mind
plate
bog
-eyed (u.m.)
trot (v.)
boil
down (n., u.m.)
off (n., u.m.)
out (n., u.m.)

boiler	last	crumb	**bride**	**brown**
-off	leg	earner	bed	back
-out	lick	fruit	bowl	-eyed (u.m.)
plate	strap	liner	cake	out (n., u.m.)
works	**bore**	plate	chamber	print
boiling#house	hole	seller	cup	**brush**
bold	safe	stuff	groom	ball
face (printing)	sight	winner	knot	#holder
-spirited (u.m.)	**bosom**	**break**	lace	off (n., u.m.)
bolt	-deep (u.m.)	away (n., u.m.)	maiden	-treat (v.)
cutter	-folded (u.m.)	ax	stake	**brusher**
head	-making (u.m.)	back (n., u.m.)	**bridge**	-off
hole	**bottle**	bone (fever)	builder	-up
-shaped (u.m.)	-fed (u.m.)	down (n., u.m.)	head	**buck**
strake	neck	-even (u.m.)	pot	eye
bomb	-nosed (u.m.)	fast	tree	-eyed (u.m.)
drop	bottom#land	fast#room	briefcase	horn
fall	boughpot	front	**bright**	hound
shell	**bow**	-in (n., u.m.)	-colored (u.m.)	passer
sight	back	neck	-eyed (u.m.)	plate
thrower	bent	off (n., u.m.)	**brilliant**	pot
-throwing (u.m.)	grace	out (n., u.m.)	-cut (u.m.)	saw
bondslave	head	point	-green (u.m.)	shot
bone	knot	through (n.,	brine-soaked	skinned
ache	legged	u.m.)	(u.m.)	stall
black	-necked (u.m.)	up (n., u.m.)	bringer-up	stay
breaker	pin	wind	**bristle**	stove
-bred (u.m.)	shot	**breaker**	cone (u.m.)	tooth
-dry (u.m.)	sprit	-down	-pointed (u.m.)	wagon
-eater	stave	-off	**broad**	wash
-hard (u.m.)	string	-up	acre	bucket-shaped
head	wow	**breast**	ax	(u.m.)
lace	**box**	band	band (radio) (n.,	**buff**
meal	car	beam	u.m.)	-tipped (u.m.)
set	haul	bone	-beamed (u.m.)	-yellow (u.m.)
shaker	head (printing)	-deep (u.m.)	brim	**bug**
-white (u.m.)	truck	-fed (u.m.)	cast	bear
boobytrap	**boxer**	-high (u.m.)	cloth	bite
boogie-woogie	-off	hook	head	-eyed (u.m.)
book	-up	mark	leaf (n.)	buildup (n., u.m.)
binder	**brachio** (c.f.)	pin	-leaved (u.m.)	**built**
case	*all one word*	plate	loom	-in (u.m.)
dealer	**brachy** (c.f.)	plow	minded	-up (u.m.)
fair	*all one word*	rail	-mouthed (u.m.)	bulb-tee (u.m.)
-fed (u.m.)	**brain**	rope	share (n., v.)	**bulbo** (c.f.)
fold	cap	**breath**	sheet (n.)	*all one word*
-learned (u.m.)	child	-blown (u.m.)	side	**bulk**
-lined (u.m.)	-cracked (u.m.)	-tainted (u.m.)	sword	head
list	fag	taking	wife	-pile (v.)
lore	pan	**breech**	woven	weigh (v.)
lover	sick	block	**broken**	**bull**
mark	-spun (u.m.)	cloth	-down (u.m.)	baiting
mobile	storm	loader	-legged (u.m.)	dog
plate	-tired (u.m.)	-loading (u.m.)	-mouthed (u.m.)	doze
rack	wash	lock	**bromo** (c.f.)	-faced (u.m.)
rest	**brake**	pin	*all one word*	fight
sale	drum	plug	**bronchio** (c.f.)	frog
seller	head	sight	*all one word*	head
shelf	meter	**breeze**	**broncho** (c.f.)	-mouthed
stack	shoe	-borne (u.m.)	*all one word*	(u.m.)
stall	brandnew (u.m.)	-lifted (u.m.)	broncobuster	neck
stamp	**brandy**	-swept (u.m.)	**bronze**	nose
stand	-burnt (u.m.)	**bribe**	-clad (u.m.)	pen
stitch	wine	-free (u.m.)	-covered (u.m.)	ring
-stitching (u.m.)	**brass**	giver	-red (u.m.)	toad
-taught (u.m.)	-armed (u.m.)	taker	**broom**	-voiced (u.m.)
wright	-bold (u.m.)	bric-a-brac	-leaved (u.m.)	whack
boom	-smith	**brick**	-making (u.m.)	whip
-ended (u.m.)	works	bat	stick	bullethead
town	**brave**	-built (u.m.)	**brother**	**bull's**
truck	-looking (u.m.)	-colored (u.m.)	-german	-eye
boondoggling	-minded (u.m.)	kiln	hood	(nonliteral)
boot	**brazen**	layer	-in-law	-foot
black	-browed (u.m.)	liner	**brow**	**bumble**
hose	face	mason	beat	bee
jack	**bread**	-red (u.m.)	point	foot
lace	basket	setter	post	kite

bung
  hole
  start
burn
  -in (n., u.m.)
  out (n., u.m.)
  up (n., u.m.)
burned-over (u.m.)
burner-off
burnt
  -out (u.m.)
  -up (u.m.)
bus
  driver

fare
  #girl
bush
  beater
  buck
  fighter
  -grown (u.m.)
  hammer
  -headed (u.m.)
  -leaguer
  ranger
  whacker
  wife
bustup (n., u.m.)

busy
  body
  -fingered (u.m.)
  head
butt
  -joint (v.)
  saw
  stock
  strap
  -weld (v.)
butter
  ball
  -colored (u.m.)
  fat

fingers
  head
  milk
  mouth
  nut
  print
  -rigged (u.m.)
  scotch
  -smooth (u.m.)
  wife
  -yellow (u.m.)
button
  -eared (u.m.)
  -headed (u.m.)

hold
  hole
  hook
  mold
buzzerphone
by
  -and-by
  -by
  -the-way (n., u.m.)
  -your-leave (n., u.m.)
  rest one word

C

C
  -sharp
  -star
  -tube
cab
  driver
  fare
  #owner
  stand
cabbagehead
cable-laid (u.m.)
caco (c.f.)
  all one word
cage#bird
cake
  baker
  bread
  -eater
  mixer
  -mixing (u.m.)
  pan
  walk
calci (c.f.)
  all one word
calk-weld (v.)
call
  back (n., u.m.)
  down (n., u.m.)
  -in (n., u.m.)
  note
  -off (n., u.m.)
  out (n., u.m.)
  -over (n., u.m.)
  up (n., u.m.)
camshaft
camel
  back (rubber)
  -backed (u.m.)
  driver
  -faced (u.m.)
camel's-hair (u.m.)
camp
  fire
  ground
  stool
can
  capper
  not
canalside
candle
  bomb
  -foot
  -hour
  lighter
  lit
  -meter
  -shaped (u.m.)
  stand
  stick
  wick

wright
candystick
cane
  -backed (u.m.)
  brake
  crusher
  cutter
canker
  -eaten (u.m.)
  -mouthed (u.m.)
cannonball
canvas-covered (u.m.)
cap
  -flash (v.)
  nut
  screw
  sheaf
  shore
car
  barn
  break
  builder
  fare
  goose
  hop
  lot
  -mile
  pool
  port
  sick
  wash
carbo (c.f.)
  all one word
carbol (c.f.)
  all one word
carcino (c.f.)
  all one word
card
  case
  -index (u.m., v.)
  player
  sharp
  stock
cardio (c.f.)
  -aortic
  rest one word
care
  free
  -laden (u.m.)
  taker
  -tired (u.m.)
  worn
carpet
  bagger
  beater
  -cleaning (u.m.)
  -covered (u.m.)
  fitter
  layer

  -smooth (u.m.)
  -sweeping (u.m.)
  weaver
  -weaving (u.m.)
  web
  woven
carpo (c.f.)
  -olecranal
  rest one word
carriage-making (u.m.)
carrot
  -colored (u.m.)
  head (nonliteral)
  juice
  top (nonliteral)
carry
  all (n., u.m.)
  around (n., u.m.)
  back (n., u.m.)
  forward (n.)
  -in (n., u.m.)
  out (n., u.m.)
cart
  wheel (coin)
  whip
  wright
case
  bearer
  finding
  hammer
  harden
  lot
  mated
caser-in
cash-flow
cast
  away (n., u.m.)
  back (n., u.m.)
  -by (u.m.)
  off (n., u.m.)
  out (n., u.m.)
  -ridden (u.m.)
  -weld (v.)
caster
  -off
  -out
castlebuilder (nonliteral)
cat
  back
  beam
  block
  call
  -eyed (u.m.)
  face (n.)
  fall
  footed

gut
  head
  hole
  -ion
  nap
  nip
  -o'-nine-tails
  stitch
  walk
catch
  all (n., u.m.)
  -as-catch-can (u.m.)
  cry
  penny
  plate
  up (n., u.m.)
  weight
  word
cater
  corner
  wauling
cat's
  -eye (nonliteral)
  -paw (nonliteral)
cattle
  #boat
  feed
  -raising (u.m.)
  yak
cauliflower
  -eared (u.m.)
  #ware
cave
  dweller
  -dwelling (u.m.)
  #fish
  -in (n., u.m.)
cease-fire (n., u.m.)
cedar-colored (u.m.)
celi (c.f.)
  all one word
celio (c.f.)
  all one word
cement
  -covered (u.m.)
  mason
  -temper (v.)
census-taking (u.m.)
center
  #field (sports)
  head (printing)
  most
  -second
centi (c.f.)
  all one word
centimeter-gram-second

centri (c.f.)
  all one word
centro (c.f.)
  all one word
cephalo (c.f.)
  all one word
cerato (c.f.)
  all one word
cerebro (c.f.)
  -ocular
  rest one word
cervico (c.f.)
  -occipital
  -orbicular
  rest one word
cess
  pipe
  pit
  pool
chaffcutter
chain
  -driven (u.m.)
  stitch
chair
  fast
  mender
  person
  -shaped (u.m.)
  warmer
chalk
  cutter
  -white (u.m.)
chapfallen
chapelgoing
char
  broiler
  coal
  pit
charge
  #book
  off (n., u.m.)
  out (n., u.m.)
chattermark
cheapskate
check
  bite
  hook
  -in (n., u.m.)
  list
  mark
  nut
  off (n., u.m.)
  out (n., u.m.)
  passer (n.)
  point
  rack
  rail
  rein
  ring
  roll
  rope

row
sheet
strap
string
up (n., u.m.)
washer
weigher
checker
-in
-off
-out
-up
cheek
bone
strap
cheerleader
cheese
burger
cake
cloth
curd
cutter
head
lip
parer
plate
chemico (c.f.)
all one word
chemo (c.f.)
all one word
cherry
-colored (u.m.)
stone
(nonliteral)
#stone (literal)
chestnut
-colored (u.m.)
-red (u.m.)
chicken
bill
-billed (u.m.)
#breast
breasted
feed
heart
pox
#yard
chief
#justice
-justiceship
#mate
child
bearing
bed
birth
crowing
hood
kind
life
-minded (u.m.)
ridden
wife
chill-cast (u.m., v.)
chin
band
-bearded (u.m.)
-chin
cloth
cough
-high (u.m.)
rest
strap
china
-blue (u.m.)
#shop
Chinatown
chipmunk

chiro (c.f.)
all one word
chisel
-cut (u.m.)
-edged (u.m.)
#maker
chitchat
chitter-chatter
chloro (c.f.)
all one word
chock
ablock
-full (u.m.)
chocolate
-brown (u.m.)
-coated (u.m.)
#maker
choir#master
choke
bore
damp
out (n., u.m.)
point
strap
chole (c.f.)
all one word
chondro (c.f.)
-osseous
rest one word
chop
-chop
stick
chowchow
Christ
-given (u.m.)
-inspired (u.m.)
chromo (c.f.)
all one word
chrono (c.f.)
all one word
chuck
hole
plate
wagon
chucklehead
chunkhead
churchgoer
churn
-butted (u.m.)
milk
cigar
case
cutter
-shaped (u.m.)
cigarette
#holder
#maker
-making (u.m.)
cine (c.f.)
all one word
circum (pref.)
arctic, pacific,
etc.
-Saturnal, etc.
rest one word
cirro (c.f.)
all one word
cis (pref.)
alpine
atlantic
-trans (u.m.)
rest one word
city
-born (u.m.)
-bred (u.m.)
folk
#man

scape
clam
bake
shell
clampdown (n.,
u.m.)
clap
net
trap
clasphook
class-conscious
(u.m.)
claw
bar
-footed (u.m.)
hammer
hatchet
-tailed (u.m.)
clay
bank
-colored (u.m.)
pan
pit
works
clean
-cut (u.m.)
handed
out (n., u.m.)
-shaved (u.m.)
-smelling (u.m.)
up (n., u.m.)
clear
cole
-cut (u.m.)
cut (forestry)
(n., v.)
-eyed (u.m.)
-sighted (u.m.)
up (n., u.m.)
wing
cleft
-footed (u.m.)
-graft (v.)
cliff
dweller
-dwelling (u.m.)
hanger
side
top
-worn (u.m.)
climbpath
clinch-built (u.m.)
clink-clank
clinker-built
(u.m.)
clip
-clop
-edged (u.m.)
sheet
clipper-built (u.m.)
cloak-and-dagger
(n., u.m.)
clock
case
face
-minded (u.m.)
setter
watcher
clod
head
hopping
pate
close
bred
-connected (u.m.)
cross
-cut (u.m.)

down (n.)
-fertilize (v.)
fisted
handed
-knit
minded
mouthed
out (n., u.m.)
up (n., u.m.)
closed
-circuit (u.m.)
#shop
cloth-backed
(u.m.)
clothes
bag
basket
brush
horse
pin
press
rack
cloud
base
burst
cap
-hidden (u.m.)
clover
bloom
leaf
seed
sick
club
foot
hand
haul
mobile
ridden
root
-shaped (u.m.)
co (pref.)
-op
exist, operate,
etc.
rest one word
coach
-and-four
builder
whip
coal
bag
bed
bin
-black (u.m.)
breaker
dealer
digger
-faced (u.m.)
hole
-laden (u.m.)
#loader
pit
rake
sack (astron.
only)
shed
ship
coastside
coat
hanger
rack
tailed

cock
bill
brain
crow
eye
fight
head
pit
spur
sure
-tailed (u.m.)
up (n., u.m.)
cockleshell
cockscomb
cod
bank
fishing
head
pitchings
smack
coffee
break
cake
-colored (u.m.)
-growing
(u.m.)
pot
cofferdam
coffin-headed
(u.m.)
cogwheel
coin-operated
(u.m.)
cold
blooded
-chisel (v.)
cuts
-draw (v.)
finch
-flow (v.)
-forge (v.)
frame
-hammer (v.)
-hammered
(u.m.)
pack
-press (v.)
-roll (v.)
-rolled (u.m.)
-short (u.m.)
-shortness
-shoulder (v.)
type (printing)
-work (v.)
cole
seed
slaw
coli (c.f.)
all one word
collar
bag
band
bone
colo (c.f.)
all one word
color
bearer
blind
#blindness
fast
-free (u.m.)
#line
type (printing)
(n.)
-washed (u.m.)
comb-toothed
(u.m.)

come	husk	**crack**	-brush (v.)	tree
-along (tool)	loft	down (n., u.m.)	-carve (v.)	under (n., u.m.)
back (n., u.m.)	meal	jaw	-channel (u.m.)	-vote
-between (n.)	stalk	pot	-check	walk
down (n.)	starch	-the-whip (n., u.m.)	-claim	web
-off (n., u.m.)	**corner**	up (n., u.m.)	-compound (v.)	wind
-on (n., u.m.)	bind	**cradle**	-connect (v.)	word
-out (n.)	post	side	-country (u.m.)	**crow**
-outer	corpsmember	song	-cultivate (v.)	bait
uppance	**costo** (c.f.)	**cranio** (c.f.)	current	bar
comic#book	**cotton**	all one word	-curve (math.)	foot
commander#in	-clad (u.m.)	**crank**	(n.)	**crow's**
#chief	-covered (u.m.)	case	cut	-foot (nonliteral)
common	-growing (u.m.)	-driven (u.m.)	-date (v.)	-nest (nonliteral)
place	#mill	pin	-drain (v.)	crownbar
#sense (n.)	mouth (snake)	pit	-dye (v.)	crybaby
sense (u.m.)	packer	shaft	-dyeing (n.)	**crypto** (c.f.)
weal	seed	crapehanger	-examine (v.)	-Christian, etc.
wealth	sick	crashdive (v.)	-eye (n., u.m.)	rest one word
companionship	**countdown** (n., u.m.)	crawlup (n., u.m.)	-eyed (u.m.)	**crystal**
cone	**counter**	**crazy**	fall	-clear (u.m.)
-shaped (u.m.)	#check (banking)	bone	feed	-girded (u.m.)
speaker	#septum	cat	-fertile (u.m.)	-smooth (u.m.)
conference#room	-off	**cream**	-fertilize (v.)	cubbyhole
Congressman#at	act,	cake	-fiber (u.m.)	**cumulo** (c.f.)
#Large	propaganda,	-colored (u.m.)	file	all one word
contra (pref.)	etc.	creditworthiness	fire	**cup**
-acting	as combining	**creek**	flow	bearer
-approach	form, one	bed	foot	cake
-ion	word	side	-grained (u.m.)	ful
rest one word	**country**	**creep**	hair	head
cook	-born (u.m.)	hole	hand	**curb**
off (n., u.m.)	-bred (u.m.)	mouse	hatch	side
out (n., u.m.)	folk	crepe#de#chine	haul	stoner
shack	people	crestfallen	head	cure-all (n., u.m.)
stove	side	**crew**	-immunity	**curly**
cooped	**court**	cut	-index (u.m.)	head
-in (u.m.)	bred	member	-interrogate (v.)	locks (n.)
-up (u.m.)	-martial	cribstrap	-interrogatory	currycomb
cop	ship	**crime**	-invite (v.)	cussword
#out (v.)	**cousin**	fighter	legged	**custom**
out (n.)	-german	wave	legs	-built (u.m.)
copper	hood	crisscross	-level (v.)	-made (u.m.)
-bottomed (u.m.)	-in-law	**crook**	-license (v.)	-tailored (u.m.)
-colored (u.m.)	**cover**	all one word	lift (v.)	**cut**
head	alls	**crooked**	lock	away (n., u.m.)
-headed (u.m.)	let	-foot (n.)	lots	back (n., u.m.)
nose	side	-legged (u.m.)	mark	glass
plate	up (n., u.m.)	-nosed (u.m.)	member	-in (n., u.m.)
-plated (u.m.)	**cow**	-toothed (u.m.)	patch	off (n., u.m.)
works	barn	**crop**	path	out (n., u.m.)
copy	bell	-bound (u.m.)	plow (v.)	rate (u.m.)
cat	catcher	-haired (u.m.)	-pollinate (v.)	throat
cutter	-eyed (u.m.)	head	-purpose (n.)	-toothed (u.m.)
desk	gate	-year	-question	-under (u.m.)
fitter	hand	**cross**	rail	-up (n., u.m.)
holding	herd	-appeal	-reaction	**cutter**
reader	hide	arm	-refer (v.)	-built (u.m.)
right	hitch	band	-reference	-down
coral	lick	bar	road	head
-beaded (u.m.)	path	beam	row	-off
-red (u.m.)	pen	bearer	-service	-out
cork	pox	bedded	-shaft	-rigged (u.m.)
-lined (u.m.)	puncher	belt	-slide	-up
screw	shed	bench	-staff	cuttlebone
corn	sucker	-bidding	-sterile	**cyano** (c.f.)
bin	**crab**	bill (bird)	-stitch	all one word
bread	cake	#bill (legal)	-stone	cyclecar
cake	catcher	bind	-stratification	**cyclo** (c.f.)
cob	eater	bolt	-sue (v.)	-olefin
cracker	faced	bond	-surge (v.)	rest one word
crib	hole	bones	talk	**cysto** (c.f.)
crusher	meat	bred	tie	all one word
cutter	stick	breed	town	**cyto** (c.f.)
dodger		-bridge (v.)	track	all one word
-fed (u.m.)			trail	

D

D
-day
-major
-plus-4-day
dairy
-fed (u.m.)
-made (u.m.)
damp
proofing
-stained (u.m.)
damping-off (n., u.m.)
dancehall
danger # line
dare
-all (n., u.m.)
devil
say
dark
-eyed (u.m.)
horse
(nonliteral)
-skinned (u.m.)
dash
plate
wheel
data
bank
base
date
lined
mark
daughter-in-law
dawn
-gray (u.m.)
streak
day
beam
bed
break
-bright (u.m.)
dawn
dream
-fly (aviation) (v.)
-flying (u.m.)
going
lighted
lit
long (u.m.)
mark
side
star
-to-day (u.m.)
de (pref.)
-air
icer
-ion
centralize,
energize, etc.
rest one word
dead
-alive
beat (n.)
born
-burn (v.)
-cold (u.m.)
-dip (v.)
-drunk (u.m.)
-ender
eye (n.)
-eyed (u.m.)
fall
head
-heated (u.m.)
-heater

-heavy (u.m.)
latch
load
lock
melt
pan
pay
-roast (v.)
weight (n., u.m.)
deaf
-mute
-muteness
death
bed
blow
day
-divided (u.m.)
-doom (v.)
house
-struck (u.m.)
trap
watch
-weary (u.m.)
deckhand
deep
-affected (u.m.)
-cut (u.m.)
-felt (u.m.)
-freeze (u.m., v.)
-frying (u.m.)
going
-grown (u.m.)
-laid (u.m.)
most
mouthed
-rooted (u.m.)
-seated (u.m.)
-set (u.m.)
-sunk (u.m.)
-voiced (u.m.)
deer
drive (n.)
-eyed (u.m.)
food
herd
horn
hound
meat
stalker
stand
dehydr(o) (c.f.)
all one word
demi (pref.)
-Christian, etc.
-incognito
rest one word
dermato (c.f.)
all one word
desert-bred (u.m.)
desk # room
dessertspoon
deutero (c.f.)
all one word
devil
-devil
dog (a marine)
-inspired (u.m.)
-ridden (u.m.)
dew
beam
cap
-clad (u.m.)
claw
damp
-drenched (u.m.)

drop
fall
-fed (u.m.)
-laden (u.m.)
lap
point
dextro (c.f.)
all one word
di (pref.)
all one word
dia (pref.)
all one word
diamond
back
-backed (u.m.)
-shaped (u.m.)
diazo (c.f.)
-oxide
rest one word
dice
cup
play
die
-away (u.m.)
back
case
-cast (u.m., v.)
caster
-cut (u.m., v.)
cutter
hard (n., u.m.)
head
proof (philately)
(n.)
setter
sinker
-square (u.m.)
stock
diesel
-driven (u.m.)
-electric (u.m.)
dillydally
dim
-lighted (u.m.)
lit
out (n., u.m.)
diner-out
ding
bat
dong
dining # room
dinitro (c.f.)
spray
rest one word
dip
-dye (v.)
-grained (u.m.)
head
stick
dipper-in
direct
-connected
(u.m.)
-indirect
direction-finding
(u.m.)
dirt
-cheap (u.m.)
fast
-incrusted (u.m.)
plate
dirty
-faced (u.m.)
-minded (u.m.)
work

dis (pref.)
all one word
dish
cloth
pan
rack
rag
washer
wiper
disk
jockey
pack
plow
-shaped (u.m.)
ditch
bank
digger
rider
side
dittograph
dive-bomb (v.)
do
-all (n., u.m.)
-gooder
-little (n., u.m.)
-nothing (n.,
u.m.)
dock
hand
head
side
dog
bite
-bitten (u.m.)
breeder
cart
catcher
-drawn (u.m.)
-ear (v.)
-eared (u.m.)
face (soldier)
-faced (u.m.)
fall
fight
food
-headed (u.m.)
hole
leg
owner
race
shore
sled
-tired (u.m.)
tooth
-toothed (u.m.)
trick
trot
watch
-weary (u.m.)
doll
face
-faced (u.m.)
dollyhead
donkey
back
-drawn (u.m.)
-eared (u.m.)
doomsday
door
bed
bell
case
check
frame
head

jamb
knob
mat
nail
plate
post
-shaped (u.m.)
sill
step
stop
dope
passer
pusher
sheet
dorsi (c.f.)
all one word
dorso (c.f.)
-occipital
rest one word
double
-barrel (n., u.m.)
-barreled (u.m.)
-bitt (v.)
-breasted (u.m.)
-charge (v.)
check (n., v.)
checked (u.m.,
v.)
-chinned (u.m.)
cross
(nonliteral)
deal (v.)
-decker
-distilled (u.m.)
-duty (u.m.)
-dye (v.)
-edged (u.m.)
-ender
-entendre
handed
-headed (u.m.)
header
-jointed
-leaded (u.m.)
-quick (u.m.)
talk
tone (printing)
tree
-trouble
-up (u.m., v.)
work
dough
-colored (u.m.)
face
-faced (u.m.)
head
mixer
nut
down
beat
by
cast
check
coast
come
-covered (u.m.)
crier
cry
curved
cut
dale
draft
drag
face
fall

feed
filled
flow
fold
grade
gradient
growth
hanging
haul
hill
lead
lock (n.)
look
most
payment
pour
rate
right
river
rush
shore
side
sitting
slip
slope
-soft (u.m.)
spout
stage
stairs
state
stream
street
stroke
sun (adv., u.m.)
swing
take
throw
thrust
town
trampling
trend
trodden
turn
valley
weigh
weight
wind

draft
  age (allowance)
  #age
  -exempt (u.m.)
drag
  bar
  bolt
  net
  pipe
  rope
  saw
  staff
  wire
dragger
  -down
  -in
  -out
  -up
dragon
  -eyed (u.m.)
  #piece
drain
  cleaner
  pipe
  plug
  tile
draw
  -arch (n.)
  arm
  back
  bar
  beam
  bench
  bolt
  bore
  bridge
  cut
  down (n., u.m.)
  file
  gate
  gear
  glove
  head
  horse
  knife
  knot
  link
  loom

  net
  off (n., u.m.)
  out (n., u.m.)
  pin
  plate
  point
  sheet
  span
  stop
  string
  tongs
  tube
drawer
  -down
  -in
  -off
  -out
drawing
  #board
  #room
dream
  -haunted (u.m.)
  lore
  world
dressup (n., u.m.)
dressing #room
drift
  #boat
  bolt
  meter
  -mining (u.m.)
  pin
  wind
drill
  case
  -like
  stock
drip
  cock
  -drip
  -dry (u.m., v.)
  sheet
  stick
drive
  away (n., u.m.)
  belt
  bolt
  cap

  head
  -in (n., u.m.)
  pipe
  screw
drop
  away (n., u.m.)
  bolt
  -forge (v.)
  front
  hammer
  head
  kick
  leaf (n., u.m.)
  leg
  off (n., u.m.)
  out (n., u.m.)
  sonde
  stitch
drug
  -addicted (u.m.)
  mixer
  passer
  pusher
  seller
drum
  beat
  fire
  head
  stick
  -up (n., u.m.)
dry
  -burnt (u.m.)
  clean
  -cure (v.)
  dock
  -dye (v.)
  -farm (v.)
  farming (n., u.m.)
  lot
  -pack (u.m., v.)
  -rotted (u.m.)
  -salt (v.)
  wash
duck
  bill
  -billed (u.m.)
  blind

  foot (tool)
  -footed (u.m.)
  pin
  pond
  walk
due
  -in (n., u.m.)
  out (n., u.m.)
duffelbag
dug
  out (n.)
  -up (u.m.)
dull
  -edged (u.m.)
  head
  -looking (u.m.)
  -witted (u.m.)
dumdum
dumb
  bell
  head
  waiter
dump
  car
  cart
dunderhead
duo (c.f.)
  all one word
dust
  bag
  bin
  brush
  cloth
  -covered (u.m.)
  fall
  -gray (u.m.)
  -laden (u.m.)
  pan
  storm
duty-free (u.m.)
dwelling #house
dye
  mixer
  stuff
  works
dys (pref.)
  all one word

E

ear
  ache
  cap
  drop
  drum
  flap
  guard
  hole
  lap
  mark
  phone
  -piercing (u.m.)
  plug
  ring
  screw
  shot
  sore
  splitting
  tab
  wax
  wig
  witness
earth
  bank
  born
  -bred (u.m.)

  fall
  fast
  -fed (u.m.)
  fill
  grubber
  #house
  kin
  lit
  mover
  nut
  quake
  -shaking (u.m.)
  slide
  -stained (u.m.)
  wall
east
  -central (u.m.)
  going
  -northeast
  -sider
  -southeast
Eastertide
easy
  going
  mark (n.)
  -rising (u.m.)

  -spoken (u.m.)
eavesdrop
ebbtide
edge
  #plane
  shot
  ways
eel
  cake
  catcher
  fare
  pot
  pout
  spear
egg
  beater (all meanings)
  cup
  eater
  fruit
  head (nonliteral)
  hot (n.)
  nog
  plant
  -shaped (u.m.)

  shell
  -white (u.m.)
eight
  -angled (u.m.)
  fold
  penny (nail)
  -ply (u.m.)
  score
  -wheeler
elbowchair
elder
  #brother
  brotherhood
  brotherly
  -leaved (u.m.)
electro (c.f.)
  -optics
  -osmosis
  -ultrafiltration
  rest one word
embryo (c.f.)
  all one word
empty
  handed
  -looking (u.m.)

en
  #banc
  #gros
  #route
encephalo (c.f.)
  all one word
end
  -all (n., u.m.)
  bell
  brain
  gate
  lap
  long
  -match (v.)
  matcher
  -measure (v.)
  most
  -shrink (v.)
  ways
ender
  -on
  -up
endo (c.f.)
  all one word
engine
  #shop

-sized (u.m.)
work
#worker
#yard
entero (c.f.)
  all one word
entry #book
envelope
#holder
#maker
epi (pref.)
  all one word
equi (c.f.)
  -gram-molar
  rest one word
ere
  long
  now
erythro (c.f.)
  all one word
even
  glow
  handed
  minded
  -numbered (u.m.)
  song
  -tempered (u.m.)

tide
ever
  -abiding (u.m.)
  bearing
  blooming
  -constant (u.m.)
  -fertile (u.m.)
  glade
  going
  green
  lasting
  more
  -normal (u.m.)
  -present (u.m.)
  -ready (u.m.)
  sporting (biol.)
  which
every
  day (n., u.m.)
  #day (each day)
  how
  one (all)
  #one
    (distributive)
  #time
evil
  doer

-eyed (u.m.)
-faced (u.m.)
-looking (u.m.)
  minded (u.m.)
  sayer
  speaker
  wishing
ex
  #cathedra
  cathedral
  communicate
  -Governor
  #libris
  #officio
  #post #facto
  #rights
  -serviceman
  -trader
extra
  -alimentary
  -American
  bold
  -Britannic
  -condensed
    (u.m.)
  curricular
  -fine (u.m.)

hazardous
judicial
-large (u.m.)
-long (u.m.)
marginal
mural
ordinary
polar
-strong (u.m.)
territorial
vascular
eye
  ball
  bank
  bar
  blink
  -blurred (u.m.)
  bolt
  brow
  -conscious (u.m.)
  cup
  flap
  glance
  glass
  hole
  lash
  lens

lid
mark
-minded (u.m.)
peep
pit
point
service
shade
shield
shot
sick
sight
sore
spot
-spotted (u.m.)
stalk
strain
string
tooth
wash
#weariness
wink
witness

F

F
-flat
-horn
-sharp
fable
#book
teller
face
  about (n., u.m., v.)
  -arbor (v.)
  cloth
  -harden (v.)
  -hardened (u.m.)
  lifting
  mark
  -on (n., u.m.)
  plate
  up (n., u.m.)
fact
  finding
  sheet
fade
  away (n., u.m.)
  -in (n., u.m.)
  out (n., u.m.)
fail-safe
faint
  heart
  -voiced (u.m.)
fair
  ground
  -lead (n., u.m.)
  minded
  play
  -skinned (u.m.)
fairy
  folk
  hood
  tale
faithbreaker
fall
  away (n., u.m.)
  back (n., u.m.)
  -in (n., u.m.)
  out (n., u.m.)
  -plow (v.)

-sow (v.)
trap
fallow #land
false
  -bottomed (u.m.)
  -faced (u.m.)
  hood
  -tongued (u.m.)
fame
  -crowned (u.m.)
  -thirsty (u.m.)
fan
  back
  bearer
  fare
  fold
  foot
  -jet
  -leaved (u.m.)
  marker
  -shaped (u.m.)
  -tailed (u.m.)
fancy
  -free (u.m.)
  -loose (u.m.)
  -woven (u.m.)
  -wrought (u.m.)
far
  -aloft (u.m.)
  away (n., u.m.)
  -borne (u.m.)
  -distant (u.m.)
  -eastern (u.m.)
  -famed (u.m.)
  fetched
  flung (u.m.)
  gone
  -off (u.m.)
  -reaching (u.m.)
  seeing
  -seen (u.m.)
  -set (u.m.)
  sight
farm
  -bred (u.m.)
  hand
  hold

people
place
stead
fashion
  -led (u.m.)
  #piece (naut.)
  -setting (u.m.)
fast
  -anchored (u.m.)
  back
  -dyed (u.m.)
  going
  hold
  -moving (u.m.)
  -read (v.)
  -reading (u.m.)
  #time (daylight
    saving)
fat
  back
  -bellied (u.m.)
  -free (u.m.)
  head
  -soluble (u.m.)
father
  -confessor
  -in-law
fault
  finder
  slip
faux #pas
fear
  -free (u.m.)
  nought
  -pursued (u.m.)
  -shaken (u.m.)
feather
  bed (v.)
  bone
  brain
  edge
  -footed (u.m.)
  head
  -leaved (u.m.)
  stitch
  -stitched (u.m.)
  -stitching

-tongue (v.)
weight
wing (moth)
fed-up (u.m.)
feeble
  -bodied (u.m.)
  minded
feed
  back (n., u.m.)
  bag
  bin
  crusher
  cutter
  head
  lot
  mixer
  pipe
  rack
  stuff
feeder
  -in
  -up
fellow
  craft
  ship
  rest two words
felt
  cutter
  -lined (u.m.)
  packer
fenbank
fencepost
fern
  -clad (u.m.)
  leaf
  -leaved (u.m.)
ferro (c.f.)
  -carbon-titanium
  -uranium
  rest one word
fever
  less
  -stricken (u.m.)
  trap
  -warm (u.m.)
fiber
  -faced (u.m.)

glass
stitch
Fiberglas
  (copyright)
fibro (c.f.)
  -osteoma
  rest one word
fickleminded
  (u.m.)
fiddle
  back
  -faddle
  head
  -shaped (u.m.)
  stick
  string
field
  ball
  glass
  goal
  -strip
fierce
  -eyed (u.m.)
  -looking (u.m.)
fiery
  -flaming (u.m.)
  -hot (u.m.)
  -red (u.m.)
  -tempered (u.m.)
fig
  bar
  eater
  leaf
  shell
figure
  head
  -of-eight (u.m.)
  #work (printing)
file
  card
  -hard (u.m.)
  setter
  -soft (u.m.)
fill
  -in (n., u.m.)
  out (n., u.m.)
  -up (n., u.m.)

filler
  cap
  -in
  -out
  -up
film
  cutter
  goer
  going
  slide
  strip
  -struck (u.m.)
fin
  back
  -shaped (u.m.)
fine
  -cut (u.m., v.)
  -draw (v.)
  -drawn (u.m.)
  -featured (u.m.)
  -looking (u.m.)
  -set (u.m.)
finger
  breadth
  -cut (u.m.)
  hold
  hole
  hook
  mark
  nail
  parted
  post
  print
  shell
  spin
  stall
  tip
fire
  arm
  back (n.)
  ball
  bell
  bolt
  bomb
  brand
  brat
  break
  brick
  -burnt (u.m.)
  -clad (u.m.)
  coat
  cracker
  crest
  -cure (v.)
  damp
  -eater
  fall
  fang
  fighter
  guard
  -hardened (u.m.)
  hose
  lit
  pit
  place
  plow
  plug
  -polish (v.)
  -red (u.m.)
  -resistant (u.m.)
  safe
  side
  spout
  trap
  truck
  wall
  warden

firm
  -footed (u.m.)
  -set (u.m.)
  -up (n., u.m.)
first
  -aider
  -born (u.m.)
  -class (u.m.)
  comer
  hand (u.m.)
  -made (u.m.)
  -named (u.m.)
  -nighter
  -rate (u.m.)
  -rater
fish
  back
  bed
  -bellied (u.m.)
  bolt
  bone
  bowl
  cake
  eater
  eye
  -eyed (u.m.)
  fall
  -fed (u.m.)
  food
  garth
  hook
  -joint (v.)
  kill
  meal
  mouth
  plate
  pond
  pool
  pot
  pound
  trap
  weir
  works
fisher
  folk
  people
fishyback (n., u.m.)
fit
  out (n.)
  strip
five
  bar
  fold
  -ply (u.m.)
  -pointed (u.m.)
  -reeler
  score
  -shooter
flag
  bearer
  pole
  post
  -raising (u.m.)
  ship
  -signal (v.)
  staff
  stick
flame
  -colored (u.m.)
  -cut (v.)
  out (n.)
  thrower
flannelmouth
flap
  cake
  doodle

  -eared (u.m.)
  jack
flare
  back (n., u.m.)
  out (n., u.m.)
  path
  up (n., u.m.)
flash
  back (n., u.m.)
  bulb
  card
  cube
  gun
  lamp
  pan
  point
flat
  back
    (bookbinding)
  bed (printing)
  -bottomed (u.m.)
  car
  -compound (v.)
  fold
  foot (n.)
  hat
  head
  iron
  nose
  out (n., u.m.)
  -rolled (u.m.)
  sawn
  top
  -topped (u.m.)
  woods
flax
  drop
  -leaved (u.m.)
  -polled (u.m.)
  seed
  wife
flea
  bite
  -bitten (u.m.)
fleet
  foot
  -footed (u.m.)
  wing
flesh
  brush
  hook
  -pink (u.m.)
  pot
fleur-de-lis
flight
  crew
  -hour
  path
  -test (v.)
flimflam
flip
  -flap
  -flop
  -up (n., u.m.)
flood
  cock
  flow
  gate
  lamp
  lighting
  mark
  tide
  wall
floor
  beam
  cloth
  head

  lamp
  mat
  mop
  space
  stain
  walker
  -waxing (u.m.)
flour
  bag
  bin
  #mill
  sack
flow
  chart
  meter
  off (n., u.m.)
  sheet
  through
flower
  bed
  bud
  -crowned (u.m.)
  #grower
  -hung (u.m.)
  pot
  -scented (u.m.)
  #shop
flue-cure (v.)
fluid
  -compressed (u.m.)
  extract (pharm.) (n.)
  glycerate
fluo (c.f.)
    all one word
fluoro (c.f.)
    all one word
flush
  -cut (u.m.)
  -decked (u.m.)
  -decker
  gate
fluvio (c.f.)
    all one word
fly
  away
  back
  ball
  -bitten (u.m.)
  blow
  blown
  -by-night (n., u.m.)
  catcher
  eater
  -fish (v.)
  -fisher
  -fisherman
  #fishing
  flap
  -free (u.m.)
  leaf
  paper
  sheet
  speck
  -specked (u.m.)
  tier
  trap
  weight
  wheel
  winch
flying
  #boat
  #fish
foam
  bow

  -crested (u.m.)
  -white (u.m.)
fog
  born
  bow
  dog
  eater
  -hidden (u.m.)
  horn
  -ridden (u.m.)
fold
  -in
  up (n., u.m.)
folk
  free (u.m.)
  lore
  song
follow
  -on
  through (n., u.m.)
  up (n., u.m.)
follower-up
food
  packer
  sick
  stuff
foolhardy
foolscap
foot
  -and-mouth (u.m.)
  ball
  band
  bath
  blower
  brake
  breadth
  bridge
  -candle
  fall
  -free (u.m.)
  gear
  -grain
  hill
  hold
  lambert
  licker
  lining
  locker
  loose
  mark
  note
  pad
  path
  pick
  plate
  -pound
  -pound-second
  print
  race
  rail
  rest
  rope
  scald
  -second
  slogger
  sore
  stalk
  stall
  step
  stick
  stock
  stool
  -ton
  walk
  wall

-weary (u.m.)
worn
for (pref.)
  all one word
fore
  -age
  -and-aft (n., u.m.)
  -and-after (n.)
  -edge
  -end
  -exercise
  rest one word
forest
  -clad (u.m.)
  -covered (u.m.)
  #land
  side
fork
  head
  lift
  -pronged (u.m.)
  -tailed (u.m.)
form
  fitting
  #work (printing)
forth
  coming
  right
  with
fortuneteller
forty-niner
foul
  #line

-looking (u.m.)
mouthed
-spoken (u.m.)
-tongued (u.m.)
up (n., u.m.)
foundry#proof (printing)
fountainhead
four
  -bagger
  -ball (u.m.)
  -eyed (u.m.)
  flusher
  fold
  -footed (u.m.)
  -in-hand (n., u.m.)
  -masted (u.m.)
  -master
  penny (nail)
  -ply (u.m.)
  score
  some
  square
  -wheeler
fox
  -faced (u.m.)
  hole
  hound
  skinned
  tailed
  trot
fracto (c.f.)
  all one word

frameup (n., u.m.)
free
  booter
  born
  drop
  -for-all (n., u.m.)
  -grown (u.m.)
  hand (drawing)
  handed
  hold
  lance
  loader
  -minded
  masonry
  -spoken (u.m.)
  standing (u.m.)
  thinker
  trader
  wheel (u.m., v.)
  wheeler (n.)
  #will (n.)
  will (u.m.)
freeze
  down (n., u.m.)
  out (n., u.m.)
  up (n., u.m.)
freight
  #house
  -mile
  #room
french-minded (u.m.)
fresh
  -looking (u.m.)

-painted (u.m.)
frog
  belly
  eater
  -eyed (u.m.)
  face
  mouth
  nose
  pond
  tongue
    (medicine)
front
  -end (u.m.)
  -focused (u.m.)
  runner
  stall
  -wheel (u.m.)
fronto (c.f.)
  -occipital
  -orbital
  rest one word
frost
  bite
  bow
  -free (u.m.)
  -hardy (u.m.)
  -heaving (u.m.)
  -killed (u.m.)
  lamp
fruit
  cake
  #fly
  growing
  #shop

stalk
frying#pan
fuel
  #line
  #oil
full
  back
  -bellied (u.m.)
  blood
  -bound (u.m.)
  face
  -fashioned (u.m.)
  -flowering (u.m.)
  -grown (u.m.)
  -handed (u.m.)
  -headed (u.m.)
  -lined (u.m.)
  #load
  mouth
  -strength (u.m.)
  -time (u.m.)
fundraising
funlover
funnel
  form
  -shaped (u.m.)
fur
  -clad (u.m.)
  coat
  -lined (u.m.)
  -trimmed (u.m.)
fuseplug

G

G
  -major
  -man
  -minor
  -sharp
gabfest
gad
  about (n., u.m.)
  fly
gaff-topsail
gag
  -check (v.)
  root
gaugepin
gain
  say
  -sharing (u.m.)
galact(o) (c.f.)
  all one word
gallbladder
galley
  #proof (printing)
  -west (u.m.)
galvano (c.f.)
  all one word
game
  bag
  cock
gang
  boss
  plank
  saw
gapeseed
garnet-brown (u.m)
gas
  bag
  bomb
  -driven (u.m.)
  -fired (u.m.)

firing
fitter
-heated (u.m.)
-laden (u.m.)
lamp
lighted
line (auto)
#line (people queue)
lock
meter
works
gastro (c.f.)
  -omental
  rest one word
gate
  leg (u.m.)
  pin
  post
  tender
  works
gay
  cat
  -colored (u.m.)
  #dog
  -looking (u.m.)
gear
  case
  -driven (u.m.)
  fitter
  -operated (u.m.)
  set
  shift
  wheel
gelatin
  -coated (u.m.)
  -making (u.m.)
gelatino (c.f.)
  bromide
  chloride

gem
  cutter
  -set (u.m.)
  #stone
genito (c.f.)
  all one word
gentle
  folk
  -looking (u.m.)
  -mannered (u.m.)
  mouthed
  -spoken (u.m.)
geo (c.f.)
  all one word
germ-free (u.m.)
gerrymander
get
  -at-able
  away (n., u.m.)
  off (n., u.m.)
  -together (n., u.m.)
  up (n., u.m.)
ghost
  -haunted (u.m.)
  write (v.)
giddy
  brain
  head
  -paced (u.m.)
gilt-edge (u.m.)
gin-run (u.m.)
ginger
  bread
  -colored (u.m.)
  snap
  spice
give
  -and-take (n., u.m.)

away (n., u.m.)
glacio (c.f.)
  all one word
glad
  -cheered (u.m.)
  -sad
glass
  blower
  cutter
  -eater
  -eyed (u.m.)
  -hard (u.m.)
  works
glauco (c.f.)
  all one word
glidepath
globetrotter
glosso (c.f.)
  all one word
glow
  lamp
  meter
gluc(o) (c.f.)
  all one word
glue
  pot
  stock
glycero (c.f.)
  all one word
glyco (c.f.)
  all one word
go
  -ahead (n., u.m.)
  -around (n., u.m.)
  -as-you-please (u.m.)
  -back (n., u.m.)
  -between (n.)
  by (n.)

cart
-devil (n.)
-getter
-getting (n., u.m.)
-off (n., u.m.)
goalpost
goat
  -bearded (u.m.)
  -drunk (u.m.)
  -eyed (u.m.)
  herd
goat's
  -hair
  -horn
God
  -conscious (u.m.)
  -fearing (u.m.)
  -forsaken (u.m.)
  -given (u.m.)
  head
  -man
  -ordained (u.m.)
  -sent (u.m.)
  -sped (u.m.)
  speed
  -taught (u.m.)
god
  child
  daughter
  father
  head
  hood
  less
  mother
  parent
  send
  ship
  son
  sonship
goggle-eyed (u.m.)

goings-on
gold
  beater
  brick (swindle)
#brick (of real
    gold)
  -bright (u.m.)
  -brown (u.m.)
  digger
  -filled (u.m.)
  foil
  -inlaid (u.m.)
  leaf
  plate (v.)
  -plated (u.m.)
  -plating (u.m.)
  smithing
  -wrought (u.m.)
golden
  -fingered (u.m.)
  -headed (u.m.)
  mouthed
good
  bye
  -fellowship
  -for-nothing (n., u.m.)
  -looker
  -looking (u.m.)
  -natured (u.m.)
#will (kindness)
  will (salable asset)
goose
  bone
  -cackle
  -eyed (u.m.)
  flesh
  -footed (u.m.)
  herd
  mouth
  neck
  pimples
  rump
  step
  wing

gospel
  like
  -true (u.m.)
gourdhead
Government (U.S. or foreign)
  -in-exile
  -owned (u.m.)
  wide
  governmentwide (State, city, etc.)
grab
  -all (n., u.m.)
  hook
  rope
grade
  finder
  mark
grain
  -cut (u.m.)
  -laden (u.m.)
  mark
  sick
gram
  -fast (u.m.)
  -meter
  -molecular
  -negative (u.m.)
  -positive (u.m.)
grand
  aunt
  child, etc.
  stand
grant-in-aid
grape
  fruit
  juice
  -leaved (u.m.)
  seed
  stalk
  vine
graphalloy
grapho (c.f)
    all one word
grass
  -clad (u.m.)

-covered (u.m.)
  cutter
  flat
  -green (u.m.)
  hop
  nut
  plot
  roots (nonliteral)
#roots (literal)
  widow
grave
  clothes
  digger
  side
  stead
gravel-blind (u.m.)
gray
  back (n., u.m.)
  beard (n.)
  -clad (u.m.)
  coat (n.)
  -eyed (u.m.)
  -haired (u.m.)
  head
  -headed (u.m.)
  out (n., u.m.)
great
  -aunt
  coat
  -eared (u.m.)
  -grandchild, etc.
  -headed (u.m.)
  heart
  mouthed
green
  back (n., u.m.)
  belt (community)
  -clad (u.m.)
  -eyed (u.m.)
  gage (plum)
  gill
  grocer
  horn
  -leaved (u.m.)

sand (geology)
  sick
  stuff
  sward
  town (community)
#wood (literal)
  wood (forest) (nonliteral)
greyhound
gridiron
griddlecake
grip
  sack
  wheel
gross-minded (u.m.)
ground
  hog
  mass
  nut
  path
  plot
  -sluicer
  speed
  wave
#water
  group-connect (v.)
  grownup (n., u.m.)
  grubstake
guard
  plate
  rail
guestchamber
guidepost
guided-missile (u.m.)
guider-in
gum
  boil
  chewer
  digger
  drop
  -gum
  lac
  -saline (n.)
  shoe

gun
  bearer
  blast
  builder
  cotton
  crew
  deck
  fight
  fire
  flint
  lock
  paper
  pit
  play
  point
  powder
  rack
  -rivet (v.)
  runner
  shot
  -shy (u.m.)
  sight
  stock
  wale
gut
  less
  string
gutter
  blood
  -bred (u.m.)
  snipe
  spout
gymno (c.f.)
    all one word
gyneco (c.f.)
    all one word
gyro
#horizon
#mechanism
#pelorus
  plane, compass, etc.

H

H
  -bar
  -beam
  -bomb
  -hour
  -piece
hack
  barrow
  hammer
  log
  saw
hailstorm
hair
  band
  breadth
  brush
  -check (n.)
  cloth
  cut (n.)
  do
  dresser
  -fibered (u.m.)
  lock
  pin
  space (printing)
  splitting
  spring
  streak

  stroke (printing)
half
  -and-half (n., u.m.)
  -afraid
  -alive
  -angry
  back (football)
  -backed (u.m.)
  -baked (u.m.)
  blood (n.)
  -bound (u.m.)
  -bred (u.m.)
  breed
  caste
  -clear
  cock (v.)
  cocked (nonliteral)
  -dark
  deck
  -decked (u.m.)
  -decker
  -feed (v.)
  -hourly (u.m.)
  -life
#load
  -loaded (u.m.)

  -mast
  -miler
  -monthly (u.m.)
  -on (n., u.m.)
  pace
  penny
  -ripe
  -shy
  -sole (v.)
  staff
  stitch
  -strength (u.m.)
  title
  tone (printing)
  track
  -true
  -truth
  -weekly (u.m.)
  wit
  -witted (u.m.)
  -yearly (u.m.)
hallmark
ham
  shackle
  string
hammer
  cloth
  dress (v.)

  -hard (u.m.)
  -harden (v.)
  -hardened (u.m.)
  head
  lock
  toe
  -weld (v.)
  -wrought (u.m.)
hand
  bag
  ball
  bank (v.)
  barrow
  bill
  -bound (u.m.)
  bow
  brake
  breadth
  brush
  -built (u.m.)
  car
  -carry (v.)
  cart
  -carve (v.)
  clap
  clasp
  -clean (v.)
  crank

  cuff
  -cut (v.)
  -embroidered (u.m.)
  -fed (v.)
  fold
  grasp
  grenade
  grip
  guard
  gun
  -high (u.m.)
  hold
  hole
  -in-hand (u.m.)
  kerchief
  -knit (v.)
  -knitter
  laid
  -letter (v.)
  lift (truck)
  liner
  made
  -me-down (n., u.m.)
  mix (v.)
  mold (n.)
  mower

off (n., u.m.)
out (n., u.m.)
pick (v.)
post
press
print
rail
reading
saw
scrape (v.)
set
shake
spade
spike
splice
split
spring
spun
-stamp (v.)
stand
stitch
stroke
stuff
-tailored (u.m.)
tap
tool
-tooled (u.m.)
-tooling (u.m.)
truck
weave
wheel
worked
woven
write (v.)
written
wrought
handie-talkie
handlebar
hang
  dog
  nail
  net
  out (n., u.m.)
  up (n.)
hanger
-back
-on
-up
happy-go-lucky
hara-kiri
harborside
hard
-and-fast (u.m.)
  back (beetle)
-baked (u.m.)
-bitten (u.m)
-boiled (u.m.)
  case
  core
  fist (n.)
  handed
  hat (n.)
  head
-hit (u.m.)
-looking (u.m.)
  mouthed
  nose
  pan
-pressed (u.m.)
-set (u.m.)
  ship
  spun
  stand
  tack
  top (auto)
-won (u.m.)
#work

-working (u.m.)
  wrought
hare
  brain
  foot
  hound
  lip
-mad (u.m.)
harness-making
  (u.m.)
harum-scarum
has-been (n.)
hashmark
hat
  band
  brim
  brush
  cleaner
  pin
  rack
  rail
  stand
hatchet-faced
  (u.m.)
haul
  about (n., u.m.)
  away (n., u.m.)
  back (n.)
have-not (n., u.m.)
haversack
hawk
  bill
-billed (u.m.)
-nosed (u.m.)
hawse
  hole
  pipe
hay
  band
  cap
  cart
  cock
  fork
  lift
  loft
  market
  mow
  rack
  rake
  rick
-scented (u.m.)
  seed
  stack
  wire
hazel
-eyed (u.m.)
  nut
he-man
head
  ache
  achy
  band
  bander
  block
  cap
  chair
  cheese
  chute
  cloth
  dress
-ender
  first
  frame
  gate
  gear
  hunter
  lamp

  ledge
  lighting
  liner
  lock
  long
  mold
  most
  note
-on (u.m.)
  phone
  plate
  post
  quarters
  rail
  reach
  rest
  ring
  rope
  set
  shake
  sill
  space
  spin
  spring
  stall
  stand
  start
  stick
  stock
  stream
  strong
  wall
  waiter
  wind
header-up
heal-all (n., u.m.)
heart
  ache
  aching
  beat
  block
  blood
  break
  burn
  deep
  felt
  free (u.m.)
  grief
  heavy
  leaf
-leaved (u.m.)
  nut
  quake
  seed
  sick
  sore
  string
  struck
  throb
-throbbing (u.m.)
-weary (u.m.)
hearth
  rug
  warming
heat
  drops
-resistant (u.m.)
  stroke
  treat (v.)
-treating (u.m.)
heaven
-inspired (u.m.)
-sent (u.m.)
heaver
-off
-out
-over

heavy
  back
-duty (u.m.)
-eyed (u.m.)
-footed (u.m.)
  handed
-looking (u.m.)
-set (u.m.)
#water
  weight (n., u.m.)
hecto (c.f.)
  all one word
hedge
  born
  breaker
  hog
  hop
  pig
  row
heel
  ball
  band
  block
  cap
  fast
  grip
  pad
  path
  plate
  post
  print
  ring
  stay
  strap
  tap
helio (c.f.)
  all one word
hell
  bender
  bent
  born
  bred
  cat
-dark (u.m.)
  diver
  dog
  fire
  hole
  hound
-red (u.m.)
  ship
helpmeet
helter-skelter
hemstitch
hema (c.f.)
  all one word
hemato (c.f.)
  all one word
hemi (pref.)
  all one word
hemo (c.f.)
  all one word
hemp
  seed
  string
hen
  bill
  coop
-feathered
  (u.m.)
  pecked
  roost
hence
  forth
  forward
hepato (c.f.)
  all one word

hepta (c.f.)
  all one word
here
  about
  after
  at
  by
  from
  in
  inabove
  inafter
  inbefore
  into
  of
  on
  to
  tofore
  under
  unto
  upon
  with
herringbone
hetero (c.f.)
-ousia, etc.
  rest one word
hexa (c.f.)
  all one word
hi
-fi
  jack
hide
-and-seek (n.,
  u.m.)
  away (n., u.m.)
  out (n., u.m.)
high
  ball
  binder
  born
  bred
  brow
  (nonliteral)
-caliber (u.m.)
-class (u.m.)
  flier (n.)
  flying (u.m.)
-foreheaded
  (u.m.)
  handed
-hat (v.)
  jinks
  lander
#light (literal)
  light (nonlit.)
-minded (u.m.)
-power (u.m.)
-pressure
  (u.m., v.)
-priced (u.m.)
#proof
-reaching (u.m.)
-rigger (n.)
  rise (building)
  road
#seas
-speed (u.m.)
  stepper
-tension (u.m.)
-up (u.m.)
#water
higher-up (n.)
hill
  billy
  culture
  (farming)
  side
  top

hind
  brain
  cast
  gut (n.)
  head
  leg
  most
  quarter
  saddle
  sight
  wing
hip
  bone
  mold
  shot
hippo (c.f.)
  all one word
histo (c.f.)
  all one word
hit
  -and-miss (u.m.)
  -and-run (u.m.)
  -or-miss (u.m.)
hitchhiker
hoarfrost
hoary-haired
  (u.m.)
hob
  goblin
  nail
  nob
hobbyhorse
hocus-pocus
hodgepodge
hog
  back
  -backed (u.m.)
  -faced (u.m.)
  fat
  frame
  hide
  nose (machine)
  -nosed (u.m.)
  pen
  sty
  -tie (v.)
  wash
  -wild (u.m.)
hog's-back (geol.)
hogshead
hoistaway (n.)
hold
  all (n., u.m.)
  back (n., u.m.)
  -clear (n., u.m.)
  down (n., u.m.)
  fast (n., u.m.)
  off (n., u.m.)
  out (n., u.m.)

up (n., u.m.)
holder
  -forth
  -on
  -up
hole
  -high (u.m.)
  through
hollow
  back
    (bookbinding)
hoof
  -backed (u.m.)
  -eyed (u.m.)
  faced
  -ground (u.m.)
holo (c.f.)
  all one word
home
  -baked (u.m.)
  body
  born
  bred
  brew
  builder
  comer
  -fed (u.m.)
  felt
  folk
  freeze (u.m., v.)
  front
  furnishings (n.)
  grown
  lander
  life
  made
  plate
  seeker
  sick
  spun
  stead
  stretch
  town
  woven
homeo (c.f.)
  all one word
homo
  # legalis
  # sapiens
homo (c.f.)
  -ousia, etc.
  rest one word
honey
  -colored (u.m.)
  comb
  dew
  drop
  eater
  -laden (u.m.)
  lipped

moon
  mouthed
  pot
  sucker
  sweet
honor # man
hood
  cap
  mold
  wink
hoof
  beat
  mark
  print
  -printed (u.m.)
hook
  ladder
  nose
  -nosed (u.m.)
  pin
  up (n., u.m.)
hooker
  -off
  -on
  -out
  -over
  -up
hoopstick
hop
  about (n., u.m.)
  off (n., u.m.)
  scotch
  toad
hopper
  burn
  dozer
horehound
hormono (c.f.)
  all one word
horn
  bill
  blende
  blower
  -eyed (u.m.)
  pipe
  stay
  tip
hornyhanded
horse
  back
  breaker
  car
  cloth
  dealer
  fair
  fight
  flesh
  hair
  head

herd
hide
hoof
  -hour
  jockey
  laugh
  meat
  mint
  play
  pond
  power-hour
  power-year
  pox
  race
  # sense (n.)
  shoe
  thief
  whip
hot
  bed
  blood
  -blooded (u.m.)
  brain
  cake
  -cold
  dog
  foot
  head (n.)
  -mix (u.m.)
  pack
  patch
  plate
  -press (v.)
  rod (nonliteral)
  -roll (v.)
  -rolled (u.m.)
  spot
  -work (v.)
houndshark
hourglass
house
  breaking
  broken
  builder
  cleaner
  -cleaning (u.m.)
  coat
  dress
  father
  furnishing(s) (n.)
  guest
  hold
  husband
  mother
  parent
  pest
  -raising (u.m.)
  ridden
  top

trailer
wares
warming
wife
wright
how
  -do-you-do (n.)
  ever
  soever
hub
  cap
  -deep (u.m.)
humankind
humble
  bee
  -looking (u.m.)
  mouthed
  -spirited (u.m.)
humdrum
humero (c.f.)
  -olecranal
  rest one word
hump
  back
  -shouldered
    (u.m.)
humpty-dumpty
hunchback
hundred
  fold
  -legged (u.m.)
  -percenter
  -pounder
  weight
hung-up (u.m.)
hunger
  -mad (u.m.)
  -worn (u.m.)
hurly-burly
hush
  -hush
  up (n., u.m.)
hydro (c.f.)
  electric, plant,
    power, etc.
  # station
  rest one word
hygro (c.f.)
  all one word
hyper (pref.)
  -Dorian, etc.
  rest one word
hypo (c.f.)
  all one word
hystero (c.f.)
  -oophorectomy
  -salpingo-oopho-
    rectomy
  rest one word

I

I
  -bar
  -beam
  -iron
  -rail
ice
  berg
  blind
  # blindness
  blink
  block
  bone
  breaker
  cap
  -clad (u.m.)

-cold (u.m.)
  -cooled (u.m.)
  -covered (u.m.)
  fall
  # fishing
  floe (island)
  flow
    (current)
  -free (u.m.)
  melt
  pack
  plant
  plow
  quake
  # water

ichthyo (c.f.)
  all one word
ideo (c.f.)
  -unit
  rest one word
idle
  headed
  -looking (u.m.)
  -minded (u.m.)
ileo (c.f.)
  all one word
ilio (c.f.)
  all one word
ill
  -advised (u.m.)

-being (n.)
  -born (u.m.)
  -bred (u.m.)
  # breeding (n.)
  -doing (n., u.m.)
  -fated (u.m.)
  -humored (u.m.)
  -looking (u.m.)
  -treat (v.)
  -use (v.)
  -wisher
  -wishing (u.m.)
in
  -and-in (u.m.)
  -and-out (u.m.)

-and-outer
  -being (u.m.)
  -flight (u.m.)
  -house
  -law (n.)
  asmuch, sofar
  # re, # rem,
    # situ, etc.
in (pref.)
  active (u.m.)
  depth (u.m.)
  hospital (u.m.)
  migration (u.m.)
  service (u.m.),
    etc.

inch
-deep (u.m.)
-long (u.m.)
meal
-pound
-ton
index-digest
indigo
-blue (u.m.)
-carmine (u.m.)
Indo (c.f.)
chinese
-European, etc.
infra (pref.)
-anal
-auricular
-axillary

-esophageal
-umbilical
rest one word
inguino (c.f.)
all one word
ink
-black (u.m.)
mixer
pot
slinger
spot
-spotted (u.m)
stain
stand
well
inner
-city (u.m.)

#man
spring
ino (c.f.)
all one word
insect-borne
(u.m.)
inter (pref.)
-American, etc.
rest one word
intra (pref.)
-atomic, etc.
rest one word
intro (pref.)
all one word
Irish
-American (u.m.)
-born (u.m.)

iron
back
-braced (u.m.)
clad
fisted
-free (u.m.)
handed
hard
-lined (u.m.)
mold
-red (u.m.)
shod
shot (mineral)
(u.m.)
#shot (golf)
side
works

ironer-up
island
-born (u.m.)
-dotted (u.m.)
iso (c.f.)
-octane
-oleic
-osmosis
rest one word
ivory
-tinted (u.m.)
type (photog.)
-white (u.m.)
ivy
-clad (u.m.)
-covered (u.m.)

J

J-bolt
jack
ass
hammer
head
-in-the-box
knife
-of-all-trades
-o'-lantern
-plane (v.)
pot
rabbit
screw
shaft
snipe
stay
straw
tar

jam
nut
packed
jaw
bone
breaker
foot
-locked (u.m.)
twister
jay
hawk
walk
jelly
bean
roll
jerry
-build (v.)
builder

-built (u.m.)
jet
black (u.m.)
liner
port
-powered (u.m.)
prop
-propelled (u.m.)
stream
wash
jewel
-bright (u.m.)
-studded (u.m.)
jew's-harp
jib
head
-o-jib
stay

jig
-a-jig
back
-drill (v.)
saw
job
seeker
#shop
joggle#piece
joint#owner
joulemeter
joy
hop
killer
ride
stick
jump
off (n., u.m.)

rock
jungle
-clad (u.m.)
-covered (u.m.)
side
junkpile
jury
#box
-fixing (u.m.)
-rigged (u.m.)
juxta (c.f.)
-ampullar
-articular
rest one word

K

K
-ration
-term
keel
block
fat
haul
-laying (u.m.)
#line
keepsake
kerato (c.f.)
all one word
kettle
drum
stitch
key
bolt
hole
lock
note
punch
ring
seat

stop
word
kick
about (n., u.m.)
back (n., u.m.)
-in (n., u.m.)
off (n., u.m.)
out (n., u.m.)
up (n., u.m.)
killjoy
kiln
-dry (u.m., v.)
eye
hole
rib
stick
tree
kilo (pref.)
gram-meter
voltampere
watthour
rest one word
kindheart

king
bolt
head
hood
hunter
pin
kins
folk
people
kiss-off (n., u.m.)
kite
flier
flying
knapsack
knee
-braced (u.m.)
brush
cap
-deep (u.m.)
-high (u.m.)
hole
pad
pan

strap
knick
knack
point
knight
-errant
head
hood
knitback
knob
kerrie
stick
knock
about (n., u.m.)
away (n., u.m.)
down (n., u.m.)
-knee (n.)
-kneed (u.m.)
off (n., u.m.)
-on (n., u.m.)
out (n., u.m.)
up (n., u.m.)

knocker
-off
-up
knot
hole
horn
know
-all (n., u.m.)
-how (n., u.m.)
-it-all (n., u.m.)
-little (n., u.m.)
-nothing (n.,
u.m.)
knuckle
bone
-deep (u.m.)
-kneed (u.m.)
Ku#Klux#Klan

L

L
-bar
-beam
-block
-shaped
-square
labio (c.f.)
all one word
laborsaving

lace
-edged (u.m.)
#edging
wing (insect)
-winged (u.m.)
worked
lackluster
ladder-backed
(u.m.)

lady
beetle
finger
killer
ship
lake
bed
front
lander

shore
side
lameduck
(nonliteral)
(n., u.m.)
lamp
black
-blown (u.m.)
-foot

hole
-hour
#house
lighter
lit
post
shade
stand
wick

land
#base
-based (u.m.)
#bird
fall
fast
fill
flood
form
grabber
-grant (u.m.)
holding
lady
locked
look
lord
lubber
mark
mass
mine
-poor (u.m.)
right
scape
sick
side
slide
slip
spout
storm
wash
wire
wrack
lantern-jawed (u.m.)
lap
belt
-lap
robe
streak
weld (v.)
-welded (u.m.)
-welding (u.m.)
large
-eyed
-handed (u.m.)
-minded (u.m.)
mouthed
-scale (u.m.)
lark
-colored (u.m.)
spur
laryngo (c.f.)
  all one word
last
-born (u.m.)
-cited (u.m.)
-ditcher
-named (u.m.)
latch
bolt
key
string
late
-born (u.m.)
comer
-lamented (u.m.)
-maturing (u.m.)
latero (c.f.)
  all one word
lath-backed (u.m.)
lathe-bore (v.)
latter
-day (u.m.)
most
laughingstock
laundry#room

law
-abiding (u.m.)
breaker
-fettered (u.m.)
giver
suit
lawnmower
lay
away (n., u.m.)
back (n., u.m.)
-by (n.)
down (n., u.m.)
-minded (u.m.)
off (n., u.m.)
on (n., u.m.)
out (n., u.m.)
up (n., u.m.)
layer
-on
-out
-over
-up
lazy
bones
boots
legs
lead
-alpha
-burn (v.)
-filled (u.m.)
-gray (u.m.)
-in (n., u.m.)
line
#line (medical, naut. only)
off (n., u.m.)
out (n., u.m.)
leaden
-eyed (u.m.)
pated
-souled (u.m.)
leader#line
leaf
bud
-clad (u.m.)
-eating (u.m.)
-red (u.m.)
-shaped (u.m.)
stalk
lean
-faced (u.m.)
-looking (u.m.)
-to (n., u.m.)
leapfrog
lease
back (n., u.m.)
hold
leather
back
-backed (u.m.)
-bound (u.m.)
-brown (u.m.)
-covered (u.m.)
head
neck
side
leavetaking
lee-bow (v.)
leech
eater
#rope
left
-bank (v.)
#field (sports)
-hand (u.m.)
-handed (u.m.)
-hander

most
-sided (u.m.)
wing (political)
leg
band
puller
rope (v.)
lend-lease
lepto (c.f.)
  all one word
let
down (n., u.m.)
off (n., u.m.)
up (n., u.m.)
letter
drop
gram
head
-perfect (u.m.)
press
space
leuc(o) (c.f.)
  all one word
liberal-minded (u.m.)
lieutenant
#colonel
-colonelcy
#governor
-governorship
life
belt
blood
drop
float
giver
guard
hold
jacket
long
raft
ring
saver
-size (u.m.)
-sized (u.m.)
span
spring
stream
style
tide
vest
weary (u.m.)
lift-off (n., u.m.)
light
-armed (u.m.)
-clad (u.m.)
-colored (u.m.)
-drab (u.m.)
-draft (u.m.)
face (printing)
-footed (u.m.)
handed
house#keeping (nautical)
#housekeeping (domestic)
mouthed
-producing (u.m.)
ship
-struck (u.m.)
weight (n., u.m.)
-year
lighter-than-air (u.m.)
like
-looking (u.m.)
-minded (u.m.)

lily
handed
-shaped (u.m.)
-white (u.m.)
lime
juice
kiln
lighter
pit
quat
wash
linch
bolt
pin
line
-bred (u.m.)
-breed (v.)
casting
crew
cut (printing)
finder
up (n., u.m.)
walker
link
up (n., u.m.)
#up (v.)
lion
-bold (u.m.)
-headed (u.m.)
-maned (u.m.)
lip
read
service
stick
listener-in
litho (c.f.)
-offset
  rest one word
little
-known (u.m.)
neck (clam)
-used (u.m.)
live
#load
long
stock
#wire
wire (nonliteral)
liver
-brown (u.m.)
-colored (u.m.)
wurst
living#room
loadmeter
loanword
lob
fig
lolly
lobster-tailed (u.m.)
lock
fast
hole
jaw
nut
out (n., u.m.)
pin
ring
step
stitch
up (n., u.m.)
washer
locker#room
lode
star
stuff

log
jam
roll
sheet
loggerhead
logo (c.f.)
  all one word
long
-awaited (u.m.)
beard (n.)
-bearded (u.m.)
-billed (u.m.)
bow
cloth
-distance (u.m.)
-drawn (u.m.)
felt
hair (n.)
-haired (u.m.)
hand (nonlit.)
-handed (u.m.)
-handled (u.m.)
head (n.)
horn (cattle)
-horned (u.m.)
leaf
-leaved (u.m.)
-legged (u.m.)
legs (n.)
-lived (u.m.)
mouthed
-necked (u.m.)
nose (n.)
-nosed (u.m.)
-past (u.m.)
play (records)
playing (u.m.)
run (u.m.)
spun
standing (u.m.)
stitch
wave (radio)
ways
wool (sheep)
look
down (n., u.m.)
-in (n., u.m.)
out (n., u.m.)
through (n., u.m.)
looker-on
loop
hole
stitch
loose
leaf (u.m.)
mouthed
-tongued (u.m.)
lop
-eared (u.m.)
sided
loud
mouthed
speaker (radio)
-voiced (u.m.)
love
born
-inspired (u.m.)
lorn
seat
sick
low
born
bred
brow (nonlit.)
browed (nonliteral)

-built (u.m.)
down (n., u.m.)
-downer
-lander
-lived (u.m.)
-lying (u.m.)

-power (u.m.)
-pressure (u.m.)
#water
lower
  case (printing)

most
lug
  bolt
  mark
  sail
lukewarm

lumber
  jack
  #room
lumbo (c.f.)
  -ovarian
  rest one word

lumen-hour
lung
  -grown (u.m.)
  motor
lying-in (n., u.m.)

M

M-day
macebearer
machine
  -finished (u.m.)
  gun
  -hour
  -made (u.m.)
  #shop
  #work
macro (c.f.)
  all one word
mad
  brain
  cap
made
  -over (u.m.)
  -up (u.m.)
magnetite
  -basalt
  -olivinite
  -spinellite
magneto (c.f.)
  -optics
  rest one word
mahjong
maid
  #of#honor
  servant
maiden
  hair
  head
  hood
mail
  bag
  clad
  clerk
  guard
  -order (u.m.)
  pouch
  truck
main
  frame
  mast
  pin
  sail
  sheet
  spring
  stay
  stream
    (nonliteral)
  top
  topmost
  #yard
major
  -domo
  -leaguer
  -minor
make
  -believe (n., u.m.)
  fast (n.)
  ready (printing)
  shift
  up (n., u.m.)
  weight
maker
  -off
  -up
making#up

mal (c.f.)
  all one word
man
  back
  -child
  -created (u.m.)
  -day
  eater
  -fashion (u.m.)
  -grown (u.m.)
  handle
  hater
  -high (u.m.)
  hole
  hood
  -hour
  killer
  kind
  made (u.m.)
  -minute
  -of-war (ship)
  rope
  servant
  -size (u.m.)
  slaughter
  slayer
  stealer
  stopper
  trap
  -woman
  -year
manic-depressive
manifold
mantel
  shelf
  tree
many
  -colored (u.m.)
  -folded (u.m.)
  plies
  -sided (u.m.)
map
  reader
  tack
marble
  head
  -looking (u.m.)
  -topped (u.m.)
  -white (u.m.)
mare's
  -nest
  -tail
mark
  down (n., u.m.)
  off (n., u.m.)
  shot
  up (n., u.m.)
marker
  -down
  -off
  -up
marketplace
marrowbone
marsh
  buck
  mallow
    (confection)
  #mallow (plant)

mass
  -minded (u.m.)
  -produce (v.)
mast
  -brown (u.m.)
  head
master
  #at#arms
  mind
  #of#ceremonies
  ship
  #workman
mat-covered (u.m.)
match
  head
  -lined (u.m.)
  mark
  safe
  stick
maxi (n.)
maxi (pref.)
  all one word
May
  #Day
  -day (u.m.)
  pole
  tide
may
  be (adv.)
  beetle
  day (distress
    call)
  hap
mealymouth
mean
  -acting (u.m.)
  -spirited (u.m.)
  time
    (meanwhile)
  #time
    (astronomical)
  tone (u.m.)
  while
meat
  ball
  cutter
  -eater
  -fed (u.m.)
  hook
  -hungry (u.m.)
  packer
  works
  wrapper
mechanico (c.f.)
  all one word
medico (c.f.)
  all one word
medio (c.f.)
  all one word
medium
  -brown (u.m.)
  -size(d) (u.m.)
  weight (n., u.m.)
meek
  -eyed (u.m.)
  -spirited (u.m.)
meetingplace
megalo (c.f.)
  all one word

melon
  -laden (u.m.)
  -shaped (u.m.)
melt
  down (n., u.m.)
  water
men
  folk
  kind
meningo (c.f.)
  all one word
merry
  -go-round
  meeting
  -minded (u.m.)
meshbag
meso (c.f.)
  all one word
mess
  hall
  kit
  tin
  -up (n., u.m.)
meta (pref.)
  all one word
metal
  ammonium
  -clad (u.m.)
  -coated (u.m.)
  -lined (u.m.)
  works
meter
  -amperes
  gram
  -kilogram
  -kilogram-second
  -millimeter
metro (c.f.)
  all one word
mezzo
  graph
  relievo
  soprano
  tint
micro (c.f.)
  -organism
  rest one word
mid (c.f.)
  -American, etc.
  -April
  day
  -decade
  -dish
  -ice
  -1958
  -Pacific, etc.
  -Victorian, etc.
  rest one word
middle
  -aged (u.m.)
  breaker
  brow (nonlit.)
  -burst (v.)
  buster
  most
  -of-the-roader
  -sized (u.m.)

splitter
weight
midi (n.)
midi (pref.)
  all one word
mighty-handed
  (u.m.)
mil-foot
mild
  -cured (u.m.)
  -spoken (u.m.)
mile
  -long (u.m.)
  -ohm
  post
  -pound
  -ton
  -wide (u.m.)
milk
  -fed (u.m.)
  head
  shake
  shed
  sick
  sop
  -white (u.m.)
mill
  cake
  course
  dam
  feed
  hand
  -headed (u.m.)
  pond
  post
  race
  ring
  stock
  stream
  wright
milli (c.f.)
  gram-hour
  rest one word
mincemeat
mind
  -healing (u.m.)
  reader
  set (n.)
  sight
mine
  layer
  ship
  sweeper
  thrower
  works
mini (n.)
mini (pref.)
  all one word
minor-leaguer
minute#book
mirror
  -faced (u.m.)
  scope
mis (pref.)
  all one word
mist
  bow
  -clad (u.m.)

-covered (u.m.)	pot	struck	cade	flow
fall	shine	tide	car	guard
miter	**mono** (c.f.)	walker	coach	head
#box	-ideistic	-white (u.m.)	cycle	hole
-lock (v.)	-iodo	moosecall	-driven (u.m.)	lark
mix	-iodohydrin	**mop**	drome	sill
blood	-ion	head	jet	slinger
up (n.)	-ousian	stick	-minded (u.m.)	-splashed (u.m.)
mixing#room	*rest one word*	up (n., u.m.)	ship	stain
mizzenmast	**month**	mopper-up	truck	sucker
mock	end	mopping-up (u.m.)	van	track
-heroic (u.m.)	long (u.m.)	morningtide	moundbuilder	muddlehead
up (n., u.m.)	**moon**	**mosquito**	**mountain**	**mule**
mocker-up	beam	#boat	-high (u.m.)	back
mocking	bill	-free (u.m.)	side	skinner
stock	blind	**moss**	top	**multi** (c.f.)
-up (u.m.)	#blindness	back	-walled (u.m.)	*all one word*
mold	blink	-clad (u.m.)	**mouse**	multiple-purpose
made (u.m.)	born	-green (u.m.)	-brown (u.m.)	(u.m.)
#shop	-bright (u.m.)	-grown (u.m.)	-eared (u.m.)	**music**
mole	calf	head	-eaten (u.m.)	lover
catcher	down	-lined (u.m.)	hole	-mad (u.m.)
-eyed (u.m.)	eye	most-favored-	trap	**musico** (c.f.)
head	face	nation (u.m.)	**mouth**	*all one word*
heap	gazing	**moth**	-filling (u.m.)	**musk**
hill	glow	ball	-made (u.m.)	melon
money	head	-eaten (u.m.)	wash	rat
bag	lighter	hole	**muck**	**mutton**
changer	lit	**mother**	rake (v.)	#chop (meat)
getter	-mad (u.m.)	hood	sweat	chop (shape)
grubber	path	-in-law	**muco** (c.f.)	fist
lender	rise	-of-pearl	*all one word*	head
-mad (u.m.)	sail	**moto** (c.f.)	**mud**	**myria** (c.f.)
saver	set	*all one word*	bank	*all one word*
monkey	shade	**motor**	bath	**mytho** (c.f.)
-faced (u.m.)	shine	bike	cap	*all one word*
nut	shot	bus	-colored (u.m.)	**myxo** (c.f.)
pod	sick	cab	flat	*all one word*

N

nail	**neck**	braider	reader	**nimble**
bin	band	-veined (u.m.)	reel	-fingered (u.m.)
brush	bone	**nettle**	sheet	footed
head	-breaking	fire	stand	**nimbostratus**
-headed (u.m.)	(u.m.)	foot	story	(clouds)
print	cloth	some	teller	**nine**
puller	-deep (u.m.)	**neuro** (c.f.)	**nick**	fold
rod	fast	*all one word*	-eared (u.m.)	holes
-shaped (u.m.)	guard	**never**	name	-lived (u.m.)
-studded (u.m.)	-high (u.m.)	-ending (u.m.)	**nickel**	penny (nail)
name	hole	more	plate (v.)	pin
-calling (u.m.)	lace	theless	-plated (u.m.)	score
-dropping (u.m.)	mold	**new**	-plating (u.m.)	**nitro** (c.f.)
plate	tie	born	type	-hydro-carbon
sake	**necro** (c.f.)	-car (u.m.)	**night**	*rest one word*
narco (c.f.)	*all one word*	comer	-black (u.m.)	**no**
all one word	**needle**	-created (u.m.)	cap	-account (n.,
narrow	bill	fangled	-clad (u.m.)	u.m.)
heartedness	case	-fashioned (u.m.)	clothes	-fault
-mouthed (u.m.)	-made (u.m.)	-front (v.)	club	-good (n., u.m.)
minded	point	-made (u.m.)	dress	-hitter (n.)
naso (c.f.)	-shaped (u.m.)	-mown (u.m.)	fall	how
-occipital	-sharp (u.m.)	-rich (u.m.)	-fly (aviation)	#man's land
-orbital	worked	newlywed	(v.)	-par (u.m.)
rest one word	ne'er-do-well	**news**	-flying (u.m.)	-par-value (u.m.)
native-born	**neo** (c.f.)	case	gown	-show (n., u.m.)
(u.m.)	-Greek, etc.	cast	-grown (u.m.)	-thoroughfare
navy-blue (u.m.)	*rest one word*	clip	hawk	(n.)
near	**nephro** (c.f.)	dealer	long (u.m.)	whit
-acquainted	*all one word*	-greedy (u.m.)	mare	**noble**
(u.m.)	**nerve**	letter	shade	-born (u.m.)
-bordering (u.m.)	ache	paper	shirt	-featured (u.m.)
by	-celled (u.m.)	paper#work	side	heartedness
-miss	-racked (u.m.)	paper#worker	tide	-looking (u.m.)
sighted	**net**	photo	-veiled (u.m.)	-minded (u.m.)
neat's-foot (u.m.)	ball	print	walker	nol-pros (v.)

non
-civil-service
(u.m.)
-European, etc.
-pros (v.)
#sequitur, etc.
-tumor-bearing
(u.m.)
*as prefix, one
word*
none
such
theless

noon
day
tide
north
-central
(u.m.)
east
going
most
-northeast
-sider

nose
bag
bleed
bone
dive
down (n., u.m.)
gay
guard
-high (u.m.)
hole
-led (u.m.)
pipe

ring
-thumbing (u.m.)
up (n., u.m.)
wheel
notehead
notwithstanding
novel
-reading (u.m.)
#writer
-writing (u.m.)
nucleo (c.f.)
all one word

nut
breaker
-brown (u.m.)
cake
cracker
hatch
hook
pecker
pick
-shaped (u.m.)
shell
sweet

O

oak
-beamed (u.m.)
-clad (u.m.)
-green (u.m.)
-leaved (u.m.)
oar
-footed (u.m.)
lock
oat
bin
cake
-fed (u.m.)
meal
seed
oathbreaker
oblong
-elliptic (u.m.)
-leaved (u.m.)
-linear (u.m.)
-ovate (u.m.)
-shaped (u.m.)
-triangular
(u.m.)
occipito (c.f.)
-otic
rest one word
ocean
-born (u.m.)
-girdled (u.m.)
going
side
-spanning (u.m.)
octo (c.f.)
all one word
odd
-jobber
-job man
-looking (u.m.)
-numbered (u.m.)
off
-and on (u.m.)
beat
cast
center (u.m.)
color (u.m.)
-colored (u.m.)
cut (printing)
day
-fall (v.)
-flavor (n., u.m.)
-flow
-go (n.)
going
grade
hand
-hours
loading
look

-lying (u.m.)
peak
print
put
-reckoning (n.)
saddle
scape
scour
scum
-season
set
shoot
shore
side
-sorts (n.)
spring
stage
street
take
-the-record (u.m.)
type
-wheel (n.)
-wheeler (n.)
-white (u.m.)
office
#boy
seeker
-seeking (u.m.)
oftentimes
ofttimes
ohm
-ammeter
meter
-mile
oil
cake
can
cloth
coat
cup
-driven (u.m.)
-fed (u.m.)
-forming (u.m.)
-harden (v.)
hole
meal
paper
proofing
seed
skinned
-soaked (u.m.)
spill
stove
-temper (v.)
tightness
old
-fashioned (u.m.)
-fogy (u.m.)

-growing (u.m.)
-looking (u.m.)
#maid
-maidish (u.m.)
#man
-new
style (printing)
timer
#woman
-young
oleo
#butter
#gear
#oil
#strut
*as combining
form, one
word*
olive
-brown (u.m.)
-clad (u.m.)
-drab (u.m.)
-growing (u.m.)
-skinned (u.m.)
wood
#wood (color)
omni (c.f.)
-ignorant
rest one word
on
-and-off (n., u.m.)
-go (n.)
going
*noun, adjective,
one word*
once
-over (n.)
-run (u.m.)
one
-acter
-armed (u.m.)
-decker
-eyed (u.m.)
fold
-half
-handed (u.m.)
ness
-piece (u.m.)
self
-sided (u.m.)
-sidedness
signed (u.m.)
-step (dance)
-striper
time (formerly)
(u.m.)
-time (one
action) (u.m.)

-two-three
-way (u.m.)
onion peel
open
-air (u.m.)
-armed (u.m.)
-back (u.m.)
-backed (u.m.)
band (yarn)
cast
cut (mining)
-faced (u.m.)
handed
#house
minded
mouthed
#shop
side (u.m.)
-sided (u.m.)
worked
opera
goer
going
#house
ophthalmo (c.f.)
all one word
orange
ade
colored (u.m.)
peel
-red (u.m.)
stick
orchard #house
orderly #room
organo (c.f.)
all one word
ornitho (c.f.)
all one word
orrisroot
ortho (c.f.)
all one word
osteo (c.f.)
all one word
oto (c.f.)
all one word
out
-and-out (u.m.)
-and-outer (n.)
-loud (u.m.)
-Machiavelli, etc.
migration
-of-date (u.m.)
-of-door(s) (u.m.)
-of-State (u.m.)
-of-the-way
(u.m.)
-to-out (u.m.)
*as prefix, one
word*

outer
-city (u.m.)
#man
most
outward
-bound (u.m.)
-bounder
ovate
-acuminate
(u.m.)
-oblong (u.m.)
ovato (c.f.)
-oblong
-orbicular
rest one word
oven
baked
dried
peel
over
age (surplus)
age (older) (n.,
u.m.)
all (all
meanings)
-the-counter
(u.m.)
*as combining
form, one
word*
owl-eyed (u.m.)
ox
biter
blood (color)
bow
brake
cart
cheek
eye
-eyed (u.m.)
gall
harrow
hide
horn
shoe
oxy (c.f.)
all one word
oyster
bed
root
seed
shell
-white (u.m.)

P

pace-setting
  (u.m.)
pachy (c.f.)
  all one word
pack
  builder
  cloth
  horse
  -laden (u.m.)
  sack
  saddle
  staff
  thread
  up (n., u.m.)
packing#box
pad
  cloth
  lock
  tree
paddlefoot
page
  -for-page (u.m.)
  #proof (printing)
painkiller
painstaking
paint
  brush
  mixer
  pot
  stained (u.m.)
pale
  belly
  -blue (u.m.)
  buck
  -cheeked (u.m.)
  face (n.)
  -faced (u.m.)
  -looking (u.m.)
  -reddish (u.m.)
paleo (c.f.)
  -Christian, etc.
  rest one word
pallbearer
palm
  -green (u.m.)
  -shaded (u.m.)
palmi (c.f.)
  all one word
pan
  -American, etc.
  -broil (v.)
  #ice
  rest one word
Pan
  #American
    Union
    (official name)
  hellenic
panel-lined
  (u.m.)
panic-stricken
  (u.m.)
panto (c.f.)
  all one word
panty hose
paper
  back (n.)
  #box
  cutter
  hanger
  shell (n., u.m.)
  -shelled (u.m.)
  -thin (u.m.)
  weight
  -white (u.m.)

papier#mache
para (c.f. or pref.)
  -aminobenzoic
  -analgesia
  -anesthesia
  #red
  rest one word
parcel-plate (v.)
parchment
  -covered (u.m.)
  #maker
  -making (u.m.)
parieto (c.f.)
  -occipital
  rest one word
parimutuel
part
  -finished (u.m.)
  #owner
  -time (u.m.)
  -timer (n.)
  #way
parti (c.f.)
  all one word
party#line
parvi (c.f.)
  all one word
pass
  back (n.)
  key
  out (n., u.m.)
  port
  through
  word
passenger-mile
passer(s)-by
passion
  -driven (u.m.)
  -feeding (u.m.)
  -filled (u.m.)
paste
  down (n., u.m.)
  pot
  up (n., u.m.)
patent-in-fee
path
  breaker
  finder
patho (c.f.)
  all one word
patri (c.f.)
  all one word
pattycake
pawnbroker
pay
  back (n., u.m.)
  check
  day
  dirt
  off (n., u.m.)
  out (n., u.m.)
  roll
  sheet
  -TV
pea
  coat
  cod
  -green (u.m.)
  jacket
  nut
  shooter
  -sized (u.m.)
  stick
peace
  -blessed (u.m.)

  breaker
  -loving (u.m.)
peach
  bloom
  blow (color)
  -colored (u.m.)
pear-shaped
  (u.m.)
pearl
  -eyed (u.m.)
  fishing
  -pure (u.m.)
  -set (u.m.)
  -studded (u.m.)
  -white (u.m.)
peat
  -roofed (u.m.)
  stack
pebble
  -paved (u.m.)
  -strewn (u.m.)
peeloff (n., u.m.)
peep
  eye
  hole
  show
  sight
pegleg
pellmell
pen
  -cancel (v.)
  head
  knife
  manship
  point
  pusher
  rack
  script
  -shaped (u.m.)
  stock
  trough
pencil
  #box
  -mark (v.)
penny
  -a-liner
  pincher
  weight
  winkle
  worth
pent-up (u.m.)
penta (c.f.)
  -acetate
  rest one word
peptalk
pepper
  corn
  mint
  pot
  -red (u.m.)
per
  cent
  #centum
  compound
    (chemical)
  current
    (botanical)
  #diem
  salt (chemical)
  #se
  sulfide
peri (pref.)
  -insular
  rest one word
permafrost

pest
  hole
  -ridden (u.m.)
petcock
peternet
petro (c.f.)
  -occipital
  rest one word
pharmaco (c.f.)
  -oryctology
  rest one word
pharyngo (c.f.)
  -esophageal
  -oral
  rest one word
phase
  meter
  out (n., u.m.)
  -wound (u.m.)
pheno (c.f.)
  all one word
philo (c.f.)
  -French, etc.
  rest one word
phlebo (c.f.)
  all one word
phono (c.f.)
  all one word
phospho (c.f.)
  all one word
photo (c.f.)
  -offset
  -oxidation
  -oxidative
  rest one word
phreno (c.f.)
  all one word
phrasemark
  (music)
phyllo (c.f.)
  all one word
phylo (c.f.)
  all one word
physico (c.f.)
  all one word
physio (c.f.)
  all one word
phyto (c.f.)
  all one word
piano
  forte
  graph
  player
pick
  aback
  ax
  lock
  -me-up (n., u.m.)
  off (n., u.m.)
  over (n., u.m.)
  #over (v.)
  pocket
  pole
  shaft
  up (n., u.m.)
picker-up
picket#line
pickle-cured (u.m.)
picture
  #book
  #writing
pie
  bald
  crust
  -eater

  -eyed
  marker
  pan
  plant
  -stuffed (u.m.)
piece
  -dye (v.)
  meal
  mold
piezo (c.f.)
  -oscillator
  rest one word
pig
  -back (v.)
  -backed (u.m.)
  -bellied (u.m.)
  belly
  -eyed (u.m.)
  face
  -faced (u.m.)
  foot
  -footed (u.m.)
  headed
  herd
  out
  pen
  root
  stick
  sty
  tailed
  wash
pigeon
  gram
  hole
  -toed (u.m.)
  wing
piggyback
pike
  -eyed (u.m.)
  staff
pile
  driver
  -driving (u.m.)
  hammer
  up (n., u.m.)
  woven
pill
  pusher
  rolling
  taker
pillow
  case
  made
  slip
pilot
  #boat
  #light
pin
  ball
  block
  bone
  case
  cushion
  -eyed (u.m.)
  fall
  feather
  fire
  fold
  head
  hold
  hole
  hook
  lock
  paper
  point

prick
rail
setter
spot
stripe
-tailed (u.m.)
up (n., u.m.)
wheel
pinch
back
bar
beck
cock
fist
-hit (v.)
-hitter
penny
pine
apple
-bearing (u.m.)
-clad (u.m.)
-fringed (u.m.)
-shaded (u.m.)
pink
-blossomed (u.m.)
eye (n.)
-eyed (u.m.)
pipe
-drawn (u.m.)
dream
fitter
layer
lined
-shaped (u.m.)
stem
walker
welder
pisci (c.f.)
  all one word
pistol-whipped (v.)
pistonhead
pit
-eyed (u.m.)
fall
head
-headed (u.m.)
hole
mark
-marked (u.m.)
-rotted (u.m.)
saw
side
pitch
-black (u.m.)
blende
#box
-colored (u.m.)
-dark (u.m.)
fork
hole
-lined (u.m.)
-marked (u.m.)
out (n., u.m.)
up (n., u.m.)
place
card
kick
plague-infested
  (u.m.)
plain
back (fabric)
-bodied (u.m.)
clothes (u.m.)
-headed (u.m.)
-looking (u.m.)
-spoken (u.m.)
woven (u.m.)

plane
-mile
-parallel (u.m.)
table
  (surveying)
plani (c.f.)
  all one word
plano (c.f.)
  all one word
plantlife
plate
-incased (u.m.)
layer
mark
#proof (printing)
-roll (v.)
-rolled (u.m.)
platy (c.f.)
  all one word
play
-act (v.)
back (n., u.m.)
bill
broker
day
down (n., u.m.)
fellow
goer
going
ground
off (n., u.m.)
pen
reader
script
suit
thing
wright
#yard
pleasure
-bent (u.m.)
#boat
-seeking (u.m.)
-tired (u.m.)
-weary (u.m.)
pleo (c.f.)
  all one word
pleuro (c.f.)
  all one word
plow
back (n., u.m.)
-bred (u.m.)
hand
horse
pan
point
-shaped (u.m.)
share
shoe
sole
staff
#tail
wright
plug
hole
-in (n., u.m.)
tray
-ugly (n., u.m.)
plume-crowned
  (u.m.)
pluri (c.f.)
  all one word
pluto (c.f.)
  all one word
pneumato (c.f.)
-hydato-genetic
  (u.m.)
  rest one word

pneumo (c.f.)
  all one word
pock
mark
-marked (u.m.)
-pit (v.)
pocket
book (purse)
#book (book)
-eyed (u.m.)
knife
-sized (u.m.)
-veto (v.)
poet
-artist
-painter
pointblank
poison-dipped
  (u.m.)
pole
arm
-armed (u.m.)
ax
burn
cat
-dried (u.m.)
horse
-pile (v.)
setter
-shaped (u.m.)
sitter
-stack (v.)
star
timber
trap
-vault (v.)
politico (c.f.)
-orthodox
  rest one word
poly (c.f.)
  all one word
poor
-blooded (u.m.)
farm
-spirited (u.m.)
pop
corn
eye
gun
up (n., u.m.)
poppy
-bordered (u.m.)
cock
-red (u.m.)
seed
port
fire
folio
hole
hook
manteau
-mouthed (u.m.)
side
post
#bellum
#boat
card
-Christian, etc.
#diem
-free (u.m.)
haste
#hospital
  (military)
#meridiem
#mortem (literal)
mortem (non-
  literal)

#partum
#school (military)
  audit, graduate,
  etc.
  *as prefix, one
  word*
pot
ash
bellied
boil
eye
hanger
head
herb
hole
hook
hunter
latch
lid
luck
pie
pourri
rack
shot
whiskey
potato#field
poultry
#house
#keeper
-keeping (u.m.)
#raiser
-raising (u.m.)
#yard
pound
cake
-foolish (u.m.)
-foot
worth
powder
-blue (u.m.)
#house
#mill
#room
-scorched (u.m.)
power
-driven (u.m.)
-operated (u.m.)
pack
plant
praise
-deserving (u.m.)
-spoiled (u.m.)
worthiness
pre (pref.)
-Incan, etc.
president
-elect
#pro#tempore
press
#agent
-agentry
feeder
-forge (v.)
-made (u.m.)
mark
pack (v.)
plate
#proof (printing)
preter (pref.)
  all one word
price
#cutter
-cutting (u.m.)
#fixer
-fixing (u.m.)
list
-support (u.m.)

prick
-eared (u.m.)
mark
seam
priest
hood
-prince
prime
#minister
-ministerial
  (u.m.)
-ministership
-ministry
prince
hood
-priest
print
cloth
out
script
printing
-in (n., u.m.)
-out (n., u.m.)
prison
-free (u.m.)
-made (u.m.)
prisoner-of-war
  (u.m.)
prize
fighter
taker
winner
-winning (u.m.)
pro
-Ally, etc.
#forma
#rata
#tem
#tempore
  *as prefix, one
  word*
procto (c.f.)
  all one word
profit
-and-loss (u.m.)
-sharing (u.m.)
prong
buck
-hoe (v.)
horn
-horned (u.m.)
proof
read
sheet
prop
jet
wash
proso (c.f.)
  all one word
proto (c.f.)
-Egyptian, etc.
  rest one word
proud
-looking (u.m.)
-minded (u.m.)
pseudo (c.f.)
-Messiah, etc.
-occidental
-official
-orientalism
-orthorhombic
-osteomalacia
-owner
  rest one word
psycho (c.f.)
-organic
  rest one word

ptero (c.f.)
  all one word
public
  -minded (u.m.)
  -spirited (u.m.)
pug
  nose
  -pile (v.)
pull
  back (n., u.m.)
  #box
  down (n., u.m.)
  -in (n., u.m.)
  off (n., u.m.)

-on (n., u.m.)
out (n., u.m.)
-push (u.m.)
through
  (n., u.m.)
up (n., u.m.)
puller
  -in
  -out
punch
  bowl
  card
  -drunk (u.m.)
  mark

-marked (u.m.)
out (n.)
pure
  blood
  bred
  #line (biological)
purple
  -blue (u.m.)
  -clad (u.m.)
  -colored (u.m.)
  heart (wood)
push
  button
  card

cart
  off (n., u.m.)
  -pull (u.m.)
  up (n., u.m.)
pussy
  cat
  foot
put
  back (n., u.m.)
  off (n., u.m.)
  -on (n., u.m.)
  out (n., u.m.)
  -put (n.)
  -up (n., u.m.)

putter
  -forth
  -in
  -off
  -on
  -out
  -through
  -up
pyo (c.f.)
  all one word
pyro (c.f.)
  all one word

Q

Q
  -boat
  -fever
quadri (c.f.)
  -invariant
  rest one word
quarter
  -angled (u.m.)
  back

-bloom (u.m.)
-bound (u.m.)
-breed (u.m.)
-cast (u.m.)
-cut (u.m.)
deck
-miler
pace
-phase (u.m.)

saw (v.)
staff
stretch
quartermaster
#general
-generalship
quasi
  all hyphened
queen #bee

quick
  -change (u.m., v.)
  -drawn (u.m., v.)
  freeze (u.m., v.)
  lime
  sand
  set
  silver
  step

#time
-witted (u.m.)
quin (c.f.)
  all one word
quit
  claim
  rent

R

rabbit
  -backed (u.m.)
  -eared (u.m.)
  mouth
  -mouthed (u.m.)
race
  about (n., u.m.)
  course
  goer
  horse
  track
radarscope
radio
  generally two
  words except
  the following
  forms
  frequency
  isotope
  telegraph
  telephone
radiumtherapy
rag
  bolt
  -made (u.m.)
  sorter
  tag
rail
  car
  guard
  head
  -ridden (u.m.)
  road
  setter
  splitter
  way #maker
rain
  band
  -beaten (u.m.)
  bow
  check
  coat
  drop
  fall
  -soft (u.m.)
  spout
  storm

wash
rakeoff (n., u.m.)
ram
  jet
  rod
  shackle
ranch #hand
range
  finder
  #light
  rider
rash
  -brain (u.m.)
  -headed (u.m.)
  -hearted (u.m.)
  -minded (u.m.)
rat
  bite
  catcher
  hole
  -infested (u.m.)
  -tailed (u.m.)
  -tight (u.m.)
  trap
rate
  -cutting (u.m.)
  -fixing (u.m.)
  payer
  -raising (u.m.)
  setting
rattle
  brain
  snake
  trap
raw
  boned
  -edged (u.m.)
  hide
  -looking (u.m.)
razor
  back
  -billed (u.m.)
  edge
  -keen (u.m.)
  -sharp (u.m.)
  strop
razzle-dazzle

re (pref.)
  -cover (cover
    again), -create
    (create again),
    etc.
  -cross-
    examination
  -ice
  -ink
  -redirect
    rest one word
reading #room
readout (n.)
ready
  -built (u.m.)
  -handed (u.m.)
  made (u.m.)
  -mix (u.m.)
  -witted (u.m.)
rear
  guard
  most
  view (u.m.)
  reception #room
recordbreaker
recti (c.f.)
  all one word
recto (c.f.)
  all one word
red
  bait (v.)
  -billed (u.m.)
  -blooded (u.m.)
  bone
  buck
  cap (porter)
  coat (n.)
  eye (n.)
  -eyed (u.m.)
  -faced (u.m.)
  -haired (u.m.)
  handed
  head (n.)
  -hot (u.m.)
  -legged (u.m.)
  #line (literal)
  #man

out (n., u.m.)
-skinned (u.m.)
tape (nonliteral)
#tape (literal)
-throated (u.m.)
-yellow (u.m.)
religio (c.f.)
  all one word
repair #shop
representative
  #at #large
  -elect
research #worker
resino (c.f.)
  all one word
retro (c.f.)
  -ocular
  -omental
  -operative
  -oral
    rest one word
rheo (c.f.)
  all one word
rhino (c.f.)
  all one word
rhizo (c.f.)
  all one word
rhod(o) (c.f.)
  all one word
rhomb(o) (c.f.)
  all one word
rice
  growing
  #water
rich
  -bound (u.m.)
  -clad (u.m.)
  -looking (u.m.)
ridge
  band
  pole
  top
riffraff
rifleshot
rig
  out (n., u.m.)
  -up (n., u.m.)

right
  about
  about-face
  -angle (u.m., v.)
  -angled (u.m.)
  #field (sports)
  -handed (u.m.)
  -hander
  -headed (u.m.)
  most
  -of-way
  wing
    (political)
rim
  -deep (u.m.)
  fire
  lock
  rock
ring
  -adorned (u.m.)
  -banded (u.m.)
  -billed (u.m.)
  bolt
  giver
  head
  -in (n., u.m.)
  lead (v.)
  -necked (u.m.)
  -off (n., u.m.)
  pin
  -porous (u.m.)
  -shaped (u.m.)
  side
  sight
  stand
  stick
  -tailed (u.m.)
  -up (n., u.m.)
rip
  cord
  rap
  roaring
  sack
  saw
  snorter
  tide
  -up (n., u.m.)

river
bank
bed
flow
-formed (u.m.)
front
head
scape
side
wash
-worn (u.m.)
road
bank
bed
block
builder
head
hog
map
side
-test (v.)
-weary (u.m.)
rock
abye
bottom (nonlit.)
-climbing (u.m.)
fall (n.)
-fallen (u.m.)
fill
firm
pile
-ribbed (u.m.)
shaft
slide
rod-shaped (u.m.)
roebuck
roentgeno (c.f.)
all one word

roll
about (n., u.m.)
back (n., u.m.)
call
-fed (v.)
film
off (n., u.m.)
-on (n., u.m.)
out (n., u.m.)
top
up (n., u.m.)
roller
-made (u.m.)
-milled (u.m.)
Romano (c.f.)
-canonical, etc.
-Gallic, etc.
roof
garden
top
tree
root
cap
-cutting (u.m.)
fast
hold
stalk
stock
rope
dance
layer
stitch
walk
rose
-bright (u.m.)
bud
head
-headed (u.m.)

-scented (u.m.)
-sweet (u.m.)
tan
#water
rotorship
rotten
-dry (u.m.)
-minded (u.m.)
rough
-and-ready (u.m.)
-and-tumble
(n., u.m.)
cast (u.m., v.)
-coat (v.)
-cut (u.m.)
draw (v.)
dress (v.)
dry (u.m., v.)
-face (v.)
-faced (u.m.)
hew
-legged (u.m.)
-looking (u.m.)
neck
rider
setter
shod
-sketch (v.)
stuff
tailed
#work (n.)
work (v.)
wrought
rougher
-down
-out
-up
roughing-in (u.m.)

round
about (n., u.m.)
about-face
-faced (u.m.)
head
-made (u.m.)
mouthed
nose (tool)
out (n., u.m.)
robin (petition)
seam
table (panel)
-tailed (u.m.)
-topped (u.m.)
-tripper
up (n., u.m.)
rub
-a-dub
down (n., u.m.)
rubber
band
-down
-lined (u.m.)
neck
-off
-set (u.m.)
stamp
(nonliteral)
(n., u.m., v.)
#stamp (n.)
-stamped (u.m.)
ruby
-hued (u.m.)
-red (u.m.)
-set (u.m.)
-throated (u.m.)
rudder
head

hole
post
stock
rule # of # thumb
rum
-crazed (u.m.)
runner
seller
rumpus # room
run
about (n., u.m.)
around
(n., u.m.)
away (n., u.m.)
back (n., u.m.)
by (n.)
down (n., u.m.)
-in (n., u.m.)
off (n., u.m.)
-on (n., u.m.)
out (n., u.m.)
through
(n., u.m.)
up (n., u.m.)
runner-up
rush-bottomed
(u.m.)
Russo (c.f.)
-Chinese, etc.
rest one word
rust
-brown (u.m.)
-eaten (u.m.)
proofing
-resistant (u.m.)
-stained (u.m.)
rye # field

S

S
-bend
-brake
-iron
-ray
-shaped
-trap
-wrench
saber
-legged (u.m.)
tooth
-toothed (u.m.)
sable-cloaked
(u.m.)
Sabrejet
saccharo (c.f.)
all one word
sack
bearer
cloth
#coat
-coated (u.m.)
-making (u.m.)
-shaped (u.m.)
sacro (c.f.)
all one word
sad
-eyed (u.m.)
iron
-voiced (u.m.)
saddle
back
-backed (u.m.)
bag
bow
cloth

-graft (v.)
-making (u.m.)
nose
-nosed (u.m.)
sore
-stitched (u.m.)
tree
-wire (u.m.)
safe
blower
cracker
-deposit (u.m.)
guard
hold
sage
brush
leaf
-leaved (u.m.)
sail
cloth
-dotted (u.m.)
flying
sales
clerk
manship
people
person
salmon
-colored (u.m.)
-red (u.m.)
salpingo (c.f.)
-oophorectomy
-oophoritis
-ovariotomy
-ovaritis
rest one word

salt
cellar
-cured (u.m.)
mouth
pack
pan
peter
pit
pond
shaker
spoon
sprinkler
works
salver
form
-shaped (u.m.)
sample
#book
#box
-making (u.m.)
sand
bag
bank
bar
bath
bin
blast
blown
-built (u.m.)
-buried (u.m.)
-cast (u.m., v.)
culture
fill
flea
glass
heat

hill
-hiller
hog
hole
lapper
lot
paper
pile
pipe
pit
-pump (u.m., v.)
shoe
spit
storm
table
weld (v.)
-welded (u.m.)
-welding (u.m.)
sandy-bottomed
(u.m.)
sangfroid
sans
#serif
#souci
sapphire
-blue (u.m.)
-colored (u.m.)
sarco (c.f.)
all one word
sashcord
satin
-lined (u.m.)
-smooth (u.m.)
sauce
dish
pan

sauer
braten
kraut
save-all (n., u.m.)
saw
back
belly
-billed (u.m.)
bones (n.)
buck
dust
-edged (u.m.)
setter
timber
tooth
-toothed (u.m.)
sax
cornet
horn
tuba
say
-nothing
(n., u.m.)
-so (n.)
scale
bark
down (n., u.m.)
pan
-reading (u.m.)
scapegoat
scapulo (c.f.)
all one word
scar
-clad (u.m.)
face
-faced (u.m.)

scare
 crow
 head
scarfpin
scarlet
 -breasted (u.m.)
 -red (u.m.)
scatter
 brain
 good
scene
 shifter
 wright
schisto (c.f.)
 all one word
schizo (c.f.)
 all one word
school
 bag
 #board
 bookish
 bus
 children
 day
 -made (u.m.)
 ship
 teacher
 -trained (u.m.)
scientifico (c.f.)
 all one word
scissor
 bill
 -tailed (u.m.)
 -winged (u.m.)
scissors
 hold
 -shaped (u.m.)
 #smith
sclero (c.f.)
 -oophoritis
 -optic
 rest one word
score
 card
 sheet
scot-free
Scoto (c.f.)
 -Britannic, etc.
scouthood
scrap
 basket
 works
scratch
 brush
 -brusher
 -coated (u.m.)
screen
 out (n., u.m.)
 play
screw
 ball
 bolt
 cap
 down (u.m.)
 -driven (u.m.)
 driver
 head
 hook
 jack
 -lifted (u.m.)
 nut
 ship
 -threaded (u.m.)
 -turned (u.m.)
scrollhead
scuttlebutt
scythe-shaped
 (u.m.)

sea
 #base
 -based (u.m.)
 -bathed (u.m.)
 beach
 -beaten (u.m.)
 bed
 #bird
 -blue (u.m.)
 #boat
 -born (u.m.)
 -bred (u.m.)
 coast
 -deep (u.m.)
 dog
 -driven (u.m.)
 drome
 -encircled (u.m.)
 fare (food)
 fighter
 folk
 food
 front
 goer
 going
 hound
 lane
 lift
 mark
 port
 quake
 #room
 scape
 #scout
 scouting
 shell
 shine
 shore
 sick
 side
 stroke
 #time (clock)
 wall
 wing
 worn
 worthiness
 -wrecked (u.m.)
seam
 blasting
 rend (v.)
 stitch
 weld (v.)
 -welded (u.m.)
seat
 belt
 -mile
second
 -class (u.m.)
 -degree (u.m.)
 -foot
 -guess (v.)
 hand
  (adv., u.m.)
 -rate (u.m.)
secretary
 #general
 -generalcy
 -generalship
 section #man
seesaw
seed
 bed
 cake
 case
 coat
 kin
 stalk

seer
 band
 hand
 sucker
seismo (c.f.)
 all one word
self
 dom
 hood
 less
 ness
 same
 reflexive prefix,
  use hyphen
sell
 off (n., u.m.)
 out (n., u.m.)
semi (pref.)
 annual, arid,
  etc.
 -armor-piercing
  (u.m.)
 -Christian, etc.
 -idleness,
  -indirect, etc.
send
 off (n., u.m.)
 out (n., u.m.)
senso (c.f.)
 all one word
septi (c.f.)
 all one word
septo (c.f.)
 all one word
serio (c.f.)
 all one word
sero (c.f.)
 all one word
serrate
 -ciliate (u.m.)
 -dentate (u.m.)
service
 -connected (u.m.)
servo
 accelerometer
 amplifier
 control
 mechanism
 motor
 system
sesqui (c.f.)
 all one word
set
 -aside (n., u.m.)
 back (n., u.m.)
 bolt
 down (n., u.m.)
 -fair (n.)
 head
 -in (n., u.m.)
 off (n., u.m.)
 -on (n., u.m.)
 out (n., u.m.)
 pin
 screw
 -stitched (u.m.)
 -to (n., u.m.)
 up (n., u.m.)
setter
 -forth
 -in
 -on
 -out
 -to
 -up
seven
 -branched (u.m.)

 fold
 penny (nail)
 score
 -shooter
 -up (n.)
 severalfold
shade
 -giving (u.m.)
 -grown (u.m.)
shadow
 boxing
 gram
 graph
 #line
shag
 bark
 -haired (u.m.)
shake
 down (n., u.m.) ;
 out (n., u.m.)
 up (n., u.m.)
shallow
 -draft (u.m.)
 -headed (u.m.)
shame
 -crushed (u.m.)
 faced
shank
 bone
 #mill
 shapeup (n., u.m.)
share
 bone
 broker
 cropper
 out (n., u.m.)
sharp
 -angled (u.m.)
 -cut (u.m.)
 -edged (u.m.)
 -freeze (u.m., v.)
 -freezer
 -looking (u.m.)
 -set (u.m.)
 shod
 shooter
 -tailed (u.m.)
 -witted (u.m.)
shavehook
shear
 pin
 waters
shedhand
sheep
 biter
 crook
 dip
 faced
 fold
 gate
 herder
 hook
 kill
 -kneed (u.m.,)
 nose (apple)
 pen
 shank
 shear (v.)
 shearer (n.)
 shed
 sick
 stealer
 walk
 -white (u.m.)
sheer
 off (n., u.m.)
 up (n., u.m.)

sheet
 block
 flood
 rock
 ways
shell
 back
 burst
 fire
 fishery
 hole
 -like
 shocked
shelterbelt
shield-shaped
  (u.m.)
shilly-shally
shin
 bone
 guard
 plaster
shiner-up
ship
 breaker
 broken
 broker
 builder
 lap
 mast
 owning
 -rigged (u.m.)
 shape
 side
 wreck
shipping
 #master
 #room
shirt
 band
 waist
shoe
 black
 brush
 horn
 lace
 pack
 scraper
 shine
 string
 tree
shootoff
  (n., u.m.)
shop
 breaker
 folk
 lifter
 -made (u.m.)
 mark
 -soiled (u.m.)
 talk
 walker
 window
shore
 #bird
 #boat
 fast
 going
 side
short
 -armed (u.m.)
 bread
 cake
 change (v.)
 changer
 -circuited (u.m.)
 coming
 cut (n., u.m., v.)
 fall (n.)

-fed (u.m.)
hand (writing)
-handed (u.m.)
head (whale)
horn (n., u.m.)
-horned (u.m.)
-lasting (u.m.)
leaf (u.m.)
-lived (u.m.)
rib
run (u.m.)
sighted
staff
stop
wave (radio)
shot
gun
hole
put
star
shoulder-high
(u.m.)
shovel
-headed (u.m.)
-nosed (u.m.)
show
card
case
down (n., u.m.)
off (n., u.m.)
place
through
(printing)
(n., u.m.)
up (n., u.m.)
shredout (n., u.m.)
shroud
-laid (u.m.)
plate
shunt-wound
(u.m.)
shut
away (n., u.m.)
down (n., u.m.)
eye (n., u.m.)
-in (n., u.m.)
-mouthed (u.m.)
off (n., u.m.)
out (n., u.m.)
up (u.m.)
shuttlecock
sick
bay
bed
list
side
arms
band
bone
burns
car
check
-cut (u.m.)
dress (v.)
flash
head (printing)
hill
hook
kick
lap
#light (literal)
light
(nonliteral)
#line (literal)
line (nonliteral)
long
note

plate
play
saddle
show
slip
splitting
step
stitch
-stitched (u.m.)
sway
swipe
track
walk
wall
-wheeler
winder
sight
hole
read
saver
seeing
setter
sign
off (n., u.m.)
-on (n., u.m.)
post
up (n., u.m.)
silico (c.f.)
all one word
silk
-stockinged
(u.m.)
works
siltpan
silver
-backed (u.m.)
beater
-bright (u.m.)
-gray (u.m.)
-haired (u.m.)
-lead (u.m.)
-leaved (u.m.)
plate (v.)
-plated (u.m.)
point
(drawing)
print
tip
-tongued (u.m.)
top
simon-pure (u.m.)
simple
-headed (u.m.)
-minded (u.m.)
-rooted (u.m.)
-witted (u.m.)
simulcast
sin
-born (u.m.)
-bred (u.m.)
singsong
single
bar
-breasted (u.m.)
-decker
-edged (u.m.)
handed
hood
-loader
-minded (u.m.)
-phase (u.m.)
-seater
stick
tree
sink
head
hole

Sino (c.f.)
-Japanese, etc.
sister
-german
hood
-in-law
sit
down (n., u.m.)
-downer
fast (n., u.m.)
up (n., u.m.)
sitter
-by
-out
sitting #room
sitzmark
six
-cylinder
(u.m.)
fold
penny (nail)
-ply (u.m.)
score
-shooter
-wheeler
sizeup (n., u.m.)
skid
lift (truck)
road
skin
-clad (u.m.)
deep
diver
flint
-graft (v.)
skipjack
skirtmarker
skullcap
skunk
head
top
sky
-blue (u.m.)
gazer
-high (u.m.)
jacker
lift
look (v.)
rocket
sail
scape
scraper
shine
wave
slab-sided (u.m.)
slack
-bake (v.)
-filled (u.m.)
#water
slambang
slant-eyed (u.m.)
slap
bang
dab
dash
down (n., u.m.)
happy
jack
stick
-up (n., u.m.)
slate
-blue (u.m.)
-colored (u.m.)
works
slaughter
pen
-born (u.m.)

-deserted (u.m.)
holding
pen
#worker
Slavo (c.f.)
-Hungarian, etc.
sledge
-hammered
(u.m.)
meter
sleep
-filled (u.m.)
talker
walker
sleepy
-eyed (u.m.)
head
-looking (u.m.)
sleetstorm
sleeveband
sleuthhound
slide
film
knot
sling
ball
shot
slip
along (u.m.)
back
band
case
cover
knot
-on (n., u.m.)
#proof
(printing)
proof
ring
sheet
shod
sole
step
stitch
stream
-up (n., u.m.)
washer
slit
-eyed (u.m.)
shell
slop
-molded (u.m.)
seller
slope
-faced (u.m.)
ways
slow
belly
down (n., u.m.)
-footed (u.m.)
going
-motion (u.m.)
mouthed
poke
#time
up (n., u.m.)
-witted (u.m.)
slug
-cast (v.)
caster
slum
dweller
gullion
gum
lord
slumber-bound
(u.m.)

small
#businessman
-hipped (u.m.)
mouthed
pox
-scale (u.m.)
sword
talk
town (u.m.)
smart
-alecky (u.m.)
-looking (u.m.)
-tongued (u.m.)
smashup (n., u.m.)
smearcase
smoke
-blinded (u.m.)
bomb
chaser
-dried (u.m.)
-dry (v.)
-dyed (u.m.)
-filled (u.m.)
jack
jumper
-laden (u.m.)
pot
screen
stack
smoking #room
smooth
bore
-browed (u.m.)
-cast (u.m.)
mouthed
-tongued (u.m.)
-working (u.m.)
snackbar
snail
-paced (u.m.)
-slow (u.m.)
snail's #pace
snake
bite
-bitten (u.m.)
-eater
-eyed (u.m.)
head
hole
pit
snap
back
dragon
head
hook
-on (n., u.m.)
out (n.)
ring
roll
shooter
shot
-up (u.m.)
snapper
-back
-up
snipe
bill
-nosed (u.m.)
sniperscope
snooperscope
snow
ball
bank
berg
blind
#blindness
blink

block
-blocked (u.m.)
blower
break
capped
-choked (u.m.)
clad (u.m.)
-covered (u.m.)
drift
fall
flake
melt
-melting (u.m.)
mobile
pack
pit
plow
scape
shade
shed
shine
shoe
sled
slide
slip
storm
suit
-topped (u.m.)
#water
-white (u.m.)
snuff-stained
  (u.m.)
so
-and-so
beit (n., conj.)
-called (u.m.)
-seeming (u.m.)
-so
soap
  bubble
  dish
  flakes
  rock
  stock
  suds
sober
-minded (u.m.)
  sides
social
#work
#worker
socio (c.f.)
-official
  economic, etc.
sod
  buster
  culture
#house
soda
  jerk
#water
sofa
#maker
-making (u.m.)
-ridden (u.m.)
soft
  ball
-boiled (u.m.)
  head
-pedal (v.)
-shelled (u.m.)
-soap (nonliteral)
  (v.)
-soaper
  (nonliteral)
  (n.)
-spoken (u.m.)

tack
soldier-fashion
  (u.m.)
sole
  cutter
  plate
somato (c.f.)
  all one word
some
  day
  how
  one (anyone)
#one
  (distributive)
  place (adv.)
  time (adv.)
#time (some time
  ago)
  what
son-in-law
song
  fest
  wright
sonobuoy
sooth
  fast
  sayer
sore
-eyed (u.m.)
  foot (n.)
  footed (u.m.)
  head (n., u.m.)
sorry-looking
  (u.m.)
soul
-deep (u.m.)
-searching (u.m.)
  sick
sound
-absorbing (u.m.)
#field
  film
-minded (u.m.)
  off (n., u.m.)
  track
soup
  bone
  spoon
sour
  belly
  bread
  dough (n.)
  faced
-natured (u.m.)
-sweet
south
-born (u.m.)
-central (u.m.)
  east
  going
  lander
  paw
-sider
-southeast
  west
soybean
sow
  back
  belly
space
  band
  bar
-cramped
  (u.m.)
  mark
  ship
#time

spade
-dug (u.m.)
  foot
-footed (u.m.)
-shaped (u.m.)
span
-long (u.m.)
-new (u.m.)
Spanish
-Arab
-born (u.m.)
-speaking (u.m.)
spare
-bodied (u.m.)
  rib
#room
spark
#plug (literal)
  plug (nonliteral)
speakeasy (n.)
spear
  cast
  head
-high (u.m.)
-shaped (u.m.)
spectro (c.f.)
  all one word
speech
-bereft (u.m.)
-read (v.)
speed
  boating
  letter
  trap
  up (n., u.m.)
spell
  binding
  down (n., u.m.)
-free (u.m.)
spend
-all (n.)
  thrift
spermato (c.f.)
  all one word
spermo (c.f.)
  all one word
spheno (c.f.)
-occipital
  rest one word
sphygmo (c.f.)
  all one word
spice
-burnt (u.m.)
  cake
-laden (u.m.)
spider
-legged
-spun (u.m.)
#web (n.)
  web (u.m., v.)
spike
  horn
-kill (v.)
-pitch (v.)
spin
  back
  off
spindle
-formed (u.m.)
  head
-legged (u.m.)
  legs
  shanks
spine
  bone
-broken (u.m.)
-pointed (u.m.)

spino (c.f.)
-olivary
  rest one word
spirit
-born (u.m.)
-broken (u.m.)
#writing
spit
  ball
  fire
  stick
splanchno (c.f.)
  all one word
splay
  footed
  mouthed
spleen
-born (u.m.)
  sick
-swollen (u.m.)
spleno (c.f.)
  all one word
split
  finger
  (crustacean)
  fruit
  mouth
  saw
-tongued (u.m.)
  up (n., u.m.)
spoilsport
spondylo (c.f.)
  all one word
sponge
  cake
  diver
-diving (u.m.)
-shaped (u.m.)
spongio (c.f.)
  all one word
spoolwinder
spoon
-beaked (u.m.)
-billed (u.m.)
  bread
-fed (u.m.)
-shaped (u.m.)
  ways
sporeformer
sporo (c.f.)
  all one word
spot
-checked (u.m.)
-face (v.)
  weld (v.)
  welded (u.m.)
-welding (u.m.)
spray-washed
  (u.m.)
spread
-eagle (u.m., v.)
  head
  out (n., u.m.)
-set (v.)
spring
  back
  (bookbinding)
  bok
-born (u.m.)
  buck
-clean (v.)
  finger
-grown (u.m.)
  halt
  head
-plow (v.)
-plowed (u.m.)

tide (season)
  trap
spritsail
spur
-clad (u.m.)
-driven (u.m.)
  gall
-galled (u.m.)
-heeled (u.m.)
spy
  glass
  hole
  tower
square
-bottomed (u.m.)
-built (u.m.)
-faced (u.m.)
  flipper
  head
-headed
-rigged (u.m.)
-set (u.m.)
  shooter
squeeze
-in (n., u.m.)
  out (n., u.m.)
  up (n., u.m.)
squirrel-headed
  (u.m.)
stackup (n., u.m.)
staff-herd (v.)
stag
-handled (u.m.)
  head
-headed (u.m.)
  horn
-horned (u.m.)
  hound
  hunter
stage
  coach
  hand
-struck (u.m.)
stair
  case
  head
  step
stake
  head
  out (n.)
stale-worn (u.m.)
stall
-fed (u.m.)
-feed (v.)
stand
  by (n., u.m.)
  down (n., u.m.)
  fast (n., u.m.)
-in (n., u.m.)
  off (n., u.m.)
  offish
  out (n., u.m.)
  pat
  pipe
  point
  post
  still (n., u.m.)
  up (n., u.m.)
standard
  bred
#time
staphylo (c.f.)
  all one word
star
  blind
  bright
  dust

gazer
-led (u.m.)
lit
lite (gem)
nose (mole)
shake
shine
shoot
-spangled (u.m.)
stroke
-studded (u.m.)
#time
starchworks
stark
-blind (u.m.)
-mad (u.m.)
-naked (u.m.)
-raving (u.m.)
starter-off
startup (n., u.m.)
stat (pref.)
  all one word
State
-aided (u.m.)
#line
-owned (u.m.)
state
hood
quake
side
station#house
stato (c.f.)
  all one word
statute
-barred (u.m.)
#book
stay
-at-home
  (n., u.m.)
bar
bolt
boom
lace
log
pin
plow
sail
wire
steam
boating
car
-cooked (u.m.)
-driven (u.m.)
fitter
pipe
plant
power (n.)
#powerplant
-pocket (v.)
-propelled
  (u.m.)
roll (v.)
roller (u.m., v.)
ship
table
tightness
steamer#line
steel
-blue (u.m.)
-bright (u.m.)
-cased (u.m.)
clad
-framed (u.m.)
-hard (u.m.)
head
plate
works

steep
-rising (u.m.)
-to (u.m.)
-up (u.m.)
-walled (u.m.)
steeple
chase
-high (u.m.)
jack
top
stem
head
post
sickness
winder
stencil-cutting
  (u.m.)
steno (c.f.)
  all one word
step
aunt
child, etc.
down (n., u.m.)
-in (n., u.m.)
ladder
off (n., u.m.)
-on (n., u.m.)
-up (n., u.m.)
stepping
-off (u.m.)
-out (u.m.)
stereo (c.f.)
  all one word
stern
castle
-faced (u.m.)
-heavy (u.m.)
-looking (u.m.)
most
post
#wheel
-wheeler
sterno (c.f.)
  all one word
stetho (c.f.)
  all one word
stew
pan
pot
stick
-at-it (n., u.m.)
fast (n.)
-in-the-mud
  (n., u.m.)
out (n., u.m.)
pin
-to-it-iveness
  (n.)
up (n., u.m.)
sticker
-in
-on
-up
stiff
-backed (u.m.)
neck
-necked (u.m.)
still
-admired (u.m.)
birth
born
-burn (v.)
-fish (v.)
-hunt (v.)
-recurring
  (u.m.)
stand

stink
ball
bomb
damp
pot
stir
about (n., u.m.)
fry
-up (n., u.m.)
stitch
down (n., u.m.)
up (n., u.m.)
stock
breeder
broker
feeder
holding
jobber
judging
list
pile
pot
raiser
rack
-still (u.m.)
taker
truck
wright
stoke
hold
hole
stomach
-filling (u.m.)
-shaped (u.m.)
-sick (u.m.)
-weary (u.m.)
stomato (c.f.)
  all one word
stone
biter
blind
brash
breaker
broke
brood
cast
-cold (u.m.)
crusher
cutter
-dead (u.m.)
-deaf (u.m.)
-eyed (u.m.)
hand (printing)
head
layer
lifter
mason
#proof (printing)
shot
#wall (n.)
wall (u.m., v.)
#writing
stony
-eyed (u.m.)
#land
stop
back (n.)
block
clock
cock
gap
hound
list
log
-loss (n., u.m.)
off (n., u.m.)
watch

storage#room
store
front
ship
storm
-beaten (u.m.)
cock
flow
-laden (u.m.)
-swept (u.m.)
-tossed (u.m.)
wind
storyteller
stout
-armed (u.m.)
heartedness
-minded (u.m.)
stove
brush
-heated (u.m.)
pipe
stow
away (n., u.m.)
down (n., u.m.)
straddle
back
-face (v.)
-legged (u.m.)
straight
away
-backed (u.m.)
-cut (u.m.)
edge
-edged (u.m.)
-faced (u.m.)
forward
head
-legged (u.m.)
#line
-lined (u.m.)
-out (n., u.m.)
-spoken (u.m.)
#time
-up (u.m.)
-up-and-down
  (u.m.)
strainslip
strait
-chested (u.m.)
jacket
laced
stranglehold
strap
-bolt (v.)
hanger
head
-shaped (u.m.)
watch
strato (c.f.)
  all one word
straw
berry#field
boss
-built (u.m.)
hat
-roofed (u.m.)
splitting
stack
-stuffed (u.m.)
walker
-yellow (u.m.)
stray
away (n., u.m.)
#line
mark
stream
bank

bed
flow
head
lined
side
street
-bred (u.m.)
car
cleaner
-cleaning (u.m.)
sweeper
walker
strepto (c.f.)
  all one word
stretchout
  (n., u.m.)
strike
breaker
-in (n., u.m.)
out (n., u.m.)
striker
-in
-out
string
course
halt
#proof (density)
ways
strip
cropping
tease
strong
-arm (u.m., v.)
back (nautical)
-backed (u.m.)
hold
#man
-minded (u.m.)
point (n.)
stub
runner
-toed (u.m.)
wing
stubble
#field
-mulch (u.m.)
stubbornminded
stucco-fronted
  (u.m.)
stuck
up (n., u.m.)
-upper
-uppish (u.m.)
stud
bolt
horse
mare
stupid
head
-headed (u.m.)
-looking (u.m.)
sturdy-limbed
  (u.m.)
stylo (c.f.)
  all one word
sub (pref.)
-Himalayan, etc.
machinegun
#rosa, #specie,
  etc.
-subcommittee
polar, standard,
  etc.
rest one word
subject
-object
-objectivity

subter (pref.)
  all one word
such-and-such
suck
  -egg (n., u.m.)
  hole
  -in (n., u.m.)
sugar
  cake
  cane
  -coat (v.)
  -coated (u.m.)
  -cured (u.m.)
  loaf
  plum
  spoon
  sweet
  #water
  works
sulfa (c.f.)
  all one word
sulfo (c.f.)
  all one word
sulfon (c.f.)
  all one word
sullen
  hearted
  -natured (u.m.)
summer
  -clad (u.m.)
  -dried (u.m.)
  -fallow (v.)
  -made (u.m.)
  tide
  time (season)
  #time (daylight
    saving)
sun
  -baked (u.m.)
  bath
  -bathed (u.m.)
  beam
  blind
  #blindness
  bonnet

bow
break
burn
burst
-cured (u.m.)
dial
dog
down
dress
-dried (u.m.)
-dry (v.)
fall
fast
glade
glare
glass
glow
lamp
lit
quake
ray
rise
scald
set
shade
shine
-shot (u.m.)
shower
spot
stricken
stroke
struck
tan
#time (measure)
time (dawn)
up
sunny
-looking (u.m.)
-natured (u.m.)
super (pref.)
-Christian, etc.
#high frequency
-superlative
highway,
  market, etc.

Super Bowl
supra (pref.)
-abdominal
-acromial
-aerial
anal
-angular
-arytenoid
-auditory
-auricular
-axillary
-Christian, etc.
  rest one word
sur (pref.)
  all one word
sure
-fire (u.m.)
-footed (u.m.)
-slow
surf
-battered (u.m.)
#fish
-swept (u.m.)
swallow
pipe
-tailed (u.m.)
swampside
swan
-bosomed (u.m.)
dive
herd
mark
neck
song
swansdown
swash
buckler
plate
sway
back (n., u.m.)
-backed (u.m.)
bar
-brace (v.)
swearer-in
sweatband

sweep
back (aviation)
  (n., u.m.)
forward
  (aviation)
  (n., u.m.)
stake
through
  (n., u.m.)
washer
sweet
bread
-breathed (u.m.)
brier
faced
heart
meat
mouthed
-pickle (v.)
-sour
-sweet
swell
-butted (u.m.)
head
toad
swelled-headed
  (u.m.)
swept
back (n., u.m.)
forward
  (n., u.m.)
wing (n., u.m.)
swift
foot
-footed (u.m.)
-handed (u.m.)
-running (u.m.)
swill
bowl
tub
swimsuit
swine
-backed (u.m.)
bread
head

herd
pox
sty
swing
back (n., u.m.)
bar
dingle
stock
-swang
tree
swingle
bar
tree
switch
back
blade
gear
plate
plug
rail
tender
swivel
eye
-eyed (u.m.)
-hooked (u.m.)
sword
-armed (u.m.)
bearer
bill
fishing
play
-shaped (u.m.)
stick
syn (pref.)
  all one word
synchro
cyclotron
flash
mesh
tron
Syro (c.f.)
-Arabian, etc.
phenician

T

T
-bandage
-beam
-boat
-bone
-cloth
-iron
-man
-rail
-scale (score)
-shape
-shaped
-shirt
-square
table
cloth
-cut (u.m.)
cutter
-cutting (u.m.)
fellow
-formed (u.m.)
-shaped (u.m.)
spoon
talk
top
tachy (c.f.)
  all one word
tag
-affixing (u.m.)

lock
rag
sore
tail
band
-cropped
  (u.m.)
-ender
first
foremost
gate
head
-heavy (u.m.)
hook
lamp
pin
pipe
race
spin
stock
-tied (u.m.)
twister
-up (n., u.m.)
wheel
wind
tailor
-cut (u.m.)
made (u.m.)
-suited (u.m.)

take
-all (n.)
down (n., u.m.)
-home (n., u.m.)
-in (n., u.m.)
off (n., u.m.)
out (n., u.m.)
up (n., u.m.)
taker
-down
-in
-off
-up
tale
bearer
carrier
teller
talkfest
talking-to (n.)
tall
-built (u.m.)
-looking (u.m.)
tallow
-faced (u.m.)
-pale (u.m.)
tally
#board
ho
#room

tame
-grown (u.m.)
-looking (u.m.)
tan
bark
works
tangent
-cut (v.)
-saw (v.)
tangle
foot
-haired (u.m.)
tank
ship
town
tap
bolt
dance
hole
net
off (n., u.m.)
-riveted (u.m.)
root
-tap
tape
string
-tied (u.m.)
taper
bearer

-fashion (u.m.)
-headed (u.m.)
tapestry
-covered (u.m.)
#maker
-making (u.m.)
#work
tapper-out
tar
-brand (v.)
brush
-coal (u.m.)
-dipped (u.m.)
-paved (u.m.)
pot
-roofed (u.m.)
works
tariff-protected
  (u.m.)
tarpaulin
-covered (u.m.)
#maker
-making (u.m.)
tarso (c.f.)
  all one word
tasksetter
tattletale
tauro (c.f.)
  all one word

tax
-burdened (u.m.)
eater
-exempt (u.m.)
-free (u.m.)
gatherer
-laden (u.m.)
paid
payer
-supported (u.m.)
taxi
auto
bus
cab
meter
stand
tea
ball
cake
cart
-colored (u.m.)
cup
dish
kettle
pot
-scented (u.m.)
spoon
taster
teamplay
tear
bomb
-dimmed (u.m.)
down (n., u.m.)
drop
-off (n., u.m.)
-out (n., u.m.)
pit
sheet
stain
-stained (u.m.)
teen
age (u.m.)
ager
teeter-totter
tele (c.f.)
  all one word
teleo (c.f.)
  all one word
tell
tale
truth
telo (c.f.)
  all one word
tempest-rocked
  (u.m.)
temporo (c.f.)
-occipital
  rest one word
ten
fold
penny (nail)
pins
tender
#boat
-faced (u.m.)
foot
-footed (u.m.)
footish
-handed (u.m.)
heart
loin
-looking (u.m.)
tenement#house
tent
-dotted (u.m.)
pole
-sheltered (u.m.)

terneplate
terra
#cotta
#firma
mara
terrace-fashion
  (u.m.)
test-fly (v.)
tetra (c.f.)
  all one word
thanksgiving
thatch-roofed
  (u.m.)
theater
goer
going
thenceforth
theo (c.f.)
  all one word
theologico (c.f.)
  all one word
there
about(s)
above
across
after
against
among
around
at
away
before
between
by
for
fore
from
in
inafter
inbefore
into
of
on
through
to
tofore
under
until
unto
upon
with
thermo (c.f.)
  all one word
thick
-blooded (u.m.)
head
lips
-looking (u.m.)
pated
set (n., u.m.)
skinned
skull (n.)
skulled
-tongued (u.m.)
wit
-witted (u.m.)
-wooded (u.m.)
-woven (u.m.)
thin
-clad (u.m.)
down (n., u.m.)
set (u.m.)
-voiced (u.m.)
thio (c.f.)
  all one word
third
-class (u.m.)

-degree (u.m.)
hand
  (adv., u.m.)
#house
-rate (u.m.)
-rater
thistledown
thoraco (c.f.)
  all one word
thorn
back
bill
-covered (u.m.)
-set (u.m.)
-strewn (u.m.)
thorough
-bind (v.)
bred
-dried (u.m.)
fare
going
-made (u.m.)
paced
pin
thought
-free (u.m.)
-out (u.m.)
-provoking
  (u.m.)
thousand
fold
-headed (u.m.)
-legged (u.m.)
legs (worm)
thrall
born
dom
-less
thread
bare
-leaved (u.m.)
worn
three
-bagger
-cornered (u.m.)
-dimensional
  (u.m.)
fold
-in-hand
-master
penny (nail)
-piece (u.m.)
-ply (u.m.)
score
some
-spot
-square
-striper
throat
band
cutter
latch
strap
thrombo (c.f.)
  all one word
through
out
put
throw
away (n., u.m.)
back (n., u.m.)
-in (n., u.m.)
#line
off (n., u.m.)
-on (n., u.m.)
out (n., u.m.)
-weight

thrust-pound
thumb
-made (u.m.)
mark
-marked (u.m.)
nail
print
screw
stall
string
sucker
tack
worn
thunder
bearer
blast
bolt
clap
cloud
head
peal
shower
storm
struck
thymo (c.f.)
  all one word
thyro (c.f.)
  all one word
tibio (c.f.)
  all one word
tick
seed
tacktoe
tick
tock
ticket
-selling (u.m.)
#writer
tiddlywink
tide
flat
head
mark
-marked (u.m.)
race
table
-tossed (u.m.)
waiter
-worn (u.m.)
tie
back (n.)
down (n., u.m.)
-in (n., u.m.)
-on (n., u.m.)
-out (n., u.m.)
pin
-plater
up (n., u.m.)
tierlift (truck)
tiger
eye
-striped (u.m.)
tight
-belted (u.m.)
fisted
-fitting (u.m.)
lipped
rope
-set (u.m.)
-tie (v.)
wad
wire
tile
-clad (u.m.)
-red (u.m.)
setter
works

wright
tilt
hammer
up (n.)
timber
-built (u.m.)
head
-headed (u.m.)
jack
-propped (u.m.)
wright
time
born
card
clerk
clock
-consuming
  (u.m.)
frame
-honored (u.m.)
keep (v.)
killer
lag
lock
outs (n., u.m.)
pleaser
saver
server
sheet
slip
slot
span
-stamp (v.)
study
table
taker
waster
worn
tin
-bearing (u.m.)
-capped (u.m.)
-clad (u.m.)
cup
#fish
  (torpedo)
foil
horn
kettle
-lined (u.m.)
pan
plate
-plated (u.m.)
pot
-roofed (u.m.)
type
-white (u.m.)
tinsel
-bright (u.m.)
-clad (u.m.)
-covered (u.m.)
tintblock
  (printing)
tip
burn
cart
-curled (u.m.)
head
-in (n., u.m.)
most
off (n., u.m.)
staff
stock
tank
-tap
toe
top
-up (u.m.)

tire
  changer
  dresser
  fitter
  -mile
  shaper
  some
tit
  bit
  #for#tat
titano (c.f.)
  all one word
tithe
  -free (u.m.)
  payer
  right
title
  -holding (u.m.)
  winner
  -winning (u.m.)
to
  -and-fro
  -do (n.)
toad
  back
  -bellied (u.m.)
  blind
  fish
  -green (u.m.)
  stool
tobacco
  #grower
  -growing (u.m.)
  #shop
toe
  cap
  -in (n., u.m.)
  -mark (v.)
  nail
  plate
  print
toil
  -beaten (u.m.)
  some
  -stained (u.m.)
  -weary (u.m.)
  worn
toilet#room
toll
  bar
  gate
  gatherer
  #line
  payer
  penny
  taker
tom
  cat
  foolery
  -tom
tommy
  gun
  rot
ton
  -hour
  -kilometer
  -mile
  -mileage
  -mile-day
tone
  -deaf (u.m.)
  down (n., u.m.)
  -producing (u.m.)
  up (n., u.m.)
tongue
  -baited (u.m.)
  -bound (u.m.)

-free (u.m.)
-lash (v.)
#lashing
play
-shaped (u.m.)
shot
sore
tack
tied
tip
-twisting (u.m.)
tool
  bag
  builder
  crib
  dresser
  fitter
  -grinding (u.m.)
  head
  holding
  kit
  mark
  plate
  post
  rack
  setter
  shed
  slide
  stock
tooth
  ache
  #and#nail
  -billed (u.m.)
  brush
  drawer
  mark
  -marked (u.m.)
  paste
  pick
  plate
  powder
  puller
  -pulling (u.m.)
  -set (u.m.)
  -shaped (u.m.)
  some
  wash
top
  cap (n.)
  coat
  cutter
  -drain (v.)
  dress (v.)
  flight (u.m.)
  full
  gallant
    (n., u.m.)
  -graft (v.)
  hat
  -hatted (u.m.)
  heavy
  kick
  knot
  liner
  mark
  mast
  milk
  most
  notch
    (nonliteral)
  rail
  rope
  sail
  -secret (u.m.)
  -shaped (u.m.)
  side (naut.)
  soil

topo (c.f.)
  all one word
topsy-turvy
torch
  bearer
  #holder
  lighted
  lit
torpedo
  #boat
  #room
torquemeter
toss
  pot
  up (n., u.m.)
touch
  #and#go
  back (n., u.m.)
  down (n., u.m.)
  hole
  -me-not (n., u.m.)
  pan
  reader
  up (n., u.m.)
tough
  -headed (u.m.)
  -looking (u.m.)
  -skinned (u.m.)
tow
  away
  head
  mast
  -netter
  path
  rope
tower
  -high (u.m.)
  -shaped (u.m.)
town
  -bred (u.m.)
  -dotted (u.m.)
  folk
  gate
  going
  hall
  lot
  ship
  side
  talk
  -weary (u.m.)
towns
  fellow
  people
toy
  -sized (u.m.)
  town
tracheo (c.f.)
  all one word
trachy (c.f.)
  all one word
track
  barrow
  hound
  layer
  mark
  -mile
  side
  walker
tractor-trailer
trade
  #board
  -in (n., u.m.)
  -laden (u.m.)
  -made (u.m.)
  mark
  off
tradespeople

traffic-mile
tragico (c.f.)
  all one word
trail
  blazer
  breaker
  -marked (u.m.)
  side
  sight
  -weary (u.m.)
train
  bearer
  bolt
  crew
  -mile
  shed
  sick
  stop
tram
  -borne (u.m.)
  car
  rail
  road
trans (pref.)
  alpine
  atlantic
  -Canadian, etc.
  pacific
  uranic
  rest one word
transit#time
trap
  door
  fall
  shoot
trashrack
travel
  -bent (u.m.)
  -tired (u.m.)
  -worn (u.m.)
trawlnet
treadwheel
treasure
  -filled (u.m.)
  #house
  -laden (u.m.)
treaty
  breaker
  -sealed (u.m.)
tree
  -clad (u.m.)
  #line
  -lined (u.m.)
  nail
  -ripe (u.m.)
  scape
  top
trellis-covered
    (u.m.)
trench
  back
  coat
  foot
  mouth
  -plowed (u.m.)
tri (c.f.)
  -iodide
  -ply (u.m.)
  state, etc.
  rest one word
tribespeople
tribo (c.f.)
  all one word
tricho (c.f.)
  all one word
trim
  -cut (u.m.)

-dressed (u.m.)
-looking (u.m.)
trinitro (c.f.)
  all one word
trip
  -free (u.m.)
  hammer
  wire
triple
  -acting (u.m.)
  back (sofa)
  branched (u.m.)
  -edged (u.m.)
  fold
  -tailed (u.m.)
  tree (n.)
trolley#line
troopship
tropho (c.f.)
  all one word
tropo (c.f.)
  all one word
trouble
  -free (u.m.)
  -haunted (u.m.)
  shooter
  some
truce
  breaker
  -seeking (u.m.)
truck
  driver
  -mile
  stop
true
  -aimed (u.m.)
  -blue (u.m.)
  born
  bred
  -eyed (u.m.)
  -false
  love (n., u.m.)
  penny (n.)
  #time
trunk
  back
  nose
trust
  breaking
  buster
  -controlled (u.m.)
  -ridden (u.m.)
truth
  -filled (u.m.)
  lover
  seeker
  -seeking (u.m.)
  teller
try
  -on (n., u.m.)
  out (n., u.m.)
  square
  works
tube
  -eyed (u.m.)
  -fed (u.m.)
  form (u.m.)
  head
  -nosed (u.m.)
  works
tuberculo (c.f.)
  all one word
tubo (c.f.)
  -ovarian
  rest one word
tumbledown
    (n., u.m.)

tune
out (n., u.m.)
up (n., u.m.)
tunnel
-boring (u.m.)
-shaped (u.m.)
turbo (c.f.)
-ramjet (u.m.)
rest one word
turf
-built (u.m.)
-clad (u.m.)
-covered (u.m.)
turkey
back
-red (u.m.)
Turko (c.f.)
-Greek, etc.
rest one word
turn
about (n., u.m.)
about-face
again (n., u.m.)
around
(n., u.m.)

back (n., u.m.)
buckle
cap
coat
cock
down (n., u.m.)
gate
-in (n., u.m.)
key
off (n., u.m.)
out (n., u.m.)
pike
pin
plate
screw
sheet
sole
spit
stile
stitch
table
-to (n.)
under
(n., u.m.)
up (n., u.m.)

turned
-back (u.m.)
-down (u.m.)
-in (u.m.)
-on (u.m.)
-out (u.m.)
-over (u.m.)
turner-off
turtle
back
-footed (u.m.)
neck (u.m.)
twelve
fold
penny (nail)
score
twenty
-first
fold
-one
penny (nail)
twice
-born (u.m.)
-reviewed (u.m.)
-told (u.m.)

twin
#boat
born
-engined (u.m.)
fold
-jet (u.m.)
-motor (u.m.)
-screw (u.m.)
two
-a-day (u.m.)
-along (n.)
(bookbinding)
-decker
-faced (u.m.)
fold
-handed (u.m.)
penny (nail)
-piece (u.m.)
-ply (u.m.)
score
-seater
some
-spot
-step (dance)
-striper

-suiter
-thirder
-up (n., u.m.)
-way (u.m.)
-wheeler
tympano (c.f.)
all one word
type
case
cast
cutter
face
foundry
-high (u.m.)
script
set
write (v.)
typho (c.f.)
all one word
typo (c.f.)
all one word
tyro (c.f.)
all one word

U

U
-boat
-cut
-magnet
-rail
-shaped
-tube
ultra (pref.)
-ambitious,
-atomic, etc.
-English, etc.
high # frequency
-high-speed
(u.m.)
#valorem, etc.
rest one word
un (pref.)
-American, etc.
called-for (u.m.)

heard-of (u.m.)
-ionized (u.m.)
self-conscious
sent-for (u.m.)
thought-of
(u.m.)
rest one word
under
age (deficit)
age (younger)
(n., u.m.)
#cultivation
(tillage)
cultivation
(insufficient)
#secretary
-secretaryship
*as prefix, one
word*

uni (c.f.)
-univalent
rest one word
union
-made (u.m.)
#shop
unit-set (u.m.)
up
-anchor (u.m., v.)
-and-coming
(u.m.)
#and #up
beat
coast
country
dip
end (v.)
grade
gradient

keep
lift
-over (u.m.)
rate
river
stairs
state
stream
swing
take
tight (n., u.m.)
#tight (v.)
-to-date (u.m.)
#to #date
town
trend
turn
wind

upper
case (printing)
#class
classman
crust (n., u.m.)
cut
most
urano (c.f.)
all one word
uretero (c.f.)
all one word
urethro (c.f.)
all one word
uro (c.f.)
all one word
used-car (u.m.)
utero (c.f.)
all one word

V

V
-connection
-curve
-engine
-neck
-shaped
-type
vacant
-eyed (u.m.)
-looking (u.m.)
-minded (u.m.)
vagino (c.f.)
all one word
valve
-grinding (u.m.)
-in-head (u.m.)
van
driver
guard
most
pool
vapor
-filled (u.m.)
-heating (u.m.)
vase-shaped
(u.m.)

vaso (c.f.)
all one word
vegeto (c.f.)
all one word
vein
-mining (u.m.)
-streaked (u.m.)
vellum
-bound (u.m.)
-covered (u.m.)
velvet
-crimson (u.m.)
-draped (u.m.)
-green (u.m.)
-pile (u.m.)
venthole
ventri (c.f.)
all one word
ventro (c.f.)
all one word
vertebro (c.f.)
all one word
vesico (c.f.)
all one word
vibro (c.f.)
all one word

vice
#admiral
-admiralty
#consul
-consulate
#governor
-governorship
#minister
-ministry
-presidency
#president
-president-elect
-presidential
#rector
-rectorship
regal
-regency
#regent
royal
#versa
#warden
-wardenship
Vietcong
view
finder
point

vile-natured (u.m.)
vine
-clad (u.m.)
-covered (u.m.)
dresser
growing
stalk
vinegar
-flavored (u.m.)
-hearted (u.m.)
-making (u.m.)
-tart (u.m.)
violet
-blue (u.m.)
-colored (u.m.)
-eared (u.m.)
-rayed (u.m.)
#water
violin-shaped
(u.m.)
virtue-armed
(u.m.)
viscero (c.f.)
all one word
vitreo (c.f.)
all one word

vitro (c.f.)
-clarain
-di-trina
rest one word
vivi (c.f.)
all one word
volleyball
volt
ammeter
-ampere
-coulomb
meter
ohmmeter
-second
volta (c.f.)
all one word
vote
-casting (u.m.)
getter
-getting (u.m.)
vow
-bound (u.m.)
breaker
-pledged (u.m.)
vulvo (c.f.)
all one word

W

W
-engine
-shaped
-surface
-type
wage-earning
  (u.m.)
waist
  band
  belt
  cloth
  coat
  -deep (u.m.)
  -high (u.m.)
waiting
#man
#room
#woman
walk
  around
    (n., u.m.)
  away (n., u.m.)
  -on (n., u.m.)
  out (n., u.m.)
  up (n., u.m.)
walkie-talkie
wall
  eyed
  -like
  -painting (u.m.)
  paper
  plate
  -sided (u.m.)
walled
  -in (u.m.)
  -up (u.m.)
war
  -disabled (u.m.)
  -famed (u.m.)
  fare
  head
  horse
    (nonliteral)
  -made (u.m.)
  path
  ship
  -swept (u.m.)
  #time (clock)
  time (duration)
ward
  heeler
  robe
  ship
warm
  blooded
  -clad (u.m.)
  up (n., u.m.)
warmed-over
  (u.m.)
warpsetter
wash
  basin
  basket
  bowl
  cloth
  -colored (u.m.)
  day
  down (n., u.m.)
  -in (n., u.m.)
  off (n., u.m.)
  out (n., u.m.)
  pot
  rag
  stand
  tray

trough
tub
up (n., u.m.)
washed
  -out (u.m.)
  -up (u.m.)
waste
  basket
  leaf
    (bookbinding)
  paper
  word
watch
  band
  case
  cry
  dog
  -free (u.m.)
  glass
  tower
  word
water
  bag
  bank
  bearer
  -bearing (u.m.)
  -beaten (u.m.)
  -bind (v.)
  bloom
  buck
  color
  -colored (u.m.)
  -cool (v.)
  -cooled (u.m.)
  course
  dog
  -drinking (u.m.)
  drop
  fall
  -filled (u.m.)
  finder
  flood
  flow
  fog
  -free (u.m.)
  front
  gate
  head
  hole
  horse
  -inch
  -laden (u.m.)
  lane
  leaf
  -lined (u.m.)
  locked
  log
  mark
  melon
  meter
  plant
  pot
  proofing
  quake
  -rot (v.)
  scape
  shed
  shoot
  side
  -soak (v.)
  -soaked (u.m.)
  -soluble (u.m.)
  spout
  stain
  wall

works
worn
watt
  -hour
  meter
  -second
wave
  -cut (u.m.)
  form
  guide
  -lashed (u.m.)
  length
  mark
  meter
  -moist (u.m.)
  -on (n., u.m.)
  off (n., u.m.)
  -swept (u.m.)
  -worn (u.m.)
wax
  -billed (u.m.)
  chandler
  cloth
  -coated (u.m.)
  -headed (u.m.)
  #stone
  -yellow (u.m.)
way
  back (n., u.m.)
  beam
  down (n., u.m.)
  farer
  fellow
  going
  laid
  lay
  mark
  post
  side
  -sore (u.m.)
  -up (n., u.m.)
  worn
weak
  -backed (u.m.)
  -eyed (u.m.)
  handed
  -kneed (u.m.)
  minded
  mouthed
weather
  beaten
  blown
  -borne (u.m.)
  break
  cock
  glass
  going
  -hardened (u.m.)
  #house
  -marked (u.m.)
  most
  proofing
  -stain (v.)
  strip
  -stripped (u.m.)
  worn
web
  -fingered (u.m.)
  foot
  -footed (u.m.)
wedge
  -billed (u.m.)
  -shaped (u.m.)
weed
  -choked (u.m.)

-hidden (u.m.)
hook
killer
week
  day
  end
  -ender
  -ending (u.m.)
  long (u.m.)
  -old (u.m.)
weigh
  bridge
  -in (n., u.m.)
  lock
  out (n., u.m.)
  shaft
well
  -being (n.)
  -beloved (u.m.)
  -born (u.m.)
  -bound (u.m.)
  -bred (u.m.)
  -clad (u.m.)
  -deserving (u.m.)
  -doer
  -doing (n., u.m.)
  -drained (u.m.)
  -drilling (u.m.)
  #field
  -grown (u.m.)
  head
  -headed (u.m.)
  hole
  -informed (u.m.)
  -known (u.m.)
  -looking (u.m.)
  -meaner
  -nigh (u.m.)
  -off (u.m.)
  -read (u.m.)
  -set-up (u.m.)
  -settled (u.m.)
  side
  -spoken (u.m.)
  spring
  stead
  -thought-of
    (u.m.)
  -thought-out
    (u.m.)
  -to-do (u.m.)
  -wisher
  -wishing (u.m.)
  -worn (u.m.)
welterweight
werewolf
west
  -central (u.m.)
  -faced (u.m.)
  going
  most
  -northwest
  -sider
wet
  back
  -cheeked (u.m.)
  -clean (v.)
  -nurse (v.)
  pack
  wash
whale
  back
  -backed (u.m.)
  bone
  -built (u.m.)

-headed (u.m.)
-mouthed (u.m.)
ship
wharf
#boat
hand
head
side
what
  ever
  -is-it (n.)
  not (n.)
  soever
  -you-may-call-it
    (n.)
wheat
  cake
  -colored (u.m.)
  ear
  -fed (u.m.)
  -rich (u.m.)
  stalk
wheel
  band
  barrow
  base
  chair
  -cut (u.m.)
  going
  horse
    (nonliteral)
  #load
  -made (u.m.)
  plate
  race
  spin
  stitch
  -worn (u.m.)
  wright
when
  ever
  -issued (u.m.)
  soever
where
  abouts
  after
  as
  at
  by
  for
  from
  in
  insoever
  into
  of
  on
  soever
  to
  under
  upon
  with
  withal
  wherever
which
  ever
  soever
whiffletree
whip
  cord
  crack
  -graft (v.)
  lash
  -marked (u.m.)
  post
  saw

-shaped (u.m.)	**wife**	growing	**with**	winder
socket	beater	-hardy (u.m.)	draw	**woolly**
staff	hood	pot	hold	-coated (u.m.)
stalk	killer	-red (u.m.)	in	-headed (u.m.)
stall	-ridden (u.m.)	seller	out	-looking (u.m.)
stick	**wigwag**	taster	stand	-white (u.m.)
stitch	**wild**	tester	**within**	**word**
stock	cat (n.)	vat	-bound (u.m.)	-blind (u.m.)
-tailed (u.m.)	-eyed (u.m.)	**wing**	-named (u.m.)	builder
whipper	fire	band	**woe**	catcher
-in	#land	bar	begone	-clad (u.m.)
snapper	life	beat	worn	-deaf (u.m.)
whirl	#man	bolt	**wolf**	jobber
about (n., u.m.)	wind	bone	-eyed (u.m.)	list
blast	**will**	bow	#fish	-perfect (u.m.)
pool	-less	cut	hound	play
-shaped (u.m.)	-o'-the-wisp	-footed (u.m.)	pack	seller
wind	wilt-resistant	handed	**woman**	slinger
whisk	(u.m.)	-heavy (u.m.)	folk	**work**
broom	**wind** (v.)	-loading (u.m.)	hood	aday (n., u.m.)
#tail	down (n., u.m.)	-loose (u.m.)	kind	-and-turn (u.m.)
whistlestop	up (n., u.m.)	nut	**womenfolk**	away (n., u.m.)
white	**wind**	-shaped (u.m.)	**wonder**	bag
back	bag	-shot (u.m.)	strong	basket
beard (n.)	ball	span	-struck (u.m.)	bench
#book	blown	-swift (u.m.)	**wood**	card
(diplomatic)	brace	tip	bark (color)	day
cap (n.)	breaker	top	bin	-driven (u.m.)
coat (n.)	burn	walker	bined	flow
-collar (u.m.)	catcher	wall	block	folk
comb (n.)	-chapped (u.m.)	-weary (u.m.)	-built (u.m.)	hand
corn	chill	**winter**	-cased (u.m.)	-hardened (u.m.)
-eared (u.m.)	fall	-beaten (u.m.)	chipper	horse
-eyed (u.m.)	fast	-clad (u.m.)	chopper	-hour (u.m.)
face	-fertilized (u.m.)	-fallow (v.)	chuck	housed
-faced (u.m.)	firm	-fed (u.m.)	cut	life
foot (n.)	flow	feed	grub	manship
-footed (u.m.)	gall	#green (color)	hole	out (n., u.m.)
handed	-galled (u.m.)	green (plant,	horse	pan
-hard (u.m.)	hole	etc.)	hung (u.m.)	paper
head	-hungry (u.m.)	-hardy (u.m.)	-lined (u.m.)	people
-headed (u.m.)	jammer	kill	lot	place
-hot (u.m.)	lass	-made (u.m.)	-paneled (u.m.)	saving
#line	pipe	-sown (u.m.)	pile	sheet
minded	-pollinated (u.m.)	tide	-planing (u.m.)	shoe
out (u.m., v.)	-rode (u.m.)	-worn (u.m.)	print	-shy (n., u.m.)
pot	row	**wire**	pulp	-shyness
-tailed (u.m.)	screen	bar	ranger	slip
-throated (u.m.)	-shaken (u.m.)	-caged (u.m.)	rock	space
top (n.)	-shear (u.m.)	-cut (u.m.)	shed	-stained (u.m.)
vein	shield	cutter	side	stand
wash	shock	dancer	stock	stream
who	side	draw (v.)	turner	table
ever	sleeve	-edged (u.m.)	-turning (u.m.)	up (n., u.m.)
soever	sock	hair (dog)	-walled (u.m.)	ways
whole	speed	-haired (u.m.)	wind (music)	-weary (u.m.)
-headed (u.m.)	stop	less	**wooden**	week
-hogger	storm	#line	head (n.)	worn
sale	stream	photo	-hulled (u.m.)	**working**
some	swept	puller	-weary (u.m.)	#load
whomsoever	worn	spun	**wool**	#room
wicker-woven	**window**	stitch	fell	**world**
(u.m.)	breaker	-stitched (u.m.)	gatherer	beater
wicket	-breaking (u.m.)	-tailed (u.m.)	grader	-conscious (u.m.)
keeper	-cleaning (u.m.)	tap	growing	#consciousness
keeping	-dressing (u.m.)	walker	head	#line
wide	pane	works	-laden (u.m.)	#power
-angle (u.m.)	peeper	-wound (u.m.)	-lined (u.m.)	-self
-awake (u.m.)	-shop (v.)	**wise**	pack	-weary (u.m.)
-handed (u.m.)	-shopping (u.m.)	acre	press	**worm**
mouthed	sill	crack	shearer	-eaten (u.m.)
-open (u.m.)	#work	head (n.)	shed	-eating (u.m.)
spread	**wine**	-headed (u.m.)	sorter	hole
-spreading (u.m.)	bag	-spoken (u.m.)	stock	-riddled (u.m.)
widow	-black (u.m.)	**wishbone**	washer	-ripe (u.m.)
#bird	-drinking (u.m.)	**witch-hunting**	wheel	seed
hood	glass	(u.m.)	-white (u.m.)	shaft

worn	-up (n., u.m.)	drop	writing # room	wry
down (u.m.)	wreath-crowned	fall	wrong	bill
out (u.m.)	(u.m.)	lock	doer	-billed (u.m.)
outness	wreck-free	pin	-ended (u.m.)	-faced (u.m.)
worrywart	(u.m.)	plate	-minded (u.m.)	-looking (u.m.)
worth	wring	watch	-thinking (u.m.)	-mouthed (u.m.)
while (u.m.)	bolt	write	wrought-up	neck
whileness (n.)	staff	back (n., u.m.)	(u.m.)	-set (u.m.)
wrap	wrist	-in (n., u.m.)		
around	band	off (n., u.m.)		
(n., u.m.)	bone	up (n., u.m.)		

X

X	-shaped	xantho (c.f.)	xero (c.f.)	
-body	x	*all one word*	*all one word*	
-disease	# ray (n.)	xeno (c.f.)	xylo (c.f.)	
-virus	-ray (u.m.)	*all one word*	*all one word*	

Y

Y	-deep (u.m.)	long (u.m.)	-throated (u.m.)	-toed (u.m.)
-chromosome	-long (u.m.)	-old (u.m.)	top	young
-joint	stick	-round (u.m.)	yes	eyed (u.m.)
-level	-wide (u.m.)	yellow	-man	-headed (u.m.)
-potential	yaw	back	-no	-ladylike
-shaped	meter	-backed (u.m.)	yester	-looking (u.m.)
-track	-sighted (u.m.)	-bellied (u.m.)	day	-manlike
-tube	year	belly	year	-old
Yankee-Doodle	day	-billed (u.m.)	yoke	-womanhood
yard	end	-headed (u.m.)	fellow	youthtide
arm	-hour (u.m.)	-tailed (u.m.)	mating	yuletide

Z

Z	gravity	zoo (c.f.)	zygo (c.f.)	zymo (c.f.)
-bar	zigzag	*all one word*	*all one word*	*all one word*
-chromosome	zinc	zoologico (c.f.)	zygomatico (c.f.)	
zero	-coated (u.m.)	*all one word*	-orbital	
axial	-white (u.m.)		*rest one word*	
-dimensional				
(u.m.)				

8. PUNCTUATION

8.1. Punctuation is a device used to clarify the meaning of written or printed language. Well-planned word order requires a minimum of punctuation. The trend toward less punctuation calls for skillful phrasing to avoid ambiguity and to ensure exact interpretation. The MANUAL can only offer general rules of text treatment. A rigid design or pattern of punctuation cannot be laid down, except in broad terms. The adopted style, however, must be consistent and be based on sentence structure.

8.2. The general principles governing the use of punctuation are (1) that if it does not clarify the text it should be omitted, and (2) that in the choice and placing of punctuation marks the sole aim should be to bring out more clearly the author's thought. Punctuation should aid in reading and prevent misreading.

Apostrophes and possessives

8.3. The possessive case of a singular or plural noun not ending in *s* is formed by adding an apostrophe and *s*. The possessive case of a singular or plural noun ending in *s* or with an *s* sound is formed by adding an apostrophe only. (For possessives of italicized nouns, see rule 11.6.)

man's, men's	hostess', hostesses'	Mars'
prince's, princes'	princess', princesses'	Dumas'
Essex's, Essexes'	Jones', Joneses'	Schmitz'
Co.'s, Cos.'	Jesus'	

8.4. In compound nouns, the *'s* is added to the element nearest the object possessed.

comptroller general's decision   attorney at law's fee
attorneys general's appointments   John White, Jr.'s (no comma) account
Mr. Brown of New York's motion

8.5. Joint possession is indicated by placing an apostrophe on the last element of a series, while individual or alternative possession requires the use of an apostrophe on each element of a series.

soldiers and sailors' home   Carter's or Reagan's administration
Brown & Nelson's store   Mrs. Smith's and Mrs. Allen's children
men's, women's, and children's clothing   the Army's and the Navy's work
St. Michael's Men's Club   master's and doctor's degrees
editor's or proofreader's opinion

8.6. In the use of an apostrophe in geographic names, firm names, the names of organizations and institutions, and the titles of books, the authentic form is to be followed. (Note use of "St.")

Harpers Ferry; Hells Canyon   Court of St. James's
Masters, Mates & Pilots' Association   St. Peter's Church
Dentists' Supply Co. of New York   St. Elizabeths Hospital
International Ladies' Garment Workers'   Johns Hopkins University
  Union   Hinds' Precedents
Freedmen's Hospital   *but* Martha's Vineyard

117

8.7. Generally the apostrophe should not be used after names of countries and other organized bodies ending in *s,* or after words more descriptive than possessive (not indicating personal possession), except when plural does not end in *s.*

United States control
United Nations meeting
Southern States industries
Massachusetts laws
Bureau of Ships report
Actors Equity Association
House of Representatives
  session
Teamsters Union
editors handbook

syrup producers manual
technicians guide
teachers college
merchants exchange
children's hospital
Young Men's Christian Association
but Veterans' Administration (in
  conformity with enabling statute)
Congress' attitude

8.8. Possessive pronouns do not take an apostrophe.

its   ours   theirs

8.9. Possessive indefinite or impersonal pronouns require an apostrophe.

each other's books
one's home

someone's pen
but somebody else's proposal

8.10. The singular possessive case is used in such general terms as the following:

arm's length
attorney's fees
author's alterations
confectioner's sugar

cow's milk
distiller's grain
fuller's earth
miner's inch

printer's ink
traveler's checks
writer's cramp

8.11. In addition to illustrating possession, an apostrophe is used to indicate contractions, the omission of figures or letters (see also "Courtwork," rule 17.34), and the coined plurals of letters, figures, and symbols.

don't
I've
ne'er
it's (it is) (it has)
class of '92
spirit of '76
three R's
4–H'ers
49'ers
TV'ers

the 1920's *or* the
  twenties; *not*
  the '20's *nor* 20's
but age: in her
  seventies
Btu's
OK's
MC'ing
RIF'ing
RIF'd

RIF's
YMCA's
ABC's
a's; ¶'s; 7's
T's, Y's
2 by 4's (lumber)
but 10s (yarn and thread)
4½s (bonds)
3s (golf)

8.12. The apostrophe is omitted in abbreviations, and also in shortened forms of certain other words.

Danl., *not* Dan'l
Sgt., *not* Sg't
phone

coon
possum
Frisco

Halloween
copter
but ma'am

8.13. The plural of spelled-out numbers, of words referred to as words, and of words already containing an apostrophe is formed by adding *s* or *es;* but *'s* is added to indicate the plural of words used as words if the omission of the apostrophe would cause difficulty in reading.

twos, threes, sevens
ands, ifs, and buts
ins and outs

ups and downs
whereases and
  wherefores

yeses and noes
but do's and don'ts
which's and that's

8.14. The possessive case is often used in lieu of an objective phrase even though ownership is not involved.

1 day's labor (labor for 1 day)   5 or 10 billion dollars' worth
2 hours' traveltime   for charity's sake
a stone's throw   for pity's sake
2 weeks' pay

8.15. The possessive case is not used in such expressions as the following, in which one noun modifies another.

day labor (labor by the day)   State prison
quartermaster stores   State rights

8.16. For euphony, nouns ending in *s* or *ce* and followed by a word beginning with *s* form the possessive by adding an apostrophe only.

for goodness' sake   for old times' sake   for conscience' sake
Mr. Hughes' service   for acquaintance' sake

8.17. A possessive noun used in an adjective sense requires the addition of *'s*.

He is a friend of John's   Stern's is running a sale

8.18. A noun preceding a gerund should be in the possessive case.

in the event of Mary's leaving   the ship's hovering nearby

Brace

8.19. The brace is used to show the relation of one line or group of lines to another group of lines. The point of the brace is placed toward the fewer number of lines; or if the number of lines is the same, toward the single group. For examples of braces used in tabular matter, see rule 13.26.

Supervision of timber sales.
1-hour jobs { District 1, District 7 } 1½ hours' travel ....
2-hour jobs { District 6, District 4 } . 1 hour's travel ....
3-hour jobs { District 2, District 3, District 5 } 2 hours' travel ....
Sales conducted monthly from May to July.

Brackets

Brackets, in pairs, are used—

8.20. In transcripts, congressional hearings, testimony in courtwork, etc., to enclose interpolations that are not specifically a part of the original quotation, corrections, explanations, omissions, editorial comments, or a caution that an error is reproduced literally. (For use of parentheses, see rule 8.94.)

> We found this to be true at the Government Printing Office [GPO].
> He came on the 3d [2d] of July.
> Our conference [lasted] 2 hours.
> The general [Washington] ordered him to leave.
> The paper was as follows [reads]:
> I do not know. [Continues reading:]
> [Chorus of "Mr. Chairman."]
> They fooled only themselves. [Laughter.]

Our party will always serve the people [applause] in spite of the opposition [loud applause]. (If more than one bracketed interpolation, both are included within the sentence.)

The WITNESS. He did it that way [indicating].

Q. Do you know these men [handing witness a list]?

The bill had *not* been paid. [Italic added.] *or* [Emphasis added.]

The statue [sic] was on the statute books.

The WITNESS. This matter is classified. [Deleted.]

[Deleted.]

Mr. JONES. Hold up your hands. [Show of hands.]

Answer [after examining list]. Yes; I do.

Q. [Continuing.]

A. [Reads:]

A. [Interrupting.]

[Discussion off the record.]

[Pause.]

The WITNESS [interrupting]. It is known——

Mr. JONES [continuing]. Now let us take the next item.

Mr. SMITH [presiding]. Do you mean that literally?

Mr. JONES [interposing]. Absolutely.

[The matter referred to is as follows:]

The CHAIRMAN [to Mr. Smith].

The CHAIRMAN [reading]:

Mr. KELLEY [to the chairman]. From 15 to 25 percent.

[Objected to.]

[Mr. Smith nods.]

[Mr. Smith aside.]

[Mr. Smith makes further statement off the record.]

Mr. JONES [for Mr. Smith].

A VOICE FROM AUDIENCE. Speak up.

SEVERAL VOICES. Quiet!

8.21. In bills, contracts, etc., to indicate matter that is to be omitted.

8.22. In mathematics, to denote that enclosed matter is to be treated as a unit. (For examples, see p. 156.)

8.23. When matter in brackets makes more than one paragraph, start each paragraph with a bracket and place the closing bracket at end of last paragraph.

Colon

The colon is used—

8.24. Before a final clause that extends or amplifies preceding matter. (See also rule 8.64.)

Give up conveniences; do not demand special privileges; do not stop work: these are necessary while we are at war.

Railroading is not a variety of outdoor sport: it is service.

8.25. To introduce formally any matter that forms a complete sentence, question, or quotation. (See also rule 3.43.)

The following question came up for discussion: What policy should be adopted?

He said: [If direct quotation of more than a few words follows]. (See also rule 8.36.)

There are three factors, as follows: First, military preparation; second, industrial mobilization; and third, manpower.

8.26. After a salutation.

MY DEAR SIR:
Ladies and Gentlemen:
To Whom It May Concern:

8.27. In expressing clock time.

2:40 p.m.

8.28. After introductory lines in lists, tables, and leaderwork, if subentries follow.

Seward Peninsula:
    Council district:
        Northern Light Mining Co.
        Wild Goose Trading Co.
    Fairhaven district: Alaska Dredging Association (single subitem runs in).
Seward Peninsula: Council district (single subitem runs in):
    Northern Light Mining Co.
    Wild Goose Trading Co.

8.29. In Biblical and other citations.

Luke 4:3.
I Corinthians xiii:13.
Journal of Education 3:342–358.

8.30. In bibliographic references, between place of publication and name of publisher.

Congressional Directory. Washington: U.S. Government Printing Office.

8.31. To separate book titles and subtitles.

Financial Aid for College Students: Graduate
Germany Revisited: Education in the Federal Republic

8.32. In imprints before the year (en space each side of colon).

U.S. Government Printing Office
Washington : 1984

8.33. In proportions.

Concrete mixed 5:3:1
but 5–2–1 (when so in copy)

8.34. In double colon as ratio sign.

1:2::3:6

Comma

The comma is used—

8.35. To separate two words or figures that might otherwise be misunderstood.

Instead of hundreds, thousands came.
Instead of 20, 50 came.
February 10, 1929.
In 1930, 400 men were dismissed.
To John, Smith was very kind.
What the difficulty is, is not known.
but He suggested that that committee be appointed.

8.36. Before a direct quotation of only a few words following an introductory phrase. (See also rule 8.25.)

He said, "Now or never."

8.37. To indicate the omission of a word or words.

Then we had much; now, nothing.

8.38. After each of a series of coordinate qualifying words.

short, swift streams; *but* short tributary streams

8.39. Between an introductory modifying phrase and the subject modified.

Beset by the enemy, they retreated.

8.40. Before and after *Jr., Sr., Esq., Ph.D., F.R.S. Inc.,* etc., within a sentence except where possession is indicated. (See rule 8.4.)

Henry Smith, Jr., chairman
Peter Johns, F.R.S., London
Washington, DC, schools
Motorola, Inc., factory
Alexandria, VA's waterfront

Brown, A.H., Jr. (*not* Brown, Jr., A.H.)
but John Smith 2d (*or* II); Smith, John, II
Mr. Smith, Junior, also spoke (where only last name is used)

8.41. To set off parenthetic words, phrases, or clauses.

Mr. Jefferson, who was then Secretary of State, favored the location of the National Capital at Washington.
It must be remembered, however, that the Government had no guarantee.
It is obvious, therefore, that this office cannot function.
The atom bomb, which was developed at the Manhattan project, was first used in World War II.
Their high morale might, he suggested, have caused them to put success of the team above the reputation of the college.
The restriction is laid down in title IX, chapter 8, section 15, of the code.

but:

The man who fell [restrictive clause] broke his back.
The dam that gave way [restrictive clause] was poorly constructed.
He therefore gave up the search.

8.42. To set off words or phrases in apposition or in contrast.

Mr. Green, the lawyer, spoke for the defense.
Mr. Jones, attorney for the plaintiff, signed the petition.
Mr. Smith, not Mr. Black, was elected.
James Roosevelt, Democrat, of California.

8.43. After each member within a series of three or more words, phrases, letters, or figures used with *and, or,* or *nor.*

red, white, and blue
horses, mules, and cattle; *but* horses and mules and cattle
by the bolt, by the yard, or in remnants
a, b, and c
neither snow, rain, nor heat
2 days, 3 hours, and 4 minutes (series); *but* 2 days 3 hours 4 minutes (age)

8.44. Before the conjunction in a compound sentence.

Fish, mollusks, and crustaceans were plentiful in the lakes, and turtles frequented the shores.
The boy went home alone, and his sister remained with the crowd.

8.45. After a noun or phrase in direct address.

Senator, will the measure be defeated?
Mr. Chairman, I will reply to the gentleman later.
but Yes, sir; he did see it.
No, sir; I do not recall.

8.46. After an interrogative clause, followed by a direct question.

You are sure, are you not?   You will go, will you not?

8.47. Between title of person and name of organization in the absence of the words *of* or *of the*. (See also rule 8.60.)

Chief, Division of Finance
chairman, Committee on Appropriations
colonel, 7th Cavalry
president, Yale University

8.48. Inside closing quotation mark. (See rule 8.145.)

He said "four," not "five."
"Freedom is an inherent right," he insisted.
Items marked "A," "B," and "C," inclusive, were listed.

8.49. To separate thousands, millions, etc., in numbers of four or more digits. (See also rule 8.55.)

4,230   50,491   1,250,000

8.50. After year in complete dates within sentence.

The reported dates of September 11, 1943, to June 12, 1944, were erroneous. This was reflected in the June 13, 1959, report.

but Production for June 1950 was normal. The 10 February 1980 deadline passed.

The comma is omitted—

8.51. Between superior figures or letters in footnote references.

Numerous instances may be cited.[1][2]
Data are based on October production.[a][b]

8.52. Before ZIP (zone improvement plan) Code postal-delivery number.

Government Printing Office, Washington, DC 20401
Thornburg, VA 22565-0120

8.53. Between month, holiday, or season and year in dates.

June 1938; 22d of May 1938; February and March 1938; January, February, and March 1938; January 24 A.D. 1938; 15th of June A.D. 1938; 150 B.C.; Labor Day 1966; Easter Sunday 1966; 5 January 1944 (military usage); spring 1929

8.54. Between the name and number of an organization.

Columbia Typographical Union No. 101
General U.S. Grant Post No. 25

8.55. In fractions, in decimals, and in serial numbers, except patent numbers.

$\frac{1}{2500}$
1.0947
page 2632
202-275-2303 (telephone number)
1721-1727 St. Clair Avenue
Executive Order 11242
motor No. 189463
1450 kilocycles; 1100 meters (no comma unless more than four figures, radio only)

8.56. Between two nouns one of which identifies the other.

The Children's Bureau's booklet "Infant Care" is a bestseller.

8.57. Before ampersand (&). (For exception, see rule 15.29.)

Brown, Wilson & Co.
Mine, Mill & Smelter Workers

8.58. Before abbreviations of compass directions.

6430 Princeton Dr. SW.

8.59. In bibliographies, between name of publication and volume or similar number.

American Library Association Bulletin 34:238, April 1940.

8.60. Wherever possible without danger of ambiguity.

$2 gold
$2.50 U.S. currency
$3.50 Mexican
Executive Order No. 21
General Order No. 12; *but* General Orders, No. 12

Public Law 85-1
He graduates in the year 2000 (*not* 2,000)
My age is 30 years 6 months 12 days.
John Lewis 2d (*or* II)
Murphy of Illinois; Murphy of New York
Carroll of Carrollton; Henry of Navarre (places closely identified with the persons); *but* Clyde Downs, of Maryland; President Hadley, of Yale University
James Bros. et al.; *but* James Bros., Nelson Co., et al. (last element of series)

Dash

The em dash is used—

8.61. To mark a sudden break or abrupt change in thought. (See also rule 8.95.)

He said—and no one contradicted him—"The battle is lost."
If the bill should pass—which God forbid!—the service will be wrecked.
The auditor—shall we call him a knave or a fool?—approved an inaccurate statement.

8.62. To indicate an interruption or an unfinished word or sentence. A 2-em dash will be used when the interruption is by a person other than the speaker, and a 1-em dash will show self-interruption. (Note that extracts must begin with a true paragraph. Following extracts, 10 point must start as a paragraph, as example shown.)

"Such an idea can scarcely be——"
"The word 'donation'——"
"The word 'dona'——"
"He said: "Give me lib——"
"The bill reads "repeal," not "am——"

Q. Did you see——A. No, sir.
Mr. BROWN [reading]:
The report goes on to say that—
Observe this closely—
during the fiscal year * * *

8.63. Instead of commas or parentheses, if the meaning may thus be clarified.

These are shore deposits—gravel, sand, and clay—but marine sediments underlie them.

8.64. Before a final clause that summarizes a series of ideas. (See also rule 8.24.)

Freedom of speech, freedom of worship, freedom from want, freedom from fear—these are the fundamentals of moral world order.

8.65. After an introductory phrase reading into the following lines and indicating repetition of such phrase.

I recommend—
    That we accept the rules;
    That we also publish them; and
    That we submit them for review.

8.66. With a preceding question mark, in lieu of a colon.

How can you explain this?—"Fee paid, $5."

8.67. To precede a credit line or a run-in credit or signature.

Still achieving, still pursuing,
Learn to labor and to wait.
—*Longfellow.*

Every man's work shall be made manifest.—I Corinthians 3:13.
This statement is open to question.—GERALD H. FORSYTHE.

8.68. After a run-in sidehead. (For examples, see rule 8.110.)
8.69. To separate run-in questions and answers in testimony. (See also rule 17.7.)

Q. Did he go?—A. No.

The em dash is not used—

8.70. At the beginning of any line of type, except as shown in rule 8.67.

8.71. Immediately after a comma, colon, or semicolon.

A 3-em dash is used—

8.72. In bibliographies to indicate repetition.

> POWELL, JAMES W., Jr., Hunting in Virginia's lowlands. 1972. 200 pp.
> —— Fishing off Delmarva. 1972. 28 pp.

The en dash is used—

8.73. In a combination of (1) figures, (2) capital letters, or (3) figures and capital letters. (An en dash, not a hyphen, is used, even when such terms are adjectival modifiers.) (See also rules 6.21 and 6.44.)

exhibit 6–A	WTOP–AM–FM–TV
5–20 bonds	4–H Club
DC–14; *but* Convair 340	LK–66–A(2)–74
Public Law 85–1, *but* Public Laws 85–1–	$15–$20
85–20 (note em dash between two	CBS–TV network
elements with en dashes)	AFL–CIO merger
301–942–8367 (telephone number	*but* ACF–Brill Motors Co.
including area code)	loran–C
section 12 (a)–(f)	Mig–21
I–95 (interstate)	

8.74. In the absence of the word *to* when denoting a period of time. (See also rule 12.9c.)

> 1935–37   January–June   Monday–Friday

The en dash is not used—

8.75. For *to* when the word *from* precedes the first of two related figures or expressions. (See also rules 12.9c and 13.123.)

> From January 1 to June 30, 1951; *not* from January 1–June 30, 1951.

8.76. For *and* when the word *between* precedes the first of two related figures or expressions.

> Between 1923 and 1929; *not* between 1923–29

Ellipses

8.77. Three asterisks (preferred form) or three periods, separated by en quads, are used to denote an ellipsis within a sentence, at the beginning or end of a sentence, or in two or more consecutive sentences (see also rule 8.83). To achieve faithful reproduction of excerpt material, editors using period ellipses should indicate placement of terminal period in relation to an ellipsis at the end of a sentence.

> He called * * * and left. * * * When he returned the * * *.
> * * * called * * * and left. * * * he returned the * * *.
> He called * * * and * * *. When he returned the * * *.
> He called * * * and * * * he returned the * * *. [Two or more consecutive sentences, including intervening punctuation]

8.78. Ellipses are not overrun alone at the end of a paragraph.

8.79. When both asterisks and periods for ellipsis occur in the copy and periods are not specifically requested, use asterisks throughout.

8.80. A line of asterisks (or periods) indicates an omission of one or more entire paragraphs. In 26½-pica or wider measure, a line of "stars" means seven asterisks indented 2 ems at each end of the line, with the remaining space divided evenly between the asterisks. In measures less than 26½ picas, five asterisks are used. Quotation marks are not used on line of asterisks or periods in quoted matter. Where line of asterisks ends complete quotation, no closing quote is used.

     *   *   *   *   *   *   *

8.81. Indented matter in 26½-pica or wider measure also requires a seven-asterisk line to indicate the omission of one or more entire paragraphs.

8.82. An extra indention is added in indented matter; except where there are too many varying indentions, then all the asterisks (or periods) have the same alignment.

8.83. If an omission occurs in the last part of a paragraph immediately before a line of asterisks, three asterisks are used, in addition to the line of asterisks, to indicate such an omission.

8.84. If two or more sizes of type are used on a page, 10-point asterisks are indented 2 ems, 8-point and 6-point asterisks being aligned with the 10-point asterisks.

8.85. Equalize spacing above and below an ellipsis line.

Exclamation point

8.86. The exclamation point is used to mark surprise, incredulity, admiration, appeal, or other strong emotion, which may be expressed even in a declarative or interrogative sentence.

He acknowledged the error!
How beautiful!
"Great!" he shouted. [Note omission of comma.]

What!
Who shouted, "All aboard!" [Note omission of question mark.]

8.87. In direct address, either to a person or a personified object, O is used without an exclamation point, or other punctuation; but if strong feeling is expressed, an exclamation point is placed at the end of the statement.

    O my friend, let us consider this subject impartially.
    O Lord, save Thy people!

8.88. In exclamations without direct address or appeal, *oh* is used instead of *O*, and the exclamation point is omitted.

    Oh, but the gentleman is mistaken.
    Oh dear; the time is so short.

Hyphen

The hyphen (a punctuation mark, not an element in the spelling of words) is used—

8.89. To connect the elements of certain compound words. (See "Compound Words," pp. 73-80.)

8.90. To indicate continuation of a word divided at end of a line. (See Word Division, supplement to STYLE MANUAL; for brief description of supplement, see p. 2.)

8.91. Between the letters of a spelled word.

> The Style Board changed the spelling a-l-i-n-e to a-l-i-g-n.
> Note the adoption of g-a-u-g-e to replace g-a-g-e and the addition of e-n-s-u-r-e.

8.92. To separate elements of chemical formulas. (See rule 6.44.)

The hyphen, as an element, may be used—

8.93. To represent letters deleted or illegible words in copy.

> d - - n   h - ll   Leroy Joseph B - - -

Parentheses (See rule 8.20 for use of brackets in colloquy.)

Parentheses are used—

8.94. To set off matter not intended to be part of the main statement or not a grammatical element of the sentence, yet important enough to be included. In colloquy, brackets must be used. (See rule 8.20.)

> This case (124 U.S. 329) is not relevant.
> The result (see fig. 2) is most surprising.
> The United States is the principal purchaser (by value) of these exports (23 percent in 1955 and 19 percent in 1956).

8.95. To enclose a parenthetic clause where the interruption is too great to be indicated by commas. (See also rules 8.20 and 8.61.)

> You can find it neither in French dictionaries (at any rate, not in Littré) nor in English.

8.96. To enclose an explanatory word not part of a written or printed statement.

> the Erie (PA) News; *but* the News of Erie, PA
> Portland (OR) Chamber of Commerce; *but* Washington, DC, schools.

8.97. To enclose letters or numbers designating items in a series, either at beginning of paragraphs or within a paragraph.

> The order of delivery will be: (*a*) Food, (*b*) clothing, and (*c*) tents and other housing equipment.
> You will observe that the sword is (1) old fashioned, (2) still sharp, and (3) unusually light for its size.
> Paragraph 7(B)(1)(*a*) will be found on page 6. (Note parentheses closed up (see rule 2.9).)

8.98. To enclose a figure inserted to confirm a written or printed statement given in words if double form is specifically requested. (See also rule 12.18.)

> This contract shall be completed in sixty (60) days.

8.99. A reference in parentheses at the end of a sentence is placed before the period, unless it is a complete sentence in itself.

> The specimen exhibits both phases (pl. 14, *A, B*).
> The individual cavities show great variation. (See pl. 4.)

8.100. If a sentence contains more than one parenthetic reference, the one at the end is placed before the period.

> This sandstone (see pl. 6) occurs in every county of the State (see pl. 1).

8.101. When a figure is followed by a letter in parentheses, no space is used between the figure and the opening parenthesis; but if the letter is not in parentheses and the figure is repeated with each letter, the letter is closed up with the figure.

> 15(*a*). Classes, grades, and sizes.
> 15*a*. Classes, grades, and sizes.

8.102. If both a figure and a letter in parentheses are used before each paragraph, a period and an en space are used after the closing parenthesis; if the figure is not repeated before each letter in parentheses but is used only before the first, the period is placed after the figure.

> 15(*a*). When the figure is used before the letter in each paragraph—
> 15(*b*). The period is placed after the closing parenthesis.
> 15. (*a*) When the figure is used before letter in first paragraph but not repeated with subsequent letters—
> (*b*) The period is used after the figure only.
> Sec. 12 (a) If no period is used and a letter in parentheses appears after a numbered item—
> (b) Space must be used after the number if at least one other lettered subsection is shown.

8.103. Note position of period relative to closing parenthesis:

> The vending stand sells a variety of items (sandwiches, beverages, cakes, etc.).
> The vending stand sells a variety of items (sandwiches, beverages, cakes, etc. (sometimes ice cream)).
> The vending stand sells a variety of items. (These include sandwiches, beverages, cakes, etc. (6).)

8.104. To enclose bylines in congressional work.

(By Sylvia Porter, staff writer)

8.105. When matter in parentheses makes more than one paragraph, start each paragraph with a parenthesis and place the closing parenthesis at end of last paragraph.

Period

The period is used—

8.106. After a declarative sentence that is not exclamatory or after an imperative sentence.

> Stars are suns.
> He was employed by Sampson & Co.
> Do not be late.
> On with the dance.

8.107. After an indirect question or after a question intended as a suggestion and not requiring an answer.

> Tell me how he did it.
> May we hear from you.
> May we ask prompt payment.

8.108. In place of a parenthesis after a letter or number denoting a series.

> *a.* Bread well baked.   1. Punctuate freely.
> *b.* Meat cooked rare.   2. Compound sparingly.
> *c.* Cubed apples stewed.   3. Index thoroughly.

8.109. Sometimes to indicate ellipsis. (See rule 8.77.)

8.110. After a run-in sidehead.

Conditional subjunctive.—The conditional subjunctive is required for all unreal and doubtful conditions.

2. **Peacetime preparation.**—*a.* The Chairman of the National Security Resources Board, etc.

2. *Peacetime preparation—Industrial mobilization plans.*—The Chairman of the National Security Resources Board, etc.

2. **Peacetime preparation.**—*Industrial mobilization.*—The Chairman of the National Security Resources Board, etc.

62. *Determination of types.*—*a. Statement of characteristics.*—Before types of equipment, etc.

Steps in planning for procurement.—(1) *Determination of needs.*—To plan for the procurement of such arms, etc.

62. *Determination of types.*—*(a) Statement of characteristics.*—Before, etc.

DETERMINATION OF TYPES.—**Statement of characteristics.**—Before types of, etc.

Note.—The source material was furnished.

but Source: U.S. Department of Commerce, Bureau of the Census.

8.111. Paragraphs and subparagraphs may be arranged according to the scheme below. The sequence is not fixed, and variations, in addition to the use of center and side heads or indented paragraphs, may be adopted, depending on the number of parts.

I. (Roman numeral)	(1)
A.	(a)
1.	(i) (lowercase Roman numeral)
a.	(aa)

8.112. To separate integers from decimals in a single expression.

3.75 percent $3.50 1.25 meters

8.113. In continental European languages, to indicate thousands.

1.317   72.190.175

8.114. After abbreviations, unless otherwise specified. (See "Abbreviations," p. 135.)

Apr.	NE. (Northeast)	*but* m (meter)
fig.	RR.	kc (kilocycle)
Ph.D.		NY (New York)

8.115. After legends and explanatory matter beneath illustrations. Legends without descriptive language do not receive periods.

Figure 1.—Schematic drawing.
Figure 1.—Continued.
but Figure 1 (no period)

8.116. After *Article 1, Section 1,* etc., at beginning of paragraphs. An en space is used after such terms.

A center period is sometimes used—

8.117. To indicate multiplication. (Multiplication sign preferable.)

$a \cdot b$ $(a \times b)$

The period is omitted—

8.118. After—

Lines in title pages.
Center, side, and running heads.
Continued lines.
Boxheads of tables.
Scientific, chemical, or other symbols.

This rule does not apply to abbreviation periods.

8.119. After a quotation mark that is preceded by a period. (See also rule 8.145.)

> He said, "Now or never."

8.120. After letters used as names without specific designation.

> Officer B; Subject A, etc.
> A said to B that all is well.
> Mr. A told Mr. B that the case was closed.
> Mr. X (for unknown or censored name)
> *but* Mr. A. [for Mr. Andrews]. I do not want to go.
> Mr. K. [for Mr. King]. The meeting is adjourned.

8.121. After a middle initial which is merely a letter and not an abbreviation of a name.

> Daniel D Tompkins   *but* Harry S. Truman (his
> Ross T McIntire   preference)

8.122. After a short name which is not an abbreviation of the longer form. (See also rule 9.23.)

> Alex   Ed   Sam

8.123. After Roman numerals used as ordinals.

> King George V   Apollo XII insigne   Super Bowl XVII

8.124. After words and incomplete statements listed in columns. Full-measure matter is not to be regarded as a column.

8.125. After explanatory matter set in 6 point under leaders or rules.

> ....
>   (Name)   (Address)   (Position)

8.126. Immediately before leaders, even if an abbreviation precedes the leaders.

Question mark

The question mark is used—

8.127. To indicate a direct query, even if not in the form of a question.

> Did he do it?
> He did what?
> Can the money be raised? is the question.
> Who asked, "Why?" (Note single question mark)
> "Did you hurt yourself, my son?" she asked.

8.128. To express more than one query in the same sentence.

> Can he do it? or you? or anyone?

8.129. To express doubt.

> He said the boy was 8(?) feet tall. (No space before question mark)
> The statue(?) was on the statute books.
> The scientific identification *Dorothia*? was noted.

Quotation marks

Quotation marks are used—

8.130. To enclose direct quotations. (Each part of an interrupted quotation begins and ends with quotation marks.)

> The answer is "No."
> He said, "John said, 'No.' "
> "John," said Henry, "why do you go?"

8.131. To enclose any matter following such terms as *entitled, the word, the term, marked, designated, classified, named, endorsed, cited as, referred to as,* or *signed;* but are not used to enclose expressions following the terms *known as, called, so-called,* etc., unless such expressions are misnomers or slang.

> Congress passed the act entitled "An act * * *."
> After the word "treaty," insert a comma.
> Of what does the item "Miscellaneous debts" consist?
> The column "Imports from foreign countries" was not * * *.
> The document will be marked "Exhibit No. 21"; *but* The document may be made exhibit No. 2.
> The check was endorsed "John Adamson."
> It was signed "John."
> Beryllium is known as glucinium in some European countries.
> It was called profit and loss.
> The so-called investigating body.

8.132. To enclose titles of addresses, articles, books, captions, chapter and part headings, editorials, essays, headings, headlines, hearings, motion pictures and plays (including television and radio programs), papers, short poems, reports, songs, studies, subheadings, subjects, and themes. All principal words are to be capitalized. (See also rules 3.51 and 8.136.)

> An address on "Uranium-235 in the Atomic Age"
> The article "Germany Revisited" appeared in the last issue.
> "The Conquest of Mexico," a published work (book)
> Under the caption "Long-Term Treasurys Rise"
> The subject was discussed in "Courtwork." (chapter heading)
> It will be found in "Part XI: Early Thought."
> The editorial "Haphazard Budgeting"
> "Compensation," by Emerson (essay)
> "United States To Appoint Representative to U.N." (heading for headline)
> In "Search for Paradise" (motion picture); "South Pacific" (play)
> A paper on "Constant-Pressure Combustion" was read.
> "O Captain! My Captain!" (short poem)
> The report "Atomic Energy: What It Means to the Nation"; *but* annual report of the Public Printer
> This was followed by the singing of "The Star-Spangled Banner."
> Under the subhead "Sixty Days of Turmoil" will be found * * *.
> The subject (or theme) of the conference is "Peaceful Uses of Atomic Energy."
> *also* Account 5, "Management fees."
> Under the heading "Management and Operation."
> Under the appropriation "Building of ships, Navy."

8.133. The lines of a poem should range on the left, those that rhyme taking the same indention. Poems are usually centered on the longest line; overs 3 ems; 6 points of space between stanzas.

> We care not whence they came,
> Dear in their lifeless clay.
> Whether unknown or known to fame,
> Their cause and country still the same,
> They died—and wore the gray.

8.134. At the beginning of each paragraph of a quotation, but at the end of the last paragraph only.

8.135. To enclose a letter or communication, which bears both date and signature, within a letter. (See rule 8.140.)

8.136. To enclose misnomers, slang expressions, sobriquets, coined words, or ordinary words used in an arbitrary way. (See also rule 6.26.)

> His report was "bunk."
> It was a "gentlemen's agreement."
> The "invisible government" is responsible.
> George Herman "Babe" Ruth.
> *but* He voted for the lameduck amendment.

8.137. Quotation marks will not be borne off from adjacent characters except when they precede a fraction or an apostrophe or precede or follow a superior figure or letter, in which case a thin space will be used. A thin space will also be used to separate double and single quotation marks.

Quotation marks are not used—

8.138. To enclose titles of works of art: paintings, statuary, etc.

8.139. To enclose names of newspapers or magazines.

8.140. To enclose complete letters having date and signature.

8.141. To enclose extracts that are indented or set in smaller type, or solid extracts in leaded matter; but indented matter in text that is already quoted carries quotation marks.

8.142. In indirect quotations.

> Tell her yes.
> He could not say no.

8.143. Before a display initial which begins a quoted paragraph.

8.144. The comma and the final period will be placed inside the quotation marks. Other punctuation marks should be placed inside the quotation marks only if they are a part of the matter quoted. (See rule 8.48.)

> Ruth said, "I think so."
> "The President," he said, "will veto the bill."
> The trainman shouted, "All aboard!"
> Who asked, "Why?"
> The President suggests that "an early occasion be sought * * *."
> Why call it a "gentlemen's agreement"?

8.145. In congressional and certain other classes of work showing amendments, and in courtwork with quoted language, punctuation marks are printed after the quotation marks when not a part of the quoted matter.

> Insert the words "growth", "production", and "manufacture".
> To be inserted immediately after the words "cadets, U.S. Coast Guard;".
> Change "February 1, 1983", to "June 30, 1983".
> "Insert in lieu thereof 'July 1, 1983,'."

8.146. When occurring together, quotation marks should precede the footnote reference number.

The commissioner claimed that the award was "unjustified." [1]
His exact words were: "The facts in the case prove otherwise." [2]

8.147. Quotation marks should be limited, if possible, to three sets (double, single, double).

"The question in the report is, 'Can a person who obtains his certificate of naturalization by fraud be considered a "bona fide" citizen of the United States?' "

Semicolon

The semicolon is used—

8.148. To separate clauses containing commas. (See also rule 8.151.)

Donald A. Peters, president of the First National Bank, was also a director of New York Central; Harvey D. Jones was a director of Oregon Steel Co. and New York Central; Thomas W. Harrison, chairman of the board of McBride & Co., was also on the board of Oregon Steel Co.
Reptiles, amphibians, and predatory mammals swallow their prey whole or in large pieces, bones included; waterfowl habitually take shellfish entire; and gallinaceous birds are provided with gizzards that grind up the hardest seeds.
Yes, sir; he did see it.
No, sir; I do not recall.

8.149. To separate statements that are too closely related in meaning to be written as separate sentences, and also statements of contrast.

Yes; that is right.
No; we received one-third.
It is true in peace; it is true in war.
War is destructive; peace, constructive.

8.150. To set off explanatory abbreviations or words which summarize or explain preceding matter.

The industry is related to groups that produce finished goods; i.e., electrical machinery and transportation equipment.
There were involved three metal producers; namely, Jones & Laughlin, Armco, and Kennecott.

The semicolon is not used—

8.151. Where a comma will suffice.

Regional offices are located in New York, NY, Chicago, IL, and Dallas, TX.

Single punctuation

8.152. Single punctuation is used wherever possible without ambiguity.

124 U.S. 321 (no comma)
Sir: (no dash)
Joseph replied, "It is a worthwhile effort." (no outside period)

Type

8.153. All punctuation marks, including parentheses, brackets, and superior reference figures, are set to match the type of the words which they adjoin. A lightface dash is used after a run-in boldface sidehead followed by lightface matter. Lightface brackets,

parentheses, or quotation marks shall be used when both boldface and lightface matter are enclosed.

Charts: C&GS 5101 (N.O. 18320), page 282 (see above); N.O. 93491 (Plan); page 271.

9. ABBREVIATIONS

(See also Numerals; Symbols)

9.1. Abbreviations are used to save space and to avoid distracting the mind of the reader by a needless spelling out of repetitious words or phrases.

9.2. The nature of the publication governs the extent to which abbreviations are used. In text of technical and legal publications, and in parentheses, brackets, footnotes, sidenotes, tables, leaderwork, and bibliographies, many words are frequently abbreviated. Cut-in sideheads, legends, tables of contents, and indexes follow the style of the text.

9.3. Internal and terminal punctuation in units of measure are to be omitted to conform with practice adopted by scientific, technical, and industrial groups, nationally and internationally. Where omission of terminal punctuation causes confusion; e.g., the symbol *in* (inch) mistaken for the preposition *in,* the abbreviation should be spelled out.

9.4. Standard and easily understood forms are preferable, and they should be uniform throughout a job. Abbreviations not generally known should be followed in the text by the spelled-out forms in parentheses the first time they occur; in tables and leaderwork such explanatory matter should be supplied in a footnote. As the printer cannot rewrite the copy, the author should supply these explanatory forms.

9.5. In technical matter, abbreviations for units of measure should be used only with figures; similarly, many other abbreviations should not appear in isolation; for example, energy is measured in foot-pounds, *not* energy is measured in ft·lb.

Capitals, hyphens, periods, and spacing

9.6. In general, an abbreviation follows the capitalization and hyphening of the word or words abbreviated. It is followed by a period unless otherwise indicated.

c.o.d.   St.   *but* ft·lb

9.7. Abbreviations and initials of a personal name with points are set without spaces. However, abbreviations composed of contractions and initials or numbers, will retain space.

U.S.	A.F. of L.–CIO (*or* AFL–CIO preferred)
U.S.S.R.	AT&T
U.N.	Texas A&M
U.S.C. (*but* Rev. Stat.)	R&D
B.S., LL.D., Ph.D., B.Sc.	A.D., B.C.
H.R. 116 (*but* S. 116, S. Con.	e.s.t.
Res. 116)	i.e., e.g. (*but* op. cit.)
C.A.D.C. (*but* App. D.C.)	J.F.K.
A.B. Secrest, D.D.S.	L.B.J.

9.8. Except as otherwise designated, points and spaces are omitted after initials used as shortened names of governmental agencies and of other organized bodies. "Other organized bodies" shall be interpreted to mean organized bodies that have become popularly identified with a symbol, such as MIT (Massachusetts Institute of Technology), GM (General Motors), GMAC (General Motors Acceptance Corp.), etc. (See rule 9.61.) Symbols, when they appear in copy, may be used for acts of Congress. Example: ARA (Area Redevelopment Act).

MIT	AFL–CIO
NLRB	ARC
TVA	ASTM

Geographic terms

9.9. *U.S.* (for United States) will be used when preceding the word *Government* or the name of a Government organization, except in formal writing (treaties, Executive orders, proclamations, etc.); congressional bills; legal citations and courtwork; covers and title pages unless abbreviation is requested); and in association with name or names of other countries.

U.S. Government
U.S. Congress
U.S. Department of Health and Human Resources
U.S. district court
U.S. Supreme Court (*but* Supreme Court of the United States)
U.S. Army (*but* Army of the United States)
U.S. monitor *Nantucket*
U.S.-NATO assistance
U.S.-U.S.S.R. meeting
U.S. Government efforts to control inflation must be successful if the United
      States is to have a stable economy.
but British, French, and United States Governments; United States-British talks

9.10. With the exceptions in the above rule, the abbreviation *U.S.* is used in the adjective position, but is spelled out when used as a noun.

U.S. foreign policy	*but* Foreign policy of the United
U.S. farm-support program	States
U.S. attorney	United States Code (official title)
U.S. citizen	United States Steel Corp. (legal title)

9.11. The names of foreign countries, except U.S.S.R. (to avoid too long a name), are not abbreviated.

9.12. In other than formal usage, all States of the United States, the Canal Zone, Puerto Rico, and the Virgin Islands are abbreviated immediately following any capitalized geographic term (see p. 47), including armory, arsenal, airbase, airport, barracks, depot, fort, Indian agency, military camp, national cemetery (also forest, historic site, memorial, seashore, monument, park), naval shipyard, proving ground, reservation (forest, Indian, or military), and reserve or station (military or naval).

Prince George County, VA	Richmond, VA
Mount Rainier National Forest, WA	Arlington National Cemetery, VA
Stone Mountain, GA	Aberdeen Proving Ground, MD
National Naval Medical Center,	Friendship Airport, MD
Bethesda, MD	Redstone Arsenal, AL
Mark Twain National Wildlife Refuge,	*but* Leavenworth freight yards, Kansas
IL-IA-MO (note use of hyphens here)	Altoona sidetrack, Wisconsin

9.13. The Postal Service style of two-letter State and Province abbreviations is to be used.

UNITED STATES

AL	Alabama	MD	Maryland	PA	Pennsylvania
AK	Alaska	MA	Massachusetts	RI	Rhode Island
AZ	Arizona	MI	Michigan	SC	South Carolina
AR	Arkansas	MN	Minnesota	SD	South Dakota
CA	California	MS	Mississippi	TN	Tennessee
CO	Colorado	MO	Missouri	TX	Texas
CT	Connecticut	MT	Montana	UT	Utah
DE	Delaware	NE	Nebraska	VT	Vermont
FL	Florida	NV	Nevada	VA	Virginia
GA	Georgia	NH	New Hampshire	WA	Washington
HI	Hawaii	NJ	New Jersey	WV	West Virginia
ID	Idaho	NM	New Mexico	WI	Wisconsin
IL	Illinois	NY	New York	WY	Wyoming
IN	Indiana	NC	North Carolina	CZ	Canal Zone
IA	Iowa	ND	North Dakota	DC	District of
KS	Kansas	OH	Ohio		Columbia
KY	Kentucky	OK	Oklahoma	GU	Guam
LA	Louisiana	OR	Oregon	PR	Puerto Rico
ME	Maine			VI	Virgin Islands

CANADA

AB	Alberta	NF	Newfoundland	PE	Prince Edward
BC	British Columbia	NT	Northwest		Island
LB	Labrador		Territories	PQ	Quebec
MB	Manitoba	NS	Nova Scotia	SK	Saskatchewan
NB	New Brunswick	ON	Ontario	UT	Yukon Territory

9.14. The names of other insular possessions, trust territories, and *Long Island, Staten Island,* etc., are not abbreviated.

9.15. The names of Canadian Provinces and other foreign political subdivisions are not abbreviated except as noted in rule 9.13.

Addresses. (For use of numerals in addresses, see rule 12.13.)

9.16. The words *street, avenue, place, road, square, boulevard, terrace, drive, court,* and *building,* following name or number, are abbreviated in footnotes, sidenotes, tables, leaderwork, and lists.

9.17. In addresses, a single period is used with the abbreviations *NW., SW., NE., SE.* (indicating sectional divisions of cities) following name or number. *North, South, East,* and *West* are spelled out at all times.

9.18. The word *Street* or *Avenue* as part of a name is not abbreviated even in parentheses, footnotes, sidenotes, tables, and leaderwork.

> 14th Street Bridge　　　　　　Ninth Avenue Bldg.

9.19. The words *county, fort, mount, point,* and *port* are not abbreviated. *Saint (St.)* and *Sainte (Ste.)* should be abbreviated.

Descriptions of tracts of land

9.20. If fractions are spelled out in land descriptions, *half* and *quarter* are used (not *one-half* nor *one-quarter*).

> south half of T. 47 N., R. 64 E.

9.21. In the description of tracts of public land the following abbreviations are used (periods are omitted after abbreviated compass directions that immediately precede and close up on figures):

SE¼NW¼ sec. 4, T. 12 S., R. 15 E., of the Boise Meridian
lot 6, NE¼ sec. 4, T. 6 N., R. 1 W.
N½ sec. 20, T. 7 N., R. 2 W., sixth principal meridian
Tps. 9, 10, 11, and 12 S., Rs. 12 and 13 W.
T. 2 S., Rs. 8, 9, and 10 E., sec. 26
T. 3 S., R. 1 E., sec. 34, W½E½, W½, and W½SE¼SE¼
sec. 32 (with or without a township number)

9.22. In case of an unavoidable break in a land-description symbol group at end of a line, use no hyphen and break after fraction.

Names and titles

9.23. The following forms are not always abbreviations, and copy should be followed as to periods:

Al	Ed	Will
Alex	Fred	
Ben	Sam	

9.24. In signatures the exact form used by the signer must be retained.

George Wythe   Geo. Taylor

9.25. In company and other formal names, if it is not necessary to preserve the full legal title, the forms *Bro., Bros., Co., Corp., Inc., Ltd.,* and & are used. *Association* and *Manufacturing* are not abbreviated.

Radio Corp. of America
Aluminum Co. of America
Standard Oil Co. of New Jersey
Ronald G. Brown & Bro.
Jones Bros. & Co.
American Telephone & Telegraph Co.
Norbert J. Schackmar Investment Corp.
Vic Sport Shop, Inc.
Maryland Steamship Co., Ltd.
Chesapeake & Delaware Canal
Fairmount Building & Loan Association
Electronics Manufacturing Co.
Texas College of Arts & Industries

National Barrel & Drum Association
Robert Wilson & Associates, Inc.
U.S. News & World Report
Baltimore & Ohio Railroad
Mine, Mill & Smelter Workers
but Little Theater Company
Senate Banking, Housing, and Urban Affairs Committee
Federal Savings and Loan Insurance Corporation (Federal unit)

9.26. *Company* and *Corporation* are not abbreviated in names of Federal Government units.

Panama Railroad Company   Commodity Credit Corporation

9.27. In parentheses, footnotes, sidenotes, tables, and leaderwork, abbreviate the words *railroad* and *railway (RR.* and *Ry.),* except in such names as "Washington Railway & Electric Co." and "Florida Railroad & Navigation Corp." *SS* for *steamship, MS* for *motorship,* etc., preceding name are used at all times. (See rule 11.6.)

9.28. In the names of informal companionships the word *and* is spelled out.

Gilbert and Sullivan   Currier and Ives

9.29. In other than formal usage, a civil, military, or naval title preceding a name is abbreviated if followed by Christian or given name or initial; but *Mr., Mrs., Miss, Ms., M., MM., Messrs., Mlle.,*

Mme., and *Dr.* are abbreviated with or without Christian or given name or initial.

Adj.
Adj. Gen.
Adm. (admiral)
A1c. (airman, first class)
Asst. Surg.
Brig. Gen.
Bvt. (brevet)
Capt.
Col.
Comdr.
Cpl.
CWO (chief warrant officer)
En1c. (engineman, first class)
Ens.
1st Lt.
1st Sgt.
Gen.
Gov.
Hosp. Corpsman 3c.
Hosp. Sgt.

Hosp. Steward
Insp. Gen.
Judge Adv. Gen.
Lt.
Lt. Col.
Lt. Comdr.
Lt. Gen.
Lt. Gov.
Lt. (jg.)
Maj.
Maj. Gen.
M. Sgt.
Orderly Sgt.
Ord. Sgt. (ordnance sergeant)
Passed Asst. Surg.
Pfc. (private first class)
PO (petty officer)
Prof.
Pvt.
Q.M. Gen.

Q.M. Sgt.
Rdm3c. (radarman, third class)
Rear Adm.
S1c. (seaman, first class)
2d Lt.
Sfc. (sergeant, first class)
Sgt.
Sgt. Maj.
Sp3c. (specialist, third class)
S. Sgt.
Supt.
Surg.
Surg. Gen.
T2g. (technician, second grade)
T. Sgt.
Vice Adm.
WO (warrant officer)
WO (jg.)

If requested, the following military abbreviations will be used:

ADM, admiral
BG, brigadier general
CDR, commander
COL, colonel
CPL, corporal
CAPT, captain
CPT, captain
CWO4, chief warrant officer (W-4)
ENS, ensign
LCDR, lieutenant commander
LT, lieutenant
LTC, lieutenant commander

LTG, lieutenant general
LTJG, lieutenant junior grade
2LT, second lieutenant
MAJ, major
PFC, private first class
PVT, private
RADM, radarman
SFC, sergeant first class
S4, specialist four
SGT, sergeant
VADM, vice admiral
WO1, warrant officer

9.30. Spell *Senator, Representative, commodore,* and *commandant.*

9.31. Unless preceded by *the,* abbreviate *honorable, reverend,* and *monsignor* when followed by the first name, initials, or title.

Hon. Elihu Root; the Honorable Elihu Root; the Honorable Mr. Root
the Honorables William H. Rehnquist, Lewis F. Powell, Jr., and Harry A. Blackmum
Rev. Martin Luther King, Jr.; the Reverend Dr. King; Rev. Dr. King; Reverend King (*not* Rev. King, *nor* the Reverend King)
Rt. Rev. James E. Freeman; the Right Reverend James E. Freeman; Very Rev. Henry Boyd; the Very Reverend Henry Boyd
Rt. Rev. Msgr. John Bird; the Right Reverend Monsignor John Bird

9.32. The following and similar forms are used after a name:

Esq., Jr., Sr.
2d, 3d (*or* II, III) (not preceded by comma)
Degrees: LL.D., M.A., Ph.D., etc.
Fellowships, orders, etc.: F.R.S., K.C.B., C.P.A., etc.

9.33. The abbreviation *Esq.* and other titles such as *Mr., Mrs.,* and *Dr.,* should not appear with any other title or with abbreviations indicating scholastic degrees.

John L. Smith, Esq., *not* Mr. John L. Smith, Esq., *nor* John L. Smith, Esq., A.M.; *but* James A. Jones, Jr., Esq.
Ford Maddox, A.B., Ph.D., *not* Mr. Ford Maddox, A.B., Ph.D.
George Gray, M.D., *not* Mr. George Gray, M.D., *nor* Dr. George Gray, M.D.
Dwight A. Bellinger, D.V.M.

9.34. *Sr.* and *Jr.* should not be used without Christian or given name or initials, but may be used in combination with any title. (See also rule 8.40.)

A.K. Jones, Jr., or Mr. Jones, Junior, *not* Jones, Jr., *nor* Jones, Junior.
President J.B. Nelson, Jr.

9.35. When name is followed by abbreviations designating religious and fraternal orders and scholastic and honorary degrees, their sequence is as follows: Orders, religious first; theological degrees; academic degrees earned in course; and honorary degrees in order of bestowal.

Henry L. Brown, D.D., A.M., D.Lit.
T.E. Holt, C.S.C., S.T.Lr., LL.D., Ph.D.
Samuel J. Deckelbaum, P.M.

9.36. Academic degrees standing alone may be abbreviated.

John was graduated with a B.A. degree; *but* bachelor of arts degree (lowercase if spelled out).
He earned his Ph.D. by hard work.

9.37. In addresses, signatures, and lists of names, including leaderwork but not in tables nor in centerheads, *Mr., Mrs.,* and other titles preceding a name, and *Esq., Jr., Sr., 2d,* and *3d* following a name, are set in roman caps and lowercase if the name is in caps and small caps. If the name is in caps, they are set in caps and small caps, if small caps are available—otherwise in caps and lowercase. (See also rule 16.3.)

Parts of publications

9.38. For parts of publications mentioned in parentheses, brackets, footnotes, sidenotes, list of references, synonymies, tables, and leaderwork, and followed by figures, letters, or Roman numerals, the following abbreviations are used:

app., apps. (appendix, appendixes)
art., arts. (article, articles)
bull., bulls. (bulletin, bulletins)
ch., chs. (chapter, chapters)
col., cols. (column, columns)
ed., eds. (edition, editions)
fig., figs. (figure, figures)
No., Nos. (number, numbers)
p., pp. (page, pages)
par., pars. (paragraph, paragraphs)

pl., pls. (plate, plates)
pt. pts., (part, parts)
sec., secs. (section, sections)
subch., subchs. (subchapter, subchapters)
subpar., subpars. (subparagraph, subparagraphs)
subpt., subpts. (subpart, subparts)
subsec., subsecs. (subsection, subsections)
supp., supps. (supplement, supplements)
vol., vols. (volume, volumes)

9.39. The word *article* and the word *section* are abbreviated when appearing at the beginning of a paragraph and set in caps and small caps followed by a period and an en space, except that the first of a series is spelled out.

Art. 2; Sec. 2; etc.; *but* Article 1; Section 1
Art. II; Sec. II; etc.; *but* Article I; Section I

9.40. At the beginning of a legend, the word *figure* preceding the legend number is not abbreviated.

Figure 4.—Landscape.

Terms relating to Congress

9.41. The words *Congress* and *session,* when accompanied by a numerical reference, are abbreviated in parentheses, brackets, and text footnotes. In sidenotes, lists of references, synonymies, tables, leaderwork, and footnotes to tables and leaderwork, the following abbreviations are used:

92d Cong., 1st sess.	Public Law 84, 92d Cong.
1st sess., 92d Cong.	Private Law 68, 92d Cong.

9.42. In references to bills, resolutions, documents and reports in parentheses, brackets, footnotes, sidenotes, tables, and leaderwork, the following abbreviations are used:

H.R. 416 (House bill)
S. 116 (Senate bill)
The above two examples may be used in either abbreviated or spelled-out form in text.
H. Res. 5 (House resolution)
H. Con. Res. 10 (House concurrent resolution)
H.J. Res. 21 (House joint resolution)
S. Res. 50 (Senate resolution)
S. Con. Res. 17 (Senate concurrent resolution)

S.J. Res. 45 (Senate joint resolution)
H. Conf. Rept. 10 (House conference report)
H. Doc. 35 (House document)
S. Doc. 62 (Senate document)
H. Rept. 214 (House report)
S. Rept. 410 (Senate report)
Ex. Doc. B (Executive document)
Ex. F (92d Cong., 2d sess.)
Ex. Rept. 9 (92d Cong., 1st sess.)
Misc. Doc. 16 (miscellaneous document)
Public Res. 47

9.43. References to statutes in parentheses, footnotes, sidenotes, tables, leaderwork, and congressional work are abbreviated as follows (for references in courtwork, see rule 17.12):

Rev. Stat. (Revised Statutes); 43 Rev. Stat. 801; 18 U.S.C. 38
Supp. Rev. Stat. (Supplement to the Revised Statutes)
Stat. L. (Statutes at Large)
but Public Law 85–1

Calendar divisions

9.44. Names of months followed by the day, or day and year, are abbreviated in footnotes, tables, leaderwork, and sidenotes, and in bibliographies. (See examples, rule 9.45.) *May, June,* and *July* are always spelled out. In narrow columns in tables, however, the names of months may be abbreviated even if standing alone. Preferred forms follow:

Jan.	Apr.	Oct.
Feb.	Aug.	Nov.
Mar.	Sept.	Dec.

9.45. In text only, dates as part of a citation or reference within parentheses or brackets are also abbreviated.

(Op. Atty. Gen., Dec. 4, 1985)
(Congressional Record, Sept. 25, 1981)
[From the New York Times, Mar. 4, 1978]
[From the Mar. 4 issue]
On Jan. 25 (we had commenced on Dec. 26, 1977) the work was finished. (In footnotes, tables, leaderwork, and sidenotes)
On January 25, a decision was reached (Op. Atty. Gen., Dec. 4, 1975). (Text, but with citation in parentheses)
but On January 25 (we had commenced on December 26, 1967) the work was finished. (Not a citation or reference in text)

9.46. Weekdays are not abbreviated, but the following forms are used, if necessary, in lists or in narrow columns in tables:

Sun.	Wed.	Fri.
Mon.	Thurs.	Sat.
Tues.		

9.47. The following forms are to be used when abbreviating names of time zones:

A.s.t, Atlantic standard time
A.t., Atlantic time
c.s.t., central standard time
c.t., central time
d.s.t., daylight saving (no "s") time
e.d.t., eastern daylight time
e.s.t., eastern standard time
e.t., eastern time
G.c.t., Greenwich civil time
G.m.a.t., Greenwich mean astronomical time

G.m.t., Greenwich mean time
l.s.t., local standard time
m., noon (meridies)
m.s.t., mountain standard time
m.t., mountain time
P.s.t., Pacific standard time
P.t., Pacific time
u.t., universal time

Coined words and symbols

9.48. To obtain uniform treatment in the formation of coined words and symbols, the following formula, which conforms to current usage, should be applied:

When only first letter of each word or selected words is used to make up symbol, use all caps:

APPR (Army package power reactor)
MAG (Military Advisory Group)
MIRV (multiple independently targetable reentry vehicle)
SALT (strategic arms limitation talks)
STEP (supplemental training and employment program)

Where first letters of prefixes and/or suffixes are utilized as part of established expressions, use all caps:

CPR (*cardio*pulmonary *r*esuscitation)
ESP (*e*xtrasensory *p*erception)
FLIR (*f*orward-*l*ooking *i*nfrared)

Where an acronym or abbreviated form is copyrighted or established by law, copy must be followed:

ACTION (agency of Government; not an acronym)
MarAd (*Ma*ritime *Ad*ministration)
NACo (*N*ational *A*ssociation of *Co*unties)
MEDLARS (*Med*ical *L*iterature *A*nalysis and *R*etrieval *S*ystem)

When proper names are used in shortened form any word of which uses more than first letter of each word, use caps and lowercase:

Conrail (Consolidated Rail Corporation)
Vepco (Virginia Electric Power Co.)
Inco (International Nickel Co.)
Aramco (Arabian-American Oil Co.)

In common-noun combinations made up of more than first letter of lowercased words, use lowercase:

loran (*long-range n*avigation)
sonar (*so*und *n*avigation *r*anging)
secant (*se*paration *c*ontrol of *a*ircraft by *n*onsynchronous *t*echniques)

9.49. The words *infra* and *supra* are not abbreviated.

Terms of measure

9.50. Compass directions are abbreviated as follows:

N.	S.	10° N. 25° W.
NE.	NNW.	NW. by N. ¼ W.
E.	W.	
SW.	ESE.	

9.51. The words *latitude* and *longitude,* followed by figures, are abbreviated in parentheses, brackets, footnotes, sidenotes, tables, and leaderwork, and the figures are always closed up.

lat. 52°33′05″ N.   long. 13°21′10″ E.

9.52. Avoid breaking latitude and longitude figures at end of line; space out line instead. In case of an unavoidable break at end of line, use hyphen.

9.53. Temperature and gravity are expressed in figures. When using the degree mark bump to cap letters, not against figures. Note the following abbreviations and letter symbols:

abs, absolute	API, American Petroleum Institute
Bé, Baumé	Twad, Twaddell
°C,[1] degree Celsius [2]	100 °C
°F, degree Fahrenheit	212 °F [1]
°R, degree Rankine	671.67 °R
K, kelvin	273.15 K
°API	18 °API

9.54. References to meridian in statements of time are abbreviated as follows:

10 a.m.	12 m. (noon)
2:30 p.m.	12 p.m. (midnight)

9.55. The word *o'clock* is not used with abbreviations of time. (See rule 12.9b.)

9.56. Metric unit letter symbols are set lowercase roman unless the unit name has been derived from a proper name, in which case the first letter of the symbol is capitalized (for example Pa for pascal and W for watt). The exception is the letter L for liter. The same form is used for singular and plural. The preferred symbol for *cubic centimeter* is cm^3; use *cc* only when requested.

A space is used between a figure and a unit symbol except in the case of the symbols for degree, minute, and second of plane angle.

3 m   25 °C   *but* 33°15′21″

Prefixes for multiples and submultiples				*Metric units*
E	exa (10^{18})	d	deci (10^{-1})	m, meter (for length)
P	peta (10^{15})	c	centi (10^{-2})	g, gram (for weight or mass)
T	tera (10^{12})	m	milli (10^{-3})	L, liter (for capacity)
G	giga (10^{9})	μ	micro (10^{-6})	
M	mega (10^{6})	n	nano (10^{-9})	
k	kilo (10^{3})	p	pico (10^{-12})	
h	hecto (10^{2})	f	femto (10^{-15})	
da	deka (10)	a	atto (10^{-18})	

---

[1] Without figures preceding it, °C or °F should be used only in boxheads and over figure columns in tables.

[2] Preferred form (superseding Centigrade) approved by Ninth General Conference on Weights and Measures, October 1948.

	Length		*Area*		*Volume*
km	kilometer	km²	square kilometer	km³	cubic kilometer
hm	hectometer	hm²	square hectometer	hm³	cubic hectometer
dam	dekameter	dam²	square dekameter	dam³	cubic dekameter
m	meter	m²	square meter	m³	cubic meter
dm	decimeter	dm²	square decimeter	dm³	cubic decimeter
cm	centimeter	cm²	square centimeter	cm³	cubic centimeter
mm	millimeter	mm²	square millimeter	mm³	cubic millimeter

	Weight		*Land area*		*Capacity of containers*
kg	kilogram	ha	hectare	kL	kiloliter
hg	hectogram	a	are	hL	hectoliter
dag	dekagram			daL	dekaliter
g	gram			L	liter
dg	decigram			dL	deciliter
cg	centigram			cL	centiliter
mg	milligram			mL	milliliter
µg	microgram				

9.57. A similar plan of abbreviation applies to any unit of the metric system.

A	ampere	V	volt	mH	millihenry
VA	voltampere	W	watt	µF	microfarad (one-
c	cycle (radio)	kc	kilocycle		millionth of a
F	farad	kV	kilovolt		farad)
H	henry	kVA	kilovoltampere		
J	joule	kW	kilowatt		
		mF	millifarad		

9.58. The following forms are used when units of English weight and measure and units of time are abbreviated, the same form of abbreviation being used for both singular and plural:

Length	*Area and volume*
in, inch	in^2, square inch
ft, foot	in^3, cubic inch
yd, yard	mi^2, square mile
mi, mile (statute)	ft^3, cubic foot

Time	*Weight*	*Capacity*
yr, year	gr, grain	gill(s), not abbreviated
mo, month	dr, dram	pt, pint
d, day	oz, ounce	qt, quart
h, hour	lb, pound	gal, gallon
min, minute	cwt, hundredweight	pk, peck
s, second	dwt, pennyweight	bu, bushel
	ton(s), not abbreviated	bbl, barrel
	but t, metric ton (tonne)	

9.59. In astrophysical and similar scientific matter, magnitudes and units of time may be expressed as follows, if so written in copy. (See also "Clock time," rule 12.9b.)

$$2^m_.3 \qquad 5^h3^m9^s \qquad 4.5^h$$

Money

9.60. The following are some of the abbreviations and symbols used for indicating money:

\$, dol. (dollar)	₽ (peso)
c, ct, ¢ (cent, cents)	£ (pound)
LT175 (Turkish)	s (shilling)
US\$15,000	d (pence)
Mex\$2,650	£12 16s 8d (*not* 12/16/8)

Use "US\$" if omission, in relatively rare instances, would result in confusion.

(For the abbreviations of other terms indicating foreign money, see p. 238.)

LIST OF STANDARD WORD ABBREVIATIONS

and

LIST OF LETTER SYMBOLS FOR UNITS OF MEASURE

(Standard word abbreviations, this page; standard letter symbols for units of measure, etc., pp. 150-153.)

Standard word abbreviations

(For a comprehensive list of standard abbreviations of legal and other Latin phrases, see pp. 414-417; for similar abbreviations in other languages, see section on abbreviations in the language desired, pp. 355-460.)

9.61. If abbreviations are required, use these forms:

AA, Alcoholics Anonymous
A.B. or B.A., bachelor of arts
abbr., abbreviation
abs., abstract
acct., account
ACDA, Arms Control and Disarmament Agency
ACTH, adrenocorticotropic hormone
ACTION (not an acronym, an independent agency)
A.D. (anno Domini), in the year of our Lord
ADP, automated data processing
AEF, American Expeditionary Forces
AF, audiofrequency
AFB, and similar military symbols (with name), Air Force Base
AFL–CIO, American Federation of Labor and Congress of Industrial Organizations
AID, Agency for International Development
a.k.a., also known as
A.L.R., American Law Reports
AM (no periods), amplitude modulation
A.M. (anno mundi), in the year of the world
A.M. or M.A., master of arts
a.m. (ante meridiem), before noon
Am. Repts., American Reports
AMVETS, American Veterans of World War II; Amvet(s) (individual)
antilog (no period), antilogarithm
A1 (rating)
AOA, Administration on Aging
API, American Petroleum Institute
APO (no periods), Army post office
App. D.C., District of Columbia Appeal Cases
App. Div., Appellate Division
APPR, Army package power reactor
approx., approximately
ARC, American Red Cross
ARS, Agricultural Research Service
ASCS, Agricultural Stabilization and Conservation Service
ASME, American Society of Mechanical Engineers
A.S.N., Army service number

ASTM, American Society for Testing Materials
Atl., Atlantic Reporter; A.2d, Atlantic Reporter, second series
AUS, Army of the United States
Ave., avenue
AWACS, airborne warning and control system
a.w.l., absent with leave
a.w.o.l., absent without official leave
B.C., before Christ
BCG (bacillus Calmette-Guérin), antituberculosis vaccine
bf., boldface
BGN, Board on (not of) Geographic Names)
BIA, Bureau of Indian Affairs
BIS, Bank for International Settlements
Blatch. Pr. Cas., Blatchford's Prize Cases
Bldg., building
B.Lit(t). or Lit(t).B., bachelor of literature
BLM, Bureau of Land Management
BLS, Bureau of Labor Statistics
Blvd., boulevard
b.o., buyer's option
B.S. or B.Sc., bachelor of science
ca. (circa), about
ca, centiare
CAB, Civil Aeronautics Board
CACM, Central American Common Market
c. and s.c., caps and small caps
CAP, Civil Air Patrol
CARE, Cooperative for American Remittances to Everywhere, Inc.
c.b.d., cash before delivery
C.C.A., Circuit Court of Appeals
CCC, Commodity Credit Corporation
C.Cls., Court of Claims
C.Cls.R., Court of Claims Reports
C.C.P.A., Court of Customs and Patents Appeals
CCR, Commission on Civil Rights
CDC, Centers for Disease Control
CEA, Council of Economic Advisers
Cento, Central Treaty Organization
cf. (confer), compare, or see

CFR, Code of Federal Regulations
CFR Supp., Code of Federal Regulations Supplement
CHAMPUS, Civilian Health and Medical Program of the Uniformed Services
CIA, Central Intelligence Agency
CIC, Counterintelligence Corps
C.J. (corpus juris), body of law; Chief Justice
CLC, Cost of Living Council
CO, commanding officer
Co., company (commercial)
c.o.d., cash on delivery
COLA, cost-of-living adjustment
Comp. Dec., Comptroller's Decisions (Treasury)
Comp. Gen., Comptroller General Decisions
Comsat, communication satellite
con., continued
conelrad, control of electromagnetic radiation (civil defense)
Conrail, Consolidated Rail Corporation
Conus, continental United States
Corp., corporation (commercial)
cos (no period), cosine
cosh (no period), hyperbolic cosine
cot (no period), cotangent
coth (no period), hyperbolic cotangent
c.p., chemically pure
C.P.A., certified public accountant
CPI, Consumer Price Index
CPR, cardiopulmonary resuscitation
cr., credit; creditor
csc (no period), cosecant
csch (no period), hyperbolic cosecant
Ct., court
Dall., Dallas (U.S. Supreme Court Reports)
DAR, Daughters of the American Revolution
DAR, defense acquisition regulation
d.b.a., doing business as
d.b.h., diameter at breast height
D.D., doctor of divinity
D.D.S., doctor of dental surgery
DDT, dichlorodiphenyltrichloroethane
DEW, distant early warning (DEW line)
Dist. Ct., District Court
D.Lit(t). or Lit(t).D., doctor of literature
do. (ditto), the same
DNC, Domestic Names Committee (BGN)
DOD, Department of Defense
DOT, Department of Transportation
DP (no periods), displaced person
D.P.H., doctor of public health
D.P.Hy., doctor of public hygiene
dr., debit; debtor
Dr., doctor; drive
D.V.M., doctor of veterinary medicine
E., east
EEC, European Economic Community (Common Market)
EEOC, Equal Employment Opportunity Commission
EFTA, European Free Trade Association

EFTS, electronic funds transfer system
e.g. (exempli gratia), for example
EHF, extremely high frequency
8°, octavo
emcee, master of ceremony
e.o.m., end of month
EOP, Executive Office of the President
EPA, Environmental Protection Agency
ERP, European Recovery Program
et al. (et alii), and others
et seq. (et sequentia), and the following
etc. (et cetera), and so forth
Euratom, European Atomic Energy Community
Eurodollars, U.S. dollars used to finance foreign trade
Euromarket, European Common Market (European Economic Community)
Ex. Doc. (with letter), executive document
f., ff., and following page (pages)
FAA, Federal Aviation Administration
FAO, Food and Agriculture Organization
f.a.s., free alongside ship
FAS, Foreign Agricultural Service
FBI, Federal Bureau of Investigation
FCA, Farm Credit Administration
FCC, Federal Communications Commission
FCIC, Federal Crop Insurance Corporation
FCSC, Foreign Claims Settlement Commission
FDA, Food and Drug Administration
FDIC, Federal Deposit Insurance Corporation
Fed., Federal Reporter; F.2d, Federal Reporter, second series
FEOF, Foreign Exchange Operations Fund
FHA, Federal Housing Administration
FmHA, Farmers Home Administration
FHLBB, Federal Home Loan Bank Board
FHWA, Federal Highway Administration
FICA, Federal Insurance Contributions Act
FIPS, Federal Information Processing Standards
FLSA, Fair Labor Standards Act
FM, frequency modulation
FMC, Federal Maritime Commission
FMCS, Federal Mediation and Concilation Service
FNMA, Federal National Mortgage Association (Fannie Mae)
FNS, Food and Nutrition Service
f°, folio
f.o.b., free on board
4°, quarto
FPC, Federal Power Commission
FPO (no periods), fleet post office
FR, Federal Register (publication)
FRG, Federal Republic of Germany
FRS, Federal Reserve System

FS, Forest Service
FSLIC, Federal Savings and Loan Insurance Corporation
FSS, Federal Supply Service
F.Supp., Federal Supplement
FTC, Federal Trade Commission
FWS, Fish and Wildlife Service
GAO, General Accounting Office
GATT, General Agreement of Tariffs and Trade
GDR, German Democratic Republic
GI, general issue; Government issue
G.M.&.S., general, medical, and surgical
GNMA, Government National Mortgage Association (Ginnie Mae)
GNP, gross national product
Gov., governor
GPO, Government Printing Office
gr. wt., gross weight
GS, Geological Survey
GSA, General Services Administration
H.C., House of Commons
H. Con. Res. (with number), House concurrent resolution
H. Doc. (with number), House document
HE (no periods), high explosive
HF (no periods), high frequency
HHS, Health and Human Resources (Department of)
H.J. Res. (with number), House joint resolution
H.L., House of Lords
How., Howard (U.S. Supreme Court Reports)
H.R. (with number), House bill
H. Rept. (with number), House report
H. Res. (with number), House resolution
HUD, Housing and Urban Development
IADB, Inter-American Defense Board
IAEA, International Atomic Energy Agency
ibid. (ibidem), in the same place
ICBM, intercontinental ballistic missile
ICC, Interstate Commerce Commission
id. (idem), the same
IDA, International Development Association
i.e. (id est), that is
IF (no periods), intermediate frequency
IFC, International Finance Corporation
IMCO, Intergovernmental Maritime Consultative Organization
IMF, International Monetary Fund Inc., incorporated
INS, Immigration and Naturalization Service
Insp. Gen., Inspector General
Interpol, International Criminal Police Organization
IOU, I owe you
IQ, intelligence quotient
IRBM, intermediate range ballistic missile
IRE, Institute of Radio Engineers
IRO, International Refugee Organization
IRS, Internal Revenue Service
ITO, International Trade Organization

ITU, International Telecommunication Union; International Typographical Union
JAG, Judge Advocate General
jato, jet-assisted takeoff
J.D. (jurum doctor), doctor of laws
JOBS, Job Opportunities in the Business Sector
Jr., junior
Judge Adv. Gen., Judge Advocate General
LAFTA, Latin American Free Trade Association
lat., latitude
LC, Library of Congress
lc., lowercase
L.Ed., Lawyer's edition (U.S. Supreme Court Reports)
liq., liquid
lf., lightface
LF, low frequency
LL.B., bachelor of laws
LL.D., doctor of laws
loc. cit. (loco citato), in the place cited
log (no period), logarithm
long., longitude
loran (no periods), long-range navigation
lox (no periods), liquid oxygen
LPG, liquefied petroleum gas
Ltd., limited
Lt. Gov., lieutenant governor
M, money supply:
   M_1; M_{1B}; M_2
M., monsieur; MM., messieurs
m. (meridies), noon
M, more
MA (see MarAd)
MAC, Military Airlift Command
MAG, Military Advisory Group
MarAd, Maritime Administration
MC, Member of Congress (emcee, master of ceremonies)
M.D., doctor of medicine
MDAP, Mutual Defense Assistance Program
MediCal, Medicaid California
memo, memorandum
MF, medium frequency
MFN, most favored nation
MIA, missing in action (plural, MIA's)
Misc. Doc. (with number), miscellaneous document
Mlle., mademoiselle
Mme., madam
Mmes., mesdames
mo., month
MOS, military occupational specialty
M.P., Member of Parliament
MP, military police
Mr., mister (plural, Messrs.)
Mrs., mistress
Ms., coined feminine title (plural, Mses.)
M.S., master of science
MS., MSS., manuscript, manuscripts
MSC, Military Sealift Command
Msgr., monsignor
m.s.l., mean sea level

MTN, multilateral trade negotiations
N., north
NA., not available; not applicable
NAC., National Association of Counties
NAS, National Academy of Science
NASA, National Aeronautics and Space Administration
NATO, North Atlantic Treaty Organization
NBS, National Bureau of Standards
NCUA, National Credit Union Administration
NE., northeast
n.e.c., not elsewhere classified
n.e.s., not elsewhere specified
net wt., net weight
N.F., National Formulary
NFAH, National Foundation on the Arts and the Humanities
NIH, National Institutes of Health
n.l., natural log or logarithm
NLRB, National Labor Relations Board
No., Nos., number, numbers
NOAA, National Oceanic and Atmospheric Administration
n.o.i.b.n., not otherwise indexed by name
n.o.p., not otherwise provided (for)
n.o.s., not otherwise specified
NOS, National Ocean Service (formerly National Ocean Survey)
NOVS, National Office of Vital Statistics
NPS, National Park Service
NRC, Nuclear Regulatory Commission
NS, nuclear ship
NSA, National Shipping Authority
NSC, National Security Council
NSF, National Science Foundation
n.s.k., not specified by kind
n.s.p.f., not specifically provided for
NW., northwest
OAS, Organization of American States
OASDHI, Old-Age, Survivors, Disability, and Health Insurance Program
OASI, Old-Age and Survivors Insurance
OCD, Office of Civil Defense
OD, officer of the day
OD, overdose; OD'd, overdosed
O.D., doctor of optometry
OECD, Organization for Economic Cooperation and Development
OK, OK'd OK'ing, OK's
OMB, Office of Management and Budget
Op. Atty. Gen., Opinions of the Attorney General
op. cit. (opere citato), in the work cited
OPEC, Organization of Petroleum Exporting Countries
OSD, Office of the Secretary of Defense
OTC, Organization for Trade Cooperation
PA, public address system
Pac., Pacific Reporter; P.2d, Pacific Reporter, second series
PAC, political action committee (plural, PAC's)

Passed Asst. Surg., passed assistant surgeon
PBS, Public Building Service
Pet., Peters (U.S. Supreme Court Reports)
Ph, phenyl
Phar.D., doctor of pharmacy
Ph.B. or B.Ph, bachelor of philosophy
Ph.D., or D.Ph., doctor of philosophy
Ph.G., graduate in pharmacy
PHS, Public Health Service
PIN, personal identification number
Pl., place
p.m. (post meridiem), afternoon
P.O. Box (with number); but post office box (in general sense)
POW, prisoner of war (plural, POW's)
Private Res. (with number), private resolution
Prof., professor
pro tem (pro tempore), temporarily
P.S. (post scriptum), postscript; public school (with number)
PTA, parent-teachers' association
Public Res. (with number), public resolution
PX, post exchange
QT, on the quiet
racon, radar beacon
radar, radio detection and ranging
RAM, random access memory
Rand Corp. (research and development)
R&D, research and development
rato, rocket-assisted takeoff
Rd., road
RDT&E, research, development, testing, and evaluation
REA, Rual Electrification Administration
Rev., reverend
Rev. Stat., Revised Statutes
RF, radiofrequency
R.F.D., rural free delivery
Rh, Rhesus (blood factor)
RIF, reduction(s) in force; RIF'd, RIF'ing, RIF's
R.N., registered nurse
ROTC, Reserve Officers' Training Corps
RR., railroad
RRB, Railroad Retirement Board
Rt. Rev., right reverend
Ry., railway
S, south; Senate bill (with number)
SAC, Strategic Air Command
SAE, Society of Automotive Engineers
S&L('s), savings and loan(s)
SALT, strategic arms limitation talks
SAR, Sons of the American Revolution
SBA, Small Business Administration
sc. (scilicet), namely (see also ss)
s.c., small caps
S. Con. Res. (with number), Senate concurrent resolution
s.d. (sine die), without date
S. Doc. (with number), Senate document
SE., southeast

SEATO, Southeast Asia Treaty Organization
SEC, Securities and Exchange Commission
sec, secant
sech, hyperbolic secant
2d, 3d, second, third
SHF, superhigh frequency
shoran, short range (radio)
SI, Systeme International d' Unités
sic, thus
sin, sine
sinn, hyperbolic sine
S.J. Res. (with number), Senate joint resolution
sonar (no period), sound, navigation, and ranging
SOP, standard operating procedure
SOS, wireless distress signal
SP, shore patrol
SPAR, Coast Guard Women's Reserve (*semper paratus—always ready*)
sp. gr., specific gravity
Sq., square (street)
Sr., senior
S. Rept. (with number), Senate report
S. Res. (with number), Senate resolution
SS, steamship
ss (scilicet), namely (in law) (see also sc.)
SSA, Social Security Administration
SSS, Selective Service System
St., Ste., SS., Saint, Sainte, Saints
St., street
Stat., Statutes at Large
STP, standard temperature and pressure
Sup. Ct., Supreme Court Reporter
Supp. Rev. Stat., Supplement to the Revised Statutes
Supt., superintendent
Surg., surgeon
Surg. Gen., Surgeon General
SW., southwest
S.W.2d, Southwestern Reporter, second series
SWAT, special weapons and tactics (team)
T., Tps., township, townships
tan, tangent
tann, hyperbolic tangent
TB, tuberculosis
T.D., Treasury Decisions
Ter., terrace
t.m., true mean
TNT, trinitrotuluol
TV, television
TVA, Tennessee Valley Authority
2,4-D (insecticide)
uc, uppercase

UHF, ultrahigh frequency
UMTA, Urban Mass Transportation Administration
U.N., United Nations
Unesco, United Nations Educational, Scientific, and Cultural Organization (copyrighted form)
UNICEF, United Nations Children's Fund
U.S., U.S. Supreme Court Reports
U.S.A., United States of America
USA, U.S. Army
USAF, U.S. Air Force
U.S.C., United States Code
U.S.C.A., United States Code Annotated
U.S.C. Supp., United States Code Supplement
USCG, U.S. Coast Guard
USDA, U.S. Department of Agriculture
USES, U.S. Employment Service
U.S. 40, U.S. No. 40, U.S. Highway No. 40
USIA, U.S. Information Agency
USMC, U.S. Marine Corps
USN, U.S. Navy
USNR, U.S. Naval Reserve
U.S.P., United States Pharmacopeia
USPS, U.S. Postal Service
U.S.S., U.S. Senate; U.S. ship
U.S.S.R., Union of Soviet Socialist Republics
v. or vs. (versus), against
VA, Veterans' Administration
VAT, value added tax
VCR, video cassette recorder
VHF, very high frequency
VIP, very important person
viz (videlicet), namely
VLF, very low frequency
VTR, video tape recording
W., west
WAC, Women's Army Corps; a Wac
w.a.e., when actually employed
WAF, Women in the Air Force; a Waf
Wall., Wallace (U.S. Supreme Court Reports)
WAVES, *women accepted for volunteer emergency service*; a Wave
wf, wrong font
Wheat., Wheaton (U.S. Supreme Court Reports)
WHO, World Health Organization
WMAL, WRC, etc., radio stations
w.o.p., without pay
Yale L.J., Yale Law Journal
ZIP Code, Zone Improvement Plan Code (Postal Service)
ZIP+4, 9-digit ZIP Code

Standard letter symbols for units of measure (Note: The same form is used for singular and plural senses.)

A, ampere
Å, angstrom
a, are
a, atto (prefix, one-quintillionth)

aA, attoampere
abs, absolute (temperature and gravity)
ac, alternating current
AF, audiofrequency

Ah, ampere-hour
A/m, ampere per meter
AM, amplitude modulation
asb, apostilb
At, ampere-turn
at, atmosphere, technical
atm, atmosphere (infrequently, As)
at wt, atomic weight
au, astronomical units
avdp, avoirdupois
b, barn
B, bel
b, bit
bbl, barrel
bbl/d, barrel per day
Bd, baud
bd. ft., board foot (obsolete); use fbm
Bé, Baumé
Bev (obsolete); see GeV
Bhn, Brinell hardness number
bhp, brake horsepower
bm, board measure
bp, boiling point
Btu, British thermal unit
bu, bushel
c, ¢, ct; cent(s)
c, centi (prefix, one-hundredth)
C, coulomb
c, cycle (radio)
°C, degree Celsius
cal, calorie (also: cal$_{IT}$, International
    Table; cal$_{th}$, thermochemical)
cc. (obsolete), use cm³
cd, candela (candle obsolete)
cd/in², candela per square inch
cd/m², candela per square meter
c.f.m. (obsolete), use ft³/min
c.f.s. (obsolete), use ft³/s
cg, centigram
c·h, candela-hour
Ci, curie
cL, centiliter
cm, centimeter
c/m, cycles per minute
cm², square centimeter
cm³, cubic centimeter
cmil, circular mil
cp, candlepower
cP, centipoise
cSt, centistokes
cu ft (obsolete) use ft³
cu in (obsolete) use in³
cwt, hundredweight
D, darcy
d, day
d, deci (prefix, one-tenth)
d, pence
da, deka (prefix, 10)
dag, dekagram
daL, dekaliter
dam, dekameter
dam², square dekameter
dam³, cubic dekameter
dB, decibel
dBu, decibel unit
dc, direct current
dg, decigram
dL, deciliter

dm, decimeter
dm², square decimeter
dm³, cubic decimeter
dol, dollar
doz, dozen
dr, dram
dwt, deadweight tons
dwt, pennyweight
dyn, dyne
EHF, extremely high frequency
emf, electromotive force
emu, electromagnetic unit
erg, erg
esu, electrostatic unit
eV, electronvolt
°F, degree Fahrenheit
F, farad
f, femto (prefix, one-quadrillionth)
F, fermi (obsolete); use fm, fentometer
fbm, board foot; board foot measure
fc, footcandle
fL, footlambert
fm, femtometer
FM, frequency modulation
ft, foot
ft², square foot
ft³, cubic foot
ftH₂O, conventional foot of water
ft·lb, foot-pound
ft·lbf, foot pound-force
ft/min, foot per minute
ft²/min, square foot per minute
ft³/min, cubic foot per minute
ft-pdl, foot poundal
ft/s, foot per second
ft²/s, square foot per second
ft³/s, cubic foot per second
ft/s², foot per second squared
ft/s³, foot per second cubed
G, gauss
G, giga (prefix, 1 billion)
g, gram; acceleration of gravity
Gal, gal cm/s²
gal, gallon
gal/min, gallons per minute
gal/s, gallons per second
Gb, gilbert
g/cm³, gram per cubic centimeter
GeV, gigaelectronvolt
GHz, gigahertz (gigacycle per second)
gr, grain; gross
h, hecto (prefix, 100)
H, henry
h, hour
ha, hectare
HF, high frequency
hg, hectogram
hL, hectoliter
hm, hectometer
hm², square hectometer
hm³, cubic hectometer
hp, horsepower
hph, horsepower-hour
Hz, hertz (cycles per second)
id, inside diameter
ihp, indicated horsepower
in, inch

in^2, square inch
in^3, cubic inch
in/h, inch per hour
inH$_2$O, conventional inch of water
inHg, conventional inch of mercury
in-lb, inch-pound
in/s, inch per second
J, joule
J/K, joule per kelvin
K, kayser
K, kelvin (degree symbol improper)
k, kilo (prefix, 1,000)
k, thousand (7k = 7,000)
kc, kilocycle; see also kHz (kilohertz), kilocycles per second
kcal, kilocalory
keV, kiloelectronvolt
kG, kilogauss
kg, kilogram
kgf, kilogram-force
kHz, kilohertz (kilocycles per second)
kL, kiloliter
klbf, kilopound-force
km, kilometer
km^2, square kilometer
km^3, cubic kilometer
km/h, kilometer per hour
kn, knot (speed)
kΩ, kilohm
kt, kiloton; carat
kV, kilovolt
kVA, kilovoltampere
kvar, kilovar
kW, kilowatt
kWh, kilowatthour
L, lambert
L, liter
lb, pound
lb ap, apothecary pound
lb, avdp, avoirdupois pound
lbf, pound-force
lbf/ft, pound-force foot
lbf/ft^2, pound-force per square foot
lbf/ft^3, pound-force per cubic foot
lbf/in^2, pound-force per square inch
lb/ft, pound per foot
lb/ft^2, pound per square foot
lb/ft^3, pound per cubic foot
lct, long calcined ton
ldt, long dry ton
LF, low frequency
lin ft, linear foot
l/m, lines per minute
lm, lumen
lm/ft^2, lumen per square foot
lm/m^2, lumen per square meter
lm-s, lumen second
lm/W, lumen per watt
l/s, lines per second
L/s, liter per second
lx, lux
M, mega (prefix, 1 million)
M, million (3M = 3 million)
m, meter
m, milli (prefix, one-thousandth)
M$_1$, monetary aggregate
m^3, cubic meter
m^2, square meter

μ, micro (prefix, one-millionth)
μ, micron (name micron obsolete); use μm, micrometer
mA, milliampere
μA, microampere
mbar, millibar
μbar, microbar
Mc, megacycle; see also MHz (megahertz), megacycles per second
mc, millicycle; see also mHz (millihertz), millicycles per second
mcg, microgram (obsolete, use μg)
mD, millidarcy
meq, milliquivalent
MeV, megaelectronvolts
mF, millifarad
μF, microfarad
mG, milligauss
mg, milligram
μg, microgram
Mgal/d, million gallons per day
mH, millihenry
μH, microhenry
mho, mho (obsolete, use S, siemens)
MHz, megahertz
mHz, millihertz
mi, mile (statute)
mi^2, square mile
mi/gal, mile(s) per gallon
mi/h, mile per hour
mil, mil
min, minute (time)
μin, microinch
mL, milliliter
mm, millimeter
mm^2, square millimeter
mm^3, cubic millimeter
mμ (obsolete); see nm, nanometer
μm, micrometer
μm^2, square micrometer
μm^3, cubic micrometer
μμ, micromicron (use of compound prefixes obsolete; use pm, picometer)
μμf, micromicrofarad (use of compound prefixes obsolete; use pF)
mmHg, conventional millimeter of mercury
μmho, micromho (obsolete, use μS, microsiemens)
MΩ, megohm
mo, month
mol, mole (unit of substance)
mol wt, molecular weight
mp, melting point
ms, millisecond
μs, microsecond
Mt, megaton
mV, millivolt
μV, microvolt
MW, megawatt
mW, milliwatt
μW, microwatt
MWd/t, megawatt-days per ton
Mx, maxwell
n, nano (prefix, one-billionth)
N, newton
nA, nanoampere

nF, nanofarad
nm, nanometer (millimicron, obsolete)
N·m, newton meter
N/m², newton per square meter
nmi, nautical mile
Np, neper
ns, nanosecond
N·s/m², newton second per square meter
nt, nit
od, outside diameter
Oe, oersted (use of A/m, amperes per meter, preferred)
oz, ounce (avoirdupois)
p, pico (prefix, one-trillionth)
P, poise
Pa, pascal
pA, picoampere
pct, percent
pdl, poundal
pF, picofarad (micromicrofarad, obsolete)
pF, water-holding energy
pH, hydrogen-ion concentration
ph, phot; phase
pk, peck,
p/m, parts per million
ps, picosecond
pt, pint
pW, picowatt
qt, quart
quad, quadrillion (10¹⁵)
°R, rankine
°R, roentgen
R, degree rankine
R, degree reaumur
rad, radian
rd, rad
rem, roentgen equivalent man
r/min, revolutions per minute
rms, root mean square
r/s, revolutions per second
s, second (time)

s, shilling
S, siemens
sb, stilb
scp, spherical candlepower
s·ft, second-foot
shp, shaft horsepower
slug, slug
sr, steradian
sSf, standard saybolt fural
sSu, standard saybolt universal
stdft³, standard cubic foot (feet)
Sus, saybolt universal second(s)
T, tera (prefix, 1 trillion)
Tft³, trillion cubic feet
T, tesla
t, tonne (metric ton)
tbsp, tablespoonful
thm, therm
ton, ton
tsp, teaspoonful
Twad, twaddell
u, (unified) atomic mass unit
UHF, ultrahigh frequency
V, volt
VA, voltampere
var, var
VHF, very high frequency
V/m, volt per meter
W, watt
Wb, weber
Wh, watthour
W/(m·K), watt per meter kelvin
W/sr, watt per steradian
W/(sr·m²), watt per steradian square meter
x, unknown quantity
yd, yard
yd², square yard
yd³, cubic yard
yr, year

NOTES

10. SIGNS AND SYMBOLS

10.1. The increased use of signs and symbols and their importance in technical and scientific work have emphasized the necessity of standardization on a national basis and of the consistent use of the standard forms.

10.2. Certain symbols are well standardized—number symbols (the digits, 0, 1, 2, 3, 4, 5, 6, 7, 8, 9); letter symbols (the letters of the alphabet, a, b, c, d, etc.); and graphic symbols (the mathematical signs $+$, $-$, $\pm$, $\times$, $\div$).

10.3. The signs $+$, $-$, $\pm$, $\times$, and $\div$, etc., are closed against accompanying figures and symbols. When the $\times$ is used to indicate "crossed with" (in plant or animal breeding) or magnification, it will be separated from the accompanying words by a space.

i–vii$+$1–288 pages

The equation $A+B$

The result is 4×4

20,000$\pm$5,000

Early June $\times$ Bright (crossed with)

$\times$ 4 (magnification)

Symbols with figures

10.4. In technical publications the degree mark is used in lieu of the word *degree* following a figure denoting measurement.

10.5. Following a figure the percent symbol is used in areas where space will not allow the word *percent* to be used. The spelled form is preferred.

In that period the price rose 12, 15, and 19 percent.

10.6. Any symbol that is set close up to figures, such as the dollar mark or cent mark, is used before or after each figure in a group or series.

45 to 65 °F., *not* 45° to 65° F.

$5 to $8 price range

5′–7′ long, *not* 5–7′ long

3¢ to 5¢ (no spaces)

$\pm$2 to $\pm$7; 2°$\pm$1°

but § 12 (thin space)

from 15 to 25 percent

Letter symbols

10.7. Letter symbols are set in italic (see rule 10.8) or in roman (see rule 9.56) without periods and are capitalized only if so shown in copy, since the capitalized form may have an entirely different meaning.

Equations

10.8. In mathematical equations, use italic for all letter symbols—capitals, lowercase, small capitals, and superiors and inferiors (exponents and subscripts); use roman for figures, including superiors and inferiors.

10.9. If an equation or a mathematical expression needs to be divided, break before $+$, $-$, $=$, etc. However, the equal sign is to clear on left of other beginning mathematical signs.

10.10. A short equation in text should not be broken at the end of a line. Space out the line so that the equation will begin on the next line; or better, center the equation on a line by itself.

10.11. An equation too long for one line is set flush on the left, the second half of the equation is set flush on the right, and the two parts are balanced as nearly as possible.

10.12. Two or more equations in series are aligned on the equal signs and centered on the longest equation in the group.

10.13. Connecting words of explanation, such as *hence, therefore,* and *similarly,* are set flush left either on the same line with the equation or on a separate line.

10.14. Parentheses, braces, brackets, integral signs, and summation signs should be of the same height as the mathematical expressions they include.

10.15. Inferiors precede superiors if they appear together; but if either inferior or superior is too long, the two are aligned on left.

$$\sqrt{\Phi} = \sum_{k=0}^{m}{}_{ak}(A_k \cos k\psi + B_k \sin k\psi) \tag{1}$$

$$\frac{e}{e_0} = \frac{1}{\sqrt{\left[1 - (f/f_M)^2 + \dfrac{C_M}{c}\right]^2 + \left[\dfrac{r}{Xc_M}\right]^2}} \tag{2}$$

$$Q = A_2\rho^1 \left(\frac{p_2}{p_1}\right)^{\frac{1}{\gamma}} \left\{2gp_1v_1 \left(\frac{\gamma}{\gamma-1}\right) \left[1 - \left(\frac{p_2}{p_1}\right)^{\frac{\gamma-1}{\gamma}}\right]\right\}^{\frac{1}{2}}$$

$$= A_2 \left\{2g \frac{p_1}{v_1} \left(\frac{\gamma}{\gamma-1}\right) \left[\left(\frac{p_2}{p_1}\right)^{\frac{2}{\gamma}} - \left(\frac{p_2}{p_1}\right)^{\frac{\gamma+1}{\gamma}}\right]\right\}^{\frac{1}{2}} \tag{3}$$

$$\omega_n(x, \theta_x) = \frac{1}{\sqrt{r_1 r_2}} \int_0^x dx_2 \int_0^{x_1} dx_1 \cos n\psi_x(x_1, x_2)$$

$$\left[\frac{r_1 r_2}{p_1 p_2} (\phi_{n-1}(k_1) + \phi_{n+1}(k_1)) + 2\phi_n(k_1)\right] \tag{4}$$

$$m_{s_1 s_2} = \int_{x_{i_1}}^{x_{e_1}} dx_1 \int_{x_{i_1}}^{x_{e_2}} dx_2 \int_0^{2\pi} \frac{d\theta_1}{2\pi}$$

$$\int_0^{2\pi} \frac{d\theta_2}{2\pi} \frac{\dfrac{r_1 r_2}{p_1 p_2} \cos(\theta_2 - \theta_1) + 1}{\sqrt{(x_2 - x_1)^2 + R^2(\theta_2 - \theta_1)}}$$

$$= \int_{x_{i_1}}^{x_{e_1}} dx_1 \int_{x_{i_1}}^{x_{e_2}} dx_2 \int_0^{2\pi} \frac{d\psi}{2\pi} \frac{\dfrac{r_1 r_2}{p_1 p_2} \cos\psi + 1}{\sqrt{(x_2 - x_1)^2 + R^2(\psi)}} \tag{5}$$

$$\sum_2 (\psi_n, c_n) = 2c_2 \frac{\tan(2\psi_2 - \psi_1)}{\cos(2\psi_3 - \psi_2)} + 6c_3 \frac{\tan(2\psi_3 - \psi_2)}{\cos(2\psi_4 - \psi_3)}$$

$$+ 14c_4 \frac{\tan(2\psi_4 - \psi_3)}{\cos(2\psi_5 - \psi_4)} + \cdots$$

$$+ 2(2^{1+n} - 1)c_{n+2} \frac{\tan(2\psi_{n+2} - \psi_{n+1})}{\cos(2\psi_{n+3} - \psi_{n+2})} \cdots \tag{6}$$

Chemical symbols

10.16. The names and symbols listed below are approved by the International Union of Pure and Applied Chemistry. (See rule 6.44.)

Element	Symbol	Atomic number [1]	Atomic weight	Element	Symbol	Atomic number [1]	Atomic weight
Actinium	Ac	89	227.0278	Molybdenum	Mo	42	95.94
Aluminium	Al	13	26.98154	Neodymium	Nd	60	144.24
Americium	Am	95	(243)	Neon	Ne	10	20.179
Antimony (Stibium).	Sb	51	121.75	Neptunium	Np	93	237.0482
Argon	Ar	18	39.948	Nickel	Ni	28	58.69
Arsenic	As	33	74.9216	Niobium	Nb	41	92.9064
Astatine	At	85	(210)	Nitrogen	N	7	14.0067
Barium	Ba	56	137.33	Nobelium	No	102	(259)
Berkelium	Bk	97	(247)	Osmium	Os	76	190.2
Beryllium	Be	4	9.01218	Oxygen	O	8	15.9994
Bismuth	Bi	83	208.9804	Palladium	Pd	46	106.42
Boron	B	5	10.81	Phosphorus	P	15	30.97376
Bromine	Br	35	79.904	Platinum	Pt	78	195.08
Cadmium	Cd	48	112.41	Plutonium	Pu	94	(244)
Caesium	Cs	55	132.9054	Polonium	Po	84	(209)
Calcium	Ca	20	40.08	Potassium (Kalium).	K	19	39.0983
Californium	Cf	98	(251)	Praseodymium	Pr	59	140.9077
Carbon	C	6	12.011	Promethium	Pm	61	(145)
Cerium	Ce	58	140.12	Protactinium	Pa	91	231.0359
Chlorine	Cl	17	35.453	Radium	Ra	88	226.0254
Chromium	Cr	24	51.996	Radon	Rn	86	(222)
Cobalt	Co	27	58.9332	Rhenium	Re	75	186.207
Copper	Cu	29	63.546	Rhodium	Rh	45	102.9055
Curium	Cm	96	(247)	Rubidium	Rb	37	85.4678
Dysprosium	Dy	66	162.50	Ruthenium	Ru	44	101.07
Einsteinium	Es	99	(252)	Samarium	Sm	62	150.36
Erbium	Er	68	167.26	Scandium	Sc	21	44.9559
Europium	Eu	63	151.96	Selenium	Se	34	78.96
Fermium	Fm	100	(257)	Silicon	Si	14	28.0855
Fluorine	F	9	18.998403	Silver	Ag	47	107.8682
Francium	Fr	87	(223)	Sodium (Natrium).	Na	11	22.98977
Gadolinium	Gd	64	157.25	Strontium	Sr	38	87.62
Gallium	Ga	31	69.72	Sulfur	S	16	32.06
Germanium	Ge	32	72.59	Tantalum	Ta	73	180.9479
Gold	Au	79	196.9665	Technetium	Tc	43	(98)
Hafnium	Hf	72	178.49	Tellurium	Te	52	127.60
Helium	He	2	4.00260	Terbium	Tb	65	158.9254
Holmium	Ho	67	164.9304	Thallium	Tl	81	204.383
Hydrogen	H	1	1.00794	Thorium	Th	90	232.0381
Indium	In	49	114.82	Thulium	Tm	69	168.9342
Iodine	I	53	126.9045	Tin	Sn	50	118.69
Iridium	Ir	77	192.22	Titanium	Ti	22	47.88
Iron	Fe	26	55.847	Tungsten (Wolfram).	W	74	183.85
Krypton	Kr	36	83.80	(Unnilhexium)	(Unh)	106	(263)
Lanthanum	La	57	138.9055	(Unnilpentium)	(Unp)	105	(262)
Lawrencium	Lr	103	(260)	(Unnilquadium)	(Unq)	104	(261)
Lead	Pb	82	207.2	Uranium	U	92	238.0289
Lithium	Li	3	6.941	Vanadium	V	23	50.9415
Lutetium	Lu	71	174.967	Xenon	Xe	54	131.29
Magnesium	Mg	12	24.305	Ytterbium	Yb	70	173.04
Manganese	Mn	25	54.9380	Yttrium	Y	39	88.9059
Mendelveium	Md	101	(258)	Zinc	Zn	30	65.38
Mercury	Hg	80	200.59	Zirconium	Zr	40	91.22

[1] The atomic weights of many elements are not invariant but depend on the origin and treatment of the material. The values of atomic weight given here apply to elements as they exist naturally on Earth and to certain artificial elements. Values in parentheses are used for radioactive elements whose atomic weights cannot be quoted precisely without knowledge of the origin of the elements. The value given is the atomic mass number of the isotope of that element of longest known half life.

Standardized symbols

10.17. Symbols duly standardized by any national scientific, professional, or technical group are accepted as preferred forms within the field of the group. The issuing office desiring or requiring the use of such standardized symbols should see that copy is prepared accordingly.

Signs and symbols

10.18. This list contains some signs and symbols frequently used in printing. The forms and style of many symbols vary with the method of reproduction employed by the printer.

10.19. It is important that editors and writers clearly identify signs and symbols when they appear within a manuscript.

ACCENTS

- ˊ acute
- ˘ breve
- ¸ cedilla
- ˆ circumflex
- ¨ dieresis
- ˋ grave
- ¯ macron
- ~ tilde

ARROWS

- → direction
- ↖ direction
- ↱ direction
- ↶ direction
- ↷ direction
- ⬅ bold arrow
- ▷ open arrow
- ⇄ reversible reaction

BULLETS

- ● solid circle; bullet
- • bold center dot
- • movable accent

CHEMICAL

- ‰ salinity
- ♏ minim
- ⇅ exchange
- ↑ gas

CIRCLED SYMBOLS

- ◷ angle in circle
- ⦶ circle with parallel rule
- ◬ triangle in circle
- ⊙ dot in circle
- ◬ dot in triangle in circle
- ⊕ cross in circle
- © copyright
- ① Ceres
- ② Pallas
- ③ Juno
- ④ Vesta

CODE

- · No. 1 6 pt. code dot
- · No. 2 8 pt. code dot
- · No. 3 10 pt. code dot
- • No. 4 8 pt. code dot
- • No. 4 10 pt. code dot
- – No. 1 6 pt. code dash
- – No. 2 8 pt. code dash
- — No. 3 10 pt. code dash
- ▬ No. 4 8 pt. code dash
- ▬ No. 4 10 pt. code dash

COMPASS

- ° degree
- °. degree with period
- ′ minute
- ′. minute with period
- ″ second
- ″. second with period
- ″̲ canceled second

DECORATIVE

- ✚ bold cross
- ✠ cross patte
- ■ cross patte
- ⌘ cross patte
- ✿ (184 N)
- ⚿ key
- ⚲ (206 N)
- ¶ paragraph

ELECTRICAL

- ℜ reluctance
- ↔ reaction goes both right and left
- ↕ reaction goes both up and down
- ↕ reversible
- → direction of flow; yields
- → direct current
- ⇆ electrical current
- ⇆ reversible reaction
- ⇄ reversible reaction
- ⇆ alternating current
- ⇄ alternating current
- ⇌ reversible reaction beginning at left
- ⇋ reversible reaction beginning at right
- Ω ohm; omega
- MΩ megohm; omega
- μΩ microohm; mu omega
- ω angular frequency, solid angle; omega
- Φ magnetic flux; phi
- Ψ dielectric flux; electrostatic flux; psi
- γ conductivity; gamma

ELECTRICAL—Con.

ρ resistivity; rho
Λ equivalent conductivity
HP horsepower

MATHEMATICAL

— vinculum (above
letters)
÷ geometrical proportion
−: difference, excess
‖ parallel
‖s parallels
≠ not parallels
| | absolute value
· multiplied by
: is to; ratio
÷ divided by
∴ therefore; hence
∵ because
:: proportion; as
≪ is dominated by
> greater than
⊏ greater than
≥ greater than or equal
to
≧ greater than or equal
to
≷ greater than or less
than
≯ is not greater than
< less than
⊐ less than
≶ less than or greater
than
≮ is not less than
⋖ smaller than
≤ less than or equal to
≦ less than or equal to
≧ or ≥ greater than or
equal to
≶ equal to or less than
≣ equal to or less than
≸ is not greater than
equal to or less than
≷ equal to or greater
than
≹ is not less than equal
to or greater than
⊥ equilateral
⊥ perpendicular to
⊢ assertion sign
≑ approaches

MATHEMATICAL—Con.

≑ approaches a limit
⩗ equal angles
≠ not equal to
≡ identical with
≢ not identical with
⑅ score
≈ or ≑ nearly equal to
= equal to
∼ difference
≃ perspective to
≅ congruent to approxi-
mately equal
≏ difference between
⟠ geometrically equiva-
lent to
⊂ included in
⊃ excluded from
⊆ is contained in
∪ logical sum or union
∩ logical product or in-
tersection
√ radical
√ root
∛ square root
∛ cube root
∜ fourth root
∜ fifth root
∛ sixth root
π pi
ε base (2.718) of natural
system of loga-
rithms; epsilon
ε is a member of; di-
electric constant;
mean error; epsilon
+ plus
+ bold plus
− minus
− bold minus
/ shill(ing); slash;
virgule
± plus or minus
∓ minus or plus
× multiplied by
= bold equal
number
℞ per
% percent
∫ integral
| single bond
\ single bond
/ single bond

MATHEMATICAL—Con.

‖ double bond
⑊ double bond
∥ double bond
⬡ benzene ring
∂ or δ differential; variation
∂ Italian differential
→ approaches limit of
∼ cycle sine
∖ horizontal integral
∮ contour integral
∝ variation; varies as
Π product
Σ summation of;
sum; sigma
! or ⌊ factorial product

MEASURE

℔ pound
ʒ dram
f ʒ fluid dram
℥ ounce
f ℥ fluid ounce
O pint

MISCELLANEOUS

§ section
† dagger
‡ double dagger
% account of
℅ care of
⑅ score
¶ paragraph
þ Anglo-Saxon
₵ center line
♂ conjunction
⊥ perpendicular to
″ or " ditto
∝ variation
℞ recipe
⊐ move right
⊏ move left
○ or ⊙ or ① annual
⊙⊙ or ② biennial
∈ element of
℈ scruple
ƒ function
! exclamation mark
⊞ plus in square
♃ perennial

MISCELLANEOUS—Con.

φ	diameter
c̃	mean value of c
U	mathmodifier
⊂	mathmodifier
⊡	dot in square
△	dot in triangle
⊠	station mark
@	at

MONEY

¢	cent
¥	yen
£	pound sterling
₥	mills

MUSIC

♮	natural
♭	flat
♯	sharp

PLANETS

☿	Mercury
♀	Venus
⊕	Earth
♂	Mars
♃	Jupiter
♄	Saturn
♅	Uranus
♆	Neptune
♇	Pluto
☊	dragon's head, ascending node
☋	dragon's tail, descending node
☌	conjunction
☍	opposition
☉ or ⊙	Sun
♘	Sun's lower limb
♙	Sun's upper limb
◍	solar corona
⊕	solar halo
◍	Moon
●	new Moon
☽	first quarter
◑	first quarter
◕	third quarter
◐	last quarter
☾	last quarter
◑	last quarter
○	full Moon
⊕	full Moon

PLANETS—Con.

☽	eclipse of Moon
☌	lunar halo
☋	lunar corona
⚳	Ceres
⚴	Juno

PUNCTUATION

{ }	braces
[ ]	brackets
( )	parentheses
⟨ ⟩	square parentheses; angle brackets
¡	Spanish open quote
¿	Spanish open quote

SEX

♂ or ♂	male
☐	male, in charts
♀	female
○	female, in charts
☿	hermaphrodite

SHAPES

♦	solid diamond
◇	open diamond
○	circle
▲	solid triangle
△	triangle
☐	square
■	solid square
▱	parallelogram
▭	rectangle
▤	double rectangle
★	solid star
☆	open star
∟	right angle
∠	angle
√	check
✔	check
ß	German ss
ß	italic German ss
👈	solid index
👉	solid index
☜	index
☞	index

GEOLOGIC SYSTEMS [1]

Q	Quaternary
T	Tertiary
K	Cretaceous
J	Jurassic
Ŧ	Triassic
P	Permian
P	Pennsylvanian
M	Mississippian
D	Devonian
S	Silurian
O	Ordovician
Є	Cambrian
pЄ	Precambrian
C	Carboniferous

VERTICAL

|	5 unit vertical
|	8 point vertical
|	9 unit vertical

WEATHER

T	thunder
⚡	thunderstorm; sheet lightning
⟨	sheet lightning
↓	precipitate
◍	rain
←	floating ice crystals
↔	ice needles
▲	hail
⊗	sleet
∾	glazed frost
⊔	hoarfrost
V	frostwork
✳	snow or sextile
⊠	snow on ground
⊹	drifting snow (low)
≡	fog
∞	haze
⌂	Aurora

ZODIAC

♈	Aries; Ram
♉	Taurus; Bull
♊	Gemini; Twins
♋	Cancer; Crab
♌	Leo; Lion
♍	Virgo; Virgin
♎	Libra; Balance
♏	Scorpio; Scorpion
♐	Sagittarius; Archer
♑	Capricornus; Goat
♒	Aquarius; Water bearer
♓	Pisces; Fishes

[1] Standard letter symbols used by the Geological Survey on geologic maps. Capital letter indicates the system and one or more lowercased letters designate the formation and member where used.

11. ITALIC

(See also Courtwork; Symbols; Datelines, Addresses, and Signatures)

11.1. Italic is sometimes used to differentiate or to give greater prominence to words, phrases, etc. However, an excessive amount of italic defeats this purpose, and its use in general work should be restricted as indicated.

Emphasis, foreign words, titles of publications

11.2. Italic is not used for mere emphasis, foreign words, or the titles of publications unless it is specially requested and the copy is edited therefor.

11.3. In nonlegal work, *ante, post, infra,* and *supra* are italicized only when part of a legal citation. Otherwise these terms, as well as the abbreviations *id, ibid., op. cit., et seq.,* and other foreign words, phrases, and their abbreviations, are printed in roman. (See also rule 17.8.)

11.4. When "emphasis supplied," "emphasis added," or "emphasis ours" appears in copy, it should not be changed; but "underscore supplied" should be changed to "italic supplied."

11.5. When copy is submitted with instructions to set "all roman (no italic)," these instructions will not apply to *Ordered, Resolved, Be it enacted,* etc.; titles following signatures or addresses; or the parts of datelines which are always set in italic.

Names of aircraft and vessels

11.6. The names of aircraft, vessels, and spacecraft are italicized unless otherwise indicated. In lists set in columns and in stubs and reading columns of tables consisting entirely of such names they will be set in roman. Missiles and rockets will be caps and lowercase and will not be italicized.

SS *America;* the liner *America*
the *Friendship*
the Bermuda *Clipper*
U.S.S. *Nautilus* (submarine)
U.S.S. *Wisconsin*
ex-U.S.S. *Savannah*
USCGS (U.S. Coast and Geodetic Survey) ship *Pathfinder*
C.S.N. *Virginia*
CG cutter *Thetus*
the *U–7*
destroyer *31*
H.M.S. *Hornet*
HS (hydrofoil ship) *Denison*
MS (motorship) *Richard*
FPV (free piston vessel) *James*

GTS (gas turbine ship) *Alexander*
NS (nuclear ship) *Savannah*
MV (motor vessel) *Havtroll*
Freedom 7; Friendship 7 (U.S. spaceships)
West Virginia class or type
the *Missouri*'s (roman "s") turret
the *U–7*'s (roman "s") deck
F–18 *Hornet*
F–15 *Eagle*
but Air Force One (President's plane)
B–50 (type of plane)
DD–882
LST–1155
Mig; Mig-21
PT–109

11.7. Names of vessels are quoted in matter printed in other than lowercase roman.

Sinking of the "Lusitania"   Sɪɴᴋɪɴɢ ᴏғ ᴛʜᴇ "Lᴜsɪᴛᴀɴɪᴀ"
Sinking of the "Lusitania"   SINKING OF THE "LUSITANIA"

Names of legal cases. (See rule 17.12.)

11.8. The names of legal cases are italicized, except the *v.* When requested, the names of such cases may be set in roman with italic *v.* In matter set in italic, legal cases are set in roman with the *v.* being set roman.

"The Hornet" and "The Hood," 124 F.2d   *John Doe* v. *Richard Roe*
    45   *but* John Doe against Richard Roe
Smith v. *Brown et al.*   the *Cement* case
Smith Bros. case (172 App. Div. 149)   Sᴍɪᴛʜ *v.* Bʀᴏᴡɴ ᴇᴛ ᴀʟ. (heading)
Smith Bros. case, *supra*   SMITH v. BROWN ET AL.
Smith Bros. case   (heading)
As cited in *Smith Bros.*   *Durham* rule
     Brown decision

Scientific names

11.9. The scientific names of genera, subgenera, species, and subspecies (varieties) are italicized, but are set in roman in italic matter; the names of groups of higher rank than genera (phyla, classes, orders, families, tribes, etc.) are printed in roman.

> *A.s. perpallidus*
> *Dorothia*? sp. (roman "?")
> *Tsuga canadensis*
> *Cypripedium parviflorum* var. *pubescens*
> the genera *Quercus* and *Liriodendron*
> the family Leguminosae; the family Nessiteras rhombopteryx
> *Measurements of specimens of* Cyanoderma erythroptera neocara

11.10. Quotation marks should be used in place of italic for scientific names appearing in lines set in caps, caps and small caps, or boldface, even if there is italic type available in the series.

Words and letters

11.11. The words *Resolved, Resolved further, Provided, Provided, however, Provided further, And provided further,* and *ordered,* in bills, acts, resolutions, and formal contracts and agreements are italicized; also the words *To be continued, Continued on p. —, Continued from p. —,* and *See* and *see also* (in indexes and tables of contents only).

> *Resolved,* That (resolution)
> *Resolved by the Senate and House of Representatives of the United States of America in Congress assembled,* That
> [To be continued] (centered; no period)
> [*Continued from p. 3*] (centered; no period)
> *see also* Mechanical data (index entry)

11.12. All letters (caps, small caps, lowercase, superiors, and inferiors) used as symbols are italicized (except as provided by rule 8.120), but in italic matter roman letters are used. Chemical sym-

bols (even in italic matter) and certain other standardized symbols
are set in roman. (See also rules 6.44 and 10.8.)

nth degree; x dollars

$$D \div 0.025 V_m{}^{2.7} = 0.042/G - 1 V_m{}^{2.7}$$

$$5Cu_2S.2(Cu,Fe,Zn)S.2Sb_2S_3O_4$$

11.13. Letter designations in mathematical and scientific matter,
except chemical symbols, are italicized.

11.14. Letter symbols used in legends to illustrations, drawings,
etc., or in text as references to such material, are set in italic without periods and are capitalized if so shown in copy.

11.15. Letters (*a*), (*b*), (*c*), etc., and *a*, *b*, *c*, etc., used to indicate
sections or paragraphs, are italicized in general work but not in
laws and other legal documents.

NOTES

12. NUMERALS

(See also Tabular Work; Leaderwork)

12.1. Most rules for the use of numerals are based on the general principle that the reader comprehends numerals more readily than numerical word expressions, particularly in technical, scientific, or statistical matter. However, for special reasons numbers are spelled out in indicated instances.

12.2. The following rules cover the most common conditions that require a choice between the use of numerals and words. Some of them, however, are based on typographic appearance rather than on the general principle stated above.

12.3. Arabic numerals are generally preferable to the use of Roman numerals.

NUMBERS EXPRESSED IN FIGURES (rules 12.4 to 12.15)

12.4. A figure is used for a single number of *10* or more with the exception of the first word of the sentence. (See also rules 12.9, 12.23.)

50 ballots	24 horses	about 40 men
10 guns	nearly 10 miles	10 times as large

Numbers and numbers in series

12.5. When 2 or more numbers appear in a sentence and 1 of them is *10* or more, figures are used for each number. See supporting rule 12.6.

Each of 15 major commodities (9 metal and 6 nonmetal) was in supply.
but Each of nine major commodities (five metal and four nonmetal) was in supply.

Petroleum came from 16 fields, of which 8 were discovered in 1956.
but Petroleum came from nine fields, of which eight were discovered in 1956.

That man has 3 suits, 2 pairs of shoes, and 12 pairs of socks.
but That man has three suits, two pairs of shoes, and four hats.

Of the 13 engine producers, 6 were farm equipment manufacturers, 6 were principally engaged in the production of other types of machinery, and 1 was not classified in the machinery industry.
but Only nine of these were among the large manufacturing companies, and only three were among the largest concerns.

There were three 6-room houses, five 4-room houses, and three 2-room cottages, and they were built by 20 men. (See rule 12.21.)
There were three six-room houses, five four-room houses, and three two-room cottages, and they were built by nine men.
Only 4 companies in the metals group appear on the list, whereas the 1947 census shows at least 4,400 establishments.
but If two columns of sums of money add or subtract one into the other and one carries points and ciphers, the other should also carry points and ciphers.
At the hearing, only one Senator and one Congressman testified.
There are four or five things which can be done.

12.6. A unit of measurement, time, or money (as defined in rule 12.9), which is always expressed in figures, does not affect the use of figures for other numerical expressions within a sentence.

Each of the five girls earned 75 cents an hour.
Each of the 15 girls earned 75 cents an hour.
A team of four men ran the 1-mile relay in 3 minutes 20 seconds.
This usually requires from two to five washes and a total time of 2 to 4 hours.
This usually requires 9 to 12 washes and a total time of 2 to 4 hours.
The contractor, one engineer, and one surveyor inspected the 1-mile road.
but There were two six-room houses, three four-room houses, and four two-room cottages, and they were built by nine men in thirty 5-day weeks. (See rule 12.21.)

12.7. Figures are used for serial numbers.

Bulletin 725
Document 71
pages 352–357
lines 5 and 6
paragraph 1
chapter 2

290 U.S. 325
Genesis 39:20
202-275-2348 (telephone number)
the year 1931
1721–1727 St. Clair Avenue
but Letters Patent No. 2,189,463

12.8. A colon preceding figures does not affect their use.

The result was as follows: 12 voted yea, 4 dissented.
The result was as follows: nine voted yea, four dissented.

Measurement and time

12.9. Units of measurement and time, actual or implied, are expressed in figures.

a. Age:
6 years old
52 years 10 months 6 days
a 3-year-old
at the age of 3 (*years* implied)

b. Clock time (see also Time):
4:30 p.m.
10 o'clock *or* 10 p.m. (*not* 10 o'clock p.m.; 2 p.m. in the afternoon; 10:00 p.m.); 12 m. (noon); 12 p.m. (midnight); this p.m.; in the p.m.
half past 4
4^h30^m *or* 4.5^h, in scientific work, if so written in copy
0025, 2359 (astronomical and military time)
08:31:04 (stopwatch reading)

c. Dates:
June 1985 (*not* June, 1985); June 29, 1985 (*not* June 29th, 1985)
March 6 to April 15, 1935 (*not* March 6, 1935, to April 15, 1935)
May, June, and July 1965 (*but* June and July 1965)
15 April 1951 (military)
4th of July (*but* Fourth of July, meaning the holiday)
the 1st [day] of the month (*but* the last of April or the first [part] of May, not referring to specific days)
in the year 2000 (*not* 2,000)

In referring to a fiscal year, consecutive years, or a continuous period of 2 years or more, when contracted, the forms 1900–11, 1906–38, 1931–32, 1801–2, 1875–79 are used (*but* upon change of century, 1895–1914 and to avoid three ciphers together, 1900–1901). For two or more separate years not representing a continuous period, a comma is used instead of a dash (1875, 1879); if the word *from* precedes the year or the word *inclusive* follows it, the second year is not shortened and the word *to* is used in lieu of the dash (from 1933 to 1936; 1935 to 1936, inclusive).

In dates, *A.D.* precedes the year (A.D. 937); *B.C.* follows the year (254 B.C.).

d. Decimals: In text a cipher should be supplied before a decimal point if there is no unit, and ciphers should be omitted after a decimal point unless they indicate exact measurement.

0.25 inch; 1.25 inches
silver 0.900 fine
specific gravity 0.9547
gauge height 10.0 feet

but .30 caliber (meaning 0.30 inch, bore of small arms); 30 calibers (length)

e. Degrees, etc. (spaces omitted):
longitude 77°04′06″ E.
latitude 49°26′14″ N.
35°30′; 35°30′ N.
a polariscopic test of 85°
an angle of 57°
strike N. 16° E.
dip 47° W. *or* 47° N. 31° W.

25.5′ (preferred); *also* 25′.5 *or* 25.′5, as in copy
but two degrees of justice;
12 degrees of freedom
32d degree Mason
150 million degrees Fahrenheit

f. Game scores:
1 up (golf)
3 to 2 (baseball)

7 to 6 (football), etc.
2 all (tie)

g. Market quotations:
4½ percent bonds
Treasury bonds sell at 95
Metropolitan Railroad, 109

gold is 109
wheat at 2.30
sugar, .03; *not* 0.03

h. Mathematical expressions:
multiplied by 3   divided by 6

a factor of 2

i. Measurements:
7 meters
about 10 yards
8 by 12 inches
8- by 12-inch page
2 feet by 1 foot 8 inches by
   1 foot 3 inches
2 by 4 (lumber) (*not* 2 x 4 or 2×4)
1½ miles
6 acres
9 bushels
1 gallon
3 ems
20/20 (vision)

30/30 (rifle)
12 gauge shotgun
2,500 horsepower
15 cubic yards
6-pounder
80 foot-pounds
10s (for yarns and threads)
f/2.5 (camera focal length)
but tenpenny nail; fourfold; three-ply; five votes; six bales; two dozen; one gross; zero miles; seven-story building (see also rule 12.22)

j. Money:
$3.65; $0.75; 75 cents; 0.5 cent
$3 (*not* $3.00) per 200 pounds
75 cents apiece
Rs32,25,644 (Indian rupees)
2.5 francs *or* fr2.5
£2 4s. 6d.

T£175
65 yen
₱265
but two pennies, three quarters, one half, six bits, etc.

k. Percentage:
12 percent; 25.5 percent; 0.5 percent (*or* one-half of 1 percent)
3.65 bonds; 3.65s; 5–20 bonds; 5–20s; 4½s; 3s (see also rule 8.11)
50–50 (colloquial expression)
5 percentage points
an 1100-percent rise

l. Proportion:
1 to 4   1–3–5   1:62,500

m. Time (see also Clock time):
6 hours 8 minutes 20 seconds
10 years 3 months 29 days
7 minutes
8 days
4 weeks
1 month
3 fiscal years

1 calendar year
but four centuries; three decades; three quarters (9 months)
statistics of any one year
in a year or two
four afternoons
one-half hour

n. Unit modifiers:

5-day week	10-million-peso loan
8-year-old wine	a 5-percent increase
8-hour day	20th-century progress
10-foot pole	*but* two-story house
½-inch pipe	five-man board
5-foot-wide entrance	$20 million airfield

o. Vitamins B_{12}, B_T, A_1, etc.

Ordinal numbers

12.10. Except as indicated in rules 12.11 and 12.19, and also for day preceding month, figures are used in text and footnotes to text for serial ordinal numbers beginning with *10th*. In tables, leaderwork, footnotes to tables and leaderwork, and in sidenotes, figures are used at all times. Military units are expressed in figures at all times when not the beginning of sentence, except *Corps*. (For ordinals in addresses, see rule 12.13.)

29th of May, *but* May 29	323d Fighter Wing
First Congress; 82d Congress	12th Regiment
ninth century; 20th century	9th Naval District
Second Congressional District;	7th Fleet
20th Congressional District	7th Air Force
seventh region; 17th region	7th Task Force
eighth parallel; 38th parallel	
fifth ward; 12th ward	*but* XII Corps (Army usage)
ninth birthday; 66th birthday	Court of Appeals for the Tenth
first grade; 11th grade	Circuit
1st Army	Seventeenth Decennial Census
1st Calvary Division	(title)

12.11. When ordinals appear in juxtaposition and one of them is *10th* or more, figures are used for such ordinal numbers.

This legislation was passed in the 1st session of the 92d Congress.
He served in the 9th and 10th Congresses.
From the 1st to the 92d Congress.
He represented the 1st, 4th, and 13th wards.
We read the 8th and 12th chapters.
but The district comprised the first and second precincts.
He represented the first, third, and fourth regions.
The report was the sixth in a series of 14.

12.12. Ordinals and numerals appearing in a sentence are treated according to the separate rules dealing with ordinals and numerals standing alone or in a group. (See rules 12.4, 12.5, and 12.24.)

The fourth group contained three items.
The fourth group contained 12 items.
The 8th and 10th groups contained three and four items, respectively.
The eighth and ninth groups contained 9 and 12 items, respectively.

12.13. Beginning with *10th*, figures are used in text matter for numbered streets, avenues, etc., but in tables, leaderwork, footnotes to tables and leaderwork, and sidenotes, figures are used at all times and *street, avenue,* etc., are abbreviated. (See also rule 9.16.)

First Street NW.; *also* in parentheses: (Fifth Street) (13th Street); 810 West 12th Street; North First Street; 1021 121st Street; 2031 18th Street North; 711 Fifth Avenue; 518 10th Avenue; 51–35 61st Avenue

Punctuation

12.14. The comma is used in a number containing four or more digits, except in serial numbers, common and decimal fractions, as-

tronomical and military time, and kilocycles and meters of not more than four figures pertaining to radio.

Chemical formulas

12.15. In chemical formulas full-sized figures are used before the symbol or group of symbols to which they relate, and inferior figures are used after the symbol. (See also rules 6.44 and 10.16.)

$$6PbS\cdot(Ag,Cu)_2S\cdot2As_2S_3O_4$$

NUMBERS SPELLED OUT (rules 12.16 to 12.28)

12.16. Numerals are spelled out at the beginning of a sentence or head. Rephrase a sentence or head to avoid beginning with figures. (See rule 12.25 for related numbers.)

Five years ago * * *; *not* 5 years ago * * *
Five hundred and fifty men are employed * * *; *not* 550 men are employed * * *
"Five-Year Plan Announced"; *not* "5-Year Plan Announced" (head)
Although 1965 may seem far off, it * * *; *not* 1965 may seem far off, it * * *
Employees numbering 207,843 * * *; *not* 207,843 * * * employees * * *
Benefits amounting to $69,603,566 * * *; *not* $69,603,566 worth of benefits * * *

1958 REPORT *change to* THE 1958 REPORT

$3,000 BUDGETED *change to* THE SUM OF $3,000 BUDGETED

4 MILLION JOBLESS *change to* JOBLESS NUMBER 4 MILLION

12.17. In testimony, hearings, transcripts, and Q. and A. matter, figures are used immediately following Q. and A. or name of interrogator or witness for years (e.g., 1958), sums of money, decimals, street numbers, and for numerical expressions beginning with *101*.

Mr. BIRCH, Junior. 1977 was a good year.
Mr. BELL. $1 per share was the return. Two dollars in 1956 was the alltime high. Nineteen hundred and seventy-eight may be another story.
Colonel DAVIS. 92 cents.
Mr. SMITH. 12.8 people.
Mr. JONES. 1240 Pennsylvania Avenue NW., Washington, DC 20004.
Mr. SMITH. Ninety-eight persons.
Q. 101 years? *But* Q. One hundred years?
A. 200 years.
Mr. SMITH. Ten-year average would be how much?

12.18. A spelled-out number should not be repeated in figures, except in legal documents. In such instances use these forms:

five (5) dollars, *not* five dollars (5)
ten dollars ($10), *not* ten ($10) dollars

12.19. Numbers appearing as part of proper names or mentioned in connection with serious and dignified subjects such as Executive orders, legal proclamations, and in formal writing are spelled out.

Three Rivers, PA, Fifteenmile Creek, etc.
the Thirteen Original States
in the year nineteen hundred and eighty-four
the Ninety-eighth Congress
millions for defense but not one cent for tribute
threescore years and ten
Ten Commandments
Air Force One (Presidential plane)

12.20. Numbers larger than *1,000,* if spelled out, should be in the following form:

two thousand and twenty
one thousand eight hundred and fifty
one hundred and fifty-two thousand three hundred and five
eighteen hundred and fifty (serial number)

12.21. Numbers of less than *100* preceding a compound modifier containing a figure are spelled out.

two ¾-inch boards   *but* 120 8-inch boards
twelve 6-inch guns   three four-room houses

12.22. Indefinite expressions are spelled out.

the seventies; the early seventies;   *but* 1 to 3 million
  but the early 1870's *or* 1970's   mid-1971; mid-1970's
in his eighties, *not* his '80's *nor* 80's   40-odd people; nine-odd people
midthirties (age, years, money)   40-plus people
a thousand and one reasons   100-odd people
between two and three hundred horses [1]   3½-fold; 250-fold; 2.5-fold/41-fold
twelvefold; thirteenfold; fortyfold;
  hundredfold; twentyfold to thirtyfold
  (see rule 6.23)

The use of such words as *nearly, about, around, approximately,* etc., do not constitute indefinite expressions.

The bass weighed about 6 pounds.   She was nearly 80 years old.

12.23. Except as indicated in rules 12.5 and 12.9, a number less than *10* is spelled out within a sentence.

six horses   *but* 3½ cans
five wells   2½ times *or* 2.5 times
eight times as large

12.24. For typographic appearance and easy grasp of large numbers beginning with *million,* the word *million* or *billion* is used.

The following are guides to treatment of figures as submitted in copy. If copy reads—

$12,000,000, *change* to $12 million
2,750,000 dollars, *change* to $2,750 million
2.7 million dollars, *change* to $2.7 million
2⅜ million dollars, *change* to $2⅜ million
two and one-half million dollars, *change* to $2½ million
a hundred cows, *change* to 100 cows
a thousand dollars, *change* to $1,000
a million and a half, *change* to 1½ million
two thousand million dollars, *change* to $2,000 million
less than a million dollars, *change* to less than $1 million
but $2,700,000, *do not change* to $2.7 million
also $10 to $20 million; 10 or 20 million; between 10 and 20 million
4 millions of assets
amounting to 4 millions
$1,270,000
$1,270,200,000
$2¾ billion; $2.75 billion; $2,750 million
$500,000 to $1 million
300,000; *not* 300 thousand
$½ billion to $1¼ billion (note full figure with second fraction); $1¼ to $1½ billion.
three-quarters of a billion dollars
5 or 10 billion dollars' worth (see rule 8.14)

[1] Better: Between 200 and 300 horses.

12.25. Related numbers appearing at the beginning of a sentence, separated by no more than three words, are treated alike.

Fifty or sixty more miles away is snowclad Mount McKinley.
Sixty and, quite often, seventy listeners responded.
Fifty or, in some instances, almost 60 applications were filed.

Fractions

12.26. Fractions standing alone, or if followed by *of a* or *of an,* are generally spelled out. (See also rule 12.28.)

three-fourths of an inch;
   not ¾ inch *nor* ¾ of an inch
one-half inch
one-half of a farm; *not* ½ of a farm
one-fourth inch
seventh-tenths of 1 percent
or, if copy so reads:
   three-quarters of an inch
   half an inch
   a quarter of an inch

one-tenth
one-hundredth
two one-hundredths
one-thousandth
five one-thousandths
thirty-five one-thousandths
but ½ to 1¾ pages
½-inch pipe
½-inch-diameter pipe
3½ cans; 2½ times

12.27. Fractions (¼, ½, ¾, ⅜, ⅝, ⅞, $\frac{1}{2954}$) or the shilling mark with full-sized figures (1/4, 1/2954) may be used only when either is specifically requested. A comma should not be used in any part of a built-up fraction of four or more digits or in decimals.

12.28. Fractions are used in a unit modifier.

   ½-inch pipe; *not* one-half-inch pipe   ¼-mile run   ⅞-point rise

ROMAN NUMERALS

12.29. A repeated letter repeats its value; a letter placed after one of greater value adds to it; a letter placed before one of greater value subtracts from it; a dashline over a letter denotes multiplied by 1,000.

I	1	XXIX	29	LXXV	75	DC	600
II	2	XXX	30	LXXIX	79	DCC	700
III	3	XXXV	35	LXXX	80	DCCC	800
IV	4	XXXIX	39	LXXXV	85	CM	900
V	5	XL	40	LXXXIX	89	M	1,000
VI	6	XLV	45	XC	90	MD	1,500
VII	7	XLIX	49	XCV	95	MM	2,000
VIII	8	L	50	XCIX	99	MMM	3,000
IX	9	LV	55	C	100	MMMM or M$\overline{\text{V}}$	4,000
X	10	LIX	59	CL	150	$\overline{\text{V}}$	5,000
XV	15	LX	60	CC	200	$\overline{\text{M}}$	1,000,000
XIX	19	LXV	65	CCC	300		
XX	20	LXIX	69	CD	400		
XXV	25	LXX	70	D	500		

Dates

MDC	1600	MCMX	1910	MCML	1950
MDCC	1700	MCMXX	1920	MCMLX	1960
MDCCC	1800	MCMXXX	1930	MCMLXX	1970
MCM or MDCCCC	1900	MCMXL	1940	MCMLXXX	1980

NOTES

13. TABULAR WORK

(See also Abbreviations; Leaderwork)

(See pp. 192–193 for sample table and tabular terms)

13.1. The object of a table is to present in a concise and orderly manner information that cannot be presented so clearly in any other way.

13.2. Tabular material should be kept as simple as possible, so that the meaning of the data can be easily grasped by the user.

13.3. Tables shall be set without down (vertical) rules when there is at least an em space between columns, except where: (1) In the judgment of the Government Printing Office down rules are required for clarity; (2) the agency has indicated on the copy they are to be used. The mere presence of down rules in copy or enclosed sample is not considered a request that down rules be used. The publication dictates the type size used in setting tables. The Congressional Record is set 6 on 7. The balance of congressional work sets 7 on 8.

Abbreviations

13.4. To avoid burdening tabular text, commonly known abbreviations (see rule 9.61 and abbreviation rules) are used in tables. Metric and unit-of-measurement abbreviations (p. 150) are used with figures.

13.5. The names of months (except May, June, and July) when followed by the day are abbreviated; otherwise months are spelled. However, in narrow reading columns or boxheads consisting solely of single months, the months may be abbreviated.

13.6. The words *street, avenue, place, road, square, boulevard, terrace, drive, court,* and *building,* following name or number, are abbreviated. For the numbered streets, avenues, etc., figures are used.

13.7. Abbreviate the words *United States* if preceding the word *Government,* the name of any Government organization, or as an adjective generally. (See rules 9.9–9.10.)

13.8. Use the abbreviations *RR.* and *Ry.* following name (except as indicated in rule 9.27), and *SS, MS,* etc., preceding name.

13.9. Use *lat.* and *long.* with figures.

13.10. Abbreviate, when followed by figures, the various parts of publications, as *article, part, section,* etc. (See rule 9.38.)

13.11. Use, generally, such abbreviations and contractions as *98th Cong., 1st sess., H. Res. 5, H.J. Res. 21, S. Doc. 62, S. Rept. 410* (see rules 9.42–9.43), *Rev. Stat.,* etc.

13.12. In columns containing names of persons, copy is followed as to abbreviations of given names.

13.13. Periods are not used after abbreviations followed by leaders, but are used before footnote references.

Bearoff (normally an en space)

13.14. An en space is used for all bearoffs.

13.15. In a crowded table, when down rules are necessary, the bearoff may be reduced in figure columns.

13.16. Fractions are set flush right to the bearoff of the allotted column width, and not aligned. (See example, p. 184.)

13.17. Mathematical signs, parentheses, fractions, and brackets are set with a normal bearoff.

Boxheads

Horizontal

13.18. Periods are omitted after all boxheads, but a dash is used after any boxhead which reads into the matter following.

13.19. Boxheads run crosswise.

13.20. Boxheads are set solid, even in leaded tables.

13.21. Boxheads are centered horizontally and vertically.

Down-Rule Style (See Rule 13.3)

Sex and age	Employed boys and girls whose work records were obtained						
	Total		Time of year at beginning work [depth of this box does not influence the depth of box on left]				
			June to August		September to May		
	Number	Distribution (percent)	Number	Distribution (percent)	Number	Distribution (percent)	Not reported
Boys (12 to 14)..........	3,869	45.5	1,415	9.6	2,405	15.8	49

No-Down-Rule Style (Preferred)

TABLE 9.—*Mine production of gold, silver, copper, lead, and zinc in 1953*

Class of material	Short tons	Gold (fine ounces)	Silver (fine ounces)	Copper (pounds)	Lead (pounds)	Zinc (pounds)
	Concentrate shipped to smelters and recoverable metals					
Copper............................	220,346	763	70,357	14,242,346	9,950	6,260
Lead	3,931	392	48,326	72,500	5,044,750	290,980
Zinc	25,159	269	41,078	263,400	581,590	26,441,270
Total:						
1953......................	249,436	1,424	159,756	14,578,246	5,636,290	26,738,510
1952......................	367,430	1,789	432,122	10,622,155	13,544,875	101,923,060
	Crude material shipped to smelters					
Dry gold, dry gold-silver ore....	134	52	2,839	2,200	....	....
Copper:						
Crude ore............................	107,270	844	39,861	2,442,882	124,100	2,200
Slag...................................	421	10	165	285,421	....	....
Lead....................................	528	12	1,693	5,950	110,870	300
Mill cleanings (lead-zinc)..........	31	....	254	1,450	8,100	4,300
Total:						
1953......................	125,749	919	45,444	30,375,754	249,710	6,890
1952......................	166,184	1,042	47,176	41,601,845	497,125	26,940

13.22. In parallel tables, and when so prepared in divide tables, a spanner head that is divided is repeated on subsequent pages with the word *Continued*. (See pp. 194–195.)

13.23. In referring to quantity of things, the word *Number* in boxheads is spelled if possible.

13.24. Column numbers or letters in parentheses may be set under boxheads, and are separated by a quadline below the deepest head. (If alignment of parentheses is required within the table, use brackets in boxhead.) These column references align across the table. Units of quantity are set in parentheses within boxheads.

No-Down-Rule Style (Preferred)

States	Department of Agriculture				Department of Commerce		
	Commodity Credit Corporation, value of commodities donated	Special school milk program [1]	Value of commodities distributed within States	Disaster loans, etc. (payments to assist States in furnishing hay in drought-stricken areas)	Civil Aeronautics Administration—Federal airport program—regular grants	Bureau of Public Roads: Highway construction	
						Regular grants [2]	Emergency grants [3]
	(1)	(2)	(3)	(4)	(5)	(6)	(7)
Alabama......	$4,730,154	$1,520,362	$7,970,875	....	$79,284	$1,176,401	$247,515
Alaska..........	393,484	269,274	591,487	....	297,266	12,366,106	472,749
Arizona........	4,545,983	823,136	6,512,639	....	127,749	9,317,853	....

13.25. Leaders may be supplied in a column consisting entirely of symbols or years or dates or any combination of these.

Braces

13.26. Braces are avoided if possible; if used, they are placed in the left-hand bearoff of the column braced, or to the right of down rules, and should extend to the complete depth of the group, including overruns.

No-Down-Rule Style (Preferred)

New Jersey..................................		659,425	659,425	62.35	....	649,374	62.35
New York..............................							
Pennsylvania, Delaware, Maryland, and the District of Columbia	[1] 2,900,499		(1) 2,900,499	{ 66.56 { 39.73 }	[1] 3,312,610	3,312,610	{ 66.92 { 39.64
Tennessee.............................				{ 47.24	....		
Virginia................................		23,187	....	{ 54.32			{ 53.60
South Dakota......................		640	....	51.03	19,718	19,718	{ 46.00
Texas.....................................				{ 51.50			{ 52.50
Oklahoma		5,453	....	45.02	208	208	47.10
Utah.....................................		326,500	....	54.97	355,006	355,006	54.47

Down-Rule Style (See Rule 13.3)

New Jersey		659,425	659,425	62.35		649,374	62.35
New York							
Pennsylvania, Delaware, Maryland, and the District of Columbia	[1] 2,900,499	([2])	2,900,499	{ 66.56 / 39.73	[1] 3,312,610	3,312,610	{ 66.92 / 39.64
Tennessee				{ 47.24			{ 53.60
Virginia	23,187		23,187	54.32			46.00
South Dakota	640		[1] 640	51.03	19,718	19,718	52.50
Texas				{ 51.50			
Oklahoma	5,453		5,453	45.02	208	208	47.10
Utah	326,500		326,500	54.97	355,006	355,006	54.47

Centerheads, flush entries, and subentries

13.27. Heads follow the style of the tables as to the use of figures and abbreviations.

13.28. Heads and headnotes over parallel tables center over the two-page spread of tables, except short lines. In heads over parallel tables, words are not divided between pages. (See pp. 194–195.)

13.29. In divide tables that are made up parallel, the heads and headnotes are set over parallel tables; the heads and the headnotes repeat on each succeeding page; the word *Continued* is used on the head only.

13.30. Punctuation is omitted after centerheads. Flush entries and subentries over subordinate items are followed by a colon (single subentry to run in, preserving the colon), but a dash is used instead of a colon when the entry reads into the matter below. (See also rules 13.101–13.102.)

No-Down-Rule Style (Preferred)

25	Miscellaneous powerplant equipment	245,040.37
26	Roads, railroads, and bridges	275,900.34
	Total	520,940.71

TRANSMISSION PLANT

42	Structures and improvements	26,253.53
43	Station equipment	966,164.41
	Total	992,417.94

GENERAL PLANT

General plant:	
Norris	753,248.97
Other	15,335.81
Total	768,584.78
Grand total	2,281,943.43

13.31. In reading columns if centerhead clears reading matter below at least an em and there are leaders, no space is used under the head; if there are no leaders below and centerhead clears at least an em, the space is omitted; if it clears less than an em, a space is used. (See also rule 13.32.) However, if an overrun, rule, etc., in another column, or in the same column, creates a blank space above the head, the extra space is not added.

13.32. Units of quantity and years used as heads in reading and figure columns are set in italic with space above and no space below. If italic is not available in a font, a space is used both above and below the year.

No-Down-Rule Style (Preferred)

1941								
Oct. 1.........	35.6	15	Jan. 16.......	45.2	15	May 8..........	46.5	15
Oct. 31.......	45.0	15	Feb. 4..........	50.2	15	May 22.......	45.1	18
Nov. 14.......	40.9	18	Feb. 17.......	43.4	15	June 9.........	47.1	14
Dec. 24.......	41.7	15	Mar. 4.........	45.6	15	June 24.......	48.2	16
			Mar. 19.......	42.7	15	July 9..........	46.6	17
1942			Apr. 2..........	40.9	15	July 24.......	45.9	16
Jan. 3..........	43.9	15	Apr. 28.......	47.7	13	Aug. 6.........	46.5	16

Down-Rule Style (See Rule 13.3)

1941								
Oct. 1..........	35.6	15	Jan. 16.......	45.2	15	May 8.........	46.5	15
Oct. 31.......	45.0	15	Feb. 4..........	50.2	15	May 22.......	45.1	18
Nov. 14.......	40.9	18	Feb. 17.......	43.4	15	June 9........	47.1	14
Dec. 24.......	41.7	15	Mar. 4.......	45.6	15	June 24......	48.2	19
			Mar. 19.......	42.7	15	July 9.........	46.6	17
1942			Apr. 2..........	40.9	15	July 24.......	45.9	16
Jan. 3.........	43.9	15	Apr. 28.......	47.7	13	Aug. 6........	46.5	16

13.33. Where the logical construction of a table requires, it is permissible to insert subheads between table-width cross rules, or between rules spanning all columns, except stub, within the table, to indicate the data to which they refer.

No-Down-Rule Style (Preferred)

C-302	Chehalis silty clay loam.	1	PK..........	2.58	9.13	1.62	0.255	2.21	0.95
			PKCa	2.45	8.78	1.24	.257	2.30	.95
			NPKCa ..	2.54	10.08	.54	.240	2.07	.89

SOILS DERIVED FROM ORGANIC MATERIAL

C-303	Peat	1	Check.....	3.31	7.77	1.41	0.268	1.14	0.55
			P..............	3.14	6.66	1.42	.358	.83	.73
			PK..........	3.92	7.25	1.49	.310	1.78	.59
			PKCa	3.84	8.44	1.40	.289	1.83	.64

Down-Rule Style (See Rule 13.3)

C-302	Chehalis silty clay loam.	1	PK..........	2.58	9.13	1.62	0.255	2.21	0.95
			PKCa.....	2.45	8.78	1.24	.257	2.30	.95
			NPKCa..	2.54	10.08	.54	.240	2.07	.89

SOILS DERIVED FROM ORGANIC MATERIAL

C-303	Peat...........................	1	Check.....	3.31	7.77	1.41	0.268	1.14	0.55
			P.............	3.14	6.66	1.42	.358	.83	.73
			PK..........	3.92	7.25	1.49	.310	1.78	.59
			PKCa	3.84	8.44	1.40	.289	1.83	.64

Ciphers

13.34. Where the first number in a column or under a cross rule is wholly a decimal, a cipher is added at the left of its decimal point. A cipher used alone in a money or other decimal column is placed in the unit row and is not followed by a period. In mixed units the cipher repeats before decimals unless group totals.

No-Down-Rule Style (Preferred)

January............................	+26.4	0	0	0	0	0	[1]+$0.7	27.1 $\neq$	+40.4
February...........................	+66.7	0	0	0	0	0	−.9	65.8+	+98.1
March	+143.1	+2.6	−7.5	0	0	0	+12.4	150.6	+224.1
April..................................	+168.4	+6.9	+19.1	−1.1	+1.7	+4.4	+33.0	194.2+	+289.5

Down-Rule Style (See Rule 13.3)

January............................	+26.4	0	0	0	0	0	[1]+$0.7	27.1+	+40.4
February...........................	+66.7	0	0	0	0	0	−.9	65.8+	+98.1
March	+143.1	+2.6	−7.5	0	0	0	+12.4	150.6	+224.1
April	+168.4	+6.9	+19.1	−1.1	+1.7	+4.4	+33.0	194.2+	+289.5

13.35. In columns containing both dollars and cents, ciphers will be supplied on right of decimal point in the absence of figures.

13.36. Where column consists of single decimal, supply a cipher on the right, unless the decimal is a cipher.

```
0.6
0
3.0
4.2
5.0
```

13.37. Where column has mixed decimals of two or more places, do not supply ciphers but follow copy.

```
0.22453
1.263
4
2.60
3.4567
78
12.6
──────────
102.14423
```

13.38. Copy is followed in the use of the word *None* or a cipher to indicate *None* in figure columns. If neither one appears in the copy, leaders are inserted, unless a clear is specifically requested.

13.39. In columns of figures under the heading £ *s d*, if a whole number of pounds is given, one cipher is supplied under *s* and one under *d;* if only shillings are given, one cipher is supplied under *d*.

13.40. In columns of figures under *Ft In*, if only feet are given, supply cipher under *In;* if only inches are given, clear under *Ft;* if ciphers are used for *None*, place one cipher under both *Ft* and *In*.

13.41. In any column containing sums of money, the period and ciphers are omitted if the column consists entirely of whole dollars.

Continued heads

13.42. In continued lines an em dash is used between the head and the word *Continued*. No period is carried after a continued line.

13.43. Continued heads over tables will be worded exactly like table heading. Notes above tables are repeated; footnote references are repeated in boxheads and in continued lines.

Dashes or rules

13.44. Rules are not carried in reading columns or columns consisting of serial or tracing numbers, but are carried through all figure columns.

13.45. Parallel rules are used to cut off figures from other figures below that are added or subtracted; also generally above a grand total. (For examples, see rules 13.31, 13.60, and 13.105.)

Ditto (do.)

13.46. The abbreviation *do.* is used in reading columns only, lowercased and preceded by leaders when there is matter in preceding column. If ditto marks are requested, opening quotes will be used.

13.47. Capitalize *Do.* in first and last columns.

13.48. To achieve consistency in the treatment of *do.*, tracing columns are counted as the first and last columns of table.

13.49. All *do.*'s should be uniform throughout column; if any one is lowercased, all in the column should be lowercased and preceded by leaders. (For examples see pp. 192–193.)

13.50. In mixed columns made up of figure and reading-matter items, *do.* is used only under the latter items.

13.51. *Do.* is not used—

    (1) In a figure or symbol column;

    (2) In the first line under a centerhead in the column in which the centerhead occurs;

    (3) Under a line of leaders or a rule;

    (4) Under an item italicized or set in boldface type for a specific reason (italic or boldface *do.* is never used; item is repeated);

    (5) Under an abbreviated unit of quantity or other abbreviations;

    (6) Under a braced group; and

    (7) Under words of three letters or less.

13.52. *Do.* is used, however, under a clear space and under the word *None* in a reading column.

13.53. *Do.* does not apply to a reference mark on the preceding item. The reference mark, if needed, is added to *do.* (See table, pp. 192–193.)

13.54. Leaders are not used before *Do.* in the first column or before or after *Do.* in the last column.

13.55. In a first and/or last column 6 ems or less in width, a 1-em space is used before *Do.* In all other columns 6 ems or less in width, six periods are used. Bearoff is not included.

13.56. In a first and/or last column more that 6 ems in width, 2 ems of space are used before *Do.* In all other columns more than 6 ems in width, six periods are used. Bearoff space is not included. If the preceding line is indented, the indention of *Do.* is increased accordingly.

13.57. *Do.* under an indented item in an inside reading column, with or without matter in preceding column, is preceded by six periods which are indented to align with item above.

Divide tables. (See "Parallel and divide tables," p. 186.)

Dollar mark

13.58. The dollar mark or any other money symbol is placed close to the figure; it is used only at the head of the table and under cross rules when the same unit of value applies to the entire column.

13.59. In columns containing mixed amounts (as money, tons, gallons, etc.), the dollar mark, pound mark, peso mark, or other symbol, as required, is repeated before each sum of money.

13.60. If several sums of money are grouped together, they are separated from the nonmoney group by a parallel rule, and the symbol is placed on the first figure of the separated group only.

No-Down-Rule Style (Preferred)

	1958	1967
Water supply available (gallons)	4,000,000	3,000,000
Wheat production (bushels)	9,000,000	8,000,000
Operations:		
Water-dispatching operations	$442,496	$396,800
Malaria control	571,040	426,600
Plant protection	134,971	58,320
Total	1,148,507	881,720
Number of plants	642	525
Percent of budget	96.8	78.8

NOTE.—Preliminary figures.

Source: U.S. Department of Commerce, Bureau of the Census.

13.61. In a double money column, dollar marks are used in the first group of figures only; en dashes are aligned. (See also rule 13.123.)

$7–$9
10–12
314–316
1,014–1,016

13.62. The dollar mark is omitted from a first item consisting of a cipher.

0	*but*	$0.12
$300		13.43
500		15.07
700		23.18

13.63. The dollar mark should be repeated in stub or reading columns.

0 to $0.99 ....
$1 to $24 ....
$25 to $49 ....
$50 to $74 ....

Double-up tables

13.64. A hairline rule is used to separate the two parts of a double-up table. If down rules are necessary, a parallel rule is used to separate the two parts.

No-Down-Rule Style (Preferred)

TABLE 14.—*Production of crude petroleum, 1962–63, by districts and fields, in thousand barrels*

[Oil & Gas Journal]

District and field	1962	1963	District and field	1962	1963
Southeast:			Lovington and East...........	1,136	2,472½
Arrowhead........................	809	953½	Other	14,648	22,183
Do	1,353	1,162	Northwest [2]	566	755
Hare......................................	2,027	2,047			
Hobbs....................................	(1)	(1)	Total.................................	22,174	31,042
Langlie-Mattix	1,635	1,669			

[1] Included in "Other" fields.
[2] Bureau of Mines data.

Source: U.S. Department of Commerce, Bureau of the Census.

Down-Rule Style (See Rule 13.3)

TABLE 14.—*Production of crude petroleum, 1962–63, by districts and fields, in thousand barrels*

[Oil & Gas Journal]

District and field	1962	1963	District and field	1962	1963
Southeast:			Lovington and East	1,136	2,472½
Arrowhead	809	953½	Other	14,648	22,183
Do	(1,353)	1,162	Northwest [2]	566	755
Hare	2,027	2,047			
Hobbs	(1)	(1)	Total	22,174	31,042
Langlie-Mattix	1,635	1,669			

Figure columns

13.65. Figures align on right. To conserve space in a table the bearoff may be reduced in figure columns only. There is no bearoff on leaders. (See rule 13.26.)

13.66. In a crowded table, when down rules are used, the bearoff may be reduced. It is preferable to retain the bearoff. The whole table, including all parts of a divided table, must be treated alike. (For example, see rule 13.26.)

13.67. Figures in parentheses align if so required.

13.68. In double rows of figures in a single column, connected by a dash, a plus, or minus sign, and in dates appearing in the form *2–12–43*, the dashes or signs are aligned.

13.69. Plus or minus signs at the left of figures are placed against the figures regardless of alignment; plus and minus signs at the right of figures are cleared. (For example, see rule 13.34.)

13.70. Words and Roman numerals in figure columns are aligned on the right with the figures, without periods.

No-Down-Rule Style (Preferred)

Median value of livestock	$224	$62
Median value of machinery	$54	Small
Median value of furniture	$211	$100
Possessing automobiles (percent)	25	17
Median age (years)		5.5
Median value		$144
Fraternal membership:		
Men	IV	486
Women		None

Down-Rule Style (See Rule 13.3)

Median value of livestock	$224	$82
Median value of machinery	$54	Small
Median value of furniture	$211	$100
Possessing automobiles (percent)	25	17
Median age (years)		5.5
Median value		$144
Fraternal membership:		
Men	IV	486
Women		None

13.71. For symbols and letters in columns, see rules 13.127–13.128.

13.72. Figures (including decimal and common fractions) expressing mixed units of quantity (feet, dollars, etc.) and figures in parentheses are aligned on the right.

13.73. Decimal points are aligned except in columns containing numbers that refer to mixed units (such as pounds, dollars, and percentage) and have irregular decimals.

13.74. It is preferred that all columns in a table consisting entirely of figure columns be centered.

Footnotes and references

13.75. Footnotes to tables are numbered independently from footnotes to text.

13.76. Superior figures are used for footnote references, beginning with 1 in each table.

13.77. If figures might lead to ambiguity (for example, in connection with a chemical formula), asterisks, daggers, or italic superior letters, etc., may be used.

13.78. When items carry several reference marks, the superior-figure reference precedes an asterisk, dagger, or similar character used for reference. (See rule 15.15.) These, in the same sequence, precede mathematical signs. A thin space is used to bear off an asterisk, dagger, or similar character.

13.79. Footnote references are repeated in boxheads or in continued lines over tables.

13.80. References to footnotes are numbered consecutively across the page from left to right, and across both pages in a parallel table. (For examples, see pp. 192–195.)

13.81. Footnotes to a parallel table begin on the even page unless there are no references on that page. With references on each page, footnotes are made up in approximately equal depth on both pages.

13.82. In a divide table, references to footnotes are numbered consecutively across and down the first part of the divide, then similarly in the second part.

13.83. Footnote references are placed at the right in reading columns and symbol columns, and at the left in figure columns (also at the left of such words as *None* in figure columns), and are separated by a thin space. (See table, pp. 192–193.)

13.84. Two or more footnote references occurring together are separated by spaces, not commas. (For example, see rule 13.133.)

13.85. In a figure column, a footnote reference standing alone is set in parentheses and flushed right. In a reading column, it is set at the left in parentheses and is followed by leaders, but in the last column it is followed by a period, as if it were a word. In a symbol column it is set at left and cleared.

13.86. Numbered footnotes are placed immediately beneath the table. If a sign or letter reference in the heading of a table is to be followed, it is not changed to become the first numbered reference mark. The footnote to it precedes all other footnotes.

13.87. For better makeup or appearance, footnotes may be placed at the end of a lengthy table. A line reading "Footnotes at end of table." is supplied.

13.88. If the footnotes to both table and text fall together at the bottom of a page, the footnotes to the table are placed above the footnotes to the text, and the two groups are separated by a 50-point rule flush left; but if there are footnotes to the text and none to the table, the 50-point rule is retained.

13.89. Footnotes to cut-in and indented tables and tables in rules are set full measure, except when footnotes are short, they can be set in 1 em under indented table.

13.90. Footnotes are set as paragraphs, but two or more short footnotes should be combined into one line, separated by not less than 2 ems. (See rule 2.20.)

13.91. The footnotes and notes to tables are set solid.

13.92. Footnotes and notes to tables and boxheads are set the same size, but not smaller than 6 point.

13.93. Footnotes to tables follow tabular style in the use of abbreviations, figures, etc.

13.94. In footnotes, numbers are expressed in figures, even at the beginning of a note or sentence. (For fractions, see rule 13.98.)

13.95. If a footnote consists entirely or partly of a table or leaderwork, it should always be preceded by introductory matter carrying the reference number; if necessary, the copy preparer should add an introductory line, such as "[1] See the following table:".

13.96. An explanatory paragraph without specific reference but belonging to the table rather than to the text follows the footnotes, if any, and is separated from them or from the table by space.

Fractions

13.97. All fractions are set flush right to the bearoff.

No-Down-Rule Style (Preferred)

Total length .... $40\frac{3}{4}$	41	0.42	43	44	0.455	46	47	48	½ in.
Sleeve length .... $10\frac{5}{8}$	10	10	10	11	11	11	11	11	1 in.
Armhole length .... $8\frac{5}{8}$	$8\frac{1}{2}$	9	$9\frac{1}{2}$	$9\frac{1}{2}$	10	$10\frac{1}{2}$	$10\frac{1}{2}$	11	1 in.
Sleeve cuff length (if cuff $5\frac{1}{2}$	$5\frac{1}{2}$	$5\frac{1}{2}$	$5\frac{7}{12}$	$5\frac{1}{2}$	$5\frac{7}{12}$	$5\frac{1}{2}$	$5\frac{1}{2}$	$5\frac{1}{2}$	Maximum.
is used).									
Neck opening .... $26\frac{1}{2}$	26	$27\frac{17}{32}$	$28\frac{15}{32}$	28	$29\frac{17}{32}$	30	30	31	2 in.
Waist:									
7, 8, 9, 10 cut .... $23\frac{1}{2}$	24	$25\frac{1}{2}$	$27\frac{15}{32}$	28	$29\frac{1}{2}$	31	32	$33\frac{1}{2}$	6 pct.
11, 12, 14 cut .... $22\frac{1}{2}$	$23\frac{1}{2}$	25	$26\frac{1}{2}$	$27\frac{1}{2}$	29	$30\frac{1}{2}$	$31\frac{1}{2}$	33	6 pct.

13.98. Fractions standing alone are expressed in figures, even at the beginning of a line, but not at the beginning of a footnote.

Headnotes

13.99. Headnotes should be set lowercase, but not smaller than 6 point, bracketed, and period omitted at end, even if the statement is a complete sentence; but periods should not be omitted internally if required by sentence structure.

13.100. Headnotes are repeated under continued heads but the word *Continued* is not added to the headnote.

Indentions and overruns

Subentries

13.101. The indention of subentries is determined by the width of the stub or reading column. Subentries in columns more than 15 ems wide are indented in 2-em units; in columns 15 ems or less, with short entry lines and few overruns, 2-em indentions are also used. All overruns are indented 1 em more.

13.102. Subentries in columns of 15 ems or less are indented in 1-em units. Overruns are indented 1 em more.

Total, mean, and average lines

13.103. All total (also mean and average) lines are indented 3 ems. In very narrow stub columns, total lines may be reduced to 1- or 2-em indentions, depending on length of line.

13.104. Where overrun of item above conflicts, the total line is indented 1 em more. Runovers of total lines are also 1 em more.

13.105. It is not necessary to maintain uniform indention of the word *Total* throughout the same table. The word *Total* is supplied when not in copy.

No-Down-Rule Style (Preferred)

Wide stub column—subentries 2 ems	Total, all banks	National banks	Non-national banks	Building associations
ASSETS				
Loans and discounts:				
Loans to banks	$74,518	$1,267,493	$947,289	$135,619
Commercial and industrial loans	2,753,456	450,916	211,597	18,949
Total (total lines generally indent 3 ems)	2,827,974	718,409	1,158,886	154,568
Real estate loans:				
Secured by farmland	12,532	29,854	186,228	19,044
Secured by residential property other than rural and farm	1,011,856	167,765	1,554,084	3,172,837
Total (indent 1 em more to avoid conflict with line above)	1,024,388	194,619	1,740,312	3,191,881
Securities:				
U.S. Government obligations:				
Direct obligations:				
U.S. savings bonds	1,149,764	3,285,721	2,361,796	23,506
Nonmarketable bonds (including investment series A–1965)	242,500	490,677	732,689	167,735
Total (indent 1 em more than runover above)	1,392,264	3,776,398	3,094,485	191,241

Italic

13.106. Names of vessels and aircraft (except in columns consisting entirely of such names), titles of legal cases (except *v.* for *versus*), and certain scientific terms are set in italic. The word "Total" and headings in the column do not affect the application of this rule. In gothic typefaces without italic, quotes are allowed.

13.107. Set "See" and "See also" in roman. (See rule 15.21.)

Leaders

13.108. Leaders run across the entire table except that they are omitted from a last reading column. (For example, see table, pp. 192–193.)

13.109. The style of leadering is guided by two rules: (1) Tables with a single reading column leader from the bottom line, and (2) tables with any combination of more than one reading or symbol column leader from the top line.

13.110. If leadering from the top line, overruns end with a period. (For example, see table, pp. 192–193.)

13.111. A column of dates is regarded as a reading column only if leaders are added; in all other cases it is treated as a figure column.

13.112. In parallel tables and in tables with tracing figures on left and right of page, leader from top line. (See pp. 192–193.)

Numerals in tables

13.113. Figures, ordinals, and fractions are used in all parts of a table, except fractions which will be spelled out at the beginning of a footnote. (See also rules 13.94, 13.98, and 13.126.)

Overruns. (See "Indentions and overruns.")

Parallel and divide tables

Parallel tables. (For examples, see pp. 194–195.)

13.114. Parallel tables are set in pairs of pages, beginning on a left-hand page and running across to facing right-hand page; leader from the top line.

13.115. Heads and headnotes center across the pair of pages, with 2-em hanging indention for three or more lines when combined measure exceeds 30 picas in width. Two-line heads are set across the pair of pages. A single-line head or headnote is divided evenly, each part set flush right and left, respectively. Words are not divided between pages.

13.116. Boxheads are set as described on pages 174–175. Boxheads and horizontal rules align across both pages.

13.117. Boxheads are not divided but are repeated, with *Continued* added.

13.118. Vertical rules are used on the right of even pages and on the left of odd pages only when down rules are used.

13.119. Tracing figures are carried through from the outside columns of both pages and are set to "leader from the top line."

Divide tables

13.120. In divide tables that are made up parallel, with stub column repeated, the head and headnote repeat on each succeeding page, with *Continued* added to the head only.

No-Down-Rule Style (Preferred)

TABLE 1.—*Data available in Source Book of Statistics of Income from corporation returns for the years 1965–66*

[Excludes consolidated returns of inactive corporations]

Division and State	All industries	Agriculture, forestry, and fishery	Mining	Construction	Manufacturing	Transportation, communication, and other public utilities	Wholesale and retail trade
United States..............	34,627,905	7,988,243	902,061	2,032,023	8,250,690	2,768,267	5,509,228
New England	328,287	54,315	841	20,801	118,074	22,664	50,112
Maine...............................	204,215	38,756	533	11,906	68,160	15,062	31,473
New Hampshire..............	124,072	15,559	308	8,895	49,914	7,602	18,639
Middle Atlantic	7,059,570	442,137	235,385	453,940	2,210,034	700,217	1,329,225
New York.........................	3,521,163	206,354	8,614	235,763	968,453	363,343	739,295

No-Down-Rule Style (Preferred)

TABLE 1.—*Data available in Source Book of Statistics of Income from corporation returns for the years 1965–66*—Continued

[Excludes consolidated returns of inactive corporations]

Division and State	Finance, insurance, and real estate	Business and repair service	Personal service	Amusement, recreation, and related services	Professional and related services	Government	Industry not reported
United States.............	1,013,297	789,377	1,133,585	316,063	1,472,453	1,414,069	450,570
New England........................	5,900	9,369	10,973	2,310	13,815	13,735	6,376
Maine	3,586	5,179	6,504	1,457	8,253	9,295	4,029
New Hampshire	2,314	3,170	4,469	853	5,562	4,440	2,347
Middle Atlantic....................	341,574	183,586	290,986	14,541	374,017	309,017	123,832
New York	216,106	101,091	172,664	47,231	212,765	182,687	65,807

13.121. Tables with tracing figures or stub, or both, repeating on the left of odd pages, are divide tables and not parallel tables. Over such tables the heads are repeated, with *Continued* added. Outside vertical rules are not used.

Reading columns

13.122. Figures or combinations of figures and letters used to form a reading column align on left and are followed by leaders. *Do.* is not used under such items.

13.123. The en dash is not to be used for *to* in a reading column; if both occur, change to *to* throughout.

13.124. Cut-in items following a colon are indented 2 ems.

13.125. Run in single entry under colon line; retain the colon.

13.126. Numerical terms, including numbered streets, avenues, etc., are expressed in figures, even at the beginning of an item. (See also rules 9.16 and 12.13.)

Symbol columns

13.127. A column consisting entirely of letters, letters and figures, symbols, or signs, or any combination of these, is called a symbol column. It should be set flush left and cleared, except when it takes the place of the stub, it should then be leadered. No closing period is used when such column is the last column. Blank lines in a last column are cleared. *Do.* is not used in a symbol column.

No-Down-Rule Style (Preferred)

Symbol	Typical commercial designation	Army product symbol	Filing order symbol	General description	Specification symbol
GM(2)	Gasoline and diesel engine oil, SAE10 and SAE10W grades.	OR10	A	Fuel, grease, chassis, or soap base.	G.&D.
CG	Ball and roller bearing grease.	4l-X-59	N	Extreme pressure..................	BR
CW [1]	Wheel-bearing grease.......... OE20 [2]		X	......do..	WBG [3]
	Grease not typified...			Further tests being conducted.	
G090	Universal gear lubricant..... S.&T.		B	Water-pump grease...............	80D
	(Stub or reading column)			(Reading column)	

13.128. Columns composed of both symbols and figures are treated as figure columns and are set flush right. In case of blank lines in a last column, leaders will be used as in figure columns.

No-Down-Rule Style (Preferred)

Symbol or catalog number	Typical commercial designation	Symbol or product number	Symbol or filing order symbol	General description	Symbol or specification number
WBD	Chassis grease, cup grease, under pressure.	961	A	Especially adapted to very cold climates.	1359
14L88	Water-power bearing grease.....	SWA	352	Under moderate pressure......................	
5190	Exposed gear chain lubricant..	12L	N	High-speed use.............................	AE10
	E.P. hypoid lubricant	863	X	For experimental use only	NXL
376	Special grade for marine use..................		468	Free flowing in any weather ...	749
	(Stub or reading column)			(Reading column)	

Tables without rules

13.129. It is preferable to set all tables alike; that is, without either down rules or cross rules and with roman boxheads. When so indicated on copy, by ordering agency, tabular matter may be set without rules, with italic boxheads. The same arrangement and bearoff for figures prevails as in ruled tables; that is, neither leaders nor rules bear off.

13.130. Column heads over figure columns in 6- or 8-point tables are set in 6-point italic, solid.

13.131. Horizontal rules (spanner) used between a spread or upper level column heading carried over two or more lower level column headings are set continuous and without break, from left to right, between the two levels of such headings.

TABLE 9.—*Changes in fixed assets and related allowances*

		Fixed assets				
	Balance June 30, 1966 (table 9-a)	*Investment*		*Operations*		
		Current additions	*Adjustments*	*Transfers*	*Retirements*	*Balance June 30, 1966*
Supporting and general facilities:						
Transportation and utilities:						
Panama Railroad	$12,123,197	$306	....	($539)	($284,358)	$11,838,606
Motor Transportation Division	2,242,999	122,597	....	2,143	(147,561)	2,220,178
Steamship line	13,653,989	10,247	....			13,664,236
Power system	19,364,373	366,311	....	(342)	(290,174)	19,440,168
Communication system	2,739,012	151,819	($113,261)	....	(26,100)	2,751,470
Water system and hydroelectric facilities	10,590,820	104,039	....	1,661	(48,920)	10,647,600
Total, transportation and utilities	60,714,390	755,319	(113,261)	2,923	(797,113)	60,562,258
Employee service and facilities:						
Commissary Division	7,012,701	105,952	(130,891)	21,777	(36,418)	6,973,121
Service centers	3,684,670	29,086	....	530	(230,276)	3,484,010
Housing Division	35,729,465	(10,336)	....	(485,548)	(937,916)	34,295,665
Total employee service and facilities	46,426,836	124,702	(130,891)	(463,241)	(1,204,610)	44,752,796
Grand total	107,141,236	880,021	(244,152)	(466,164)	(2,001,723)	105,315,054

13.132. More than one figure column, also illustrating use of dollar mark, rule, bearoff, etc.

For property purchased from—
Central Pipeline Distributing Co.:
  Capital stock issued recorded amount $75,000
  Undetermined consideration recorded 341
Pan American Bonded Pipeline Co.: Recorded money outlay ... 3,476
M.J. Mitchell: Recorded money outlay 730
R. Lacy, Inc., and Lynch Refining Co.:
  Recorded money outlay $157,000
  Note issued 100,000
  Subtotal 257,000
Less value of oil in lines and salvaged construction material 26,555 230,445 $309,992

For construction, improvements, and replacements, recorded money outlay 522

For construction work in progress, recorded money outlay 933,605

Total 1,244,119

	Quantity (million cubic feet)	Value at point of consumption
Use:		
Residential	34,842	$21,218,778
Commercial	14,404	5,257,468
Industrial:		
Field (drilling, pumping, etc.)	144,052	10,419,000
All other industrial:		
Fuel for petroleum refineries	96,702	
Other, including electric utility plants	346,704	61,440,000
Total	636,704	98,335,246

	Estimated		
	1953	1957	Change
General account:			
Receipts	$64,800	$69,800	+$5,000
Expenditures	(70,300)	(67,100)	(−3,200)
Net improvement, 1957 over 1953			1,800
Deduct 1953 deficit			1,500
Net surplus, estimated for 1957			300

[In U.S.-dollar equivalent]

Balance with the Treasury Department July 1, 1954		$165,367,704.85
Receipts:		
Collections	$564,944,502.99	
Return from agency accounts of currencies advanced for liquidation of obligations incurred prior to July 1, 1953	4,450,577.07	
Total receipts		569,395,080.06
Total available		734,762,784.91

Total, mean, and average lines. (See rules 13.103–13.105.)

Units of quantity

13.133. Units of quantity in stub columns are set in lowercase in plural form and placed in parentheses.

No-Down-Rule Style (Preferred)

Coke (short tons)	4,468,437	[1] 25,526,646	5,080,403	[2] 29,519,871
Diatomite	([1 2 3])	([1])	([1])	([1 2 3])
Emery (pounds)	765	6,828	1,046	9,349
Feldspar (crude) (long tons)	([1])	([1])	([1])	([1])
Ferroalloys (short tons)	183,465	[2] 18,388,766	259,303	[2] 30,719,756

13.134. Units of quantity and other words as headings over figure columns are used at the beginning of a table or at the head of a continued page or continued column in a double-up table.

13.135. Over figure columns, units of quantity and other words used as headings, and the abbreviations *a.m.* and *p.m.*, if not included in the boxheads, are set in italic and are placed immediately above the figures, without periods other than abbreviating periods. In congressional work (gothic), or at any time when italic is not available, these units should be placed in the boxheads in parentheses. Any well-known abbreviation will be used to save an overrun, but if one unit of quantity is abbreviated, all in the same table will be abbreviated. If units change in a column, the new units are set in italic with space above and no space below. The space is placed both above and below only when there is no italic available. (See examples, pp. 192–193.)

Quoted tabular work

13.136. When a table is part of quoted matter, quotation marks will open on each centerhead on top of table, on first centered boxhead then on each footnote paragraph, and if table is end of quoted matter, quotation marks close at end of footnotes. If there are no footnotes and the table is the end of the quotation, quotation marks close at end of last item.

DEFINITION AND PARTS OF A TABLE

To define and describe fully all of the many parts, terms, and details which enter into tabular presentation is difficult to explain in a few words or to understand readily without an accompanying visual example. The example shown is directed at those concerned with the construction and makeup of tables, with guidelines identifying tabular terms and details. Many of the terms can be applied to any form of tabular matter.

TABLE 10.—*Heading or headline*

[Headnote or bracket line]

	Stubhead	Column head	Spanner head[1]: Coal	Spanner head[1]: Coke	Subspanner head: Car-loads more than other years	Subspanner head: Wood	Reading column head	Reading column head
	CENTERHEAD	*Millions of dollars*	*Tons*	*Tons*	*Number*	*Thousands of pounds*		
1	Lead or caption line[2] ...	[3] 900	150	191	246	1,987	Feb. 12, 1958.....	Reading column.[4]
2	Wheat and other grains.	189	257	250	379	1,235	May 9, 1957	
3	Lumber and mill work..	326	382	177	584	1,742	Dec. 31, 1957.....	
4	......do.[5]	573	176	263	129	1,963	......do.................	Do.[6]
5	Total line..............	1,988	965	881	1,338	6,927	....	([7]).
	CENTERHEAD							
6	Lead or caption line	1,057	([8])	286	2,673	1,891	July 19, 1958	Same reading column with a runover.
7	Mining equipment	321	156	112	1,114	3,821	May 3, 1958	Do.
8	......do..............................	769	....	....	....	....	....	
9	([9])..................................	258	387	596	342	2,297	June 15, 1958 ...	Reading column.
10	Total line..............	2,405	543	994	4,129	8,009	....	

Labels at the left of the table, from top to bottom:

- *The panel*
- *Head rule—usually hairline and single*
- *Boxhead*
- *Boxhead cutoff rule—usually hairline and single*
- *Centerline in stub column*
- *The line*
- *Ditto or "do" line*
- *Single rule*
- *Parallel rule*
- *Block or group*
- *Total line*
- *Cutoff rule*

Labels at the right of the table:

- *Units of quantity over figure columns—italic*
- *Clear*
- *Field or body*
- *Leader line*

Labels under the braces below the table:

- *Stub column*
- *Figures bear off*
- *Reading column*

Cutoff rule

2 READING COLUMNS
(Leader from top line)

1 Dairy products:							
2 In ctns (pounds)	1,485,692	380	462	3,624	Mar. 3, 1958	Reading column.	1
3 In cans (pounds)	263,491	198	3,762	5,783	Dec. 17, 1957	Do.	2
4 Clay products (other than pottery, refractories) (boxes).	325,000	621	4,111	1,926	Nov. 26, 1957	Do.	3
							4
5 Ferrous alloys (tons)	163,381	556	276	1,985	112,812	...do	Same reading column.
							5

Colon line

Subentry

Flush line

Runover indention

If tracer-figure (line number) column is used on right, preceding column will carry leaders to adjacent cast and leader from top

1 READING COLUMN
(Leader from bottom line)

1 A short line (boxes)	13,092	748	365	2,421	986	7,654,000	5,137
2 A long, crowded line (thousands of tons)	5,692	345	721	2,679	3,542	962,111	4,728
3 A very long line that runs over (crate)	386,591	475	582	13,563	12,297	82,129	18,591,763

Foot or bottom rule usually hairline and single

Tracer-figure (line number) column

Footnotes or reference lines

1 Reference number in boxheading.
2 Reference number followed by leaders in stub or inside reading column.
3 Reference number in figure column.
4 Reference number in last or outside reading column.
5 Reference number following "do" in inside reading column.
6 Reference number following "Do." in last or outside reading column.
7 Reference number standing alone in last or outside reading column, enclosed in parentheses followed by period "(7),," and quadded out to end of line.
8 Reference number standing alone in figure column, enclosed in parentheses (8).
9 Reference number standing alone in inside reading column, enclosed in parentheses (9), and leadered out to cast on right.

NOTE.—If no tracer-figure column is used on the left of table and the stub or reading column is set flush, "Do." will be capitalized and leadered out to cast on right.

No-Down-Rule Style (Preferred)

PARALLEL

CHART I.—*Data available in the Source Book of Statistics*

[For list of major and minor

NOTE.—Under each classification data are shown (1) in composite,

Fiscal year or month	Budget receipts and expenditures [1]			Trust account and other transactions, net receipts, or expenditures (—) [4]	Clearing account [5]
	Net receipts [2]	Expenditures [3]	Surplus, or deficit (—)		
1932	$1,923,913,117	$4,659,202,825	−$2,735,289,708	[11] −$5,178,050	
1933	2,021,212,943	4,622,865,028	−2,601,652,085	−5,009,989	
1934	3,064,267,912	6,693,899,854	−3,629,631,943	834,880,108	

NOTE.—References to footnotes are numbered across parallel pages from left to right and top to bottom.

No-Down-Rule Style (Preferred)

PARALLEL TABLE WITH

TABLE 6.—*Corporation returns with balance sheets,[1] 1949, by total assets returns with no net income:[3] Number of returns, selected assets and deficit, and dividends paid in cash and assets other than own stock;*

[Total assets classes and money

		Major industrial groups				
		Finance, insurance, real estate, and lessors of real property in 1957			Services	
		Insurance carriers, agencies, and agents— Insurance agents and brokers	Real estate, except lessors of real property other than buildings	Lessors of real property, except buildings	Total services	Hotels and other lodging places
1	Number of returns [4]	5,341	76,010	3,589	29,468	3,584
	Receipts:					
2	Gross sales [7]		23,089		1,314,378	437,633
3	Gross receipts from operations [8]	349,983	1,065,196		5,823,484	714,254
	Interest on Government obligations (less amortizable bond premium):					
4	Wholly taxable [9]	373	3,631	4,084	4,075	1,194
5	Subject to surtax only [10]	24	314	70	123	8
6	Wholly tax exempt [11]	17	621	117	652	12

NOTE.—Preparers of parallel tables will indicate the width of 1 page immediately adjacent the instruction

TABLE

of Income from corporation returns for the years 1926–66

industrial groups, see chart II]

(2) for returns with net income, and (3) for returns with no net income

Public debt, net increase or decrease (−)	Cash balance in account of the Treasurer of the United States, net increase or decrease (−)	Cash balance in account of the Treasurer of the United States	Amount, end of period			
				Debt outstanding [6]		
			Public debt [7]	Guaranteed obligations [8]	Total [9]	Subject to limitation [10]
$2,685,720	−$54,746,805	$417,197,178	$19,487,002	....	$19,487,002	([12])
3,051,670	445,008,042	862,205,221	22,538,672	....	22,538,672	([12])
4,514,468	1,719,717,020	2,581,922,240	27,053,141	$680,767,817	27,733,909	([12])

TRACING FIGURES

classes, and by major industrial groups,[2] for returns with net income and liabilities, selected receipts, compiled net profit or net loss, net income or also, for returns with net income, the income tax

figures in thousands of dollars]

	Major industrial groups—Continued						
	Services—Continued						
Personal services	Business services	Automotive repair services and garages	Miscellaneous repair services, hand trades	Motion pictures	Amusement, except motion pictures	Other services, including schools	Nature of business not allocable
[5] 6,689	6,067	2,488	[6] 1,190	3,558	2,822	3,070	902 1
312,555	181,732	113,906	88,304	72,602	51,215	56,431	57,971 2
865,090	1,599,119	157,940	113,000	1,480,924	431,053	462,104	17,938 3
259	734	126	24	1,041	358	339	41 4
11	69	1	3	7	6	18	15 5
[12] 34	40	1	....	542	2	21	23 6

"parallel table." In the example above, the table should be rubberstamped "parallel table 26½ picas."

14. LEADERWORK

(See also Abbreviations; Tabular Work)

14.1. Leaderwork is a simple form of tabular work without boxheads or rules and is separated from text by 4 points of space above and below in solid matter and 6 points of space in leaded matter. It consists of a reading (stub) column and a figure column, leadered from the bottom line. It may also consist of two reading columns, aligning on the top line. In general, leaderwork (except indexes and tables of contents, which are set the same style as text) is governed by the same rules of style as tabular work. Unless otherwise indicated, leaderwork is set in 8 point. The period is omitted immediately before leaders. (See also "Tables without rules," p. 188.)

Bearoff

14.2. No bearoff is required at the right in a single reading column.

Columns

14.3. A figure column is at least an en quad wider than the largest group of figures, but not less than 3 ems in single columns and 2 ems in double-up columns. Total rules are to be the full width of all figure columns.

	[1]*Pounds*
Year: 1952	655,939
Fiscal year:	
1954	368,233
1955	100,000
Total	1,124,172

[1] Certain production methods require the use of an 8-point italic centered heading here.

14.4. Where both columns are reading columns, they are separated by an em space.

Particulars	*Artist*
To the French Government:	
The entire collection of French paintings on loan, with the exception of Mlle. DuBourg (Mme. Fantin-Latour).	Degas.
Avant la Course	Do.
To Col. Axel H. Oxholm, Washington, DC:	
Martha Washington, George Washington, and Thomas Jefferson.	Attributed to Jonathan E. Earl, Los Angeles, CA.
Roses	Renoir.
Do	Forain.
Roses in a Chinese Vase and Sculpture by Maillol.	Vuillard.
Maternity	Gauguin.

Continued heads

14.5. The use of continued lines is no longer in effect.

Ditto

14.6. The abbreviation *do.* is indented and capitalized in stub. It is capitalized and cleared in last reading column. (See rules 14.4 and 14.20.)

Dollar mark and ciphers

14.7. The dollar mark or any other money symbol is used at the beginning of each statement.

14.8. In a column containing mixed amounts (as money, tons, gallons, etc.) the figures are aligned on the right, and the dollar mark or other symbol is repeated before each sum of money. If several sums of money are grouped and added to make a total, they are separated from the nonmoney group by a parallel rule, and the symbol is placed on the first figure of the separated group only. (See rule 13.60.)

14.9. If two columns of sums of money add or subtract one into the other and one carries points and ciphers, the other should also carry points and ciphers.

Flush items and subheads

14.10. Flush items clear the figure column.
14.11. Subheads are centered in full measure.

Footnotes

14.12. Footnotes to leaderwork follow the style of footnotes to tables. (See "Footnotes and references," p. 183.)

14.13. Footnote references begin with 1 in each leadered grouping, and footnotes are placed at end, separated from it by 4 points of space. Separate notes from matter following by not less than 6 points of space.

14.14. If the leaderwork runs over from one page to another, they will be placed at the bottom of the leadered material.[1]

Units of quantity

14.15. Units of quantity or other words over a stub or figure column are set italic.

14.16. The example below shows the style to be observed where there is a short colon line at left. In case of only one subentry, run in with colon line and preserve the colon.

Baltimore & Ohio RR.:
   Freight carried: *Tons*
      May 50,000
      June 52,000
   Coal carried 90,000
Dixie RR.: Freight carried Jan. 1, 1978, including freight carried by all its subsidiaries .... [1] 2,000

[1] Livestock not included.

---

[1] If footnotes to leaderwork and text fall at bottom of page, leaderwork footnotes are placed above text footnotes. The two groups are separated by a 50-point rule.

14.17. If there is no colon line, the style is as follows:

Freight carried by the Dixie RR. and the Baltimore & Ohio RR. in May .... *Tons* 71,500

14.18. Explanatory matter is set in 6 point under leaders (note omission of period):

....
      (Name)   (Address)   (Position)

14.19. In blank forms, leaders used in place of complete words to be supplied are preceded and followed by a space.

On this .... day of .... 19......

14.20. In half measure doubled up, units of quantity are aligned across the page. (See also rule 15.22.)

Seedlings:

	Inches		*Inches*
Black locust	27	Osage-orange	20
Honey locust	16	Catalpa	16
Green ash	7	Black walnut	10

14.21. Mixed units of quantity and amounts and words in figure column are set as follows:

Capital invested	$8,000
Value of implements and stock	$3,000
Land under cultivation (acres)	128.6
Orchard (acres)	21.4
Forest land (square miles)	50
Livestock:	
Horses:	
Number	8
Value	$1,500
Cows:	
Number	18
Estimated weekly production of butter per milk cow (pounds)	7½
Hogs:	
Number	46
Loss from cholera	None

NOTES

15. TEXT FOOTNOTES, INDEXES, AND CONTENTS

FOOTNOTES AND REFERENCE MARKS

(For footnotes in tabular work, see p. 183.)

15.1. Except as noted under "Abbreviations" (p. 135), footnotes to text follow the style of text.

15.2. In a publication divided into chapters, sections, or articles, each beginning a new page, text footnotes begin with 1 in each such division. In a publication without such divisional grouping, footnotes are numbered consecutively from 1 to 99, and then begin with 1 again. However, in supplemental sections, such as appendixes and bibliographies, which are not parts of the publication proper, footnotes begin with 1.

15.3. Copy preparers must see that references and footnotes are plainly marked and must also indicate the measure if footnotes are to be doubled up.

15.4. On a job that is not completed, the last footnote number must be given to the supervisor, who will record it so that there will be no question as to next footnote number.

15.5. If a reference is repeated on another page, it should carry the original footnote; but to avoid repetition of a long note, the copy preparer may use the words "See footnote 3 (6, etc.) on p.—" instead of the entire footnote.

15.6. Unless copy is otherwise marked: (1) Footnotes to 12-point text (except 12-point briefs) are set in 8 point; (2) footnotes to 11-point text are set in 8 point, except in Supreme Court reports, in which they are set in 9 point; (3) footnotes to 10- and 8-point text are set in 7 point. (See also "Courtwork," p. 215.)

15.7. Footnotes are set as paragraphs at the bottom of the page and are separated from the text by a 50-point rule, flush on the left, with no less than 2 points of space above and below the rule.

15.8. Footnotes to indented matter (other than excerpt footnotes) are set full measure. (See also rule 13.89.)

15.9. To achieve faithful reproduction of indented excerpt material (particularly legal work) containing original footnotes, these footnotes are also indented and placed at bottom of excerpt, separated by 6 points of space. No side dash is used. Reference numbers are not changed to fit numbering sequence of text footnotes.

15.10. Footnotes must always begin on the page carrying the reference. The breaking over of a footnote from one page to the next should be avoided.[1]

15.11. Footnotes to charts, graphs, and other illustrations should be placed immediately beneath such illustrative material.

---

[1] When a footnote breaks from an odd (right-hand) page to an even (left-hand) page, the word (*Continued*) will be placed flush right below the last line where the break occurs. The usual 50-point dash is used above each part. Where break occurs on facing pages; i.e., from even page to odd page, do not use (*Continued*) lines.

15.12. A cutoff dash is not required between the chart or graph and the footnotes.

15.13. For reference marks use: (1) Roman superior figures, (2) italic superior letters, and (3) symbols. Superior figures (preferred), letters, and symbols are separated from the words to which they apply by thin spaces, unless immediately preceded by periods or commas.

15.14. Where reference figures might lead to ambiguity (for example, in matter containing exponents), asterisks, daggers, etc., or italic superior letters may be used.

15.15. When symbols or signs are used for footnote reference marks, their sequence should be (*) asterisk, (†) dagger, (‡) double dagger, and (§) section mark. Should more symbols be needed, these may be doubled or tripled, but for simplicity and greater readability, it is preferable to extend the assortment by adding other single-character symbols.

15.16. Symbols with commonly established other meanings likely to produce confusion, such as the percent mark (%) and the number mark (#), should not be used.

15.17. To avoid possible confusion with numerals and letters frequently occurring in charts and graphs, it is preferable in such instances to use symbols as reference marks.

15.18. When items carry several reference marks, the superior-figure reference precedes an asterisk, dagger, or similar character used for reference.

15.19. A superior reference mark follows all punctuation marks except a dash, but falls inside a closing parenthesis or bracket if applying only to matter within the parentheses or brackets.

15.20. Two or more superior footnote references occurring together are separated by thin spaces.

INDEXES AND TABLES OF CONTENTS

15.21. Indexes and tables of contents are set in the same style as the text, except that *See* and *see also* are set in italic.

15.22. *Page, section, paragraph,* etc., over figure columns are set in roman, flush on right.

454   ANNUAL REPORT OF THE SECRETARY OF THE TREASURY

Notes—Continued
   Treasury:
      Marketable: Page
         Exchanges.. 459

456   ANNUAL REPORT OF THE SECRETARY OF THE TREASURY

Notes—Continued   Page
   Treasury.. 459

15.23. Where a word occurs in an index page column, either alone or with a figure, it is set flush on the right. If the word extends back into the leaders, it is preceded by an en space.

Page
Explanatory diagram.. Frontispiece
General instructions.. VIII
Capitalization (*see also* Abbreviations)................................... 16
Correct imposition (diagram) .... Facing 34

15.24. For better appearance, Roman numerals should be set in small caps in the figure columns of tables of contents and indexes.

15.25. In indexes set with leaders, if the page numbers will not fit in the leader line, the first number only is set in that line and the other numbers are overrun. If the entry makes three or more lines and the last line of figures is not full, do not use a period at the end.

If page folios overrun due to an excessive amount of figures use this form 220, 224, 227, 230, 240

And this way when overrun folios make two or more lines................................ 220, 224–225, 230–240, 245, 246, 250–255, 258, 300, 320, 330, 350, 360, 370, 380, 390, 400, 410–500, 510, 520, 530, 540, 550, 560, 570, 580, 590, 600–620, 630, 640, 650, 660, 670, 680, 690, 700

(For examples of item indentions in reading column of indexes set with leaders, see index in this MANUAL.)

15.26. Overrun page numbers are indented 3½ ems in measures not over 20 picas and 7 ems in wider measures, more than one line being used if necessary. These indentions are increased as necessary to not less than 2 ems more than the line immediately above or below.

15.27. When copy specifies that all overs are to be a certain number of ems, the runovers of the figure column shall be held in 2 ems more than the specified indention.

15.28. Examples of block-type indexes:

Example 1

Medical officer, radiological defense, 3
Medicolegal dosage, 44
Military Liaison Committee, 4
Monitoring, 58
  Air, 62
  Personnel, 59
    Civilian, 60
    Military, 59
  Sea, 61
  Ship, 61
Monitors, radiological defense, 3

NEPA, 29
NEPS; project, 30
Neutron(s), 16
  Flux, 41
Nuclear binding energy, 22
Nuclear energy, release of, 23

Example 2

Brazil—Continued
  Exchange restrictions—Continued
    Williams mission (*see als.*) Williams, John H., special mission), efforts in connection with exchange control situation, 586–588
    Trade agreement with United States, proposed:
    Draft text, 558–567
    Proposals for:
      Inclusion of clauses relating to exchange control operation, 550, 551, 557
      Joint United States-Brazilian declaration of policy: Brazilian attitude, 553, 569, 570, 572–574; information concerning, 550, 551, 552

15.29. In index entries the following forms are used:

    Brown, A.H., Jr. (*not* Brown, Jr., A.H.)
    Brown, A.H., & Sons (*not* Brown & Sons, A.H.)
    Brown, A.H., Co. (*not* Brown Co., A.H.)
    Brown, A.H., & Sons Co. (*not* Brown & Sons Co., A.H.)

15.30. In a table of contents, where *chapter, plate,* or *figure* is followed by a number and period, an en space is used after the period. The periods are aligned on the right.

15.31. Subheads in indexes and tables of contents are centered in the full measure.

15.32. In contents set in combination of two sizes of lightface type, or in combination of boldface and lightface type, all leaders and page numbers will be set in lightface roman type. Contents set entirely in boldface will use boldface page numbers. All page numbers will be set in the predominant size.

16. DATELINES, ADDRESSES, AND SIGNATURES

16.1. The general principle involved in the typography of datelines, addresses, and signatures is that they should be so set as to stand out clearly from the body of the letter or paper which they accompany. This is accomplished by using caps and small caps and italic, as set forth below. Other typographic details are designed to ensure uniformity and good appearance. Street addresses and ZIP Code numbers are not to be used. (But in certain lists which carry ZIP Code numbers regular spacing will be used preceding ZIP Code.) Certain general instructions apply alike to datelines, addresses, and signatures.

General instructions

16.2. Principal words in datelines, addresses, and titles accompanying signatures are capitalized.

16.3. *Mr., Mrs., Miss, Ms.,* and all other titles preceding a name, and *Esq., Jr., Sr.,* and *2d* following a name in address and signature lines, are set in roman caps and lowercase if the name is in caps and small caps or caps and lowercase; if the name is in caps, they are set in caps and small caps, if small caps are available—otherwise in caps and lowercase. (See also rule 9.37.)

Spacing

16.4. At least 2 points of space should appear between dateline and text or address, address and text, text and signature, and signature and address. (See examples, rule 16.26.)

DATELINES

16.5. Datelines at the beginning of a letter or paper are set at the right side of the page, the originating office in caps and small caps, the place name and date in italic; if the originating office is not given, the place name is set in caps and small caps and the date in italic; if only the date is given, it is set in caps and small caps. Such datelines are indented from the right 1 em for a single line; 3 ems and 1 em, successively, for two lines; and 5 ems, 3 ems, and 1

em, successively, for three lines. In measures 30 picas or wider, these indentions are increased by 1 em.

THE WHITE HOUSE,☐☐☐
Washington, DC, January 1, 1983.☐

THE WHITE HOUSE, *July 30, 1983.*☐

TREASURY DEPARTMENT,☐☐☐☐☐
OFFICE OF THE TREASURER,☐☐☐
Washington, DC, January 1, 1983.☐

TREASURY DEPARTMENT, *July 30, 1983.*☐

DEPARTMENT OF COMMERCE,☐☐☐
July 30, 1983.☐

FAIRFAX COUNTY, VA.☐

OFFICE OF JOHN SMITH & Co.,☐☐☐
New York, NY, June 6, 1983.☐

WASHINGTON, *May 20, 1983—10 a.m.*☐

THURSDAY, MAY 8, 1983—2 P.M.☐

JANUARY 24, 1983.☐

WASHINGTON, *November 29, 1983* ☐☐☐
[Received December 6, 1983].☐

ON BOARD U.S.S. "CONNECTICUT,"☐☐☐
January 21, 1983.☐

OFFICE OF THE COMMISSIONERS OF THE☐☐☐☐☐
DISTRICT OF COLUMBIA,☐☐☐
Washington, January 6, 1983.☐

16.6. Congressional hearings:

MONDAY, OCTOBER 24, 1983[1]

HOUSE OF REPRESENTATIVES,☐☐☐☐☐☐☐
SUBCOMMITTEE ON IMMIGRATION,☐☐☐☐☐
COMMITTEE ON THE JUDICIARY,☐☐☐
Washington, DC.☐

U.S. SENATE,☐☐☐☐☐
COMMITTEE ON ARMED SERVICES,☐☐☐
Washington, DC.☐

CONGRESS OF THE UNITED STATES,☐☐☐☐☐
JOINT COMMITTEE ON PRINTING,☐☐☐
Washington, DC.☐

16.7. Datelines at the end of a letter or paper, either above or below signature, are set on left in caps and small caps for the place and italic for the date. When the word *dated* is used, dateline is set in roman caps and lowercase.

☐MAY 7, 1983.

☐STEUBENVILLE, OH.

☐STEUBENVILLE, OH, *July 1, 1983.*

☐Dated July 1, 1983.

☐Dated Albany, March 12, 1983.

---

[1] Normally, dates in House hearings on appropriation bills are set on right in 10-point caps and small caps.

NOTE.—The U.S. Government Correspondence Manual offers proper forms of addresses, salutations and closings. (See "Bibliography," p. 3.)

16.8. Datelines in newspaper extracts are set at the beginning of the paragraph, the place name in caps and small caps and the date in roman caps and lowercase, followed by a period and a 1-em dash.

☐ABOARD SS "HOPE," April 3, 1983.—

☐NEW YORK, NY, August 21, 1983.—A dispatch received here from * * *.

ADDRESSES

16.9. Addresses are set flush left at the beginning of a letter or paper in congressional work (or at end in formal usage). (See examples, rule 16.26.)

16.10. At beginning or at end:

To SMITH & JONES and
☐BROWN & GREEN, Esqs.,
Attorneys for Claimant

(Attention of Mr. Green).

Hon. HOWARD H. BAKER,
U.S. Senate.

Hon. JIM WRIGHT,
U.S. House of Representatives. (Collective address).

The PRESIDENT,
The White House.

16.11. A long title following an address is set in italic caps and lowercase, the first line flush left and right, overruns indented 2 ems to clear a following 1-em paragraph indention.

Hon. HUBERT H. HUMPHREY,
Chairman, Subcommittee on Reorganization of the Committee on Government Opera-
☐☐*tions, U.S. Senate, Washington, DC.*

16.12. The name or title forming the first line of the address is set in caps and small caps, but *Mr., Mrs.,* or other title preceding a name, and *Esq., Jr., Sr.,* or *2d* following a name, are set in roman caps and lowercase; the matter following is set in italic. The words *U.S. Army* or *U.S. Navy* immediately following a name are set in roman caps and lowercase in the same line as the name.

Maj. Gen. EDWARD M. MARKHAM, Jr., U.S. Army,
Chief of Engineers.

CHIEF OF ENGINEERS, U.S. ARMY. (Full title, all caps and small caps.)

Maj. Gen. EDWARD M. MARKHAM,
Chief of Engineers, U.S. Army,
Washington, DC.

Hon. RALPH R. ROBERTS,
Clerk of the House of Representatives.

Hon. JOHN L. MCCLELLAN,
U.S. Senator, Washington, DC.

Hon. CHARLES POTTER,
Senate Office Building, Washington, DC.

The COMMITTEE ON APPROPRIATIONS,
House of Representatives.

16.13. General (or collective) addresses are set in italic caps and lowercase, flush left, with overruns indented 2 ems and ending with a colon, except when followed by a salutation, in which case a period is used.

16.14. Examples of general addresses when not followed by salutation (note the use of colon at end of italic line):

To the Officers and Members of the Daughters of the American Revolution,
□□*Washington, DC.:*

To the American Diplomatic and Consular Officers:

To Whom It May Concern:

Collectors of Customs:

To the Congress of the United States:

16.15. Example of general address when followed by salutation (note the use of period at end of italic line):

Senate and House of Representatives:
□Gentlemen: You are hereby * * *.

16.16. Examples illustrating other types of addresses:

To the Editor:

To John L. Nelson, *Greeting:*

To John L. Nelson, *Birmingham, AL, Greeting:*

To the Clerk of the House of Representatives:

Chief of Engineers
(Through the Division Engineer).
□My Dear Sir: I have the honor * * *.
□Mr. Reed: I have the honor * * *.
□Dear Mr. Reed: I have the honor * * *.

Lt. (jg.) John Smith,
Navy Department:
□The care shown by you * * *.

State of New York,
County of New York, ss:
□Before me this day appeared * * *.

District of Columbia, *ss:*
□Before me this day appeared * * *.

Envelope addresses

U.S. House of Representatives
Committee on Education and Labor
Room 429, House Office Building
Washington, DC 20515

SIGNATURES

16.17. Signatures, preceded by an em dash, are sometimes run in with last line of text. (See also rule 8.67.)

16.18. Signatures are set at the right side of the page. They are indented 1 em for a single line; 3 ems and 1 em, successively, for two lines; and 5 ems, 3 ems and 1 em, successively, for three lines. In measures 30 picas or wider, these indentions are increased by 1 em. (See examples, rule 16.26.)

16.19. The name or names are set in caps and small caps; *Mr., Mrs.,* and all other titles preceding a name, and *Esq., Jr., Sr.,* and *2d* following a name, are set in roman caps and lowercase; the title following name is set in italic. Signatures as they appear in copy must be followed in regard to abbreviations.

16.20. If name and title make more than half a line, they are set as two lines.

16.21. Two to eight independent signatures, with or without titles, are aligned on the left, at approximately the center of the measure.

> W.H. SOUTHERLAND.
> JAMES G. GREEN.
> WM. C. WILSON.
>
> WARREN H. ATHERTON.
> ALBERT J. HAYES.
> THOMAS C. KINKAID,
> > Commander, U.S. Navy (Retired).□
>
> DAVID SARNOFF, Chairman.

16.22. More than eight signatures, with or without titles, are set full measure, roman caps and lowercase, run in, indented 5 and 7 ems in measures of 26½ picas or wider; in measures less than 26½ picas, indent 2 and 3 ems.

⬜⬜⬜⬜Brown, Shipley & Co.; Denniston, Cross & Co.; Fruhling & Groschen, ⬜⬜⬜⬜⬜⬜Attorneys; C.J. Hambro & Sons; Hardy, Nathan & Co.; Heilbut, ⬜⬜⬜⬜⬜⬜Symons & Co.; Harrison Bros. & Co., by George Harrison; ⬜⬜⬜⬜⬜⬜Hoare, Miller & Co.; Thomas Eaton Co.

16.23. The punctuation of closing phrases is governed by the sense. A detached complimentary close is made a new paragraph.

16.24. Examples of various kinds of signatures:

> UNITED STATES IMPROVEMENT CO.,
> (By) JOHN SMITH, Secretary.
>
> TEXARKANA TEXTILE MERCHANTS &
> > MANUFACTURERS' ASSOCIATION,
> JOHN L. JONES, Secretary.
>
> TEXARKANA TEXTILE MERCHANTS &
> > MANUFACTURERS' ASSOCIATION,
> HUBERT P. STONEGARTEN,
> > Board Member and Secretary.□
>
> JOHN L. PENN, Solicitor
> (Per) FREDERICK VAN DYNE,
> > Assistant Solicitor.□
>
> > JOHN W. SMITH⬜⬜⬜
> > (And 25 others).□
>
> > JOHN SMITH,⬜⬜⬜⬜
> > Lieutenant Governor⬜⬜⬜
> > (For the Governor of Maine).□
>
> NORTH AMERICAN ICE CO.,
> G.Y. ATLEE, Secretary.
>
> > JOHN [his thumbmark] SMITH.□
>
> CLARENCE CANNON,
> AUGUST H. ANDRESEN,
> > Managers on the Part of the House.□
>
> CARTER GLASS,
> CARL HAYDEN,
> > Managers on the Part of the Senate.□

□I am, very respectfully, yours,

> (Signed)□FRED C. KLEINSCHMIDT,⬜⬜⬜
> > Assistant Clerk, Court of Claims.□

□On behalf of the Philadelphia Chamber of Commerce:
> GEO. W. PHILIPS.
> SAML. CAMPBELL.

□I have the honor to be,
□□□Very respectfully, your obedient servant,
                    (Signed)□John R. King
                    (Typed)□JOHN R. KING,
                                        Secretary.□

                              or

                    (S)□John R. King
                    JOHN R. KING,
                                        Secretary.□

□Hoping to hear from you soon, I have the honor to be,
□□□Very respectfully, your obedient servant,
                              HENRY L. JONES, M.D.□

                    MARY J. JONES
                    Mrs. Henry T. Jones.

□Attest:
                              RICHARD ROE, *Notary Public.*□

□By the Governor:
                              NATHANIEL COX, *Secretary of State.*□

□Approved.
                              JOHN SMITH, *Governor.*□

□By the President:
                              CORDELL HULL, *Secretary of State.*□

□Respectfully submitted.
                              L.A. WRIGHT, *U.S. Indian Agent.*□

□□□Yours truly,
                              Capt. JAMES STALEY, Jr.,□□□
                                        Superintendent.□

□□□Respectfully yours,
                              J.B. ELLIS.□

□□□Very respectfully,
                              A.F. CALDWELL, *U.S. Indian Agent.*□

16.25. In quoted matter:
□□□"Very respectfully,

                    "KENNETH ADAMS.
                    "JOHN STEPHEN.
                    "BEVERLY RYAN.
                    "WILLIAM ARNOLD.
                    "M.T. JENKINSON.
                    "ALBERT WARD."

16.26. Examples of various kinds of datelines, addresses, and signatures:

Re weather reports submitted by the International Advisory Committee of the □□Weather Council.

Mr. WILLIAM E. JONES, Jr.,
Chairman, Commerce Committee,
Washington, DC.

□DEAR MR. JONES: We have been in contact with your office, etc.
                              PAUL S. REED,□□□□□
                                    Executive Director,□□□
                              National Information Bureau.□

□NEW YORK, *August 19, 1983.*
     or, if copy—
□AUGUST 19, 1983.

LINCOLN PARK, MI, *February 15, 1983.*☐

Re Romeo O. Umanos, Susanna M. Umanos, case No. S–254, Immigration and Natu-
☐☐ralization Service, application pending.
Hon. FRANCIS E. WALTER,
Chairman, Subcommittee on Immigration,
Committee on the Judiciary, Washington, DC.

☐DEAR MR. WALTER: You have for some time * * *.
☐☐☐Sincerely yours,

CHARLES A. BRANDT,☐☐☐
Architectural Designer.☐

Hon. FRANCIS E. WALTER,
Chairman, Subcommittee on Immigration of the Committee on the Judiciary, House
☐☐*of Representatives, Washington, DC.*
☐DEAR MR. WALTER: You have for some time * * *.

U.S. DEPARTMENT OF COMMERCE,☐☐☐☐☐
WEATHER BUREAU,☐☐☐
Washington, March 3, 1983.☐
Hon. CHARLES E. CHAMBERLAIN,
House of Representatives,
Washington, DC.
☐DEAR MR. CHAMBERLAIN: We will be glad to
give you any further information desired.
☐☐☐Sincerely yours,
F.W. REICHELDERFER,☐☐☐
Chief of Bureau.☐

NEW YORK, NY, *February 10, 1983.*☐

To: All supervisory employees of production plants, northern and eastern divisions,
☐☐New York State.
From: Production manager.
Subject: Regulations concerning vacations, health and welfare plans, and wage con-
☐☐tract negotiations.
☐It has come to our attention that the time * * *.

WASHINGTON, DC, *May 16, 1983.*☐

The Honorable the SECRETARY OF THE NAVY.
☐DEAR MR. SECRETARY: This is in response to your letter * * *.
☐☐☐Very sincerely yours,

[SEAL]☐RONALD REAGAN.☐

EAST LANSING, MI, *June 10, 1983.*☐

To Whom It May Concern:
☐I have known Kyu Yawp Lee for 7 years and am glad to testify as to his fine char-
acter. He has been employed * * *.
☐Wishing you success in your difficult and highly important job, we are,
☐☐☐Sincerely yours,
ELWIN J. GLEASON.
MILDRED T. GLEASON.

MARCH 10, 1983.☐

Hon. STROM THURMOND,
Chairman, Committee on the Judiciary,
U.S. Senate, Washington, DC.

☐DEAR SENATOR: In response to your request for a report relative to * * *.
☐☐☐Sincerely,

J.M. SWING, *Commissioner.*☐

VETERANS' ADMINISTRATION,☐☐☐☐☐☐☐
OFFICE OF THE ADMINISTRATOR OF☐☐☐☐☐
VETERANS' AFFAIRS,☐☐☐
Washington, DC.☐

Hon. STROM THURMOND,
Chairman, Committee on the Judiciary,
U.S. Senate, Washington, DC.

☐DEAR SENATOR THURMOND: Further reference is made to your reply * * *.
☐☐☐Sincerely yours,

JOHN S. PATTERSON,☐☐☐☐☐☐☐
Deputy Administrator☐☐☐☐☐
(For and in the absence of☐☐☐
H.V. Higley, Administrator).☐

WASHINGTON, DC, *September 16, 1983.*☐

Mr. WILLIAM E. JONES, Jr.,
Special Assistant to the Attorney General, Attorney for Howard Sutherland, Direc-
☐☐*tor, Office of Alien Property.*

☐DEAR MR. JONES: In reply to your letter * * *.
☐☐☐Yours truly,

(Signed)☐THOMAS E. RHODES,☐☐☐
Special Assistant to the Attorney General.☐

☐P.S.—A special word of thanks to you from J.R. Brown for your fine help.

T.E.R.☐

TOKYO, JAPAN, *November 13, 1983.*☐

U.S. DEPARTMENT OF JUSTICE,
IMMIGRATION AND NATURALIZATION SERVICE,
Detroit, MI.

☐GENTLEMEN: This letter will testify to the personal character * * *.
☐☐☐Very truly yours,

Mrs. GRACE C. LOHR,☐☐☐☐☐
Inspector General Section, HQ, AFFE,☐☐☐
APO 343, San Francisco, CA.☐

16.27. The word *seal* appearing with the signature of a notary or of an organized body, such as a company, is spaced 1 em from the signature. The word *seal* is to be set in small caps and bracketed. (See rule 16.28.)

[SEAL]☐RICHARD ROE,☐☐☐
Notary Public.☐

[SEAL]☐J.M. WILBER.☐

[SEAL]☐BARTLETT, ROBINS & Co.☐

16.28. Presidential proclamations after May 23, 1967, do not utilize the seal except when they pertain to treaties, conventions, protocols, or other international agreements. Copy will be followed literally with respect to the inclusion of *and* between elements of numerical expressions.

Now, THEREFORE, I, RICHARD NIXON, President of the United States of America, do hereby designate Saturday, September 23, 1972, as National Hunting and Fishing Day.

    *   *   *   *   *   *   *   *

IN WITNESS WHEREOF, I have hereunto set my hand this second day of May, in the year of our Lord nineteen hundred seventy-two, and of the Independence of the United States of America the one hundred ninety-sixth.

RICHARD NIXON.☐

NOTES

17. COURTWORK

(See also Capitalization; General Instructions; Italic)

17.1. Courtwork differs in style from other work only as set forth in this section; otherwise the style prescribed in the preceding sections will be followed.

Briefs, decisions, exhibits, and opinions

17.2. In general, copy is printed "Fol. lit."

17.3. Titles of legal cases are italicized.

17.4. Single punctuation is used in citations wherever possible.

17.5. When "emphasis supplied," "emphasis added," or "emphasis ours" appears in copy, it should not be changed; but "underscore supplied" should be changed to "italic supplied."

17.6. When *Question* and *Answer* are spelled out in copy, set in separate paragraphs.

17.7. In National Labor Relations Board transcript, the abbreviated forms *Q.* and *A.* are always used, run in, and the question and its answer are connected by an em dash.

17.8. The words *infra* and *supra* are italicized. Copy is followed for the use of italic in Latin legal terms and abbreviations, in addition to italic used for emphasis.

17.9. In the titles of cases the first word and all principal words are capitalized, but not such terms as *defendant* and *appellee.*

17.10. In the titles of cases copy is followed as to use of figures and abbreviations.

17.11. Abbreviations in names of legal cases are to be followed literally in all classes of work.

17.12. The following examples indicate the capitalization, italic, small caps, abbreviations, etc., generally used, except the word *case,* which is set in italic only when so indicated in copy.

Defendant John Smith; *but* the defendant, John Smith

The *Legal Tender* cases

In Clarke's case, the court said * * *

In the case of Clarke

Clarke's case (14 How. 14)

WALLACE, J., delivered the opinion

Brown's case, 14 Hun 14 (N.Y. 1838)

In *Roe* v. *Doe,* the court ruled * * *

In *Ex parte 74,* the court said * * *

(*Ex parte 74,* 58 I.C.C. 220)

In the *Fifteen Percent Rate Increase* case, the court decided * * *

In the case of Jones against Robinson (A general or casual reference to a case)

In *Jones* v. *Robinson,* 122 U.S. 329 (1929)

In *In re Robinson,* 19 Wall. (18 U.S.) 304 (1910), the Court * * *

John Brown, Jr. v. *Edwin Smith*

Smith & Brown, Inc. v. *Commissioner*

Commissioner, etc. v. *Klein Chain Co.*

Dunham Towing & Wrecking Co. v. *Bassett* (the *Aksel Monson* case)

United States v. *12 Diamond Rings*

The United States v. *Forty Hogsheads of Tobacco*

Stat., Rev. Stat., Stat. L., or R.S., as written

Bowman Act, 22 Stat. 50 (1939)

Act of August 5, 1953 (67 Stat. 588; 18 U.S.C. 1162 (*or* U.S.C., title 18, sec. 1162))

Act of August 5, 1882, Supp. Rev. Stat. sec. [*or* §] 284; Rev. Stat. sec. [*or* §] 15

Public Law 250, 84th Cong., 2d sess. (67 Stat. 623)

Public Law 85–143, Aug. 14, 1957

30 U.S.C., 1952 ed., Supp. II, sec. 184 (C.A.D.C. 1941) [Appeals, Dist. of Columbia] (D.D.C. 1955) [District Court, Dist. of Columbia]
164 Fed. 205 (N.D. W. Va. 1949)
117 F. Supp, 463 (N.D. Del. 1949)
9 Pac. 735 (Mont. 1935)
9 P. 2d 1095 (Wash. 1932)
44 Atl. 317 (Del. 1899)
37 A. 2d 10 (Del. 1944)
259 S.W. 57 (Mo. 1957)
14 Fed. Cas. 143, No. 7621 (C.C.N.D. Ill. 1876)
34 Comp. Gen. 230 (1954)
132 Ct. Cl. 645 (1955)
43 CFR 192.1 [Code of Federal Regulations]
43 CFR, 1940 ed., 192.14

43 CFR, 1940 ed., Cum. Supp., 19.14
21 F.R. 623 [Federal Register]
United States v. *Eller*, 114 F. Supp. 284 (N.D.N.C.), *rev'd* 208 F. (2d) (or (2) (*but* do not supply parentheses on "2d" if not in copy)) 716 (4th Cir. 1953), cert. denied, 347 U.S. 934 (1954)
United States ex rel. Smith v. *Jones*
In the Matter of Jones
8 Wigmore, *Evidence* § 2195 (3d ed. 1940)
Cf. Thomas v. *Jones, supra*
Smith et al. v. *Jones, infra*
Restatement, Second, *Agency* § 103
2 Moore, *Federal Practice* 9.2 at 1162, footnote 15
Legislative History:
I Leg. Hist. 983 (1949)
II Leg. Hist. 1001 (1959)

17.13. In citations of single lines, the period is inserted at the end of each line.

17.14. If citations are run in, semicolons are used.

17.15. The following forms show punctuation and spacing required:

1. X Q.	4. R. X Q.	24. Q.	46th. Cross-int.
X Ques. 1.	Re X Q. 1.	24. Question.	46. Cross-int.
1. Add. direct.	R. X Int. 1.	X Q. 1.	46. Cross-ques.
2. R.D.Q.	X Int. 1.	24. Int.	46. C. Int.
3. R.R.D.Q.	X 20.	5 Re X Q.	46th. C. Int.
3. Re D.Q.	24. X.	Re-R. X Q. 5.	Answer to cross-int. 1.
2. Re-R.D.Q.		24th. Cross-ques.	Question 1.

17.16. When spelled out, use the following forms:

cross-examination
cross-interrogatory
re-cross-examination

redirect examination
re-direct examination

17.17. Brackets, not parentheses, are used (in transcripts, congressional hearings, testimony in courtwork, etc.) to enclose interpolations that are not specifically a part of the original quotation, corrections, explanations, omissions, editorial comments, or to caution that an error is reproduced literally.

17.18. If the entire sentence is in brackets, the punctuation should be within the brackets.

17.19. The following examples illustrate the use of brackets, other punctuation, and spacing. (See also rule 8.20.)

At end of sentence: [Laughter.]; within sentence: [laughter]
The paper was as follows [reads]:
I do not know. [Continues reading:]
The CHAIRMAN [to Mr. Smith].
Mr. KELLEY [to the chairman].
SEVERAL VOICES. Order!
The WITNESS. He did it that way [indicating].

By the COMMISSIONER:

Q. Do you know these men [handing witness a list]?
[Objected to.]
A. [After examining list.] Yes; I do.
Q. Did you see——A. No, sir.
Q. [Interrupting.] But why?—A. I really cannot say.
Q. What did you say?—A. It was the *City of Para.*
Q. The *City of* what? Did you say *Paris?*—A. No; I said *City*——
Q. Well, *Paris* or *Para;* it does not matter.

Question [continuing].
Answer [reads].

By Mr. SMITH:

17.20. In text, a parenthetic citation at the end of a sentence is included within the sentence unless it forms a sentence in itself or unless copy is specifically marked otherwise; but if a sentence contains more than one parenthetic reference, the one at the end is placed before the period.

This statement is made by the defendant. [See exhibit 1.]
This statement is made in the claimant's brief [p. 65].
This statement is made by the defendant [exhibit 1], but its accuracy is open to doubt [see exhibit 29].
That case has *not* been decided. [Italic ours.]

17.21. Only one cut-in is used in courtwork. Text matter that is an excerpt from law or a citation of language used as an argument and not a part of the brief proper is indented 3 ems on the left and separated from the preceding and following full-measure matter by 3 leads. Other matter that follows a colon is quoted.

17.22. Footnote matter following a colon does not indent. It is quoted and set full measure.

17.23. All footnotes in 12-point briefs are set 10-point leaded, and extracts in footnotes are set full measure and are quoted.

17.24. The following differences in capitalization and in the use of quotation marks should be noted:

The said paper was marked "Defendant's Exhibit No. 4" [exact title].
The defendant's exhibit No. 4 was thereupon placed on file.

17.25. The following capitalization is followed in all courtwork:

Circuit Court	Court of Appeals	Southern District
Circuit Court for the Southern District	Court of Customs and Patent Appeals	Sixth Circuit
Circuit Court of the United States for the Southern District of New York	Court of Claims	Superior Court
	District Court	Supreme Bench
	Emergency Court of Appeals	Tax Court
County Court	John Smith, U.S. marshal for the Northern District	

17.26. Unless otherwise indicated, covers and captions in briefs are single leaded at all times. Signatures are also single leaded, even in briefs set double leaded.

Supreme Court records

17.27. Paragraphs are made of answers in Q. and A. matter.

17.28. The folio number is flush in the same line as the first word of the folio and in a cut-in 3 ems square (unless there are 10 points of white space above or below). Indentions of paragraphs, etc., are in addition to the 3-em cut-in. In hanging indentions of headings the extra indention is carried to the end of the heading. (See p. 246.)

17.29. A cut-in folio is not used opposite a paragraph reading "Endorsement on cover."

17.30. Copy is followed literally, including capitalization (initial capitalization of words), punctuation (including compounding), and obscene language, but not italic.

17.31. Italic letters are used only to indicate errors in spelling (for example, *c*urely for surely), except in the names of persons and firms, in geographic names, and in foreign words that are not law terms. These and errors in syntax are not corrected. Roman letters are used to indicate errors in words set in italic.

17.32. In typewritten records manifest errors of the typewriter are corrected (for example, if one letter has been struck over another or if a space appears where a letter was obviously intended to be); but if a word is used in the wrong place (for example, *in* for *on; boot* for *boat*), it is not changed nor set in italic.

17.33. Words having the sanction of any dictionary are permissible, and the spelling is not changed.

17.34. An apostrophe is used to indicate the omission of one or more letters in a word; but in well-established abbreviations, the period is used instead of an apostrophe.

17.35. Doublets are indicated by italicizing the repeated words or lines.

17.36. A 3-em quad is used to indicate the omission of one or more words.

17.37. The names of vessels are set in roman, quoted.

17.38. The titles of cases are set in roman, including the abbreviation of *versus*.

17.39. The word *The* is capitalized in names of legal cases as follows:

> the said The B. & O. RR. Co.
> The Sun v. The Globe
> The City of Washington v. The B. & O. RR. Co.
> the defendant, The Davies County Bank

17.40. Printing Office editorial marks must be erased before the copy is returned to the originating office. Copy preparers should make only necessary marks thereon, and those lightly, with a soft pencil. Cut-in folios should not be indicated on copy. All instructions are entered on the preparer's instruction sheet. The folio numbers on copy are picked up. Any matter preceding or following an original folio is marked, in pencil, with the jacket number followed by lowercase letters (e.g., J. 12–345a, J. 12–345b, etc., to the end).

17.41. Preparers must indicate on the instruction sheet such information as 11-point type, solid or leaded, cut-in folios, etc.

17.42. The following abbreviations of the names of reporters are used in citations of U.S. Supreme Court Reports:

Name	*Abbreviation*
Cranch	Cranch
Dallas	Dall. or Dal.
Howard	How.
Peters	Pet.
U.S. Reports	U.S.
Wallace	Wall.
Wheaton	Wheat.

[Cover for briefs]

No. 49112

In the United States Court of Claims

OTIS THORNTON, INDIVIDUALLY, AND OTIS THORNTON
AS THE SURVIVING MEMBER OF AND IN BEHALF OF
BOSWELL-KAHN-THORNTON COMMISSION CO. AND
KAHN AND THORNTON COMMISSION CO., PLAINTIFF

v.

UNITED STATES OF AMERICA, DEFENDANT

BRIEF FOR THE UNITED STATES

HOLMES BALDRIDGE,
Assistant Attorney General,
ANDREW D. SHARPE,
ELLIS N. SLACK,
Special Assistants to the Attorney General,
JOHN A. REES, Jr.,
Attorney.

BREAKDOWN OF DISPLAY HEADS IN BRIEFS

Supreme Court

8-POINT IONIC CAPS

I

12-POINT SMALL CAPS

10-POINT SMALL CAPS

10-point lowercase italic

10-point lowercase

12-point lowercase italic (run-in sidehead)

Circuit courts

8-POINT IONIC CAPS [1]

I. 10-point Century bold lowercase, first up

A. 8-point Century bold lowercase, first up

1. 8-point Century bold lowercase italic, first up (with roman figure "1")

a. *12-point lowercase italic* (centered or run-in sidehead)

12-point lowercase (centered or run-in sidehead)

---

[1] Second Circuit, 10-point Century bold Caps.

[Cover for briefs]

No. 738

In the Supreme Court of the United States

OCTOBER TERM, 1966

BIG LAKE OIL COMPANY, PETITIONER
[3 leads]
v.
[3 leads]
D. B. HEINER, COLLECTOR OF INTERNAL REVENUE FOR THE TWENTY-THIRD DISTRICT OF PENNSYLVANIA

ON PETITION FOR WRIT OF CERTIORARI TO THE UNITED STATES COURT OF APPEALS FOR THE THIRD CIRCUIT

BRIEF FOR THE RESPONDENT IN OPPOSITION

[Caption for briefs]

In the Supreme Court of the United States

OCTOBER TERM, 1966

No. 738

BIG LAKE OIL COMPANY, PETITIONER
v.
D. B. HEINER, COLLECTOR OF INTERNAL REVENUE FOR THE TWENTY-THIRD DISTRICT OF PENNSYLVANIA

ON PETITION FOR WRIT OF CERTIORARI TO THE UNITED STATES COURT OF APPEALS FOR THE THIRD CIRCUIT

BRIEF FOR THE RESPONDENT IN OPPOSITION

In briefs, agencies may request ZIP Code numbers in a signature on cover and at end of brief.

JOHN SMITH,
Attorney,
Department of Justice,
Washington, D.C. 20530.

[Cover for Circuit Court briefs]

No. 11266

In the [1] United States Court of Appeals for the [1] Sixth Circuit

[Case number is carried at this point in captions over text]

NATIONAL LABOR RELATIONS BOARD, PETITIONER

v.

S. H. KRESS & COMPANY, RESPONDENT

ON PETITION FOR ENFORCEMENT OF AN ORDER OF THE NATIONAL LABOR RELATIONS BOARD [2]

BRIEF FOR THE NATIONAL LABOR RELATIONS BOARD [3]

GEORGE J. BOTT, [4]
General Counsel,
SAMUEL M. SINGER,
ROBERT G. JOHNSON,
Attorneys,
National Labor Relations Board.

To be argued by :
MARCEL MALLET-PREVOST,
Attorney. [5]

---

[1] "In the" and "for the" are not used in briefs for the Tenth Circuit, except for Tax Division briefs, in which these words are to be supplied. They are also to be supplied in briefs for all other circuit courts.
[2] In briefs for Second Circuit, set in 10-point italic.
[3] In briefs for Second Circuit, set in 12-point Century bold if one line and in 12-point Cheltenham bold condensed to avoid two lines.
[4] In briefs for Second Circuit, set name in 12-point caps and small caps and title in italic.
[5] In Second Circuit briefs, set in 12 point.

NOTES

1. Unless otherwise specified (see note 4), all courtwork is set 25 picas wide, 12-point double leaded, except briefs (including cover) which may be set 11-point single leaded to avoid excess length. Transcripts are set 11-point single leaded, including cover.
2. Indexes for 12-point briefs are set 10-point single leaded ; 11-point briefs, 8-point leaded.
3. Footnotes for 12-point briefs are set in 10 point ; 10-point briefs, 8 point ; and 11-point Supreme Court reports, 9 point.
4. Tenth Circuit briefs are set 30 picas wide.
5. Tables are set 8-point leaded, with 8-point solid boxheads.

[Cover for briefs]

BRIEF FOR RESPONDENT

United States Court of Appeals

FOR THE DISTRICT OF COLUMBIA CIRCUIT

No. 10530

IDAHO POWER COMPANY, PETITIONER

v.

FEDERAL POWER COMMISSION, RESPONDENT

ON PETITION TO REVIEW ORDERS OF THE FEDERAL POWER
COMMISSION

BRADFORD ROSS,
General Counsel,
WILLARD W. GATCHELL,
Assistant General Counsel,
JOHN C. MASON,
Attorney,
Counsel for Respondent,
Federal Power Commission, Washington, D.C.

EXAMPLES OF CUT-IN AND RUN-IN FOLIOS
(See rules 17.28–17.29)

11 In Supreme Court of District of Columbia

be considered, in justice and equity as a loss sustained by the corpo-
☐☐☐ration in producing or in preparing to produce pyrites.
25 The respondent says that the Secretary of the Interior did hear,
consider, and determine that question, and that he found as a
matter of fact that the Pratts were entitled to receive the * * *.

[224]☐LONNIE SMETHERS [Board witness].

[225] DIRECT EXAMINATION

[107]☐☐☐By Mr. SMITH:

[126]☐Q. Did you ever see Mr. Dougherty or Mr. Gullion come out?

Q. Then, it is your testimony, is it, that the time you got up, and the
machinery was shut down?—[109] A. Yes, sir.

Q. Yes; tell us about it?—A. We started out with a certain number, I
believe it was 12 packers * * * Gullion would [127] hire them * * *.

he had been doing in the past, and that was about where that con-
versa-[204]tion was left; and so far as the office employees are * * *.

In the United States Court of Customs and Patent Appeals

Patent Appeal No. 5648

IN RE HARKER H. HITTSON—IMPROVEMENT IN ROAD GRADER

BRIEF FOR THE COMMISSIONER OF PATENTS

W. W. COCHRAN,
Solicitor, U.S. Patent Office.

E. L. REYNOLDS,
Of Counsel.

SUPREME COURT OF THE UNITED STATES

No. 295.—OCTOBER TERM, 1960.

Colonel Henry S. Robertson, President, Army Review Board, Petitioner,

v.

Robert H. Chambers.

On Writ of Certiorari to the United States Court of Appeals for the District of Columbia Circuit.

[April 9, 1961.]

MR. JUSTICE DOUGLAS delivered the opinion of the Court.

Respondent, a former captain in the Army, was honorably discharged for physical disability and without retirement pay, as the result of a decision by an Army Retiring

[Court of Claims—Reports ¹²]

In the United States Court of Claims

No. 284–63

(Filed Oct. 24, 1966)

ANDREW ALFORD v. THE UNITED STATES

REPORT OF COMMISSIONER TO THE COURT*

Loren K. Olson, attorney of record for plaintiff. *Richard H. Speidel* and *Charles Hieken*, of counsel.

Michael T. Platt, with whom was *Assistant Attorney General John W. Douglas*, for defendant.

OPINION

LANE, *Commissioner:* This is a patent suit under Title 28 U.S.C. § 1498, in which plaintiff seeks to recover reasonable

*　　*　　*　　*　　*　　*　　*

Respectfully submitted,

[Supreme Court—Transcripts of record]

SUPREME COURT OF THE UNITED STATES

OCTOBER TERM, 1966

No. 439

JAMES C. DAVIS, DIRECTOR GENERAL OF RAILROADS, AND AGENT UNDER SECTION 206 OF TRANSPORTATION ACT OF 1920, PETITIONER

vs.

MRS. MAUDE E. GREEN, ADMINISTRATRIX OF THE ESTATE OF JESSE GREEN, DECEASED

ON PETITION FOR WRIT OF CERTIORARI TO THE SUPREME COURT OF THE STATE OF MISSISSIPPI

INDEX

[Set index in 8-point leaded]

---

*The opinion, findings of fact, and recommended conclusion of law are submitted under the order of reference and Rule 57(a).

¹ Decisions follow same general style.

² Footnotes and references are followed even if numbers are duplicated on same page. Place first footnote near reference, second footnote at bottom of page.

United States Court of Appeals
[3 leads]
FOR THE DISTRICT OF COLUMBIA CIRCUIT

No. 6430

ROBERT N. HARPER, APPELLANT
[3 leads]
v.
[3 leads]
AUGUSTUS P. CRENSHAW, JR., AND JO V. MORGAN, AS ADMINIS-
TRATORS OF THE ESTATE OF AUGUSTUS P. CRENSHAW, DECEASED;
GEORGE W. LIPSCOMB; ET AL.

Appeal from the United States District Court for the District of
Columbia

Argued October 16, 1937—Decided January 20, 1938

William C. Sullivan, of Washington, D.C., for appellant.
*George C. Gertman, Roger J. Whiteford, Arthur P. Drury, Hugh
Hay O'Bear, James O'D. Moran, A. Coulter Wells, W. N. Tobriner,
Leon Tobriner, Selig C. Brez, Benjamin S. Minor,* and *H. Prescott
Gatley,* all of Washington, D.C., for appellees.

Before MARTIN, Chief Justice, and ROBB, VAN ORSDEL, GRONER,
and STEPHENS, Associate Justices [1]

MARTIN, *Chief Justice:* This appeal is taken from an order and
decree of the lower court sustaining a motion to dismiss the bill of
complaint filed in that court by the appellant as plaintiff against
the various appellees as defendants.

In the bill the plaintiff, Harper, alleges in substance that * * *

*   *   *   *   *   *   *

Reversed and remanded.

A true copy.
Test: [2]

[2 slugs]
*Clerk, U.S. Court of Appeals
for the District of Columbia.*

---

[1] *C.J.* and *JJ.* when in copy.
[2] As in copy.

NOTE.—Headings will be prepared in accordance with this sample, and copy of opinion proper will be
followed literally, but titles of cases will be italicized, using roman "v." for *versus.* Quotations, which in the
copy are indented, will be set in 8 point, full measure, enclosed in quotation marks if so in copy. Do not
cut or mutilate copy in any way.

[Opinions—Circuit Courts of Appeals, all circuits]

UNITED STATES COURT OF APPEALS FOR THE [1] FOURTH CIRCUIT

No. 3747

THE UNITED STATES OF AMERICA, APPELLANT
[3 leads]
v.
[3 leads]
LOUISE EARWOOD, AS GUARDIAN OF THOMAS CALEB EARWOOD AND MAE EARWOOD, APPELLEES

Appeal from the District Court of the United States for the Southern District of West Virginia, at Huntington. At law

Argued January 14, 1938—Decided April 2, 1938 [2]

March 22, 1938 [2]

Before NORTHCOTT and SOPER, Circuit Judges, and GLENN, District Judge

Mr. *W. N. Ivie*, U.S. Attorney (Mr. *Cleveland Cabler*, Regional Attorney, Veterans' Bureau, and Mr. *G. T. Sullis*, Assistant U.S. Attorney, were with him on the brief), for appellant.
Mr. *W. R. Donham* and Mr. *W. W. Shepherd* filed brief for appellees.

Opinion of the court [3]

NORTHCOTT, *Circuit Judge:* This is an action at law brought in the District Court of the United States for the Southern District of West

*　　　*　　　*　　　*　　　*　　　*　　　*

The judgment is reversed and the cause is remanded for further and not inconsistent proceedings.

Affirmed.

A true copy.
Teste: [2]

[Two slugs]
*Clerk of the U.S. Circuit Court of
Appeals for the Fourth Circuit.*

---

[1] Supply "for the" when not in copy
[2] As in copy.
[3] Do not supply if not in copy.

18. USEFUL TABLES

GEOLOGIC TERMS

[With suggestions by U.S. Geological Survey]

For capitalization, compounding, and use of quotations in geologic terms, copy is to be followed. The list below exemplifies common usage of both rock and time terms. The term *red beds* has been used to designate certain rocks of mixed lithologic character that are predominantly red; as a unit modifier the use should be *red-bed*. The terms lower, middle, and upper (referring to rocks) are capitalized only as indicated in the list (Upper Devonian, lower Tertiary, lower Paleozoic); similarly, the terms early, middle, and late (referring to time) are capitalized only as indicated. A formal geologic term is capitalized: Devonian System, Pliocene Series, San Rafael Group, Morrison Formation, Fayetteville Shale, Wedington Sandstone Member, Wisconsin Glaciation, Tazewell Stade. (Geologic terms quoted verbatim from published material should be left as the original author used them; however, it should be made clear that the usage is that of the original author.) A structural term such as arch, anticline, syncline, dome, uplift, or basin is not capitalized even if preceded by a name: Cincinnati arch, Cedar Creek anticline, Ozark uplift, Michigan basin. (A physiographic term that is preceded by a name is capitalized: Bighorn Basin, Half Dome.)

Alexandrian	glacial:	Mississippian:	Permian:
Animikie	interglacial	Upper, Late	Upper, Late
Atoka	postglacial	Lower, Early	Lower, Early
Belt	preglacial	Missouri	Pleistocene
Cambrian:	Glenarm	Mohawkian	Pliocene:
Upper, Late	Grand Canyon	Morrow	upper, late
Middle, Middle	Grenville	Niagara	middle, middle
Lower, Early	Guadalupe	Ochoa	lower, early
Carboniferous	Gulf	Ocoee	Precambrian:
Systems	Gunnison River	Oligocene:	upper
Cayuga	Holocene	upper, late	middle
Cenozoic	Jurassic:	middle, middle	lower
Cincinnatian	Upper, Late	lower, early	Quaternary
Chester	Middle, Middle	Osage	red beds
Coahuila	Lower, Early	Ordovician:	Shasta
Comanche	Keweenawan	Upper, Late	Silurian:
Cretaceous:	Kinderhook	Middle, Middle	Upper, Late
Upper, Late	Leonard	Lower, Early	Middle, Middle
Lower, Early	Little Willow	Pahrump	Lower, Early
Des Moines	Llano	Paleocene:	St. Croixan
Devonian:	Meramec	upper, late	Tertiary
Upper, Late	Mesozoic:	middle, middle	Triassic:
Middle, Middle	pre-Mesozoic	lower, early	Upper, Late
Lower, Early	post-Mesozoic	Paleozoic	Middle, Middle
Eocene:	Miocene:	Pennsylvanian:	Lower, Early
upper, late	upper, late	Upper, Late	Virgil
middle, middle	middle, middle	Middle, Middle	Wolfcamp
lower, early	lower, early	Lower, Early	Yavapai

PHYSIOGRAPHIC TERMS

[With suggestions by U.S. Geological Survey]

The following table lists physical divisions of the United States approved by the Association of American Geographers and should be used as a guide to capitalization. The general terms *province* and *section*, used in the common-noun sense, are not capitalized; the other terms are proper names and are therefore capitalized.

CHAPTER 18

PHYSICAL DIVISIONS OF THE UNITED STATES

Major division	Province	Section
Laurentian Upland	Superior Upland	
Atlantic Plain	Continental Shelf	
	Coastal Plain	Embayed section.
		Sea Island section.
		Floridian section.
		East Gulf Coastal Plain.
		Mississippi Alluvial Plain.
		West Gulf Coastal Plain.
Appalachian Highlands	Piedmont province	Piedmont Upland.
		Piedmont Lowland.
	Blue Ridge province	Northern; Southern section.
	Valley and Ridge province	Tennessee section.
		Middle section.
		Hudson Valley.
	St. Lawrence Valley	Champlain section.
		Northern section.
	Appalachian Plateaus	Mohawk section.
		Catskill section.
		Southern New York section.
		Allegheny Mountain section.
		Kanawha section.
		Cumberland Plateau.
		Cumberland Mountain section.
	New England province	Seaboard Lowland.
		New England Upland.
		White Mountain section.
		Green Mountain section.
		Taconic section.
	Adirondack province	
Interior Plains	Interior Low Plateaus	Highland Rim.
		Lexington Plain.
		Nashville Basin.
	Central Lowland	Eastern lake section.
		Western lake section.
		Wisconsin Driftless section.
		Till Plains.
		Dissected Till Plains.
		Osage Plains.
	Great Plains	Missouri Plateau, glaciated.
		Missouri Plateau, unglaciated.
		Black Hills.
		High Plains.
		Plains Border.
		Colorado Piedmont.
		Raton section.
		Pecos Valley.
		Edwards Plateau.
		Central Texas section.
Interior Highlands	Ozark Plateaus	Springfield-Salem Plateaus.
		Boston "Mountains."
	Ouachita province	Arkansas Valley.
		Ouachita Mountains.
Rocky Mountain System	Southern Rocky Mountain	
	Wyoming Basin	
	Middle Rocky Mountains	
	Northern Rocky Mountains	
Intermontane Plateaus	Columbia Plateaus	Walla Walla Plateau.
		Blue Mountain section.
		Payette section.
		Snake River Plain.
		Harney section.
	Colorado Plateaus	High Plateaus of Utah.
		Uinta Basin.
		Canyon Lands.
		Navajo section.
		Grand Canyon section.
		Datil section.
	Basin and Range province	Great Basin.
		Sonoran Desert.
		Salton Trough.
		Mexican Highland.
		Sacramento section.
Pacific Mountain System	Sierra-Cascade Mountains	Northern Cascade Mountains.
		Middle Cascade Mountains.
		Southern Cascade Mountains.
		Sierra Nevada.
	Pacific Border province	Puget Trough.
		Olympic Mountains.
		Oregon Coast Range.
		Klamath Mountains.
		California Trough.
		California Coast Ranges.
		Los Angeles Ranges.
	Lower Californian province	

PRINCIPAL AND GUIDE MERIDIANS AND BASE LINES OF THE UNITED STATES

First, second, etc., standard parallel.
First, second, etc., guide meridian.
First, second, etc., principal meridian.
Auxiliary (first, second, etc.) meridian.
Ashley Guide Meridian. (Utah)
Beaverhead Guide Meridian. (Montana)
Belt Mountain Guide Meridian. (Montana)
Big Hole Guide Meridian. (Montana)
Bitterroot Guide Meridian. (Montana)
Black Hills base line. (South Dakota)
Black Hills Guide Meridian. (South Dakota)
Boise Meridian. (Idaho)
Boulder Guide Meridian. (Montana)
Browning Guide Meridian. (Montana)
Buffalo Creek Guide Meridian. (Montana)
Carson River Guide Meridian. (Nevada)
Castle Valley Guide Meridian. (Utah)
Chickasaw Meridian. (Mississippi)
Choctaw base line. (Mississippi)
Choctaw Meridian. (Mississippi)
Cimarron Meridian. (Oklahoma)
Colorado Guide Meridian. (Utah)
Columbia Guide Meridian. (Washington)
Colville Guide Meridian. (Washington)
Copper River Meridian. (Alaska)
Coulson Guide Meridian. (Montana)
Deer Lodge Guide Meridian. (Montana)
Deschutes Meridian. (Oregon)
Emery Valley Guide Meridian. (Utah)
Fairbanks Meridian. (Alaska)
Flathead Guide Meridian. (Montana)
Fort Belknap Guide Meridian. (Montana)
Fremont Valley Guide Meridian. (Utah)
Gila and Salt River Meridian. (Arizona)
Grand River Guide Meridian. (Utah)
Grande Ronde Guide Meridian. (Oregon)
Green River Guide Meridian. (Utah)
Haystack Butte Guide Meridian. (Montana)
Helena Guide Meridian. (Montana)
Henry Mountain Guide Meridian. (Utah)
Horse Plains Guide Meridian. (Montana)
Humboldt Meridian. (California)
Humboldt River Guide Meridian. (Nevada)
Huntsville Meridian. (Alabama-Mississippi)
Indian Meridian. (Oklahoma)
Jefferson Guide Meridian. (Montana)
Judith Guide Meridian. (Montana)

Kanab Guide Meridian. (Utah)
Kolob Guide Meridian. (Utah)
Little Porcupine Guide Meridian. (Montana)
Louisiana Meridian. (Louisiana)
Maginnis Guide Meridian. (Montana)
Michigan Meridian. (Michigan-Ohio)
Mount Diablo base line. (California-Nevada)
Mount Diablo Meridian. (California-Nevada)
Musselshell Guide Meridian. (Montana)
Navajo base line. (Arizona-New Mexico)
Navajo Meridian. (Arizona-New Mexico)
New Mexico Guide Meridian. (New Mexico-Colorado)
New Mexico Principal Meridian. (New Mexico-Colorado)
Panguitch Guide Meridian. (Utah)
Passamari Guide Meridian. (Montana)
Pine Valley Guide Meridian. (Utah)
Principal Meridian. (Montana)
Red Rock Guide Meridian. (Montana)
Reese River Guide Meridian. (Nevada)
Ruby Valley Guide Meridian. (Nevada)
St. Helena Meridian. (Louisiana)
St. Stephens base line. (Alabama-Mississippi)
St. Stephens Meridian. (Alabama-Mississippi)
Salt Lake Meridian. (Utah)
San Bernardino base line. (California)
San Bernardino Meridian. (California)
Sevier Lake Guide Meridian. (Utah)
Seward Meridian. (Alaska)
Shields River Guide Meridian. (Montana)
Smith River Guide Meridian. (Montana)
Snake Valley Guide Meridian. (Utah)
Square Butte Guide Meridian. (Montana)
Sweet Grass Guide Meridian. (Montana)
Tallahassee Meridian. (Florida)
Teton Guide Meridian. (Montana)
Uinta Special Meridian. (Utah)
Ute Principal Meridian. (Colorado)
Valley Creek Guide Meridian. (Montana)
Wah Wah Guide Meridian. (Utah)
Washington Meridian. (Mississippi)
Willamette Meridian. (Oregon-Washington)
Willow Springs Guide Meridian. (Utah)
Wind River Meridian. (Wyoming)
Yantic Guide Meridian. (Montana)
Yellowstone Guide Meridian. (Montana)

PRINCIPAL FOREIGN COUNTRIES, TITLES OF CHIEFS OF STATE, NAMES OF LEGISLATIVE BODIES, ETC., AS OF MARCH 1983

[With suggestions by the Department of State and the Board on Geographic Names]

Country	Chief of state	Legislative body	Form of government	Capital
Afghanistan	King	Revolutionary Council; Council of Ministers	Democratic Republic	Kabul (Kabul).
Albania	President of the Presidium	People's Assembly (unicameral)	People's Republic	Tirana (Tiranë).
Algeria	President	National Assembly (suspended)	Republic	Algiers.
Andorra	Bishop of Urgel (Spain). President of the French Republic.	General Council of the Valleys (unicameral)	Coprincipality	Andorra.
Angola	President	National Assembly (planned)	People's Republic	Luanda.
Antigua and Barbuda	Queen represented by Governor General.	Parliament	Parliamentary State	Saint Johns.
Argentina	President	National Congress: Senate, Chamber of Deputies (dissolved).	Republic	Buenos Aires.
Australia	Queen represented by Governor General.	Federal Parliament: Senate, House of Representatives.	Commonwealth	Canberra.
Austria	President	Parliament: Federal Council (Bundesrat), National Council (Nationalrat).	Federal Republic	Vienna (Wien).
Bahamas, The	Queen represented by Governor General.	Parliament: Senate, House of Assembly	Commonwealth	Nassau.
Bahrain	King	None	Traditional Monarchy	Manama.
Bangladesh	President	Constituent Assembly (unicameral)	Republic	Dacca.
Barbados	Queen represented by Governor General.	Parliament: Senate, House of Assembly	Parliamentary State	Bridgetown.
Belgium	King	Parliament: Senate, Chamber of Representatives.	Constitutional Monarchy	Brussels (Bruxelles, Brussel).
Belize	Queen represented by Governor General.	National Assembly: Senate, House of Representatives.	Parliamentary State	Belmopan.
Benin (formerly Dahomey)	President	National Revolutionary Assembly	Military (Revolutionary Assembly).	Porto-Novo.
Bhutan	King	National Assembly (unicameral)	Monarchy	Thimphu; Paro, administrative capital.
Bolivia	President	Congress: Senate, Chamber of Deputies	Republic	Sucre, legal capital; La Paz, seat of government.
Botswana	do	National Assembly (unicameral)	do	Gaborone.
Brazil	do	Congress: Senate, Chamber of Deputies	Federative Republic	Brasilia.
Bulgaria	President of the Presidium	National Assembly (unicameral)	People's Republic	Sofia (Sofiya).
Burma	President	People's Assembly (unicameral)	Socialist Republic	Rangoon.
Burundi	do	None	Republic	Bujumbura.
Cameroon	do	National Assembly (unicameral)	do	Yaounde.
Canada	Queen represented by Governor General.	Parliament: Senate, House of Commons.	Parliamentary State	Ottawa.
Cape Verde	President	National Assembly (unicameral)	Republic	Praia.
Central African Republic	do	National Assembly (unicameral) (dissolved).	do	Bangui.
Ceylon (see Sri Lanka).				
Chad	do	National Assembly (dissolved)	do	N'Djamena.
Chile	do	National Congress (dissolved)	do	Santiago.
China	Chairman, National People's Congress.	National People's Congress	People's Republic	Beijing.
Colombia	President	Congress: Senate, House of Representatives	Republic	Bogotá.
Comoros	do	None	do	Moroni.

Country	Head of State	Legislature	Form of Government	Capital
Congo	President	Council of State	People's Republic	Brazzaville.
Costa Rica	do	Legislative Assembly (unicameral)	do	San José.
Cuba	do	National Assembly of People's Power	Socialist Republic	Havana (La Habana).
Cyprus	do	House of Representatives (unicameral)	Republic	Nicosia.
Czechoslovakia	do	Federal Assembly: Chamber of the People, Chamber of the Nations.	Socialist Republic	Prague.
Dahomey (see Benin).				
Denmark	King	Parliament	Constitutional Monarchy	Copenhagen.
Djibouti	President	Parliament: Chamber of Deputies (unicameral)	Republic	Djibouti.
Dominica	do	House of Assembly (unicameral)	Commonwealth	Roseau.
Dominican Republic	do	Congress: Senate, Chamber of Deputies	Republic	Santo Domingo.
Ecuador	do	National Congress (unicameral)	do	Quito.
Egypt	do	People's Assembly (unicameral)	do	Cairo.
El Salvador	do	Constituent Assembly	do	San Salvador.
Equatorial Guinea	do	Legislature (suspended)	Republic	Malabo.
Estonia [1]	Head of State	Parliament (dissolved)	do	Tallinn.
Ethiopia	do	Parliament: Senate, House of Representatives.	Military	Addis Ababa.
Fiji	Queen (represented by Governor-General).		Parliamentary State	Suva.
Finland	President	Parliament (Eduskunta) (unicameral)	Republic	Helsinki.
France	do	Parliament: Senate, National Assembly	do	Paris.
Gabon	do	National Assembly (unicameral)	do	Libreville.
Gambia, The	do	House of Representatives (unicameral)	do	Banjul.
German Democratic Republic.	Chairman, Council of State.	People's Chamber (unicameral)	Socialist Republic	East Berlin. [3]
Germany, Federal Republic of [2]	do	Parliament: Federal Council (Bundesrat), Federal Assembly (Bundestag).	Federal Republic	Bonn.
Ghana	President (suspended)	Parliament (unicameral)	Republic	Accra.
Greece	President	Parliament (Vouli) (unicameral) (suspended)	Parliamentary Republic.	Athens.
Grenada	Queen (represented by Governor-General).	Parliament (suspended)	Commonwealth	Saint Georges.
Guatemala	President	Congress (unicameral)	Republic	Guatemala.
Guinea	do	National Assembly (unicameral)	do	Conakry.
Guinea-Bissau	do	National People's Assembly (dissolved).	do	Bissau.
Guyana	do	Parliament: National Assembly (unicameral).	do	Georgetown.
Haiti	do	Legislative Chamber (unicameral)	do	Port-au-Prince.
Honduras	President of the Presidential Council.	Congress (unicameral)	do	Tegucigalpa.
Hungary	President	National Assembly (unicameral)	People's Republic	Budapest.
Iceland	President	Parliament (Althing): Upper Chamber (Efi Deild), Lower Chamber (Neore Deild).	Republic	Reykjavik.
India	do	Parliament: Council of States (Rajya Sabha), House of the People (Lok Sabha).	do	New Delhi.
Indonesia	do	Parliament: People's Consultative Assembly	do	Jakarta.
Iran	President	Parliament (Majlis) (unicameral)	Islamic Republic	Tehran.
Iraq	do	Revolutionary Command Council	Republic	Baghdad.
Ireland	do	National Parliament (Oireachtas): Senate (Seaned Eireann), House of Representatives (Dail Eireann).	do	Dublin.
Israel	do	Parliament (Knesset) (unicameral)	do	Tel Aviv. [4]
Italy	do	Parliament: Senate, Chamber of Deputies.	do	Rome.
Ivory Coast	do	National Assembly (unicameral)	do	Abidjan.
Jamaica	Queen (represented by Governor-General).	Parliament: Senate, House of Representatives.	Parliamentary State	Kingston.
Japan	Emperor	Diet: House of Councillors, House of Representatives.	Constitutional Monarchy	Tokyo.

PRINCIPAL FOREIGN COUNTRIES, TITLES OF CHIEFS OF STATE, NAMES OF LEGISLATIVE BODIES, ETC., AS OF MARCH 1983—Continued

[With suggestions by the Department of State and the Board on Geographic Names]

Country	Chief of state	Legislative body	Form of government	Capital
Jordan	King	National Assembly: Senate, Chamber of Deputies		Amman.
Kampuchea				Phnom Penh.
Kenya	President	National Assembly (unicameral)	Republic	Nairobi.
Kiribati	do	Parliament (unicameral)	do	Tarawa.
Korea, North	do	Supreme People's Assembly	People's Republic	Pyongyang.
Korea, South	do	National Assembly (unicameral)	Republic	Seoul.
Kuwait	Amir	do	Constitutional Monarchy	Kuwait.
Laos	President	Supreme People's Assembly	People's Republic	Vientiane.
Latvia [1]			Republic	Riga (Riga).
Lebanon	President	Chamber of Deputies (unicameral)	do	Beirut.
Lesotho	King	Parliament: Senate, National Assembly (dissolved).	Constitutional Monarchy	Maseru.
Liberia	President	Congress: Senate, House of Representatives (dissolved)	Republic	Monrovia.
Libya	Chief of State	General Peoples' Congress	do	Tripoli.[5]
Liechtenstein	Prince	Diet (unicameral)	Constitutional Monarchy	Vaduz.
Lithuania[1]			Republic	Kaunas.
Luxembourg	Grand Duke	Parliament: Chamber of Deputies, Council of State.	Constitutional Monarchy	Luxembourg.
Madagascar	President	National Popular Assembly	Republic	Antananarivo.
Malawi	do	National Assembly (unicameral)	do	Lilongwe.
Malaysia	Paramount Ruler	Parliament: Senate, House of Representatives.	Constitutional Monarchy	Kuala Lumpur.
Maldives, Republic of the	President	National Legislature (Majlis) (unicameral)	Republic	Male.
Mali	do	National Assembly (unicameral)	do	Bamako.
Malta	do	House of Representatives (unicameral).	do	Valletta.
Mauritania	do	National Assembly (unicameral) dissolved	Islamic Republic	Nouakchott.
Mauritius	Queen	Legislative Assembly (unicameral).	Parliamentary State.	Port Louis.
Mexico	President	Congress: Chamber of Deputies	Federal Republic	Mexico (Ciudad de México).
Monaco	Prince	National Council (unicameral)	Constitutional Monarchy	Monaco.
Mongolia	Chairman, Presidium, People's Great Hural.	People's Great Hural (National Assembly) (unicameral)	People's Republic	Ulaanbaatar.
Morocco	King	Legislature (unicameral)	Constitutional Monarchy	Rabat.
Mozambique	President	People's Assembly (unicameral)	People's Republic	Maputo.
Nauru	do	Parliament (unicameral)	Republic	Yaren.
Nepal	King	National Assembly (Panchayat) (unicameral)	Constitutional Monarchy	Katmandu.
Netherlands	Queen	States-General: First-Chamber, Second-Chamber.	do	Capital, Amsterdam. Seat of government, The Hague.
New Zealand	Queen (represented by Governor General).	Parliament: House of Representatives (unicameral)	Parliamentary State	Wellington.
Nicaragua	Coordinator, Junta of the Government of National Reconstruction.	Congress: Senate, Chamber of Deputies (suspended)	Republic	Managua.
Niger	President	National Assembly (unicameral) (suspended)	do	Niamey.
Nigeria	do	Parliament: Senate, House of Representatives.	Federal Republic	Lagos.
Norway	King	Parliament (Storting: Lagting, Odelsting[4]	Constitutional Monarchy	Oslo.
Oman	Sultan	Absolute Monarchy	Sultanate.[6]	Muscat.
Pakistan	President (suspended)	Parliament: Senate, National Assembly (suspended).	Islamic Republic	Islamabad.
Panama	President	Legislature (unicameral).	Republic	Panama.

Country	Chief of State	Legislature	Form of State	Capital
Papua New Guinea	Queen (represented by Governor General)	Parliament (unicameral)	Parliamentary State	Port Moresby
Paraguay	President	Congress: Senate, Chamber of Deputies	Republic	Asuncion
Peru	do.	do.	do.	Lima
Philippines	President	National Assembly (unicameral)	Republic	Manila
Poland	President of Council of State	Parliament (Sejm) (unicameral)	People's Republic	Warsaw
Portugal	President	Assembly of the Republic (unicameral)	Republic	Lisbon
Qatar	Amir	Advisory Council	Traditional Emirate	Doha
Romania	President of Council of State	Grand National Assembly (unicameral)	Socialist Republic	Bucharest
Rwanda	President	National Assembly (unicameral)	Republic	Kigali
Saint Lucia	Queen (represented by Governor General)	Parliament: Senate, House of Assembly	Parliamentary State	Castries
Saint Vincent and the Grenadines	do.	House of Assembly (unicameral)	do.	Kingstown
San Marino	Captains-Regent	Grand and General Council (unicameral)	Republic	San Marino
Sao Tome and Principe	President	National Popular Assembly (unicameral)	do.	Sao Tome
Saudi Arabia	King	Absolute Monarchy	Monarchy	Riyadh
Senegal	President	National Assembly (unicameral)	Republic	Dakar
Seychelles	do.	People's Assembly (unicameral)	do.	Victoria
Sierra Leone	do.	House of Representatives (unicameral)	do.	Freetown
Singapore	do.	Parliament (unicameral)	do.	Singapore
Solomon Islands	Queen (represented by Governor General)	Legislative Assembly (unicameral)	Parliamentary State	Honiara
Somalia	President	National Assembly	Republic	Mogadishu
South Africa	do.	Parliament: Senate, House of Assembly	do.	Pretoria. Legislative capital, Capetown.
Spain [7]	King	Cortes: Senate, Congress of Deputies	Monarchy	Madrid
Sri Lanka	President	Parliament (unicameral)	Republic	Colombo
Sudan	do.	People's Assembly (unicameral)	do.	Khartoum
Suriname	do.	Parliament (unicameral)	do.	Paramaribo
Swaziland	King	House of Assembly, Senate	Constitutional Monarchy	Mbabane
Sweden	do.	Parliament (Riksdag) (unicameral)	do.	Stockholm
Switzerland	President	Federal Assembly (Bundesversammlung): Council of States (Standerat), National Council (Nationalrat)	Confederation	Bern
Syria	do.	People's Council	Republic	Damascus
Tanzania	do.	National Assembly (unicameral)	do.	Dar es Salaam
Thailand	King	do.	Constitutional Monarchy	Bangkok
Togo	President	National Assembly (unicameral)	Republic	Lomé
Tonga	King	Legislative Assembly (unicameral)	Constitutional Monarchy	Nuku'alofa
Trinidad and Tobago	President	Parliament: Senate, House of Representatives	Parliamentary State	Port-of-Spain
Tunisia	do.	National Assembly (unicameral)	Republic	Tunis
Turkey	do.	Grand National Assembly: Senate of the Republic, National Assembly	do.	Ankara
Tuvalu	Queen (represented by Governor General)	House of Assembly (unicameral)	Parliamentary State	Funafuti
Uganda	President	National Assembly (unicameral)	do.	Kampala
Union of Soviet Socialist Republics	Chairman of the Presidium of Supreme Soviet	Supreme Soviet: Soviet of the Union, Soviet of Nationalities	Federation of Soviet Republics	Moscow
United Arab Emirates	President	Supreme Council of Rulers; National Assembly	Federation of Emirates	Abu Dhabi
United Kingdom	Queen	Parliament: House of Lords, House of Commons	Constitutional Monarchy	London
Upper Volta	President	National Assembly (unicameral)	Republic	Ouagadougou
Uruguay	President	General Assembly: Senate, Chamber of Deputies (suspended)	do.	Montevideo
Vanuatu	Prime Minister	Representative Assembly (unicameral)	do.	

PRINCIPAL FOREIGN COUNTRIES, TITLES OF CHIEFS OF STATE, NAMES OF LEGISLATIVE BODIES, ETC., AS OF MARCH 1983—Continued

[With suggestions by the Department of State and the Board on Geographic Names]

Country	Chief of state	Legislative body	Form of government	Capital
Vatican City	Pope	None	Papacy	Vatican City.
Venezuela	President	Congress: Senate, Chamber of Deputies	Republic	Caracas.
Vietnam	do	None	Socialist Republic	Hanoi.
Western Samoa	Head of State	Legislative Assembly	Constitutional Monarchy	Apia.
Yemen (Aden)	Chairman, Supreme People's Council	Supreme People's Council	Republic	Aden.
Yemen (Sanaa)	President	Assembly, Republican Council (suspended)	do	Sanaa.
Yugoslavia	Presidium	Assembly: Federal Council, Council of the Republic and Provinces	Federal Socialist Republic	Belgrade.
Zaire	do	Legislative Council (unicameral)	Republic	Kinshasa.
Zambia	do	National Assembly (unicameral)	do	Lusaka.
Zimbabwe	do	Parliament: Senate, House of Assembly	Parliamentary State	Harare.

[1] The United States has not recognized the Soviet regime in Estonia, Lativa, and Lithuania. [2] In this table, the items in the entry for Germany apply to the Federal Republic of Germany, the government established in Western Germany. This government achieved sovereignty on May 5, 1955, under terms of the Paris treaties. The government for Berlin functions in the American, British, and French sectors of occupation of Berlin, under authority of the Allied Kommandatura. [3] The GDR has located the seat of its government in the Eastern Sector of Berlin. However, Greater Berlin, including all four occupied sections, retains its Four Power juridical status. [4] In 1950, the Israel Parliament Proclaimed Jerusalem as the capital. The United States does not recognize Jerusalem as the capital and the U.S. Embassy continues to be located in Tel Aviv. [5] Officially Banghaz is a co-capital, but there are no central government operations there at the present time. [6] No accurate English equivalents. [7] The Law of Succession, July 27, 1947, declared that Spain was constituted a Kingdom.

NOUNS AND ADJECTIVES DENOTING NATIONALITY

[Revised with suggestions by the Department of State]

Country or region	Noun (plural ending in parentheses)	Adjective
Afghanistan	Afghan(s)	Afghan.
Albania	Albanian(s)	Albanian.
Algeria	Algerian(s)	Algerian.
Andorra	Andorran(s)	Andorran.
Angola	Angolan(s)	Angolan.
Antigua and Barbuda	Antiguan(s)	Antiguan.
Argentina	Argentine(s)	Argentine.
Australia	Australian(s)	Australian.
Austria	Austrian(s)	Austrian.
Bahamas, The	Bahamian(s)	Bahamian.
Bahrain (State of)	Bahraini(s)	Bahraini.
Bangladesh	Bangladeshi(s)	Bangladesh.
Barbados	Barbadian(s)	Barbadian.
Belgium	Belgian(s)	Belgian.
Belize	Belizean(s)	Belizean.
Benin	Beninese (singular, plural)	Beninese.
Bermuda	Bermudan(s)	Bermudan.
Bhutan	Bhutanese (singular, plural)	Bhutanese.
Bolivia	Bolivian(s)	Bolivian.
Botswana	Motswana (singular), Botswana (plural).	Botswana.
Brazil	Brazilian(s)	Brazilian.
Brunei	Bruneian(s)	Bruneian.
Bulgaria	Bulgarian(s)	Bulgarian.
Burma	Burman(s)	Burmese.
Burundi	Burundian(s)	Burundi.
Cameroon	Cameroonian(s)	Cameroonian.
Canada	Canadian(s)	Canadian.
Cape Verde	Cape Verdean(s)	Cape Verdean.
Central African Republic	Central African(s)	Central African.
Chad	Chadian(s)	Chadian.
Chile	Chilean(s)	Chilean.
China	Chinese (singular, plural)	Chinese.
Colombia	Colombian(s)	Colombian.
Comoro Islands	Comoran(s)	Comoran.
Congo	Congolese (singular, plural)	Congolese or Congo.
Cook Islands	Cook Islander(s)	Cook Islander.
Costa Rica	Costa Rican(s)	Costa Rican.
Cuba	Cuban(s)	Cuban.
Cyprus	Cypriot(s)	Cypriot.
Czechoslovakia	Czechoslovak(s)	Czechoslovak.
Denmark	Dane(s)	Danish.
Djibouti	Afar(s), Issa(s)	Afar, Issa.
Dominica	Dominican(s)	Dominican.
Dominican Republic	....do....	Do.
Ecuador	Ecuadorean(s)	Ecuadorean.
Egypt	Egyptian(s)	Egyptian.
El Salvador	Salvadoran(s)	Salvadoran.
Equatorial Guinea	Equatorial Guinean(s)	Equatorial Guinean.
Estonia	Estonian(s)	Estonian.
Ethiopia	Ethiopian(s)	Ethiopian.
Falkland Islands	Falkland Islander(s)	Falkland Island.
Faroe Islands	Faroese (singular, plural)	Faroese.
Fiji	Fijian(s)	Fijian.
Finland	Finn(s)	Finnish.
France	Frenchman(men)	French.
French Guiana	French Guianese (singular, plural)	French Guiana.
French Polynesia	French Polynesian(s)	French Polynesian.
Gabon	Gabonese (singular, plural)	Gabonese.
Gambia, Republic of The	Gambian(s)	Gambian.
German Democratic Republic	German(s)	German.
Germany, Federal Republic of	German(s)	German.
Ghana	Ghanaian(s)	Ghanaian.
Gibraltar	Gibraltarian(s)	Gibraltar.
Greece	Greek(s)	Greek.
Greenland	Greenlander(s)	Greenlandic.
Grenada	Grenadian(s)	Grenadian.
Guadeloupe	Guadeloupian(s)	Guadeloupe.
Guatemala	Guatemalan(s)	Guatemalan.
Guinea	Guinean(s)	Guinea.
Guinea-Bissau	Guinean(s)	Guinean.
Guyana	Guyanese (singular, plural)	Guyanese.
Haiti	Haitian(s)	Haitian.
Honduras	Honduran(s)	Honduran.
Hong Kong		Hong Kong.
Hungary	Hungarian(s)	Hungarian.
Iceland	Icelander(s)	Icelandic.
India	Indian(s)	Indian.
Indonesia	Indonesian(s)	Indonesian.
Iran	Iranian(s)	Iranian.
Iraq	Iraqi(s)	Iraqi.
Ireland	Irishman(men), Irish (collective, plural).	Irish.

NOUNS AND ADJECTIVES DENOTING NATIONALITY—Continued

[Revised with suggestions by the Department of State]

Country or region	Noun (plural ending in parentheses)	Adjective
Israel	Israeli(s)	Israeli.
Italy	Italian(s)	Italian.
Ivory Coast	Ivorian(s)	Ivorain.
Jamaica	Jamaican(s)	Jamaican.
Japan	Japanese (singular, plural)	Japanese.
Jordan	Jordanian(s)	Jordanian.
Kampuchea	Kampuchean(s)	Kampuchean
Kenya	Kenyan(s)	Kenyan.
Khmer Republic	Cambodian(s) or Khmer (singular, plural).	Cambodian or Khmer.
Kiribati	Kiribatian(s)	Kiribati
Korea	Korean(s)	Korean.
Kuwait	Kuwait(s)	Kuwaiti.
Laos	Lao or Laotian (singular), Laotians (plural).	Lao or Laotian.
Latvia	Latvian(s)	Latvian.
Lebanon	Lebanese (singular, plural)	Lebanese.
Lesotho	Masotho (singular), Basotho (plural)	Basotho.
Liberia	Liberian(s)	Liberian.
Libya	Libyan(s)	Libyan.
Liechtenstein	Liechtensteiner(s)	Liechtenstein.
Lithuania	Lithuanian(s)	Lithuanian.
Luxembourg	Luxembourger(s)	Luxembourg.
Macau	Macanese (singular, plural)	Macau.
Madagascar	Malagasy (singular, plural)	Malagasy.
Malawi	Malawian(s)	Malawian.
Malaysia	Malaysian(s)	Malaysian.
Maldives	Maldivian(s)	Maldivian.
Mali	Malian(s)	Malian.
Malta	Maltese (singular, plural)	Maltese.
Martinique	Martiniquais (singular, plural)	Martiniquais
Mauritania	Mauritanian(s)	Mauritanian.
Mauritius	Mauritian(s)	Mauritian.
Mexico	Mexican(s)	Mexican.
Monaco	Monacan(s), Monegasque(s)	Monacan or Monegasque.
Mongolia	Mongolian(s)	Mongolian
Morocco	Moroccan(s)	Moroccan.
Mozambique	Mozambican(s)	Mozambican.
Nauru	Nauruan(s)	Nauruan.
Nepal	Nepalese (singular, plural)	Nepalese.
Netherlands	Netherlander(s)	Netherlands.
Netherlands Antilles	Netherlands Antillean(s)	Netherlands Antillean.
New Caledonia	New Caledonian(s)	New Caledonian.
New Zealand	New Zealander(s)	New Zealand.
Nicaragua	Nicaraguan(s)	Nicaraguan.
Niger	Nigerois (singular, plural)	Niger.
Nigeria	Nigerien(s) (singular, plural)	Nigerian.
Norway	Norwegian(s)	Norwegian.
Oman	Omani(s)	Omani.
Pakistan	Pakistani(s)	Pakistani.
Panama	Panamanian(s)	Panamanian.
Papua New Guinea	Papua New Guinean(s)	Papua New Guinean.
Paraguay	Paraguayan(s)	Paraguayan.
Peru	Peruvian(s)	Peruvian.
Philippines	Filipino(s)	Philippine.
Poland	Pole(s)	Polish.
Portugal	Portuguese (singular, plural)	Portuguese.
Qatar	Qatari(s)	Qatari.
Reunion	Reunionese (singular, plural)	Reunionese.
Romania	Romanian(s)	Romanian.
Rwanda	Rwandan(s)	Rwandan.
St. Christopher-Nevis	Kittsian(s), Nevisian(s)	Kittsian, Nevisian.
St. Lucia	St. Lucian(s)	St. Lucian.
Sao Tome e Principe	Sao Tomean(s)	Sao Tomean.
St. Vincent and The Grenadines	St. Vincentian(s) or Vincentian(s)	St. Vincentian or Vincentian.
San Marino	Sanmarinese (singular, plural)	Sanmarinese.
Saudi Arabia	Saudi(s)	Saudi Arabian or Saudi.
Senegal	Senegalese (singular, plural)	Senegalese.
Seychelles	Seychellois (singular, plural)	Seychelles.
Sierra Leone	Sierra Leonean(s)	Sierra Leonean.
Singapore	Singaporean(s)	Singapore.
Solomon Islands	Solomon Islander(s)	Solomon Islander.
Somalia	Somali (singular, plural)	Somali.
South Africa	South African(s)	South African.
Spain	Spaniard(s)	Spanish.
Sri Lanka	Sri Lankan(s)	Sri Lankan.
Sudan	Sudanese (singular, plural)	Sudanese.
Suriname	Surinamer(s)	Surinamese.
Swaziland	Swazi (singular, plural)	Swazi.
Sweden	Swede(s)	Swedish.
Switzerland	Swiss (singular, plural)	Swiss.
Syria	Syrian(s)	Syrian.
Taiwan	Chinese (singular, plural)	Chinese.

NOUNS AND ADJECTIVES DENOTING NATIONALITY—Continued

[Revised with suggestions by the Department of State]

Country or region	Noun (plural ending in parentheses)	Adjective
Tanzania	Tanzanian(s)	Tanzanian.
Thailand	Thai (singular, plural)	Thai.
Togo	Togolese (singular, plural)	Togolese.
Tonga	Tongan(s)	Tongan.
Trindad and Tobago	Trinidadian(s), Tobagan(s)	Trinidadian; Tobagar.
Tunisia	Tunisian(s)	Tunisian.
Turkey	Turk(s)	Turkish.
Tuvalu	Tuvaluan(s)	Tuvaluan.
Uganda	Ugandan(s)	Ugandan.
Union of Soviet Socialist Republics	Soviet(s)	Soviet.
United Arab Emirates	Emirian(s)	Emirian.
United Kingdom	Briton(s), British (collective plural)	British.
United States of America	American(s)	American.
Upper Volta	Upper Voltan(s)	Upper Voltan.
Uruguay	Uruguayan(s)	Uruguayan.
Vanuatu	Vanuatuan(s)	Vanuatuan.
Vatican City		
Venezuela	Venezuelan(s)	Venezuelan.
Vietnam	Vietnamese (singular, plural)	Vietnamese.
Wallis and Futuna Islands	Wallisian(s), Futunan(s) or Wallis and Futuna Islander(s).	Wallisian, Futunan or Wallis and Futuna Islander.
Western Samoa	Western Samoan(s)	Western Samoa.
Yemen (Aden)	Yemini (singular, plural)	Yemeni.
Yemen (Sanaa)	Yemeni(s)	Do.
Yugoslavia	Yugoslav(s)	Yugoslav.
Zaire	Zairian(s)	Zairian.
Zambia	Zambian(s)	Zambian.
Zimbabwe	Zimbabwean(s)	Zimbabwean.

CHAPTER 18

FOREIGN MONEY

[Based on list of currency units and abbreviations provided by the International Monetary Fund and the Department of State]

Country or area	Basic monetary unit		Principal fractional unit	
	Name	Symbol	Name	Abbreviation or symbol
Afghanistan	Afghani	Af	Pul	
Albania	Lek	L	Quintar	
Algeria	Dinar	DA	Centime	
Andorra	French franc	Fr. F.	French centime	
	Spanish peseta	Sp. Ptas.¹	Spanish centimo	
Angola	Kwanza	Kz	Lwei	
Antigua and Barbuda	Dollar	EC$	Cent	
Argentina	Peso	M$N	Centavo	Ctvo.
Australia	Dollar	A$	Cent	
Austria	Schilling	S	Groschen	
Bahamas, The	Dollar	B$	Cent	
Bahrain	Dinar	BD	Fil	
Bangladesh	Taka	Tk	Paise	
Barbados	Dollar	Bds$	Cent	
Belgium	Franc	BF	Centime	
Belize	Dollar	$B	Cent	
Benin	Franc	CFAF	Centime	
Bermuda	Dollar	$B	Cent	
Bhutan	Ngultruns	N	Tikchung	
Bolivia	Peso Boliviana	$b	Centavo	Ctvo.
Botswana	Pula	P	Thebe	
Brazil	New cruzeiro	NCr$	Centavo	Ctvo.
Brunei	Dollar	B$	Cent	
Bulgaria	Lev	L	Stotinka	
Burma	Kyat	K	Pya	
Burundi	Franc	FBu	Centime	
Cameroon	Franc	CFAF	....do	
Canada	Dollar	$ or Can$	Cent	C, ct.
Cape Verde	Escudo	C.V. Esc	Centavo	
Central African Republic	Franc	CFAF	Centime	
Chad	Franc	CFAF	....do	
Chile	Peso	Ch$	Centavo	
China	Yuan	¥	Fen	
Colombia	Peso	Col$	Centavo	Ctvo.
Comoros	Franc	CFAF	Centime	
Congo	....do	CFAF	....do	
Cook Islands	New Zealand dollar	NZ$	Cent	
Costa Rica	Colon	¢	Centimo	Ctmo.
Cuba	Peso	$	Centavo	Ctvo.
Cyprus	Pound	£ or £C	Mil	
Czechoslovakia	Koruna	Kcs	Haler	
Dahomey	Franc	CFAF	Centime	
Denmark	Krone	DKr	Øre	
Djibouti	Franc	DF	Centime	
Dominica	Dollar	EC$	Cent	
Dominican Republic	Peso	RD$	Centavo	Ctvo.
Ecuador	Sucre	S/	....do	Ctvo.
Egypt	Pound	£E	Piaster	
El Salvador	Colon	¢	Centavo	Ctvo.
Equartorial Guinea	Ekuele	EK	Centimo	
Estonia	Ruble		Kopek	
Ethiopia	Birr	EB	Cent	
Falkland Islands	Pound	£	Shilling	
Faroe Islands	Danish krone	DKr	Øre	
Fiji	Dollar	$F	Cent	
Finland	Finnmark	Fimr	Penni	Pia.
France	Franc	F	Centime	
French Guiana	....do	F	....do	
French Polynesia	....do	CFPF	....do	
Gabon	....do	CFAF	....do	
Gambia, The	Dalasi	DD	Butut	
German Democratic Republic.	Mark	DME	Pfennig	Pf.
Ghana	Cedi	¢	Pesewa	P.
Gibraltar	Pound	£	Shilling	
Greece	Drachma	Dr	Lepton	
Greenland	Danish krone	DKr	Øre	
Grenada	Dollar	EC$	Cent	
Guadeloupe	Franc	F	Centime	
Guatamala	Quetzal	Q	Centavo	Ctvo.
Guinea	Syli	GS	Cauri	
Guyana	Dollar	G$	Cent	
Haiti	Gourde	G	Centime	
Honduras	Lempira	L	Centavo	Ctvo.
Hong Kong	Dollar	HK$	Cent	
Hungary	Forint	Ft	Filler	
Iceland	Krona	IKr	Eyrir	
India	Rupee	Rs	Paisa	

FOREIGN MONEY—Continued

[Based on list of currency units and abbreviations provided by the International Monetary Fund and the Department of State]

Country or area	Basic monetary unit		Principal fractional unit	
	Name	Symbol	Name	Abbreviation or symbol
Indonesia	Rupiah	Rp	Sen	
Iran	Rial	Rls [2]	Dinar	
Iraq	Dinar	ID	Fil	
Ireland	Pound	£ or £Ir	Shilling	S., d.
Israel	Shekel	I£	Agrirot	
Italy	Lira	Lit	Centesimo	Ctmo.
Ivory Coast	Franc	CFAF	Centime	
Jamaica	Dollar	J$	Cent	
Japan	Yen	¥	Sen	
Jordan	Dinar	JD	Fil	
Kampuchea	Riel	KR		
Kenya	Shilling	K Sh	Cent	
Kiribati	Australian dollar	A$	....do	
Korea	Chon	W	Chun	
Kuwait	Dinar	KD	Fil	
Laos	Kip	K	At	
Latvia	Ruble	R	Kopek	
Lebanon	Pound	LL	Piaster	
Lesotho	Rand	R	Cent	
Liberia	Dollar	$	....do	
Libya	Dinar	LD	Milleme	
Liechtenstein	Swiss franc	Sw F	Centime	
Lithuania	Ruble	R	Kopek	
Luxembourg	Franc	Lux F	Centime	
Macao	Pataca	P	Avo	
Madagascar	Franc	FMG	Centime	
Malawi	Kwacha	K	Tambal	
Malaysia	Ringgits	M$	Sen	
Maldives	Rupee	Mal Re	Lari	
Mali	Franc	MF		
Malta	Pound	£M	Cent	
Martinique	Franc	F	Centime	
Mauritania	Ouguiya	UM	Khoum	
Mauritius	Rupee	Mau Rs [3]	Cent	
Mexico	Peso	Mex$	Centavo	Ctvo.
Monaco	French franc	Fr	Centime	
Mongolia	Tugrik	Tug	Möngö	
Montserrat	Dollar	EC$	Cent	
Morocco	Dirham	DH	Centime	
Mozambique	Escudo	M. Esc	Centavo	
Nauru	Australian dollar	$A	Cent	
Nepal	Rupee	NRs [1]	Pice	
Netherlands	Guilder	f.	Cent	
Netherlands Antilles	....do	NAE	....do	
New Caledonia	Franc	CFPF	Centime	
New Zealand	Dollar	$NZ	Cent	
Nicaragua	Cordoba	C$	Centavo	Ctvo.
Niger	Franc	CFAF	Centime	
Nigeria	Naira	₦	Kobo	k.
Norway	Krone	NKr	Øre	
Oman	Riyal	ORls	Baiza	
Pakistan	Rupee	PRs	Paisa	
Panama	Balboa	B	Centesimo	Ctmo.
Paraguay	Guarani	G	Centimo	Ctmo.
Papua New Guinea	Kina	K	Toea	
Peru	Sol	S/	Cer.tavo	Ctvo.
Philippines	Peso	₱	....do	Ctvo.
Poland	Zloty	Zl	Grosz	
Portugal	Escudo	Esc	Centavo	
Qatar	Riyal	QRls	Dirham	
Reunion	French franc	F	Centime	
Romania	Leu	L	Ban	
Rwanda	Franc	RF	Centime	
St. Christopher-Nevis	Dollar	EC$	Cent	
St. Lucia	....do	EC$	....do	
St. Pierre and Miquelon	Franc	CFAF	Centime	
St. Vincent and the Grenadines.	Dollar	EC$	Cent	
San Marino	Italian lira	Lit	Centesimo	
Sao Tome e Principe	Dobra	Db	Centavo	
Saudi Arabia	Riyal	SRls [2]	Halala	
Senegal	Franc	CFAF	Centime	
Seychelles	Rupee	Sey Rs [3]	Cent	
Sierra Leone	Leone	Le	....do	
Singapore	Dollar	S$	....do	
Solomon Islands	Dollar	SI$	....do	
Somalia	Shilling	So. Sh.	....do	
South Africa	Rand	R	Cent	

FOREIGN MONEY—Continued

[Based on list of currency units and abbreviations provided by the International Monetary Fund and the Department of State]

Country or area	Basic monetary unit		Principal fractional unit	
	Name	Symbol	Name	Abbreviation or symbol
Spain	Peseta	Ptas [1]	Centimo	
Sri Lanka	Rupee	Cey Rs [3]	Cent	
Sudan	Pound	£S	Piaster	
Suriname	Guilder	Sur. f.	Cent	
Swaziland	Lilangeni (emalangeni, plural).	E	...do	
Sweden	Krona	SKr	Öre	
Switzerland	Franc	SwF	Centime	
Syria	Pound	£Syr	Piaster	
Tanzania	Shilling	T Sh	Cent	
Thailand	Baht	B	Satang	
Taiwan	New Taiwan dollar	NT$	Cent	
Togo	Franc	CFAF	Centime	
Tonga	Pa'anga	T$	Seniti	
Trinidad and Tobago	Dollar	TT$	Cent	
Tunisia	Dinar	D	Millime	
Turkey	Lira	TL	Kurus	
Tuvalu	Australian dollar	A$	Cent	
Uganda	Shilling	U Sh	...do	
U.S.S.R.	Ruble	R	Kopek	
United Arab Emirates	Dirham	UD	Fil	
United Kingdom	Pound	£ or £ stg.	Shilling	S., d.
United States	Dollar	$ or US$	Cent	
Upper Volta	Franc	CFAF	Centime	
Uruguay	Peso	N$	Centesimo	
Vanatu	Franc	FNH	Centime	
Vatican City	Italian lira	Lit	Centesimo Ctmo.	
Venezuela	Bolivar	Bs	Centimo	
Vietnam	Dông	VND	Hao	
Wallis and Futuna	Franc	CFPF	Centime	
Western Samoa	Tala	WS$	Cent	
Yemen (Aden)	Dinar	SYD	Fil	
Yemen (Sanaa)	Rial	Y Rls [2]	...do	
Yugoslavia	Dinar	Din	Para	
Zaire	Zaire	Z	Likuta	
Zambia	Kwacha	K	Ngwee	S., d.
Zimbabwe	Dollar	Z$	Cent	

[1] Singular: Pta.
[2] Singular: Rl.
[3] Singular: Re.

METRIC TABLES

LENGTH

Myriameter (obs.)	10,000 meters	6.2137 miles	Meter	1 meter	39.37 inches.
Kilometer	1,000 meters	0.62137 mile	Decimeter	0.1 meter	3.937 inches.
Hectometer	100 meters	328 feet 1 inch	Centimeter	0.01 meter	0.3937 inch.
Dekameter	10 meters	393.7 inches	Millimeter	0.001 meter	0.0394 inch.

AREA

Hectare	10,000 square meters	2.471 acres.
Are	100 square meters	119.6 square yards.
Centiare	1 square meter	1,550 square inches.

WEIGHT

Name	Number of grams	Volume of water corresponding to weight	Avoirdupois weight of water
Metric ton, millier or tonneau	1,000,000	1 cubic meter	2,204.6 pounds.
Kilogram or kilo	1,000	1 liter	2.2046 pounds.
Hectogram	100	1 deciliter	3.5274 ounces.
Dekagram	10	10 cubic centimeters	0.3527 ounce.
Gram	1	1 cubic centimeter	15.432 grains.
Decigram	.1	0.1 cubic centimeter	1.5432 grains.
Centigram	.01	10 cubic millimeters	0.1543 grain.
Milligram	.001	1 cubic millimeter	0.0154 grain.

CAPACITY

Name	Number of liters	Metric cubic measure	United States measure	British measure
Kiloliter or stere	1,000	1 cubic meter	1.308 cubic yards	1.308 cubic yards.
Hectoliter	100	0.1 cubic meter	2.838 bushels; 26,417 gallons.	2.75 bushels; 22.00 gallons.
Dekaliter	10	10 cubic decimeters	1.135 pecks; 2.6417 gallons.	8.80 quarts; 2.200 gallons.
Liter	1	1 cubic decimeter	0.908 dry quart; 1.0567 liquid quarts.	0.880 quart.
Deciliter	.1	0.1 cubic decimeter	6.1023 cubic inches; 0.845 gill.	0.704 gill.
Centiliter	.01	10 cubic centimeters	0.6102 cubic inch; 0.338 fluid ounce.	0.352 fluid ounce
Milliliter	.001	1 cubic centimeter	0.061 cubic inch; 0.271 fluid dram.	0.284 fluid dram.

COMMON MEASURES AND THEIR METRIC EQUIVALENTS

Common measure	Equivalent	Common measure	Equivalent
Inch	2.54 centimeters.	Dry quart, United States	1.101 liters.
Foot	0.3048 meter.	Quart, imperial	1.136 liters.
Yard	0.9144 meter.	Gallon, United States	3.785 liters.
Rod	5.029 meters.	Gallon, imperial	4.546 liters.
Mile	1.6093 kilometers.	Peck, United States	8.810 liters.
Square inch	6.452 square centimeters.	Peck, imperial	9.092 liters.
Square foot	0.0929 square meter.	Bushel, United States	35.24 liters.
Square yard	0.836 square meter.	Bushel, imperial	36.37 liters.
Square rod	25.29 square meters.	Ounce, avoirdupois	28.35 grams.
Acre	0.4047 hectare.	Pound, avoirdupois	0.4536 kilogram.
Square mile	259 hectares.	Ton, long	1.0160 metric tons.
Cubic inch	16.39 cubic centimeters.	Ton, short	0.9072 metric ton.
Cubic foot	0.0283 cubic meter.	Grain	0.0648 gram.
Cubic yard	0.7646 cubic meter.	Ounce, troy	31.103 grams.
Cord	3.625 steres.	Pound, troy	0.3732 kilogram.
Liquid quart, United States	0.9463 liter.		

METRIC TABLES—Continued

U.S. EQUIVALENTS OF THE PRINCIPAL WEIGHTS AND MEASURES USED IN FOREIGN AGRICULTURAL STATISTICS

[With suggestions by the Department of Agriculture]

Weight or measure	Country	Weight or measure	Country
1 ardeb = 1.98 hectoliters = 5.6189 Winchester or United States bushels.	Egypt.	1 koku = 4.9602 imperial bushels = 5.1192 Winchester bushels.	Japan.
1 arroba = 25 pounds, avoirdupois.	Cuba.	1 koku = 47.655 United States standard gallons.	Japan.
1 batman = 6.5 pounds, avoirdupois.	Iran.	1 kwan = 8.2673 pounds, avoirdupois.	Do.
1 bouw = 7,096.5 square meters = 1.754 acres.	Indonesia.	1 liter = 0.028378 Winchester bushel = 0.26418 United States gallon.	(2).
1 cantar = 44.928 kilograms = 99.049 pounds, avoirdupois.	Egypt.	1 manzana = 1.7266 acres..........	Guatemala.
1 catty (kati) = 1⅓ pounds, avoirdupois.	China.	1 maund = 82.2857 pounds, avoirdupois.	British India.
1 central = 100 pounds, avoirdupois.	United States, Canada, Union of South Africa.[1]	1 mesana = 0.6397 acre.............	Cuba.
		1 morgen = 2.1165 acres............	Union of South Africa.
1 centner = 110.23 pounds, avoirdupois.	Denmark.	1 mow = 0.1518 acre (varying)..	China.
1 chetvert = 5.9568 Winchester bushels.	Union of Soviet Socialist Republics.	1 oke = 1.248 kilograms = 2.751 pounds, avoirdupois.	Egypt.
1 cho = 2.4506 acres....................	Japan.	1 oke = 2.822 pounds, avoirdupois.	Greece.
1 dekar = 0.2471 acre	Norway.	1 picul = 133⅓ pounds, avoirdupois.	China.
1 dessiatine = 2.6997 acres........	Union of Soviet Socialist Republics.	1 picul = 61.761 kilograms = 136.16 pounds, avoirdupois.	Indonesia.
1 donum = 0.227 acre	Turkey.	1 picul = 132.28 pounds, avoirdupois.	Japan.
1 doppelzentner = 220.46 pounds, avoirdupois.	Germany.	1 pood = 36.1128 pounds, avoirdupois.	Union of Soviet Socialist Republics.
1 feddan = 1.038 acres...............	Egypt.	1 pound, Great Venetian = 1.0582 pounds, avoirdupois.	Greece.
1 hectare = 2.471 acres...............	(2).	1 quintal (double centner, or metric centner) = 220.46 pounds, avoirdupois.	(2).
1 hectoliter = 2.8378 Winchester bushels.	(2).		
1 hectoliter = 26.418 United States gallons.	(2).	1 quarter = 8 imperial bushels = 8.2564 Winchester bushels.	United Kingdom.
1 hundredweight (long) = 112 pounds, avoirdupois.	United Kingdom, Australia.[1]	1 rai = 0.3954 acre......................	Thailand.
1 hundredweight (or cental) = 100 pounds, avoirdupois.	United States, Canada, Union of South Africa.[1]	1 Russian pound = ¹⁄₄₀ pood = 0.90282 pound, avoirdupois.	Union of Soviet Socialist Republics.
1 imperial bushel = 1.03205 Winchester bushels.	United Kingdom, Canada, Australia, Union of South Africa.[1]	1 stremma (royal) = 0.2471 acre.	Greece.
1 imperial gallon = 1.2009 United States gallons.	Do.[1]	1 tan (or picul) = 133⅓ pounds, avoirdupois.	China.
1 joch (cadastral hold, or cadastral arpent) = 1.422 acres.	Hungary.	1 ton (long) = 2,240 pounds, avoidupois.	United States (foreign trade) and United Kingdom.
1 kilogram = 2.2046 pounds, avoirdupois.	(2).	1 ton (metric) = 2,204.6 pounds, avoirdupois.	(2).
1 kin = 1.3228 pounds, avoirdupois.	Japan.	1 ton (short) = 2,000 pounds, avoirdupois.	United States (internal trade) and Canada (foreign trade).
1 ko = 2.3966 acres.....................	Formosa.	1 zentner = 110.23 pounds, avoirdupois.	Germany.

[1] List of countries given may not be complete.   [2] Metric system.

Note.—The values given are believed to be carried to a sufficient number of decimal places to meet the purpose for which the units may be used.

PICAS REDUCED TO INCHES

Picas	Inches	Picas	Inches	Picas	Inches	Picas	Inches	Picas	Inches	Picas	Inches
1	0.166	18	2.988	35	5.811	52	8.634	69	11.457	86	14.279
2	.332	19	3.154	36	5.977	53	8.800	70	11.623	87	14.445
3	.498	20	3.320	37	6.143	54	8.966	71	11.789	88	14.611
4	.664	21	3.487	38	6.309	55	9.132	72	11.955	89	14.778
5	.830	22	3.653	39	6.475	56	9.298	73	12.121	90	14.944
6	.996	23	3.819	40	6.641	57	9.464	74	12.287	91	15.110
7	1.162	24	3.985	41	6.807	58	9.630	75	12.453	92	15.276
8	1.328	25	4.151	42	6.973	59	9.796	76	12.619	93	15.442
9	1.494	26	4.317	43	7.139	60	9.962	77	12.785	94	15.608
10	1.660	27	4.483	44	7.306	61	10.128	78	12.951	95	15.774
11	1.826	28	4.649	45	7.472	62	10.294	79	13.117	96	15.940
12	1.992	29	4.815	46	7.638	63	10.460	80	13.283	97	16.106
13	2.158	30	4.981	47	7.804	64	10.626	81	13.449	98	16.272
14	2.324	31	5.147	48	7.970	65	10.792	82	13.615	99	16.438
15	2.490	32	5.313	49	8.136	66	10.959	83	13.781	100	16.604
16	2.656	33	5.479	50	8.302	67	11.125	84	13.947	125	20.750
17	2.822	34	5.645	51	8.468	68	11.291	85	14.113	150	24.900

INCREASE OF TEXT BY SPACING

If lines are spaced 2 points—
6-point type is increased one-third.
8-point type is increased one-fourth.
10-point type is increased one-fifth.
11-point type is increased two-elevenths.
12-point type is increased one-sixth.

NUMBER OF WORDS AND EMS TO THE SQUARE INCH

Size of type	Number of words		Number of ems	Size of type	Number of words		Number of ems
	Solid	Leaded [1]			Solid	Leaded [1]	
14 point	11	8	26½	8 point	32	23	81
12 point	14	11	36	6 point	47	34	144
11 point	17	14	43	5 point	69	50	207
10 point	21	16	52				

[1] "Leaded" refers to 2 points of space between lines.

NOTES

19. COUNTIES

Following the practice of modern-day geographers and cartographers the genitive apostrophe is not used in county names.

Note the orthography of names of the following counties:

Allegany in Maryland and New York
Alleghany in North Carolina and Virginia
Allegheny in Pennsylvania
Andrew in Missouri
Andrews in Texas
Aransas in Texas
Arkansas in Arkansas
Barber in Kansas
Barbour in Alabama and West Virginia
Brevard in Florida
Broward in Florida
Brooke in West Virginia
Brooks in Georgia and Texas
Brown in all States
Bulloch in Georgia
Bullock in Alabama
Burnet in Texas
Burnett in Wisconsin
Cheboygan in Michigan; Sheboygan in Wisconsin
Clarke in Alabama, Georgia, Iowa, Mississippi, and Virginia; all others Clark
Coffee in Alabama, Georgia, and Tennessee
Coffey in Kansas
Coal in Oklahoma
Cole in Missouri
Coles in Illinois
Cook in Illinois and Minnesota
Cooke in Texas
Davidson in North Carolina and Tennessee
Davie in North Carolina
Daviess in Indiana, Kentucky, and Missouri
Davis in Iowa and Utah
Davison in South Dakota
De Kalb in Alabama, Georgia, Illinois, and Indiana
DeKalb in Tennessee
Dickenson in Virginia
Dickinson in Iowa, Kansas, and Michigan
Dickson in Tennessee
Douglas in all States
Forrest in Mississippi; Forest in others
Glascock in Georgia
Glasscock in Texas
Green in Kentucky and Wisconsin; all others Greene
Harford in Maryland

Hartford in Connecticut
Huntingdon in Pennsylvania
Huntington in Indiana
Johnston in North Carolina and Oklahoma; all others Johnson
Kanabec in Minnesota
Kennebec in Maine
Kearney in Nebraska
Kearny in Kansas
Lawrence in all States
Linn in Iowa, Kansas, Missouri, and Oregon
Lynn in Texas
Loudon in Tennessee
Loudoun in Virginia
Manatee in Florida
Manistee in Michigan
Merced in California; Mercer elsewhere
Morton in Kansas
Norton in Kansas
Muscogee in Georgia
Muskogee in Oklahoma
Park in Colorado and Montana
Parke in Indiana
Pottawatomie in Kansas and Oklahoma
Pottawattamie in Iowa
Sanders in Montana
Saunders in Nebraska
Smyth in Virginia; all others Smith
Stafford in Virginia
Strafford in New Hampshire
Stanley in South Dakota
Stanly in North Carolina
Stark in Illinois, North Dakota, and Ohio
Starke in Indiana
Stephens in Georgia, Oklahoma, and Texas
Stevens in Kansas, Minnesota, and Washington
Storey in Nevada
Story in Iowa
Terrell in Georgia and Texas
Tyrrell in North Carolina
Tooele in Utah
Toole in Montana
Vermillion in Indiana; all others Vermilion
Woods in Oklahoma; all others Wood
Wyandot in Ohio
Wyandotte in Kansas

ALABAMA (67 counties)

Autauga	Blount	Chambers	Clarke	Colbert
Baldwin	Bullock	Cherokee	Clay	Conecuh
Barbour	Butler	Chilton	Cleburne	Coosa
Bibb	Calhoun	Choctaw	Coffee	Covington

245

Crenshaw
Cullman
Dale
Dallas
De Kalb
Elmore
Escambia
Etowah
Fayette
Franklin

Geneva
Greene
Hale
Henry
Houston
Jackson
Jefferson
Lamar
Lauderdale
Lawrence

Lee
Limestone
Lowndes
Macon
Madison
Marengo
Marion
Marshall
Mobile
Monroe

Montgomery
Morgan
Perry
Pickens
Pike
Randolph
Russell
St. Clair
Shelby
Sumter

Talladega
Tallapoosa
Tuscaloosa
Walker
Washington
Wilcox
Winston

ALASKA ((*) signifies boroughs, all others are Census divisions)

Aleutian Islands
Anchorage*
Bethel
Bristol Bay*
Dillingham
Fairbanks North
    Star*

Haines*
Juneau*
Kenai Peninsula*
Ketchikan
    Gateway*
Kobuk
Kodiak Island*

Matanuska-
    Susitna*
Nome
North Slope*
Prince of Wales-
    Outer
    Ketchikan

Sitka*
Skagway-Yakutat-
    Angoon
Southeast
    Fairbanks
Valdez-Cordova
Wade Hampton

Wrangell-
    Petersburg
Yukon-Koyukuk

ARIZONA (15 counties)

Apache
Cochise
Coconino

Gila
Graham
Greenlee

La Paz
Maricopa
Mohave

Navajo
Pima
Pinal

Santa Cruz
Yavapai
Yuma

ARKANSAS (75 counties)

Arkansas
Ashley
Baxter
Benton
Boone
Bradley
Calhoun
Carroll
Chicot
Clark
Clay
Cleburne
Cleveland
Columbia
Conway

Craighead
Crawford
Crittenden
Cross
Dallas
Desha
Drew
Faulkner
Franklin
Fulton
Garland
Grant
Greene
Hempstead
Hot Spring

Howard
Independence
Izard
Jackson
Jefferson
Johnson
Lafayette
Lawrence
Lee
Lincoln
Little River
Logan
Lonoke
Madison
Marion

Miller
Mississippi
Monroe
Montgomery
Nevada
Newton
Ouachita
Perry
Phillips
Pike
Poinsett
Polk
Pope
Prairie
Pulaski

Randolph
St. Francis
Saline
Scott
Searcy
Sebastian
Sevier
Sharp
Stone
Union
Van Buren
Washington
White
Woodruff
Yell

CALIFORNIA (58 counties)

Alameda
Alpine
Amador
Butte
Calaveras
Colusa
Contra Costa
Del Norte
El Dorado
Fresno
Glenn
Humboldt

Imperial
Inyo
Kern
Kings
Lake
Lassen
Los Angeles
Madera
Marin
Mariposa
Mendocino
Merced

Modoc
Mono
Monterey
Napa
Nevada
Orange
Placer
Plumas
Riverside
Sacramento
San Benito
San Bernardino

San Diego
San Francisco
San Joaquin
San Luis Obispo
San Mateo
Santa Barbara
Santa Clara
Santa Cruz
Shasta
Sierra
Siskiyou
Solano

Sonoma
Stanislaus
Sutter
Tehama
Trinity
Tulare
Tuolumne
Ventura
Yolo
Yuba

COLORADO (63 counties)

Adams
Alamosa
Arapahoe
Archuleta
Baca
Bent
Boulder
Chaffee
Cheyenne
Clear Creek
Conejos
Costilla
Crowley

Custer
Delta
Denver
Dolores
Douglas
Eagle
Elbert
El Paso
Fremont
Garfield
Gilpin
Grand
Gunnison

Hinsdale
Huerfano
Jackson
Jefferson
Kiowa
Kit Carson
Lake
La Plata
Larimer
Las Animas
Lincoln
Logan
Mesa

Mineral
Moffat
Montezuma
Montrose
Morgan
Otero
Ouray
Park
Phillips
Pitkin
Prowers
Pueblo
Rio Blanco

Rio Grande
Routt
Saguache
San Juan
San Miguel
Sedgwick
Summit
Teller
Washington
Weld
Yuma

CONNECTICUT (8 counties)

Fairfield	Litchfield	New Haven	Tolland
Hartford	Middlesex	New London	Windham

DELAWARE (3 counties)

Kent	New Castle	Sussex

DISTRICT OF COLUMBIA (single entity)

FLORIDA (67 counties)

Alachua	Dixie	Hillsborough	Martin	Santa Rosa
Baker	Duval	Holmes	Monroe	Sarasota
Bay	Escambia	Indian River	Nassau	Seminole
Bradford	Flagler	Jackson	Okaloosa	Sumter
Brevard	Franklin	Jefferson	Okeechobee	Suwannee
Broward	Gadsden	Lafayette	Orange	Taylor
Calhoun	Gilchrist	Lake	Osceola	Union
Charlotte	Glades	Lee	Palm Beach	Volusia
Citrus	Gulf	Leon	Pasco	Wakulla
Clay	Hamilton	Levy	Pinellas	Walton
Collier	Hardee	Liberty	Polk	Washington
Columbia	Hendry	Madison	Putnam	
Dade	Hernando	Manatee	St. Johns	
De Soto	Highlands	Marion	St. Lucie	

GEORGIA (159 counties)

Appling	Cobb	Grady	Madison	Sumter
Atkinson	Coffee	Greene	Marion	Talbot
Bacon	Colquitt	Gwinnett	Meriwether	Taliaferro
Baker	Columbia	Habersham	Miller	Tattnall
Baldwin	Cook	Hall	Mitchell	Taylor
Banks	Coweta	Hancock	Monroe	Telfair
Barrow	Crawford	Haralson	Montgomery	Terrell
Bartow	Crisp	Harris	Morgan	Thomas
Ben Hill	Dade	Hart	Murray	Tift
Berrien	Dawson	Heard	Muscogee	Toombs
Bibb	Decatur	Henry	Newton	Towns
Bleckley	De Kalb	Houston	Oconee	Treutlen
Brantley	Dodge	Irwin	Oglethorpe	Troup
Brooks	Dooly	Jackson	Paulding	Turner
Bryan	Dougherty	Jasper	Peach	Twiggs
Bulloch	Douglas	Jeff Davis	Pickens	Union
Burke	Early	Jefferson	Pierce	Upson
Butts	Echols	Jenkins	Pike	Walker
Calhoun	Effingham	Johnson	Polk	Walton
Camden	Elbert	Jones	Pulaski	Ware
Candler	Emanuel	Lamar	Putnam	Warren
Carroll	Evans	Lanier	Quitman	Washington
Catoosa	Fannin	Laurens	Rabun	Wayne
Charlton	Fayette	Lee	Randolph	Webster
Chatham	Floyd	Liberty	Richmond	Wheeler
Chattahoochee	Forsyth	Lincoln	Rockdale	White
Chattooga	Franklin	Long	Schley	Whitfield
Cherokee	Fulton	Lowndes	Screven	Wilcox
Clarke	Gilmer	Lumpkin	Seminole	Wilkes
Clay	Glascock	McDuffie	Spalding	Wilkinson
Clayton	Glynn	McIntosh	Stephens	Worth
Clinch	Gordon	Macon	Stewart	

HAWAII (5 counties)

Hawaii	Honolulu	Kalawao	Kauai	Maui

IDAHO (44 counties)

Ada	Bonneville	Custer	Kootenai	Owyhee
Adams	Boundary	Elmore	Latah	Payette
Bannock	Butte	Franklin	Lemhi	Power
Bear Lake	Camas	Fremont	Lewis	Shoshone
Benewah	Canyon	Gem	Lincoln	Teton
Bingham	Caribou	Gooding	Madison	Twin Falls
Blaine	Cassia	Idaho	Minidoka	Valley
Boise	Clark	Jefferson	Nez Perce	Washington
Bonner	Clearwater	Jerome	Oneida	

ILLINOIS (102 counties)

Adams	Du Page	Jo Daviess	Massac	Schuyler
Alexander	Edgar	Johnson	Menard	Scott
Bond	Edwards	Kane	Mercer	Shelby
Boone	Effingham	Kankakee	Monroe	Stark
Brown	Fayette	Kendall	Montgomery	Stephenson
Bureau	Ford	Knox	Morgan	Tazewell
Calhoun	Franklin	Lake	Moultrie	Union
Carroll	Fulton	La Salle	Ogle	Vermilion
Cass	Gallatin	Lawrence	Peoria	Wabash
Champaign	Greene	Lee	Perry	Waren
Christian	Grundy	Livingston	Piatt	Washington
Clark	Hamilton	Logan	Pike	Wayne
Clay	Hancock	McDonough	Pope	White
Clinton	Hardin	McHenry	Pulaski	Whiteside
Coles	Henderson	McLean	Putnam	Will
Cook	Henry	Macon	Randolph	Williamson
Crawford	Iroquois	Macoupin	Richland	Winnebago
Cumberland	Jackson	Madison	Rock Island	Woodford
De Kalb	Jasper	Marion	St. Clair	
De Witt	Jefferson	Marshall	Saline	
Douglas	Jersey	Mason	Sangamon	

INDIANA (92 counties)

Adams	Elkhart	Jefferson	Ohio	Sullivan
Allen	Fayette	Jennings	Orange	Switzerland
Bartholomew	Floyd	Johnson	Owen	Tippecanoe
Benton	Fountain	Knox	Parke	Tipton
Blackford	Franklin	Kosciusko	Perry	Union
Boone	Fulton	LaGrange	Pike	Vanderburgh
Brown	Gibson	Lake	Porter	Vermillion
Carroll	Grant	La Porte	Posey	Vigo
Cass	Greene	Lawrence	Pulaski	Wabash
Clark	Hamilton	Madison	Putnam	Warren
Clay	Hancock	Marion	Randolph	Warrick
Clinton	Harrison	Marshall	Ripley	Washington
Crawford	Hendricks	Martin	Rush	Wayne
Daviess	Henry	Miami	St. Joseph	Wells
Dearborn	Howard	Monroe	Scott	White
Decatur	Huntington	Montgomery	Shelby	Whitley
De Kalb	Jackson	Morgan	Spencer	
Delaware	Jasper	Newton	Starke	
Dubois	Jay	Noble	Steuben	

IOWA (99 counties)

Adair	Clay	Hancock	Madison	Sac
Adams	Clayton	Hardin	Mahaska	Scott
Allamakee	Clinton	Harrison	Marion	Shelby
Appanoose	Crawford	Henry	Marshall	Sioux
Audubon	Dallas	Howard	Mills	Story
Benton	Davis	Humboldt	Mitchell	Tama
Black Hawk	Decatur	Ida	Monona	Taylor
Boone	Delaware	Iowa	Monroe	Union
Bremer	Des Moines	Jackson	Montgomery	Van Buren
Buchanan	Dickinson	Jasper	Muscatine	Wapello
Buena Vista	Dubuque	Jefferson	O'Brien	Warren
Butler	Emmet	Johnson	Osceola	Washington
Calhoun	Fayette	Jones	Page	Wayne
Carroll	Floyd	Keokuk	Palo Alto	Webster
Cass	Franklin	Kossuth	Plymouth	Winnebago
Cedar	Fremont	Lee	Pocahontas	Winneshiek
Cerro Gordo	Greene	Linn	Polk	Woodbury
Cherokee	Grundy	Louisa	Pottawattamie	Worth
Chickasaw	Guthrie	Lucas	Poweshiek	Wright
Clarke	Hamilton	Lyon	Ringgold	

KANSAS (105 counties)

Allen	Butler	Cloud	Doniphan	Ford
Anderson	Chase	Coffey	Douglas	Franklin
Atchison	Chautauqua	Comanche	Edwards	Geary
Barber	Cherokee	Cowley	Elk	Gove
Barton	Cheyenne	Crawford	Ellis	Graham
Bourbon	Clark	Decatur	Ellsworth	Grant
Brown	Clay	Dickinson	Finney	Gray

Greeley	Labette	Morris	Reno	Smith
Greenwood	Lane	Morton	Republic	Stafford
Hamilton	Leavenworth	Nemaha	Rice	Stanton
Harper	Lincoln	Neosho	Riley	Stevens
Harvey	Linn	Ness	Rooks	Sumner
Haskell	Logan	Norton	Rush	Thomas
Hodgeman	Lyon	Osage	Russell	Trego
Jackson	McPherson	Osborne	Saline	Wabaunsee
Jefferson	Marion	Ottawa	Scott	Wallace
Jewell	Marshall	Pawnee	Sedgwick	Washington
Johnson	Meade	Phillips	Seward	Wichita
Kearny	Miami	Pottawatomie	Shawnee	Wilson
Kingman	Mitchell	Pratt	Sheridan	Woodson
Kiowa	Montgomery	Rawlins	Sherman	Wyandotte

KENTUCKY (120 counties)

Adair	Clark	Harrison	McCracken	Perry
Allen	Clay	Hart	McCreary	Pike
Anderson	Clinton	Henderson	McLean	Powell
Ballard	Crittenden	Henry	Madison	Pulaski
Barren	Cumberland	Hickman	Magoffin	Robertson
Bath	Daviess	Hopkins	Marion	Rockcastle
Bell	Edmonson	Jackson	Marshall	Rowan
Boone	Elliott	Jefferson	Martin	Russell
Bourbon	Estill	Jessamine	Mason	Scott
Boyd	Fayette	Johnson	Meade	Shelby
Boyle	Fleming	Kenton	Menifee	Simpson
Bracken	Floyd	Knott	Mercer	Spencer
Breathitt	Franklin	Knox	Metcalfe	Taylor
Breckinridge	Fulton	Larue	Monroe	Todd
Bullitt	Gallatin	Laurel	Montgomery	Trigg
Butler	Garrard	Lawrence	Morgan	Trimble
Caldwell	Grant	Lee	Muhlenberg	Union
Calloway	Graves	Leslie	Nelson	Warren
Campbell	Grayson	Letcher	Nicholas	Washington
Carlisle	Green	Lewis	Ohio	Wayne
Carroll	Greenup	Lincoln	Oldham	Webster
Carter	Hancock	Livingston	Owen	Whitley
Casey	Hardin	Logan	Owsley	Wolfe
Christian	Harlan	Lyon	Pendleton	Woodford

LOUISIANA (64 parishes)

Acadia	Claiborne	Jefferson Davis	Rapides	St. Tammany
Allen	Concordia	Lafayette	Red River	Tangipahoa
Ascension	De Soto	Lafourche	Richland	Tensas
Assumption	East Baton Rouge	La Salle	Sabine	Terrebonne
Avoyelles	East Carroll	Lincoln	St. Bernard	Union
Beauregard	East Feliciana	Livingston	St. Charles	Vermilion
Bienville	Evangeline	Madison	St. Helena	Vernon
Bossier	Franklin	Morehouse	St. James	Washington
Caddo	Grant	Natchitoches	St. John the	Webster
Calcasieu	Iberia	Orleans	Baptist	West Baton Roug
Caldwell	Iberville	Ouachita	St. Landry	West Carroll
Cameron	Jackson	Plaquemines	St. Martin	West Feliciana
Catahoula	Jefferson	Pointe Coupee	St. Mary	Winn

MAINE (16 counties)

Androscoggin	Hancock	Oxford	Somerset
Aroostook	Kennebec	Penobscot	Waldo
Cumberland	Knox	Piscataquis	Washington
Franklin	Lincoln	Sagadahoc	York

MARYLAND (23 counties)

Allegany	Carroll	Garrett	Prince Georges	Washington
Anne Arundel	Cecil	Harford	Queen Annes	Wicomico
Baltimore	Charles	Howard	St. Marys	Worcester
Calvert	Dorchester	Kent	Somerset	
Caroline	Frederick	Montgomery	Talbot	

MASSACHUSETTS (14 counties)

Barnstable	Dukes	Hampden	Nantucket	Suffolk
Berkshire	Essex	Hampshire	Norfolk	Worcester
Bristol	Franklin	Middlesex	Plymouth	

MICHIGAN (83 counties)

Alcona	Clare	Iosco	Marquette	Otsego
Alger	Clinton	Iron	Mason	Ottawa
Allegan	Crawford	Isabella	Mecosta	Presque Isle
Alpena	Delta	Jackson	Menominee	Roscommon
Antrim	Dickinson	Kalamazoo	Midland	Saginaw
Arenac	Eaton	Kalkaska	Missaukee	St. Clair
Baraga	Emmet	Kent	Monroe	St. Joseph
Barry	Genesee	Keweenaw	Montcalm	Sanilac
Bay	Gladwin	Lake	Montmorency	Schoolcraft
Benzie	Gogebic	Lapeer	Muskegon	Shiawassee
Berrien	Grand Traverse	Leelanau	Newaygo	Tuscola
Branch	Gratiot	Lenawee	Oakland	Van Buren
Calhoun	Hillsdale	Livingston	Oceana	Washtenaw
Cass	Houghton	Luce	Ogemaw	Wayne
Charlevoix	Huron	Mackinac	Ontonagon	Wexford
Cheboygan	Ingham	Macomb	Osceola	
Chippewa	Ionia	Manistee	Oscoda	

MINNESOTA (87 counties)

Aitkin	Dakota	Lac qui Parle	Olmsted	Stearns
Anoka	Dodge	Lake	Otter Tail	Steele
Becker	Douglas	Lake of the Woods	Pennington	Stevens
Beltrami	Faribault	Le Sueur	Pine	Swift
Benton	Fillmore	Lincoln	Pipestone	Todd
Big Stone	Freeborn	Lyon	Polk	Traverse
Blue Earth	Goodhue	McLeod	Pope	Wabasha
Brown	Grant	Mahnomen	Ramsey	Wadena
Carlton	Hennepin	Marshall	Red Lake	Waseca
Carver	Houston	Martin	Redwood	Washington
Cass	Hubbard	Meeker	Renville	Watonwan
Chippewa	Isanti	Mille Lacs	Rice	Wilkin
Chisago	Itasca	Morrison	Rock	Winona
Clay	Jackson	Mower	Roseau	Wright
Clearwater	Kanabec	Murray	St Louis	Yellow Medicine
Cook	Kandiyohi	Nicollet	Scott	
Cottonwood	Kittson	Nobles	Sherburne	
Crow Wing	Koochiching	Norman	Sibley	

MISSISSIPPI (82 counties)

Adams	Forrest	Kemper	Noxubee	Tate
Alcorn	Franklin	Lafayette	Oktibbeha	Tippah
Amite	George	Lamar	Panola	Tishomingo
Attala	Greene	Lauderdale	Pearl River	Tunica
Benton	Grenada	Lawrence	Perry	Union
Bolivar	Hancock	Leake	Pike	Walthall
Calhoun	Harrison	Lee	Pontotoc	Warren
Carroll	Hinds	Leflore	Prentiss	Washington
Chickasaw	Holmes	Lincoln	Quitman	Wayne
Choctaw	Humphreys	Lowndes	Rankin	Webster
Claiborne	Issaquena	Madison	Scott	Wilkinson
Clarke	Itawamba	Marion	Sharkey	Winston
Clay	Jackson	Marshall	Simpson	Yalobusha
Coahoma	Jasper	Monroe	Smith	Yazoo
Copiah	Jefferson	Montgomery	Stone	
Covington	Jefferson Davis	Neshoba	Sunflower	
DeSoto	Jones	Newton	Tallahatchie	

MISSOURI (114 counties)

Adair	Cape Girardeau	Daviess	Howell	Macon
Andrew	Carroll	De Kalb	Iron	Madison
Atchison	Carter	Dent	Jackson	Maries
Audrain	Cass	Douglas	Jasper	Marion
Barry	Cedar	Dunklin	Jefferson	Mercer
Barton	Chariton	Franklin	Johnson	Miller
Bates	Christian	Gasconade	Knox	Mississippi
Benton	Clark	Gentry	Laclede	Moniteau
Bollinger	Clay	Greene	Lafayette	Monroe
Boone	Clinton	Grundy	Lawrence	Montgomery
Buchanan	Cole	Harrison	Lewis	Morgan
Butler	Cooper	Henry	Lincoln	New Madrid
Caldwell	Crawford	Hickory	Linn	Newton
Callaway	Dade	Holt	Livingston	Nodaway
Camden	Dallas	Howard	McDonald	Oregon

Osage	Polk	St. Charles	Scott	Vernon
Ozark	Pulaski	St. Clair	Shannon	Warren
Pemiscot	Putnam	St. Francois	Shelby	Washington
Perry	Ralls	Ste. Genevieve	Stoddard	Wayne
Pettis	Randolph	St. Louis	Stone	Webster
Phelps	Ray	Saline	Sullivan	Worth
Pike	Reynolds	Schuyler	Taney	Wright
Platte	Ripley	Scotland	Texas	

MONTANA (56 counties)

Beaverhead	Fallon	Lewis and Clark	Pondera	Sweet Grass
Big Horn	Fergus	Liberty	Powder River	Teton
Blaine	Flathead	Lincoln	Powell	Toole
Broadwater	Gallatin	McCone	Prairie	Treasure
Carbon	Garfield	Madison	Ravalli	Valley
Carter	Glacier	Meagher	Richland	Wheatland
Cascade	Golden Valley	Mineral	Roosevelt	Wibaux
Chouteau	Granite	Missoula	Rosebud	Yellowstone
Custer	Hill	Musselshell	Sanders	
Daniels	Jefferson	Park	Sheridan	
Dawson	Judith Basin	Petroleum	Silver Bow	
Deer Lodge	Lake	Phillips	Stillwater	

NEBRASKA (93 counties)

Adams	Cuming	Greeley	Loup	Sarpy
Antelope	Custer	Hall	McPherson	Saunders
Arthur	Dakota	Hamilton	Madison	Scotts Bluff
Banner	Dawes	Harlan	Merrick	Seward
Blaine	Dawson	Hayes	Morrill	Sheridan
Boone	Deuel	Hitchcock	Nance	Sherman
Box Butte	Dixon	Holt	Nemaha	Sieoux
Boyd	Dodge	Hooker	Nuckolls	Stanton
Brown	Douglas	Howard	Otoe	Thayer
Buffalo	Dundy	Jefferson	Pawnee	Thomas
Burt	Fillmore	Johnson	Perkins	Thurston
Butler	Franklin	Kearney	Phelps	Valley
Cass	Frontier	Keith	Pierce	Washington
Cedar	Furnas	Keya Paha	Platte	Wayne
Chase	Gage	Kimball	Polk	Webster
Cherry	Garden	Knox	Red Willow	Wheeler
Cheyenne	Garfield	Lancaster	Richardson	York
Clay	Gosper	Lincoln	Rock	
Colfax	Grant	Logan	Saline	

NEVADA (16 counties)

Churchill	Esmeralda	Lincoln	Pershing
Clark	Eureka	Lyon	Storey
Douglas	Humboldt	Mineral	Washoe
Elko	Lander	Nye	White Pine

NEW HAMPSHIRE (10 counties)

Belknap	Cheshire	Grafton	Merrimack	Strafford
Carroll	Coos	Hillsborough	Rockingham	Sullivan

NEW JERSEY (21 counties)

Atlantic	Cumberland	Mercer	Passaic	Warren
Bergen	Essex	Middlesex	Salem	
Burlington	Gloucester	Monmouth	Somerset	
Camden	Hudson	Morris	Sussex	
Cape May	Hunterdon	Ocean	Union	

NEW MEXICO (33 counties)

Bernalillo	Dona Ana	Lincoln	Rio Arriba	Socorro
Catron	Eddy	Los Alamos	Roosevelt	Taos
Chaves	Grant	Luna	Sandoval	Torrance
Cibola	Guadalupe	McKinley	San Juan	Union
Colfax	Harding	Mora	San Miguel	Valencia
Curry	Hidalgo	Otero	Santa Fe	
De Baca	Lea	Quay	Sierra	

NEW YORK (62 counties)

Albany	Dutchess	Madison	Putnam	Sullivan
Allegany	Erie	Monroe	Queens	Tioga
Bronx	Essex	Montgomery	Rensselaer	Tompkins
Broome	Franklin	Nassau	Richmond	Ulster
Cattaraugus	Fulton	New York	Rockland	Warren
Cayuga	Genesee	Niagara	St. Lawrence	Washington
Chautauqua	Greene	Oneida	Saratoga	Wayne
Chemung	Hamilton	Onandaga	Schenectady	Westchester
Chenango	Kerkimer	Ontario	Schoharie	Wyoming
Clinton	Jefferson	Orange	Schuyler	Yates
Columbia	Kings	Orleans	Seneca	
Cortland	Lewis	Oswego	Steuben	
Delaware	Livingston	Otsego	Suffolk	

NORTH CAROLINA (100 counties)

Alamance	Chowan	Guilford	Mitchell	Rutherford
Alexander	Clay	Halifax	Montgomery	Sampson
Alleghany	Cleveland	Harnett	Moore	Scotland
Anson	Columbus	Haywood	Nash	Stanly
Ashe	Craven	Henderson	New Hanover	Stokes
Avery	Cumberland	Hertford	Northampton	Surry
Beaufort	Currituck	Hoke	Onslow	Swain
Bertie	Dare	Hyde	Orange	Transylvania
Bladen	Davidson	Iredell	Pamlico	Tyrrell
Brunswick	Davie	Jackson	Pasquotank	Union
Buncombe	Duplin	Johnston	Pender	Vance
Burke	Durham	Jones	Perquimans	Wake
Cabarrus	Edgecombe	Lee	Person	Warren
Caldwell	Forsyth	Lenoir	Pitt	Washington
Camden	Franklin	Lincoln	Polk	Watauga
Carteret	Gaston	McDowell	Randolph	Wayne
Caswell	Gates	Macon	Richmond	Wilkes
Catawba	Graham	Madison	Robeson	Wilson
Chatham	Granville	Martin	Rockingham	Yadkin
Cherokee	Greene	Mecklenburg	Rowan	Yancey

NORTH DAKOTA (53 counties)

Adams	Divide	La Moure	Pembina	Stark
Barnes	Dunn	Logan	Pierce	Steele
Benson	Eddy	McHenry	Ramsey	Stutsman
Billings	Emmons	McIntosh	Ransom	Towner
Bottineau	Foster	McKenzie	Renville	Traill
Bowman	Golden Valley	McLean	Richland	Walsh
Burke	Grand Forks	Mercer	Rolette	Ward
Burleigh	Grant	Morton	Sargent	Wells
Cass	Griggs	Mountrail	Sheridan	Williams
Cavalier	Hettinger	Nelson	Sioux	
Dickey	Kidder	Oliver	Slope	

OHIO (88 counties)

Adams	Darke	Hocking	Miami	Scioto
Allen	Defiance	Holmes	Monroe	Seneca
Ashland	Delaware	Huron	Montgomery	Shelby
Ashtabula	Erie	Jackson	Morgan	Stark
Athens	Fairfield	Jefferson	Morrow	Summit
Auglaize	Fayette	Knox	Muskingum	Trumbull
Belmont	Franklin	Lake	Noble	Tuscarawas
Brown	Fulton	Lawrence	Ottawa	Union
Butler	Gallia	Licking	Paulding	Van Wert
Carroll	Geauga	Logan	Perry	Vinton
Champaign	Greene	Lorain	Pickaway	Warren
Clark	Guernsey	Lucas	Pike	Washington
Clermont	Hamilton	Madison	Portage	Wayne
Clinton	Hancock	Mahoning	Preble	Williams
Columbiana	Hardin	Marion	Putnam	Wood
Coshocton	Harrison	Medina	Richland	Wyandot
Crawford	Henry	Meigs	Ross	
Cuyahoga	Highland	Mercen	Sandusky	

OKLAHOMA (77 counties)

Adair	Atoka	Beckham	Bryan	Canadian
Alfalfa	Beaver	Blaine	Caddo	Carter

Cherokee	Garvin	Latimer	Nowata	Seminole
Choctaw	Grady	Le Flore	Okfuskee	Sequoyah
Cimarron	Grant	Lincoln	Oklahoma	Stephens
Cleveland	Greer	Logan	Okmulgee	Texas
Coal	Harmon	Love	Osage	Tillman
Comanche	Harper	McClain	Ottawa	Tulsa
Cotton	Haskell	McCurtain	Pawnee	Wagoner
Craig	Hughes	McIntosh	Payne	Washington
Creek	Jackson	Major	Pittsburg	Washita
Custer	Jefferson	Marshall	Pontotoc	Woods
Delaware	Johnston	Mayes	Pottawatomie	Woodward
Dewey	Kay	Murray	Pushmataha	
Ellis	Kingfisher	Muskogee	Roger Mills	
Garfield	Kiowa	Noble	Rogers	

OREGON (36 counties)

Baker	Deschutes	Josephine	Morrow	Wasco
Benton	Douglas	Klamath	Multnomah	Washington
Clackamas	Gilliam	Lake	Polk	Wheeler
Clatsop	Grant	Lane	Sherman	Yamhill
Columbia	Harney	Lincoln	Tillamook	
Coos	Hood River	Linn	Umatilla	
Crook	Jackson	Malheur	Union	
Curry	Jefferson	Marion	Wallowa	

PENNSYLVANIA (67 counties)

Adams	Chester	Fulton	Mercer	Sullivan
Allegheny	Clarion	Greene	Mifflin	Susquehanna
Armstrong	Clearfield	Huntingdon	Monroe	Tioga
Beaver	Clinton	Indiana	Montgomery	Union
Bedford	Columbia	Jefferson	Montour	Venango
Berks	Crawford	Juniata	Northampton	Warren
Blair	Cumberland	Lackawanna	Northumberland	Washington
Bradford	Dauphin	Lancaster	Perry	Wayne
Bucks	Delaware	Lawrence	Philadelphia	Westmoreland
Butler	Elk	Lebanon	Pike	Wyoming
Cambria	Erie	Lehigh	Potter	York
Cameron	Fayette	Luzerne	Schuylkill	
Carbon	Forest	Lycoming	Snyder	
Centre	Franklin	McKean	Somerset	

PUERTO RICO (78 municipios)

Adjuntas	Cataño	Gurabo	Maunabo	San Juan
Aguada	Cayey	Hatillo	Mayagüz	San Lorenzo
Aguadilla	Ceiba	Hormigueros	Moca	San Sebastián
Aguas Buenas	Ciales	Humacao	Morovis	Santa Isabel
Aibonito	Cidra	Isabela	Naguabo	Toa Alta
Añasco	Coamo	Jayuya	Naranjito	Toa Baja
Arecibo	Comerío	Juana Díaz	Orocovis	Trujillo Alto
Arroyo	Corozal	Juncos	Patillas	Utuado
Barceloneta	Culebra	Lajas	Peñuelas	Vega Alta
Barranquitas	Dorado	Lares	Ponce	Vega Baja
Bayamón	Fajardo	Las Marías	Quebradillas	Vieques
Cabo Rojo	Florida	Las Piedras	Rincón	Villalba
Caguas	Gúanica	Loíza	Río Grande	Yabucoa
Camuy	Guayama	Luquillo	Sabana Grande	Yauco
Canóvanas	Guayanilla	Manatí	Salinas	
Carolina	Guaynabo	Maricao	San Germán	

RHODE ISLAND (5 counties)

Bristol	Kent	Newport	Providence	Washington

SAMOA, AMERICAN (5 entities: districts* and islands)

Eastern*	Manu'a*	Rose	Swains	Western*

SOUTH CAROLINA (46 counties)

Abbeville	Beaufort	Chesterfield	Edgefield	Hampton
Aiken	Berkeley	Clarendon	Fairfield	Horry
Allendale	Calhoun	Colleton	Florence	Jasper
Anderson	Charleston	Darlington	Georgetown	Kershaw
Bamberg	Cherokee	Dillon	Greenville	Lancaster
Barnwell	Chester	Dorchester	Greenwood	Laurens

Lee	Marlboro	Pickens	Sumter
Lexington	Newberry	Richland	Union
McCormick	Oconee	Saluda	Williamsburg
Marion	Orangeburg	Spartanburg	York

SOUTH DAKOTA (66 counties)

Aurora	Corson	Hand	McCook	Spink
Beadle	Custer	Hanson	McPherson	Stanley
Bennett	Davison	Harding	Marshall	Sully
Bon Homme	Day	Hughes	Meade	Todd
Brookings	Deuel	Hutchinson	Mellette	Tripp
Brown	Dewey	Hyde	Miner	Turner
Brule	Douglas	Jackson	Minnehaha	Union
Buffalo	Edmunds	Jerauld	Moody	Walworth
Butte	Fall River	Jones	Pennington	Washabaugh
Campbell	Faulk	Kingsbury	Perkins	Yankton
Charles Mix	Grant	Lake	Potter	Ziebach
Clark	Gregory	Lawrence	Roberts	
Clay	Haakon	Lincoln	Sanborn	
Codington	Hamlin	Lyman	Shannon	

TENNESSEE (95 counties)

Anderson	Decatur	Henderson	Marion	Sequatchie
Bedford	DeKalb	Henry	Marshall	Sevier
Benton	Dickson	Hickman	Maury	Shelby
Bledsoe	Dyer	Houston	Meigs	Smith
Blount	Fayette	Humphreys	Monroe	Stewart
Bradley	Fentress	Jackson	Montgomery	Sullivan
Campbell	Franklin	Jefferson	Moore	Sumner
Cannon	Gibson	Johnson	Morgan	Tipton
Carroll	Giles	Knox	Obion	Trousdale
Carter	Grainger	Lake	Overton	Unicoi
Cheatham	Greene	Lauderdale	Perry	Union
Chester	Grundy	Lawrence	Pickett	Van Buren
Claiborne	Hamblen	Lewis	Polk	Warren
Clay	Hamilton	Lincoln	Putnam	Washington
Cocke	Hancock	Loudon	Rhea	Wayne
Coffee	Hardeman	McMinn	Roane	Weakley
Crockett	Hardin	McNairy	Robertson	White
Cumberland	Hawkins	Macon	Rutherford	Williamson
Davidson	Haywood	Madison	Scott	Wilson

TEXAS (254 counties)

Anderson	Camp	Dickens	Guadalupe	Jim Wells
Andrews	Carson	Dimmit	Hale	Jonson
Angelina	Cass	Donley	Hall	Jones
Aransas	Castro	Duval	Hamilton	Karnes
Archer	Chambers	Eastland	Hansford	Kaufman
Armstrong	Cherokee	Ector	Hardeman	Kendall
Atascosa	Childress	Edwards	Hardin	Kenedy
Austin	Clay	Ellis	Harris	Kent
Bailey	Cochran	El Paso	Harrison	Kerr
Bandera	Coke	Erath	Hartley	Kimble
Bastrop	Coleman	Falls	Haskell	King
Baylor	Collin	Fannin	Hays	Kinney
Bee	Collingsworth	Fayette	Hemphill	Kleberg
Bell	Colorado	Fisher	Henderson	Knox
Bexar	Comal	Floyd	Hidalgo	Lamar
Blanco	Comanche	Foard	Hill	Lamb
Borden	Concho	Fort Bend	Hockley	Lampasas
Bosque	Cooke	Franklin	Hood	La Salle
Bowie	Coryell	Freestone	Hopkins	Lavaca
Brazoria	Cottle	Frio	Houston	Lee
Brazos	Crane	Gaines	Howard	Leon
Brewster	Crockett	Galveston	Hudspeth	Liberty
Briscoe	Crosby	Garza	Hunt	Limestone
Brooks	Culberson	Gillespie	Hutchinson	Lipscomb
Brown	Dallam	Glasscock	Irion	Live Oak
Burleson	Dallas	Goliad	Jack	Llano
Burnet	Dawson	Gonzales	Jackson	Loving
Caldwell	Deaf Smith	Gray	Jasper	Lubbock
Calhoun	Delta	Grayson	Jeff Davis	Lynn
Callahan	Denton	Gregg	Jefferson	McCulloch
Cameron	De Witt	Grimes	Jim Hogg	McLennan

McMullen	Newton	Refugio	Sterling	Walker
Madison	Nolam	Roberts	Stonewall	Waller
Marion	Nueces	Robertson	Sutton	Ward
Martin	Ochiltree	Rockwall	Swisher	Washington
Mason	Oldham	Runnels	Tarrant	Webb
Matagorda	Orange	Rusk	Taylor	Wharton
Maverick	Palo Pinto	Sabine	Terrell	Wheeler
Medina	Panola	San Augustine	Terry	Wichita
Menard	Parker	San Jacinto	Throckmorton	Wilbarger
Midland	Parmer	San Patricio	Titus	Willacy
Milam	Pecos	San Saba	Tom Green	Williamson
Mills	Polk	Schleicher	Travis	Wilson
Mitchell	Potter	Scurry	Trinity	Winkler
Montague	Presidio	Shackelford	Tyler	Wise
Montgomery	Rains	Shelby	Upshur	Wood
Moore	Randall	Sherman	Upton	Yoakum
Morris	Reagan	Smith	Uvalde	Young
Motley	Real	Somervell	Val Verde	Zapata
Nacogdoches	Red River	Starr	Van Zandt	Zavala
Navarro	Reeves	Stephens	Victoria	

TRUST TERRITORY OF THE PACIFIC ISLANDS (6 districts)

Kosrae	Palau	Truk
Marshall Islands	Ponape	Yap

UTAH (29 counties)

Beaver	Duchesne	Kane	San Juan	Utah
Box Elder	Emery	Millard	Sanpete	Wasatch
Cache	Garfield	Morgan	Sevier	Washington
Carbon	Grand	Piute	Summit	Wayne
Daggett	Iron	Rich	Tooele	Weber
Davis	Jaub	Salt Lake	Uintah	

VERMONT (14 counties)

Addison	Chittenden	Grand Isle	Orleans	Windham
Bennington	Essex	Lamoille	Rutland	Windsor
Caledonia	Franklin	Orange	Washington	

VIRGINIA (95 counties)

Accomack	Charlotte	Greene	Mecklenburg	Roanoke
Albemarle	Chesterfield	Greensville	Middlesex	Rockbridge
Alleghany	Clarke	Halifax	Montgomery	Rockingham
Amelia	Craig	Hanover	Nelson	Russell
Amherst	Culpeper	Henrico	New Kent	Scott
Appomattox	Cumberland	Henry	Northampton	Shenandoah
Arlington	Dickenson	Highland	Northumberland	Smyth
Augusta	Dinwiddie	Isle of Wight	Nottoway	Southhampton
Bath	Essex	James City	Orange	Spotsylvania
Bedford	Fairfax	King and Queen	Page	Stafford
Bland	Fauquier	King George	Patrick	Surry
Botetourt	Floyd	King William	Pittsylvania	Sussex
Brunswick	Fluvanna	Lancaster	Powhatan	Tazewell
Buchanan	Franklin	Lee	Prince Edward	Warren
Buckingham	Frederick	Loudoun	Prince George	Washington
Campbell	Giles	Louisa	Prince William	Westmoreland
Caroline	Gloucester	Lunenburg	Pulaski	Wise
Carroll	Goochland	Madison	Rappahannock	Wythe
Charles City	Grayson	Mathews	Richmond	York

VIRGIN ISLANDS (3 islands)

St. Croix	St. Thomas	St. John

WASHINGTON (39 counties)

Adams	Douglas	King	Pacific	Stevens
Asotin	Ferry	Kitsap	Pend Oreille	Thurston
Benton	Franklin	Kittitas	Pierce	Wahkiakum
Chelan	Garfield	Klickitat	San Juan	Walla Walla
Clallam	Grant	Lewis	Skagit	Whatcom
Clark	Grays Harbor	Lincoln	Skamania	Whitman
Columbia	Island	Mason	Snohomish	Yakima
Cowlitz	Jefferson	Okanogan	Spokane	

WEST VIRGINIA (55 counties)

Barbour	Grant	Logan	Nicholas	Summers
Berkeley	Greenbrier	McDowell	Ohio	Taylor
Boone	Hampshire	Marion	Pendleton	Tucker
Braxton	Hancock	Marshall	Pleasants	Tyler
Brooke	Hardy	Mason	Pocahontas	Upshur
Cabell	Harrison	Mercer	Preston	Wayne
Calhoun	Jackson	Mineral	Putnam	Webster
Clay	Jefferson	Mingo	Raleigh	Wetzel
Doddridge	Kanawha	Monongalia	Randolph	Wirt
Fayette	Lewis	Monroe	Ritchie	Wood
Gilmer	Lincoln	Morgan	Roane	Wyoming

WISCONSIN (72 counties)

Adams	Douglas	Kewaunee	Ozaukee	Taylor
Ashland	Dunn	La Crosse	Pepin	Trempealeau
Barron	Eau Claire	Lafayette	Pierce	Vernon
Bayfield	Florence	Langlade	Polk	Vilas
Brown	Fond du Lac	Lincoln	Portage	Walworth
Buffalo	Forest	Manitowoc	Price	Washburn
Burnett	Grant	Marathon	Racine	Washington
Calumet	Green	Marinette	Richland	Waukesha
Chippewa	Green Lake	Marquette	Rock	Waupaca
Clark	Iowa	Menominee	Rusk	Waushara
Columbia	Iron	Milwaukee	St. Croix	Winnebago
Crawford	Jackson	Monroe	Sauk	Wood
Dane	Jefferson	Oconto	Sawyer	
Dodge	Juneau	Oneida	Shawano	
Door	Kenosha	Outagamie	Sheboygan	

WYOMING (23 counties)

Albany	Crook	Laramie	Platte	Uinta
Big Horn	Fremont	Lincoln	Sheridan	Washakie
Campbell	Goshen	Natrona	Sublette	Weston
Carbon	Hot Springs	Niobrara	Sweetwater	
Converse	Johnson	Park	Teton	

20. PLANT AND INSECT NAMES

PLANT NAMES AND ADJECTIVE FORMS

20.1. The following list of plant names, some of which vary in form from those given in Webster's Third International Dictionary, has been compiled with the cooperation of the Department of Agriculture. The name of the kinds of agricultural and vegetable crops are given in the "Rules and Regulations Under the Federal Seed Act."

20.2. In general, derivatives of proper names with acquired independent common meaning are not capitalized. (See rule 3.4.) However, in plant names, if the capital letter is retained, either the hyphened or the two-word form is used, depending on predominant usage. Such names as English ivy, Dutchmans-pipe, Cupids-dart, flower-of-Jove, and apple-of-Peru retain the capital letter. On the other hand, such names as Charlie, Jack, and Susan lose their capital letter in fanciful names; e.g., creeping-charlie, jack-in-a-box, and browneyedsusan.

20.3. The apostrophe is omitted in names with a possessive element; thus: babysbreath, Grays iily, devils-paintbrush, etc.

20.4. To indicate preferred usage, there are also included adjective forms, such as nightblooming, straightstem, three-color, two-wing, etc., not by themselves plant names.

20.5. Except as indicated in the list, plant names ending in *bane, bark, bean, berry, bine, brush, cup, fern, flower, grass, leaf, lily, nut, pea, plant, pod, root, seed, thorn, tree, vine, weed, wood,* and *wort* are printed solid, unless the preceding word is a proper name which retains its capitalized form. (See rule 20.2.) All such one-word forms were excluded from the list, along with two-word forms listed in Webster's Third.

Aarons-beard	alfilaria	antelope-brush	Australian-pea
addersmouth	alpencress	Apache-plume	autumn-crocus
adderstongue	Alpine-azalea	apple-of-Peru	avalanche-lily
adzuki bean	Amazon-lily	Arab-primrose	awl-leaf
African-violet	anatto-tree	arar-tree	
airpotato	angel-trumpet	atamasco lily	

baby-blue-eyes	bastardbox	bigtooth	black-eyed-susan
babysbreath	batterdock	birdeye bean	blackfoot
babytears	baycedar	birdpepper	blackjoint
baldhip	beak-rush	birdseye	blacklaurel
baldrush	bearcabbage	birdsfoot	black-mangrove
ballmustard	bears-tail	birdsnest	blackpurple
balm-of-Gilead	beavertail	bishops-cap	blackspot
balsamapple	beebalm	bishops-hood	blackstem
balsam-of-Peru	beefsteak-plant	bittercress	black-salsify
balsam-pear	bee-sage	bittervetch	bladder-senna
banana-shrub	beggarticks	blackbead	blade-apple
Barbados-cherry	belladonna-lily	blackberry-lily	blazing-star
barestem	bigcone-spruce	blackbox	bleedingheart
barnyardgrass	bigfruit	black-bryony	blistercress
barrenground	bigmoon	blackbud	bloodball
barren-strawberry	bigstem	black-calabash	bloodred

257

fieldcress
fieldmadder
field # pea
figmarigold
finetooth
firemoss
firepink
fishhooks
fishpoison-tree
five-blade

five-coil
five-finger
five-stamen
flamboyant-tree
flamepoppy
flameray
floatingheart
floptop
Florida-boxwood
flowerfence

flowering-rush
flower-of-an-hour
flower-of-Jove
fogfruit
forget-me-not
four-color
four-o'clock
four-stamen
four-wing
foxchop

foxfeet
foxglove
foxtailgrass
Franciscan-nightshade
fringebell
fringe-orchid
frogfoot
fullers # teasel
fullmoon

gallwind
garambullo
garden # bean
garden # pea
gayfeather
gaywings
ghostpipe
giantfennel
giantgroundsel
gill-over-the-ground
giltedge
globe-amaranth
globe-cone
globedaisy
globemallow
globethistle
globe-tulip
glorybower
goatsbeard
goatsrue
goldband
goldbeard
goldblotch
golddust

goldedge
golden-aster
goldenback
goldenball
goldenbeard
goldenbowl
goldenchain
golden-eyed-grass
goldenfeather
goldenfleece
goldenglow
golden-larch
goldenlocks
goldenmoon
goldenpert
goldenplume
golden-rain-tree
goldenrod
goldenseal
golden-shower
goldenstar
goldentop
goldentuft
goldentwig

goldenwave
goldenyarrow
goldeye-grass
goldfields
goldhair
Goldie (fern, etc.)
goldmoss
goldspot
goldstripe
goldthread
goldtip
goldtwig
goldvein
good-King-Henry
gooseberry-tree
goosefoot
goosetongue
grains-of-paradise
grapehyacinth
grass-pink
grasswidow
gravel-bind
graybox
grays (lily, etc.)

Greek-valerian
green-ebony
greenfire
greenheart
green-net
greenscale
greensides
greenstem
greenthread
greentwig
greenvein
groundcedar
groundcherry
ground-ivy
groundpine
groundsmoke
Guiana-chestnut
gumbo-limbo
gum-myrtle
gunbright
guttapercha

hairgrass
hairyhead
halfhigh
halfmoon
halfskirt
hardbeam
hard-iron
hardshell
harebell
harebottle
hares-ear-mustard
harestail
hartstongue

hawksbeard
healbite
heartpetal
hedgehog-coneflower
hedgemustard
hedgestraw
heronbill
Hicks (yew, etc.)
Himalaya-berry
Himalaya-honeysuckle
Hinds (walnut, etc.)
hoarycress
hogpeanut

hogsfennel
hollowstem
hollyaster
hollygrape
honeybell
honeybind
honeybloom
hopsage
hornpoppy
horsebalm
horsechestnut
horse-eye
horsegentian

horsemint
horse-nettle
horse-pipe
horseradish
horseradish-tree
horsetail-tree
houndstongue
house-amaryllis
houseleek
hummingbird-trumpet
hyacinth-bean
hydrangea-vine

incense-cedar
India-almond
India-elm
India-hawthorn
India-mulberry

Indian-fig
Indian-physic
Indian-pipe
Indian-potato
indiantobacco

Indian-warrior
Indian-wheat
ivory-leaves
ivy-arum
ivybells

ivy-gourd
ivy-vine

jaburan
jackfrost
jackfruit
Jacobs-rod
jambolan-plum
Jersey-tea

Jerusalem-artichoke
Jerusalem-cherry
Jerusalem-oak
Jerusalem-sage
Jerusalem-thorn
jobs-tears

joe-pye-weed
jointfir
jointvetch
Josephs-coat
Joshua-tree
Judas-tree

jungle-plum
junglerice
Jupiters-beard

kafircorn
karanda
Kartaba (iris, etc.)
kasumi (cherry, etc.)

katsura-tree
kauri-pine
kei-apple
kidney bean

kidneyvetch
kittentails
kohlrabi
kolomikta

kousa
kudzu
kwanso (daylily, etc.)
kyushu (azalea, etc.)

Labrador-tea
lacquer-tree
ladies-tresses
ladybell
ladyslipper

ladysmantle
ladysthumb
lambsquarters
lap-love
largetooth

lavender-cotton
leaf-flower
lemon-verbena
lignum vitae
lilybasket

lily-of-the-valley
lions-ear
little-pickles
live-ever
liveforever

liver-balsam
living-rock
loblolly-bay
loggerheads

London-pride
longbarb
longcluster
longlip

long-spine
long-stalk
Longs (grapes, etc.)
longtube

lookingglass
loveman

Madden-cherry
Madeira-bay
Magdalena mock
    (orange, etc.)
mahala-mats
maidenhair-tree
Malabar-nut
Malabar-plum
Malay-apple
malu-creeper
mame (cherry, etc.)
mandacaru
Mangles (everlasting,
    etc.)
marestail
Mardin (iris, etc.)
Maries (fir, etc.)
marshcress
marsh-elder
marshfire
marshmallow

Martens (selaginella,
    etc.)
Mascarene (grass, etc.)
matilija-poppy
Matreed
matrimonyvine
mayapple
maybloom
maypear
Mays (brake, etc.)
meadowbeauty
meadowfoam
meadowrue
mealymat
Meiwa (kumquat, etc.)
merrybells
Mexican-buckeye
Mexican-clover
Mexican-orange
Mexican-star
mexicantea

Michaelmas-daisy
milkthistle
milkvetch
mistmaiden
miyama
mock-cucumber
mockorange
mockstrawberry
Molucca-balm
momi
monkeycomb
monkeypuzzle
monks-hood-vine
monreale
Moores (agapanthus,
    etc.)
moosetongue
morningglory
moso
mosquitotrap
moss # rose

moth # bean
moth-orchid
mountainash
mountain-bluet
mountain-dandelion
mountainheath
mountain-holly
mountain-laurel
mountain-lilac
mountain-mint
mouse-ear
mousetail
Moyes (rose, etc.)
mudbank
mullein
mung # bean
mundi-root
Mupin (cotoneaster,
    etc.)
muskphlox
myrtle-of-the-river

Narbonne (flax, etc.)
narihira
Natal-ebony
navy # bean

needleandthread
needlerush
netvein
nightblooming

nightjasmine
nightphlox
nimblewill
ningala

Nippon-bells
nodfruit
nosesmart

Oconee-bells
oldman (fern, etc.)
one-spike

orange-eye
orange-jasmine
orange-rose

organpipe
orobus
otaksa

owlclover
oxeye-daisy

painted-cup
palma # dulce
paloblanco
pansy-orchid
paper-mulberry
paradise-tree
Parsons (arborvitae,
    etc.)
partridgefoot
pawpaw
pear-hip
pearlfruit
pearl-stripe
peatpink
pea-tree
pennyrot
pheasanteye
pinebarren
pinemat

pinkbells
pink-edge
pinkscale
pink-shell
pinkshower
pink-star
pinkstem
pinkstripe
pinkwax
pinpillow
pinpoint
pinxterbloom
plumepoppy
plum-pine
poets (narcissus, etc.)
pointvetch
poison-hemlock
poison-ivy
poison-oak

poison-sumac
poisonvetch
pond-apple
pondcypress
ponyfoot
poor-robins-plantain
popglove
poppy-mallow
Portugal-laurel
possumhaw
Potts (tritonia, etc.)
prairie-clover
prairie-gentian
prairie-mallow
prairie-smoke
pricklepoppy
prickly-thrift
pricktimber
pride-of-Madeira

primrose-willow
princesfeather
princesplume
princess-pine
puckneedle
purplebell
purplecane
purplecone
purple-eye
purple-lady
purplenet
purple-spot
purplestem
purple-stripe
purplewreath
pussy-ears
pussypaws
pussytoes

quakerladies
Queen-Annes-lace

queen-of-the-night

Queensland-nut

quill-leaf

rabbitear
rabbitfoot
rabbittail
raggedrobin
ramshead
Rangoon-creeper
rattlesnake-plaintain
rattlesnake-root
redbead
redbox
red-devil
redflesh
redflowering
redhelmet
redmaids

red-osier
redpepper
redrim
redscale
redshanks
redshoot
redspot
redspray
redspur
redstem
redtip
redtwig
red-white-and-blue-
    flower
Reeves (spirea, etc.)

rice # bean
ricepaper-plant
Rivers (beech, etc.)
rockbeauty
rockbrake
rockcress
rockjasmine
rockmat
rockpurslane
rockspray
rosa-montana
rosarypea
rose-acacia
rosegay
rose-gentian

rose-of-heaven
rose-of-Jericho
rosepink
rose-ring
roundbud
round-eared
roundheart
roundlobe
roundtop
runningpine
Russian-olive
Russian-thistle

sacred-lily
saffron-plum
sagerose
St. Augustinegrass
St.-Bernards-lily
St.-Brunos-lily
St.-James-lily
St. Johns (coontie, etc.)
St.-Johnswort
salad-rocket
saltmarsh
saltmeadow
salt-tree
sandheath
sandmint
sandmyrtle
sandreed
sandverbena
sappan
sapsuck-bush
satinpoppy
saw-palmetto
sawpetal
scarboro-lily
scarlet-bugler
scarletfunnel
scarletplume
scorpion-senna
Scotch-broom
scouringrush
screwpine
scurf-pea
sea-buckthorn
seaholly
seakale
sea-lavender
seamoss
sea-onion
seaplum
sea-urchin
seawife

selfheal
Seneca-snakeroot
senna-pea
sensitive-pea
seven-lobe
seven-stars
seven-year-apple
sharp-lobe
sharpscale
shell # bean
shepherdspurse
shooting-star
shortbeak
shortcluster
short-hair
short-spine
shrub-althea
sidebells
side-oats
silk-oak
silktassel-bush
silverbell
silverdust
silver-edge
silverline
silvermargin
silvernerve
silverplume
silverpurple
silverstar .
silvervein
singhara-nut
six-weeks
skunkcabbage
skyblue
skydrop
Smalls (penstemon, etc.)
snailclover
snakebeard
snakegourd

snakepipe
snap # bean
snowcloud
snowgarland
snowhill
snowpoppy
snow-wreath
soapbloom
Solomon-plume
Solomons-seal
sourclover
southernplume
sowthistle
Spanish-bayonet
Spanish-dagger
Spanish-moss
spanishneedles
spectacle-pod
speedwell
spider-orchid
spiderweb
spikeheath
spike-sedge
spine-date
spinemallow
spongegourd
springbeauty
spurgall
spurge-nettle
spurge-olive
spur-valerian
squaw-apple
squawcarpet
squirrelcorn
squirting-cucumber
star-apple
starbur
star-gooseberry
starjasmine
starthistle
stiffstem

stinging-nettle
stinkbell
stonebreak
stonegall
stonemint
straightstem
strawberry-blite
strawberry-tree
string # bean
sugar-apple
sugar # beet
sugarbird
sugar # pea
sugar-root
summer-cypress
summer-fir
summer-hyacinth
summersweet
sunn-hemp
sunray
Surinam-cherry
swampbay
swampcandle
swamp-laurel
swamp-pink
swamp-privet
swan-orchid
sweet-anise
sweetbay
sweet-calabash
sweetclover
sweetgale
sweetpotato
sweetshrub
sweetspire
sweet-sultan
sweetvetch
sweetwater
sweet-william
Syrian privet

tailgrape
tangletail
tansymustard
tansy-ragwort
tea-olive
Teas (catalpa, etc.)
teaselgourd
tea-tree
telegraphplant
Tennessee-indigo
tepary # bean
Texas-plume
thickspike
thintail
thornapple

thoroughgrowth
threadstalk
three-coil
three-color
three-lobe
three-seed
three-spine
three-tip
throughgrow
tickclover
tick-trefoil
tidemarsh
tigerfoot
tigertail
tipu-tree

tonka-bean
toringo
towelgourd
trailing-arbutus
travelers-joy
travelers-tree
treacle-mustard
treebeard
treehair
treemallow
treepoppy
tree-spirea
tree-tomato
true-dwarf (box)
tumblemustard

tung-oil tree
turbantop
turkeymullein
turkeysbeard
Turks-cap
Turks-rug
turnip-chervil
twinbloom
twist-arum
twocolor
two-groove
two-row
two-wing

umbrella-pine
umbrella-sedge

umbrella-tree

undergreen

urd # bean

valley-mahogany
Vanhoutte (elm, etc.)

vegetable-oyster
Venus-button

vi-apple
vinespinach

virgins-bower

wakerobin
walkingstick
wallcress
wandering-Jew
watercreeper
water-elm
waterhemlock
waterhemp

waterlemon
waterlocust
watermarigold
waterparsnip
waterpepper
wasterpoppy
watershrub
water-snowflake

watersoldier
waterstar
waterwillow
waxgourd
wayfaring-tree
weakleaf
weavers-broom
wedgescale

Welsh-poppy
whisperingbells
whitebud
white-cedar
white-edge
white-eye
white-ironwood
whitemat

white-sapote   wingstem   witchbells   woodsorrel
whitespike   winter-aconite   wolftail   woodwaxen
whitespot   wintercress   woodbetony   woollybutt
whitestem   winterfat   wood-gossip   woollyhead
whitestripe   winterhazel   woodland-star   woolwitch
wildcelery   wintersweet   woodnymph   woundwort
wildgoose   wirelettuce   woodrush
wild-indigo   wirestem   Woods (rose, etc.)

yate-tree   yellow-edge   yellownet   yellowvein
Yeddo-hawthorn   yelloweye   yellow-oleander   yellow-vetch
yellowband   yellow-eyed-grass   yellow-poplar   yerba-buena
yellowbeard   yellowflag   yellow-rocket   yerba-del-venado
yellowbell   yellowflax   yellowspot   yerba-santa
yellow-cedar   yellowfruit   yellowstripe   Youngs (cypress, etc.)
yellowcress   yellowheart   yellowtip

AQUATIC WEEDS (ANNUAL AND PERENNIAL)

alligatorweed   ducksalad (see also   pithophora   sprangletop, bearded
arrowarum   mud-plantain,   pondweed   sweetflag
arrowhead   waterstargrass)   American   toothcup
  California   duckweed   curlyleaf   torpedograss
  coastal   common   fineleaf
  common   giant   flatleaf   ulva
  delta   star   flatstem   umbrellaplant (see also
  dwarf   floating   flatsedge)
azolla   egeria   giant   smallflower
  Atlantic   elodea (see also egeria)   horned   tall
  Pacific   Illinois
    flatsedge (see also   largeleaf   vallisneria
bladderwort   umbrellaplant)   leafy   vaucheria
  common   jointed   narrowleaf
  floating   redroot   ribbonleaf   waterbuttercup
  leafy   floatingfern   Richardson   white
  purple   frogbit   sago   yellow
bluejoint   small   waterchestnut
bogbean, common   goldenclub   waterthread   watercress
bulrush   whitestem   watergrass, southern
  American   horsetail   waterhyacinth
  California   giant   redroot   waterhyssop
  green   water   restem   Carolina
  hardstem   hydrodictyon   reed, common   Eisen
  river   rosemallow   waterlettuce
  roughseed   knotgrass   swamp   waterlily
  softstem   woolly   banana
  woolgrass   lizardtail   rush   fragrant
burhead   loosestrife   Baltic   white
burreed   purple   brownhead   watermeal
  giant   swamp   needle   watermilfoil
  greenfruit   lotus, American   shore   watermilfoil (see also
  narrowleaf   soft   parrotfeather)
  threesquare   maidencane   broadleaf
  water   mallow, seashore   saltgrass, seashore   eurasian
    mannagrass, water   salvinia   northern
cabomba   marshmarigold   sawgrass, smooth   waterplantain
cattail   marsilea (see   sedge   common
  blue   pepperwort)   bull   narrowleaf
  common   mudplantain (see also   Nebraska   waterprimrose
  narrowleaf   ducksalad,   ripgut   California
  southern   waterstargrass)   rough   creeping
chara   sugargrass   perennial
cladophora   naiad   water   winged
coontail   hollyleaf   widefruit   waterpurslane
  common   slender   smartweed   watershield
  prickly   southern   dotted   waterstargrass (see
cordgrass   napiergrass   marshpepper   also ducksalad,
  big   nitella   water   mudplantain)
  Florida   spatterdock   waterstarwort
  saltmeadow   paragrass (see   spikerush   waterwillow
  smooth   herbaceous weeds)   blunt   waterwort
cutgrass   parrotfeather (see also   creeping   American
  giant   watermilfoil)   dwarf   small
  rice   paspalum, water   gulfcoast   widgeongrass
  southern   pennywort, water   slender   wildrice, annual
    pepperwort   squarestem
    pickerelweed   spirogyra

WOODY PLANTS

abutilon, hairy
acacia (see also
  guajillo, huisache,
  whitethorn)
  blackbrush
  catclaw
agarito
agave, Schott
albizzia, silktree

alder
  American green
  hazel
  red
  Sitka
  speckled
  white
allthorn
apple
arrowwood

ash
  black
  blue
  Carolina
  green
  Oregon
  pumpkin
  velvet
  white

aspen (see also
  cottonwood,
  poplar)
  bigtooth
  quaking
azalea (see also
  rhododendron)
  piedmont
  western

baccharis (see also
  coyotebrush,
  desert broom,
  yerba-de-pasmo)
  eastern
  seepwillow
  willow
baldcypress
barberry (see also
  mahonia,
  oregongrape)
  American
  Colorado
  European
  Japanese
basswood
  American
  white
bayberry, northern
bean, precatory
bearberry
beargrass
bearmat

beautyberry, American
beech, American
birch
  gray
  paper
  river
  sweet
  water
  yellow
bird-of-paradise
bitterbrush
blackberry (see also
  dewberry,
  raspberry,
  salmonberry,
  thimbleberry)
  Allegheny
  European
  evergreen
  Hawaiian
  Himalaya
  grapeleaf
blackbush

blackgum
blackhaw, rusty (see
  also viburnum)
blueberry (see also
  huckleberry)
  box
  lowbush
  ovalleaf
boxelder
broom
  desert
  French
  Scotch
  Spanish
buckbrush (see also
  snowberry)
buckeye
  California
  Ohio
  painted
  red
  Texas
  yellow

buckthorn
  aldar
  California
  Carolina
  cascara
  European
  hollyleaf
buffaloberry
  russet
  silver
bumelia
  buckthorn
  gum
bur, Sacramento
burrobush
burroweed (see also
  goldenweed,
  jimmyweed)
bush, wait-a-minute
  (see wait-a-minute-
  bush)
butternut
buttonbush, common

camelthorn
canotia
caperbush, smooth
catalpa
  northern
  southern
catsclaw
ceanothus (see also
  whitethorn)
  bigpod
  blueblossom
  deerbrush
  jimbrush
  Lemmons
  redstem
  San Diego
  snowbrush
  spiny
  squawcarpet
  varnishleaf
  wedgeleaf
cedar (see also
  redcedar,
  saltcedar)
  incense
  northern white
  Port Orford
chamise, redshank

cherry (see also
  chokecherry)
  bitter
  black
  pin
  sour
  sweet
chestnut, American
chinaberry
chinquapin
  Allegheny
  California
  golden
  trailing
chokeberry
  black
  red
chokecherry (see also
  cherry)
  black
  common
  western
cholla (see also
  pricklypear,
  tasajillo)
  jumping
  spiny
  staghorn
  walkingstick

christmas berry
cinquefoil, shrubby
clematis
  Virginia
  western
clerodendron, fragrant
coffeetree, Kentucky
colima
colubrina, Texas
condalia
  bluewood
  lotebush
copperweed
cottonwood (see also
  aspen, poplar)
  black
  eastern
  Fremont
  plains
  Rio Grande
  swamp
coyotebrush (see also
  baccharis)
coyotillo
crabapple
  prairie
  southern
  sweet

cranberry
  mountain
  small
creeper, Virginia
creosotebush
crossvine
crotalaria
  fuzzy
  striped
  tawny
cucumbertree
currant (see also
  gooseberry)
  American black
  nutmeg
  redflowered
  Sierra
  skunk
  sticky
  stink
  swamp black
  swamp red
  trailing
  wax
  western black

dangleberry
deerberry, common
devils-walkingstick

dewberry (see also
  raspberry)
  northern
  southern

dogwood
  flowering
  Pacific
  redosier

roughleaf
roundleaf
western

sugarberry (see also grenjeno, hackberry)

sumac
evergreen
fragrant
laurel
little leaf
prairie
poison
shining
skunkbush
smooth
staghorn
sugar

supplejack, Alabama
sweetfern
sweetgum
sycamore, American

tallowtree
tamarack (see also larch)
tamarisk (see also saltcedar)
athel
French

tanoak, scrub
tarbush
tasajillo (see also cholla)
tea, Labrador
tephrosia
thimbleberry, western

titi
tobacco, tree
tree-of-heaven
treebine, ivy
trema, Florida
trumpetcreeper
trumpetflower

tuliptree
tupelo
swamp
water
turpentinebrush

vervain, nettleleaf
viburnum (see also blackhaw)

arrowwood
hobblebush

mapleleaf
Rafinesque
sweet

vine, Maderia

wahoo, eastern
wait-a-minute-bush
walnut (see also butternut)
black
river
waltheria, Florida
wattle, black

waxmyrtle
Pacific
southern
whitebrush
whitehorn
chaparral
Chihuahua
mountain

willow
Bebb
black
ditchbank
meadow
Pacific
peachleaf
red

sandbar
ward
whiplash
white
yellow
witchhazel
common
southern

yaupon, deciduous (see also gallberry, holly)
yerbasanta
California
narrowleaf

woolly
yellowwood
yerba-de-pasmo (see also baccharis)
yew

Florida
Pacific
yucca (see also soap-weed
soaptree

Torrey

INSECT NAMES

20.6. The following list of insect names is taken from the list of names approved by the Entomological Society of America and the Department of Agriculture's Insect Identification and Beneficial Insect Introduction Institute and serves as a guide to compounding for these specialized terms.

20.7. Except as indicated in the list, names ending in *bug, fly, hopper, roach,* and *worm* are set solid; names with a final element of *ant, aphid, beetle, borer, caterpillar, louse, maggot, midge, miner, mite, mosquito, moth, roller, scale, thrips, tick,* and *weevil* are set as two words.

abbreviated wireworm
acacia psyllid
achemon sphinx
acuminate scale
acute-angled fungus
  beetle
aerial yellowjacket
African mole cricket
ailanthus webworm
alder bark beetle
alder flea beetle
alder spittlebug
alfalfa blotch
  leafminer
alfalfa caterpillar
alfalfa gall midge
alfalfa leafcutting bee
alfalfa leaftier
alfalfa looper
alfalfa plant bug
alfalfa seed chalcid
alfalfa snout beetle
alfalfa webworm

alfalfa weevil
alkali bee
Allegheny mound ant
Allegheny spruce
  beetle
almond moth
aloe mite
American aspen beetle
American black flour
  beetle
American cockroach
American dagger moth
American dog tick
American grasshopper
American hornet moth
American house dust
  mite
American plum borer
American spider beetle
Angora goat biting
  louse
Angoumois grain moth
angularwinged katydid

angulate leafhopper
apple-and-thorn
  skeletonizer
apple aphid
apple bark borer
apple barkminer
apple blotch leafminer
apple curculio
apple flea weevil
apple fruitminer
apple fruit moth
apple grain aphid
apple leafhopper
apple maggot
apple mealybug
apple red bug
apple rust mite
apple seed chalcid
apple sucker
apple twig beetle
apple twig borer
appleleaf skeletonizer
appleleaf trumpet
  miner

araucaria aphid
arborvitae leafminer
arborvitae weevil
Argentine ant
argus tortoise beetle
army cutworm
armyworm
artichoke plume moth
ashgray blister beetle
ash plant bug
Asiatic garden beetle
Asiatic oak weevil
Asiatic rice borer
Asiatic rose scale
asparagus beetle
asparagus miner
asparagus spider mite
aspen blotchminer
aspen leaf beetle
aster leafhopper
aster leafminer
Australian cockroach
Australian fern weevil
Australian mantid

Australian rat flea
Australian spider
  beetle

Australianpine borer
avocado brown mite
avocado red mite

avocado whitefly
azalea bark scale
azalea lace bug

azalea leafminer
azalea plant bug
azalea whitefly

bagworm
Bahaman swallowtail
baldcypress coneworm
baldfaced hornet
balsam fir sawfly
balsam fir sawyer
balsam gall midge
balsam shootboring
  sawfly
balsam twig aphid
balsam woolly adelgid
bamboo borer
bamboo mealybug
bamboo powderpost
  beetle
bamboo spider mite
banana aphid
banana root borer
banana skipper
banded alder borer
banded ash clearwing
banded cucumber
  beetle
banded greenhouse
  thrips
banded hickory borer
banded sunflower
  moth
banded wood snail
banded woollybear
bandedwing whitefly
Banks grass mite
banyan aphid
Barber brown lacewing
barberpole caterpillar
barley jointworn
barnacle scale
basswood lace bug
basswood leafminer
basswood leafroller
beachgrass scale
bean aphid
bean butterfly
bean capsid
bean fly
bean leaf beetle
bean leafroller
bean leafskeletonizer
bean pod borer
bean stalk weevil
bean thrips
bean weevil
Beardsley leafhopper
bed bug

beech blight aphid
beech scale
beet armyworm
beet leaf beetle
beet leafhopper
beet leafminer
beet webworm
bella moth
Bermudagrass mite
bertha armyworm
bidens borer
bigheaded ant
bigheaded grasshopper
birch bark beetle
birch casebearer
birch leafminer
birch sawfly
birch skeletonizer
birch tubemaker
bird tick
black army cutworm
black blister beetle
black blow fly
black carpenter ant
black carpet beetle
black cherry aphid
black cherry fruit fly
black citrus aphid
black cockroach wasp
black cutworm
black dung beetle
black earwig
black elm bark weevil
black flower thrips
black fungus beetle
black grain stem
  sawfly
black horse fly
black hunter thrips
black imported fire ant
black lady beetle
black larder beetle
black peach aphid
black pecan aphid
black pineleaf scale
black potter wasp
black scale
black soldier fly
black stink bug
black turfgrass
  ataenius
black twig borer
black swallowtail
black thread scale

avocado whitefly
azalea bark scale
azalea lace bug

black turpentine beetle
black vine weevil
black walnut curculio
black widow spider
black witch
blackbellied clerid
blackberry skeletonizer
Blackburn butterfly
blackfaced leafhopper
blackheaded ash
  sawfly
blackheaded fireworm
blackheaded pine
  sawfly
blackhorned pine borer
blackhorned tree
  cricket
blackjacket
blacklegged tick
blacklegged tortoise
  beetle
blackmargined aphid
blister coneworm
bloodsucking conenose
blue cactus borer
blue horntail
blue soldier fly
blueberry bud mite
blueberry case bearer
blueberry flea beetle
blueberry maggot
blueberry thrips
blueberry tip midge
bluegrass billbug
bluegrass webworm
bluntnosed cranberry
  leafhopper
body louse
Boisduval scale
boll weevil
bollworm
booklouse
boxelder aphid
boxelder bug
boxelder leafroller
boxelder psyllid
boxelder twig borer
boxwood leafminer
boxwood psyllid
bramble leafhopper
Brasilian leafhopper
bristly cutworm
bristly roseslug
broad mite

broadbean weevil
broadhorned flour
  beetle
broadnecked root borer
broadnosed grain
  weevil
broadwinged katydid
bromegrass seed midge
bronze appletree
  weevil
bronze birch borer
bronze leaf beetle
bronze poplar borer
bronzed cutworm
brown chicken louse
brown citrus aphid
brown cockroach
brown cotton leafworm
brown dog tick
brown dung beetle
brown flour mite
brown garden snail
brown house moth
brown mite
brown pineapple scale
brown recluse spider
brown saltmarsh
  mosquito
brown soft scale
brown spider beetle
brown stink bug
brown wheat mite
brown widow spider
brownbanded
  cockroach
brownheaded jack pine
  sawfly
brownheaded ash
  sawfly
brownlegged grain
  mite
browntail moth
Bruce spanworm
buck moth
buckthorn aphid
buffalograss webworm
buffalo treehopper
bulb mite
bulb scale mite
bumble flower beetle
bumelia fruit fly
burdock borer
Burmeister mantid
butternut curculio

cabbage aphid
cabbage curculio
cabbage looper
cabbage maggot
cabbage seedpod weevil
cabbage seedstalk
  curculio
cabbage webworm
cactus moth
cactus scale
cadelle
Caledonia seed bug
calico scale
California fivespined
  ips
California flatheaded
  borer

California harvester
  ant
California oakworm
California pear sawfly
California prionus
California red scale
California saltmarsh
  mosquito
California tortoiseshell
camellia scale
camphor scale
camphor thrips
caragana aphid
caragana blister beetle
caragana plant bug
Caribbean black scale
Caribbean pod borer

carmine spider mite
carnation maggot
carnation tip maggot
Carolina conifer aphid
Carolina grasshopper
Carolina mantid
carpenter bee
carpenterworm
carpet beetle
carpet moth
carrot beetle
carrot rust fly
carrot weevil
casemaking clothes
  moth
catalpa midge
catalpa sphinx

cat flea
cat follicle mite
cat louse
cattle biting louse
cattle follicle mite
cattle itch mite
cattle tail louse
cattle tick
Cayenne tick
ceanothus silk moth
cecropia moth
cedartree borer
celery aphid
celery leaftier
celery looper
cereal leaf beetle
chaff scale

European honeysuckle
  leafroller
European hornet
European house dust
  mite
European mantid

European mouse flea
European peach scale
European pine sawfly
European pine shoot
  moth
European red mite

European spruce beetle
European spruce
  sawfly
European wheat stem
  sawfly

eyed click beetle
eyespotted bud moth

face fly
fall armyworm
fall cankerworm
fall webworm
false celery leaftier
false chinch bug
false German
  cockroach
false hemlock looper
false potato beetle
false stable fly
feather mite
fern aphid
fern caterpillar
fern scale
field crickets
fiery hunter
fiery skiper

fig mite
fig scale
fig wasp
Fijian ginger weevil
filament bearer
filbert aphid
filbert bud mite
filbert weevil
filbertworm
fir cone looper
fire ant
firebrat
fir engraver
fir seed moth
firtree borer
flat grain beetle
flatheaded appletree
  borer

flatheaded cone borer
flatheaded fir borer
flax bollworm
Fletcher scale
floodwater mosquito
Florida carpenter ant
Florida fern caterpillar
Florida harvester ant
Florida red scale
Florida wax scale
flower thrips
fluff louse
follicle mite
forage looper
Forbes scale
foreign grain beetle
forest day mosquito
forest tent caterpillar

forest tree termite
forktailed bush katydid
Formosan
  subterranean
  termite
fourlined plant bug
fourspotted spider mite
fourspotted tree cricket
fowl tick
foxglove aphid
frigate bird fly
fringed orchid aphid
frit fly
fruittree leafroller
Fuller rose beetle
furniture beetle
furniture carpet beetle

gallmaking maple
  borer
garden fleahopper
garden millipede
garden springtail
garden symphylan
garden webworm
gardenia bud mite
genista caterpillar
German cockroach
giant African snail
giant bark aphid
giant Hawaiian
  dragonfly
giant stag beetle
giant water bug
Giffard whitefly
ginger maggot
gladiolus thrips
glassy cutworm
globose scale
globular spider beetle
gloomy scale
Glover scale
goat biting louse
goat follicle mite
goat sucking louse
golden buprestid
golden cricket wasp
golden oak scale
golden paper wasp

golden spider beetle
golden tortoise beetle
goldeneye lacewing
goldenglow aphid
gooseberry fruitworm
gooseberry witchbroom
  aphid
goose body louse
gorse seed weevil
gophertortoise tick
grain mite
grain rust mite
grain thrips
granary weevil
granulate cutworm
grape berry moth
grape blossom midge
grape cane gallmaker
grape colaspis
grape curculio
grape erineum mite
grape flea beetle
grape leaffolder
grape mealybug
grape phylloxera
grape plume moth
grape root borer
grape rootworm
grape sawfly
grape scale
grape seed chalcid

grape trunk borer
grape whitefly
grapeleaf skeletonizer
grapevine aphid
grapevine looper
grass fleahopper
grass mite
grass sawfly
grass scolytid
grass sharpshooter
grass sheathminer
  complex
grass thrips
grass webworm
grasshopper bee fly
grasshopper maggots
gray garden slug
gray lawn leafhopper
gray pineapple
  mealybug
gray sugarcane
  mealybug
gray willow leaf beetle
graybanded leafroller
great ash spinx
Great Basin wireworm
greater wax moth
greedy scale
green budworm
green cloverworm
green fruitworm

green garden looper
green sphinx
green June beetle
green peach aphid
green rose chafer
green scale
green shield scale
green spruce aphid
green stink bug
greenbug
greenheaded spruce
  sawfly
greenhouse leaftier
greenhouse orthezia
greenhouse slug
greenhouse stone
  cricket
greenhouse thrips
greenhouse whitefly
greenstriped
  grasshopper
greenstriped
  mapleworm
gregarious oak
  leafminer
ground mealybug
Guinea ant
guinea feather louse
Gulf Coast tick
Gulf wireworm
gypsy moth

hackberry engraver
hackberry lace bug
hackberry nipplegall
  maker
hag moth
hairy chinch bug
hairy fungus beetle
hairy maggot blow fly
hairy rove beetle
hairy spider beetle
Hall scale
hard maple budminer
harlequin bug
harlequin cockroach
hau leafminer
Hawaiian antlion
Hawaiian beet
  webworm

Hawaiian bud moth
Hawaiian carpenter
  ant
Hawaiian flower thrips
Hawaiian grass thrips
Hawaiian pelagic
  water strider
Hawaiian sphinx
hawthorn lace bug
hazelnut weevil
head louse
heath spittlebug
hellgrammite
hemispherical scale
hemlock borer
hemlock looper
hemlock sawfly

hemlock scale
Hessian fly
hibiscus leafminer
hibiscus mealybug
hibiscus whitefly
hickory bark beetle
hickory horned devil
hickory leafroller
hickory plant bug
hickory shuckworm
hickory tussock moth
hide beetle
High Plains
  grasshopper
hog follicle mite
hog louse
holly leafminer

holly scale
hollyhock plant bug
hollyhock weevil
honey bee
honey bee mite
honeylocust plant bug
honeysuckle leafminer
honeysuckle sawfly
hop aphid
hop flea beetle
hop looper
hop plant bug
horned passalus
horned squash bug
hornet moth
hornets
horn fly
horse biting louse

horse bot fly
horse follicle mite
horse sucking louse
horseradish flea beetle

house centipede
house cricket
house fly
house mite

house mouse mite
household casebearer
human flea
hunting billbug

hyaline grass bug

ilima leafminer
ilima moth
imbricated snout
  beetle
immigrant acacia
  weevil
imperial moth

imported cabbageworm
imported crucifer
  weevil
imported currantworm
imported longhorned
  weevil

imported willow leaf
  beetle
incense-cedar wasp
Indianmeal moth
inornate scale
introduced pine sawfly
io moth

iris borer
iris thrips
iris weevil
Italian pear scale
itch mite
ivy aphid

jack pine budworm
jack pine sawfly
jack pine tip beetle
Japanese beetle

Japanese broadwinged
  katydid
Japanese grasshopper

Jeffrey pine beetle
Jerusalem cricket
juniper midge

juniper scale
juniper tip midge
juniper webworm

Kamehameha butterfly
keyhole wasp
khapra beetle
kiawe bean weevil

kiawe flower moth
kiawe roundheaded
  borer
kiawe scolytid

Kirkaldy whitefly
Klamathweed beetle
koa bug
koa haole seed weevil

koa moth
koa seedworm
kou leafworm

Lange metalmark
lantana cerambycid
lantana defoliator
  caterpillar
lantana gall fly
lantana hispid
lantana lace bug
lantana leaf beetle
lantana leafminer
lantana leaftier
lantana plume moth
lantana seed fly
lantana stick
  caterpillar
lappet moth
larch aphid
larch casebearer
larch sawfly
larder beetle
large aspen tortrix
large bigeyed bug
large brown spider
large chestnut weevil
large chicken louse
large cottony scale
large duck louse
large kissing bug
large milkweed bug
large red slug
large turkey louse
larger black flour
  beetle

larger canna leafroller
larger elm leaf beetle
larger grain borer
larger Hawaiian
  cutworm
larger lantana
  butterfly
larger pale trogiid
larger shothole borer
larger yellow ant
larkspur leafminer
  complex
latania scale
latrine fly
lawn armyworm
lawn leafhopper
leadcable borer
leaf crumpler
leaffooted assassin bug
leaffooted bug
leaffooted pine seed
  bug
leek moth
leopard moth
lespedeza webworm
lesser appleworm
lesser brown scorpion
lesser bud moth
lesser bulb fly
lesser canna leafroller

lesser clover leaf
  weevil
lesser cornstalk borer
lesser ensign wasp
lesser follicle mite
lesser grain borer
lesser lawn leafhopper
lesser mealworm
lesser orchid weevil
lesser peachtree borer
lesser wax moth
lettuce root aphid
light brown apple
  moth
lilac borer
lilac leafminer
lily bulb thrips
lily weevil
limabean pod borer
limabean vine borer
linden borer
linden looper
lined click beetle
lined spittlebug
lined stalk borer
lion beetle
litchi fruit moth
litchi mite
little black ant
little carpenterworm

little fire ant
little green leafhopper
little house fly
little yellow ant
loblolly pine sawfly
locust borer
locust leafminer
locust leafroller
locust twig borer
lodgepole cone beetle
lodgepole needleminer
lodgepole pine beetle
lodgepole sawfly
lodgepole terminal
  weevil
lone star tick
long brown scale
longheaded flour beetle
longleaf pine
  seedworm
longlegged ant
longnosed cattle louse
longtailed fruit fly
  parasite
longtailed mealybug
lotis blue
Louisiana red crayfish
lowland tree termite
lubber grasshopper
luna moth

Macao paper wasp
Madeira cockroach
magnolia scale
maize billbug
maize weevil
mango bark beetle
mango bud mite
mango flower beetle
mango shoot
  caterpillar
mango spider mite
mango weevil
maple bladdergall mite
maple callus borer
maple leafcutter
maple petiole borer
maple trumpet
  skeletonizer

margined blister beetle
marsh slug
masked hunter
mauna loa bean beetle
McDaniel spider mite
meadow plant bug
meadow spittlebug
meal moth
mealybug destroyer
mealy plum aphid
Mediterranean flour
  moth
Mediterranean fruit
  fly
melon aphid
melon fly
melonworm

merchant grain beetle
Mexican bean beetle
Mexican bean weevil
Mexican black scale

Mexican corn
  rootworm
Mexican fruit fly
Mexican leafroller
Mexican mealybug
Mexican pine beetle
migratory grasshopper
mimosa webworm
mining scale
mint aphid
minute egg parasite
minute pirate bug

mission blue
mold mite
monarch butterfly
monkeypod moth
monkeypod
  roundheaded borer
Monterey pine cone
  beetle
Morrill lace bug
Monterey pine resin
  midge
Monterey pine weevil
Mormon cricket
morningglory
  leafminer
mossyrose gall wasp
mottled tortoise beetle
mountain-ash sawfly

mountain leafhooper
mountain pine beetle
mountain pine
  coneworm

mourningcloak
  butterfly
mulberry whitefly

mullein thrips

Nantucket pine tip
  moth
narcissus bulb fly
narrownecked grain
  beetle
narrowwinged mantid
native elm bark beetle
native holly leafminer
navel orangeworm
negro bug

Nevada sage
  grasshopper
New Guinea sugarcane
  weevil
new house borer
New York weevil
nigra scale
northeastern sawyer
northern cattle grub
northern corn
  rootworm

northern fowl mite
northern house
  mosquito
northern masked
  chafer
northern mole cricket
northern pine weevil
northern pitch twig
  moth
northern rat flea

northwest coast
  mosquito
Norway maple aphid
nose bot fly
nutgrass armyworm
nutgrass billbug
nutgrass borer moth
nutgrass weevil
Nuttall blister beetle

oak clearwing moth
oak lace bug
oak leafroller
oak leaftier
oak lecanium
oak sapling borer
oak skeletonizer
oak timberworm
oak webworm
obliquebanded
  leafroller
obscure mealybug
obscure root weevil
obscure scale
oceanic burrower bug
oceanic embiid

oceanic field cricket
odd beetle
odorous house ant
old house borer
oleander aphid
oleander hawk moth
oleander pit scale
oleander scale
olive fruit fly
olive scale
omnivorous leaftier
omnivorous looper
onespotted stink bug
onion aphid
onion bulb fly

onion maggot
onion plant bug
onion thrips
orange spiny whitefly
orange tortrix
orangedog
orangehumped
  mapleworm
orangestriped
  oakworm
orangetailed potter
  wasp
orchid aphid
orchidfly
Oregon fir sawyer

Oregon wireworm
oriental beetle
oriental cockroach
oriental fruit fly
oriental fruit moth
oriental house fly
oriental moth
oriental rat flea
oriental stink bug
ornate aphid
orthezia lady beetle
oval guineapig louse
oxalis spider mite
oxalis whitefly
oystershell scale

Pacific beetle
  cockroach
Pacific Coast tick
Pacific Coast
  wireworm
Pacific cockroach
Pacific dampwood
  termite
Pacific flatheaded
  borer
Pacific kissing bug
Pacific pelagic water
  strider
Pacific spider mite
Pacific tent caterpillar
Pacific willow leaf
  beetle
Packard grasshopper
painted beauty
painted hickory borer
painted lady
painted leafhopper
painted maple aphid
pale damsel bug
pale juniper webworm
pale leaf spider
pale leafcutting bee
pale legume bug
pale tussock moth
pale western cutworm
pales weevil
palesided cutworm
palestriped flea beetle
palm mealybug
palmerworm
palm leafskeletonizer
pandanus mealybug
pandora moth
papaya fruit fly
paper wasps
parasitic grain wasp

parlatoria date scale
parsleyworm
parsnip webworm
pavement ant
pea aphid
pea leafminer
pea leaf weevil
pea moth
pea weevil
peach bark beetle
peach silver mite
peach twig borer
peachtree borer
pear midge
pear plant bug
pear psylla
pear rust mite
pear sawfly
pear thrips
pearleaf blister mite
pecan bud moth
pecan carpenterworm
pecan cigar casebearer
pecan leaf casebearer
pecan leaf phylloxera
pecan leafroll mite
peacan leaf scorch
  mite
pecan nut casebearer
pecan phylloxera
pecan serpentine
  leafminer
pecan spittlebug
pecan weevil
pepper-and-salt moth
peppergrass beetle
pepper maggot
pepper weevil
periodical cicada
persimmon borer
persimmon psylla

phantom hemlock
  looper
Pharaoh ant
Philippine katydid
phlox plant bug
pickleworm
pigeon fly
pigeon tremex
pine bark adelgid
pine bud mite
pine butterfly
pine candle moth
pine chafer
pine colaspis
pine conelet looper
pine engraver
pine false webworm
pine gall weevil
pine leaf adelgid
pine needleminer
pine needle scale
pine needle
  sheathminer
pine root collar weevil
pine root tip weevil
pine rosette mite
pine spittlebug
pine tortoise scale
pine tube moth
pine tussock moth
pine webworm
pineapple false spider
  mite
pineapple mealybug
pineapple scale
pineapple tarsonemid
pineapple weevil
pinevine swallowtail
pink bollworm
pink scavenger
  caterpillar

pink sugarcane
  mealybug
pinkstriped oakworm
pinkwinged
  grasshopper
pinon cone beetle
pistol casebearer
pitch mass borer
pitch pine tip moth
pitch twig moth
pitch-eating weevil
pitcherplant mosquito
plains false wireworm
plaster beetle
plum curculio
plum gouger
plum leafhopper
plum rust mite
plum webspinning
  sawfly
plumeria borer
plumeria whitefly
poinciana looper
polyphemus moth
ponderosa pine bark
  borer
ponderosa pine cone
  beetle
poplar borer
poplar-and-willow
  borer
poplar leaffolding
  sawfly
poplar petiolegall
  aphid
poplar tentmaker
poplar twig gall aphid
poplar vagabond aphid
portulaca leafmining
  weevil
potato aphid

southern masked
   chafer
southern mole cricket
southern pine beetle
southern pine
   coneworm
southern pine root
   weevil
southern pine sawyer
southern potato
   wireworm
southern red mite
southwestern corn
   borer
southwestern Hercules
   beetle
southwestern pine tip
   moth
southwestern squash
   vine borer
southwestern tent
   caterpillar
sow thistle aphid
soybean looper
soybean thrips
Spanishfly
spider mite destroyer
spicebush swallowtail
spinach flea beetle
spinach leafminer
spined assassin bug
spined rat louse
spined soldier bug
spined stilt bug
spiny assassin bug
spiny oakworm
spinybacked spider
spirea aphid
spotted alfalfa aphid
spotted asparagus
   beetle

spotted beet webworm
spotted blister beetle
spotted cucumber
   beetle
spotted cutworm
spotted garden slug
spotted hairy fungus
   beetle
spotted Mediterranean
   cockroach
spotted pine sawyer
spotted tentiform
   leafminer
spotted tussock moth
spottedwinged antlion
spring cankerworm
spruce aphid
spruce beetle
spruce bud midge
spruce bud moth
spruce bud scale
spruce budworm
spruce coneworm
spruce mealybug
spruce needleminer
spruce seed moth
spruce spider mite
squarenecked grain
   beetle
squarenosed fungus
   beetle
squash beetle
squash bug
squash vine borer
stable fly
stalk borer
star jasmine thrips
steelblue lady beetle
Stevens leafhopper
sticktight flea

stinging rose
   caterpillar
stink beetle
stored nut moth
straw itch mite
strawberry aphid
strawberry bud weevil
strawberry crown
   borer
strawberry crown
   moth
strawberry
   crownminer
strawberry leafroller
strawberry root aphid
strawberry root weevil
strawberry rootworm
strawberry sap beetle
strawberry spider mite
strawberry whitefly
striped alder sawfly
striped ambrosia beetle
striped blister beetle
striped cucumber
   beetle
striped cutworm
striped earwig
striped flea beetle
striped garden
   caterpillar
striped horse fly
striped mealybug
subtropical pine tip
   moth
subulina snail
suckfly
sugar maple borer
sugar pine cone beetle
sugarbeet crown borer
sugarbeet root aphid

sugarbeet root maggot
sugarbeet wireworm
sugarcane aphid
sugarcane beetle
sugarcane borer
sugarcane bud moth
sugarcane delphacid
sugarcane leaf mite
sugarcane leafroller
sugarcane stalk mite
sugarcane thrips
sunflower beetle
sunflower bud moth
sunflower maggot
sunflower moth
sunflower seed midge
sunflower spittlebug
superb plant bug
Surinam cockroach
Swaine jack pine
   sawfly
swallow bug
sweetclover aphid
sweetclover root borer
sweetclover weevil
sweetfern leaf
   casebearer
sweetpotato flea beetle
sweetpotato hornworm
sweetpotato leaf beetle
sweetpotato leafminer
sweetpotato leafroller
sweetpotato vine borer
sweetpotato weevil
sweetpotato whitefly
sycamore lace bug
sycamore tussock moth

Tahitian coconut
   weevil
tamarind weevil
tamarisk leafhopper
tarnished plant bug
tawny garden slug
tea scale
tenlined June beetle
tenspotted lady beetle
terrapin scale
tessallated scale
Texas citrus mite
Texas leafcutting ant
thief ant
thirteenspotted lady
   beetle
thistle aphid
thread bug
threebanded
   leafhopper
threecornered alfalfa
   hopper
threelined leafroller

threelined potato
   beetle
threespotted flea beetle
threestriped blister
   beetle
threestriped lady
   beetle
throat bot fly
thurberia weevil
tiger swallowtail
tilehorned prionus
tipdwarf mite
toad bug
tobacco budworm
tobacco flea beetle
tobacco hornworm
tobacco moth
tobacco stalk borer
tobacco thrips
tobacco wireworm
tomato bug
tomato fruitworm
tomato hornworm

tomato pinworm
tomato psyllid
tomato russet mite
toothed flea beetle
torsalo
transparentwinged
   plant bug
transverse lady beetle
trefoil seed chalcid
tropical fowl mite
tropical horse tick
tropical rat louse
tropical rat mite
tropical sod webworm
tuber flea beetle
tule beetle
tulip bulb aphid
tuliptree aphid
tuliptree scale
tumid spider mite
tupelo leafminer
turkey chigger
turkey gnat

turnip aphid
turnip maggot
turpentine borer
twicestabbed lady
   beetle
twig girdler
twig pruner
twobanded fungus
   beetle
twobanded Japanese
   weevil
twolined chestnut
   borer
twolined spittlebug
twomarked treehopper
twospotted lady beetle
twospotted spider mite
twospotted stink bug
twostriped grasshopper
twostriped
   walkingstick

uglynest caterpillar

unicorn caterpillar

vagabond crambus
vagrant grasshopper
Van Duzee treehopper
vanda thrips
variable oakleaf
   caterpillar

varied carpet beetle
variegated cutworm
vedalia
vegetable leafminer
vegetable weevil
velvetbean caterpillar

verbena bud moth
vespiform thrips
vetch bruchid
vexans mosquito
viburnum aphid
viceroy

violet aphid
violet sawfly
Virginia pine sawfly
Virginiacreeper
   leafhopper
Virginiacreeper sphinx

21. CONGRESSIONAL RECORD

LAWS AND RULES FOR PUBLICATION OF THE CONGRESSIONAL RECORD

CODE OF LAWS OF THE UNITED STATES

TITLE 44, SECTION 901. CONGRESSIONAL RECORD: ARRANGEMENT, STYLE, CONTENTS, AND INDEXES.—The Joint Committee on Printing shall control the arrangement and style of the CONGRESSIONAL RECORD, and while providing that it shall be substantially a verbatim report of proceedings, shall take all needed action for the reduction of unnecessary bulk. It shall provide for the publication of an index of the CONGRESSIONAL RECORD semimonthly during and at the close of sessions of Congress. (Oct. 22, 1968, c. 9, 82 Stat. 1255.)

TITLE 44, SECTION 904. CONGRESSIONAL RECORD: MAPS; DIAGRAMS; ILLUSTRATIONS.—Maps, diagrams, or illustrations may not be inserted in the RECORD without the approval of the Joint Committee on Printing. (Oct. 22, 1968, c. 9, 82 Stat. 1256.)

GENERAL RULES

The rules governing document work apply to the Congressional Record, except as may be noted herein. The same general style should be followed in the permanent Record (bound Record) as is used in the daily Record. All should familiarize themselves with the exceptions and the forms peculiar to the Record.

Daily and permanent Record texts are set in 8-point type on a 9-point body. Extracts are set in 7-point type on an 8-point body and stamped "FIC & punc." Quoted matter in 8 point is to be treated as "FIC & punc."

An F-dash will be used preceding 8-point cap lines in proceedings in Senate and House.

All 7-point extracts and poetry will carry 2 points of space above and below.

All extracts are set 7 point unless otherwise ordered by the Joint Committee on Printing.

Except as noted below, all communications from the President must be set in 8 point, but if such communications contain extracts, etc., the extracts are set in 7 point.

An address of the President delivered outside of Congress or referred to as an extract is set in 7 point.

A letter from the President to the Senate is set in 7 point when any form of treaty is enclosed that is to be printed in the Record in connection therewith. The letter is set in 7 point whether the treaty follows or precedes it or is separated from it by intervening matter.

In all quoted amendments and excerpts of bills and in reprinting bills, the style and copy as printed in the bill, will be followed, as these data are picked up and converted, and no rekeying is required. Bill titles as used in Record briefs and History of Bills will follow Record style.

Profanity, obscene wording, or extreme vulgarisms are to be deleted and a 3-em dash substituted therefor.

Instructions covering the measure and the size and kind of type for parallel columns in the Record will be at the discretion of the preparer in charge of the Record.

In correcting proof, operators must exercise great care.

Extreme caution must be used in making corrections in copy, and no important change will be made without authority.

Observe the lists of names of Senators and Representatives, committees of both Houses, and duplicate names. Changes caused by death, resignation, or otherwise must be noted. There is no excuse for error in the spelling of names of Senators,

Representatives, or department officials. In case of doubt, the Congressional Directory will be the authority.

Datelines should be followed on Extensions of Remarks. If any question arises as to the proper date to be used, the preparer in charge of the Record in the markup section must be consulted.

Indented matter in leaderwork will be 1 em only.

Queries must not be made on proofs. In case of doubt, readers will consult the Referee.

CAPITALIZATION

(See also Guide to Capitalization, p. 35)

If the name of the Congressional Record is mentioned, it must be set in caps and small caps and never abbreviated, even when appearing in citations.

The name of a Senator or a Representative preceding his direct remarks is set in caps and is followed by a period with equal spacing to be used.

The name of a Senator or a Representative used in connection with a bill or other paper—that is, in an adjectival sense—is lowercased, as the Hawkins bill, the Fish amendment, etc.; but FISH's amendment, etc.

The names of Members and Members-elect of both branches of the Congress, including those of the Vice President and Speaker, will be printed in caps and small caps if mention is made of them, except in "FIC and punc." matter.

Deceased Members' names will be set in caps and small caps in eulogies only on the first day the House or Senate is in session following death of Member, in a speech carrying date when Member was eulogized, or on memorial day in Senate and House. Eulogy day in one House will be treated the same in the other.

Certificates of Senators-elect of a succeeding Congress are usually presented to the current Congress, and in such cases the names of the Senators-elect must be in caps and small caps.

Names of Members of Congress must be set in caps and lowercase in votes, in lists set in columns, in the list of standing and select committees, in contested-election cases, in lists of pairs, and in all parts of tabular matter (head, body, and footnotes). (See under Pairs, p. 284.)

Observe that the names of all persons not certified Members of Congress are to be set in caps and lowercase; that is, names of secretaries, clerks, messengers, and others.

Names of proposed boards, commissions, services, etc., are capitalized.

Capitalize principal words and quote after each of the following terms: *Address, article, book, caption, chapter heading, editorial, essay, heading, headline, motion picture* or *play* (including TV or radio program), *paper, poem, report, song, subheading, subject, theme,* etc. Also, following the word *entitled,* except with reference to bill titles which are treated as follows: "A bill (or an act) transferring certain functions of the Price Administrator to the Petroleum Administrator for War," etc. (See rules 355, 8.131.)

CONTRACTIONS

Do not change well-founded historical utterances or expressions made popular by continued use on television, radio, or in the press. Use quotation marks and say, "Don't shoot until you see the whites of their eyes," "Let's look at the record." Follow contractions in 7-point extracts and when quoted in 8-point text or when used as a heading over 8-point data when it is the title of the article in 7 point. The abbreviation *etc.* must be made to read *and so forth* (et cetera if so worded), except in extracts and headings.

FIGURES

The general rules set forth under "Numerals" (p. 165) will apply to the use of figures in the Record.

Figures appearing in copy as "20 billion 428 million, 125 thousand dollars" should be converted to figures, as "$20,428,125,000."

In a Member's language (8 point), when numbered items are used, they are to read *first, second, third,* etc. In 7-point excerpts, either the numerals *1, 2, 3* or the words *first, second, third* may be used.

For ordinal numbers, follow rules 12.10–12.12.

TABULAR MATTER AND LEADERWORK

Record tables may be set either one or three columns in width, as follows:
  One-column table: 14 picas (168 points).
  Three-column table: 43½ picas (522 points). Footnote(s) will be set 43½ picas.
  All short footnotes should be run in with 2 ems between each.

ITALIC

Italic, boldface, caps, or small caps shall not be used for emphasis; nor shall unusual indentions be used. This does not apply to literally reproduced quotations from historical, legal, or official documents. If italic other than restricted herein is desired, the words should be underscored and "Fol. ital." written on each folio. Do not construe this to apply to *"Provided," "Provided further," "Ordered," "Resolved," "Be it enacted, etc.,"* titles following signatures or addresses, or the part of datelines which should be set in italic.

Names of vessels must be set in italic, except in headings, where they will be quoted.

The prayer delivered in either House must be set in 8-point roman. If prefaced or followed by a quotation from the Bible, such quotation must be set in 8-point italic. Extracts from the Bible or other literature contained in the body of the prayer will be set in 8-point roman and quoted.

When general or passing mention is made of a case, the title is set in roman, as Smith Bros. case, in 7 and 8 point. When a specific citation is indicated and reference follows, use italic for title, as *Smith Bros.* case (172 App. Div. 149).

Titles of cases are always set in italic if followed by references; but, except as in casual use noted above, titles in 7-point matter are italicized in "versus" cases whether or not references follow, as *United States* v. *Jones Lumber Co.,* but follow copy if it is marked "FIC and punc." See page 162 for other examples.

In 8-point matter, when only the title of a case is given, set in roman, as United States versus 12 Diamond Rings.

When *versus* is used in other than legal phrases and for the purposes of showing contrast, it is not abbreviated or set in italic, as "airplanes versus battleships."

For contested-election cases, see page 304.

For other examples of legal cases and references, see rules 9.45 and 17.12.

MISCELLANEOUS

Do not quote any communication carrying date and signature. However, a letter (or other communication) bearing both date and signature that appears within a letter shall be quoted.

Do not put quotation marks on centerheads in 7-point extracts unless centerheads belong to original matter.

In newspaper extracts, put place and date at beginning of paragraph. Use caps and small caps for name of place and roman lowercase for spelled-out date. Connect date and extract by a period and an em dash. If date and place are credited in a bracket line above extract, they need not be used again at the beginning of paragraph. (See p. 286 under "Credits.")

Each *Whereas* in a preamble must begin a new paragraph. The *Therefore be it* must be preceded by a colon and be run in with the last *Whereas. Be it* will run in with the word *Therefore,* but must not be supplied when not in copy. Note the following:

Whereas it has been deemed advisable to, etc.: Therefore be it
Resolved, That the committee, etc.

In the titles of legal cases copy is followed as to spelling, abbreviations, and use of figures.

Use single punctuation in citations of cases and statutes:
  United States v. *12 Diamond Rings* (124 U.S. 329; R.S. p. 310, sec. 1748).
  Indent asterisk lines 2 ems on each side. Use five asterisks.

If a title is used as part of the name of an organization, vessel, etc., spell; thus, General U.S. Grant Post No. 76, Grand Army of the Republic.

The order of subdivision of the Constitution of the United States is as follows: article I, section 2, clause 3.

If an exhibit appears at the end of a speech, the head *Exhibit* is set in 7-point caps and small caps.

In extracts containing votes the names must be run in, as Mrs. Smith of Nebraska, AuCoin, and Clay, etc.

In a Senator's or a Representative's remarks, when amendments, sections, etc., are referred to by number, use *No.* before the figure even though *number* appears in copy. However, if intervening words separate the number and the term it identifies, use *numbered.* For example, Senate amendments Nos. 187 and 188, amendments of the Senate numbered 187 and 188; bill sections Nos. 10 and 11, sections of the bill numbered 10 and 11.

In text references to Senate and House reports and in executive and miscellaneous documents, the *No.* must always be supplied if not in copy; thus, House Report No. 98–75, Executive Document No. 98–20, Miscellaneous Document No. 37.

In headings and text references to resolutions and memorials, the *No.* is not used. Examples: *House Resolution 46, House Joint Memorial 3, Resolution 4.*

In gross or en gros

When a bill comes to final action, in the presentment of amendments collectively for a vote, either the term *"in gross"* or the French equivalent *"en gros"* may be used.

USE OF CAPS AND SMALL CAPS

[Names of Senators and Members are set in caps and small caps when in parentheses, brackets, leaderwork, or tabular matter.]

Mr. BAKER. (Name all caps when visitor addresses Senate or House.)

On motion by (or of) Mr. LONG of Maryland, it was, etc.

The VICE PRESIDENT resumed the chair.

The PRESIDING OFFICER (Mr. HEINZ in the chair). Shall the bill pass?

The SPEAKER called the House to order.

Mr. MITCHELL'S amendment was adopted.

Mr. BROWN of California took the floor and yielded to Mr. GRANT.

During the rollcall,

Mr. CLAUSEN said: If not paired, I would vote "no" on this bill.

A MEMBER. And debate it afterward.

SEVERAL SENATORS. I object.

Mr. KENNEDY, Mr. NUNN (and others). Let it be read.

Mr. JACKSON (and others). Yes.

Mrs. HAWKINS (and other Members). No.

Mr. SMITH of Oklahoma objected.

The ACTING SECRETARY. In line 11, after the word *"Provided"*, it is proposed, etc.

Mr. SPENCE was recognized, and yielded his time to Mr. FLORIO.

Mr. CRANSTON, a Senator from the State of California, appeared in his seat today.

[When two Members from the same State have the same surname, full name is used.]

Mr. WILLIAM COYNE and Mr. JAMES COYNE rose to a point of order.

The SPEAKER proceeded to put the question on the motion of Mr. YATES.

The CHAIRMAN appointed Mr. WALKER and Mr. TAYLOR as tellers.

Mr. CONTE. I desire to withdraw my vote of "no" and vote "present."

The Clerk (House) called the name of Mr. MURTHA, and he answered "present."

The clerk (Senate) read Mr. GLENN'S amendment.

The legislative clerk will read it.

The LEGISLATIVE CLERK. This bill will * * *.

Mr. ADDABBO entered the Chamber.

The Secretary proceeded to call the roll, and Mr. DOLE answered "aye."

Mr. McDONALD entered the Chamber and answered to his name.

Mr. HOYER and Mr. MYERS entered the Chamber and answered to their names.

After some delay, Mr. KENNEDY entered the Chamber and answered to his name.

[Extracts that consist of colloquies will use caps and small caps for names of persons speaking, as shown below:]

Mr. STIGLER. I think this bill is so well understood that no time will be required for its discussion.

Mrs. NORTON. Does this bill come from the Committee on Armed Services?

The SPEAKER. It does.

SPECIAL ORDERS GRANTED

By unanimous consent, permission to address the House, following

the legislative program and any special orders heretofore entered, was granted to:

Mr. REUSS, for 1 hour, on Wednesday, February 2.

Mr. GONZALEZ (at the request of Mr. REUSS), for 1 hour, on February 2.

Mr. ANNUNZIO, today, for 10 minutes.

(The following Members (at the request of Mr. GINN) and to revise and extend their remarks and include therein extraneous matter:)

Mr. KEMP, for 5 minutes, today.

Mr. MILLER of Ohio, for 5 minutes, today.

Mr. FINDLEY, for 30 minutes, today.

[Note the following double action:]

(Mr. GRAMM asked and was given permission to extend his remarks at this point in the RECORD and to include extraneous matter.)

[Mr. GRAMM's remarks will appear hereafter in the Extensions of Remarks.]

(Mr. GRAMM asked and was given permission to extend his remarks at this point in the RECORD and to include extraneous matter.)

[Mr. GRAMM's remarks will appear hereafter in the Extensions of Remarks.]

PUNCTUATION

Mr. PACKWOOD. Mr. President, I call up my amendment which is identified as "unprinted amendment No. 1296," and ask that it be stated.

The bill was reported to the Senate as amended, and the amendment was concurred in.

The bill was reported to the Senate without amendment, ordered to be engrossed for a third reading, read the third time, and passed.

The bill was ordered to be engrossed for a third reading, read the third time, and passed.

The bill as amended was ordered to be engrossed and read a third time; and being engrossed, it was accordingly read the third time and passed.

The bill was ordered to a third reading, and it was accordingly read the third time and passed.

The bill was ordered to a third reading, was read the third time, and passed.

[Use this form when title of bill is given:]

The bill was ordered to be engrossed and read a third time, was read the third time, and passed.

The title was amended so as to read: "A bill for the relief of Maude S. Burman."

A motion to reconsider was laid on the table. [House.]

[Use this form when title of bill is not given:]

The bill was ordered to be engrossed and read a third time, was read the third time, and passed, and a motion to reconsider was laid on the table. [House.]

The bill was ordered to be engrossed and read a third time, was read the third time, and passed.

The amendments were ordered to be engrossed and the bill to be read a third time.

The amendment was agreed to, and the bill as amended was ordered to be engrossed and read a third time; and being engrossed, it was accordingly read the third time and passed.

There was no objection, and, by unanimous consent, the Senate proceeded, etc.

The question was taken, and the motion was agreed to.

The question being taken, the motion was agreed to.

There being no objection, the Senate, as in Committee of the Whole, proceeded to consider the bill, which had been reported from the Committee on Agriculture and Forestry with amendments.

The Secretary read the bill; and there being no objection, the Senate, as in Committee of the Whole, proceeded to its consideration.

Ordered to lie on the table and to be printed.

During the delivery of Mr. SMITH's speech.

As in executive session,

The Secretary read the bill; and, by unanimous consent, the Senate, as in Committee of the Whole, proceeded to its consideration.

Mr. LENT, by unanimous consent, was granted leave to withdraw from the files of the House, without leaving copies, the papers in the case of John Jones, no adverse report having been made thereon.

Mr. YATES. Regular order! [or division.]

Mr. WRIGHT. Regular order, Mr. Chairman.

My friend, the Senator from Massachusetts, said it was a mistake.

Mr. SARBANES addressed the Senate. After having spoken for 35 minutes.

Mr. MATHIAS. Mr. President, if the Senator will yield for a moment.

After the second call of the roll,

Mr. WAXMAN. Mr. Speaker, that has been agreed to.

―――

Mr. COUGHLIN. Mr. Chairman, I move to strike the requisite number of words.

(Mr. COUGHLIN asked and was given permission to revise and extend his remarks.)

[Note use of interrogation mark in the following:]

Mr. DOLE. Mr. President, what does this mean?—

We have never received a dollar of this amount.

―――

A resolution of the Senate of the State of California: to the Committee on Interior and Insular Affairs:

"SENATE RESOLUTION 126

"Resolution relative to flood control and water conservation projects

"Whereas the great storms of December 1964 caused widespread flooding along the Sacramento River and its tributaries; and

"Whereas this flooding caused extensive damage along the Sacramento River and its tributaries in Tehama and Shasta Counties; and

"Whereas these projects could be integrated with the Federal Central Valley project: Now, therefore, be it

"*Resolved by the Senate of the State of California,* That the Congress of the United States, the U.S. Army Corps of Engineers, and the Bureau of Reclamation are respectfully * * *".

[Note use of italic in title of cases:]

* * * This is the occasion America did not have to consider what other options might guarantee maternal safety while protecting the unborn. This is our national opportunity to reconsider *Roe* v. *Wade,* 410 U.S. 113 (1973).

Roe against Wade and its companion case, *Doe* v. *Bolton,* 410 U.S. 179, (1973) granted abortion the elevated status of a fundamental constitutional right and invalidated almost all effective restrictions on abortion throughout the 9 months of pregnancy.* * *

PARENTHESES AND BRACKETS

This legislation would exempt certain defined Central Intelligence Agency [CIA] operational files from the search and review process of the Freedom of Information Act [FOIA], thus permitting the agency to respond much more quickly to those FOIA requests which are at all likely to result in the release of information.

[Acronyms are to be bracketed as shown above.]

Mr. WRIGHT. Mr. Speaker, I now yield 5 minutes to the gentleman from Maryland [Mr. MITCHELL].

(Mr. WILLIAMS of Ohio asked and was given permission to revise and extend his remarks in the RECORD.)

Mr. TAYLOR. There is no "may not" about it. Here is the form in which they are printed.

Mr. FARY. I am in hopes we shall be able to secure a vote on the bill tonight.

["Vote! Vote!"]

Mr. YATES. The Chair rather gets me on that question. [Laughter.] I did not rise. [Cries of "Vote! Vote!"]

Mr. KASTEN (one of the tellers). I do not desire to press the point that no quorum has voted.

The CHAIRMAN [after a pause]. If no gentleman claims the floor, the Clerk will proceed with the reading of the bill.

Mr. CLAUSEN. Then he is endeavoring to restrict the liberty of the individual in the disbursement of his own money. [Applause on the Republican side.]

Mr. KENNEDY. Mr. Speaker, I desire to ask unanimous consent that the time of the gentleman—— [Cries of "Regular order!"]

Mr. McCORMACK was recognized and said: I will yield 3 additional minutes to the gentleman from Ohio.

Lay on, Macduff;
And damn'd be him that first cries,
"Hold, enough!"

[Laughter.]

The SPEAKER. Is there objection to the consideration of this bill at this time? [After a pause.] There is no objection.

The CHAIRMAN [rapping with his gavel]. Debate is exhausted.

Mr. JONES of Oklahoma [reading]:

Mr. JONES of Oklahoma. Yes. [Reading:]

When in the course of human events, etc.

[Mr. REED of New York addressed the House. His remarks will appear hereafter in the Extensions of Remarks.]

[Or the following, which this Office is authorized to insert, observing that 2 points of space are used on each side of "withhold" lines:]

[Mr. RANDOLPH addressed the Senate. His remarks will appear hereafter in the Extensions of Remarks.]

[Mr. DERWINSKI addressed the Committee [or House]. His remarks will appear hereafter in the Extensions of Remarks.]

[Names of Senators or Representatives appearing in remarks of other Members of Congress must be enclosed in brackets, except in listing of tellers or when some other title than "Mr." is used, as in the following examples:]

Mrs. SMITH of Nebraska. The gentleman from Washington [Mr. FOLEY] stated that he would support the measure.

Mr. CLAY. The gentleman from Maryland, Dr. LONG, stated that he would support the measure.

In Senate copy a Senator is referred to as "the Senator from —— [Mr. ——]." Do not supply name and brackets if name does not appear in copy.

Whenever in House copy Members are referred to as "Mr. WINN of Kansas," etc., copy shall be changed to read "the gentleman from Kansas [Mr. WINN]."

Note that brackets are used only when *Mr.* appears in copy.

See also use of *Mr.* in explanation of votes under "Pairs," p. ——.

When Members are referred to as "Representative HOYER," "PHILIP M. CRANE," "Congressman PICKLE," etc., change copy to read "the gentleman from Maryland, Representative HOYER," "the gentleman from Illinois, PHILIP M. CRANE," "the gentleman from Texas, Congressman PICKLE." *The gentleman from*, with the name of State, must be supplied when not in copy.

VOTING IN THE HOUSE AND IN COMMITTEE OF THE WHOLE

Note that a dash is used only when a comma is necessary to separate the ayes and noes. If only the ayes or the noes are given, no punctuation is to be used. If the word *and* is used to connect the ayes and noes, as *ayes 52 and noes 65*, or *52 ayes and 65 noes*, the dash is omitted after the word *were* or *being.*

On the question of ordering the yeas and nays there were 18 ayes and 88 noes.

The House divided; and there were—ayes 52, noes 65.

So (no further count being called for) the amendment of Mr. SMITH of Virginia was not agreed to.

So (two-thirds having voted in favor thereof) the rules were suspended, and the bill was passed.

So (two-thirds not having voted in favor thereof) the motion was rejected.

The CHAIRMAN. The gentleman raises the point of no quorum. The Chair will count. [After counting.] Two hundred and seventeen present, a quorum. The noes have it, and the amendment is rejected.

The question being taken on the motion of Mr. BUSH to suspend the rules and pass the bill, it was agreed to (two-thirds voting in favor thereof).

So (the affirmative not being one-fifth of the whole vote) the yeas and nays were not ordered.

The question was taken by a viva voce vote, and the Speaker announced that two-thirds appeared to have voted in the affirmative and [after a pause] that the bill was passed.

So (two-thirds voting in favor thereof) the motion to suspend the rules was agreed to, and the bill was passed.

Two-thirds voting in favor thereof, the rules were suspended, and the bill was passed.

The question was taken; and (two-thirds having voted in favor thereof) the rules were suspended and the bill, as amended, was passed.

The question was taken; and (two-thirds having voted in favor thereof) the rules were suspended and the bill was passed.

The yeas and nays were ordered, there being 43 in the affirmative, more than one-fifth of the last vote.

The question being taken on Mr. KENNEDY's motion, there were—ayes 18, noes 35.

The question being taken on concurring in the amendments of the Senate, there were—ayes 101, noes 5.

The question was taken; and on a division [demanded by Mr. FRENZEL] there were—ayes 17, noes 29.

Mr. FRENZEL. Mr. Chairman, I demand a recorded vote, and pending that, I make the point of order that a quorum is not present.

The CHAIRMAN. Evidently a quorum is not present.

The Chair announces that pursuant to clause 2, rule XXIII, he will vacate proceedings under the call when a quorum of the Committee appears.

Members will record their presence by electronic device.

The call was taken by electronic device.

□ 1700

[The above box followed by a four-digit number indicates floor time in the House.]

QUORUM CALL VACATED

The CHAIRMAN. One hundred Members have appeared. A quorum of the Committee of the Whole is present. Pursuant to rule XXIII, clause 2, further proceedings under

the call shall be considered as vacated.

The Committee will resume its business.

The pending business is the demand of the gentleman from Minnesota [Mr. FRENZEL] for a recorded vote.

A recorded vote was refused.

So the amendment to the amendment offered as a substitute for the amendment was rejected.

The CHAIRMAN. The question is on the amendment offered by the gentleman from Oklahoma [Mr. ENGLISH] as a substitute for the amendment offered by the gentleman from South Dakota [Mr. DASCHLE].

The question was taken; and the Chairman announced that the noes appeared to have it.

RECORDED VOTE

Mr. ENGLISH. Mr. Chairman, I demand a recorded vote.

A recorded vote was ordered.

The vote was taken by electronic device, and there were—ayes 223, noes 162, answered "present" 1, not voting 47, as follows:

[Roll No. 275]

AYES—223

Addabbo	Dowdy	Howard
Akaka	Duncan	Hoyer
Albosta	Dwyer	Hubbard
Anderson	Dyson	Huckaby
Andrews	Eckart	Hunter

NOES—162

Alexander	Fish	Miller (CA)
Annunzio	Foley	Mineta
Archer	Forsythe	Moakley
Atkinson	Fountain	Molinari
Beard	Frank	Mollohan

ANSWERED "PRESENT"—1

Brown (OH)

NOT VOTING—47

Ashbrook	Clay	Garcia
Bafalis	Collins (TX)	Gilman
Barnard	Corcoran	Gingrich

[The Speaker's vote is recorded only in the "Ayes" or "Noes." It is never recorded as "not voting."]

So the amendment offered as a substitute for the amendment was agreed to.

The result of the vote was announced as above recorded.

VOTING BY YEAS AND NAYS

Senate

QUORUM CALL

The clerk will call the roll.

The assistant legislative clerk proceeded to call the roll, and the following Senators entered the Chamber and answered to their names:

[Quorum No. 42]

Baker	Dodd	Kassebaum
Biden	Dole	Kasten
Bradley	Domenici	Long
Brady	East	Lugar
Bumpers	Garn	Packwood
Byrd	Gorton	Stennis
Harry F., Jr.	Grassley	Thurmond
Cannon	Hart	Tower
Cochran	Helms	Warner

The PRESIDING OFFICER. A quorum is not present.

Mr. BAKER. Mr. President, I move that the Sergeant at Arms be instructed to require the attendance of absent Senators, and I ask for the yeas and nays on the motion.

The PRESIDING OFFICER. Is there a sufficient second? There is a sufficient second.

The yeas and nays were ordered.

The PRESIDING OFFICER. The question is on agreeing to the motion of the Senator from Tennessee. On this question the yeas and nays have been ordered, and the clerk will call the roll.

The assistant legislative clerk called the roll.

Mr. STEVENS. I announce that the Senator from New York [Mr. D'AMATO] is necessarily absent.

Mr. CRANSTON. I announce that the Senator from Florida [Mr. CHILES], the Senator from Massachusetts [Mr. KENNEDY], the Senator from Montana [Mr. MELCHER], and the Senator from West Virginia [Mr. RANDOLPH] are necessarily absent.

The PRESIDING OFFICER [Mr. ANDREWS]. Are there any other Senators in the Chamber who desire to vote?

The result was announced—yeas 90, nays 5, as follows:

[Rollcall Vote No. 229 Leg.]

YEAS—90

Abdnor	Exon	Metzenbaum
Andrews	Ford	Mitchell
Armstrong	Garn	Moynihan
Baker	Glenn	Murkowski
Baucus	Gorton	Nickles

NAYS—5

Goldwater	Proxmire	Weicker
Johnston	Quayle	

NOT VOTING—5

Chiles	Kennedy	Randolph
D'Amato	Melcher	

So the motion was agreed to.

The PRESIDING OFFICER. Are there any other Senators in the Chamber wishing to vote?

The result was announced—yeas 97, nays 0, as follows:

[Rollcall Vote No. 87 Ex.]

YEAS—97

Abdnor	Goldwater	Moynihan
Andrews	Gorton	Murkowski
Armstrong	Grassley	Nickles
Baker	Hart	Nunn
Baucus	Hatch	Packwood
Bentsen	Hatfield	Percy
Biden	Hawkins	Pressler

NAYS—0

NOT VOTING—3

DeConcini	Hollings	Pell

So the nomination was confirmed.

The PRESIDING OFFICER. Are there any other Senators in the Chamber wishing to vote?

The yeas and nays resulted—yeas 94, nays 4, as follows:

[Rollcall Vote No. 159—Ex. W—96-1.
160—Ex. A—96-2,
161—Ex. P—96-2, and
162—Treaty Doc. No. 97-5]

YEAS—94

Abdnor	Goldwater	Murkowski
Andrews	Gorton	Nickles
Armstrong	Grassley	Nunn
Baker	Hart	Packwood
Baucus	Hatch	Pell

NAYS—4

East	Humphrey
Helms	Symms

NOT VOTING—2

Glenn	Hollings

The PRESIDING OFFICER. Two-thirds of the Senators present and voting having voted in the affirmative, the resolution of ratification are agreed to.

House

Mr. HOWARD. Mr. Speaker, on that I demand the yeas and nays.

The yeas and nays were ordered.

The vote was taken by electronic device, and there were—yeas 288, nays 123, not voting 22, as follows:

[Roll No. 267]

YEAS—288

Addabbo	Brodhead	Dellums
Akaka	Brooks	DeNardis
Albosta	Broomfield	Dicks
Alexander	Brown (CA)	Dingell
Anderson	Brown (OH)	Dixon
Andrews	Burgener	Donnelly

NAYS—123

Archer	Gramm	Martin (IL)
Bafalis	Grisham	Martin (NC)
Bailey (MO)	Hall, Ralph	Martin (NY)
Bethune	Hall, Sam	McCollum
Bliley	Hamilton	McDonald

NOT VOTING—22

Ashbrook	Lundine	Rangel
Aspin	Madigan	Rudd
Beard	McCloskey	Skelton

[If the Speaker votes, his name is not used, but at the end of the "yeas" or "nays," according to his vote, insert: "The Speaker."]

PAIRS

[The word *with* must always be used in pairs in the House, not *and*; and copy must be altered to conform thereto, as Mr. Smith with Mr. Jones—*not* Mr. Smith and Mr. Jones. Note use of lowercase for names in list of pairs in House.]

The Clerk announced the following pairs:

On this vote:

Mr. Hefner for, with Mr. Richmond against.

Until further notice:

Mr. Biaggi with Mr. Jeffords.
Mr. Florio with Mr. Horton.
Mr. Mitchell of Maryland with Mr. Kemp.
Mr. Rangel with Mr. Simon.
Mr. Fascell with Mr. Minish.
Mr. Volkmer with Mr. Harkin.
Mr. Andrews with Mr. Savage.

Messrs. EMERSON, EVANS of Georgia, and MARLENEE changed their votes from "nay" to "yea."

So the bill was passed.

The result of the vote was announced as above recorded.

A motion to reconsider was laid on the table.

Mr. CRAIG. Mr. Speaker, I voted, but, being paired with the gentleman from Pennsylvania, Mr. SCOTT, I withdraw my vote.

Mr. WRIGHT. Mr. Speaker, I have a pair with the gentleman from Missouri, Mr. TAYLOR, who, if present, would have voted "yea." I voted "nay." I withdraw my vote and vote "present."

[In House pairs do not use parentheses when Members are referred to by name. In Senate pairs observe following use of parentheses:]

Mr. CANNON (when his name was called). I am paired on this question with the senior Senator from Massachusetts [Mr. KENNEDY]. If he were here, I should vote "yea."

CALL OF THE HOUSE

Mr. MURTHA. Mr. Speaker, I move a call of the House.

A call of the House was ordered.

The call was taken by electronic device and the following Members responded to their names:

[Roll No. 281]

Addabbo	Anderson	Conte
Akaka	Annunzio	Courter
Albosta	Applegate	Coyne, James
Alexander	Ashbrook	Coyne, William
Craig	Flippo	Ford (TN)
Crane, Daniel	Foglietta	Forsythe
Crane, Philip	Foley	Fountain
Crockett	Ford (MI)	Fowler

[No reference will be made of the names of those not voting.]

□ 1840

The CHAIRMAN. Three hundred ninety-three Members have answered to their names, a quorum is present, and the Committee will resume its business.

FORMS OF TITLES

[Always in roman lowercase, flush and hang 1 em, if more than two lines.]

H.J. Res. 2

Joint resolution authorizing the Secretary of the Treasury to issue 2 per centum bonds or certificates in exchange for bonds bearing a higher rate of interest

Resolved by the Senate and House of Representatives of the United States of America in Congress assembled, That the Secretary of the Treasury be, and he is hereby, etc.

H.R. 4487

A bill to authorize the Rock Island and Southwestern Railway Company to construct a bridge over the Mississippi River at New Boston, State of Illinois

Be it enacted by the Senate and House of Representatives of the United States of America in Congress assembled, That it shall be lawful for the Rock Island and Southwestern Railway Company, a corporation organized under the general incorporations, etc.

H.J. Res. —

Joint resolution proposing an amendment to the Constitution providing for the election of certain United States officers by the people

Resolved by the Senate and House of Representatives of the United States of America in Congress assembled (two-thirds of each House concurring therein), That the following amendment to the Constitution of the United States be proposed to, etc.

MEMORIAL OF THE SETTLERS OF SOUTHERN COLORADO

To the Senate and House of Representatives of the United States in Congress Assembled:

The undersigned Executive Committee of the Settlers of Southern Colorado, living on what is called the Las Animas grant, would respectfully represent, etc.

ADDRESSES AND SIGNATURES

[No line spacing, street addresses, or ZIP Code numbers are to be used in communications in the Record]

The Honorable the SECRETARY OF THE ⊡⊡NAVY.

⊡DEAR MR. SECRETARY: This is in response to your letter, etc.

⊡⊡⊡Very sincerely yours,

RONALD REAGAN.⊡

COLUMBIA, MO,⊡⊡⊡
January 17, 1981.⊡

Hon. MORGAN M. MOULDER,
*Cannon House Office Building,
Washington, DC:*

⊡The President's farm message of today

*   *   *   *   *

farmers and prevent the spread of this depression to every part of our country.

MISSOURI FARMERS
ASSOCIATION,
F.V. HEINKEL,
President.

JANUARY 20, 1966.⊡

Hon. JOHN B. CONNALLY, Jr.,
*The Secretary of the Treasury, Department of the Treasury, Washington,
⊡⊡DC.*

⊡DEAR MR. SECRETARY: Mindful of the tremendous workload, etc.

I would appreciate your comment on the foregoing proposal.

Your proposal seems to be in the best interest of all concerned.

⊡⊡⊡Sincerely yours,

HERBERT ZELENKO,⊡⊡⊡
Member of Congress.⊡

ALEXANDRIA, MN,⊡⊡⊡
November 17, 1971.⊡

Hon. WALTER MONDALE,
*Senate Office Building,
Washington, DC:*

⊡We oppose the nomination of Earl Butz for Secretary of Agriculture because he resists family farms.

RAYMOND WAGNER.⊡

⊡BRANDON, MN.

JANUARY 17, 1972.⊡

Re resignation from committee.

Hon. CARL ALBERT,
*The Speaker, U.S. House of Representa-
⊡⊡tives, U.S. Capitol, Washington, DC.*

⊡DEAR MR. SPEAKER: Having changed my politics from Republican to Democratic, etc.

⊡With my best wishes.

⊡⊡⊡Sincerely,

VINCENT J. DELLAY.⊡

U.S. SENATE,⊡⊡⊡⊡
PRESIDENT PRO TEMPORE,⊡⊡⊡
Washington, DC, March 17, 1972.⊡

To the Senate:

⊡Being temporarily absent from the Senate, I appoint Hon. MIKE MANSFIELD, a Senator from the State of Montana, to

perform the duties of the Chair during my absence.

ALLEN J. ELLENDER,☐☐☐
President pro tempore.☐

———

MARCH 28, 1972.☐
☐I hereby designate the Honorable CHARLES A. VANIK to act as Speaker pro tempore today.

CARL ALBERT,☐☐☐☐
Speaker of the House of☐☐☐
Representatives.☐

———

☐☐THE INTERNATIONAL UNION OF☐☐☐ ☐☐☐UNITED BREWERY, FLOUR, CE-☐☐☐ ☐☐☐REAL, SOFT DRINKS & DISTILL-☐☐☐ ☐☐☐ERY WORKERS OF AMERICA,
Cincinnati, OH, March 25, 1966.☐
To the Senate of the United States.
To the U.S. House of Representatives.
☐HONORABLE SIRS: April 7, 1966, being the 25th anniversary of the modification, etc.

[Two to eight independent signatures, with or without titles, are aligned on the left.]

To the Honorable Senate and House of
☐☐*Representatives of the United States*
☐☐*of America Now Assembled at Wash-*
☐☐*ington, DC:*
☐The undersigned, officers of the Navy of the United States, respectfully show unto your honorable bodies, etc.

JAMES G. GREEN.
W.H. SOUTHERLAND.
F.F. FLETCHER.
C.C. WILSON.

———

☐Respectfully submitted,
KARL F. FELLER,
International President.
THOMAS RUSCH,
Director of Organization.
ARTHUR GILDEA,
Secretary-Treasurer.☐
JOSEPH E. BRADY,
Director of Legislation.

[More than eight signatures, with or without titles, are set full measure, caps and lowercase, run in, indented 2 and 3 ems, as follows:]

☐☐Gene H. Rosenblum, Cochairman; ☐☐☐Paul H. Ray, Cochairman; Cynthia ☐☐☐Asplund, James Pedersen, George Doty; Thomas St. Martin; Joan O'Neill; Lloyd Moosebrugger; Sam Kaplan; Ronald Nemer; Dean Potter; Philip Archer; Thomas McDonough; Mrs. Lloyd Moosebrugger, Minnesota Young Democratic Civil Rights Committee.

———

JOHN SMITH,☐☐☐☐
Lieutenant Governor☐☐☐
(For the Governor of Maine).☐

———

TEXARKANA TEXTILE
MERCHANTS &
MANUFACTURERS'
ASSOCIATION,
JOHN L. JONES,
Secretary.

———

V.J. ADDUCI,☐☐☐☐
Colonel, U.S. Air Force☐☐☐
☐☐(For and in the absence of Joe W. ☐☐☐Kelly, Major General, U.S. Air ☐☐☐Force).

CREDITS

[From the Sacramento (CA) Bee, July 22, 1983]

THE KISSINGER SMOKE SCREEN
(By C. K. McClatchy)

The Reagan administration has embarked on a dangerously aggressive, confrontational policy in Latin America that should be sending shock waves of anger and fear through the American public. Thus far, however, the opposition has been muted by a combination of the administration's anti-Communist rhetoric and public relations molasses.

[From the Wall Street Journal, Aug. 1, 1983]

THE SKY HASN'T FALLEN

Backers of the proposal to increase the U.S. contribution to the International Monetary Fund by $8.4 billion staved off several attacks in the House Friday, but the bill still faces an uncertain future. It has been languishing in the House for nearly three months, and the 40 or so amendments still awaiting it testify to the difficulty of putting together a winning coalition.

POETRY

If poetry is quoted, each stanza should start with quotation marks, but only the last stanza should end with them. The lines of the poem should range on the left, those that rhyme taking the same indention, and the quotation marks should be cleared. Poems are flush left; overs 3 ems; 2 points of space between stanzas, and 2 points of space above and below.

Eisd, O Eisd!
(Listen, O Listen!)

Oft in the still of a moment's dream,
 A fleeting glimpse I see
Of a giant of a man from a foreign
  land,
 And he stares back at me.

And I shake my head to clear my eye,
 And I try my pulse to slow.
But his steady glance and lordly stance
 Bring me an inner glow.

His clothes are strange—worn loose and
  free;
 His features warm and clean;
A dagger thrust close by his knee,
 And his plaid MacArthur green.

Son of Arthur? Is this then he
 Whose name I bear so long?
Is this the man from that phantom clan,
 Heard in a piper's song?

Can kith and kin all count his flesh
 As if it were their own?
Can that sure smile fail to beguile
 Pretenders to his throne?

What is this call I feel to go,
 That stirs my restless feet?
Has the cross of fire instilled desire
 To march, to join, to meet?

As pipes and drums echo command—
 Grandfather Mountain's call—
A ghostly hand from a distant land
 Beckons to us all!

EXTRACTS

[NOTE.—Extracts must begin with a true paragraph. Following extracts, 8-point text must start as a paragraph.]

[Extracts must be set in 7 point unless ordered otherwise by the Joint Committee on Printing and the operator will be expected to set them so, whether marked or not, if the copy clearly indicates that they are extracts. This does not refer to a casual quotation of a few words or a quotation that would not make more than one line of 7 point. The beginning of the 7-point extract must start with a true paragraph; 8 point is always a paragraph.]

Mr. BENNETT. Let us see what that is:

The stipulations of this treaty are to be a full settlement of all claims of said Creek Nation for damages and losses of every kind growing out of the late rebellion—

I do not think he means that—

and all expenditures by the United States of annuities in clothing and feeding refugee and destitute Indians since the diversion of annuities for that purpose consequent upon the late war with the so-called Confederate States; and the Creeks hereby ratify and confirm—

What?—

all such diversions of annuities heretofore made from the funds of the Creek Nation by the United States; and the United States agree that no annuities—

And so forth. I believe that shows clearly the purpose of the treaty.

[Note, as above, that following an excerpt, the 8 point must begin with a paragraph.]

[An address of the President delivered outside of Congress or referred to as an extract will be set in 7 point.]

SCHEME OF TEXT HEADINGS

[For spacing of headings, see under "General rules," p. 275]

	8 point
Single head	8-point caps.
With 1 class of subhead	{ 8-point caps. / 7-point small caps.
	7 point
Single head	7-point caps and small caps.
With 1 class of subhead	{ 7-point caps and small caps. / 7-point small caps.
With 2 classes of subheads	{ 7-point caps and small caps. / 7-point small caps. / 7-point italic lowercase.
With 3 or 4 classes of subheads	{ 7-point caps and small caps. / 7-point small caps. / 7-point italic lowercase. / 7-point roman caps and lowercase. / 7-point roman lowercase.

USE OF DOUBLE HEADS

This is something which has been entirely overlooked by the * * *.

ANALYSIS OF SPECIFIC PROVISIONS OF THE COMMITTEE BILL

AMENDMENTS CHANGING THE INTERSTATE COMMERCE PROVISIONS OF THE ACT

As the law stands today, it applies only to an employee who * * *.

EXECUTIVE PROGRAM

ESTATE TAX CONVENTION WITH CANADA

ADDITIONAL COSPONSORS OF BILLS AND JOINT RESOLUTIONS

S. 659

AMENDMENTS SUBMITTED

RECIPROCAL TRADE AGREEMENTS

SPECTER AMENDMENT NO. 1194

HEADS USED IN EXTENSIONS OF REMARKS

DEPARTMENT OF DEFENSE AUTHORIZATION ACT, 1983

SPEECH OF

HON. JOHN CONYERS, JR.

OF MICHIGAN

IN THE HOUSE OF REPRESENTATIVES

Thursday, July 22, 1982

The House in Committee of the Whole House on the State of the Union had under consideration the bill (H.R. 6030) to authorize appropriations for fiscal year 1983 for the Armed Forces * * *

[The words "Speech of" are to be used only when on copy and is an indication that that particular Extension of Remarks is to be inserted in the proceedings of the bound Record of the date used in the heading.]

MISSING CHILDREN

HON. ORRIN G. HATCH

OF UTAH

IN THE SENATE OF THE UNITED STATES

Monday, January 3, 1983

● Mr. HATCH. Mr. President, I rise before this distinguished assembly to focus additional attention on the tragedy of missing children. The Department of Health and Human Services has estimated that approximately 1.3 million children disappear each year. A significant number do not leave of their own accord.* * *

CONGRESSIONAL PROCEEDINGS

SENATE

MONDAY, AUGUST 2, 1982

(Legislative day of Monday, July 12, 1982) [1]

The Senate met at 10 a.m., on the expiration of the recess, and * * *.

[Above line to be used only when Senate is in recess.]

The Senate met at 12 noon, and was called to order by the President pro tempore [Mr. THURMOND].

[Note.—Entire prayer set in 8 point.]

PRAYER

The Chaplain, the Reverend Richard C. Halverson, LL.D., D.D., offered the following prayer:

Let us pray:

Lord, Thou hast been our dwelling place in all generations. Before the mountains were brought forth, or ever Thou hadst formed the earth and the world, from everlasting to everlasting Thou art God.—Psalm 90: 1-2 RSV.

Almighty God, eternal Father, make Thy presence felt in this place today. Grant that all who do business here may experience a fresh touch from Thee. As the Senators enter into this very full week, help them to have a perspective which sees the parts in light of the whole. Free them from the tyranny of urgency which makes it impossible to see the forest for the trees. Help them not to allow the transitory to obliterate the transcendent. Give them vision which sees the temporary in light of the permanent, the temporal in light of the eternal.

Guide them to decisions which will honor Thee and bless the people. In Jesus' name. Amen.

APPOINTMENT OF ACTING PRESIDENT PRO TEMPORE

The PRESIDING OFFICER. The clerk will please read a communication to the Senate from the President pro tempore [Mr. THURMOND].

The assistant legislative clerk read the following letter:

U.S. SENATE,
PRESIDENT PRO TEMPORE,
Washington, DC, April 15, 1982.

To the Senate:

Under the provisions of rule I, section 3, of the Standing Rules of the Senate, I hereby appoint the Honorable S.I. HAYAKAWA, a Senator from the State of California, to perform the duties of the Chair.

STROM THURMOND,
President pro tempore.

Mr. HAYAKAWA thereupon assumed the chair as Acting President pro tempore.

RECOGNITION OF THE MAJORITY LEADER

The ACTING PRESIDENT pro tempore. The majority leader is recognized.

THE JOURNAL

Mr. BAKER. Mr. President, I ask unanimous consent that the Journal of the proceedings of the Senate be approved to date.

The ACTING PRESIDENT pro tempore. Without objection, it is so ordered.

JOINT SESSION OF THE TWO HOUSES—MESSAGE OF THE PRESIDENT OF THE UNITED STATES (H. DOC. NO. 98-1)

The PRESIDENT pro tempore. Under the previous order, the Senate will now proceed to the Hall of the House of Representatives.

Thereupon, at 8:38 p.m., the Senate, preceded by the Sergeant at Arms, Howard Liebengood; the Assistant Secretary of the Senate, Marilyn E. Courtot; and the President pro tempore (Mr. THURMOND), proceeded to the Hall of the House of Representatives to hear the ad-

[1] To be used only when the Senate is in recess.

dress by the President of the United States, Ronald Reagan.

(The address by the President of the United States, this day delivered by him to the joint session of the two Houses of Congress, appears in the proceedings of the House of Representatives in today's RECORD.)

ORDER FOR ROUTINE MORNING BUSINESS

Mr. STEVENS. Mr. President, I ask unanimous consent that following the time for the two leaders under the standing order and the special order for Senator SPECTER, there be a period for the transaction of routine morning business, not to exceed 30 minutes, in which Senators may make speeches for not to exceed 3 minutes each.

The PRESIDING OFFICER [Mr. CHAFEE]. Without objection, it is so ordered.

MESSAGES FROM THE PRESIDENT

Messages from the President of the United States were communicated to the Senate by Mr. Saunders, one of his secretaries.

EXECUTIVE MESSAGES REFERRED

As in executive session, the Acting President pro tempore laid before the Senate messages from the President of the United States submitting a sundry nomination which was referred to the Committee on Armed Services.

(The nomination received today is printed at the end of the Senate proceedings.)

BUDGET OF THE DISTRICT OF COLUMBIA—MESSAGE FROM THE PRESIDENT—PM 126

The PRESIDING OFFICER laid before the Senate the following message from the President of the United States, together with an accompanying document; which was referred to the Committee on Governmental Affairs:

To the Congress of the United States:

In accordance with the District of Columbia Self-Government and Governmental Reorganization Act, I am transmitting the 1983 Budget of the District of Columbia.

I am informed that the proposals for Federal payments to the District of Columbia reflected in this document are consistent with those shown in the 1983 Budget of the United States submitted to the Congress on February 8, 1982.

RONALD REAGAN.☐
☐THE WHITE HOUSE, *April 15, 1982.*

EXECUTIVE AND OTHER COMMUNICATIONS

The following communications were laid before the Senate, together with accompanying papers, reports, and documents, which were referred as indicated:

EC–3155. A communication from the Secretary of Health and Human Services transmitting a draft of proposed legislation to incorporate the supplemental food programs into the maternal and child health block grant; to the Committee on Agriculture, Nutrition, and Forestry.

PRESIDENTIAL APPROVALS

A message from the President of the United States reported that he had approved and signed the following acts and joint resolution:

On July 19, 1982:
S. 2651. An act to extend the expiration date of section 252 of the Energy Policy and Conservation Act.

ENROLLED BILLS AND JOINT RESOLUTION SIGNED

The message further announced that the Speaker pro tempore of the House had affixed his signature to the following enrolled bills and joint resolution, and they were signed by the Acting President pro tempore:

S. 171. An act for the relief of Arthur A. Schipke;
S. 518. An act for the relief of Robert T. Groom, Daisy Groom, and Margaret Groom Turpin; and

HOUSE BILLS AND JOINT RESOLUTIONS REFERRED OR PLACED ON THE CALENDAR

The following bills and joint resolutions were severally read twice by their titles and referred, or ordered to be placed on the calendar, as indicated:

H.R. 1408. An act to amend section 301 (a)(1) of the Agricultural Adjustment Act of 1938, as amended, and the first sentence of paragraph (1) of section 2 of the Agricultural Adjustment Act of 1933, as amended, and as reenacted and amended by the Agricultural Marketing Agreement Act of 1937, approved June 3, 1937, as amended, so as to include the cost of all farm labor in determining the parity price of agricultural commodities; to the calendar; and

H.R. 777. An act to amend an act entitled "An act to regulate the hours of employment and safeguard the health of females employed in the District of Columbia," approved February 24, 1914.

MESSAGES FROM THE HOUSE

At 2:11 p.m., a message from the House of Representatives was delivered by Mr. Berry, one of its reading clerks, announced that the Speaker had signed the following enrolled bills and joint resolution:

S. 272. An act to improve small business access to Federal procurement information.

H.J. Res. 338. Joint resolution to correct Public Law 98-63 due to an error in the enrollment of H.R. 3069.

The bills and joint resolution were subsequently signed by the President pro tempore (Mr THURMOND).

At 3:18 p.m., a message from the House of Representatives was delivered by Ms. Goetz, one of its reading clerks, announced that the House agrees to the amendments of the Senate to the bill (H.R. 2355).

PETITIONS AND MEMORIALS

The following petitions and memorials were laid before the Senate and were referred or ordered to lie on the table as indicated:

POM-724. A resolution adopted by the Legislature of the State of Arizona; to the Committee on Banking, Housing, and Urban Affairs.

"HOUSE CONCURRENT MEMORIAL 2002

"Whereas article I, section 8, Constitution of the United States, provides that only the Congress of the United States shall have the power 'to borrow money on the credit of the United States;' and

"Whereas, article I, section 8, Constitution of the United States, directs that only the Congress of the United States is permitted 'to coin money and regulate the value thereof;' and

"Whereas, the Federal Reserve Act of 1913 transferred the power to borrow money on the credit of the United States to a consortium of private bankers in violation of the prohibitions of article I, section 8, Constitution of the United States; and

"Whereas, the Congress of the United States is without authority to delegate any powers which it has received under the Constitution of the United States established by the people of the United States; and

"Whereas, article I, section 1, Constitution of the United States, provides that 'all legislative Powers herein granted shall be vested in a Congress of the United States, which shall consist of a Senate and House of Representatives'; and

"Whereas, the Federal Reserve Act of 1913 was imposed upon the People of the State of Arizona in violation of the provisions of article I, section 1, Constitution of the United States."

REPORTS OF COMMITTEES

The following reports of committees were submitted:

By Mr. PACKWOOD, from the Committee on Commerce, Science, and Transportation, with an amendment in the nature of a substitute and an amendment to the title:

S. 2172. A bill to amend the Communications Act of 1934 (Rept. No. 97-518).

EXECUTIVE REPORTS OF COMMITTEES

The following executive reports of committees were submitted:

By Mr. GARN, from the Committee on Banking, Housing and Urban Affairs:

Ralph D. DeNunzio, of Connecticut, to be a Director of the Securities Investor Protection Corporation for a term expiring December 31, 1982;

David F. Goldberg, of Illinois, to be a Director of the Securities Investor Protection Corporation for a term expiring December 31, 1984; and

Roger A. Yurchuck, of Ohio, to be a Director of the Securities Investor Pro-

tection Corporation for a term expiring December 31, 1984.

INTRODUCTION OF BILLS AND JOINT RESOLUTIONS

The following bills and joint resolutions were introduced, read the first and second time by unanimous consent, and referred as indicated:

By Mr. HUMPHREY (for himself, Mr. RUDMAN, Mr. STAFFORD, Mr. WEICKER, Mr. TSONGAS, Mr. KENNEDY, Mr. DODD, and Mr. LEAHY):

S. 2835. A bill to grant the consent and approval of the Congress to an interstate agreement or compact relating to the restoration of Atlantic salmon in the Connecticut River Basin, and to allow the Secretary of Commerce and the Secretary of the Interior to participate as members in a Connecticut River Atlantic Salmon Commission; to the Committee on the Judiciary.

SUBMISSION OF CONCURRENT AND SENATE RESOLUTIONS

The following concurrent resolutions and Senate resolutions were read, and referred (or acted upon), as indicated:

By Mr. MATTINGLY (for himself, Mr. KENNEDY, Mr. HUMPHREY, and Mr. CHAFEE):

S. Con. Res. 62. A concurrent resolution to direct the Commissioner of Social Security and the Secretary of Health and Human Services to develop a plan outlining the steps which might be taken to correct the social security benefit disparity known as the notch problem; to the Committee on Finance.

By Mr. D'AMATO:

S. Res. 446. Resolution to honor Michael R. Masone; to the Committee on the Judiciary.

STATEMENTS ON INTRODUCED BILLS AND JOINT RESOLUTIONS

By Mr. QUAYLE:

S. 1778. A bill to provide for a block grant to States for health planning activities, and for other purposes; to the Committee on Labor and Human Resources.

HEALTH PLANNING BLOCK GRANT ACT OF 1983

● Mr. QUAYLE. Mr. President, I introduce S. 1778, a bill to establish a block grant to the States to support health planning.

The latest authorization for the Federal health planning program expired at the conclusion of the last fiscal year. The program has been funded under a continuing resolution despite the fact that it has not been reauthorized. Health planning has been useful in many States in containing health care costs and assuring equitable access to health services. It is important that the Federal Government continue to encourage health planning on the State and local levels but the current health planning law should be replaced.●

AMENDMENTS SUBMITTED

DEPARTMENT OF THE INTERIOR APPROPRIATIONS, 1984

McCLURE AMENDMENT NO. 2110

Mr. McCLURE proposed an amendment to the bill (H.R. 3363) making appropriations for the Department of the Interior and related agencies for the fiscal year ending September 30, 1984, and for other purposes, as follows:

On page 81, line 14, before the period insert the following:

"Provided, That all of the restrictions and limitations set forth in 16 U.S.C. 839(j)(1), shall apply to any contracts or obligations entered into by the Administrator pursuant to this provision"

EXON AMENDMENT NO. 2111

Mr. EXON proposed an amendment to the bill, H.R. 3363, supra, as follows:

At the appropriate place in the bill insert the following:

That notwithstanding any other provision of law, the Secretary of the Interior (hereinafter in this Act referred to as • • •.

ADDITIONAL STATEMENTS

NATIONAL PARALYZED VETERANS RECOGNITION DAY

● Mr. STAFFORD. Mr. President, I am pleased today to call attention here to the fact that this is National Paralyzed Veterans Recognition Day. Legislation to establish this observance was signed by the President on August 1 (Public Law 98–62). In the Senate, the legislation was designated Senate Joint Resolution 106 and authored by the distinguished chairman of the Veterans' Affairs Committee, Senator SIMPSON. I am proud to have been a cosponsor.●

CONCLUSION OF MORNING BUSINESS

The PRESIDING OFFICER. Is there further morning business?

If not, morning business is closed.

BLANCHE H. KARSCH, ADMINISTRATRIX OF THE ESTATE OF KATE E. HAMILTON—VETO MESSAGE (S. DOC. NO. 108)

The VICE PRESIDENT laid before the Senate the following veto message from the President of the United States, which was read, and with the accompanying bill, referred to the Committee on the Judiciary and ordered to be printed:

To the Senate:

I return herewith, without my approval, S. 514, entitled "An act for the relief of Blanche H. Karsch, administratrix of the estate of Kate E. Hamilton."

I know of no circumstances which would justify the exception made by S. 514 to the long-continued policy of Congress, and do not believe that the field of special legislation should be opened * * *

HARRY S. TRUMAN.□

THE WHITE HOUSE, *March 17, 1952.*

[The above to be 8 point "FIC & punc."]

[When communications from the President contain extracts, etc., such extracts must be in 7 point.]

REPORT ON CLASSIFIED INFORMATION (S. DOC. NO. 107)

Mr. LODGE. Mr. President, the Committee on Armed Services of the Senate has recently requested the Office of Public Relations of the Department of the Navy to submit to it a report on classified information. The Department of the Navy has complied with the request, and I now present the report and ask that it be published as a Senate document.

The VICE PRESIDENT. Without objection, the report will be printed as a document as requested by the Senator from Massachusetts.

PAWNEE INDIANS v. THE UNITED STATES (S. DOC. NO. 311)

The VICE PRESIDENT laid before the Senate a communication from the Assistant Clerk of the Court of Claims, transmitting a certified copy of the findings of fact and conclusion filed by the court in the cause of The Pawnee Tribe of Indians against The United States, which was referred to the Committee on Finance and ordered to be printed.

[Note the insertion of (*S. Doc. No. —*) in cases where papers are ordered to be printed as a document. To be inserted only when *ordered to be printed* or its equivalent is in copy.]

Third reading and passage of a bill

MISSOURI RIVER BRIDGE NEAR ST. CHARLES, MO

The bill (S. 4174) to extend the times for commencing and completing the construction of a bridge across the Missouri River at or near St. Charles, MO, was considered, ordered to be engrossed for a third reading, read the third time, and passed, as follows:

S. 4174

Be it enacted by the Senate and House of Representatives of the United States of America in Congress assembled, That the times for commencing and completing the construction of the bridge across the Missouri River, etc.

Amendment, third reading, and passage of a bill

GOVERNMENT OF THE TERRITORY OF HAWAII

The Senate proceeded to consider the bill (S. 1881) to amend an act entitled "An act to provide a government for the Territory of Hawaii," approved April 30, 1900, as amended, to establish a Hawaiian Homes Commission, and for other purposes, which had been reported from the Committee on Interior and Insular Affairs with amendments.

The first amendment was, on page 4, line 22, to strike out "Keaaupaha" and insert "Keaaukaha".

The amendment was agreed to.

The next amendment was, on page 6, line 19, after the figure "(1)", to insert "by further authorization of Congress and", so as to make the paragraph read:

(1) by further authorization of Congress and for a period of five years after the first meeting of the Hawaiian Homes Commission only those lands situated on the island of Molokai, etc.

The amendment was agreed to.

The bill was ordered to be engrossed for a third reading, read the third time, and passed.

Forms of amendments

The joint resolution (S.J. Res. 4) requesting the President to negotiate a treaty or treaties for the protection of salmon in certain parts of the Pacific Ocean was announced as next in order.

Mr. McFARLAND. Mr. President I have just had an opportunity to examine this joint resolution. I offer this amendment.

The PRESIDING OFFICER. The Secretary will state the amendment offered by the Senator from Arizona.

The READING CLERK. On page 1, line 11, it is proposed to strike out the words "both within and", so as to make the joint resolution read:

Resolved by the Senate and House of Representatives of the United States of America in Congress assembled, That the President of the United States be, and he is hereby, requested to negotiate on behalf of the United States, as promptly as is practicable, etc.

Mr. BRIDGES. Mr. President, I observe in the report of the bill by the chairman of the Foreign Relations Committee that it is reported as a Senate joint resolution. I ask for a modification of it so that it will be a Senate resolution instead of a Senate joint resolution.

The LEGISLATIVE CLERK. It is proposed to strike out "S.J. Res. 4" and insert "S. Res. 85".

The PRESIDING OFFICER. Is there objection to the modification? The Chair hears none, and it will be so modified.

Mr. McFARLAND. Would it not be necessary to change the resolving clause also? The resolving clause reads:

Resolved by the Senate and House of Representatives of the United States of America in Congress assembled,

Mr. BRIDGES. Yes, Mr. President; it should read simply "Resolved". I ask that that change be made.

The LEGISLATIVE CLERK. On page 1, lines 1 and 2, it is proposed to strike out all after the word "Resolved".

The amendment was agreed to.

The VICE PRESIDENT. The next amendment will be stated.

The ASSISTANT SECRETARY. On page 2, line 13, after the word "pound", insert the words "except rice cleaned for use in the manufacture of canned foods", so as to read:

Rice, cleaned, 9 cents per pound, except rice cleaned for use in the manufacture of canned foods.

The VICE PRESIDENT. The question is on agreeing to the amendment.

The amendment was agreed to.

The next amendment was, on page 151, to strike out:

Steamer *Phalarope*: Master, $1,500; engineer, $1,200; fireman, $780; two seamen at $810 each; cook, $870; in all $5,970.

The amendment was agreed to.

[Note use of words, figures, and punctuation in the following:]

The next amendment was, on page 34, in line 9, under the heading "Employees' Compensation Commission", before the word "assistants", to strike out "five" and insert "three"; in line 10, after the word "clerks" and before the words "of class 3", to strike out "seven" and insert "five"; in line 11, before the words "of class 2", to strike out "twelve" and insert "nine"; in the same line, before the words "of class 1", to strike out "twentyseven" and insert "twenty"; in line 12, before the words "at $1,000 each", to strike out "three" and insert "two"; and in line 18, to strike out "$124,940" and insert "$102,590", so as to read:

EMPLOYEES' COMPENSATION COMMISSION

Salaries: Three Commissioners at $4,000 each; secretary, $2,750; attorney, $4,000; chief statistician, $3,000; chief of accounts, $2,500; accountant, $2,250; claim examiners—chief $2,250, assistant $2,000, assistant $1,800, three assistants at $1,600 each; special agents—two at $1,800 each, two at $1,600 each; clerks—five of class 3; nine of class 2, twenty of class 1, two at $1,000 each; in all $102,590.

Mr. HOLLAND submitted an amendment intended to be proposed by him to the sundry civil appropriation bill, which was ordered to lie on the table and to be printed, as follows:

Add a new section, as follows:
"That the President of the Senate appoint three Members of the Senate; and the Speaker of the House three Members of the House."

The Senate resumed the consideration of the bill (H.R. 4075) to limit the immigration of aliens into the United States.

Mr. HARRY F. BYRD, JR. Mr. President, I offer an amendment, which I send to the desk.

The VICE PRESIDENT. The amendment will be stated.

The ASSISTANT SECRETARY. On page 9, line 3, it is proposed to amend by striking out "3" and inserting "1", so that it will read:

SEC. 2. (a) That the number of aliens of any nationality who may be admitted under the immigration laws to the United States in any fiscal year shall be limited to 1 per centum of the number of foreign-born persons of such nationality resident in the United States.

The VICE PRESIDENT. The question is on agreeing to the amendment offered by the Senator from Virginia to the amendment of the committee.

The amendment to the amendment was rejected.

The PRESIDING OFFICER. The question is, Shall the bill pass?

Mr. THYE. I ask for the yeas and nays on the passage of the bill.

Mr. GEORGE. Let us have the yeas and nays.

The yeas and nays were ordered, and the reading clerk proceeded to call the roll.

Mr. LONG (when his name was called). I am paired with the senior Senator from New Hampshire [Mr. BRIDGES]. I am informed that if he were present he would vote as I intend to vote on the passage of the bill. I therefore feel at liberty to vote, and vote "yea."

Mr. SALTONSTALL. I desire to announce that the Senator from Nebraska [Mr. BUTLER], the senior Senator from New Hampshire [Mr. BRIDGES], and the Senator from Delaware [Mr. WILLIAMS] would vote for the bill if present. They are necessarily absent.

The result was announced—yeas 78, nays 1, as follows:

YEAS—78

Aiken	Gillette	Long
Dirksen	Green	Nixon

NAY—1

Ives

NOT VOTING—17

Bricker	Kilgore	Robertson
Byrd	Long	Taft

EXECUTIVE SESSION

The PRESIDING OFFICER. The Senate will now proceed to executive session. There will now be 5 minutes debate on Calendar Order No. 156, which the clerk will state.

EXECUTIVE SESSION

Mr. BAKER. Mr. President, I ask unanimous consent that the Senate now go into executive session for the purpose of considering those nominations on page 2, with the ex-

ception of Calendar No. 43; those nominations on page 3, with the exception of Calendar Order No. 46; all of the nominations on page 4, and all of the nominations on page 5.

The PRESIDING OFFICER. Without objection, it is so ordered.

LEGISLATIVE SESSION

Mr. BAKER. Mr. President, I ask unanimous consent that the Senate now return to legislative session.

The PRESIDING OFFICER. Without objection, it is so ordered.

[An executive session usually being open, the following precedes the recess or adjournment heading:]

TREATY OF ARBITRATION AND CONCILIATION WITH SWITZERLAND

The Chief Clerk proceeded to read Executive B, a treaty of arbitration and conciliation with Switzerland, signed at Washington on March 17, 1952, which was considered as in Committee of the Whole, and is as follows:

To the Senate of the United States:
To the end that I may receive the advice and consent of the Senate to ratification, I transmit herewith a treaty of arbitration and conciliation between the United States and Switzerland, signed at Washington on March 17, 1952.

HARRY S. TRUMAN.□
THE WHITE HOUSE, *March 17, 1952.*

[A letter from the President to the Senate is set in 7-point type when any form of treaty is enclosed that is to be printed in the Record in connection therewith. The letter is set in 7-point type whether the treaty follows or precedes it or is separated from it by intervening matter.]

RECESS UNTIL TOMORROW AT 10:30 A.M.

Mr. BAKER. Mr. President, I know of no further business to come before the Senate. I move, in accordance with the order previously entered, that the Senate stand in recess until the hour of 10:30 a.m. tomorrow.

The motion was agreed to and, at 7:20 p.m., the Senate recessed until Wednesday, November 18, 1981, at 10:30 a.m.

[After the recess or adjournment heading the following appears:]

NOMINATIONS

Executive nominations received by the Senate March 17 (legislative day of March 9), 1966:

[Under heading *Postmaster,* omit the State subheading if only one nomination or confirmation is given. Under the heads *Nominations, Confirmations, Withdrawal,* and *Rejection,* the following scheme for subheads is to be followed:

[Heads indicating service, or branch or department of Government—7-point caps and small caps.

[Subheads indicating subdivision or type of service—7-point small caps.

[Subheads indicating new rank of appointee—7-point italic.]

[NOTE.—Nominations will be set as indicated on copy when it is received—last name first or first name first—as in executive nominations.]

DIPLOMATIC AND FOREIGN SERVICE

Merlin E. Smith, of Ohio, to be a Foreign Service officer, unclassified, a vice consul of career, and a secretary in the diplomatic service of the United States of America.

THE JUDICIARY

Tom C. Clark of Texas, to be Assistant Attorney General of the United States, vice Hon. Thurman Arnold, resigned.

Hugh B. Cox, of the District of Columbia, to be Assistant Attorney General of the United States; new position.

TEMPORARY APPOINTMENT IN THE ARMY OF THE UNITED STATES

Lt. Gen. Henry Harley Arnold (major general, U.S. Army), Army of the United States.

APPOINTMENTS, BY TRANSFER, IN THE REGULAR ARMY OF THE UNITED STATES

TO ORDNANCE DEPARTMENT

Lt. Col. George DeVere Barnes, Quartermaster Corps (temporary colonel), with rank from January 11, 1952.

IN THE AIR FORCE

To be brigadier general

Maj. Gen. Harry George Armstrong, 209A, (colonel U.S. Air Force), Air Force of the United States, medical.

Brig. Gen. John Ferral McBlain, 203A (colonel, U.S. Air Force), Air Force of the United States.

To be major general

Brig. Gen. Herbert R. Temple, Jr., 557-32-7721.

IN THE AIR FORCE

The following Air National Guard of the United States officers for promotion in the Reserve of the Air Force under the provisions of section 593(a) title 10 of the United States Code, as amended.

LINE OF THE AIR FORCE

To be lieutenant colonel

Maj. Clayton B. Anderson, 503-56-3340.

Maj. George C. Arvanetaki, 041-26-0819.

Maj. George D. Brooks, 407-42-0022.

Maj. Raymond A. Cline, Jr., 159-28-9276.

SUPPLY CORPS
Captain

Alwine, Paul R., Jr.

Barr, Charles V.

Bartuska, Anthony John

Bentson, Gordon J.

Bolin, James H.

Booth, Henry Adolph, Jr.

MEDICAL CORPS

Maj. Pomp T. Carney, 427-66-3233

Maj. Gerald D. Loos, 503-40-6401

Maj. Hugh E. McGee, Jr., 145-30-9499

IN THE ARMY

The following-named officers for appointment in the Regular Army of the United States, in their active duty grades, under the provisions of title 10, United States Code, sections 531, 532, and 533:

Colonel

Porter, Robert O., 541-34-2316

Lieutenant colonel

Smith, Edward F., 146-32-1660

Major

Davis, Rudy P., 534-40-4313

Herod, Herbert L., 533-28-5599

Jones, Lafayette, Jr., 226-56-9538

Captain

Duque, George M., 046-40-2668

CONFIRMATIONS

Executive nominations confirmed by the Senate February 9, 1972:

NATIONAL COMMISSION ON LIBRARIES AND INFORMATION SCIENCE

Harold C. Crotty, of Michigan, to be a member of the National Commission on Libraries and Information Science for the remainder of the term expiring July 19, 1972.

NATIONAL LABOR RELATIONS BOARD

John A. Penello, of Maryland, to be a member of the National Labor Relations Board for the term of 5 years expiring August 27, 1976.

IN THE ARMY
TEMPORARY APPOINTMENT IN THE ARMY OF THE UNITED STATES
To be brigadier general

William Edward Raab Covell

Albert Jesse Browning

APPOINTMENTS IN THE REGULAR ARMY
To be chaplain, with rank of first lieutenant, to rank from date of appointment

Charles Edwin Brown, Jr.

John Porter Fellows III

To be first lieutenant, Medical Corps, with rank from date of appointment

Charles Herman Ransom

IN THE NAVY
PROMOTIONS IN THE REGULAR SERVICE
To be captain

Cornelius Flynn	Charles W. Styer
Armit C. Thomas	Thomas L. Sprague
Edmund E. Brady, Jr.	Einar R. Johnson, Jr.

To be assistant dental surgeon

Estes W. Murphy

IN THE MARINE CORPS
TEMPORARY SERVICE
To be brigadier general, Marine Corps Reserve

Littleton, W.T. Waller, Jr.

To be lieutenant colonel

George A. Williams

To be second lieutenant

John D. Hayes	John J. Kalen
Dudley R. Carr	William E. Lunn

ADJOURNMENT UNTIL MONDAY, SEPTEMBER 12, 1983

Mr. BAKER. Mr. President, no other matter is cleared for action by either side. The time for the transaction of routine morning business has long since expired, as has the patience of most Senators.

In view of that, Mr. President, I move, in accordance with the provisions of House Concurrent Resolution 153 the Senate now do adjourn until September 12 at 12 noon.

The motion was agreed to; and the Senate, at 7:03 p.m., adjourned until Monday, September 12, 1983, at 12 noon.

HOUSE OF REPRESENTATIVES

TUESDAY, MAY 25, 1982

The House met at 12 o'clock noon and was called to order by the Speaker pro tempore [Mr. FOLEY].

DESIGNATION OF SPEAKER PRO TEMPORE

The SPEAKER pro tempore laid before the House the following communication from the Speaker.

WASHINGTON, DC,
June 23, 1983.

I hereby designate the Honorable THOMAS S. FOLEY to act as Speaker pro tempore on Monday, June 27, 1983.

THOMAS P. O'NEILL, JR.,
Speaker of the House of Representatives.

PRAYER

The Chaplain, Rev. James David Ford, D.D., offered the following prayer:

O sing to the Lord a new song, for He has done marvelous things!— Psalm 98: 1.

O Lord, You have been with us all our days and blessed us with gifts both great and small. We give thanks that when our spirits were low, You gave new strength, and when we were discouraged, You gave new hope. As You have promised to Your people a new song of joy and peace, so enable us to commit ourselves to the way of truth that we may be ministers of righteousness and heralds of peace in our own day and time. Amen.

THE JOURNAL

The SPEAKER. The Chair has examined the Journal of the last day's proceedings and announces to the House his approval thereof.

Pursuant to clause 1, rule I, the Journal stands approved.

SWEARING IN OF MEMBERS

The SPEAKER. The Chair understands there are some Members present who desire to take the oath at this time. Will those Members who have not taken the oath of office kindly step to the well.

The Speaker administered the oath of office to the following Members-elect:

OATH OF OFFICE OF MEMBER

The oath of office required by the sixth article of the Constitution of the United States, and as provided by section 3 of the act of May 13, 1884 (23 Stat. 22), to be administered to Members of the House of Representatives, the text of which is carried in section 1757 of title XIX of the Revised Statutes of the United States and being as follows:

"I, A B, do solemnly swear (or affirm) that I will support and defend the Constitution of the United States against all enemies foreign and domestic; that I will bear true faith and allegiance to the same; that I take this obligation freely without any mental reservation or purpose of evasion; and that I will well and faithfully discharge the duties of the office on which I am about to enter. So help me God."

has been subscribed to in person and filed in duplicate with the Clerk of the House of Representatives by the following Member of the 92d Congress, pursuant to Public Law 412 of the 80th Congress entitled "An act to amend section 30 of the Revised Statutes of the United States" (2 U.S.C. 25), approved February 18, 1948:

RICHARD W. MALLARY, at Large District of Vermont.

MESSAGE FROM THE SENATE

A message from the Senate by Mr. Sparrow, one of its clerks, announced that the Senate had passed without amendment a concurrent resolution of the House of the following title:

H. Con. Res. 290. Concurrent resolution reaffirming that deposits, up to the statutorily prescribed amount, in federally insured depository institutions are

backed by the full faith and credit of the United States.

The message also announced that the Senate had passed a bill of the following title, in which the concurrence of the House is requested:

S. 2158. An act to amend title 23, United States Code, to authorize and direct the payment of an incentive grant for highway safety programs to any State in the first fiscal year during which the State adopts provisions relating to driving while intoxicated; to establish a national driver register, and for other purposes.

The message also announced that the Secretary be directed to request the House of Representatives to return to the Senate the bill (S. 907) entitled "An act to amend sections 351 and 1751 of title 18 of the United States Code to provide penalties for crimes against Cabinet officers, Supreme Court Justices, and Presidential staff members, and for other purposes."

[Observe that bills from the Senate to the House read *An act.* If the copy should read *A bill,* change to *An act* in conformity with this rule, and place number first. Note also the following forms:]

The message also announced that the Senate had passed a joint resolution (S.J. Res. 20) making available the sum of $150,000 for the construction, etc.

The message also announced that the Senate had adopted the following resolution:

S. Res. 209

Resolved, That the Senate has heard with profound sorrow the announcement of the death of Hon. Henry B. Steagall, late a Representative from the State of Alabama, etc.

MESSAGE FROM THE PRESIDENT

A message in writing from the President of the United States was communicated to the House by Mr. Leomar, one of his secretaries, who also informed the House that on the following dates the President approved and signed bills and a joint resolution of the House of the following titles:

On June 2, 1971:

H.R. 4209. An act to amend the Revised Organic Act of the Virgin Islands.

On June 4, 1971:

H.R. 5765. An act to extend for 6 months the time for filing the comprehensive report of the Commission on the Organization of the Government of the District of Columbia; and

H.J. Res. 583. Joint resolution designating the last full week in July of 1971 as "National Star Route Mail Carriers Week."

[Observe that bills coming from the President take the form of *An act.* This rule must be followed invariably, even if the copy reads *A bill.*]

AT LAST—SOME GOOD NEWS IN SOCIAL SECURITY

(Mr. PICKLE asked and was given permission to address the House for 1 minute and to revise and extend his remarks.)

Mr. PICKLE. Mr. Speaker, last Friday, for the first time since the early 1970's * * *.

MRS. VIRGINIA THRIFT

Mr. COUDERT. Mr. Speaker, by direction of the Committee on House Administration, I offer a privileged resolution (H. Res. 321) and ask for its immediate consideration.

The Clerk read as follows:

H. Res. 321

Resolved, That there shall be paid out of the contingent fund of the House to Mrs. Virginia Thrift, widow of Chester R. Thrift, late an employee of the House, an amount equal to six months' salary compensation at the rate he was receiving at the time of his death, and an additional amount not to exceed $250 to defray funeral expenses of the said Chester R. Thrift.

The resolution was agreed to.

A motion to reconsider was laid on the table.

BILLS PRESENTED TO THE PRESIDENT

Mr. KLEIN, from the Committee on Rules, reported that that committee did on this day present to the President, for his approval, bills of the House of the following titles:

H.R. 3331. An act for the relief of Harry L. Smith; and

H.R. 3366. An act to amend section 409 of the Interstate Commerce Act, relating

to joint rates of freight forwarders and common carriers by motor vehicle.

ENROLLED BILLS SIGNED

Mr. HAYS, from the Committee on House Administration, reported that that committee had examined and found truly enrolled bills of the House of the following titles, which were thereupon signed by the Speaker:

H.R. 4209. An act to amend the Revised Organic Act of the Virgin Islands; and

H.R. 8190. An act making supplemental appropriations for the fiscal year ending June 30, 1971, and for other purposes.

THE PRIVATE CALENDAR

The SPEAKER. The Clerk will call the first bill on the Private Calendar.

JOHN SIMS

The Clerk called the first bill on the Private Calendar, H.R. 399, for the relief of John Sims.

There being no objection, the Clerk read the bill, as follows:

H.R. 399

Be it enacted by the Senate and House of Representatives of the United States of America in Congress assembled, That the Secretary of the Treasury is authorized and directed to pay to John Sims, Mobile, Alabama, the sum of $5,000.

The SPEAKER. The gentleman from Florida offers an amendment, which the Clerk will report.

The Clerk read as follows:

Amendment by Mr. SIKES: In line 4, after the word "pay", add a comma and the following words: "out of any money in the Treasury not otherwise appropriated".

The SPEAKER. The question is on agreeing to the amendment.

The amendment was agreed to.

On motion of Mr. SIKES, a motion to reconsider the vote by which the bill was passed was laid on [*not* upon] the table.

SENATE BILLS REFERRED

Bills of the Senate of the following titles were taken from the Speaker's table and, under the rule, referred as follows:

S. 962. An act for the relief of Mr. and Mrs. Frank Holehan; to the Committee on the Judiciary; and

S. 1077. An act for the relief of William A. Haag; to the Committee on the Judiciary.

[In the reference of Senate acts to House committees the name of the committee will be repeated after each act, though there may be several acts referred to the same committee.]

COMMITTEE OF THE WHOLE HOUSE ON THE STATE OF THE UNION

RAIL SAFETY AND SERVICE IMPROVEMENT ACT OF 1982

The SPEAKER. Pursuant to House Resolution 336 and rule XXIII, the Chair declares the House in the Committee of the Whole House on the State of the Union for the consideration of the bill (H.R. 6308), to insure rail safety, provide for the preservation of rail service, transfer responsibility for the Northeast corridor improvement project to Amtrak * * *.

The SPEAKER pro tempore. The Chair designates the gentleman from Massachusetts [Mr. FRANK] as Chairman of the Committee of the Whole and requests the gentleman from New York, Mr. McHUGH, to assume the chair temporarily.

IN THE COMMITTEE OF THE WHOLE

Accordingly the House resolved itself into the Committee of the Whole House on the State of the Union for the consideration of the bill, H.R. 6308, with Mr. McHUGH, Chairman pro tempore, in the chair.

The Clerk read the title of the bill.

The CHAIRMAN pro tempore. Pursuant to the rule, the first reading of the bill is dispensed with.

Under the rule, the gentleman from New Jersey [Mr. FLORIO] will be recognized for 30 minutes and the gentleman from New York [Mr. LENT] will be recognized for 30 minutes.

The CHAIRMAN. Pursuant to the rule, the text of H.R. 6911 shall be considered by titles as an original bill for the purpose of amendment under the 5-minute rule in lieu of the amendments recommended by the Committees on Energy and Commerce and Interior and Insular Affairs. Each title shall be considered as having been read.

The Clerk will designate section 1.

The Clerk read as follows:

That this Act may be referred to as the "Rail Safety and Service Improvement Act of 1982".

The CHAIRMAN. Are there any amendments to section 1? If not, the Clerk will designate title I.

The text of title I is as follows:

AMENDMENT OFFERED BY MR. SIMON

Mr. SIMON. Mr. Chairman, I offer an amendment.

The Clerk read as follows:

Amendment offered by Mr. SIMON: Page 2, line 4, strike out "a new subsection as follows" and insert in lieu thereof "the following new subsections".

Page 2, line 16, strike out the quotation mark and the period which follows it.

Page 2, after line 16, insert the following:

"(j) The Secretary shall within 30 days report to Congress on whether it should issue rules, regulations, orders, and standards to require that the leading car of any railroad train in operation after July 1, 1983, be equipped with an acceptable form of mounted oscillating light.".

Mr. SIMON. Mr. Chairman, I would like to take my 5 minutes just to explain this situation, though I believe the amendment may be acceptable.

The CHAIRMAN. Under the rule, the Committee rises.

Accordingly the Committee rose; and the Speaker pro tempore [Mr. MURTHA] having assumed the chair, Mr. FRANK, Chairman of the Committee of the Whole House on the State of the Union, reported that that Committee, having had under consideration the bill (H.R. 6308) to insure rail safety, provide for the preservation of rail service, transfer responsibility for the Northeast corridor improvement project to Amtrak, and for other purposes, pursuant to House Resolution 546, reported the bill back to the House with an amendment adopted by the Committee of the Whole.

The SPEAKER pro tempore. Under the rule, the previous question is ordered.

Is a separate vote demanded on any amendment to the amendment in the nature of a substitute adopted by the Committee of the Whole? If not, the question is on the amendment.

The amendment was agreed to.

The bill was ordered to be engrossed and read a third time, was read the third time, and passed.

The title of the bill was amended so as to read: "A bill to insure rail safety, provide for the preservation of rail service, insure the completion of the Northeast corridor improvement project, and for other purposes."

A motion to reconsider was laid on the table.

(Mr. ARCHER asked and was given permission to revise and extend his remarks.)

Mr. ARCHER. Mr. Chairman, at a time when the United States is suffering from a serious balance-of-payments deficit, it is in my opinion * * *.

The CHAIRMAN. The question is on the amendment offered by the gentleman from Texas [Mr. ARCHER].

The question was taken; and on a division (demanded by Mr. ARCHER) there were—ayes 36, noes 33.

COMMITTEE AMENDMENT

The CHAIRMAN. The Clerk will report the next committee amendment.

The Clerk read as follows:

Committee amendment: Page 2, line 5, strike out the quotation mark and insert the following:

"SEC. 12. The Secretary of the Treasury shall instruct the United States * * *

Mr. WRIGHT (during the reading). Mr. Chairman, this is the same amendment that was passed in the two preceding bills. It deals with narcotics. I do not think there is any objection to it.

I ask unanimous consent that further reading of the amendment be dispensed with, that it be printed in the RECORD, and be open to amendment.

The CHAIRMAN. Is there objection to the request of the gentleman from Texas?

There was no objection.

The CHAIRMAN. The question is on the amendment offered by the gentleman from Texas [Mr. GONZALEZ].

The amendment was agreed to.

The CHAIRMAN. Under the rule, the Committee rises.

Accordingly the Committee rose; and the Speaker having resumed the chair, Mr. NEDZI, Chairman of the Committee of the Whole House on the State of the Union, reported that that Committee having had under consideration the bill (S. 2010) to provide for increased participation by the United States in the International Development Association, pursuant to House Resolution 786, he reported the bill back to the House with sundry amendments adopted by the Committee of the Whole.

Conference report and statement

Conference reports and statements to be set in 7 point.

Use 3-point space before and after conference report and statement.

In the House the names of Members are to be first.

Follow copy literally in the report. Observe the form *Amendments numbered 1, 2, 3, etc.,* and when the amendment is to make an independent paragraph, the phrase *And the Senate* [or *House*] *agree to the same* will be a paragraph by itself; otherwise it will be run in after the amendment with a semicolon. Examples of each are given in the report following.

In the statement change *numbered,* when in copy, to *No.,* as *amendment No. 1,* but do not supply *No.* or *amendment* if omitted in copy; otherwise regular style will prevail.

(See pp. 344–346 for styles of conference report set as House report and as Senate document.)

CONFERENCE REPORT (H. REPT. NO. 97-747)

The committee of conference on the disagreeing votes of the two Houses on the amendments of the Senate to the bill (H.R. 6863) making supplemental appropriations for the fiscal year ending September 30, 1982, and for other purposes, having met, after full and free conference, have agreed to recommend and do recommend to their respective Houses as follows:

That the Senate recede from its amendments numbered 7, 9, 14, 31, 38, 39, 40, 52, 53, 56, 75, 76, 80, 81, 94, 102, 109, 116, 118, 129, 133, 141, 142, 148, 152, 154, 155, 162, 163, 164, 171, 173, 179, and 181.

That the House recede from its disagreement to the amendments of the

Senate numbered 20, 23, 25, 26, 28, 30, 32, 33, 34, 35, 36, 46, 48, 54, 61, 68, 70, 77, 78, 79, 87, 99, 101, 104, 105, 106, 110, 111, 125, 127, 134, 136, 139, 156, 157, 165, 167, 168, 170, 174, 175, and 176, and agree to the same.

Amendment numbered 16:

That the House recede from its disagreement to the amendment of the Senate numbered 16, and agree to the same with an amendment, as follows:

In lieu of the sum proposed by said amendment insert *$4,400,000*; and the Senate agree to the same.

Amendment numbered 27:

That the House recede from its disagreement to the amendment of the Senate numbered 27, and agree to the same with an amendment, as follows:

In lieu of the sum proposed by said amendment insert *$53,700,000*; and the Senate agree to the same.

JOHN T. MYERS
(except amendments
54 and 177),
CLARENCE E. MILLER,
LAWRENCE COUGHLIN,
JACK F. KEMP,
GEORGE M. O'BRIEN,
Managers on the Part of the House.

JOHN C. STENNIS,
DANIEL K. INOUYE,
ERNEST F. HOLLINGS,
THOMAS F. EAGLETON,
LAWTON CHILES,
J. BENNETT JOHNSTON,
WALTER D.
HUDDLESTON,
PATRICK J. LEAHY,
DENNIS DeCONCINI,
Managers on the Part of the Senate.

JOINT EXPLANATORY STATEMENT OF THE COMMITTEE OF CONFERENCE

The managers on the part of the House and the Senate at the conference on the disagreeing votes of the two Houses on the amendments of the Senate to the bill (H.R. 6863), making supplemental appropriations for the fiscal year 1982, rescinding certain budget authority, and for other purposes, submit the following joint statement to the House and the Senate in explanation of the effect of the action agreed upon by the managers and recommended in the accompanying conference report:

TITLE I
CHAPTER I—DEPARTMENT OF AGRICULTURE
SOIL CONSERVATION SERVICE
CONSERVATION OPERATIONS

Amendment No. 1: Reported in technical disagreement. The managers on the part of the House will offer a motion to recede and concur in the amendment of the Senate which allows the Soil Conservation Service to exchange a parcel of land in Bellingham, Washington, for other land.

In lieu of the matter inserted by said amendment, insert the following:

Food and Nutrition Service

child nutrition programs

If the funds available for Nutrition Education and Training grants authorized under section 19 of the Child Nutrition Act of 1966, as amended, require a ratable reduction in those grants, the minimum grant for each State shall be $50,000.

The managers on the part of the Senate will move to concur in the amendment of the House to the amendment of the Senate.

Committee on Agriculture: Solely for consideration of the title I of the House bill and title I of the Senate amendment:

E DE LA GARZA,
THOMAS S. FOLEY,
DAVID R. BOWEN,
FRED RICHMOND,
BILL WAMPLER,
PAUL FINDLEY
(on all matters
except as listed
below),
TOM HAGEDORN
(on all matters
except as listed
below),

Amendments

[As figures are used in bills to express sums of money, dates, paragraph numbers, etc., amendments involving such expressions must be set in figures thus: Strike out "$840" and insert "$1,000", etc. For other enumerations in bill style, see rule 2.13, p. 2.47.]

EMANUEL F. LENKERSDORF

The Clerk called the bill (H.R. 2520) for the relief of Emanuel F. Lenkersdorf.

There being no objection, the Clerk read the bill as follows:

H.R. 2520

Be it enacted by the Senate and House of Representatives of the United States of America in Congress assembled, That for the purposes of the Immigration and Nationality Act, Emanuel F. Lenkersdorf shall be held and considered to have been lawfully admitted to the United States for permanent residence as of the date of the enactment of this Act, upon payment of the required visa fee. Upon the granting of permanent residence to such alien as provided for in this Act, the Secretary of State shall instruct the proper officer to deduct one number

from the total number of immigrant visas and conditional entries which are made available to natives of the country of the alien's birth under paragraphs (1) through (8) of section 203(a) of the Immigration and Nationality Act.

With the following committee amendment:

On page 2, strike lines 4 through 6 and insert in lieu thereof: "which are made available to natives of the country of the alien's birth under section 203(a) of the Immigration and Nationality Act or, if applicable, from the total number of such visas which are made available to such natives under section 202(e) of such Act.".

The committee amendment was agreed to.

The bill was ordered to be engrossed and read a third time, was read the third time, and passed, and a motion to reconsider was laid on the table.

CONTESTED ELECTION, CARTER AGAINST LeCOMPTE—MESSAGE FROM THE CLERK OF THE HOUSE OF REPRESENTATIVES (H. DOC. NO. 235)

The SPEAKER laid before the House the following message from the Clerk of the House of Representatives, which was read and, with the accompanying papers, referred to the Committee on House Administration:

AUGUST 23, 1957.
The Honorable the SPEAKER,
House of Representatives.

SIR: I have the honor to lay before the House of Representatives the contest for a seat in the House of Representatives from the Fourth Congressional District of the State of Iowa, Steven V. Carter against Karl M. LeCompte, notice of which has been filed in the office of the Clerk of the House; and also transmit herewith original testimony, papers, and documents relating thereto.

LEAVE OF ABSENCE

By unanimous consent, leave of absence was granted to:

Mr. YATES (at the request of Mr. FOLEY), on account of illness in the family.

Mr. BROYHILL (at the request of Mr. MICHEL), for today, on account of a death in the family.

Mr. D'AMOURS (at the request of Mr. WRIGHT), for today, on account of a death in the family.

SPECIAL ORDERS GRANTED

By unanimous consent, permission to address the House, following the legislative program and any special orders heretofore entered, was granted to:

(The following Members (at the request of Mr. GINGRICH) to revise and extend their remarks and include extraneous material:)

Mr. BETHUNE, for 60 minutes, today.

Mr. MARTIN of North Carolina, for 30 minutes, today.

EXTENSION OF REMARKS

By unanimous consent, permission to revise and extend remarks was granted to:

Mr. ECKART, to revise and extend his remarks on H.R. 6324 at the conclusion of general debate.

(The following Members (at the request of Mr. GINGRICH) and to include extraneous matter:)

Mr. MICHEL.

Mr. MADIGAN in two instances.

ADJOURNMENT

Mr. ANDREWS. Mr. Speaker, I move that the House do now adjourn.

The motion was agreed to; accordingly (at 6 o'clock and 9 minutes p.m.), the House adjourned until tomorrow, Wednesday, August 18, 1982, at 10 a.m.

RECESS

The SPEAKER pro tempore. Pursuant to the order of the House of December 17, 1982, the Chair declares a recess subject to the call of the Chair. Bells will be rung 15 minutes prior to the reconvening of the House.

Accordingly (at 5 o'clock and 56 minutes p.m.), the House stood in recess subject to the call of the Chair.

☐ 2130
AFTER RECESS

The recess having expired, the House was called to order by the Speaker pro tempore [Mr. NATCHER] at 9 o'clock and 35 minutes p.m.

[Follow copy as to expressing time of adjournment as 6 o'clock and 25 minutes p.m., or *6:25 p.m.* If necessary, the headings Recess and Adjournment must be supplied in House and Senate copy.]

MOTION TO DISCHARGE COMMITTEE
MARCH 17, 1952.

To the CLERK OF THE HOUSE OF REPRESENTATIVES:

Pursuant to clause 4 of rule XXVII, I, PERCY J. PRIEST, move to discharge the Committee on Banking and Currency from the consideration of the bill (H.R. 2887) entitled "A bill transferring certain functions of the Price Administrator, with respect to petroleum and petroleum products, to the Petroleum Administrator for War," which was referred to said committee March 7, 1952, in support of which motion the undersigned Members of the House of Representatives affix their signatures, to wit:

1. Percy J. Priest.
2. Oren Harris.
217. William E. Hess.
218. James G. Polk.

This motion was entered upon the Journal, entered in the CONGRESSIONAL RECORD with signatures thereto, and referred to the Calendar of Motions To Discharge Committees, February 21, 1952.

House briefs

[The briefs follow at end of day's proceedings. Heads and dashes to be used as shown here.]

EXECUTIVE COMMUNICATIONS, ETC.

Under clause 2 of rule XXIV, executive communications were taken from the Speaker's table and referred as follows:

4593. A communication from the President of the United States, transmitting proposed requests for transfer authority and appropriation language for fiscal year 1982, amended appropriation requests, and amended appropriation language for fiscal year 1983 (H. Doc. No. 97-228); to the Committee on Appropriations and ordered to be printed.

4594. A letter from the Assistant Secretary of Defense (Comptroller), transmitting notice of the proposed obligation of $4.8 million in the Navy stock fund for war reserve stocks, pursuant to section 734, Public Law 97-114; to the Committee on Appropriations.

4595. A letter from the Director for Facility Requirements and Resources, Department of Defense, transmitting notice of the location, nature, and estimated cost of various construction projects proposed to be undertaken by the Naval and Marine Corps Reserve, pursuant to 10 U.S.C. 2233a(1); to the Committee on Armed Services.

4596. A letter from the Assistant Secretary of the Navy (Shipbuilding and Logistics), transmitting notice of the proposed conversion to contractor performance of the administrative telephone services function at the Naval Coastal Systems Center, Panama City, pursuant to section 502(b) of Public Law 96-342; to the Committee on Armed Services.

[Use the following form if only one communication is submitted—8 point:]

194. Under clause 2 of rule XXIV, a letter from the Secretary of the Treasury, transmitting a statement of the estimated cost of revised central heating, lighting, and powerplant project, Washington, D.C. (H. Doc. No. 97-102), was taken from the Speaker's table, referred to the Committee on Public Works, and ordered to be printed.

[Note the insertion of (*H. Doc. No. —*) in cases where papers are ordered to be printed as a document. To be inserted only when *ordered to be printed* or its equivalent appears in copy.]

REPORTS OF COMMITTEES ON PUBLIC BILLS AND RESOLUTIONS

Under clause 2 of rule XIII, reports of committees were delivered to the Clerk for printing and reference to the proper calendar, as follows:

Mr. DINGELL: Committee on Energy and Commerce. H.R. 5008. A bill to amend the Communications Act of 1934 to make certain technical revisions regarding the administration of such act, and for other purposes; with an amendment (Rept. No. 97-751). Referred to the Committee of the Whole House on the State of the Union.

REPORTS OF COMMITTEES ON PRIVATE BILLS AND RESOLUTIONS

Under clause 2 of rule XIII, reports of committees were delivered to the Clerk for printing and reference to the proper calendar, as follows:

Mr. GLICKMAN: Committee on the Judiciary. H.R. 3171. A bill for the relief of Dr. David Pass (Rept. No. 97–440). Referred to Committee of the Whole House.

Mr. KINDNESS: Committee on the Judiciary. H.R. 3835. A bill for the relief of Rutherford K. Clarke and his wife, Ida T. Clarke (Rept. No. 97–441). Referred to Committee of the Whole House.

Mr. MOORHEAD: Committee on the Judiciary. H.R. 4350. A bill for the relief of Arthur J. Grauf (Rept. No. 97–442). Referred to the Committee of the Whole House.

[Use above form also when only one report is submitted.]

ADVERSE REPORTS

Under clause 2 of rule XIII,

Mr. WALTER: Committee on the Judiciary. H.R. 3347. A bill for the relief of Edward Dietrich, a veteran of the World War (Rept. No. 89–1054). Laid on the table.

Mr. STANLEY: Committee on House Administration. House Resolution 188. Resolution to provide for printing of 1,000 additional copies of the hearings held before the Committee on Banking and Currency of the House on the bill H.R. 10517, entitled "For increasing and stabilizing the price level of commodities, and for other purposes" (Rept. No. 92–1035). Ordered to be printed.

[Use above form also when only one report is submitted.]

PUBLIC BILLS AND RESOLUTIONS

Under clause 5 of rule X and clause 4 of rule XXII, public bills and resolutions were introduced and severally referred as follows:

By Mr. GAYDOS (for himself, Mr. REGULA, Mr. BENJAMIN, Mr. MURTHA, Mr. FARY, Mr. MURPHY, Mr. FORSYTHE, Mr. MOLLOHAN, Mr. WALKER, Mr. RAHALL, and Mr. PORTER):

H.R. 5727. A bill to amend the Trade Act of 1974 to restore the authority of the President with respect to reciprocal nondiscriminatory treatment; to the Committee on Ways and Means.

[Use the following form when only one bill or resolution is submitted:]

Under clause 1 of rule XXII,

Mr. LANTOS introduced a bill (H.R. 6766) for the relief of Shanna Teresa Milich; which was referred to the Committee on the Judiciary.

MEMORIALS

Under clause 4 of rule XXII, memorials were presented and referred as follows:

[Use the following form when submitted by the Speaker if *By the Speaker* is not in copy:]

200. By the SPEAKER: Memorial of the Senate of the Commonwealth of Massachusetts, relative to the persecution of Soviet Jews; to the Committee on Foreign Affairs.

201. Also, memorial of the Legislature of the State of Oklahoma, relative to the development of Oklahoma's water resources; to the Committee on Interior and Insular Affairs.

202. Also, memorial of the Legislature of the State of Alabama, relative to the posthumous restoration of Robert E. Lee's citizenship; to the Committee on the Judiciary.

[Use the following form when only one memorial is submitted:]

Under clause 4 of rule XXII,

203. The SPEAKER presented a memorial of the Legislature of the State of Rhode Island, ratifying the proposed amendment to the Constitution of the United States extending the right to vote to citizens 18 years of age and older; to the Committee on the Judiciary.

PRIVATE BILLS AND RESOLUTIONS

Under clause 1 of rule XXII, private bills and resolutions were introduced and severally referred as follows:

By Mr. ATKINSON:

H.R. 6583. A bill for the relief of Mohamed Tejpar and Nargis Tejpar; to the Committee on the Judiciary.

By Mr. AuCOIN:

H.R. 6584. A bill for the relief of Celia Maarit Halle; to the Committee on the Judiciary.

By Mr. MOTTL:

H.R. 6585. A bill for the relief of Roy Gonsenhauser, Rachele Gonsenhauser, and Eve Gonsenhauser; to the Committee on the Judiciary.

By Mr. SANTINI:

H.R. 6586. A bill for the relief of the estate of Nell J. Redfield; to the Committee on the Judiciary.

ADDITIONAL SPONSORS

Under clause 4 of rule XXII, sponsors were added to public bills and resolutions as follows:

H.R. 756: Mr. KEMP.

H.R. 757: Mr. KEMP.

H.R. 767: Mr. FAZIO.

H.R. 768: Mr. GOODLING.

H.R. 1368: Mr. SIMON.

H.R. 1918: Mr. LUKEN.

H.R. 2034: Mr. ROUSSELOT, Mr. EMERY, and Mrs. COLLINS of Illinois.

H.R. 3526: Mr. ZABLOCKI.

H.R. 4280: Mr. GUNDERSON, Mr. DAN DANIEL, Mr. TAUKE, Mr. RINALDO, and Mr. YOUNG of Florida.

H.R. 4912: Mr. FOGLIETTA and Mr. AKAKA.

H.R. 5038: Mr. GINGRICH.

H.R. 5242: Mr. McDONALD, Mr. CORCORAN, Mr. MITCHELL of New York, Mr. DANIEL B. CRANE, Mr. ROBERTS of South Dakota, Mr. ALEXANDER, Mr. KEMP, Mr. CHAPPIE, Mr. APPLEGATE, Mr. KRAMER, Mr. OXLEY, and Mr. MYERS.

PETITIONS, ETC.

Under clause 1 of rule XXII, petitions and papers were laid on the Clerk's desk and referred as follows:

468. By the SPEAKER: Petition of Board of County Commissioners, Citrus County, Inverness, FL, relative to defense contracts; to the Committee on Armed Services.

469. Also, petition of the Transport Workers Union of America, Railroad Division, relative to railroad retirement funds; to the Committee on Energy and Commerce.

470. Also, petition of the Monroe County Legislature, Rochester, NY, relative to nuclear weapons; to the Committee on Foreign Affairs.

AMENDMENTS

Under clause 6 of rule XXIII, proposed amendments were submitted as follows:

H.R. 6030

By Mr. WEISS:

—Page 2, line 12, strike out "$2,948,500,000" and insert in lieu thereof "$1,682,040,000".

—Page 8, after line 12, insert the following new section:

PROHIBITION OF PROCUREMENT OF NUCLEAR WARHEADS

SEC. 109. None of the funds authorized by this title shall be available for procurement of nuclear warheads.

Resolution headings

There being no objection, the resolution was referred to the Committee on Public Works, and ordered to be printed in the RECORD, as follows:

RESOLUTION 78-58-59

Resolution memorializing the Senate of the United States expressing opposition to H.R. 2, Chicago water diversion bill

Whereas H.R. 2 concerning the diversion of water from Lake Michigan to the Chicago Canal has recently passed the House of Representatives: Now, therefore, be it

Resolved by the mayor and Common Council of the City of Sheboygan, That by this resolution it go on record as opposing said diversion of water from Lake Michigan as contemplated in H.R. 2, and request that the Senators of the State of Wisconsin, to wit: the Honorable William Proxmire and the Honorable Alexander Wiley vote in opposition to said measure and do all that is possible to secure the defeat of said legislation.

There being no objection, the resolution was ordered to be printed in the RECORD, as follows:

RESOLUTION OF NEW YORK CHAPTER, ASSOCIATION OF THE U.S. ARMY

Whereas it has been proposed that the size of the U.S. Army be reduced below its present figure, which figure is deemed to be too low, etc.

RESOLUTION OF FRANK A. JOHNSON POST NO. 758, AMERICAN LEGION, JOHNSON CITY, NY

Whereas the railroads have played an important role in the development of this community and the Nation, both in peacetime and in times of national emergency, etc.

CONGRESSIONAL RECORD INDEX

GENERAL INSTRUCTIONS

Set in 7 point on 8 point, Record measure (168 points, 14 picas).
In bound Record index, use red page numbers as shown on copy.
Cap lines and italic lines are set flush left.
Entries are indented 1 em, with overs 2 ems.
Bill introductions are to be identified as to sponsor or cosponsor.
Bullet following page number in biweekly index identifies unspoken material.
Bullet is not used in bound Record index.
Pages are identified as S (Senate), H (House), and E (Extensions).
Pages in bound Record index are entered numerically, without S, H, or E prefixes.
Entries must follow correct Record data base locators.
Correct hierarchy must be followed using level 1, 2, 3, and 4 tags in succession.

ABBREVIATIONS AND ACRONYMS

(for use on notation of content line)

ABBREVIATIONS:

Streets: St.; Ave.; Ct.; Dr.; Blvd.; Rd.; Sq.; Ter.

Names: Jr.; Sr.; II (etc.)

Businesses: Co.; Corp. (this includes all Federal corporations); Inc.; Ltd.; Bros.

Dept. of Agriculture	Sec. of Agriculture.
Dept. of Commerce	Sec. of Commerce.
Dept. of Defense	Sec. of Defense.
Dept. of Energy	Sec. of Energy.
Dept. of Health and Human Services	Sec. of Health and . . .
Dept. of Housing and Urban Development	Sec. of Housing and . . .
Dept. of the Interior	Sec. of the Interior.
Dept. of Justice	Attorney General.
Dept. of Labor	Sec. of Labor.
Dept. of State	Sec. of State.
Dept. of the Treasury	Sec. of the Treasury.
Dept. of Transportation	Sec. of Transportation.

States: See page 137, GPO STYLE MANUAL, section 9.13.

ACRONYMS:

Agency for International Development	AID
Aid to families with dependent children	AFDC
American Bar Association	ABA
American Bar Association Journal	ABA Journal
American Broadcasting Co	ABC
American Civil Liberties Union	ACLU
American Federation of Labor and Congress of Industrial Organizations	AFL–CIO
American Medical Association	AMA
American Medical Association Report	AMA Report
Arms Control and Disarmament Agency	ACDA
British Broadcasting Corp	BBC
Bureau of Indian Affairs	BIA
Bureau of Land Management	BLM
Bureau of Labor Statistics	BLS
Central Intelligence Agency	CIA
Civil Aeronautics Board	CAB
Columbia Broadcasting Co	CBS
Commodity Credit Corp	CCC

CHAPTER 21

Commodity Futures Trading Commission .... CFTC
Comprehensive Employment and Training Act .... CETA
Congressional Budget Office .... CBO
Consumer Product Safety Commission .... CPSC
Daughters of the American Revolution .... DAR
Defense Civil Preparedness Agency .... DCPA
Defense Intelligence Agency .... DIA
Disabled American Veterans .... DAV
Domestic international sales corporation .... DISC
Drug Enforcement Administration .... DEA
Earth Resources Observation Systems .... EROS
Employee Retirement Income Security Act .... ERISA
Environmental Protection Agency .... EPA
Equal Employment Opportunity Commission .... EEOC
Equal rights amendment .... ERA
European Economic Community .... EEC
Export-Import Bank .... Eximbank
Federal Aviation Administration .... FAA
Federal Bureau of Investigation .... FBI
Federal Communications Commission .... FCC
Federal Crop Insurance Corp .... FCIC
Federal Deposit Insurance Corp .... FDIC
Federal Election Commission .... FEC
Federal Emergency Management Agency .... FEMA
Federal Energy Administration .... FEA
Federal Insurance Contribution Act .... FICA
Federal National Mortgage Association (Fannie Mae) .... FNMA
Federal Power Commission .... FPC
Federal Savings and Loan Insurance Corp .... FSLIC
Federal Trade Commission .... FTC
Food and Drug Administration .... FDA
General Accounting Office .... GAO
General Agreement on Tariffs and Trade .... GATT
General Services Administration .... GSA
General Motors Corp .... GMC
Government Printing Office .... GPO
Grand Old Party (Republican Party) .... GOP
Gross national product .... GNP
Immigration and Naturalization Service .... INS
Internal Revenue Service .... IRS
International Business Machines Corp .... IBM
International Communication Agency .... ICA
International Criminal Police Organization .... Interpol
International Development Bank .... IDB
International Monetary Fund .... IMF
International Trade Commission .... ITC
Interstate Commerce Commission ICC
Law Enforcement Assistance Administration .... LEAA
Legal Services Corp .... LSC
Missing in action .... MIA('s)
National Aeronautics and Space Administration .... NASA
National Association for the Advancement of Colored People .... NAACP
National Broadcasting Co .... NBC
National Bureau of Standards .... NBS
National Institutes of Health .... NIH
National Labor Relations Board .... NLRB
National Oceanic and Atmospheric Administration .... NOAA
National Railroad Passenger Corp .... Amtrak
National Security Council .... NSC
National Science Foundation .... NSF
National Transportation Safety Board .... NTSB
North Atlantic Treaty Organization .... NATO
Nuclear Regulatory Commission .... NRC
Occupational Safety and Health Administration .... OSHA
Office of Economic Opportunity .... OEO
Office of Management and Budget .... OMB
Office of Personnel Management .... OPM

Office of Technology Assessment	OTA
Organization of American States	OAS
Organization of Petroleum Exporting Countries	OPEC
Overseas Private Investment Corp	OPIC
Palestine Liberation Organization	PLO
Parent-Teachers Association	PTA
Prisoner(s) of war	POW('s)
Public Broadcasting Service	PBS
Reserve Officers' Training Corps	ROTC
Rural Electrification Administration	REA
Securities Exchange Commission	SEC
Small Business Administration	SBA
Strategic Arms Limitation Talks	SALT
Strategic Arms Reduction Talks	START
Supplemental security income	SSI
Tennessee Valley Authority	TVA
Unidentified flying object(s)	UFO('s)
United Auto Workers	UAW
United Nations Children's Fund	UNICEF
United Nations Educational Scientific and Cultural Organization	UNESCO
United States Information Agency	USIA
Veterans' Administration	VA
Veterans of Foreign Wars	VFW
Volunteers in Service to America	VISTA
Water and Power Resources Service	WPRS
Women Accepted for Volunteer Emergency Service	WAVES
Women's Army Corps	WAC
World Health Organization	WHO
Young Men's Christian Association	YMCA
Young Women's Christian Association	YWCA

SPACING

Biweekly Record index folioed in upper right and left corner; no extra spacing.
Bound Record index folioed in upper right and left corner; no extra spacing.
History of Bills folioed in upper right and left corner using H.B. numbers; no extra spacing.
Bound History of Bills folioed in upper right and left corner, first folio numerically higher than the last folio of index; no extra spacing.

CAPITALIZATION

Guide for Capitalization

Capitalize principal words of titles after the following format classifications:

Abstract	Homily
Address	Hymn
Advertisement	Memorandum
Analysis	Message
Appendix	Nomination
Article or editorial	Oath of office
Biography	Ode
Book review	Pamphlet
Book, booklet	Paper
Brochure	Platform
Composition	Poem
Designated act Pres pro tem	Prayerbook
Document	Preface
Election of Member	Report
Essay	Report to constituents
Eulogy	Resume
Factsheet	Seminar
Foreword	Sermon
Former Members	Song
Granted	Statement
History	Study

Summary
Survey
Symposium
Synopsis
Testimony

Transcript
Treaty
Tributes to retiring Member
TV program

Lowercase after these format classifications:

Affidavit
Agenda
Agreement
Amendment
Announcement
Appointment
Award
Bills and resolutions
Brief
Briefing
Broadcast
Bulletin
Cable
Certificate of election
Chronology
Citation
Cloture motion
Colloquy
Commentary
Comments
Communications from
Communique
Comparison
Compendium
Confirmation
Court decision
Court order
Critique
Decision
Declaration
Dedication
Definition
Description
Designation
Dialog
Digest
Dispatch
Endorsement
Example
Executive order
Exhibit
Explanation
Financial statement
Guideline
Interview
Introduction
Invocation
Journal
Letter

List
Litany
Mailgram
Manifesto
Memorial
Motion
Newsletter
Notice
Obituary
Opinion
Order
Outline
Petition
Press conference
Press release
Proceedings
Proclamation
Program
Project
Proposal
Provision
Questionnaire
Questions and answers
Quotation
Recorded
Regulations
Remarks by, on
Remarks in House
Remarks in Senate
Resignation
Resolutions
Result
Review
Rollcall
Rollcall vote
Rules
Rulings
Schedule
Subpoena
Table
Telegram
Telephone conversation
Test
Text of
Tribute
Veto
Vignette
Voting record

PUNCTUATION

Comma precedes folio figures.

If numbers of several bills are given, use this form: S. 24, 2586; H.R. 217, 2887, etc.; that is, do not repeat S. or H.R. with each number. Separate the Senate and House bills with a semicolon: S. 24; H.R. 217.

In consecutive numbers (more than two) use an en dash to connect first with last: S46–S48, 518–520.

Quotes are used for book titles.

A 3-em dash is used as a ditto for word or words leading up to colon: example:
Taxation: farm property

——tuition
——withholding

ROMAN AND ITALIC

Use italic for Members of Congress descriptive data: ABDNOR, JAMES *(a Senator
from South Dakota)*; ACKERMAN, GARY L. *(a Representative from New York)*.

Names of vessels in italic: *Brooklyn* (U.S.S.); *Savannah* (nuclear ship); *Columbia*
(space shuttle).

FLUSH CAP LINES

All cap lines are separate entries. They are set flush with overs indented 2 ems.
Examples:

ABNOR, JAMES *(a Senator from South Dakota)*
ACKERMAN, GARY L. *(a Representative from New York)*
PRESIDENT OF THE UNITED STATES (Ronald Reagan)
VICE PRESIDENT OF THE UNITED STATES (George Bush)
COMMITTEE ON PUBLIC WORKS AND TRANSPORTATION (House)
COMMITTEE ON PUBLIC WORKS (Senate)
FARMS *see* AGRICULTURE
SENATE *see also* COMMITTEES OF THE SENATE; HOUSE OF REPRESENTATIVES; LEGISLA-
    TIVE BRANCH OF THE GOVERNMENT; MEMBERS OF CONGRESS; VOTES IN SENATE
DEPARTMENT OF THE INTERIOR *see also* SECRETARY OF THE INTERIOR
PRESIDENTIAL APPOINTMENTS
VOTES IN HOUSE
VOTES IN SENATE

Style of Biweekly Index

No. XIX

Congressional Record Index

PROCEEDINGS AND DEBATES OF THE 98ᵗʰ CONGRESS, FIRST SESSION

Vol. 129   **NOVEMBER 14 TO DECEMBER 14, 1983**   *Nos. 157 to 162*

NOTE.—For debate and action on bills and resolutions see "History of Bills and Resolutions" at end of Index, under numbers referred to in Index entry.

DATES AND PAGES INCLUDED IN INDEX XIX

November 14	S16049–S16121	H9775–H9832	E5501–E5518
November 15	S16123–S16241	H9833–H9945	E5519–E5580
November 16	S16243–S16343	H9947–H10083	E5581–E5638
November 16 (Pt. 2)	S16345–S16410	H10085–H10142	....
November 17	S16411–S16547	H10143–H10194	E5639–E5663
November 17 (Pt. 2)	S16549–S16750	H10195–H10425	E5665–E5675
November 18	S16751–S16782	H10427–H10469	E5677–E5696
November 18 (Pt. 2)	S16783–S16950	H10471–H10585	E5697–E5748
November 18 (Pt. 3)	S16951–S17121	H10587–H10661	E5749–E5799
November 18 (Pt. 4)	S17123–S17193	....	E5801–E5926
December 14	....	....	....

ABDNOR, JAMES *(a Senator from South Dakota)*
Amendments offered by, to
Social Security Act: amend (H.R. 1900), S3352, S3611, S3663, S3675
Unemployment: emergency expenditures for humanitarian assistance (H.R. 1718), S2854
Appointments
Conferee: H.R. 1718, emergency expenditures relative to unemployment, S3266
Articles and editorials
Republic Airlines Has Launched Aggressive Tactics for Stronger East-West Network, Bill Sweetman, Airline Executive (magazine), S2813•
Bills and resolutions introduced by
Rivers and harbors: improvement projects (see S. 947), S3973
Bills and resolutions introduced by, as cosponsor
Army Reserve Day: designate (see S.J. Res. 31), S2938
Conservation of soil and water: tax credit (see S. 152), S3663
Education: meetings of students in public secondary schools (see S. 815), S2914
Enterprise Zone Employment and Development Act: enact (see S. 863), S3400
Family Week: designate (see S.J. Res. 45), S3432
Labor unions: prosecution of extortion (see S. 462), S4036
Lumber industry: termination, extension, or modification of certain contracts (see S. 916), S3796
Railroads: tax-free revenue bonds for line rehabilitation (see S. 928), S3973
REA: exempt from certain fees, entities receiving financial assistance (see S. 508), S2803
School prayer: constitutional amendment (see S.J. Res. 73), S3973
Sweden: commemorate anniversary of signing of Treaty of Amity and Commerce (see S.J. Res. 64), S3283
Weather stations: closing procedures (see S. 890), S3823
Letters
Yankton Sioux Indian Reservation irrigation construction (sundry), S3247, S3248
Remarks by, on
Agriculture: decrease in food prices, S4059•
Community development: block grants, S2910
Deep Draft Navigation Act: introduction (S. 865), S3466•
Economic conditions: decrease in food prices, S4059•
Republic Airlines: economic recovery, S2813•
Rivers and harbors: improvement projects (S. 947), S3985•

Social Security Act: conference report on H.R. 1900, S4098
Subcommittee on Water Resources: notices of hearings, S2804
Unemployment: conference report on H.R. 1718, S3633•
——emergency expenditures for humanitarian assistance (H.R. 1718), S2786, S2844, S2854, S2855, S2910, S3247, S3248
Water Resources Development Act: enact (S. 947), S3985•
Tables
Percent farm value of retail food costs, 1982, S4059•
Targeted unemployment assistance under amendment to H.R. 1718, S2854, S2855
Texts of
S. 947, Water Resources Development Act, S3986•
ABELSON, PHILIP H.
Articles and editorials
International Competition in High Technology, E1345
ABERDEEN (SD) AMERICAN NEWS
Articles and editorials
WEB Could Use Financial Shot in the Arm and Should Get It, S3249
ABORTION
Articles and editorials
Abortion Paradox—A Live Baby, H1680
Live Births in Abortions Stir Wisconsin, H1680
Bills and resolutions
Constitution: amend (see H.J. Res. 223)
Remarks in House
Laws: reform, H1680
Live births: incidences, H1680
ABRANZON, ZINA AND ARKADY
Remarks in House
Soviet Union: efforts to emigrate, E1337
ABU-RAS, NEHAD M.
Bills and resolutions
Relief (see S. 931)
ACID DEPOSITION REPORTING ACT
Bills and resolutions
Enact (see S. 877)
Remarks in Senate
Introduction (S. 877), S3649
Texts of
S. 877, provisions, S3650
ACKERMAN, GARY L. *(a Representative from New York)*
Bills and resolutions introduced by, as cosponsor
Armed Forces: authorize the transport to the place of burial of members entitled to retired or retainer pay (see H.R. 1104), H1266
Civil Service retirement: take steps to ensure integrity (see H. Res. 135), H1562
Emergency shelters: homeless financial assistance (see H.R. 1950), H1811

Equal rights for men and women: amend Constitution (see H.J. Res. 1), H1688

Federal Aviation Act: transportation of controlled substances (see H.R. 1580), H1811

Handicapped: employment discrimination (see H.R. 1200), H1197

National Atomic Veterans' Day: designate (see H.J. Res. 210), H1463

National Drug Abuse Education Week: designate (see H.J. Res. 215), H1687

National Mental Health Counselors Week: designate (see H.J. Res. 102), H1156

Petroleum: amend Export Administration Act (see H.R. 1197), H1810

Petroleum companies: provide that overcharges be available for low-income energy assistance (see H.R. 1531), H1688

Revenue sharing: amend code (see H.R. 1930), H1811

Scharansky, Anatoly: Soviet Union should allow to emigrate (see H. Res. 67), H1267

History of bills and resolutions in biweekly index

In history of bills, sequence is: Senate bills, Senate joint resolutions, Senate concurrent resolutions, and Senate resolutions; then House bills, House joint resolutions, House concurrent resolutions, and House resolutions: S. 14, S.J. Res. 7, S. Con. Res. 26, S. Res. 5, H. 980, H.J. Res. 9, H. Con. Res. 16, and H. Res. 50.

SENATE BILLS

S. 1—A bill to implement the consensus recommendations of the National Commission on Social Security Reform; to the Committee on Finance.
By Mr. DOLE (for himself, Mr. Moynihan, Mr. Heinz, Mr. Baker, Mr. Stevens, Mr. Laxalt, Mr. Danforth, Mr. Kennedy, Mr. Bentsen, Mr. Murkowski, and Mr. Stafford), S89
Amendment, S1173, S2945
Cosponsors added, S1238
Reported with amendments (S. Rept. 98-23), S2676

S. 4—A bill to provide assistance and coordination in the provision of child-care services for children living in homes with working parents and for other purposes; to the Committee on Labor and Human Resources.
By Mr. CRANSTON (for himself and Mr. Riegle), S89
Cosponsors added, S1957, S2937

S. 11—A bill to amend title 38, United States Code, to establish a Veterans'

Administration Advisory Committee on Women Veterans; to improve various aspects of Veterans' Administration health-care programs; to extend the period for Vietnam-era veterans to request counseling under the Veterans' Administration readjustment counseling program; to promote the recruitment and retention of certain health-care personnel in the Veterans' Administration's Department of Medicine and Surgery; to express the sense of the Congress with respect to the role of the Administrator of Veterans' Affairs; to require the Administrator of Veterans' Affairs to conduct an epidemiological study of long-term health effects in veterans of exposure to ionizing radiation from nuclear test detonations; and for other purposes; to the Committee on Veterans' Affairs.
By Mr. CRANSTON (for himself, Mr. Randolph, Mr. Matsunaga, Mr. Mitchell, and Mr. DeConcini), S89
Cosponsors added, S2018, S4036

S. 13—A bill to amend the Internal Revenue Code of 1954 to decrease the holding period for long-term capital gains treatment from 1 year to 6 months; to the Committee on Finance.
By Mr. DOLE (for himself, Mr. Long, Mr. Danforth, Mr. Bentsen, Mr. Baker, Mr. Wallop, Mr. Symms, Mr. Jepsen, Mr. D'Amato, and Mr. Thurmond), S89
Cosponsors added, S1087, S1120, S1367, S1753, S2218, S4036

S. 16—A bill to amend the Internal Revenue Code of 1954 to provide for the establishment of, and the deduction of contributions to, education savings accounts; to the Committee on Finance.
By Mr. DOLE (for himself, Mr. Long, and Mr. Bentsen), S89
Cosponsors added, S733, S1087, S1120, S1367, S4036

S. 17—A bill to expand and improve the domestic commodity distribution program; to the Committee on Agriculture, Nutrition, and Forestry.
By Mr. DOLE (for himself, Mr. Hatfield, Mr. Jepsen, Mr. Moynihan, Mr. Dixon, Mr. Riegle, Mr. Levin, Mr. Danforth, Mr. Domenici, and Mr. Andrews), S89
Cosponsors added, S838, S1087, S1172, S1463, S1626, S1753, S1957, S2018, S2218, S3431
Reported with amendments (S. Rept. 98-21), S2430

S. 19—A bill to amend the Employee Retirement Income Security Act of 1974 and the Internal Revenue Code of 1954 to assure equality of economic

opportunities for women and men under retirement plans; to the Committee on Finance.

By Mr. DOLE (for himself, Mr. Long, Mr. Heinz, Mr. Danforth, and Mr. Wallop), S89

Cosponsors added, S838, S1087, S1367, S1558, S4036

S. 20—A bill to provide for a 2-year budget process, and for other purposes; to the Committee on the Budget and the Committee on Governmental Affairs, jointly, pursuant to the order of August 4, 1977, with instructions that if one committee reports, the other has 30 days of continuous session to report or be discharged.

By Mr. ROTH, S89

Cosponsors added, S3431

S. 24—A bill to provide emergency credit assistance to farmers, and for other purposes; to the Committee on Agriculture, Nutrition, and Forestry.

By Mr. HUDDLESTON (for himself, Mr. Boren, Mr. Zorinsky, Mr. Pryor, Mr. Heflin, Mr. Baucus, Mr. Bumpers, Mr. DeConcini, Mr. Exon, Mr. Glenn, Mr. Nunn, Mr. Riegle, Mr. Kennedy, Mr. Bentsen, Mr. Levin, and Mr. Burdick), S89

Cosponsors added, S924, S1172, S1238, S1463, S2802

Reported with amendments (S. Rept. 98-28), S3399

S. 32—A bill to amend title 17 of the United States Code with respect to rental, lease, or lending of sound recordings; to the Committee on the Judiciary.

By Mr. MATHIAS (for himself, Mr. Melcher, Mr. Cranston, and Mr. Baker), S90

Cosponsors added, S734, S1238, S1559, S3663

S. 50—A bill to provide access to trade remedies to small businesses, and for other purposes; to the Committee on Finance.

By Mr. COHEN (for himself and Mr. Mitchell), S90

Cosponsors added, S4036

S. 53—A bill to amend the Omnibus Crime Control and Safe Streets Act of 1968; to the Committee on the Judiciary.

By Mr. SPECTER (for himself, Mr. Heflin, Mr. Kennedy, Mr. Baucus, Mr. Biden, and Mr. Mathias), S90

Cosponsors added, S2802

S. 57—A bill to amend title 18 of the United States Code relating to the sexual exploitation of children; to the Committee on the Judiciary.

By Mr. SPECTER (for himself, Mr. Heflin, and Mrs. Hawkins), S90

Cosponsors added, S3528, S3663

S. 61—An original bill to designate a "Nancy Hanks Center" and the "Old Post Office Building" in Washington, D.C., and for other purposes; from the Committee on Environment and Public Works; placed on the calendar.

By Mr. STAFFORD, S91

Reported (no written report), S89

Passed Senate, S369

Passed House, H2489

Examined and signed in the Senate, S970

Presented to the President, S970

Examined and signed in the House, H325

Approved [Public Law 98-1], S3282

S. 89—A bill to amend the Saccharin Study and Labeling Act; to the Committee on Labor and Human Resources.

By Mr. HATCH, S91

Reported (S. Rept. 98-32), S3795

S. 102—A bill to require the Administrator of General Services to notify States of the availability of surplus real property and to convey at reduced cost certain surplus real property for public park or public recreational use to State and local governments; to the Committee on Governmental Affairs.

By Mr. PELL (for himself, Mr. Chafee and Mr. Moynihan), S92

SENATE JOINT RESOLUTIONS

S.J. Res. 1—Joint resolution proposing an amendment to the Constitution of the United States with respect to fixing the compensation of Members of the Congress; to the Committee on the Judiciary.

By Mr. LONG (for himself, Mr. Baker, Mr. Chiles, Mr. Cranston, Mr. Dole, and Mr. Moynihan), S95

Cosponsors added, S1753, S8467, S9345

S.J. Res. 3—Joint resolution to amend the Constitution to establish legislative authority in Congress and the States with respect to abortion; to the Committee on the Judiciary.

By Mr. HATCH (for himself, Mr. Nickles, Mr. Boschwitz, Mr. Denton, Mr. Zorinsky, Mr. Humphrey, and Mr. Eagleton), S95

Cosponsors added, S1088, S5803, S5887, S6759, S8923, S9186

Reported with amendments (S. Rept. 98-149), S7798

Debated, S9076, S9249, S9264, S9265, S9303, S9581

Failed of passage under suspension of the rules, S9310

22. SENATE AND HOUSE JOURNALS

GENERAL RULES

The Journals are set in 8 point on 9-point body (except votes, which are 6 point on 7-point body and appear in columns), Record measure, and as a rule Record style prevails.

Messages from the President are set in 8 point, and extracts in same are quoted.

Abbreviate States as provided in rule 9.13, except in amendments, which must be set bill style.

In amendments, matter stricken out must be set in roman, quoted; and matter inserted must be set in italic, bill style. Amendment of title of bill is set in roman, bill style, quoted, unless part of all amended and italicized bill. (Same applies in conference report.)

Omit comma between name of Senator or Representative and State in duplicate names, thus: Mr. Sarbanes of Maryland.

In the Journals names of Members are set in caps or in caps and small caps as in the Record.

For abbreviations of bills, resolutions, etc., see rule 9.42.

Indented matter will be the same as in the bills except the indentions will be in 1-em increments, instead of bill style which is 2-em increments.

Except for first day of session (Senate Journal), each new day will be separated by an F dash and 2 inches of space.

The bold dateline in the House Journal carries the session number enclosed in parenthesis. Each item within that day carries a bold paragraph symbol, the day of session, a point, and the item number. The paragraph symbol and the item number will print as ears on each page.

SENATE

[Observe punctuation and paragraphing]

WEDNESDAY, JUNE 23, 1982

(Legislative day of Tuesday, June 8, 1982)

The PRESIDENT pro tempore called the Senate to order at 9 o'clock and 30 minutes a.m., and the Chaplain offered a prayer.

THE JOURNAL

On motion by Mr. BAKER, and by unanimous consent,

The Journal of the proceedings of Tuesday, June 22, 1982, was approved.

ENROLLED BILL SIGNED

The Secretary reported that he had examined and found truly enrolled the bill (S. 1519) to designate certain national wildlife refuge lands.

The PRESIDENT pro tempore signed the same.

AUTHORITY FOR CERTAIN COMMITTEES TO MEET

On motion by Mr. BAKER, and by unanimous consent,

Ordered, That the following committees be authorized to meet during the sessions of the Senate indicated:

The Committee on Agriculture, Nutrition, and Forestry, at 10 o'clock a.m. today and at 2 o'clock p.m. tomorrow, relative to the food stamp program.

RECOGNITION OF MR. CHILES

Pursuant to the order of yesterday,

Mr. CHILES was recognized; and concluded his remarks.

TRANSACTION OF ROUTINE MORNING BUSINESS

Pursuant to the order of yesterday,

317

The Senate proceeded to the transaction of routine morning business.

PROPOSED RESCISSION AND PROPOSED DEFERRAL

The PRESIDENT pro tempore laid before the Senate the following message from the President of the United States; which, together with accompanying reports, pursuant to the order of January 30, 1975, was referred jointly to the Committee on Appropriations, the Committee on the Budget, and the Committee on Energy and Natural Resources:

To the Congress of the United States:

In accordance with the Impoundment Control Act of 1974, I herewith report a proposal to rescind $8 million in budget authority previously provided to the Office of the Federal Inspector of the Alaska Natural Gas Transportation System. In addition, I am reporting a new deferral of $3.6 million in funds appropriated to the Office of the Solicitor and Office of the Secretary of the Department of the Interior.

The details of the rescission proposal and deferral are contained in the attached report.

RONALD REAGAN.
THE WHITE HOUSE, *June 23, 1982.*

REPORTS OF COMMITTEES

The following reports were submitted:

By Mr. PACKWOOD, from the Committee on Commerce, Science, and Transportation, with amendments:

H.R. 3816. An act to improve the operation of the fishermen's contingency fund established to compensate commercial fishermen for damages resulting from oil and gas exploration, development, and production in areas of the Outer Continental Shelf.

By Mr. THURMOND, from the Committee on the Judiciary, with an amendment:

S. 1880. An act to amend the manufacturing clause of the copyright law.

By Mr. THURMOND, from the Committee on the Judiciary, with amendments and an amendment to the title:

S.J. Res. 183. Joint resolution to authorize and request the President to issue a proclamation designating October 19 through October 25, 1982, as "Lupus Awareness Week."

INTRODUCTION OF BILLS AND JOINT RESOLUTIONS

The following bills and joint resolutions were introduced, read the first and second times by unanimous consent, and referred, placed on the calendar, held at the desk, or acted upon, as indicated:

By Mr. HART:

S. 2663. A bill to authorize a national program of improving the quality of education; to the Committee on Labor and Human Resources.

By Mr. HATCH (for himself, Mr. THURMOND, Mr. DeCONCINI, Mr. GRASSLEY, Mr. LEAHY, and Mr. MATHIAS):

S. 2671. A bill to provide for the establishment of a Commission on the Bicentennial of the Constitution; to the Committee on the Judiciary.

The Speaker of the House of Representatives having signed two enrolled bills, viz, S. 1881 and H.R. 5622, I am directed to bring the same to the Senate for the signature of its President.

Resolved by the House of Representatives (the Senate concurring), That the final report of the Select Committee on Foreign Aid be printed as a House document, and that five thousand additional copies of volume I be printed, of which three thousand copies shall be for the use of the House of Representatives, to be distributed by the House folding room and two thousand copies shall be for the use of the Select Committee on Foreign Aid.

When said concurrent resolution was considered,

The following amendments, recommended by the Committee on House Administration, were agreed to:

[Do not close italic insert with a period unless it is part of the amendment.]

Page 1, line 2, after "That", insert *there be printed six thousand five hundred copies of*

Page 1, line 3, strike out "be printed as a House document and" and insert *(House Report Numbered 1845)*

Page 1, line 4, strike out "that five thousand additional copies of volume I be printed".

Page 1, line 6, strike out "Representatives to be distributed by the House" and insert *Representatives,*

The following amendments, recommended by the Committee on Ways and Means, were agreed to:

Page 1, line 6, strike out "July 1, 1956" and insert *April 1, 1956*

Page 2, line 2, strike out "July 1956" and insert *April 1956*

The bill, as amended, was ordered to be engrossed and read a third time, was read a third time by title, and passed.

[Note use of roman type and quotes for title amendment.]

By unanimous consent, the title was amended so as to read: "A bill to provide wage credits under title II of the Social Security Act for military service before April 1956, and to permit application for lump-sum benefits under such title to be made within two years after interment or reinterment in the case of servicemen dying overseas before April 1956".

The following amendments, recommended by the Committee on House Administration, were agreed to:

Line 1, after "That", insert *effective January 4, 1955,*

Line 2, strike out "H. Res. 88" and insert: *H. Res. 118*

The title was amended so as to read: "A resolution to provide funds for studies and investigations to be conducted pursuant to H. Res. 118".

ORDER FOR TRANSACTION OF ROUTINE MORNING BUSINESS

On motion by Mr. BAKER, and by unanimous consent,

Ordered, That today, after the recognition of Senators under special orders, there be a period for the transaction of routine morning business for not to exceed 30 minutes, during which Senators may speak for not to exceed 5 minutes each.

ORDERS FOR RECESS OR ADJOURNMENT UNTIL 9:30 A.M. TOMORROW, AND FROM TOMORROW UNTIL 11 A.M. NEXT TUESDAY

On motion by Mr. BAKER, and by unanimous consent,

Ordered, That when the Senate concludes its business today, it recess or adjourn until 9:30 o'clock a.m. tomorrow.

Ordered further, That when the Senate concludes its business tomorrow, it recess or adjourn until 11 o'clock a.m. next Tuesday (June 29, 1982).

BILL H.R. 6645 PLACED ON CALENDAR

On motion by Mr. BAKER, and by unanimous consent,

Ordered, That the pending bill (H.R. 6645) making urgent supplemental appropriations for the fiscal year ending September 30, 1982, and for other purposes, be placed on the calendar.

ENERGY POLICY AND CONSERVATION ACT EXTENSION

On the request of Mr. BAKER, The PRESIDING OFFICER (Mr. WARNER in the chair) laid before the Senate the amendment (in the nature of a substitute) received from the House of Representatives for concurrence to the text of the bill (S. 2332) to amend the Energy Policy and Conservation Act to extend certain authorities relating to the International Energy Program, to provide for the Nation's energy emergency preparedness, and for other purposes, together with the amendment to the title thereof, providing that the same read: "An Act to amend the Energy Policy and Conservation Act to extend certain authorities relating to the international energy program, and for other purposes".

On motion by Mr. BAKER,

Resolved, That the Senate disagree to the amendments of the House of Representatives to the bill, and ask a conference with the House on the disagreeing votes of the two Houses thereon.

Ordered, That the conferees on the part of the Senate be appointed by the Presiding Officer; and

The PRESIDING OFFICER appointed Mr. McCLURE, Mr. WEICKER, Mr. WARNER, Mr. JACKSON, Mr. JOHNSTON, Mr. FORD, and Mr. METZENBAUM.

MESSAGE FROM THE HOUSE

A message from the House of Representatives, by Mr. Berry, one of its clerks:

Mr. President: The Speaker of the House of Representatives having signed two enrolled bills, viz, H.R. 1482 and H.R. 3863, I am directed to bring the same to the Senate for the signature of its President.

ENROLLED BILLS SIGNED

The Secretary reported that he had examined and found truly enrolled the following bills:

H.R. 1482. An act for the relief of Christina Boltz Sidders; and

H.R. 3863. An act to amend the Poultry Inspection Act to increase the number of turkeys which may be slaughtered and processed without inspection under such act, and for other purposes.

The VICE PRESIDENT signed the same.

RECOGNITION OF CERTAIN SENATORS

Pursuant to the order of yesterday,

The following Senators were recognized; and concluded their remarks: Mr. COHEN, Mr. LEVIN, and Mr. BUMPERS.

MESSAGE FROM THE HOUSE

A message from the House of Representatives, by Mr. Gregory, one of its clerks:

Mr. President: The House of Representatives has passed the following bills and joint resolution, in which it requests the concurrence of the Senate:

H.R. 5879. An act to amend chapter 2 of title IV of the Immigration and Nationality act to extend for 1 year the authorization of appropriations for refugee assistance, and for other purposes;

H.R. 6681. An act to authorize humanitarian assistance for the people of Lebanon; and

HOUSE BILL REFERRED

The bill H.R. 5879, received from the House of Representatives for concurrence, was read the first and second times, by unanimous consent, and referred to the Committee on the Judiciary.

RECOGNITION OF MR. CHILES

Pursuant to the order of yesterday,

Mr. CHILES was recognized; and concluded his remarks.

TRANSACTION OF ROUTINE MORNING BUSINESS

Pursuant to the order of today,

The Senate proceeded to the transaction of routine morning business.

PETITIONS AND MEMORIALS

The following petitions and memorials were laid before the Senate, and were referred or ordered to lie on the table, as indicated:

POM-973. A resolution adopted by the House of Representatives of the State of Michigan urging Congress to maintain current funding for the National Center on Child Abuse and Neglect; to the Committee on Appropriations.

POM-974. A resolution adopted by the House of Representatives of the State of Oklahoma urging Congress to direct that a ship be named in honor of the State of Oklahoma; to the Committee on Armed Services.

POM-975. A joint resolution adopted by the Legislature of the State of California supporting amendment of the Mortgage Subsidy Bond Tax Act of 1980 to permit interim financing of any duration obtained by a Cal-Vet purchaser to qualify under that act for refinancing with Cal-Vet bond funds; to the Committee on Banking, Housing, and Urban Affairs.

COMMENDATION OF PHILIP A. LOOMIS, JR.

Mr. GARN (for himself, Mr. TOWER, Mr. D'AMATO, Mr. PROXMIRE, and Mr. SARBANES) submitted a resolution (S. Res. 417) commending Philip A. Loomis, Jr.

The Senate proceeded, by unanimous consent, to consider the resolution.

The question being on agreeing to the resolution.

After debate,

No amendment being proposed,

The resolution was agreed to, together with the accompanying preamble.

On motion by Mr. GARN to reconsider the vote agreeing to the resolution.

On motion by Mr. BAKER,

The motion to reconsider was laid on the table.

TEMPORARY INCREASE IN PUBLIC DEBT LIMIT

Under the authority of the order of yesterday,

On the request of Mr. BAKER,

The PRESIDING OFFICER (Mr. GORTON in the chair) laid before the Senate the joint resolution (H.J. Res. 519) to provide for a temporary increase in the public debt limit, received from the House of Representatives for concurrence, which was deemed read the first and second times.

MESSAGE FROM THE HOUSE

A message from the House of Representatives, by Mr. Berry, one of its clerks:

Mr. President: The House of Representatives has passed the bill (S. 2332) to amend the Energy Policy and Conservation Act to extend certain authorities relating to the international energy program, to provide for the Nation's energy emergency preparedness, and for other purposes, with amendments, in which it requests the concurrence of the Senate.

The House has receded from its amendment to the amendment of the Senate numbered 62 to the bill (H.R. 5922) making urgent supplemental appropriations for the fiscal year ending September 30, 1982, and for other purposes, and has agreed thereto.

The Senate resumed the consideration of the joint resolution H.J. Res. 519.

The question being on the passage of the joint resolution.

Pending debate,

On motion by Mr. CHAFEE,

The yeas and nays, being desired by one-fifth of the Senators present, were ordered on the question of the passage of the joint resolution.

After debate,

No amendment being proposed,

Ordered, That the joint resolution be read a third time.

The joint resolution was read the third time, by unanimous consent.

On the question, Shall the joint resolution pass?

It was determined in the affirmative................ | Yeas ... 49 / Nays ... 39

[No. 198 Leg.]

Senators who voted in the affirmative are—

Abdnor	Garn	Percy
Andrews	Gorton	Pressler
Baker	Hatfield	Quayle
Bentsen	Hawkins	Roth
Boschwitz	Hayakawa	Rudman
Burdick	Jackson	Schmitt
Chafee	Kassebaum	Simpson
Cochran	Kasten	Specter
Cohen	Laxalt	Stennis
D'Amato	Levin	Stevens
Danforth	Long	Thurmond
Denton	Lugar	Tower
Dole	Mathias	Wallop
Domenici	McClure	Warner
Durenberger	Murkowski	Weicker
Eagleton	Packwood	
East	Pell	

Senators who voted in the negative are—

Armstrong	Hart	Metzenbaum
Baucus	Heflin	Mitchell
Biden	Helms	Moynihan
Boren	Hollings	Nickles
Bradley	Huddleston	Nunn
Chiles	Humphrey	Proxmire
DeConcini	Inouye	Randolph
Dixon	Jepsen	Riegle
Dodd	Kennedy	Sarbanes
Exon	Leahy	Sasser
Ford	Matsunaga	Symms
Glenn	Mattingly	Tsongas
Grassley	Melcher	Zorinsky

So it was

Resolved, That the joint resolution do pass.

On motion by Mr. BAKER to reconsider the vote on the passage of the joint resolution.

On motion by Mr. CHAFEE,

The motion to reconsider was laid on the table.

REPORTS OF COMMITTEES

The following reports were submitted:

By Mr. THURMOND, from the Committee on the Judiciary, with amendments:

S. 1739. A bill to amend the Military Personnel and Civilian Employees' Claims Act of 1964 to increase from $15,000 to $25,000 the maximum amount that the United States may pay in settlement of a claim under that Act (Rept. No. 97–482).

By Mr. HELMS, from the Committee on Agriculture, Nutrition, and Forestry:

H.R. 6590. An act to provide for the operation of the tobacco price support and production adjustment program in such a manner as to result in no net cost to taxpayers, to limit increases in the support price for tobacco, and for other purposes.

INTRODUCTION OF BILLS AND JOINT RESOLUTIONS

The following bills and joint resolutions were introduced, read the first and second times by unanimous consent, and referred, placed on the calendar, held at the desk, or acted upon, as indicated:

By Mr. LEVIN (for himself, Mr. COHEN, and Mr. KASTEN):

S. 2674. A bill to amend title II of the Social Security Act to require a finding of medical improvement when disability benefits are terminated, to provide for a review and right to personal appearance prior to termination of disability benefits, to provide for uniform standards in determining disability, to provide continued payment of disability benefits during the appeals process, and for other purposes; to the Committee on the Judiciary.

SUBMISSION OF CONCURRENT RESOLUTIONS AND (SIMPLE) RESOLUTIONS

The following concurrent resolutions and (simple) resolutions were submitted, and referred, placed on the calendar, held at the desk, or acted upon, as indicated:

By Mr. ARMSTRONG (for himself, Mrs. HAWKINS, Mr. THURMOND, Mr. MATTINGLY, Mr. HELMS, Mr. SYMMS, and Mr. KASTEN):

S. Con. Res. 109. Concurrent resolution expressing the sense of the Congress that legislation should be passed in order to make the Government Printing Office more cost-effective and efficient; to the Committee on Governmental Affairs.

By Mr. TSONGAS (for himself, Mrs. KASSEBAUM, Mr. KENNEDY, Mr. MOYNIHAN, Mr. D'AMATO, Mr. LEVIN, Mr. DODD, Mr. SARBANES, Mr. INOUYE, and Mr. CRANSTON):

S. Con. Res. 110. Concurrent resolution expressing the sense of the Congress respecting the Secretary of State's recommending continuing extended voluntary departure status for Ethiopian nationals in the United States; to the Committee on the Judiciary.

ORDERS FOR RECESS UNTIL 11 A.M. TOMORROW, AND FOR PROGRAM

On motion by Mr. BAKER, and by unanimous consent,

Ordered, That when the Senate concludes its business today, it recess until 11 o'clock a.m. tomorrow.

Ordered further, That on tomorrow, after the recognition of the majority and minority leaders, the following Senators be recognized for not to exceed 15 minutes each: Mr. COHEN, Mr. LEVIN, Mr. BUMPERS, and Mr. CHILES.

AUTHORITY FOR CERTAIN MOTIONS DURING RECESS

On motion by Mr. BAKER, and by unanimous consent,

Ordered, That during the recess of the Senate following the conclusion of business today until 11 o'clock a.m. tomorrow, the Secretary of the Senate be authorized to receive messages from the House of Representatives, and that the Vice President and the President pro tempore be authorized to sign duly enrolled bills and joint resolutions.

[Note the use of the F dash and 2 inches of space ending each day's proceedings. This space is used for any additions that may be made to the proceedings.]

RECESS

On motion by Mr. BAKER,
At 7 o'clock and 59 minutes p.m.,

The Senate, under its order of today, recessed until 11 o'clock a.m. tomorrow.

THURSDAY, JUNE 24, 1982

(Legislative day of Tuesday, June 8, 1982)

The PRESIDENT pro tempore called the Senate to order at 11 o'clock a.m., and the Chaplain offered a prayer.

THE JOURNAL

On motion by Mr. GARN, and by unanimous consent,

The Journal of the proceedings of Wednesday, June 23, 1982, was approved.

MESSAGE FROM THE HOUSE RECEIVED DURING RECESS

Under the authority of the order of Wednesday, June 23, 1982,

HOUSE

[Observe the punctuation and paragraphing and that datelines are set in Century bold caps centered. Follow Record style in the treatment of names of Members of Congress.]

MONDAY, JUNE 21, 1982 (72)

¶72.1 The House was called to order by the Speaker pro tempore, Mr. WRIGHT, who laid before the House the following communication:

WASHINGTON, DC, *June 17, 1982.*

I hereby designate the Honorable JIM WRIGHT to act as Speaker pro tempore on Monday, June 21, 1982.

THOMAS P. O'NEILL, Jr., *Speaker, House of Representatives.*

¶72.2 APPROVAL OF THE JOURNAL

The SPEAKER pro tempore, Mr. WRIGHT, announced he had examined and approved the Journal of the proceedings of Thursday, June 17, 1982.

Pursuant to clause 1, rule I, the Journal was approved.

¶72.3 COMMUNICATIONS

Executive and other communications, pursuant to clause 2, rule XXIV, were referred as follows:

4189. A communication from the President of the United States, transmitting proposed supplemental appropriations for the fiscal year 1982 and an amendment to the request for appropriations for the fiscal year 1983 for the Department of the Treasury (H. Doc. No. 97-201); to the Committee on Appropriations and ordered to be printed.

4190. A letter from the Acting Director, Defense Security Assistance Agency transmitting a report on the impact on U.S. readiness of the Navy's proposed sale of certain defense equipment to the United Kingdom (Transmittal No. 82-69), pursuant to section 813 of Public Law 94-106; to the Committee on Armed Services.

[Use the following form if only one executive communication is transmitted:]

An executive communication, pursuant to clause 2, rule XXIV, was referred as follows:

¶72.4 MESSAGE FROM THE SENATE

A message from the Senate by Mr. Sparrow, one of its clerks, announced that the Senate had passed with an amendment in which the concurrence of the House is requested, a bill of the House of the following title:

H.R. 3112. An act to amend the Voting Rights Act of 1965 to extend the effect of certain provisions, and for other purposes.

¶72.5 CONSENT CALENDAR

Pursuant to clause 4, rule XIII,

The SPEAKER pro tempore, Mr. WRIGHT, directed the Consent Calendar to be called.

When,

¶72.6 BILL PASSED

By unanimous consent, the Committee of the Whole House on the State of the Union was discharged from further consideration of the bill of the Senate of the following title, when said bill was considered, read twice, ordered to be read a third time, was read a third time by title, and passed:

S. 1519. A bill to designate certain national wildlife refuge lands.

Ordered, That the Clerk notify the Senate thereof.

¶72.7 BILL PASSED OVER

By unanimous consent, the bill of the following title was passed over without prejudice and retained its place on the Consent Calendar:

H.R. 5081. A bill to declare that the United States holds certain lands in trust for the Washoe Tribe of Nevada and California and to transfer certain other lands to the administration of the United States Forest Service.

¶72.8 COMMUNICATION FROM THE CLERK—MESSAGE FROM THE PRESIDENT—ADMINISTRATION ON AGING

The SPEAKER pro tempore, Mr. WRIGHT, laid before the House a communication, which was read as follows:

WASHINGTON, DC,
June 21, 1982.

Hon. THOMAS P. O'NEILL, Jr.,
Speaker, House of Representatives, Washington, D.C.

DEAR MR. SPEAKER: Pursuant to the permission granted in the Rules of the House of Representatives, I have the honor to transmit a sealed envelope from The White House, received in the Clerk's Office at 1:25 p.m. on Friday, June 18, 1982 and said to contain a Message from the President wherein he transmits the 1981 Annual Report of the Administration on Aging of the Department of Health and Human Services.

With kind regards, I am,

Sincerely,

EDMUND L. HENSHAW, Jr.,
Clerk, House of Representatives.

Mr. HOPKINS demanded a second.

By unanimous consent, a second was considered as ordered.

After debate,

The question being put, viva voce,

Will the House suspend the rules and pass said bill, as amended?

Ordered, That the Clerk request the concurrence of the Senate in said bill.

¶72.9 MESSAGE FROM THE PRESIDENT

A message in writing from the President of the United States was communicated to the House by Mr. Saunders, one of his secretaries.

¶72.10 WAIVING CERTAIN POINTS OF ORDER AGAINST THE CONFERENCE REPORT ON H.R. 5922

Mr. LONG of Louisiana, by direction of the Committee on Rules, called up the following resolution (H. Res. 502):

Resolved, That upon the adoption of this resolution it shall be in order, section 311(a) of the Congressional Budget Act of 1974 (Public Law 93–344) to the contrary notwithstanding, to consider the conference report on the bill (H.R. 5922) making urgent supplemental appropriations for the fiscal year ending September 30, 1982, and for other purposes, to consider any amendment reported from said conference in disagreement, and to consider any motion to dispose of any of said amendments which the managers have stated their intention in the joint statement of managers to offer. It shall be in order to consider a motion to recede and to concur in Senate amendment numbered 62, reported from conference in disagreement, with an amendment printed in the Congressional Record of June 15, 1982, by Representative FAZIO, and all points of order against said amendment for failure to comply with the provisions of clause 7, rule XVI, are hereby waived.

Mr. BARNES moved to recommit the bill (H.R. 9999) to the Committee on Appropriations with instructions to report the same back forthwith, with the following amendment:

On page 24, lines 8 to 17, strike out the first proviso, and insert *Provided, That the Director of the Budget finds it necessary to meet increased costs*

On motion of Mr. MITCHELL, by unanimous consent, the previous question was ordered on the motion to recommit.

The question being put, viva voce, Will the House recommit said bill?

The motion to recommit was not agreed to.

The question being put, viva voce, Will the House pass said bill?

So the bill was passed.

A motion to reconsider the vote whereby said bill was passed was, by unanimous consent, laid on the table.

AMENDMENTS

When said resolution was considered,

The following amendments, recommended by the Committee on House Administration, were agreed to:

Line 1, strike out "affective" and insert *effective*

Line 4, strike out "$5,000" and insert *$2,500*

The resolution, as amended, was then agreed to.

A motion to reconsider the vote whereby said resolution, as amended was agreed to was, by unanimous consent, laid on the table.

The House then proceeded to the consideration of the following amendments of the Senate in disagreement (Nos. 7, 7½, 11, 13, 32, 46, 52, 54, 56, 63, 74, 76, 77, and 85):

Senate amendment No. 7: Page 10, line 10, after "responsibility", insert : *Provided further, That not to exceed $2,700,000 of the amount herein appropriated may be transferred to the Department of the Navy*

Senate amendment No. 7½: Page 10, line 10, after "responsibility", insert : *Provided further, That no* part of this appropriation or contract authorization shall be used—

(A) to start any new construction project for which an estimate was not included in the budget for the current fiscal year; or

(B) to start any new construction project the currently estimated cost of which exceeds the estimated cost included therefor in such budget;

unless the Director of the Bureau of the Budget specifically approves the start of such construction project;

The committee of conference on the disagreeing votes of the two Houses on the amendment of the House to the bill (S. 1479) to discontinue the operation of village delivery service in second-class post offices, having met, after full and free conference, have agreed to recommend and do recommend to their respective Houses as follows:

That the House recede from its disagreement to the amendments of the Senate numbered 1, 3, 5, 6, 9, 19, 23, 25, 26, 27, 29, 30, 31, 33, 35, 37, 38, 39, 40, 46, 48, 49, 50, 53, 55, 56, 59, 63, 77, 83, 84, and 85, and agree to the same.

Amendment numbered 2: That the House recede from its disagreement to the amendment of the Senate numbered 2, and agree to the same with an amendment as follows: In lieu of the matter inserted by said amendment insert the following: *including not to exceed $2,365 for necessary per diem and traveling expenses in connection therewith*; and the Senate agree to the same.

The committee of conference report in disagreement amendments numbered 8, 10, 11, 12, 13, 14, 15, 16, 18, 32, 54, 60, 62, 79, 80, and 87.

That the Senate recede from its disagreement to the amendment of the House.

AUGUSTUS F. HAWKINS
(except as to
amendment No. 3),
MICHAEL D. BARNES,
BARBARA A. MIKULSKI,
Managers on the Part of the House.
CLAIBORNE PELL,
ROBERT C. BYRD,
JOHN GLENN,
Managers on the Part of the Senate.

A quorum not being present,

The roll was called under clause 4, rule XV, and the call was taken by electronic device.

When there appeared { Yeas ... 257 / Nays ... 155

¶72.11

[Roll No. 146]

YEAS—347

Akaka	Bereuter	Campbell
Alexander	Bethune	Carman
Anderson	Bevill	Carney
Andrews	Bingham	Cheney
Annunzio	Blanchard	Clinger
Anthony	Bliley	Coats
Archer	Boner	Coleman
Ashbrook	Bonker	Collins (TX)
Aspin	Brinkley	Conable
AuCoin	Brooks	Conte
Bailey (PA)	Brown (CO)	Corcoran
Bedell	Broyhill	Coughlin
Benedict	Butler	Courter
Bennett	Byron	

When said resolution was considered.

After debate,

On motion of Mr. Long of Louisiana, the previous question was ordered on the resolution its adoption or rejection.

The question being put, viva voce,

Will the House agree to said resolution?

Mr. DANNEMEYER demanded that the vote be taken by the yeas and nays, which demand was supported by one-fifth of the Members present, so the yeas and nays were ordered.

The vote was taken by electronic device.

It was decided in the { Yeas ... 257 / affirmative .... { Nays ... 155

¶72.12

[Roll No. 147]

YEAS—337

Addabbo	Fascell	Martin (NY)
Akaka	Fazio	Martinez
Albosta	Fenwick	Mavroules
Alexander	Ferraro	Mazzoli
Anderson	Fiedler	McClory
Annunzio	Fields	McCloskey

The SPEAKER pro tempore, Mr. BROOKS, laid before the House a message from the President, which was read as follows:

To the Congress of the United States:

In accordance with the Magnuson Fishery Conservation and Management Act of 1976 (Public Law 94–265; 16 U.S.C. 1801), I transmit herewith an exchange of diplomatic notes, together with the present agreement, extending the governing international fishery agreement between the United States and Poland, signed at Washington on August 2, 1976, until July 1, 1983. The exchange of notes together with the present agreement constitute a governing international fishery agreement within the requirements of section 201(c) of the act.

I urge that the Congress give favorable consideration to this extension at an early date. Several U.S. fishing interests have urged prompt consideration of this agreement, and I therefore recommend that the Congress consider issuance of a joint resolution to bring this agreement into force before the agreement expires on July 1, 1982.

RONALD REAGAN.

THE WHITE HOUSE, *June 21, 1982.*

By unanimous consent, the message, together with the accompanying papers, was referred to the Committee on Merchant Marine and Fisheries and ordered to be printed (H. Doc. 97–200).

¶72.13 REFUGEE ASSISTANCE

On motion of Mr. MAZZOLI, pursuant to House Resolution 499, the House resolved itself into the Committee of the Whole House on the State of the Union for the consideration of the bill (H.R. 5879) to amend the Immigration and Nationality Act to extend for 3 years the authorization for appropriations for refugee assistance, to make certain improvements in the operation of the program, and for other purposes; and after some time spent therein,

The SPEAKER pro tempore, Mr. SAM B. HALL, Jr., assumed the chair.

When Mr. BRINKLEY, Chairman, reported that the Committee, having had under consideration said bill, had come to no resolution thereon.

And then,

¶72.14 ADJOURNMENT

On motion of Mr. MAZZOLI, at 2 o'clock and 10 minutes p.m., the House adjourned.

¶72.15 REPORTS OF COMMITTEE ON PUBLIC BILLS AND RESOLUTIONS

Under clause 2 of rule XIII, reports of committees were delivered to the Clerk for printing and reference to the proper calendar, as follows:

[Pursuant to the order of the House of June 17, 1982, the following report was filed on June 18, 1982]

Mr. DE LA GARZA: Committee on Agriculture. H.R. 6590. A bill to provide for the operation of the tobacco price support and production adjustment program in such a manner as to result in no net cost to taxpayers, to limit increases in the support price for tobacco, and for other purposes; with an amendment (Rept. No. 97–613). Referred to the Committee of the Whole House on the State of the Union.

Mr. DINGELL: Committee on Energy and Commerce. H.R. 5447. A bill to extend the Commodity Exchange Act, and for other purposes; with amendments (Rept. No. 97–565, Pt. II). Referred to the Committee of the Whole House on the State of the Union.

¶72.16 PUBLIC BILLS AND RESOLUTIONS

Under clause 5 of rule X and clause 4 of rule XXII, public bills and resolutions were introduced and severally referred as follows:

By Mr. EVANS of Iowa:
H.R. 6642. A bill to provide that lands set aside or diverted must lie within contiguous counties; to the Committee on Agriculture.

By Mr. FISH:
H.R. 6643. A bill entitled the "Mass Transportation Act of 1982"; to the Committee on Public Works and Transportation.

H.J. Res. 515. Joint resolution designating July 1, 1982, as "Camp Smith Centennial Day"; to the Committee on Post Office and Civil Service.

¶72.17 MEMORIALS

Under clause 4 of rule XXII,

413. The SPEAKER presented a memorial of the Senate of the State of Alaska, relative to Alaska canned salmon; to the Committee on Foreign Affairs.

By Mr. TRIBLE:
H.R. 6615. A bill to amend the Impoundment Control Act of 1974 respecting the rescission of budget authority; to the Committee on Rules.

By Mr. SABO (for himself, Mr. GINGRICH, Mr. LEHMAN, Mr. DOUGHERTY, Mr. GRAY, Mr. FAZIO, Mr. RATCHFORD, Mr. GEJDENSON, Mrs. KENNELLY, Mr. OBERSTAR, Mr. MILLER of California, Mr. HOYER, and Ms. FERRARO):

H.R. 6616. A bill to amend the Internal Revenue Code of 1954 to provide an exclusion from gross income for that portion of a governmental pension received by an individual which does not exceed the maximum amount payable as benefits under title II of the Social Security Act minus the amount of any such benefits, actually received by such individual, and for other purposes; to the Committee on Ways and Means.

¶72.18 MEMORIALS

Under clause 4 of rule XXII, memorials were presented and referred as follows:

410. By the SPEAKER: Memorial of the Legislature of the State of California, relative to the KTW bullet; to the Committee on the Judiciary.

411. Also, memorial of the Legislature of the State of Delaware, relative to jurisdictions of Federal courts; to the Committee on the Judiciary.

412. Also, memorial of the Legislature of the State of California, relative to veterans' farm and home loan bonds; to the Committee on Ways and Means.

¶72.19 REPORTED BILLS SEQUENTIALLY REFERRED

Under clause 5 of rule X, bills and reports were delivered to the Clerk for printing, and bills referred as follows:

Mr. JONES of North Carolina: Committee on Merchant Marine

and Fisheries. H.R. 4374. A bill to improve the international ocean commerce transportation system of the United States; with an amendment. Referred to the Committee on the Judiciary for a period ending not later than July 30, 1982, for consideration of such provisions of the bill and amendment as fall within that committee's jurisdiction under clause 1(m), rule X (Rept. No. 97–611, Pt 1). Ordered to be printed.

¶72.20 PUBLIC BILLS AND RESOLUTIONS

Under clause 5 of rule X and clause 4 of rule XXII, public bills and resolutions were introduced and severally referred as follows:

By Mr. ZABLOCKI (by request):

H.R. 6603. A bill to authorize the President to furnish emergency assistance to alleviate the human suffering arising from the strife in Lebanon; to the Committee on Foreign Affairs.

By Mr. BEDELL (for himself and Mr. REUSS):

H.R. 6604. A bill to discourage tax-motivated corporate acquisitions by eliminating certain tax benefits which may be derived through such acquisitions; to the Committee on Ways and Means.

By Mr. DICKINSON (for himself, Mr. BRINKLEY, Mr. EDWARDS of Alabama, Mr. FLIPPO, Mr. GINGRICH, Mr. GINN, Mr. HATCHER, Mr. NICHOLS, Mr. SHELBY, and Mr. SMITH of Alabama):

H.R. 6609. A bill to authorize and direct the Secretary of the Army, acting through the Chief of Engineers, to remove obstructions to navigation from the Apalachicola-Chattahoochee-Flint waterway system, Alabama, Florida, and Georgia, and to maintain the authorized navigable depths of the system, and for other purposes; to the Committee on Public Works and Transportation.

¶72.21 ADDITIONAL SPONSORS

Under clause 4 of rule XXII, sponsors were added to public bills and resolutions as follows:

H.R. 4433: Mr. NELLIGAN.

H.R. 4890: Mr. SHELBY.

H.R. 5525: Mr. BLILEY, Mr. WEBER of Ohio, and Mr. KOGOVSEK.

H.R. 5583: Mr. LOWRY of Washington.

H.R. 5608: Mr. WOLPE and Mrs. KENNELLY.

H.R. 5653: Mr. SKEEN, Mr. ANDERSON, Mr. SEIBERLING, Mr. HANCE, Mrs. SCHNEIDER, and Mr. McKINNEY.

H.R. 5969: Mr. GRAY, Mr. HUCKABY, Mr. STOKES, and Mrs. COLLINS of Illinois.

¶72.22 PETITIONS, ETC.

Under clause 1 of rule XXII, petitions and papers were laid on the Clerk's desk and referred as follows:

488. The SPEAKER presented a petition of the board of directors of the Steel Valley School District, Munhall, PA., relative to steel import limitations; to the Committee on Ways and Means.

23. NOMINATIONS, REPORTS, HEARINGS

NOMINATIONS

GENERAL RULES

Nominations are picked up from the Record and converted by format change to conform to the style of the nominations.

Both regular and advance nominations are set 28½ picas wide and are made up to a maximum depth of 64 picas.

All nominations take a nomination number which is set in 10-point Century with a right-hand (closing) bracket only and placed flush left in the upper left-hand corner.

Regular nominations take current date, but the legislative day is added only when necessary. Advance nominations do not carry a date. (Sample of each form is shown on following pages.)

In withdrawals, follow the date on copy and also the wording of the dateline.

Spell everything except year, day of month, section, page, paragraph numbers, and any serial number where the word *numbered* is used or implied.

Omit the words *I nominate* in all nominations, no matter how or where written in copy.

Those that are to be grouped (a number of names printed as one nomination) are nominations to or promotions in the Coast Guard, Coast and Geodetic Survey, Public Health Service, military service, naval service, and consular service (except where consul, minister, or ambassador is named to a specific country).

If nomination contains an explanatory note, enclose note in parentheses and place just before the blank dateline at bottom.

Single or multiple nominations for Air Force, Army, Navy, and Marine Corps promotions to rank of general (admiral, Navy) and civilian are set in 10-point Century full-measure (28½-pica) paragraph style.

All nominations for military appointments from the rank of second lieutenant (ensign, Navy) up to and including that of lieutenant colonel (commander, Navy) are set in 7-point Ionic on 8-point body.

If name is followed by *Jr., Sr.,* or *III,* set as follows: John D. Smith, Jr., John D. Smith III. If last name is printed first, set: Smith, John D., Jr., or Smith, John D., III.

Names without serial numbers are set 7 picas wide, flush left, and arranged in four columns.

Names without serial numbers, with three names spelled out, and names with serial numbers are set 14 picas wide, flush left and doubled up. No periods after name.

Because of computer limitations, when a large number of names are printed in any one category, the alphabets will be separated by an F dash.

Serial numbers with eight digits do not carry en dashes (00000000). Serial numbers with nine digits do carry en dashes (000–00–0000).

Note that the word *confirmed* is set in italic in the recommendation line. (See sample, p. 386.)

Reinstatement, Reappointment, or similar statement, if a sentence at the end of a nomination, is placed in parentheses.

The President's signature indicates the end of a nomination, but is printed only in a withdrawal, a withdrawal and nomination combined, or a message. The President's signature does not print in a nomination or nominations.

Capitalize the word *Arm* when synonymous with *Corps,* as Cavalry Arm, Infantry Arm, etc.

A nomination confirmed without reference to a committee is printed as a message only.

Messages

Style of messages are the same as a regular nomination except for the change of heading and signature at the end of the message. (See samples in the following pages.)

Data picked up from nominations and messages for insertion in the executive journal must be made solid except for spacing around heads. 10 points of space above and 8 points of space below 10-point heads and 8 points above and 6 points below 8-point heads.

Note the use of the words *I nominate* in paragraphs in the messages.

All regular nominations carry the words *I nominate* paragraph style. All advance nominations carry the words *I nominate* in the same manner except those from the Navy in which they are flushed right.

No less than 22 picas (one-third of a page) must be allowed for the President's signature at the end of all advance nominations and messages.

Samples of use of *I nominate:*
For list of names,

I nominate—
The following, etc.

For single nominations,

The following, etc.

For advance Navy only,

I nominate

NOTE.—See sample for Nominations not confirmed printed at the end of the year, in the following pages. Prints as a message with a special heading and is inserted in the executive journal after it is printed.

SAMPLE 1

[Regular nomination]

PN379]

NOMINATION REFERENCE AND REPORT

IN EXECUTIVE SESSION,
SENATE OF THE UNITED STATES,
January 3, 1982.

Ordered, That the following nomination be referred to the Committee on Foreign Relations:

Louis H. Burns, Junior, of Louisiana, to be Foreign Service officer, class 5, vice Henry Mooney, resigned.

, 1982

Reported by Mr.   with the

recommendation that the nomination be *confirmed.*

SAMPLE 2

[Regular nomination]

PN972]

NOMINATION REFERENCE AND REPORT

As in Executive Session,
Senate of the United States,
January 28, 1982.

Ordered, That the following nominations be referred to the Committee on Armed Services:

The following-named temporary captains of the Reserve of the U.S. Navy for permanent promotion to the grade of captain in the line and staff corps, as indicated, pursuant to the provisions of title 10, United States Code, section 5912:

LINE

Chop, Raymond E.   Coyle, Francis X.   Jackson, Harry B.   Veto, Timothy A.

MEDICAL CORPS

Barnwell, Grady G.,   Brownlow, Bradley   Novak, Edward A.,   Smith, Peter R.

The following-named temporary commanders of the Reserve of the U.S. Navy for permanent promotion to the grade of commander in the line and staff corps, as indicated, pursuant to the provisions of title 10, United States Code, section 5912.

LINE

Clough, Geoffrey A.	Jackson, John D.	Pate, James W., Jr.	Robinson, Welford
Dyer, Bruce P.	Jacobsen, James D.	Poust, Roy N.	Schubarth, Paul T.
Isenberg, Michael	Manning, Dennis B.	Rawls, Hugh M., Jr.	Shepard, Donald W.

To be lieutenant colonel

Abrams, Bernard L., 340-18-9755
Albea, John M., 411-36-3941
Albeida, Louis, 527-83-8330
Bartlett, William G., 220-32-3879

Buchanan, Millicent K., 267-42-0648
Lockwood, Richard A., 441-26-1962
Lopez, Francisco, 197-32-9099
Mortel, Demosthenes, A., 138-32-1753

The following persons for appointment as a Reserve of the Air Force, in the grade indicated, under the provisions of sections 593, title 10, United States Code.

LINE OF THE AIR FORCE

To be lieutenant colonel

Ulrich, Donald R., 151-28-7268
Webb, Dean R., Jr., 277-34-9247

The following persons for appointment as Reserve of the Air Force (ANGUS) in the grade indicated, under the provisions of sections 593 and 8351, title 10, United States Code, with a view to designation under the provisions of section 8067, title 10, United States Code, to perform the duties indicated.

MEDICAL CORPS

To be lieutenant colonel

Curry, Leon E., 256-50-6109
Davis, Henry F., 568-44-9181

Wilson, James A., 203-26-930
Wittke, Paul E., 366-36-3050

SAMPLE 3

[Regular nomination]

PN915]

NOMINATION REFERENCE AND REPORT

As in Executive Session,
Senate of the United States,
December 15 (legislative day, December 10), 1981. [1]

Ordered, That the following nominations be referred to the Committee on Armed Services:

The following officers for appointment in the Regular Air Force under the provisions of section 531, title 10, United States Code, with a view to designation under the provisions of section 8067, title 10, United States Code, to perform the duties indicated, and with grades and dates of rank to be determined by the Secretary of the Air Force in accordance with section 533, title 10, United States Code.

CHAPLAIN

Boyle, James F., 185-24-8176
Cuneo, James J., 524-44-4362
Curry, James A., 249-48-0525
Gwinn, Andrew O., 248-50-1990

Moore, Thermon E., 257-42-1393
Page, William G., 425-46-2832
Robinson, Robert E., 181-26-4741
Ross, Robert J., 033-20-6063

NURSE CORPS

Adamczyk, Leonore M., 154-28-2362
Bagley, Alvin E., 531-40-8496
Betz, Coralie S., 301-34-9251
Bishop, Mary E., 215-28-1900

Kew, James R., 014-30-4562
Kingham, Sandra K., 287-32-9185
Kulow, David S., 293-30-3797
Lagomarsino, Sarah L., 545-54-3995

The following cadet, U.S. Air Force Academy, for appointment in the Regular Air Force, under the provisions of section 9353(b) and 531, title 10, United States Code, with grade indicated and date of rank to be determined by the Secretary of the Air Force.

LINE OF THE AIR FORCE

To be second lieutenant

Sinclair, Lori A., 542-24-5579

The following persons for appointement as Reserve of the Air Force, in grade indicated, under the provisons of section 593, title 10, United States Code, with a view to designation under the provisions of section 8067, title 10, United States Code, to perform the duties indicated.

MEDICAL CORPS

To be colonel

Dunn, James R., Jr., 250-18-5397   Zimmerman, Raymond, 058-30-0850

---

[1] Note legislative day within the release date.

PN1359]

NOMINATION REFERENCE AND REPORT

SENATE OF THE UNITED STATES,[1]
August 31, 1982.
(Under authority of the order of the
Senate of August 20, 1982.)

Ordered, That the following nominations be referred to the Committee on Armed Services:

The following-named officers of the Marine Corps Reserve for permanent appointment to the grade of lieutenant colonel under provisions of title 10, United States Code, section 5912, subject to qualification therefor as provided by law:

Adamson, James C., 9727
Allen, George F., Jr., 8614
Allen, James W., III, 6998
Allen, Charles R., Jr., 8622

Ande, Robert V., 1618
Anderson, Peder A., 3820
Anderson, Ralph C., 7924
Anderson, Delane E., Jr., 6410

, 1982.

Reported by Mr.   with the

recommendation that the nominations be *confirmed.*

[1] Note.—No Executive Session line.

SAMPLE 4

[Advance nomination]

PN426]

NOMINATION REFERENCE AND REPORT

IN EXECUTIVE SESSION,
SENATE OF THE UNITED STATES,
[Advance nominations carry no date. Leave blank space.]

Ordered, That the following nominations be referred to the Committee on Armed Services:

The following-named (Naval Reserve Officer Training Corps) graduates for permanent appointment to the grade of second lieutenant in the Marine Corps, subject to the qualifications therefor as provided by law:

Adams, David L.
Adang, Thomas C.
Aldrige, Michael E.
Anderson, James E.

Anderson, Wilbur
Andres, Paul A.
Ellis, Dan S.
Elwood, Hugh T.

Field, Alan J.
Fleming, Ronald R.
Lilienthal, John M.
Long, Jerry E.

Lotto, James C.
Lund, Daniel E.
Roach, Jay W.
Roan, Richard W.

SAMPLE 5

WITHDRAWAL [1]

The following message from the President, withdrawing a nomination, was ordered to lie on the table:

PN436]

THE WHITE HOUSE, *January 15, 1951.*

To the Senate of the United States:

I withdraw the nomination of the following-named officer, which was submitted to the Senate on January 10, 1951:

Ordnance Department

Captain Arthur Grant Mack, Junior, Cavalry, with rank from October 19, 1950.

HARRY S. TRUMAN.

[If copy for this form shows reference to a committee, leave off the reference. If there is more than one withdrawal, make the head and following paragraph read in the plural. The head and the paragraph go at beginning of first withdrawal only.]

SAMPLE 6

MESSAGES [2]

[Observe the forms of *I nominate.* The messages are made up from the Nomination Reference and Report forms and carry no display heading. A 3-inch "sink" is put at top of first page.
[In Armed Services advance messages, use the following form when in copy: Par. 1. I nominate Joseph Banks, etc.]

421]

THE WHITE HOUSE, *October 10, 1982.*

To the Senate of the United States:

I nominate—

The following-named Air National Guard of the United States officers for promotion in the Reserve of the Air Force, under the appropriate provisions of section 593(a), title 10, United States Code, as amended.

LINE OF THE AIR FORCE

Major to lieutenant colonel

Philip J. Blank, 390–26–6048
Kenneth S. Dugan, 447–26–4874
Donald W. Easley, 209–22–8669
James W. Freston, 528–44–1379
Edgar J. Holt, 450–32–4735
Thomas R. Jennings, 504–24–5870

James R. Mercer, 254–36–4612
Earl W. Rose, Jr., 552–38–5714
James E. Sahr, 535–28–8644
Joseph J. Sannelia, 106–20–8390
Kenneth G. Stastewicz, 388–32–8772
John H. Stennis, 579–54–9566

RONALD REAGAN.

To the Committee on Armed Services.

---

[1] When used in Executive Journal, reset in small caps roman.
[2] The heading does not appear in the completed print.

REPORTS, DOCUMENTS, AND HEARINGS

[In either Senate or House reports follow bill style in extracts from bills. Report numbers run consecutively from first to second session, etc.]

STYLE AND FORMAT OF CONGRESSIONAL REPORTS

There are set forth below certain rules which the Government Printing Office has been authorized to follow in the makeup of congressional numbered reports:

1. All excerpts to be set in 10-point type, cut in 2 ems on each side, except as noted in paragraph 3 below. For ellipses in cut-in matter, lines of five stars are used. In matter set 13 picas, lines of three stars are used.

2. Contempt proceedings to be considered as excerpts.

3. The following are to be set in 10-point type, but not cut in:

(*a*) Letters which are readily identified as such by salutation and signature.

(*b*) Straight matter set in two columns.

(*c*) Appendixes and/or exhibits which have a heading readily identifying them as such; and

(*d*) Matter printed in compliance with the Ramseyer rule.[1]

4. All leaderwork and lists of more than six items to be set in 8-point type.

5. All tabular work to be set in 7-point type.

6. An amendment in the nature of a substitute to be set in 8-point type, but quotations from such amendment later in the report to be treated as excerpts, but set full measure (see rule 10).

7. Any committee print having a report head indicated on original copy to be set in report type and style.

8. Committee prints not having a report head indicated on original copy to be set in the old report style; that is, excerpts to be set in 8 point, full measure.

9. If a committee print set as indicated in paragraph 8 is later submitted as a report or included in a report, and the type is available for pickup, such type shall be picked up and used with format conversion to make it conform to the new type and style.

10. On matter that is cut in on the left only for purposes of breakdown, no space is used above and below, but on all matter that is cut in on both sides, two leads are used above and below. If a bill is submitted as an excerpt, it will not be squeezed because of the indentions and the limit on the number of locators.

11. On reports of immigration cases, set memorandums full measure unless preceded or followed directly by committee language. Memorandums are indented on both sides if followed by such language. Preparers should indicate the proper indention on copy.

Order of printing (Senate reports only): (1) Report, (2) minority or additional views, (3) Cordon rule[2] (last unless an appendix is used), (4) appendix (if any).

Minority views or additional views will begin a new page with 10-point cap heading.

[Sample of excerpt]

In *Palmer* v. *Mass.*, decided in 1939, which involved the reorganization of the New Haven Railroad, the Supreme Court said:

> The judicial processes in bankruptcy proceedings under section 77 are, as it were, brigaded with the administrative processes of the Commission.

---

[1] Ramseyer rule: If report has "Changes in Existing Law" use caps and small caps for heads, except for breakdown within a cap and small cap head.

[2] Cordon rule: Means that there are no "Changes in Existing Law" or the head and explanatory paragraph appears, but no actual changes; therefore all small cap heads are used as the main heads.

[Sample of an excerpt with an added excerpt]

The Interstate Commerce Commission in its report dated February 29, 1956, which is attached hereto and made a part hereof, states that it has no objection to the enactment of S. 3025, and states, in part, as follows:

> The proposed amendment, however, should be considered together with the provisions of section 959(b), title 28, United States Code, which reads as follows:
> "A trustee, receiver, or manager appointed in any cause pending in any court of the United States," etc.

[Sample of amendment]

On page 6, line 3, strike the words "and the service", strike all of lines 4, 5, and 6, and insert in lieu thereof the following:

> and, notwithstanding any other provision of law, the service credit authorized by this clause 3 of rule XIII of the Rule of the House of Representatives, change shall not—
> (A) be included in establishing eligibility for voluntary or involuntary retirement or separation from the service, under any provision of law;

[Sample of amendment]

The amendments are indicated in the bill as reported and are as follows:

On page 2, line 15, change the period to a colon and add the following:

> *Provided,* That such approaches shall include only those necessary portions of streets, avenues, and boulevards, etc.

On page 3, line 12, after "operated", insert "free of tolls".

[Sample of amendment in the nature of a substitute]

The amendment is as follows:

Strike all after the enacting clause and insert the following:

That the second paragraph under the heading "National Park Service" in the Act of July 31, 1953 (67 Stat. 261, 271), is amended to read as follows: "The Secretary of the Interior shall hereafter report in detail all proposed awards of concessions leases and contracts involving a gross annual business of $100,000 or more, or of more than five years in duration, including renewals thereof, sixty days before such awards are made, to the President of the Senate and Speaker of the House of Representatives for transmission to the appropriate committees."

[Sample of letter inserted in report]

The Department of Defense recommends enactment of the proposed legislation and the Bureau of the Budget interposes no objection as indicated by the following attached letter, which is hereby made a part of this report:

MARCH 21, 1982.

Hon. TIP O'NEILL,
Speaker of the House of Representatives,
Washington, DC.

MY DEAR MR. SPEAKER: There is forwarded herewith a draft of
legislation to amend section 303 of the Career Compensation Act of

*   *   *   *   *   *   *   *

Sincerely yours,

ROBERT H. CONN,
Assistant Secretary of the Navy
(Financial Management).

[Sample of cut-in for purposes of breakdown; no leads above or below]

Under uniform regulations prescribed by the Secretaries concerned, a member of the uniformed services who—
    (1) is retired for physical disability or placed upon the tempo-
rary disability retired list; or
    (2) is retired with pay for any other reason, or is discharged
with severance pay, immediately following at least eight years
of continuous active duty (no single break therein of more than
ninety days);
may select his home for the purposes of the travel and transportation allowances payable under this subsection, etc.

[Sample of leaderwork]

Among the 73 vessels mentioned above, 42 are classified as major
combatant ships (aircraft carriers through escort vessels), in the
following types:

Forrestal-class aircraft carriers	4
Destroyers	10
* * * * * *	
Guided-missile submarine	1
Total	42

[Sample of sectional analysis]

SECTIONAL ANALYSIS

Section 1. Increase of 1 year in constructive service for promotion
    purposes

The principal purpose of the various subsections of section 1 is to
provide a 1-year increase for medical and dental officers in service.

*   *   *   *   *   *   *

Subsection 201(a) is in effect a restatement of the existing law

This subsection authorizes the President to make regular appointments in the grade of first lieutenant through colonel in the

*   *   *   *   *   *   *

Section 2. Recognition of constructive service for pay longevity purposes—Additional annual cost, $9,577,000

Section 2 would provide additional language to the existing provisions of the Career Compensation Act relating to creditable service.

[Sample of double-column comparison (Ramseyer rule)]

CHANGES IN EXISTING LAW

In compliance with paragraph 3 of the Rules of the House of Representatives, there is herewith printed in parallel columns the text of provisions of existing law which would be repealed or amended by the various provisions of the law.

EXISTING LAW	THE BILL
Act of October 12, 1949 (63 STAT. 863) SEC. 517. (a) Section 11 of the Act of March 4, 1925, as amended by section 1(c) of the Act of June 29, 1946 (60 Stat. 343; 34 U.S.C. 701), is hereby further	That subsection 517(a) of the Act of October 12, 1949 (63 Stat. 833), is amended to read as follows: "(a) The band of the United

---

[Sample of amendment under Ramseyer rule]

CHANGES IN EXISTING LAW

In compliance with clause 3 of rule XII of the Rules of the House of Representatives, changes in existing law made by the bill, as introduced, are shown as follows (existing law proposed to be omitted is enclosed in black brackets, new matter is printed in italic, existing law in which no change is proposed is shown in roman):

EXPORT CONTROL ACT OF 1949

*   *   *   *   *   *   *

TERMINATION DATE

SEC. 12. The authority granted herein shall terminate on June 30, [1956] *1959*, or upon any prior date which the Congress by concurrent resolution or the President may designate.

[Sample of "Report [26,26]" Skeleton]

| 98TH CONGRESS | HOUSE OF REPRESENTATIVES | REPT. 98–423 |
| 1st Session | | Part 2 |

COAL PIPELINE ACT OF 1982 [1]

AUGUST 10, 1983.—Committed to the Committee of the Whole House on the State of the Union and ordered to be printed [2]

Mr. HOWARD, from the Committee on Public Works and Transportation, submitted the following

REPORT

together with

ADDITIONAL, MINORITY, AND DISSENTING VIEWS

[To accompany H.R. 4230 which on July 22, 1983, was referred jointly to the Committee on Interior and Insular Affairs and the Committee on Public Works and Transportation]

[Including cost estimate of the Congressional Budget Office]

The Committee on Public Works and Transportation, to whom was referred the bill (H.R. 4230) to facilitate the transportation of coal by pipeline across Federal and non-Federal lands, having considered the same report favorably thereon with an amendment and recommend that the bill as amended do pass. The amendment strikes out all after the enacting clause of the bill and inserts a new text which appears in italic type in the reported bill.[3]

GENERAL STATEMENT [4]

The issue of whether or not coal slurry pipelines should be allowed to utilize the Federal power of eminent domain in order to secure rights-of-way is not a new one.

---

[1] If title makes more than three lines in 10-point caps, set in 8-point caps, should the title be amended, make the heading correspond to the amended form.
[2] Must be set as indicated in copy. If illustrations accompany copy and are not ordered to be printed, do not add *with illustrations*. Return copy to Production Manager.
[3] If the wording in this paragraph is prepared in the singular form, follow.
[4] For *Senate Committee on Finance* and *House Committee on Ways and Means*, heads are set in bold caps.

Calendar No. 757 [1]

| 98TH CONGRESS
1st Session | SENATE | REPORT
98–525 |

INTERNATIONAL EXPOSITIONS

AUGUST 13 (legislative day, JULY 12), 1983.—Ordered to be printed

Mr. PERCY, from the Committee on Foreign Relations,
submitted the following

R E P O R T [2]

[To accompany H.R. 6409]

The Committee on Foreign Relations, to which was referred the bill (H.R. 6409) to provide for the participation of the United States in the 1984 Louisiana World Exposition to be held in New Orleans, Louisiana, and for other purposes, having considered the same, reports favorably thereon with an amendment and recommends that the bill as amended do pass.

In line 7, strike out the figures "$10,000" and insert in lieu thereof the figures "$5,000".[3]

---

[1] Use this type and form only on Senate reports. There is only one calendar in the Senate.
[2] Should this line read "Adverse Report," do not letterspace the words.
[3] Follow copy literally as to use of punctuation marks inside or outside of quoted words or figures.

Calendar No. 295

98TH CONGRESS *1st Session*	SENATE	REPORT 98-315

PROVIDING [1] FOR THE ADMISSION OF ALASKA INTO THE UNION

FEBRUARY 9 (legislative day, FEBRUARY 8), 1983.—Ordered to be printed

---

Mr. O'MAHONEY from the Committee on Interior and Insular Affairs, submitted the following

or

Mr. JOHNSON of Texas (for Mr. BYRD), from the Committee on, etc.

REPORT

together with

MINORITY VIEWS

[To accompany S. 50]

The Committee on Interior and Insular Affairs, to which was referred the bill (S. 50) to provide for the admission of Alaska into the Union, having considered the same, reports favorably thereon with amendments and with the recommendation that the bill as amended do pass.

PURPOSE OF THE BILL

The purpose of S. 50 is to enable the strategically situated and richly endowed Territory of Alaska to enter the Union as a State, on a free and equal basis with the present 48 States. The bill provides the legal and political means of achieving this purpose by—

---

[1] If copy reads "To provide," change to "Providing."

98TH CONGRESS 1st Session	HOUSE OF REPRESENTATIVES	REPORT 98–224

AMENDING [1] SECTION 80 OF THE HAWAIIAN ORGANIC ACT

JANUARY 3, 1983.—Referred to the House Calendar and ordered to be printed

Mr. O'BRIEN of New York, from the Committee on Interior and Insular Affairs, submitted the following

REPORT

[To accompany H.R. 5865]

The Committee on Interior and Insular Affairs, to whom was referred the bill (H.R. 5865) to amend the Hawaiian Organic Act to permit the Territorial legislature to provide for the election of members of a certain board of trustees, having considered the same, report favorably thereon with amendments and recommend that the bill as amended do pass.

The amendments are as follows:

Strike all after the enacting clause and insert in lieu thereof the following language:

That the first sentence of section 80 of the Hawaiian Organic Act, as amended (48 U.S.C. 546), is amended further by inserting immediately following the words "boards of a public character that may be created by law" the words ", except for the board of trustees of the employees' retirement system".

SEC. 2. Section 80 of the Hawaiian Organic Act, as amended (48 U.S.C. 546), is further amended by adding the following new paragraph immediately following the first paragraph thereof:

"The manner of appointment of members of the board of trustees of the employees' retirement system shall be as provided for by section 6-61, Revised Laws of Hawaii, 1955."

Amend the title so as to read:

A bill to amend section 80 of the Hawaiian Organic Act, and for other purposes.

[Note below amendment of title only]

The amendments are as follows:

The amendment to the text strikes all after the enacting clause and inserts a complete new text which is printed in italic type in the reported bill.

The amendment to the title is as follows:

Amend the title so as to read:

---

[1] If copy reads "To amend," change to "Amending."

An Act to amend the Federal Water Pollution Control Act to establish a Federal Water Pollution Control Administration, etc.

The purpose of H.R. 5865, as amended, introduced by Delegate Burns, is to amend section 80 of the Hawaiian Organic Act (48 U.S.C. 546) with reference to election of members of the board of trustees of the Territorial employees' retirement system.

The report of the Secretary of the Interior dated June 24, 1958, including a substitute bill which has been adopted by the committee, is as follows: [1]

DEPARTMENT OF THE INTERIOR,
OFFICE OF THE SECRETARY,
Washington, DC, June 24, 1958.

Hon. CLAIR ENGLE,
Chairman, Committee on Interior and Insular Affairs,
House of Representatives, Washington, DC.

DEAR MR. ENGLE: This responds to your request for the views of this Department on H.R. 5865, a bill to amend the Hawaiian Organic Act to permit the Territorial legislature to provide for the election of members of a certain board of trustees.

*   *   *   *   *   *   *

The Bureau of the Budget has advised that while there is no objection to the submission of this report to your committee, it believes the principle expressed in this legislation is undesirable.

Sincerely yours,

ROGER ERNST,
Assistant Secretary of the Interior.

A BILL To amend section 80 of the Hawaiian Organic Act, and for other purposes

Be it enacted by the Senate and House of Representatives of the United States of America in Congress assembled, That the first sentence of section 80 of the Hawaiian Organic Act, as amended (48 U.S.C. 546), is amended further by inserting immediately following the words "boards of a public character that may be created by law" the words ", except for the board of trustees of the employees' retirement system".

SEC. 2. Section 80 of the Hawaiian Organic Act, as amended (48 U.S.C. 546), is further amended by adding the following new paragraph immediately following the first paragraph thereof:

"The manner of appointment of members of the board of trustees of the employees' retirement system shall be as provided for by section 6-61, Revised Laws of Hawaii, 1955."

The Committee on Interior and Insular Affairs recommends enactment of H.R. 5865, as amended.

---

[1] If copy contains no introductory paragraph, as here shown, insert an appropriate head such as "Departmental Report(s)."

98TH CONGRESS } HOUSE OF REPRESENTATIVES { REPORT
  1st Session }   { 98-166

LEGISLATIVE APPROPRIATION BILL, 1983

JUNE 18, 1983.—Ordered to be printed

Mr. CANNON, of Missouri, from the committee of conference,
submitted the following

CONFERENCE REPORT [1]

[To accompany H.R. 11267]

The committee of conference on the disagreeing votes of the two
Houses on the amendments of the Senate to the bill (H.R. 11267)
making appropriations for the legislative branch of the Government for the fiscal year ending June 30, 1972, and for other purposes, having met, after full and free conference, have agreed to
recommend and do recommend to their respective Houses as follows:

That the Senate recede from its amendments numbered 49, 51,
62½, 65, 67, 71, 75, 77, 78, 79, 80, 94, 96, 97, 98, 99, 100, 102, and
132.

That the House recede from its disagreement to the amendments
of the Senate numbered 48, 50, and 60, and agree to the same.

Amendment numbered 60:

That the House recede from its disagreement to the amendment
of the Senate numbered 60, and agree to the same with an amendment as follows:

In lieu of the matter proposed to be inserted by the Senate
amendment insert the following:

*Sec. 210. The provisions of all Acts heretofore enacted inconsistent
with sections 207, 208, and 209 are, to the extent of such inconsist-
ency, hereby repealed, and such sections shall take effect on July 1,
1972.* [2]

And the Senate agree to the same.

Amendment numbered 150:

That the House recede from its disagreement to the amendment
of the Senate numbered 150, and agree to the same with an amendment as follows:

---

[1] See also p. 302 for style of conference report in Congressional Record, and p. 346 for style of
conference report printed as a Senate document.
[2] "Fol. lit." on amendments.

In lieu of the matter proposed to be stricken out by the Senate amendment insert a comma and the following: *and all officers and employees of the division and commission not indispensable to the service shall be dismissed*; [3] and the Senate agree to the same.

The committee of conference have not agreed on amendment numbered 46.

> WILLIAM H. BATES,
> GEORGE H. BENDER,
> LEROY JOHNSON,
> *Managers on the Part of the House.* [4]

> HARRY F. BYRD,
> WALTER F. GEORGE,
> EDWARD J. THYE,
> *Managers on the Part of the Senate.*

STATEMENT OF THE MANAGERS ON THE PART OF THE HOUSE [5]

The managers on the part of the House at the conference on the disagreeing votes of the two Houses on the amendments of the Senate to the bill (H.R. 11267) making appropriations for the legislative branch of the Government for the fiscal year ending June 30, 1959, and for other purposes, submit the following written statement in explanation of the effect of the action agreed upon by the conferees and recommended in the accompanying conference report:

Amendment No. 46: On this amendment, embracing title I of part 2 of the bill, relating to furloughs, permanent and temporary salary reductions, etc., the committee of conference have reached no agreement.

Amendments Nos. 165, 166, and 167: These amendments make changes in section and title numbers. The House recedes.

Amendment No. 168: This amendment makes the provisions of part 2 of the legislative appropriation act applicable to the appropriations available for the fiscal year 1959, whether contained in the legislative appropriation act or in acts prior or subsequent to the date of the approval of such act. The House recedes.

> H. B. SCUDDER (except
> amendment No. 19),
> JOHN F. KENNEDY,
> HARRY R. SHEPPARD,
> *Managers on the Part of the House.*

---

[3] Note use of roman semicolon.
[4] Names of House Members print first in a conference report printed as a House report.
[5] Statement of managers begins new page; in a Conference Report it begins a new odd page.

[Conference reports in Senate are printed as Senate documents. Note the following form:]

98TH CONGRESS *1st Session*	SENATE	DOCUMENT 98–79

AGRICULTURE APPROPRIATION BILL, 1983

Mr. RUSSELL,[1] from the committee of conference,
submitted [2] the following

CONFERENCE REPORT ON THE BILL (H.R. 7912) MAKING APPROPRIATIONS
FOR THE DEPARTMENT OF AGRICULTURE FOR THE FISCAL YEAR
ENDING JUNE 30, 1982

APRIL 5 (legislative day, APRIL 4), 1983.—Ordered to be printed

The committee of conference on the disagreeing votes of the two
Houses on the amendments of the Senate to the bill (H.R. 7912)
making appropriations for the Department of Agriculture for the
fiscal year ending June 30, 1982, and for other purposes, having
met, after full and free conference, have agreed to recommend and
do recommend to their respective Houses as follows:

That the Senate recede from its amendments numbered 41 and
45.

That the House recede from its disagreement to the amendments
of the Senate numbered 2, 3, 4, and 5, and agree to the same.
Amendment numbered 1:

That the House recede from its disagreement to the amendment
of the Senate numbered 1, and agree to the same as follows:

Restore the matter stricken out by said amendment, amended to
read as follows:

Public Resolution Numbered 9, Fifty-eighth Congress, first ses-
sion, approved March 14, 1904 (44 U.S.C. 290), is hereby amended by
striking out all after the resolving clause and inserting in lieu
thereof the following:

And the Senate agree to the same.

R. B. RUSSELL, Jr.,
CARL HAYDEN,
JOHN G. TOWNSEND, Jr.,
Managers on the Part of the Senate.

J. P. BUCHANAN,
JOHN TABER,
Managers on the Part of the House.

---

[1] Names of Senate Members print first in a conference report printed as a Senate document.
[2] The above form (using *presented* instead of *submitted*) will be followed in Senate documents
other than conference reports when no title page is called for.

[House Appropriation Hearing, Cover sample]

SUPPLEMENTAL APPROPRIATIONS FOR 1983

HEARINGS

BEFORE

SUBCOMMITTEES OF THE

COMMITTEE ON APPROPRIATIONS

HOUSE OF REPRESENTATIVES

NINETY-SEVENTH CONGRESS

SECOND SESSION

PART 4

Printed for the use of the Committee on Appropriations

[House Appropriation Hearing, Title Page sample]

MILITARY CONSTRUCTION APPROPRIATIONS FOR 1983

HEARINGS

BEFORE A

SUBCOMMITTEE OF THE

COMMITTEE ON APPROPRIATIONS

HOUSE OF REPRESENTATIVES

NINETY-SEVENTH CONGRESS

SECOND SESSION

SUBCOMMITTEE ON MILITARY CONSTRUCTION APPROPRIATIONS

BO GINN, Georgia, *Chairman*

TOM BEVILL, Alabama
W. G. (BILL) HEFNER, North Carolina
JOSEPH P. ADDABBO, New York
CLARENCE D. LONG, Maryland
BILL CHAPPELL, Florida
BILL ALEXANDER, Arkansas

RALPH S. REGULA, Ohio
CLAIR W. BURGENER, California
MICKEY EDWARDS, Oklahoma
TOM LOEFFLER, Texas

TERRY R. PEEL and MARK W. MURRAY, *Staff Assistants*

PART 5

Printed for the use of the Committee on Appropriations

U.S. GOVERNMENT PRINTING OFFICE
WASHINGTON : 1982

[Back Title Page sample]

COMMITTEE ON APPROPRIATIONS

JAMIE L. WHITTEN, Mississippi, *Chairman*

EDWARD P. BOLAND, Massachusetts
WILLIAM H. NATCHER, Kentucky
NEAL SMITH, Iowa
JOSEPH P. ADDABBO, New York
CLARENCE D. LONG, Maryland
SIDNEY R. YATES, Illinois
DAVID R. OBEY, Wisconsin
EDWARD R. ROYBAL, California
LOUIS STOKES, Ohio
TOM BEVILL, Alabama
BILL CHAPPELL, Florida
BILL ALEXANDER, Arkansas
JOHN P. MURTHA, Pennsylvania
BOB TRAXLER, Michigan
JOSEPH D. EARLY, Massachusetts
CHARLES WILSON, Texas
LINDY (MRS. HALE) BOGGS, Louisiana
ADAM BENJAMIN, JR., Indiana
NORMAN D. DICKS, Washington
MATTHEW F. McHUGH, New York
BO GINN, Georgia
WILLIAM LEHMAN, Florida
JACK HIGHTOWER, Texas
MARTIN OLAV SABO, Minnesota
JULIAN C. DIXON, California
VIC FAZIO, California
W. G. (BILL) HEFNER, North Carolina
LES AuCOIN, Oregon
DANIEL K. AKAKA, Hawaii
WES WATKINS, Oklahoma
WILLIAM H. GRAY III, Pennsylvania
BERNARD J. DWYER, New Jersey

SILVIO O. CONTE, Massachusetts
JOSEPH M. McDADE, Pennsylvania
JACK EDWARDS, Alabama
JOHN T. MYERS, Indiana
J. KENNETH ROBINSON, Virginia
CLARENCE E. MILLER, Ohio
LAWRENCE COUGHLIN, Pennsylvania
C. W. BILL YOUNG, Florida
JACK F. KEMP, New York
RALPH S. REGULA, Ohio
CLAIR W. BURGENER, California
GEORGE M. O'BRIEN, Illinois
VIRGINIA SMITH, Nebraska
ELDON RUDD, Arizona
CARL D. PURSELL, Michigan
MICKEY EDWARDS, Oklahoma
BOB LIVINGSTON, Louisiana
BILL GREEN, New York
TOM LOEFFLER, Texas
JERRY LEWIS, California
CARROLL A. CAMPBELL, JR., South Carolina
JOHN EDWARD PORTER, Illinois

KEITH F. MAINLAND, *Clerk and Staff Director*

(II)

SUBCOMMITTEE ON THE DEPARTMENTS OF COMMERCE, JUSTICE, AND STATE, THE JUDICIARY, AND RELATED AGENCIES

NEAL SMITH, Iowa, *Chairman*

BILL ALEXANDER, Arkansas
JOSEPH D. EARLY, Massachusetts
JACK HIGHTOWER, Texas
BERNARD J. DWYER, New Jersey

GEORGE M. O'BRIEN, Illinois
CLARENCE E. MILLER, Ohio
CARROLL A. CAMPBELL, Jr., South Carolina

JOHN G. OSTHAUS and TERRY D. BEVELS, *Staff Assistants*

TUESDAY, FEBRUARY 23, 1983.□

BOARD FOR INTERNATIONAL BROADCASTING

WITNESSES

FRANK SHAKESPEARE, CHAIRMAN

WALTER R. ROBERTS, EXECUTIVE DIRECTOR

ARTHUR D. LEVIN, FINANCIAL MANAGER

WILLIAM A. BUELL, VICE PRESIDENT, U.S. OPERATIONS RFE/RL, INC.

MICHAEL R. MARCHETTI, TREASURER AND COMPTROLLER, RFE/RL, INC.

Mr. HIGHTOWER [presiding]. Mr. Shakespeare, we have several questions concerning increased pay costs for fiscal year 1982, which we shall submit to you and ask you to answer in writing.

Mr. SHAKESPEARE. Very well, Mr. Chairman.

[The questions referred to and the answers submitted thereto, follow:]

[Note styles for questions and answers]

Questions From Mr. Hightower

IMPACT OF FISCAL YEAR 1982 PAY RAISE COSTS

Question. What are the costs associated with the October 1, 1981 4.8 percent general pay raise and the raising of the executive pay cap on January 1, 1982 for fiscal year 1982?

Answer. The pay raise for the general scale employees increased the budgeted amount by $4,826 for fiscal year 1982.

[Note the following style for questions and answers when a person is either asking or answering:]

QUESTION. How are you financing these costs?

Mr. SHAKESPEARE. The general scale increase costing $4,826 was absorbed by a turnover in one secretarial position, a position which was budgeted at the GS–6 level but filled by a GS–4 level employee who was hired to replace the former incumbent of that position. This turnover saved the Board for International Broadcasting (BIB) approximately $5,000 and allowed the BIB to absorb the $4,826 October 1, 1981 4.8 percent pay raise.

Mr. HIGHTOWER. In what program areas are you absorbing these costs?

ANSWER. Because of the BIB's ability to absorb these fiscal year 1982 costs in a manner described in the foregoing answer, it has not been necessary to absorb them in program areas.

TUESDAY, FEBRUARY 23, 1983.☐

U.S. ARMS CONTROL AND DISARMAMENT AGENCY

WITNESSES

EUGENE V. ROSTOW, DIRECTOR

WILLIAM J. MONTGOMERY, ADMINISTRATIVE DIRECTOR

ROBERT GREY, NOMINEE FOR POSITION OF DEPUTY DIRECTOR

FISCAL YEAR 1982 INCREASED PAY COSTS

Mr. DWYER [presiding]. I have several questions concerning increased pay cost requirements for the Arms Control and Disarmament Agency for fiscal year 1982.

What is the total cost of the cost-of-living pay raise granted last fall and the increase in the pay cap for senior level Government employees that was enacted in December of 1981?

Mr. ROSTOW. Bill, could you respond?

Mr. MONTGOMERY. Yes, I have that figure with me. In round numbers, the total for 1983, fiscal year 1983, is about three-quarters of a million dollars. I can give you that figure precisely here, if you will just bear with me.

WEDNESDAY, FEBRUARY 24, 1982.☐

THE JUDICIARY

COURTS OF APPEALS, DISTRICT COURTS, AND OTHER JUDICIAL SERVICES

DEFENDER SERVICES

WITNESSES

CHARLES CLARK, CHIEF JUDGE, UNITED STATES COURT OF APPEALS FOR THE FIFTH CIRCUIT

EDWARD V. GARABEDIAN, ASSISTANT DIRECTOR

Mr. DWYER [presiding]. You have a supplemental request for fiscal year 1982 in the amount of $2,350,000 for the Defender Services account. The amount currently available for fiscal year 1982 is $27,170,000. We shall insert the justification materials in support of the supplemental request at this point into the record.

[The justifications follow:]

[Senate Appropriation Hearing]

AGRICULTURE, RURAL DEVELOPMENT AND RELATED AGENCIES APPROPRIATIONS FOR FISCAL YEAR 1982

WEDNESDAY, MARCH 18, 1981

U.S. SENATE,☐☐☐☐☐
SUBCOMMITTEE OF THE COMMITTEE ON APPROPRIATIONS,☐☐☐
Washington, DC.☐

The subcommittee met at 9:40 a.m., in room 1224, Everett McKinley Dirksen Senate Office Building, Hon. Thad Cochran (chairman) presiding.

Present: Senators Cochran and Stennis.

DEPARTMENT OF AGRICULTURE

OFFICE OF THE INSPECTOR GENERAL

STATEMENT OF ROBERT E. MAGEE, ACTING INSPECTOR GENERAL

ACCOMPANIED BY:

GERALD W. PETERSON, ACTING ASSISTANT INSPECTOR GENERAL FOR AUDITING

DELMAS R. THORNSBURY, DIRECTOR, MANAGEMENT AND BUDGET STAFF

STEPHEN B. DEWHURST, BUDGET OFFICER, USDA

GENERAL ACCOUNTING OFFICE

STATEMENT OF HENRY ESCHWEGE, DIRECTOR, COMMUNITY AND ECONOMIC DEVELOPMENT DIVISION

ACCOMPANIED BY:

BRIAN P. CROWLEY, SENIOR ASSOCIATE DIRECTOR

WILLIAM E. GAHR, ASSOCIATE DIRECTOR

OLIVER W. KRUEGER, SENIOR GROUP DIRECTOR

STANLEY S. SARGOL, GROUP DIRECTOR

JOHN E. WATSON, GROUP DIRECTOR, INTERNATIONAL DIVISION

INTRODUCTION OF WITNESSES

Senator COCHRAN. The hearing will come to order.

This morning we are happy to have representatives of the Office of Inspector General and the General Accounting Office with us, and I would like to ask that all of you who are here to testify come forward. Let's all of you act as one panel, and the questions that we have will be directed to both.

SUCCESS OF AMERICAN AGRICULTURE

With a great deal of hard work, ingenuity and technology, the United States has become the most productive agricultural nation in the world. Modern agriculture, as practiced in the United States, has become a technological marvel, soundly based on advanced science and finely tuned to economic conditions. This complex enter-

prise is served by an equally sophisticated and far-reaching Department of Agriculture.

With over 120,000 employees and a program totaling over $47 billion annually, the Department serves not only farmers, but also provides assistance to the hungry in our cities and rural areas and to those in countries around the world. This Department not only assists in the development of new technologies in agricultural production, it also provides the necessary educational links to get this knowledge out to those who must apply it. From the protection of our soil and water resources to marketing the fruits of those resources, the Department serves all Americans.

INTRODUCTION OF WITNESSES

It is a great pleasure for me, this morning, to welcome to our committee, Secretary of Agriculture John Block, who is accompanied by Dick Lyng, his deputy secretary, and Mr. Dewhurst, the budget officer for the Department of Agriculture.

Gentlemen, welcome to the subcommittee. We appreciate your being here.

Before asking you for your statement, I would like now to invite Senator Eagleton to make any comments or statement that he might have.

STATEMENT OF SENATOR EAGLETON [1]

Senator EAGLETON. Thank you very much, Mr. Chairman.

I welcome this the first of our series of hearings on the fiscal year 1982 Department of Agriculture budget. I noted in a wry way as I came in the room there was a gentleman sitting in my chair. [Laughter.]

Surrounded by obsequious staff, drinking coffee. I carried in my own cup. What a difference an election makes. [Laughter.]

No; I am delighted to participate in this hearing and in the ensuing hearings. I am delighted to work with you, Mr. Chairman, and the new Secretary of Agriculture.

Of all the various subcommittees in the U.S. Senate, I think this particular subcommittee is the most bipartisan, nonpartisan subcommittee of which I know. For 4 years I worked with Senator Henry Bellmon of Oklahoma, one of the finest men I have ever known on God's Earth. We didn't always agree on every issue. We agreed, I think, 99 percent of the time.

---

[1] Name sets caps and small caps if not in the witness list, sets small caps if in the witness list.

IMPACT OF BUDGET CUTS ON FEDERAL STATISTICAL PROGRAMS

MARCH 16, 1982

HOUSE OF REPRESENTATIVES,☐☐☐☐☐☐☐
SUBCOMMITTEE ON CENSUS AND POPULATION,☐☐☐☐☐
COMMITTEE ON POST OFFICE AND CIVIL SERVICE,☐☐☐
Washington, DC.☐

☐☐HOUSE OF REPRESENTATIVES, COMMITTEE ON SCIENCE AND☐☐☐
☐☐☐TECHNOLOGY, SUBCOMMITTEE ON SCIENCE, RESEARCH☐☐☐
☐☐☐AND TECHNOLOGY, AND THE SUBCOMMITTEE ON INVESTI-☐☐☐
☐☐☐GATIONS AND OVERSIGHT [1]
Washington, DC.☐

The subcommittee met, pursuant to call, at 9:35 a.m., in room 304, Cannon House Office Building, Hon. Robert Garcia (chairman of the subcommittee) presiding.

Mr. GARCIA. Today the House Census and Population Subcommittee continues its series of hearings on the impact of the President's budget cuts on the information this Nation will have today, tomorrow, and in the future.

With that we will call up our first panel, Dr. James T. Bonnen, Department of Agricultural Economics, Michigan State University, and the director of the President's Reorganization Project for the Federal Statistical System; Dr. Stephen E. Fienberg, Department of Statistics, the Carnegie-Mellon University, and the chairman of the Committee on National Statistics in the National Academy of Sciences.

STATEMENTS OF JAMES T. BONNEN, DEPARTMENT OF AGRICULTURAL ECONOMICS, MICHIGAN STATE UNIVERSITY AND STEPHEN E. FIENBERG, DEPARTMENT OF STATISTICS, CARNEGIE-MELLON UNIVERSITY

Mr. BONNEN. Thank you, Mr. Garcia. It is a pleasure and a privilege to be here.

I have been asked to comment primarily on the central coordination of statistical planning and policy which was the focus of the study that I directed, as you mentioned.

Ours is an increasingly complex economy and society. If we do not have objective, accurate and relevant information in making decisions, our comprehension of the world will forever run behind events.

---

[1] Note style for a long committee name.

24. FOREIGN LANGUAGES

[Revision for this edition by foreign language experts at the Library of Congress, under the supervision of the Publications Office]

PURPOSE AND PLAN

The purpose of this section of the STYLE MANUAL is to provide a guide to the typography of the more important languages handled in this Office.

It has been designed to answer the needs of two categories of users:

1. Those who have very little or no knowledge at all of a language but seek to become more competent in following copy and syllabifying with at least a passing degree of accuracy; and

2. Those who have an academic knowledge of a language but lack the practical information belonging to the special field of typography, complete guidance to which is procurable only from advanced and foreign works.

To answer the needs of the former, there is presented first a sample of the language as it looks in print, followed by an adequate display of the alphabet and a helpful paragraph on special characters. This will be found fully adequate, for all practical purposes, to enable printers to follow copy competently, even though with but literal accuracy.

There is also included a brief discussion of pronunciation, so far as this can be described without special technical phonetic data, as a basis for the rules for syllabifying words in printing.

The rules for syllabifying follow, and these were formulated so that with the aid of the first four rules, which require no further knowledge of the language, a printer can syllabify with at least an 80-percent accuracy. The application of the remaining rules may require a further knowledge of the language, but these are intended essentially for the second category of users.

To answer the needs of this category fully, the rules for syllabifying are presented with utmost comprehensiveness, so that they cover all possible problems that may be encountered; and subjoined is also a selected list of illustrative word divisions, which may be used either for further study or reference. Other useful data on typography and bibliography are also included.

Dictionaries of languages other than English rarely show syllable division. This is due in part to the fact that many spelling systems are less complex than that of English, and therefore make it easier to divide words in writing according to the spoken syllable divisions. The rules stated in the following sections are intended to be summaries of the procedures actually followed by printers native to the languages.

355

DANISH

Den lille sønderjyske by, jeg kender fra barneårene, har som mange andre små og større danske byer forandret sit fysiognomi i de senere år. De små hjemmeindustrier er vokset op til store fabrikker, nye bydele har bredt sig ud over barndommens marker, og tilrejsende fremmede har fundet hjem og eksistens her.—Johan Severin Hansen, Den lille profil, p. 16, 1969.

Alphabet and pronunciation

A	a	long: *a* in man; short: *a* in hat, and before or after *r* like *a* in father, but shorter
B	b	*b*
C	c	*s* in so before *e, i, y, æ;* before *a, o, u,* or consonant, like *k,* and now generally written *k; ch* like *sh,* or rarely like *k;* now generally written *k;* sometimes as though written *tj;* combination *ci* before vowel, like *sh;* letter *c* occurs only in foreign words
D	d	*d* at beginning of words; between vowel and unstressed *e,* between vowel and *j, l, m, n,* or *r,* and in final position, like *th* in father; silent before *s* or *t,* as well as in combination *nd* and *ld* in final position and before unstressed *e;* often silent after *r* and at end of words
E	e	long: like *a* in care; short, stressed: like *e* in met; often like *e* in met, but tending toward *i* in pit; before *r,* like *a* in hat; before *g* or *j,* usually like *a* in hat; in word *de,* like *ee* in meet, but shorter; in unstressed syllables, like *a* in sofa; generally silent before *n*
F	f	*f*
G	g	*g* in go initially and before *t;* between vowel (or sometimes consonant) and unstressed *e,* at end of word, and between vowel and consonant other than *t,* it has sound which may be made by trying to pronounce *g* in go without making contact between tongue and roof of mouth
H	h	*h;* silent before *j* or *v*
I	i	long: *ee* in meet; short: *ee* in meet, but shorter; often like *e* in met, but tending toward *i* in bit
J	j	*y* in yes; silent (and now generally no longer written) after *g* or *k* followed by front vowel; in French words, like *sh*
K	k	*k*
L	l	*ll* in million
M	m	*m*
N	n	*n;* combination *ng,* like *ng* in singer; combination *nk,* like *ng* in finger
O	o	long: *o* in go; short: *o* in November; often like *aw* in law, but shorter
P	p	*p;* combination *ph* in foreign words, like *f,* and now usually written *f*

[Concluded on following page]

Q q   always followed by *v* (or *u*), combination being pronounced, and now usually written, *kv;* occurs only in foreign words

R r   sound made by scraping of air between back of tongue and roof of mouth, as in French; after vowel, its sound assumes quality of vowel

S s   *s* in sing; combination *ss*, and in foreign words *sc*, like *s* in sing; combination *sj*, like *sh;* followed by *i* plus another vowel, like *sh;* in foreign words, *sch* and *sh* are pronounced like *sh*

T t   *t*, at beginning of word; silent in word *det* and in ending *et* when unstressed; followed by *i* plus another vowel, like *sh*

U u   long: *oo* in food; short: *oo* in good; often like *o* in go, but shorter

V v   *v*, before vowel or *r* and after long vowel; after short vowel, like *oo* in food; often silent after *l*

W w   *v;* in foreign words only

X x   *ks*, or at beginning of words, like *s* in sing; now only in foreign words

Y y   long: *ee* in meet, but with lips rounded as in pronouncing *oo* in food; resembles (long) German *ü*, French *u;* short: *ee* in meet, but shorter, and with lips rounded as in pronouncing *oo* in food; resembles (short) German *ü*, French *u*

Z z   *s* in sing; occurs only in foreign words

Æ æ   long: *e* in met, but longer; short: *e* in met; before or after *r*, like *a* in hat; formerly sometimes written *ä;* in handwriting, usually *æ*

Ø ø   *a* in care, but with lips rounded as in pronouncing *oo* in food; resembles (long) German *ö*, French *eu;* formerly sometimes written *ö*

A å   long: *aw* in law, but tending toward *o* in go; short: *aw* in law, but shorter, and tending toward *o* in go; formerly written *aa*.

Special characters

Danish uses the Latin alphabet with the addition of the following special characters: *Æ æ, Ø ø,* and *Å å.*

The *c, q, w, x,* and *z* are used in words of foreign origin and in proper names.

Until quite recently, *aa* was written for *å,* and in dictionaries, indexes, telephone directories, etc., was found either preceding *a* or following it. Now the tendency is to place it at the end of the alphabet. The letter *w* is often regarded as a mere variant writing for *v,* and in dictionaries, etc., the *w*'s are then found interspersed with the *v*'s; otherwise, *w* follows *v.*

Fraktur type (German text) is scarcely in use today.

Vowels and consonants

The vowels are *a, e, i, o, u, y, æ, ø,* and *å;* the back vowels being *a, o, u,* and *å;* the front vowels *e, i, y, æ,* and *ø.* The other letters of the alphabet are consonants.

Combinations of vowel sounds (diphthongs)

aj (formerly *ai*) as *ai* in aisle	*ou* as *oo* in food
au (*av*) as *ou* in house	*ov* as *o* in go
eg as *ey* in grey	*yv* as (Danish) *y* plus *u*
ej (formerly *ei*) as *ey* in grey	*æv* as *e* in met plus *u*
eu (*ev*) as *e* in met plus *u*	*øg* as *oy* in boy
iv as *ee* in meet plus *u*	*øj* (formerly *øi*) as *oy* in boy
oi as *oy* in boy	*øv* as *ø* plus *u*

Combinations of consonantal letters (digraphs)

ch as *tj* or *sj* or *k*, depending on language of origin

cz as *tj* or *ts*, depending on language of origin

hj as *j*

hv as *v*

ng see under *n* in Alphabet and pronunciation

ph as *f*

ps as *s*

qv as *kv*

sc as *s*

sch as *sj*

sh as *sj*

sj see under *s* in Alphabet and pronunciation

th as *t*

wh as *v*

Consonantal units

Includes all the combinations given under Combinations of consonantal letters (digraphs) and the following: *gj, kj, kl, kv, lj, sk, skj, sp, spr, st, str,* and *sv.*

Rules for syllabification

1. Diphthongs, digraphs, and consonantal units may not be divided.

2. Division is made on a vowel or on a diphthong before a single consonant, a digraph, or a consonantal unit: *Ba-lance, hvi-sken, hu-stru, bøj-ning.*

3. In a group of two or more consonants, division is made before the last consonant, digraph, or consonantal unit: *af-ten, dan-ske, sek-sten, tjenst-lig, blom-stre.*

4. Division may be made between two vowels not constituting a diphthong or between a diphthong and a vowel: *fri-er, lej-er.*

5. Certain adverbial prefixes are kept intact. These are: *ad, af, an, bag, be, bi, bort, efter, er, for, fra, frem, ge, in, ind, med, mis, ned, om, op, over, paa, til, ud, ude, und, under,* and *ved: ad-splitte, af-drift, an-drag, bag-slag,* etc.

6. Certain suffixes are kept intact. These are: *agtig, artig, hed,* and *inde: barn-agtig, egen-artig, mat-hed, mester-inde.*

7. Compound words are divided according to their component parts (and each part according to rules 1 to 6), the compounding *s,* if used, going with the preceding component: *aften-avis, aften-blad, aftens-tid.*

8. Foreign words and components of foreign words (not naturalized) follow the conventions of the language of origin: *pa-triot, me-trisk, repu-blik, eks-trem, post-skriptum, Shake-speare, Wash-ington.* Under this rule are also included scientific and technical words, which editors prefer to treat etymologically: *hemi-sfære, dia-gnose.*

Illustrative word divisions

[The numbers in parentheses refer to the syllabification rules]

af-bræk-ke	(5, 3)	ned-sla-gen	(5, 2)
ame-ri-kan-ske	(2, 2, 3)	om-ar-bej-de	(5, 3, 2)
an-dra-gen-de	(5, 2, 3)	op-hæn-ge	(5, 3)
ar-kæ-o-lo-gi	(3, 4, 2, 2)	over-ens-komst	(5, 7)
be-skæf-ti-gel-se	(5, 3, 2, 3)	på-dra-ge	(5, 2)
der-ef-ter	(7, 3)	på-gæl-de	(5, 3)
egen-ar-tig	(6, 3)	pa-ra-graf	(2, 8)
eks-a-men	(8, 2)	pa-tri-o-ti-ske	(8, 4, 2, 2)
eks-em-plar	(8, 8)	re-ge-ring	(2, 2)
en-gel-ske	(3, 3)	re-pre-sen-ta-tion	(8, 2, 3, 2)
er-ind-ring	(5, 3)	re-pu-blik	(2, 8)
eu-ro-pæ-i-ske	(2, 2, 4, 2)	re-pu-bli-kan-ske	(2, 8, 2, 3, 2)
for-u-ren-te	(5, 3)	sam-men-brin-ge	(3, 7, 3)
gen-gæl-de	(3, 3)	selv-an-kla-ge	(7, 5, 2)
halv-å-rig	(7, 2)	ska-des-er-stat-ning	(2, 7, 3, 3)
hin-an-den	(7, 3)	stats-for-fat-ning	(7, 3, 3)
ind-plan-te	(5, 3)	sy-ste-ma-tisk	(2, 2, 2)
in-ter-es-sant	(3, 8, 3)	ti-den-de	(2, 3)
ka-mou-fla-ge	(2, 8, 2)	tids-reg-ning	(7, 3)
kends-ger-ning	(7, 3)	tids-skrif-te	(7, 3)
mid-ship-mand	(8, 3)	til-græn-sen-de	(5, 3, 3)
mis-tviv-le	(5, 3)	ti-pfen-nig	(7, 3)

Illustrative word divisions—Continued

tjenst-skyl-dig	(7, 3)	uor-dent-lig	(3, 3)
tre-å-rig	(7, 2)	uret-mæs-sig	(3, 3)
ty-de-lig	(2, 2)	uvil-kår-lig	(3, 3)
ud-ar-bej-de	(5, 3, 2)	vå-ben-ø-vel-se	(2, 7, 2, 3)
ude-stå-en-de	(5, 4, 3)	ved-bli-ven	(5, 2)
und-dra-ge	(5, 2)	vel-ær-vær-dig	(7, 3, 3)
un-der-of-fi-cer	(3, 5, 3, 2)	yt-rings-fri-hed	(3, 7, 6)
un-der-skri-ve	(3, 5, 2)	ærg-rel-se	(3, 3)
und-skyld-ning	(5, 3)	øn-ske-lig	(3, 2)

Stress and diacritics

Most words are stressed on the first syllable, except when they begin with a prefix such as *be-, er-, for-, ge-*, in which case the following syllable is stressed. Foreign words, especially those of French origin, are usually accented on the last, or next to the last, syllable. In compound words, the first component receives the primary stress; the second receives secondary stress.

In stressed syllables, vowels are generally long before one consonant or none, and short before two or more consonants. There are, however, many exceptions, especially in that a long vowel is often found before two or more consonants. Some monosyllables, which are generally weakly stressed in the sentence, are short, even when they end in a vowel or single consonant.

In unstressed syllables, the vowel is always short. If a word, having, when it stands alone, a long vowel, occurs unstressed in a spoken sentence, the vowel in question is pronounced short.

Characteristic of Danish is an unwritten sound, called the stød, or glottal stop; i.e., a closure of the vocal cords, followed by a sudden opening of them. The sound, resembling a slight cough, occurs often in English before stressed vowels, but speakers of English are scarcely aware of it.

The stød occurs only in stressed syllables. It is used both after vowels and after voiced consonants following a vowel. It does not occur in a word or syllable which is made up of a short vowel followed by one or more of the consonants *p, b, t, d, k, g, f*, or *s*, nor in any word or syllable ending in a short vowel. It is also usually absent from the first part of compound words, even where the uncompounded form would have a stød. Otherwise, the stød is found in all monosyllables and in some polysyllables, especially foreign loanwords. It is also found in polysyllabic second members of compounds, even where, uncompounded, the word would have no stød.

However, the presence or absence of the stød cannot be determined from the written form of the word, but must be known for each word itself, and even for each form of the word. A word which is pronounced with a stød when stressed may lose it if it is weakly stressed in a sentence.

With the exception of *đ, ä* (variants for *æ*), and *ŏ* (variant for *ø*), diacritics are used only in foreign loanwords and in certain proper names.

Capitalization

Capitalization is as in English, except that the pronouns *De, Dem,* and *Deres* are capitalized, as is the familiar form of the pronoun *I*. Formerly, all nouns were capitalized, as in German. Proper adjectives are lowercased.

Punctuation

Punctuation is practically the same as in English, except that all dependent clauses are set off by commas.

Abbreviations

adr.	adresse, address, c/o	Hds. M.	Hendes Majestæt, Her Majesty
afs.	afsender, sender	hr.	herr, sir, Mr.
ang.	angående, concerning	if.	ifølge, according to
anm.	anmærkning, remark, observation	jf., jfr.	javnfør, compare
A/S	Aktieselskab, joint-stock company	kap.	kapitel, chapter
		kgl.	kongelig, royal
bd.	bind, volume, volumes	kl.	klokken, o'clock; klasse, class
bl.a.	blandt andet, blandt andre, among other things, or others	kpt.	kaptajn, captain
		kr.	krone, crown; kroner, crowns (coin)
d.	død, dead		
d.å.	dette år, this year	m.fl.	med flere, with others, and others
d.d.	dags dato, the date of the day, this day	m.h.t.	med hensyn til, with regard to
d.m.	denne måned, this month	m.m.	med mere, et cetera, and more, and so forth
dr.	doktor, doctor		
d.v.s.	det vil sige, that is, that is to say	n.b.	nota bene, mark (notice) well
eks.	eksempel, example (illustration), e.g.	n.n.	nomen nescio, Mr. * * * Mr. such a one
etc.	et cetera, et cetera	nr.	nummer, number
f.	født, born	obs.	observer, observe
f.å.	forrige år, last year	o.s.v.	og så videre, and so forth, etc.
f.eks.	for eksempel, for instance		
ff.	følgende, the following	p.s.	postskriptum, postscript
fhv.	forhenværende, former, late	R.	ridder, knight
		red.	redaktør, editor
fig.	figur, figure	s.	side, page; sider, pages
forf.	forfatter, author	s.d.	samme dato, same date
frk.	frøken, Miss	sml.	sammenlign, compare
gl.	gammel, old	s.u.	svar udbedes, an answer is requested
H. M., Hs. M.	Hans Majestæt, His Majesty	vedr.	vedrørende, concerning

Cardinal numbers

en (een, et)	one	tredive	thirty
to	two	fyrre	
tre	three	(fyrretyve)	forty
fire	four	halvtreds	
fem	five	(halvtreds-	
seks	six	indstyve)	fifty
syv	seven	tres (tres-	
otte	eight	indstyve)	sixty
ni	nine	halvfjerds	
ti	ten	(halvfjerds-	
elleve (elve)	eleven	indstyve)	seventy
tolv	twelve	firs (firs-	
tretten	thirteen	indstyve)	eighty
fjorten	fourteen	halvfems	
femten	fifteen	(halvfems-	
seksten	sixteen	indstyve)	ninety
sytten	seventeen	hundrede	hundred
atten	eighteen	hundrede og en, etc.	one hundred and one, etc.
nitten	nineteen		
tyve	twenty	tohundrede, etc.	two hundred, etc.
en og tyve, etc.	twenty-one, etc.	tusind(e)	thousand

NOTE.—The forms in parentheses are old fashioned and are seldom used today.

Ordinal numbers

første	first	syttende	seventeenth
anden	second	attende	eighteenth
tredje	third	nittende	nineteenth
fjerde	fourth	tyvende	twentieth
femte	fifth	en og tyvende, etc.	twenty-first, etc.
sjette	sixth		
syvende	seventh	tredivte	thirtieth
ottende	eighth	fyrretyvende	fortieth
niende	ninth	halvtre(d)sindstyvende	fiftieth
tiende	tenth	tre(d)sindstyvende	sixtieth
ellevte (elvte)	eleventh	halvfjerdsindstyvende	seventieth
tolvte	twelfth	firsindstyvende	eightieth
trettende	thirteenth	halvfemsindstyvende	ninetieth
fjortende	fourteenth	hundrede og første, etc.	hundred and first, etc.
femtende	fifteenth		
sekstende	sixteenth		

NOTE.—Hundred(e) (100) and tusind(e) (1,000) have the same form for cardinals and ordinals.

Months

januar (jan.)	January	juli	July
februar (feb.)	February	august (aug.)	August
marts	March	september (sept.)	September
april (apr.)	April	oktober (okt.)	October
maj	May	november (nov.)	November
juni	June	december (dec.)	December

Days

søndag	Sunday	torsdag	Thursday
mandag	Monday	fredag	Friday
tirsdag	Tuesday	lørdag	Saturday
onsdag	Wednesday		

Seasons

forår	spring	efterår	autumn
sommer	summer	vinter	winter

Time

time	hour	måned	month
dag	day	år	year
uge	week		

REFERENCES.—Henni Forchhammer, How To Learn Danish (1932); A. Arnholtz und C. A. Reinhold, Einführung in das Dänische Lautsystem (1936); Ingeborg Stemann, Danish (1938); G. Langenscheidt og H. Henningsen, Lommeordbog Over det Danske og Tyske Sprog (1941); Johs. Magnussen, Otto Madsen og Herman Vinterberg, Dansk-Engelsk Ordbog (1943); Jeannette Dearden and Karin Stig-Nielsen, Spoken Danish (1945).

DUTCH

Nu is het duidelijk, dat het duratieve aspect in de feitelijke handeling moeilijk tot zijn recht kan komen. Men kan wel stilstaan op een plaats, maar niet stilstaan in de tijd. De enige middelen, die hier practisch ten dienste staan, zijn de herhaling en de vertraging. Van beide vindt men in allerlei godsdienstige rituelen voorbeelden.— Held: Magie, Hekserij en Toverij, Groningen (1950), p. 10.

Alphabet and pronunciation

A	a	*a* in father	O	o	*o* in often, low
B	b	*b; p* at end of words	P	p	*p*
C	c	*k; s* before *e, i, y*	Q	q	*q*
D	d	*d; t* at end of words	R	r	*r*
E	e	*e* in met; *a* in fate	S	s	*s* in sister
F	f	*f*	T	t	*t*
G	g	*ch* in German auch	U	u	*u* in sure; also almost
H	h	*h*			like *ee* in eel or like
I	i	*i* in fit, police			French *u* or German *ü*
J	j	*y* in yet; like English *z*	V	v	*v; f* at end of words
		in azure in some words	W	w	*w*
K	k	*k*	X	x	*x*
L	l	*l*	Y	y	*i* in fit
M	m	*m*	Z	z	*z; s* at end of words
N	n	*n*			

Special characters

Dutch uses the Latin alphabet; and with the exception of the circumflex and acute accents, which it uses only to a small extent, it has no special characters.

The letters *ij* are treated like a ligature. When they begin a capitalized word, both letters must be uppercased, thus: *IJsland*, Iceland; *IJverig*, zealous.

Vowels and consonants

The vowel letters are *a, e, i, o, u,* and *ij;* the remaining characters are all consonants. The so-called double vowels, *aa, ee, oo,* and *uu,* are merely lengthened sounds of their respective single forms; thus *aa* is like *aa* in Saar, *ee* like *a* in taste, *oo* like *o* in rose (never like *oo* in good), *uu* like *u* in sure. Double vowels are regarded by most grammarians as single characters rather than diphthongs.

Diphthongs

The diphthongs are pronounced approximately as follows:

aai as *ai* in aisle
au as *ou* in house
eeu as *a* in fate followed by French *u*
   or German *ü*
ei as *ai* in aisle
eu as *er* in her
ie as *ie* in pier

ieu as *eu* in reunion
ij as *ai* in aisle
oe as *oe* in shoe
oei as *uoy* in buoy
ooi as *oy* in annoy
ou as *ou* in house
ui as *urry* in furry

Digraphs

The digraphs and their sounds are:

ch like German *ch* [1]
ph as *f*
qu like English *qu*

sch as *s* plus *ch* or *s* [2]
sj as *sh* in shall
th as *t*

Rules for syllabification

1. Double vowels, diphthongs, and digraphs may not be divided.
2. Division is made on a vowel or on a diphthong before a single consonant or a digraph: *le-ven, leu-gen, la-chen, vrou-wen, le-raar*.
3. In a group of two or more consonants, division is made before the last consonant or digraph: *heb-ben, amb-ten, man-tje;* but if one of the consonants is *s* preceded by another consonant, the *s* goes over: *kor-sten, ern-stig, Pink-ster*. This rule cannot be applied to personal names, e.g.: *Bensdorp* should be: *Bens-dorp; Rijnsburger* should be: *Rijns-burger*, etc.
4. Division may be made between two vowels not constituting a diphthong or between a diphthong and a vowel: *zaai-en, knie-ën, spi-on*.
5. Certain adverbial prefixes are kept intact. These are: *aan, achter, af, be, bij, daar, door, er, ge, heen, her, in, mede, mein, mis, na, neder, neer, om, on, onder, ont, oor, op, over, samen, tegen, terug, toe, uit, ver, voor, voort, wan, weder,* and *weg: aan-vaarden, achter-eind, af-breken, be-drog,* etc.
6. Certain suffixes are kept intact. These are: *aard, aardig, achtig, heid, je, pje, schap, sche, ske, ste(n), ster,* and *tje: dronk-aard, eigen-aardig, zak-achtig, oord-je* (little place), *oor-tje* (little ear), *boom-pje, hoog-ste, bak-ster*.[3]
7. Compound words are divided according to their component parts (and each part according to rules 1 to 6): *eer-ambt, angst-kreet*. The compounding *s*, if used, is kept with the preceding component: *rijks-ambt, volks-eenheid*.
8. Foreign words and components of foreign words (not naturalized) follow the conventions of the language of origin: *repu-bliek, por-tret, Trans-atlantisch, Washington, Shake-speare*. Under this rule are also included scientific and technical words, which editors prefer to treat etymologically: *dia-gnostisch, proto-plasma;* but *interesse* has been naturalized and is divided *inte-resse*.

Illustrative word divisions

[The numbers in parentheses refer to the syllabification rules]

aam-bor-stig	(3, 3)	in-te-res-se	(3, 2, 3)
aan-prij-zen	(5, 2)	kun-ste-naar	(3, 2)
ach-ter-uit-gang	(3, 5, 5)	me-de-stan-der	(2, 5, 3)
Ame-ri-kaan-se	(2, 2, 3)	mees-ter-stuk-jes	(3, 7, 6)
Am-ster-dam	(3, 3)	mein-e-dig-heid	(5, 2, 6)
be-slis-sin-gen	(5, 3, 3)	mi-cro-me-trisch	(8, 2, 8)
bi-bli-o-theek	(8, 4, 2)	mis-brui-ken	(5, 2)
bij-een-bren-gen	(5, 7, 3)	moei-lijk-heid	(2, 6)
con-sti-tu-tie	(3, 2, 2)	na-druk-ken	(5, 3)
con-sti-tu-ti-o-neel	(3, 2, 2, 4, 2)	ne-der-knie-len	(2, 5, 2)
daar-op-vol-gend	(5, 5, 3)	Ne-der-lan-der	(2, 5, 3)
des-a-vou-e-ren	(8, 2, 4, 2)	Ne-der-land-se	(2, 5, 6)
door-draai-en	(5, 4)	neer-slach-tig	(5, 3)
En-gel-se	(3, 3)	om-stan-dig-heid	(5, 3, 6)
er-ach-ter	(5, 3)	on-der-druk-ken	(3, 5, 3)
ge-brui-ker	(5, 2)	on-er-va-ren	(5, 3, 2)
ge-meen-schap-pe-lijk	(2, 3, 3, 2)	ont-e-ren	(5, 2)
heen-snel-len	(5, 3)	oor-spron-ke-lijk	(5, 3, 2)
her-e-ni-gen	(5, 2, 2)	op-hel-de-ring	(5, 3, 2)
in-acht-ne-ming	(5, 7, 2)	op-ont-houd	(5, 5)
in-dus-trie	(3, 8)	pro-spec-tus	(8, 3)

---

[1] This sound of *ch* is for words of native origin only. In words of French origin *ch* is pronounced as in French (like *sh*) and in words of Greek origin like *ch* in *chorus*.

[2] The digraph *sch* has two sounds. At the beginning of a word and at the beginning of a syllable preceded by a prefix it is pronounced like *s* plus the Dutch *ch;* elsewhere like English *s*.

[3] The suffixes listed must be distinguished from the same letter combinations that are not suffixes and not appended to a meaningful word. Thus *ste* in *beste* is not a suffix, as *be* is not a word. Likewise *aard* in *veinzaard* and *grijnzaard* is not a suffix in the above sense, as there are no words *veinz* and *grijnz*. Properly, *veinzaard* and *grijnzaard* are derivatives of *veinzen* and *grijnzen* and are syllabified according to rule 3; i.e., *vein-zaard, grijn-zaard,* and *beste* is syllabified *bes-te*.

Illustrative word divisions—Continued

re-ge-ring	(2, 2)	uit-oe-fe-nen	(5, 2, 2)
re-pu-bliek	(2, 8)	ver-e-nig-de	(5, 2, 3)
re-pu-bli-keins	(2, 8, 2)	voor-af-gaan-de	(5, 3, 3)
sa-men-stel-ling	(2, 5, 3)	voort-breng-sel	(5, 3)
te-gen-ant-woord	(2, 5, 3)	wan-trou-wend	(5, 2)
te-rug-ei-sen	(2, 5, 2)	we-der-op-bou-wen	(2, 5, 5, 2)
tijd-schrif-ten	(7, 3)	weg-sprin-gen	(5, 3)
toe-tre-den	(5, 2)	zelf-re-ge-ring	(7, 2, 2)

Stress and diacritics

The stress in Dutch words falls on the root syllable in simple words and on the main component (usually the first) in compound words: *beSTELlen* (to order), *SCHOOLboek* (schoolbook). Words of foreign origin keep their own characteristic stress.

Diacritical marks are used to a limited extent in Dutch. The circumflex is used to indicate the contraction of two syllables into one, if the contraction is unusual: *daân* for *daden* (deeds), *liên* for *lieden* (people). The dieresis (trema) is used to indicate that the vowel over which it is placed does not form a diphthong with the preceding vowel but is pronounced separately: *zeeën* (pronounced *zay'-en*), seas; *oliën* (pronounced *olee'-en*), to oil. The acute is used to give added emphasis: *dáár is het*, there it is, but *daar is hij eindelijk*, there he is finally; *één gulden*, one guilder, but *een gulden*, a guilder.

Capitalization

Capitalization in Dutch is similar to that in English, but with the following differences:

The months, and days of the week in Dutch are written lowercase.

If the first word of a sentence is a single letter only, the word goes lowercase and the next one is capitalized: *'s Avonds is het koud*, in the evening it is cold. *'k Weet niet wat hij zegt*, I do not know what he says.

The first-person pronoun, *ik* (I), is not capitalized, but the second-person pronouns *U* (you), *Uw* (your), and *Gij* (you), are generally capitalized in personal correspondence.

The name particles *de, ten, van*, if not preceded by the Christian name, are capitalized; otherwise, lowercased.

Punctuation and hyphenation

Punctuation and hyphenation are similar to the usages in German (q.v.). The apostrophe, however, is used not only to indicate abbreviations or contractions but also to form the plural and possessive of foreign loanwords: *'n paard* (for *een paard*), a horse; *'s avonds* (for *des avonds*), in the evening: *'t huis* (for *te huis*), at home; *'k heb* (for *ik heb*), I have; *sofa's*, sofas; *Maria's*, Mary's. Quotation marks are set: „thus."

Abbreviations

A.P.	Anno Passato, in the past year; Amsterdams Peil, Amsterdam ordnance datum	jl.	jongstleden, last, ult.
		Jr.	Junior, junior
		jr.	jaar, year
		ll.	laatstleden, last, ult.
b.v.	bij voorbeeld, for example, e.g.	Mej.	Mejuffrouw, Miss
		Mevr.	Mevrouw, Mrs.
dgl.	dergelijke, such	Mij.,	Maatschappij, society, company
d.i.	dat is, that is, i.e.		
dl.	deel, part, volume	Ndl.	Nederland, the Netherlands
e.g.	eerstgenoemde, the former, the before-mentioned	nl.	namelijk, namely, viz
		n.m.	namiddag, post meridiem, p. m.
enz.	en zo voort, and so forth, etc.		
		N.V.	Naamloze Vennootschap, limited-liability company
e.v.	eerstvolgende, the following, next		
		o.a.	onder andere, among others
geb.	geboren, born, né(e); also gebonden, bound	ong.	ongeveer, about, ca.
		Opm.	Opmerking, remark
Gebr.	Gebroeders, Brothers, Bros.	p.a.	per adres, c/o
Geref.	Gereformeerde, Reformed, Calvinist	p.st.	pond sterling, pound sterling, £
Hfst.	Hoofdstuk, chapter	Sen./Sr.	Senior, senior
H.M.	Hare Majesteit, Her Majesty	vgl.	vergelijk, compare, cf.
i.p.v.	in plaats van, instead of	v.m.	voormiddag, ante meridiem, a.m.

Cardinal numbers

een	one	achttien	eighteen
twee	two	negentien	nineteen
drie	three	twintig	twenty
vier	four	eenentwintig, etc.	twenty-one, etc.
vijf	five	dertig	thirty
zes	six	veertig	forty
zeven	seven	vijftig	fifty
acht	eight	zestig	sixty
negen	nine	zeventig	seventy
tien	ten	tachtig	eighty
elf	eleven	negentig	ninety
twaalf	twelve	honderd	hundred
dertien	thirteen	honderd (en) één	one hundred and one
veertien	fourteen		
vijftien	fifteen	tweehonderd	two hundred
zestien	sixteen	duizend	thousand
zeventien	seventeen		

Ordinal numbers

eerste	first	zestiende	sixteenth
tweede	second	zeventiende	seventeenth
derde	third	achttiende	eighteenth
vierde	fourth	negentiende	nineteenth
vijfde	fifth	twintigste	twentieth
zesde	sixth	één en twintigste	twenty-first
zevende	seventh	dertigste	thirtieth
achtste	eighth	veertigste	fortieth
negende	ninth	vijftigste	fiftieth
tiende	tenth	zestigste	sixtieth
elfde	eleventh	zeventigste	seventieth
twaalfde	twelfth	tachtigste	eightieth
dertiende	thirteenth	negentigste	ninetieth
veertiende	fourteenth	honderdste	hundredth
vijftiende	fifteenth	duizendste	thousandth

Months

januari (jan.)	January	juli	July
februari (feb.)	February	augustus (aug.)	August
maart (mrt.)	March	september (sept.)	September
april (apr.)	April	october (oct.)	October
mei	May	november (nov.)	November
juni	June	december (dec.)	December

Days

zondag	Sunday	donderdag	Thursday
maandag	Monday	vrijdag	Friday
dinsdag	Tuesday	zaterdag	Saturday
woensdag	Wednesday		

Seasons

lente, voorjaar	spring	herfst, najaar	autumn
zomer	summer	winter	winter

Time

uur	hour	maand	month
dag	day	jaar	year
week	week		

REFERENCES.—E. Vrieze, De Nieuwe Spelling 1946 . . . (1946); T. G. G. Valette, Dutch Conversation Grammar (1928); F. G. Renier, Learn Dutch! A Dutch Grammar (1942); J. van Ham en S. Hofker, Beknopte Nederlandse Spraakkunst (1939); Kramer's Engels-Nederlands en Nederlands-Engels Woordenboek (1950); L. Bloomfield, Spoken Dutch (1944).

FINNISH

Läänien vaakunat. Valtioneuvosto vahvisti tammikuun 18 päivänä 1962 Suomen lääneille omat vaakunat. Vaakunoiden pohjana ovat useimmissa tapauksissa vanhat maakuntavaakunat tai niiden yhdistelmät. Niinpä Uudenmaan läänillä, Ahvenanmaalla, Kuopion läänillä ja Pohjois-Karjalan läänillä on vaakunansa pohjana vanha maakuntavaakuna. Kilpien päällä näissä on kreivikunnan kruunu, paitsi Pohjois-Karjalalla herttuakunnan kruunu. Muut vaakunat ovat yhdistelmävaakunoita.—Mitä, Missä, Milloin (1963), p. 311.

Alphabet and pronunciation

A	a	*a* in father, sofa	R	r	*r*, trilled
B	b	*b*	S	s	*s* in so
C	c	*c* in calm or in cease	T	t	*t*
D	d	*d*	U	u	*u;* as *oo* in boot, but short
E	e	*e* in met			
F	f	*f*	V	v	*v*
G	g	*g* in game	W	w	same as *v* (in archaic forms of proper names only)
H	h	*h*			
I	i	*i* in pit			
J	j	*y* in yet	X	x	*x*
K	k	*k*	Y	y	like German *ü* or like French *u*
L	l	*l*			
M	m	*m*	Z	z	*s* or *ts*
N	n	*n*	Ä	ä	*a* in hat
O	o	*o* in note, but short	Ö	ö	like German *ö* or like French *eu*
P	p	*p*			
Q	q	*q*			

With only minor exceptions, words are spelled as they are pronounced and pronounced as they are spelled. Each letter is pronounced as only one sound and each sound is spelled with only one letter. The only exception to this rule is the *n* sound (the velar nasal like *ng* in *song*) which is represented by *n* (before *k, kenkä*) or by *ng* (in *kangas* which is spelled *kaŋŋas*). It has to be remembered also that *n* followed by *p* is often pronounced *m;* and, that *s* has a transient pronunciation between English *s* and *sh*.

Finnish *h* is pronounced also at the end of a syllable which is followed by a consonant (*kahvi, lehmä*) the same way as at the beginning of a word or syllable.

Since no *f* exists in common Finnish, *coffee* was pronounced *kahvi* and adapted as such. Initial *b* is pronounced *p: pommi* (from French *bombe*), initial *d* as *t: tohtori* (from Latin *doctor*), and *g* as *k: kuvernööri* (from French *gouverneur*).

Finnish pronunciation prefers one consonant at the beginning of the word, as reflected by Finnish adaptations of foreign words: *Tukholma (Stockholm), ranta (strand)*.

Special characters

Finnish uses the Latin alphabet with the addition of the following special characters: *Ä ä* and *Ö ö*.

The letters *b, c, f, q, x,* and *z* do not occur in native Finnish words. However, the standard dictionaries, containing words of foreign origin, list them in the alphabetic order shown above.

Vowels and consonants

The vowel letters are *a, e, i, o, u, y, ä,* and *ö,* the remaining letters being all consonants. With the exception of *d, v, h,* and *j* which appear only in short versions, all Finnish sounds and their graphic counterparts may be short or long. Short sounds are represented by a single letter. Long vowels are represented by double letters: *aa, ee, ii, oo, uu, yy, ää,* and *öö;* long variants of the consonants are indicated in the same way: *gg, kk, ll, mm, nn, pp, tt,* etc.

Long variants of vowels occur in initial, middle, or final position in the context of words: *aamu, saada, kotimaa.* Long versions of consonants occur only in middle position in the context of words.

The letter *å* (of the Swedish alphabet), while not a genuine element of the Finnish, is frequently used in Finnish print, mostly in Swedish versions of Finnish proper names. Also known and used are the consonants *sh* (English *sh*) and *š* and *ž* (representing the *sh* and *zh* consonants which occur in Russian), mostly in proper names.

Diphthongs

The diphthongs and their sounds are:

ai as *ai* in aisle	*ui* like Finnish *u* plus *i*
au as *ow* in how	*uo* like Finnish *u* plus *o*
ei as *ei* in eight	*yi* like Finnish *y* plus *i*
eu like Finnish *e* plus *u*	*yö* like Finnish *y* plus *ö*
ey like Finnish *e* plus *y*	*äi* like Finnish *ä* plus *i*
ie like Finnish *i* plus *e*	*äy* like Finnish *ä* plus *y*
iu like Finnish *i* plus *u*	*öi* like Finnish *ö* plus *i*
oi as *oi* in oil	*öy* like Finnish *ö* plus *y*
ou as *ow* in low	

The diphthongs *ie, uo, yö, eu, iu, yi, ai, äy, öi,* and *öy* are sounded as indicated above; i.e., like their constituent separate letters but in quick succession, *ie, uo, yö* having the main stress on the second vowel, the others on the first. The above combinations, except those ending in *i,* are diphthongs only at the beginning of a word or of a compound constituent; elsewhere they are separate vowels and may be divided: *tapa-us, kope-us, kieli-en.*

Rules for syllabification

1. Division is made between vowels not constituting a diphthong or between a diphthong and a vowel; however, a single vowel, especially at the beginning of the word, is not separated from the rest: *lapsi-en, oi-ke-us; asi-asta, eri-ävä.*

2. Long vowels which are represented by double letters may not be divided: *maat, ku-nin-kaan, kä-teen, e-siin, syyn, teh-dään.*

3. Two vowels (members of a diphthong) at the beginning of a word or immediately following the initial consonant may not be separated: *Suo-mi, ai-na, kau-ka-na, tie-dän.*

But when two vowels come together as the result of *k* alternating with zero in consonant gradation, there is a syllable division between the vowels: *nä-en* (from *nä-ke-*), *ta-ot-tu* (from *ta-ko-*).

4. When two vowels (diphthongs) occur beyond the first syllable in the word, they may not be divided if the second vowel is *i, u,* or *y: an-tai-sin, va-rau-tui.* Otherwise, there is a syllable division between the vowels: *a-si-a, ka-tu-a, ly-hy-ät, sil-mi-ä-ni.*

5. Division is made on a vowel (short or long), or on a diphthong before a single consonant: *ka-la, kä-ve-let, ky-sy-mys; maa-ta, pii-ri, kuu-si; neu-la, tie-ni, yö-tä, kau-pun-ki, tu-le-vai-suus.*

6. Long consonants which are represented by double letters are divided: *kans-sa* (with), *tyt-tö, kuk-ka, kap-pa-le, keit-ti-ö, käyt-täy-tyy, lop-pu-ma-ton, lai-val-la, pork-ka-na.*

7. Division is made between two different consonants: *kan-sa* (nation), *piis-pa, kau-nis-ta, Tuk-hol-mas-ta.*

8. When more than two consonants appear together, division is made before the last one: *Rans-kas-ta, myrs-kyi-den.*

9. Compound words are divided according to their components: *maa-ilma, esi-isä, muinais-usko, talous-elämä, levy-laulaja, kulttuuri-rahasto.* Further divisions of each component part follow the rules as described above.

10. Finnish prefers to add a vowel (*a, o, u,* but mostly *i*) to consonant endings of foreign words including proper names: *aateli* (from German *Adel*), *markka*

(from Swedish *mark*), *karamelli* (from Spanish *caramel*), *humpuuki* (from English *humbug*), *punssi* (from English *punch*), *hattu* (from Swedish *hat*), *kirkko* (from Nordic *kirk*). In syllabification, such foreign words follow the rules applied to the original Finnish stock: *aa-te-li*, *mark-ka*, *ka-ra-mel-li*, *hum-puu-ki*, *puns-si*, *hat-tu*, *kirk-ko*.

In forms of declination the foreign words experience the same transformations as the original stock: *markat* (nominative plural for *markka*), syllabified as *mar-kat; hatun* (genitive singular for *hattu*), syllabified as *ha-tun; kirkon* (genitive singular for *kirkko*), syllabified as *kir-kon*.

11. Not adapted foreign words and names retain most of the original forms in pronunciation and orthography; however, a final *i* is added to words ending with consonants: *demokraatti* (democrat), *intrigi* (intrigue), *alkoholi* (alcohol), *kongressi* (congress), *monogrammi* (monogram). Syllabification of such words follows the general Finnish rules: *de-mok-raat-ti*, *int-ri-gi*, *al-ko-ho-li;* or, in cases of more evident etymological background, they are divided according to their original components: *kon-gressi*, *mono-grammi*.

Declination forms with closed syllables (ending with consonant) of foreign words which are adopted with long *pp*, *kk*, and *ss* in their singular nominative forms (mostly ending with *i*, i.e., with an open syllable), reduce the long consonants: *Euroopan* (from *Eurooppa*), *romantiikan* (from *romantiikka*), *monarkit* (from *monarkki*, monarch), *tansit* (from *tanssi*, adapted form of German *Tanz*). In syllabification: *Eu-roopan* (but *Eu-roop-pa*), *ro-man-tii-kan* (but *ro-man-tiik-ka*), *mo-nar-kit* (but *mo-nark-ki*), *tan-sit* (but *tans-si*).

12. Unadapted foreign words and their derivatives retain most of the original orthographic form of the basic words (for reasons of frequent reprinting or for difficulties caused when respelled in accordance with characteristics of Finnish pronunciation): *Shakespeare* and *Shakespearin elämä* (life of Shakespeare), *Budapest* and *Budapestissa* (in Budapest), *Washington* and *Washingtonista* (from Washington), *apopleksia*, *diagnostinen*. In syllabification: *Shake-speare* (but *Shake-spea-rin*), *Bu-da-pest* (but *Bu-da-pes-tis-sa*), *Wa-shing-ton* (but *Wa-shing-to-nis-ta*), *a-po-plek-si-a*, *dia-gnos-ti-nen*.

Illustrative word divisions

[The numbers in parentheses refer to the syllabification rules]

ah-dis-tan	(7, 7)	oi-ke-us-a-sia	(1, 1, 9, 5)
ai-no-as-taan	(5, 1, 7, 2)	omis-ta-ja	(1, 7, 5)
aja-tus-ai-ka	(1, 5, 9, 1)	ope-tus-ai-ne	(1, 5, 9, 5)
al-keis-o-pe-tus	(7, 4, 9, 5, 5)	osit-tai-nen	(1, 6, 5)
al-ku-o-sa	(7, 9, 5)	pam-flet-ti	(11, 6)
ame-ri-ka-lai-nen	(1, 5, 5, 5)	piis-pan-is-tuin	(2, 7, 9, 7)
bil-joo-na	(5, 2)	poik-ke-us	(3, 6, 1)
brit-ti-läi-nen	(6, 5, 5)	pääl-lik-kyys	(2, 6, 6, 2)
de-mo-kraat-ti	(5, 11, 6)	ran-gais-ta-va	(7, 4, 7)
Eng-lan-ti	(8, 7)	rau-ta-tie	(3, 9)
epä-o-leel-li-nen	(9, 5, 6, 5)	ri-kok-sel-li-nen	(5, 7, 6)
etu-oi-ke-us	(9, 5, 1)	sai-ras-a-pu	(3, 9, 5)
huo-li-mat-ta	(3, 5, 6)	sa-man-ai-kai-nen	(5, 9, 5, 5)
hy-dro-sta-tiik-ka	(11, 11, 2, 6)	sat-tu-moi-sin	(6, 5, 5)
il-man-a-la	(7, 9, 5)	sa-tun-nai-nen	(5, 6, 5)
kan-sa-lais-oi-ke-us	(7, 5, 4, 5, 1)	sei-sah-dus	(3, 7)
kan-sal-li-nen	(7, 6, 5)	se-lit-te-ly	(5, 6, 5)
kau-em-mak-si	(1, 6, 7)	sel-väs-ti	(7, 7)
ko-mi-sa-ri-us	(5, 5, 5, 1)	sem-min-kin	(6, 6)
lii-al-li-nen	(2, 6, 5)	seu-rus-te-lu	(3, 7, 5)
lu-et-te-lo	(1, 6, 5)	sih-tee-ri	(7, 2)
muu-ka-lai-nen	(2, 5, 5)	si-jais-kans-le-ri	(5, 4, 9, 8, 5)
muut-tu-ma-ton	(2, 6, 5)	Suo-ma-lai-nen	(3, 5, 5)
myön-tei-nen	(3, 4)	suo-si-ol-li-ses-ti	(3, 1, 6, 5, 7)
nais-a-sia	(3, 9, 1)	ta-val-li-nen	(5, 6, 5)
neu-vok-ki	(3, 6)	teh-taa-lai-nen	(7, 2, 5, 4)
neu-vot-te-lu	(3, 6, 5)	xe-ro-ftal-mia	(5, 11, 7)
ni-mi-kir-joi-tus	(5, 9, 7, 5)	Yh-dys-Val-lat	(7, 9)
nä-en-näi-ses-ti	(3, 6, 4, 7)		

Diacritics and stress

With the exception of *ä* and *ö*, Finnish uses no diacritics. Stress is always on the first syllable.

Capitalization

1. Long versions of vowels are capitalized by capitalization of the first letter: *Aa, Ee, Ii, Oo, Uu, Yy, Ää, Öö*. The same rule applies to diphthongs which are capitalized by the capitalization of their first graphic element: *Ai, Au, Ei, Eu, Ie, Iu, Oi, Ou, Ui, Uo, Yi, Yö, Äi, Äy, Öi, Öy*.

2. Capitalized is the Finnish name God: *Jumala* (or equivalent terms), but not its derivatives: *jumalallinen* (divine).

3. The personal pronoun (nominative second person singular) *sinä* (thou) is capitalized (*Sinä*) when referring to relatives, children, close friends (in correspondence), to God, or is used in poetry. The personal pronoun (nominative second person plural) *te* is capitalized (*Te*) when used in addressing a third person or a group of persons with a mark of respect.

4. Capitalized are both parts of a hyphenated name (proper noun) if the second part is also a proper noun: *Länsi-Saksa* (Western Germany), *Etelä-Amerikka* (South America), *Pohjois-Karjala* (Northern Carelia), *Vähä-Aasia* (Asia Minor). If the name does not refer to a recognized independent region, letters in lowercase are used: *pohjois-Suomi* (northern Finland), *itä-Ranska* (eastern France).

5. Capitalized are proper names which form part of the name of a state or church holiday: *Juhannuspäivä* or *Juhannuksen päivä* (St. John's Day or Midsummer Day), *Mikon päivä* (St. Michael's Day), *Tapanin päivä* (St. Stephen's Day), or first letters of similar days, including those of memorial days, if they are compound words: *Itsenäisyyspäivä* (Independence Day), *Pääsiäispäivä* (Easter Day, i.e., Easter Sunday), *Snellmanin päivä* (Snellman Day), etc.

6. Capitalized are names of countries: *Ranska* (France), *Englanti* (England), *Yhdysvallat* (United States), *Suomi* (Finland), but derivatives of the same names meaning nations (nationalities) or languages of the same countries appear in lowercase: *ranskalainen* (Frenchman), *englantilainen* (Englishman), *amerikkalaiset* (Americans), *suomen kieli* (Finnish language).

7. Capitalized are words indicating attributes of historical figures: *Kaarle Suuri* (Charles the Great), *Pyhä Henrik* (Henric the Saint).

8. Capitalized are all words appearing as separate parts of a proper name: *Kasvatusopillinen Korkeakoulu* (Pedagogical, i.e., Teachers' College), *Yhteiskunnallinen Korkeakoulu* (College of Social Sciences); but *Kansallisteatteri* (National Theater), *Kymijoki* (Kymi River), *Maamme-laulu* "Our Land" (the Finnish national anthem), *Neuvostoliitto* (Soviet Union), *Olympiakylä* (Olympic Village), *Senaatintalo* (Senate Building).

9. Capitalized are parts of main titles of newspapers, journals, and unique literary works (including those of linguistic monuments) and series: *Uusi Suomi* (New Finland, newspaper), *Helsingin Sanomat* (Helsinki News, newspaper), *Helsingin Kaupungin Historiallisen Museon Julkaisuja* (Publications of the Historical Museum of the City of Helsinki, series), *Historiallinen Arkisto* (Historical Archives, journal), *Uusi Testamentti* (The New Testament), *Vanha Kalevala* (Old Kalevala); but *Aleksis Kiven Seitsemän veljestä* (the Seven Brothers by Aleksis Kivi), *Taidetta ja käsityötä Kansallismuseossa* (Arts and Handicrafts in the National Museum, series).

Punctuation and hyphenation

Finnish punctuation differs from the English in the following:

1. The period indicates that a figure stands for the ordinal number: *2. partisiippi* (the second participle), but it is not applied in connection with Roman numerals: *II partisiippi*. Neither does it appear when a figure is followed by *p.* (for *päivänä*, on . . .th day): *6 p. joulukuuta*, on the 6th of December. The period is used to separate parts of determinative dates: *Urheilukatsaus 1.10.1961–30.9.1962* (Sports Survey, Oct. 1, 1961–Sept. 30, 1962).

2. A comma separates subordinated sentences in the front of conjunctions like *että* (that), *jotta* (in order that), *koska* (because), *kun* (when), *jos* (if), *vaikka* (though), and *kuin* (as). But it is not used before the conjunctions *eli* (or), *ja* (and), *sekä* (as well as, and), *tai* (or), *vai* (or), and the enclitic *-ka, -kä*.

3. The colon replaces letters (or parts of words) in abbreviations: *p:nä* (for *päivänä*, on . . .th day), *k:lo* (for *kello*, o'clock). Endings of grammatical cases are joined to figures by a colon: *Kirjasto on avoinna k:lo 10:stä 15:een ja k:lo 17:sta 21:een* (The library is open from 10 a.m. to 3 p.m. and from 5 to 9 p.m.). The abridged parts of the text have to be read as: *kymmenestä, viiteentoista, seitsemästätoista* and *kaksikymmentäyhteen*.

4. The apostrophe is used to mark the omission of a letter: *yht'äkkiä* (for *yhtä äkkiä*, suddenly). It is also used in foreign words and names ending in a vowel sound in order to clearly separate the end of the name from the Finnish

case-ending: *Loti'n* (of Loti), *Raleigh'n* (of Raleigh), *Friedrichsruh'ssa* (in Friedrichsruh).

5. The hyphen is used between two identical vowels in compound words: *raha-apu* (financial aid). Also where, in two or more compound words, one element is to be understood as common: *suomen-, saksan- ja englanninkielinen* (in Finnish, German, and English languages); *syntymäpaikka ja -aika* (place and date of birth). Hyphen is used also where one part is a figure or abbreviation: *30-vuotias* (30 years old); *palovak.-yhtiö* (for *palovakuutusyhtiö*, fire insurance company).

Abbreviations

ap. or a.p.	aamupäivällä, before noon	ns. or n.s.	niin sanottu, so called
Arv.	Arvoisa, esteemed	Nti	Neiti, Miss
ed.	edellinen, former, foregoing	nyk.	nykyinen, current
ent.	entinen, past, old	oik.	oikeastaan, really, properly, correctly, actually
e.pp.	edellä puolenpäivän, before noon	p.	penni, penniä, penny, pence; päivä, day, date
esim.	esimerkiksi, for example, e.g.		
H:ra or Hra	Herra, Mr., Sir	p.a.	paino arkki, printed sheet
ip. or i.p.	iltapäivällä, afternoon, p.m.	R:va or Rva	Rouva, madam
jne. or j. n. e.	ja niin edespäin, and so on	s. or siv.	sivu, sivulla, page, pages
		seur.	seuraava, following, next
j.pp.	jälkeen puolenpäivän, afternoon, p.m.	so. or s.o.	se on, that is, i.e.
k-lo	kello, hour, o'clock	s.v.	samana vuonna, same year
ko. or k.o.	kyseessä oleva, (being) under discussion, in question	t.	tai, or
		t.k.	tämän kuun, this month
		t.m.s.	tai muuta semmoista, and so on
ks.	katso, see, compare, cf.		
l.	eli, or	Tri	Tohtori, Doctor
m.	minuutti, minute(s)	ts. or t.s.	toisin sanoen, in other words
Maist.	Maisteri, M.A. (academic title)	Tuom.	Tuomari, Judge
mk(k).	markka(a), mark(s) (Finnish currency)	t.v.	tänä vuonna, this year
		v.	vuosi, year
mm.	muun muuassa, among others	vert. or vrt.	vertaa, compare, cf.
Muist.	Muistutus, note	v.k.	viime kuuta, viime kuun, last month, of the last month
n.	noin, about, circa		
nim.	nimittäin, namely, viz	v.k.	virkaa tekevä, acting (i.e., chief)
N:o or Nº	numero, number	y.m.	ynnä muuta, etc.

Cardinal numbers

yksi	one	kolmetoista, etc.	thirteen, etc.
kaksi	two	kaksikymmentä	twenty
kolme	three	kaksikymmentäyksi	twenty-one
neljä	four	kaksikymmentäkaksi, etc.	twenty-two, etc.
viisi	five		
kuusi	six	kolmekymmentä, etc.	thirty, etc.
seitsemän	seven	sata	hundred
kahdeksan	eight	satayksi, etc.	one hundred and one, etc.
yhdeksän	nine		
kymmenen	ten	kaksisataa	two hundred
yksitoista	eleven	tuhat	thousand
kaksitoista	twelve		

Ordinal numbers

ensimäinen	first	kahdeksas	eighth
toinen	second	yhdeksäs	tninth
kolmas	third	kymmenes	tenth
neljäs	fourth	yhdestoista	eleventh
viides	fifth	kahdestoista	twelfth
kuudes	sixth	kolmastoista, etc.	thirteenth, etc.
seitsemäs	seventh		

Ordinal numbers—Continued

kahdeskymmenes	twentieth	sadasensimmäinen, one hun-
kahdeskymmenesensimmäinen	twenty-first	etc. dred and
kahdeskymmenestoinen, etc.	twenty-	first, etc.
	second, etc.	kahdessadas two hun-
kolmaskymmenes, etc.	thirtieth, etc.	dredth
sadas	hundredth	tuhannes thousandth

Months

tammikuu	January	heinäkuu	July
helmikuu	February	elokuu	August
maaliskuu	March	syyskuu	September
huhtikuu	April	lokakuu	October
toukokuu	May	marraskuu	November
kesäkuu	June	joulukuu	December

Days

sunnuntai	Sunday	torstai	Thursday
maanantai	Monday	perjantai	Friday
tiistai	Tuesday	lauantai	Saturday
keskiviikko	Wednesday		

Seasons

kevät	spring	syksy	autumn
kesä	summer	talvi	winter

Time

tunti	hour	kuukausi	month
päivä	day	vuosi	year
viikko	week		

REFERENCES.—Maija Hellikki Aaltio, Finnish for Foreigners (1964); Vieno Severi Alanne, Finnish-English General Dictionary (1968); John Atkinson, Finnish Grammar (1969); Finnish for Travellers (Editions Berlitz, 1970); Lauri Hakulinen, The Structure and Development of the Finnish Language (1963); Meri K. Lehtinen, Basic Course in Finnish (1964); Aili Rytkönen and Augustus A. Koski, Finnish: Graded Reader (1968); Aino Vuolle, Finnish-English Dictionary (1964).

FRENCH

Maël, issu d'une famille royale de Cambrie, fut envoyé dès sa neuvième année dans l'abbaye d'Yvern, pour y étudier les lettres sacrées et profanes. A l'âge de quatorze ans, il renonça à son héritage et fit vœu de servir le Seigneur.—Anatole France, *L'Île des Pingouins*, chapter 1, opening lines.

Alphabet and pronunciation

A A	a à	}between *a* in pat and *o* in pot
A	â	*a* in hah
B	b	*b*
C	c	*c* in city before *e, i, y* (=*s*); *c* in car, elsewhere (=*k*)
Ç	ç	*c* in city (=*s*)
D	d	*d*
E	e	*e* in met when followed by two consonants, or by a single final consonant, digraph, or consonantal unit; silent when final and in *-ent*, third person plural verb ending; *e* in moment, before a single consonant, digraph, or consonantal unit, followed by a vowel
È	è	*e* in met
Ê	ê	*e* in met or there
Ë	ë	dieresis indicates that preceding vowel has its usual value and does not form a diphthong with *e*
É	é	*a* in late
F	f	*f*
G	g	*s* in pleasure (=*zh*) before *e, i, y; g* in game elsewhere
H	h	silent
I	i	*ee* in meet
Î	î	*ee* in meet
Ï	ï	*y* in yet, between vowels; *ee* in meet elsewhere
J	j	*s* in pleasure (=*zh*)
K	k	*k*
L	l	*l;* silent in a few cases—*gentil, outil, fils;* frequently letters *il* in final position, and after vowel, and *ill* before vowel pronounced like *y* in yet—*travail, fille*
M	m	*m*
N	n	*n;* -ent, third person plural verb ending, is silent
O	o	*o* in no when final; *o* in for elsewhere
Ô	ô	*o* in no
P	p	*p*
Q	q	*q* in quick (=*k*)
R	r	sound made by scraping of air between back of tongue and roof of mouth; silent when final in ending *-er*
S	s	*z* between vowels; usually silent when final; *s* elsewhere
T	t	*t* with few exceptions; usually silent when final.

[Concluded on following page]

U U	u û	like German *ü* (*ee* with lips rounded as for *oo*) in Esaü; usu-
Ú Ü	û ü	ally silent after *g* and *q* before *e*, *i*, *y*
V	v	*v*
W	w	*w* or *v*
X	x	*gz* at beginning of word (Xavier, xylophone) and sometimes between vowels (exister); otherwise *ks*
Y	y	*ee*
Z	z	*z;* usually silent when final

Special characters

French uses the Latin alphabet with the addition of the following special characters: *à, â, ç, é, è, ê, ë, ï, ô, ù, û, ü.*

Vowels and consonants

The vowel letters are *a, e, i, o, u, y;* the other letters are consonants. Vowel sounds are represented by one of the vowel letters or by a combination of two or three of them. Consonant sounds are represented by one or two consonant letters.

Combinations of two vowel letters (diphthongs)

ai, ay, ei, ey as *e* in met or there	*ou, oû, aoû* as *oo* in moon
au, eau as *o* in no	*oui* like English *we*
eu, œ, œu as *u* in fur [1]	*ui* somewhat like English *we*
oi, oy as *wa* in watt	

Combinations of two consonant letters (digraphs)

ch as *sh* in shoe; occasionally as *k*	*ph* as in English
gn as *ny* in canyon	*qu* as *k;* occasionally as *kw*
gu as *g* in give before *e, i, y;* occasionally as *gw*	*rh* as *r*
ll as *y* in yet (in *-ille*)	*th* as *t*

Sequences of vowel(s) and n or m (nasals)

In French, there are four nasal sounds. These are produced by allowing air to pass through the nose and the mouth at the same time, but without any actual sound of *m, n,* or *ng* after them. These sounds are represented by the syllables:

1. *am, an, em, en,* the vowel sound of each being like *a* in far;
2. *aim, ain, eim, ein, im, in, oin, ym, yn,* the vowel sound of each being *a* in sang;
3. *om, on,* with the vowel like *o* in song;
4. *eun, um, un,* with the vowel like *u* in sung.

Nasals occur at the end of a word or in the middle of a word before another consonant except *m* or *n: faim, bien, loin, manger, membre;* otherwise, the above combinations are not nasalized: *ananas* (pronounced *ànànà*), *nommer* (pronounced *nomé*). There are a few exceptions.

Consonantal units

In French, certain consonants followed by *l* or *r* or preceded by *s* are pronounced in the same syllable with the following vowel. These consonant groups are:

bl, br	*fl, fr*	*sc, sp, sph, squ, st*
chl, chr, cl, cr	*gl, gr*	*thr, tr*
dr	*phl, phr, pl, pr*	*vl, vr*

Rules for syllabification

In French, words are divided into syllables according to the following rules:

(1) *A consonant between two vowels commences a new syllable:*
ca-pi-tal, ca-pi-ta-li-sa-ble, ca-pi-ta-li-ser, ca-pi-ta-lis-me, ca-pi-ta-lis-te, mo-no-mé-tal-lis-te, li-bé-ra-toi-re, dé-sap-pro-vi-si-on-ne-ment, a-rith-mé-ti-que-ment,

---

[1] Note that *œ* is printed as a single piece of type when it has this pronunciation, and also in some words of Latin origin, where it is pronounced as French *e*. When *o* and *e* are printed separately, they represent separate sounds in different syllables.

an-tis-ta-tu-tai-re-ment, pri-vi-lè-ge, su-bor-don-né, su-res-ta-ries, é-ti-que-ta-ge, e-xa-mi-na-teur, e-xer-ci-ce, e-xis-ten-ce, e-xo-né-rer, i-ne-xac-te-ment, in-de-xa-ti-on, i-nu-ti-le, u-ne, u-na-ni-me-ment, vi-gueur, vi-gou-reux, vi-gou-reu-se, paie-ment, pa-ral-lé-lé-pi-pé-di-que.

(2) *Two adjoining consonants (except rule 4 digraphs) between two vowels sepa-rate into two syllables:*

ac-com-mo-der, ac-quit-te-ment, at-ter-ris-sa-ge, bail-le-res-se, chan-geant, chan-gean-te, con-cur-ren-ti-el-le, cor-res-pon-dan-ce, des-cen-dre, ex-cep-ti-on-nel-le-ment, ex-pé-di-ti-on-nai-re, in-na-vi-ga-ble, in-te-ro-cé-a-ni-que, in-ter-val-le, ir-res-pon-sa-bi-li-té, os-cil-ler, ras-seoir, re-con-nais-san-ce, res-ti-tu-er, sub-di-vi-ser, sur-taux, veil-le.

(3) *A vowel can only begin a syllable, other than an initial syllable, when preceded by another vowel:*

a-é-ro-pla-ne, a-gré-er, an-ci-en, ar-ri-è-re, bé-né-fi-ci-ai-re, ca-mi-on, ca-out-chouc, co-as-so-ci-é, co-ef-fi-ci-ent, co-ïn-ci-der, dé-pou-il-le-ment, ex-tra-or-di-nai-re, feu-il-le, in-né-go-ci-a-ble, li-er, mi-eux, na-ti-on, ou-est, ré-é-va-lu-er, ré-u-ni-on, ro-yau-me, vic-tu-ail-les, vi-e-il-lir, vi-eux, voi-li-er, vo-ya-ge.

(4) *The following digraph consonants are inseparable:*

bl: câ-blo-gram-me, chan-gea-ble, o-bli-té-rer, pu-bli-que. *Exception:* sub-lu-nai-re.

br: dé-brou-il-ler, li-bre, su-bré-car-gue. *Exception:* sub-ro-ger *and derivatives.*

ch: dis-pa-cheur, é-chan-til-lon, é-chauf-fer, gui-chet, re-cher-che.

cl: ac-cla-mer, ac-cli-ma-ter, é-clai-ra-ge, é-clu-se, ex-clu-sif.

cr: des-crip-ti-ve, é-cri-tu-re, ma-nus-crit, pres-cri-re, sous-cri-re.

dh: ré-dhi-bi-toi-re.

dr: a-dres-ser, cor-res-pon-dre, en-tre-pren-dre, or-dre.

fl: af-flux, ef-fleu-rer, in-fla-ti-on, in-flu-ent.

fr: af-fran-chir, en-cof-frer, in-dé-chif-fra-ble, ré-af-frè-te-ment, re-frap-pa-ge.

gl: ag-glo-mé-rer, a-veu-gle, é-tran-gle-ment, né-gli-gen-ce, rè-gle-ment.

gn: com-pa-gnie, é-par-gnant, ren-sei-gne-ment, si-gnal, vi-gnet-te.

gr: ag-gra-va-ti-on, dé-gros-sir, dé-ni-grer, in-té-gral, re-gret.

ph: chi-ro-gra-phai-re, dac-ty-lo-gra-phi-er, té-lé-pho-ne, u-ni-gra-phi-que.

pl: ac-com-plis-se-ment, ap-pli-ca-ti-on, com-plè-te-ment, ex-ploit.

pr: an-ti-pro-tec-ti-on-nis-te, ap-pren-dre, ex-pri-mer, pro-pri-é-té.

rh: ar-rhe-ment, ar-rhes, bi-blo-rhapt, e-nar-rher, trans-rhé-na-ne.

th: au-then-ti-que, dés-hy-po-thé-quer, hy-po-thé-cai-re, mé-tho-de.

tr: ad-mi-nis-tra-tif, cen-tre, co-di-rec-tri-ce, con-tre-si-gner, con-tres-ta-ries, il-lus-trée.

vr: a-vril, li-vrai-son, li-vre, ma-nœu-vrer, ou-vri-er.

(5) (*a*) ns, bs, *and* rs *are separable if followed by a vowel:*

con-sa-crer, con-seil-la-ble, con-si-dé-rer, in-sé-rer, in-sol-va-ble, in-suf-fi-sant, tran-sac-ti-on, tran-sat-lan-ti-que, tran-si-ter; ab-sor-ber, ob-ser-ver; per-su-a-der.

(*b*) ns, bs, *and* rs *are inseparable if followed by a consonant:*

cons-pi-rer, cons-ta-ter, cons-ti-tu-er, ins-pec-ter, ins-tal-ler, trans-cen-dant, trans-fè-re-ment, trans-port; no-nobs-tant, obs-ta-cles, subs-tan-ce; in-ters-ti-ce, pers-pec-ti-ve.

(*c*) ns *and* bs *are inseparable if followed by a consonant coupled with* r:

cons-trui-re, ins-cri-re, trans-cri-re, trans-gres-ser; abs-trac-ti-on, obs-truc-ti-on.

(*d*) ns *and* bs *are separable before* ci:

con-sci-en-ci-eux, in-sci-em-ment; ab-scis-se.

(6) (*a*) mp *and* nc *followed by* t *are inseparable:*

a-compt-te, comp-ta-ble, es-comp-ter, pré-emp-ti-on; fonc-ti-on, sanc-ti-on.

(*b*) *In all other combinations* mp *and* nc *are separable:*

em-plo-yer, em-prun-ter, im-por-tant; a-van-cer, fran-çais, fran-che, fran-co.

(7) *In writing or in print no syllable is separable which does not include a vowel;* thus, trigraph consonants are inseparable initially: scru-tin, but separable medially: ins-cru-ta-ble.

8. Foreign words and components of foreign words (not naturalized) follow the conventions of the language of origin: *alpen-stock, reichs-amt, cre-scendo, sky-scraper, Wash-ington.* Under this rule are also included scientific and technical words, which editors prefer to treat etymologically: *dia-gnostique, hémi-sphère, hémo-ptysies.*

Some of the small syllables, especially initial vowel uniliterals and final biliterals beginning with a vowel, are not usually separated from the body of the word in writing or print, but they are of importance in the pronunciation; thus, émission is pronounced *é-mi-si-on*, but the written or printed word is ordinarily only divided émis- *(end of line)* sion, not é- *(end of line)* mission, nor émissi- *(end of line)* on, though d'é- *(end of line)* mission, l'é- *(end of line)* mission, are better than d' *(end of line)* émission, l' *(end of line)* émission.

Divisions of words at the ends of lines should, of course, be avoided as far as possible, and not be carried to extremes.

Illustrative word divisions

[The numbers in parentheses refer to the syllabification rules]

ab-so-lu-ment	(2, 1, 1)	i-nex-pu-gna-ble	(1, 2, 4, 4)
abs-trac-ti-on	(4, 2, 3)	ins-pi-ra-tion	(5, 1, 1, 3)
ad-mi-nis-tra-ti-on	(2, 1, 4, 1, 3)	ins-tan-ta-née	(5, 2, 1)
a-mé-ri-cai-nes	(1, 1, 1, 1)	ins-truc-ti-on	(5, 2, 3)
an-ti-scor-bu-ti-que	(2, 2, 2, 1, 1)	in-tro-duc-ti-on	(4, 1, 2, 3)
at-mos-phé-ri-que	(2, 4, 1, 1)	Ja-ma-ï-que	(1, 3, 1)
au-to-gno-sie	(1, 4, 1)	Kam-tchat-ka	(8, 2)
bi-blio-thè-que	(4, 4, 1)	ki-lo-mé-tri-que	(1, 1, 4, 1)
bi-en-heu-reux	(3, 2, 1)	ma-la-droi-te-ment	(1, 4, 1, 1)
ca-out-chou-ter	(3, 4, 1)	ma-nus-crits	(1, 4)
cir-cons-tan-ces	(2, 5, 2)	mi-cro-sco-pi-que	(4, 2, 1, 1)
com-pri-ma-ble	(4, 1, 1)	non-ac-ti-vi-té	(1, 2, 1, 1)
cons-cien-cieu-se-ment	(5, 2, 1, 1)	no-nobs-tant	(1, 5)
cons-ti-tu-ti-on-nel	(5, 1, 1, 3, 2)	ob-jec-ti-vi-té	(2, 2, 1, 1)
des-cen-dant	(2, 2)	obli-ga-ti-on	(1, 1, 3)
des-crip-ti-on	(4, 2)	obs-cu-ri-té	(5, 1, 1)
dia-gnos-ti-quer	(4, 2, 1)	per-cep-ti-ble	(2, 2, 4)
dis-ci-pli-ner	(2, 4, 1)	pé-remp-ti-on	(1, 6, 3)
en-tr'ac-cor-der	(4, 2, 2)	pré-oc-cu-pa-ti-on	(3, 2, 1, 1, 3)
e-xé-cu-ti-ves	(1, 1, 1, 1)	pro-blè-mes	(4, 1)
ex-haus-se-ment	(2, 2, 1)	pro-pre-ment	(4, 1)
e-xo-cel-lu-lai-res	(1, 1, 2, 1, 1)	pros-crip-ti-on	(7, 2, 3)
ex-tra-or-di-nai-res	(4, 3, 2, 1, 1)	pros-pé-ri-té	(2, 1, 1)
gym-no-sper-mes	(2, 2, 2)	sub-cons-ci-en-ce	(2, 7, 3, 2)
hé-té-ro-do-xie	(1, 1, 1, 1)	su-bor-don-ner	(1, 2, 2)
hy-dro-sco-pie	(2, 2, 1)	sub-ro-ger	(4)
ig-ni-ti-on	(2, 1, 3)	subs-tan-ti-el	(7, 2, 3)

Stress and diacritics

In French, words do not have any syllabic stress, each syllable being uttered with almost equal force with a slight stress falling on the last.

The diacritics used in French are the acute, the circumflex, the grave, the dieresis (trema), and the cedilla.

The circumflex occurs on the vowels. It may indicate that an *s* followed the vowel in Old French, as in *île* from *isle*, island, and *pâté* from *paste*, paste; it may distinguish homonyms like *dû* (due) and *du* (of the); *â, ê, ô* may represent vowels longer than those spelled *a, e, o,* as in *âne, bête, môle.*

The acute accent occurs only on the *e; é* represents a close *e* sound, more like the *a* in late than the *e* in met. It will be found on an *e* followed by a single consonant or digraph or consonantal unit, followed by a vowel as in *érable, église, étrenne.* It will not be on an *e* followed by two consonants (i. e., two consonants which do not form a digraph or consonantal unit), as in *esclaves, elbeuf.* The letter *é* is common at the end of words (*été, passé*), and frequently initially, and medially as well, under the conditions already stated.

The grave accent occurs on *a, e,* and *u.* One of its functions is to distinguish homonyms: *a* (has) and *à* (to); *des* (of the) and *dès* (since); *ou* (or) and *où* (where). Far more frequent is the occurrence of *è,* indicating an open *e* sound, more like the *e* in met than the *a* in late. It occurs in one-syllable words in which mute *e* is the last letter, and a single consonant or digraph, or consonantal unit, is the next-to-last letter, as *ère, lèvre, sèche;* in word-final syllables like *-ère, -ière, -ègre, -èbre, -èvre, -èdre, -ères, -ières, -ègres,* etc.; occasionally, in a word ending in *es,* to indicate that the *e* is not silent, as in *progrès, succès.*

The dieresis occurs on the second of two consecutive vowel letters to indicate that the sequence does not have its usual value.

ai as *e* in met (*plaisir*)
ei as *e* in met (*reine*)
oi as *wa* in watt (*toi*)
œ as *u* in fur (*œil*)
gue as *g* in go plus mute *e* in vague
gui as *g* in go plus *ee* as in meet
  (*guide*); sometimes *g* as in go plus
  we as in we (*aiguille*)
aï as *a* in watt plus *ee* as in meet
  (*naïf*)

eï as *e* in met plus *ee* as in meet
oï as *o* in for plus *ee* as in meet
  (*colloïde*)
oë as *o* in for plus *a* as in late (*canoë*);
  as *o* in for plus *e* as in met (*noël*)
guë as *g* in go plus *u* as in German *ü*
  plus mute *e* (*aiguë*)
guï as *g* in go plus *u* as in German *ü*
  plus *ee* as in meet (*contiguïté*)

The cedilla occurs under the letter *c* before *a*, *o*, or *u*, to indicate that *c* is pronounced like *s*; *reçu*, received.

Capitalization

1. Capitalize the first word of sentences, phrases, verses, speeches, citations: *Un homme dit: "Je passerai la mer . . . ."*
2. After interrogation, exclamation, and suspension points when they end the sentence.
3. In proper names in general: *Jeanne, la France, la Seine.*
   a. The names designating God, the three holy persons, Jesus Christ: *Le Créateur, la Providence, le Messie, le Tout-Puissant.*
   b. The names of mythological divinities and abstractions personified by poetry or mythology, as well as the names of stars, constellations, and planets: *Jupiter, les Furies, Sirius, le Cygne.*
   c. The proper names of people, families, and dynasties: *Les Français, les Bourbons;* but *l'Etat allemand, le drapeau français.*
4. The names of holidays: *La Toussaint, à Noël:* but not the names of days or months.
5. The names that have become proper names: *L'Orateur romain* (Cicero), *la Vierge* (Virgin Mary).
6. The proper names of scholarly, political, and religious organizations, or orders of chivalry: *L'Eglise, l'Institut de France, la Chambre de représentants, l'Université catholique de Paris, l'Ordre de la Couronne.*
7. Ordinarily the cardinal points when they are used absolutely, as in: *Les peuples de l'Orient;* otherwise the lowercase is used.
8. The proper names of streets, monuments, buildings, ships, etc.: *La rue des Tuileries, le Parthénon, le Titanic.*
9. The titles of books, poems, pictures, works of art, etc.
10. Titles, such as: *Sa Majesté, Son Excellence,* when addressing the person himself.
    a. Nous, Vous, etc., in encyclicals, pastoral letters, etc.
    b. Historical events: *La Renaissance, la Révolution.*
11. The adjective is capitalized when it is intimately connected with the proper name: *Etats-Unis, la Comédie-Française, Charles le Téméraire.*
    a. When it precedes the name: *Le Saint-Office, la Sainte-Alliance.*
    b. When it accompanies a geographic term: *La mer Méditerranée.*

Punctuation and hyphenation

The period indicates the end of the sentence. It is used sometimes to give greater emphasis to a subordinate clause.
The interrogation point is used in general as in English; an indirect interrogation is never followed by an interrogation point. When an interrogative phrase is followed by an insertion, the interrogation point is placed immediately after that phrase, the sentence continuing in lower case.
The exclamation point is placed directly after the exclamation; the interjection *ô* is never used by itself, as in *O regret!*, and the exclamation point is placed after the complete exclamation.
The comma marks a brief pause. In spelled out figures the decimal part is separated from the main part by a comma (instead of a period, as in English). It must be used after the place in the date: *Paris, le 4 juin . . . .*
The comma follows salutations, such as: *Ma chère Marie, ...*
It is used before *et, ou,* or *ni* when coordinating more than two elements, such as: *Un bon financier, dit . . ., ne pleure ni ses amis, ni sa femme, ni ses enfants.*
The semicolon marks a medium long pause.
The colon is used as in English.
The suspension points are used as in English.
The quotation marks in French are written: ≪ ≫. However, *Le Grand Larousse,* in the preface to its 1960–64 edition, uses the English version: " ".
The punctuation is usually placed at the end of the quote, if the citation is a

complete phrase, as in: *Je répondis:* «*J'attends le départ.*» Otherwise " precede the punctuation, as in: *Quel homme, que ce* «*Père la Victoire*»!

The apostrophe is used to mark the omission of *a, e, i*, as in: *l'arme, d'abord, s'il vous plaît.*

The hyphen is used much more widely than in English, and care should be exercised not to mistake the marginal hyphen in copy used orthographically as one of syllabification. The various orthographic uses of the hyphen are as follows:

1. Between verbs and the pronouns in questions: *Parlez-vous?* Do you speak?
2. Between verbs and object pronouns: *Parlez-moi*, speak to me.
3. Between verbs and the participles *en, y, ce, on: Portez-leur-en*, bring them some.
4. Between the personal pronoun and the adjective *même, moi-même*, myself.
5. On each side of the euphonic *t: A-t-il?* Has he? *Parlera-t-elle?* Will she speak?
6. Before *ci* and *là: celui-ci;* and in certain expressions after *ci* and *là*, as in *ces choses là-dessus.*
7. After *entre* in all reciprocal verbs: *s'entre-tuer*, to kill one another.
8. Between *demi* and its noun: *une demi-heure*, half an hour.
9. In compound nouns and adjectives, especially with prepositional particles, as in *arc-en-ciel*, rainbow; *nouveau-né*, newborn.
10. In spelled numbers (see p. 446).
11. Between first names: *Louis-Charles-Alfred de Musset.*
12. Between the word *Saint* and the following name, when used to designate a locality, a feast-day, a street, an era, etc., but not when it concerns the Saint himself: *la rue Saint-Jacques, La Saint-Nicolas.*
13. In geographic names: *Saint-Valéry-en-Caux*, etc.
14. In certain invariable phrases: *Pêle-mêle, avant-hier*, etc.

Abbreviations

a.	accepté, accepted	R.F.	République française, French Republic
a.c.	année courante, current year		
art.	article, article	R.S.V.P.,	répondez, s'il vous plaît,
av.	avec, with	or	please answer
B.B.	billet de bank, bank note	r.s.v.p.	
c (c⁰⁵)	centime(s), centime(s)	S.A.R.	Son Altesse Royale, His Royal Highness
c.à-d.	c'est-à-dire, that is (i.e.)		
ch.	chapitre, chapter	S.E.	Son Excellence, His Excellency
ch. de f.	chemin de fer, railway		
Cie, Cⁱᵉ	compagnie, company	S.E.O.	sauf erreur ou omission, error or omission excepted
C.V.	cheval vapeur, H.P.		
C., c., cᵗᵉ	compte, account	S.M.	Sa Majesté, His Majesty
f., fr.(s)	franc, franc(s)	S.A.,	Société anonyme, similar
h.	heure, hour	Soc.	to limited liability com-
J.-C.	Jésus-Christ, Jesus Christ	anᵉ	pany
M., MM.	Monsieur, Messieurs, Mr., Messrs.	S.S.	Sa Sainteté, His Holiness
		s.v.p.	s'il vous plaît, please
Mᵐᵉ	Madame, Mrs.	t., T.	tome, book
Mⁱˡᵉ	Mademoiselle, Miss	tít.	títre, title
Mgr	monseigneur, my lord	t.s.v.p.	tournez, s'il vous plaît, please turn
N.-D.	Notre Dame, Our Lady		
N.D.L.R.	note de la rédaction, editor's note.	voy., v.	voyez, voir, see
		Vᵛᵉ	veuve, widow
p.ex.	par exemple, for example	1ᵉʳ	premier *(m.)*, first
p.f.s.a.	pour faire ses adieux, to say goodby	1ᵉʳᵉ	première *(f.)*, first
		IIᵉ, 2ᵉ	deuxième, second

Abbreviations of metric terms

Mm	mégamètre	mm³	millimètre cube	g	gramme
hkm	hectokilomètre	ha	hectare	dg	décigramme
mam	myriamètre	a	are	cg	centigramme
km	kilomètre	ca	centiare	mg	milligramme
hm	hectomètre	dast	décastère	kl	kilolitre
dam	décamètre	st	stère	hl	hectolitre
m	mètre	dst	décistère	dal	décalitre
dm	décimètre	t	tonne	l	litre
cm	centimètre	q	quintal	dl	décilitre
m²	mètre carré	kg	kilogramme	cl	centilitre
mm	millimètre	hg	hectogramme	ml	millilitre
mm²	millimètre carré	dag	décagramme		

NOTE.—It will be noted that the period is not used where the last letter in the abbreviation is the last letter of the complete word.

Cardinal numbers

un, *m.*} une, *f.*}	one	soixante et onze	seventy-one
deux	two	soixante-douze	seventy-two
trois	three	soixante-treize	seventy-three
quatre	four	soixante-quatorze	seventy-four
cinq	five	soixante-quinze	seventy-five
six	six	soixante-seize	seventy-six
sept	seven	soixante-dix-sept	seventy-seven
huit	eight	soixante-dix-huit	seventy-eight
neuf	nine	soixante-dix-neuf	seventy-nine
dix	ten	quatre-vingts	eighty
onze	eleven	quatre-vingt-un	eighty-one
douze	twelve	quatre-vingt-deux	eighty-two
treize	thirteen	quatre-vingt-trois	eighty-three
quatorze	fourteen	quatre-vingt-quatre	eighty-four
quinze	fifteen	quatre-vingt-cinq	eighty-five
seize	sixteen	quatre-vingt-six, etc.	eighty-six, etc.
dix-sept	seventeen	quatre-vingt-dix	ninety
dix-huit	eighteen	quatre-vingt-onze, etc.	ninety-one, etc.
dix-neuf	nineteen	quatre-vingt-dix-sept	ninety-seven
vingt	twenty	quatre-vingt-dix-huit	ninety-eight
vingt et un	twenty-one	quatre-vingt-dix-neuf	ninety-nine
vingt-deux, etc.	twenty-two, etc.	cent	hundred
trente	thirty	cent un, etc.	one hundred and one, etc.
trente et un	thirty-one		
trente-deux, etc.	thirty-two, etc.	deux cents, etc.	two hundred, etc.
quarante	forty	mille (mil)	thousand
cinquante	fifty	million	million
soixante	sixty	milliard	billion
soixante-dix	seventy		

Ordinal numbers

premier, *m.*} première, *f.*}	first	septième	seventh
second, *m.;* seconde, *f.*} deuxième	second	huitième	eighth
		neuvième	ninth
		dixième	tenth
troisième	third	onzième, etc.	eleventh, etc.
quatrième	fourth	vingt et unième	twenty-first
cinquième	fifth	vingt-deuxième, etc.	twenty-second, etc.
sixième	sixth	centième	hundredth

Months

janvier (janv.)	January	juillet (juil.)	July
février (fév.)	February	août	August
mars	March	septembre (sept.)	September
avril (av.)	April	octobre (oct.)	October
mai	May	novembre (nov.)	November
juin	June	décembre (déc.)	December

Days

dimanche	Sunday	jeudi	Thursday
lundi	Monday	vendredi	Friday
mardi	Tuesday	samedi	Saturday
mercredi	Wednesday		

Seasons

printemps	spring	automne	autumn
été	summer	hiver	winter

Time

seconde	second	semaine	week
minute	minute	mois	month
demi-heure	half an hour	année	year
heure	hour	saison	season
jour	day		

Sets of figures, separated in English by commas, in French are separated either by spaces, as in: 1 005; 1 000 000, or by periods as in: 1.005; 1.000.000. Percentages printed in English in lowercase are in French frequently printed in uppercase: 2 1/2 0/0.

Authors and their works are cited in the text as follows: first name (mostly by initial), last name in caps; followed by a comma, then the name of the work in italics, followed by a comma, then volume in Roman numerals, followed by a comma, then the page: p. 211, for example. If the source is a newspaper or a periodical, the name of the author appears, as above, followed by *dans* (in) *le Temps* (a newspaper), or the name of the periodical, followed by a comma and the date, as in: *7 août 1962*, followed by a comma, then p. . . .. The source appears in parentheses, and, followed if cited at the end of a sentence, by a period. Sometimes *t.* (volume) precedes the volume, and *ch.* (chapter), the chapter referred to.

REFERENCES.—Le Grand Larousse (1960–64); Maurice Grevisse, Le bon usage (8th ed.) (1964); Kettridge's Commercial and Financial Dictionary (1957); Francis M. duMont, French Grammar (College Outline Series) (Barnes & Noble); Larousse, Dictionnaire moderne français-anglais/anglais-français (1960).

GERMAN

Wenn aber auch der Charakter verschiedener Weltgegenden von allen äußeren Erscheinungen zugleich abhängt; wenn Umriß der Gebirge, Physiognomie der Pflanzen und Tiere, wenn Himmelsbläue, Wolkengestalt und Durchsichtigkeit des Luftkreises den Totaleindruck bewirken; so ist doch nicht zu leugnen, daß das Hauptbestimmende dieses Eindrucks die Pflanzendecke ist. Dem tierischen Organismus fehlt es an Masse; die Beweglichkeit der Individuen und oft ihre Kleinheit entziehen sie unseren Blicken. Die Pflanzenschöpfung dagegen wirkt durch stetige Größe auf unsere Einbildungskraft.— Alexander von Humboldt, *Ansichten der Natur*, vol. II, p. 20 f. (1849).

Alphabet and pronunciation [1]

A	a	short: *a* like *u* in cup; long: *a* in father
Ä	ä	short: *e* in bet; long: *e* in there or *a* in bad
B	b	*b;* at end of word or syllable, bulb or as *p* in lip
C	c	before *e, i, ä* and usually *y*, as *ts* in bits; before other vowels, as *c* in can (=*k*)
D	d	*d;* at end of word or syllable, as *t* in hit
E	e	short: *e* in bet; long: somewhat like *a* in gate; in unstressed syllables, like *e* in aspen
F	f	*f*
G	g	*g;* at end of word after *e, ei,* and *i,* many Germans pronounce *g* like German *ch* (see under consonant sequences)
H	h	*h;* at end of word or syllable or before consonant, merely shows that preceding vowel is long; between vowels *h* has the effect of a dieresis
I	i	short: *i* in bit; long: *ee* in meet
J	j	*y* in yes
K	k	*k*
L	l	*l* in let
M	m	*m*
N	n	*n*
O	o	short: between *o* in not and *u* in nut; long: *o* in tone
Ö	ö	short: as in French neuf; (as in fur) long (tongue in long *e* position, lips in long *o* position): *u* in hurt or *eu* in fur
P	p	*p;* after initial *s*, as *p* in spin
Q	q	*k; qu* pronounced as *kv*
R	r	*r* in three or parade; at end of word or syllable, usually as in alter
S	s	before vowel, as *z* in zoo or *s* in rose; at end of word, as *s* in miss; before *p* or *t* at beginning of word, as *sh* in ship

[Concluded on following page]

---

[1] All German vowels are pronounced short or long. German spelling does not consistently indicate vowel quantity, but two dependable conversion rules may be mentioned. A double vowel and a vowel followed by a single consonant are pronounced long; a single vowel followed by a double consonant is pronounced short. Consonant quantity is fairly stable; a double consonant does not indicate a lengthened sound.

T	t	*t;* after initial *s,* as *t* in stop
U	u	short: *oo* in cook; long: *oo* in boot
Ü	ü	short: tongue in short *u* position, lips in short *i* position; long (tongue in long *u* position, lips in long *i* position): *u* in French du
V	v	*v* or *f* at beginning of words, *f* at beginning and end of words; elsewhere usually *v*
W	w	*v*
X	x	*x* (=*ks*)
Y	y	short and long: as German *i* or German *ü; occasionally (before vowel) as *y* in yet
Z	z	*ts* in bits

Special characters

German used to be set, traditionally, in the Fraktur alphabet (German text). It was abolished for official publications in 1941 and is virtually no longer used. For information on Fraktur, see earlier editions of this Manual. The Latin alphabet, which is now generally used, has, however, retained the following special characters, called umlauts: Ä ä, Ö ö, and Ü ü.

The Fraktur alphabet employed four ligatures: ch (*ch*), ck (*ck*), ß (ß, *ss*), and tz (*tz*). However, German style when using a Latin alaphabet has retained the following usages: In syllabification, tz may be divided, ch and ß may never be divided, and ck, if division is called for, must be changed to k-k. This is because the character c may never end a word or a syllable and, hence, may not terminate a line.

When German is set in Latin characters, the only ligature employed is ß; the other ligatures are represented by their respective individual characters. When ß is not available, it may be replaced by *ss*.

Vowels and consonants

The vowels are *a, e, i, o, u,* and *y* (including the umlauts *ä, ö,* and *ü*). The other letters of the alphabet are consonants.

Vowel sequences (diphthongs)

The diphthongs and their sounds are:

aa as German long *a*	*ie* as German long *i*
ai as *ai* in aisle	*oo* as German long *o*
au as *ou* in our	*oe* as German long *o* in some proper
äu as *oi* in noise	names (as distinguished from *oe* for
ee as German long *e*	the umlaut *ö*)
ei as *ai* in aisle	*oi* as German long *o* in some proper
eu as *oi* in noise	names

To the *ie* there are a few exceptions, as in a few words *ie* is not a diphthong but the two letters are sounded separately, as *ee-uh.* These exceptions occur usually at the end of words of foreign origin, the *ie* being equivalent to the Latin *ia: Linie, Materie,* etc.

To the above diphthongs should be added also *ae, oe,* and *ue,* which are sometimes used in place of *ä, ö,* and *ü,* respectively, and are sounded as *ä, ö, ü.*

Consonant sequences (digraphs)

The digraphs and their sounds are:

ph as English *ph*=*f*   *th* as *t*
sch as *sh* in shall

The sound for *ch* may be approximated by making a strong *h* sound. In words some, *ch* is pronounced like *k*. The digraph *sch* must be distinguished from the mere coincidental juxtaposition of those letters, pronounced like *s* and *ch* separately: *biß-chen*, little bit; *Fäß-chen*, little barrel; *Häus-chen* little house.

Consonantal units

The combinations *qu* (pronounced *kv*), *st*, and *ß* are treated as consonantal units. Some editors treat *pf* as a consonantal unit, especially after another consonant; but this is not favored by Duden, Rechtschreibung der deutschen Sprache, which divides *kämp-fen*, *Karp-fen*, *rup-fen* as indicated. The rule is that *pf* is separated when followed by a vowel.

When *ß* is replaced by *ss*, *ss* is never divided.

Rules for syllabification

1. Diphthongs, digraphs, and consonantal units may not be divided with the exception of *ng*.

2. Division is made on a vowel or on a diphthong before a single consonant, a digraph, or a consonantal unit: *le-ben*, *lie-ben*, *wa-chen*, *wa-schen*, *Mei-ster*, *gro-ßen*, *Re-qui-sit*.

3. In a group of two or more consonants, division is made before the last consonant, digraph, or consonantal unit: *Mut-ter*, *Was-ser*, *stimm-ten*, *kämp-fen*, *wün-schen*, *Fen-ster*, *Pfing-sten*.

4. Division may be made between two vowels not constituting a diphthong or between a diphthong and a vowel: *Oze-an*, *Trau-ung*.

5. Certain adverbial prefixes are kept intact. These are: *ab*, *an*, *auf*, *aus*, *be*, *bei*, *durch*, *ein*, *emp*, *ent*, *er*, *fort*, *ge*, *her*, *hin*, *hinter*, *in*, *miß*, *mit*, *nach*, *nieder*, *ob*, *um*, *un*, *unter*, *ver*, *vor*, *weg*, *wider*, *wieder*, *zer*, *zu*, *zurück*, and *zusammen*: *ab-ändern*, *An-erbe*, *auf-arbeiten*, etc.

6. Certain suffixes are kept intact. These are: *artig*, *chen*, *haft*, *heit*, *schaft*, and *tum*: *eigen-artig*, *Hühn-chen*, *Knapp-heit*, *Wachs-tum*.

7. Compound words are divided according to their component parts (and each part according to rules 1 to 6): *alt-italienisch*, *Tür-angel*. The compounding *r* and *s*, if used, are kept with the preceding component: *dar-auf*, *wor-auf*, *Redens-art*, *Orts-angabe*.

8. Foreign words and components of foreign words follow the conventions of the language of origin: *Repu-blik*, *Hy-drant*, *Wash-ington*, *Shake-speare*. Under this rule are also included scientific and technical words, which editors prefer to treat etymologically: *Dia-gnose*, *Mikro-skop*.

9. When division is made on or before a syllable from which a letter was elided, the letter is restored to render the syllable integral: *glitschst* is divided *glit-schest*, *Luftschiffahrt* is divided *Luftschiff-fahrt*; and when the double consonant *ck* is divided, the *c* is changed to *k*, thus *Hacke* and *Zucker* are divided *Hak-ke* and *Zuk-ker*. It is important to bear in mind that words divided under this rule, if subsequently reset and run over, must have their original spelling restored.

10. No division should be made that results in a single letter being separated or a syllable of two letters occupying the second line. Wrong: *O-zean*, *koch-te*.

11. When, in a compound word, the first word ends with *s* and the second begins with *t*, the *st* rule does not apply: *Reichs-tag* not *Reich-stag*.

12. No division is permitted that affects the meaning adversely: *Spar-gelder* not *Spargel-der*; *Ur-instinkt* not *Urin-stinkt*.

Illustrative word divisions

[The numbers in parentheses refer to the syllabification rules]

Ab-gren-zung	(5, 2)	Nach-ord-nung	(5, 3)
ame-ri-ka-ni-sche	(2, 2, 2, 2)	ne-ben-an	(2, 7)
Amts-an-tritt	(7, 5)	nie-der-bre-chen	(2, 5, 2)
an-ord-nen	(5, 3)	nied-rig-ste	(3, 3)
Auf-pflan-zung	(5, 3)	Ober-stabs-arzt	(7, 7)
Aus-zah-lung	(5, 3)	Ob-lie-gen-heit	(5, 2, 3)
bei-tra-gen	(5, 2)	ord-nungs-mä-ßig	(3, 7, 2)
Be-ob-ach-tung	(5, 5, 3)	Orts-an-ga-be	(7, 5, 2)
Be-quem-lich-keit	(2, 3, 3)	öster-rei-chi-sche	(7, 2, 2)
bläs-chen-för-mige	(3, 7, 3, 2, 1)	ost-in-di-sche	(7, 3, 2)
dar-ein-schla-gen	(7, 5, 2)	pas-sie-ren	(3, 2)
deut-sche	(2)	pflicht-schul-dig	(7, 3)
Deutsch-land	(7)	Plan-wirt-schaft	(7, 6)
Dienst-al-ter	(7, 3)	Platz-an-wei-sung	(7, 5, 2)
durch-ar-bei-ten	(5, 3, 2)	plat-zen-de	(3, 3)
ein-spre-chen	(5, 2)	Rat-haus-saal	(7, 7)
emp-fäng-lich	(5, 3)	Rich-ter-amt	(3, 3)
eng-li-sche	(3, 2)	recht-fer-ti-gen	(7, 3, 2)
ent-spre-chen	(5, 2)	Rechts-ge-schich-te	(7, 2, 3)
er-schreck-lich	(5, 3)	re-pu-bli-ka-nisch	(2, 8, 2, 2)
eu-ro-pä-i-sche	(2, 2, 4, 2)	Sach-ver-zeich-nis	(7, 5, 3)
Far-ben-auf-trag	(3, 7, 5)	schwei-ze-ri-sche	(2, 2, 2)
Fin-ster-nis	(3, 3)	Selbst-ach-tung	(7, 3)
fort-ar-bei-ten	(5, 3, 2)	Selb-stän-dig-keit	(7, 3, 3)
fünf-und-zwan-zig	(7, 7, 3)	sy-ste-ma-ti-sche	(2, 2, 2, 2)
ge-brau-chen	(5, 2)	über-ein-kom-men	(5, 5, 3)
her-aus-zie-hen	(5, 5, 2)	um-än-dern	(5, 3)
hin-ar-bei-ten	(5, 3, 2)	un-ab-hän-gig	(5, 5, 3)
hin-ter-brin-gen	(3, 5, 3, 11)	Un-ter-ab-tei-lung	(3, 5, 5, 2)
In-an-spruch-nahme	(5, 5, 7, 3)	ver-ei-nig-te	(5, 2, 3)
in-ein-an-der	(5, 5, 3)	Vor-an-schlag	(5, 5)
In-ter-esse	(3, 8, 3, 10)	weg-schlei-chen	(5, 2)
Jah-res-tag	(3, 7)	Werk-ar-beit	(7, 3)
Ka-me-ra-den	(2, 2, 2)	wi-der-spre-chen	(2, 5, 2)
Leb-haf-tig-keit	(3, 3, 3)	Wie-der-ab-druck	(2, 5, 5)
Maß-sy-stem	(7, 2)	Wirt-schaf-ter	(6, 3)
me-di-zi-ni-sche	(2, 2, 2, 2)	zer-split-tern	(5, 3)
Miß-er-folg	(5, 3)	zu-dre-hen	(5, 2)
mit-hel-fen	(5, 3)	zu-rück-er-o-bern	(2, 5, 5, 2)
mitt-le-rer	(3, 2)	zu-sam-men-flie-ßen	(2, 3, 5, 2)

Diacritics and stress

Other than the umlauts, no diacritical marks are used in German. The chief stress falls on the root syllable in simple words (*SINGen*, to sing), and on the leading component, usually the first, in compound words (*FESTland*, mainland). Words of foreign origin have their own characteristic stress.

Capitalization

With the exception of the following, capitalization conventions are the same as in English:

1. All nouns and words used as nouns are capitalized:[1] *das Geben*, the giving; *die Armen*, the poor.

2. Proper adjectives are lowercased: *die deutsche Sprache*, the German language.

3. Adjectives derived from personal names are capitalized: *die Lutherische Übersetzung*, Luther's translation; but when used descriptively, lowercased: *die lutherische Kirche*, the Lutheran Church; *ciceronische Beredsamkeit*, Ciceronic eloquence.

4. The pronouns *Sie*, you, *Ihr*, your, and *Ihnen*, to you, are capitalized, but not *ich*, I. The pronouns *Du*, you, *Dein*, your, and their various forms are capitalized in correspondence.

In solid matter, where the umlaut on capital letters is likely to cause trouble in alinement, it will be omitted and a lowercase *e* added after the capital, as *Ae* (*Aerger*), *Oe* (*Oel*), *Ue* (*Uebel*).

[1] In the interest of simplicity, works in philology and bibliography often allow all common nouns to go lowercase.

Punctuation and hyphenation

Punctuation is practically as in English. The comma, however, is used to set off subordinate clauses of all kinds; e.g., *ich glaube, daß er kommen wird*, I believe that he will come.

In series of words made up of two parts, where one part is common to both words, the hyphen is used as follows: *Feld- und Gartenfrüchte* (field- and garden produce), the word *früchte* being common to both *Feld* and *Garten*; but *Haftpflicht-Versicherungsgesellschaft und -Versicherte* (liability-insurance company and -insured), because *Haftpflicht* is common to both *Versicherungsgesellschaft* and *Versicherte*.

Abbreviations

a.	an, am, an der, on (the), at (the)
a.a.O.	am angeführten Ort, in the place cited (loc. cit.)
Abb.	Abbildung, illustration, figure
Abk.	Abkürzung, abbreviation
Abt.	Abteilung, section
a.d.	an der, on the
a.D.	außer Dienst, retired
Adr.	Adresse, address
A.G.	Aktiengesellschaft, corporation
allg.	allgemein, general(ly)
Anm.	Anmerkung, note
Art.	Artikel, article
Aufl.	Auflage, edition
b.	bei, beim, near, with, c/o
Bd.	Band, volume
bes.	besonders, especially
betr.	betreffs, betreffend, concerning
bez.	bezüglich, respecting
Bez.	Bezirk, district
bezw., bzw.	beziehungsweise, respectively
Blg.	Beilage, enclosure
b.w.	bitte wenden, please turn page
ca.	circa, zirka, about
d.Ä.	der Ältere, Sr.
ders.	derselbe, the same
dgl.	dergleichen, the like, of that kind
d.h.	das heißt, that is, i.e.
d.i.	das ist, that is, i.e.
d.J.	der Jüngere, junior; dieses Jahres, of this year
DM	Deutsche Mark, mark (after World War II)
d.M.	dieses Monats, of the . . . instant
do.	ditto, the same
Dr.	Doktor, doctor
Dtzd.	Dutzend, dozen
einschl.	einschließlich, including, inclusive
entspr.	entsprechend, corresponding
e.V.	eingetragener Verein, incorporated society or association
ev.	evangelisch, Protestant
evtl.	eventuell, perhaps, possibly
Fa.	Firma, firm

ff.	folgende (Seiten), following (pages)
F.f.	Fortsetzung folgt, to be continued
Forts.	Fortsetzung, continuation
Frl.	Fräulein, Miss
geb.	geboren, born; gebunden, bound; geborene, née
Gebr.	Gebrüder, Brothers
gef.	gefälligst, kindly
gegr.	gegründet, founded
ges.	gesetzlich geschützt, registered trademark
gesch.	
G.m.b.H.	Gesellschaft mit beschränkter Haftung, Ltd., or Inc.
hrsg.	herausgegeben, edited or published
i.	in, im, in, in the
Ing.	Ingenieur, engineer
inkl.	inklusive, inclusive, included
insb.	insbesondere, in particular
Kap.	Kapitel, chapter
kath.	kathalisch, Catholic
Kl.	Klasse, class
lfd.	laufend, current
Lfg.	Lieferung, fascicle
M.	Mark, mark (coin)
m.E.	meines Erachtens, in my opinion
Nachf.	Nachfolger, successor(s)
nachm.	nachmittags, p.m., afternoon
näml.	nämlich, namely, i.e.
NB	(nota bene) beachte, note, remark (P.S.)
n.Chr.	nach Christus, A.D.
n.F.	neue Folge, new series
No., Nr.	Numero, number
no., ntto.	Netto, net
od.	oder, or
ö., österr.	österreichisch, Austrian
p.A.	per Adresse, care of (c/o)
Pf.	Pfennig, penny
Pfd.	Pfund, pound (lb.)
PS	Pferdestärke, horsepower
resp.	respektiv, respectively
rglm.	regelmäißg, regular

Abbreviations—Continued

S.	Seite, page	usw.	und so weiter, and so forth, etc.
s.	siehe, see (cf.)	v.	(vide) siehe, see (cf.); von, of, from, by
sel.	selig, late		
Skt., St.	Sankt, Saint	v.Chr.	vor Christus, B.C.
		Verf.	Verfasser, author
s.o.	siehe oben, see above	Verl.	Verleger, publisher
sog.	sogenannt, so called	vgl.	vergleiche, compare
Sp.	Spalte, column	v.H.	vom Hundert, percent (%)
St.	Stück, individual piece	v.J.	vorigen Jahres, of last year
staatl.	staatlich, State or Federal	v.M.	vorigen Monats, of last month
Str.	Strasse, street		
s.u.	siehe unten, see below	vorm.	vormittags, morning, a. m.
T.	Teil, part	Vors.	Vorsitzender, chairman
teilw.	teilweise, partly	w.o.	wie oben, as above
u.	und, and	Wwe.	Witwe, widow
u.a.	und andere, and others; unter anderem, among other things; unter andern, among others (inter alia)	z.	zu, zum, zur, to, to the, at
		z.B.	zum Beispiel, for example
		z.H.	zu Händen, attention of
		Ztschr.	Zeitschrift, periodical
u.a.m.	und andere mehr, and many others	z.T.	zum Teil, in part
		zus.	zusammen, together
U.A.w.g.	Um Antwort wird gebeten, an answer is requested	z.Z.	zur Zeit, at the time, acting (e.g., secretary)

Cardinal numbers

eins	one	zwanzig	twenty
zwei	two	einundzwanzig	twenty-one
drei	three	zweiundzwanzig	twenty-two
vier	four	dreiundzwanzig, etc.	twenty-three, etc.
fünf	five		
sechs	six	dreißig	thirty
sieben	seven	vierzig	forty
acht	eight	fünfzig	fifty
neun	nine	sechzig	sixty
zehn	ten	siebzig	seventy
elf	eleven	achtzig	eighty
zwölf	twelve	neunzig	ninety
dreizehn	thirteen	hundert	hundred
vierzehn	fourteen	hundertundeins	one hundred and one
fünfzehn	fifteen		
sechzehn	sixteen	hundertundzwei, etc.	one hundred and two, etc.
siebzehn	seventeen		
achtzehn	eighteen	zweihundert, etc.	two hundred, etc.
neunzehn	nineteen	tausend	thousand

Ordinal numbers

erste	first	dreizehnte, etc.	thirteenth, etc.
zweite	second	zwanzigste	twentieth
dritte	third	einundzwanzigste	twenty-first
vierte	fourth	zweiundzwanzigste, etc.	twenty-second, etc.
fünfte	fifth		
sechste	sixth	dreißigste	thirtieth, etc.
siebente	seventh	vierzigste, etc.	fortieth
achte	eighth	hundertste	hundredth
neunte	ninth	hundertunderste, etc.	one hundred and first, etc.
zehnte	tenth		
elfte	eleventh	zweihundertste	two hundredth
zwölfte	twelfth	tausendste	thousandth

After ordinal numbers a period is placed where in English the form would be 1st, 2d, etc., as *1. Heft; 2. Band.*

Months

Januar (Jan.)	January	Juli (Jul.)	July
Februar (Feb.)	February	August (Aug.)	August
März	March	September (Sept.)	September
April (Apr.)	April	Oktober (Okt.)	October
Mai	May	November (Nov.)	November
Juni (Jun.)	June	Dezember (Dez.)	December

Days

Sonntag	Sunday	Donnerstag	Thursday
Montag	Monday	Freitag	Friday
Dienstag	Tuesday	Sonnabend, Samstag	Saturday
Mittwoch	Wednesday		

Seasons

Frühling	spring	Herbst	autumn
Sommer	summer	Winter	winter

Time

Stunde	hour	Monat	month
Tag	day	Jahr	year
Woche	week		

REFERENCES.—Der Große Duden, Rechtschreibung der deutschen Sprache und der Fremdwörter nach den für das Deutsche Reich und die Schweiz gültigen amtlichen Regeln (1942); G. O. Curme, A Grammar of the German Language (1922); Karl Breul, Heath's New German and English Dictionary (1939).

GREEK (Classical)

"Ότι μὲν ὑμεῖς, ὦ ἄνδρες 'Αθηναῖοι, πεπόνθατε ὑπὸ τῶν ἐμῶν κατηγόρων, οὐκ οἶδα· ἐγὼ δ'οὖν καὶ αὐτὸς ὑπ' αὐτῶν ὀλίγου ἐμαυτοῦ ἐπελαθόμην, οὕτω πιθανῶς ἔλεγον· καίτοι ἀληθες γε ὡς ἔπος εἰπεῖν οὐδὲν εἰρήκασιν.—Plato, Apologia, 1.

Alphabet and pronunciation

Α	α	alpha	$\bar{a}$ in father; $\breve{a}$ in aha
Β	β	beta	b in bad
Γ	γ	gamma	g in go; ng in sing, before γ, κ, χ, and ξ
Δ	δ	delta	d
Ε	ε	epsilon	$\breve{e}$ in French été; e in pet
Ζ	ζ	zeta	z in daze (originally zd, or dz)
Η	η	eta	$\bar{e}$, ê in French fête, a in English fare, ä in German prägen
Θ	θ	theta	th in thin (originally aspirated t as th in hothouse)
Ι	ι	iota	$\bar{\imath}$ in machine; ĭ in pit
Κ	κ	kappa	k in kin
Λ	λ	lambda	l in let
Μ	μ	mu	m in met
Ν	ν	nu	n in now
Ξ	ξ	xi	x in lax
Ο	ο	omicron	ŏ in obey
Π	π	pi	p in pin
Ρ	ρ	rho	r in red
Σ	σ ς	sigma	s in see
Τ	τ	tau	t in tar
Υ	υ	upsilon	like German ü (ee with lips rounded as for oo) or French u
Φ	φ	phi	ph in phone (originally aspirated p, as ph in loophole
Χ	χ	chi	ch in German machen, or Scottish loch (originally aspirated k as the kh sound in blockhouse)
Ψ	ψ	psi	ps in caps
Ω	ω	omega	$\bar{o}$ in or; o in go

In transliteration from Classical Greek, the letters may be represented thus: a, b, g, d, e, z, ē, th, i, k, l, m, n, x, o, p, r, s, t, u, ph, ch, ps, ō; initial ρ is transliterated by rh, internal ρρ by rrh; υ not following α, ε, η, ι often represented by y instead of u. It was formerly customary to latinize Classical Greek names, and this custom is still followed for most ordinary names used in English literature; in doing this, the letters are transliterated as above, except: γ is represented by n before γ, κ, ξ, χ (the same applies to transliteration); η, by e, but the macron is usually omitted, giving simply e; κ, by c; υ, by y, except after α, ε, η, ι, where it is u; ω, by o, but the macron is usually omitted. The diphthong αι may be represented by i instead of ei; the diphthong ου may be represented by u instead of ou. The "rough breathing" is represented by h. In transliteration and romanization the accents and other diacritical marks are usually omitted.

387

Diphthongs

αι	*ai* in aisle	αυ	*ou* in out
ει	*ei* in veil	ευ	*e* in pet, *u* in rule; often
οι	*oi* in oil		anglicized to *u* in use
υι	German *ü*, plus *i* in machine;	ου	*ou* in soup
	often anglicized to *we* as in		
	we		

Cardinal numbers

α'	εἷς, μία, ἕν	one	ν'	πεντήκοντα	fifty
β'	δύο	two	ξ'	ἑξήκοντα	sixty
γ'	τρεῖς, τρία	three	ο'	ἑβδομήκοντα	seventy
δ'	τέσσαρες, -ρα	four	π'	ὀγδοήκοντα	eighty
ε'	πέντε	five	ϙ'	ἐνενήκοντα	ninety
ϛ'ἕξ		six	ρ'	ἑκατόν	hundred
			ρα'	ἑκατὸν καὶ εἷς, etc.	one hundred
ζ'	ἑπτά	seven			and one, etc.
η'	ὀκτώ	eight	σ'	διακόσιοι, -αι, -α	two hundred
θ'	ἐννέα	nine	τ'	τριακόσιοι, -αι, -α	three hundred
ι'	δέκα	ten	υ'	τετρακόσιοι, -αι, -α	four hundred
ια'	ἕνδεκα	eleven	φ'	πεντακόσιοι, -αι, -α	five hundred
ιβ'	δώδεκα	twelve	χ'	ἑξακόσιοι, -αι, -α	six hundred
ιγ'	τρεισκαίδεκα, etc.	thirteen, etc.	ψ'	ἑπτακόσιοι, -αι, -α	seven hundred
κ'	εἴκοσι(ν)	twenty	ω'	ὀκτακόσιοι, -αι, -α	eight hundred
κα'	εἴκοσιν εἷς, etc.	twenty-one, etc.	ϡ'	ἐννιακόσιοι, -αι, -α	nine hundred
λ'	τριάκοντα	thirty	͵α	χίλιοι, -αι, -α	thousand
μ'	τεσσαράκοντα	forty	͵ι	μύριοι, -αι, -α	ten thousand

Ordinal numbers

πρῶτος, -η, -ον	first	δέκατος		tenth
δεύτερος, -α, -ον	second	ἐνδέκατος		eleventh
τρίτος, -η, -ον	third	δωδέκατος		twelfth
τέταρτος	fourth	τρίτος καὶ δέκατος, etc.		thirteenth, etc.
πέμπτος	fifth	εἰκοστός		twentieth
ἕκτος	sixth	εἰκοστὸς πρῶτος, etc.		twenty-first,
ἕβδομος	seventh			etc.
ὄγδοος	eighth	τριακοστός, etc.		thirtieth, etc.
ἔνατος	ninth	χιλιοστός		thousandth

The *stigma* (ϛ, representing *f*), *koppa* (ϙ) and *sampi* (ϡ) are survivors of an earlier alphabet and are used only in numerical notation.

These numerals, except the cardinals from 5 to 100, are regularly declinable according to the rules of the language.

The numeral characters take an acute accent after them, from 1 to 999. To place an accent below and to the left of a character multiplies it by 1000; e.g., α'=1, ͵α=1000, ͵α ϡμδ'=1944.

Chronology

The ancient Greek communities had no uniform system of time reckoning. For the purpose of holding Olympic Games they divided time into periods of 4 years, called Olympiads, the first year of the first Olympiad beginning in the middle of the summer of 776 B.C. Each year was divided into 12 months, but there was no division into weeks. From the third century B.C. the era of the Olympiads has been introduced to historical chronology.

The seasons were called ἔαρ (ἦρ), spring; θέρος, summer; ὀπώρα, autumn, and χεῖμα (χειμών), winter.

After the rise of Roman supremacy, the Julian calendar was adopted, with the Latin month names transliterated. After the advent of Christianity, the weekly system was adopted, with names of the days as in Modern Greek.

Months

Ἑκατομβαιών	Hecatombaion	About July
Μεταγειτνιών	Metageitnion	August
Βοηδρομιών	Boëdromion	September
Πυανεψιών	Pyanepsion	October
Μαιμακτηριών	Maimacterion	November
Ποσειδεών	Poseideon	December
Ποσειδεὼν δεύτερος	Second Poseideon	In leap years only
Γαμηλιών	Gamelion	January
Ἀνθεστηριών	Anthesterion	February
Ἐλαφηβολιών	Elaphebolion	March
Μουνυχιών	Mounichion	April
Θαργηλιών	Thargelion	May
Σκιροφοριών	Skirophorion	June

These are the months of the Athenian calendar, the best known to us. Several other calendars were in use throughout the ancient Greek world, the beginning of the year falling often at other seasons.

The modern equivalents are, of course, only approximate, as the Greeks had not calculated the year as accurately as more modern mathematicians have. The first day of Hecatombaion was intended to fall upon the summer solstice, but it actually varied from the middle of June to the first week in August.

Time

ὥρα	hour		μήν	month
ἡμέρα	day		ἔτος	year
ἐβδομάς	week			

REFERENCES.—H. W. Smyth, Greek Grammar, rev. by G. M. Messing (1956); Liddell and Scott, A Greek-English Lexicon "9th" ed. (1925–40); W. Wallace, Index of Greek Ligatures and Contractions (Journal of Hellenic Studies 43, 1923); R. Proctor, The Printing of Greek in the Fifteenth Century (1900); V. Garthausen, Griechische Palaeographie. 2. Aufl., 2. Bd. (1913). E. Boisacq, Dictionnaire étymologique de la langue grecque. 4. ed. (1950); E. H. Sturtevant, Pronunciation of Greek and Latin. 2d ed. (1940).

GREEK (Modern)

'Εν πάσῃ περιπτώσει ἡ Κυβέρνησις, πρὸ τῆς νέας τροπῆς τῶν γεγονότων, εἶχε χρέος νὰ στείλῃ πρὸς πάντας εἰδοποιήσεις καὶ νὰ δώσῃ τὰς ἀπαιτουμένας ὁδηγίας.—Eleutherios G. Prebelakēs, Hē Ekstrateia tou Ibraēm Pasa eis tēn Argolida.

Alphabet and pronunciation

Α	α	𝒜 α	alpha	*a* in father; see αι, αυ, under Diphthongs
Β	б	ℬ b	beta	*v*
Γ	γ	𝒯 𝑔	gamma	*y* in yes before αι, ε, ει, η, ι, οι, υ, υι; *ng* in singer before γ, κ, ξ, χ; somewhat like *g* in go everywhere else; see γγ, γκ, under Digraphs
Δ	δ	𝒟 δ	delta	*th* in this, except in νδρ, pronounced *ndr*
Ε	ε	ℰ ε	epsilon	*e* in met; see ει, ευ, under Diphthongs
Ζ	ς	𝒵 𝒥	zeta	*z*
Η	η	ℋ 𝓃	eta	*ee* in eel; *y* in yet, when after a consonant and before a vowel; see ην, under Diphthongs
Θ	θ	𝒮 𝒮	theta	*th* in thin
Ι	ι	𝒥 ι	iota	*ee* in eel; *y* in yet when initial or after a consonant, before a vowel; see αι, ει, οι, υι, under Diphthongs
Κ	κ	𝒦 𝓊	kappa	*k*; see γκ, under Digraphs
Λ	λ	𝓛 λ	lambda	*l*
Μ	μ	𝓜 μ	mu	*m*; see μπ, under Digraphs
Ν	ν	𝒩 𝓋	nu	*n*; see ντ, under Digraphs
Ξ	ξ	𝒵 𝒥	xi	*x* (=ks)
Ο	ο	𝒪 o	omicron	*o* in for; see οι, ου, under Diphthongs
Π	π	𝒯 ϖ	pi	*p*; see μπ, under Digraphs
Ρ	ρ	𝒫 ρ	rho	*r*, somewhat like the Scotch trilled *r*
Σ	σ s¹	ℒ σ 𝒹	sigma	*z* before β, γ, δ, λ, μ, ν, ρ; *s* everywhere else

[Concluded on following page]

---

¹ The character σ is used in initial and medial positions in a word; the character s, in the final position

390

T	τ	*ϑ̆ (τ)*	tau	*t*; see *ντ, τζ, τσ*, under Digraphs
Υ	υ	*V v*	upsilon	*ee* in eel; *y* in yet, after a consonant and before a vowel; see *αυ, ευ, ηυ, ου, υι*, under Diphthongs
Φ	φ	*P p*	phi	*f*
X	χ	*X x*	chi	like a strong *h* (like German *ch*)
Ψ	ψ	*Ψ y*	psi	*ps*
Ω	ω	*W w*	omega	*o* in or

In connected speech, many phonetic changes occur: word-final *n* often drops or becomes *m*, and the first sound of the next word may change, for example, from *p* to *b*; *ts* at the beginning of a word becomes *dz* after a word ending in *n*; many other such differences in pronunciation, between an isolated word and a word in connected speech, are observable. These phenomena, however, are not reflected in the spelling.

Modern Greek uses the same alphabet as Classical Greek, but many of the letters stand for different sounds now because of the linguistic changes that have taken place since classical times. The names of the letters are given here in the usual English version of their Classical Greek form. These names are usually pronounced in English as follows: alpha (*al* as in Alfred), bayta, gamma, delta, épsilon (*o* as in don), zayta, ayta, thayta, eye-ó-ta, kappa, lamda, mew, new, zie (*ie* as in die or sigh), óm-i-kron (*o's* as in don), pie, roe, sigma, tou (*ou* as in house), yóu-psi-lon (or úp-silon), fie, kie, sie, o-máy-ga. In Modern Greek, the letter names are pronounced ahlfa, veeta, gahma, thelta (*th* as in then), eh-psee-láwn, zeeta, eeta, theeta (*th* as in thin), yoeta, kahpa, lahmvtha (*th* as in then), mee, nee, ksee, oh-mee-kráwn, pee, ro, seeg-ma, tahv, ae-psee-láwn, fee, hee, p-see, o-mée-ga.

It is suggested that for transliterating Modern Greek names, etc., the usual transliteration of the letters be used, regardless of pronunciation: *a, b, g, d, e, z, ē, th, i, k, l, m, n, x, o, p, r, s, t, u, ph, ch, ps, ō*. For *β, v* may be used if desired. (Compare with the remarks on transliteration of Classical Greek, p. 419.)

There are two quite different styles of Modern Greek: one is an extremely formal academic style, known as katharevousa; the other, called Demotic Greek, is used by everybody in daily speech, and in modern novels, stories, poetry, and some newspapers. There are considerable differences between the two styles in grammatical structure and vocabulary, but their pronunciation and spelling are largely the same.

Special characters

Some of the letters of the alphabet have variant forms: for alpha, *α* and *a*; for beta, *б* and *β*; for theta, *ϑ* and *θ*; for kappa, *κ* and *u*; for pi, *π* and *ω*; for phi, *φ* and *φ*; for psi, *ψ* and *y*. These are used interchangeably.

Some Greek letters are exactly or nearly like the corresponding Latin letters: A *a*, B *β*, E *ε*, Z, I *ι*, K *κ*, M, N, O *o*, ς, T *τ*, *v*. The other letters are characteristically Greek: Γ *γ*, Δ *δ*, ς, H *η*, Θ *θ*, Λ *λ*, *μ*, *ν*, Ξ *ξ*, Π *π*, P *ρ*, Σ *σ*, T, Φ *φ*, X *χ*, Ω *ω*.

Vowels

The vowels are *α, ε, η, ι, ο, υ*, and *ω*, including the three vowels with a subscript (*ᾳ, ῃ*, and *ῳ*), which are pronounced the same as their respective vowels without the subscript. The remaining letters are consonants.

Combinations of two vowel letters (diphthongs)

αι   as *e* in met

αυ   as *a* in watt, plus *f* before voiceless consonants (θ, κ, ζ, π, σ, τ, φ, χ, ψ); as *a* in watt, plus *v* before vowels and voiced consonants (β, γ, δ, ζ, λ, μ, ν, ρ)

ει   as *ee* in eel; *y* in yet, when after a consonant and before a vowel

ευ   as *e* in met, plus *f*, before voiceless consonants; as *e* in met, plus *v* before vowels and voiced consonants

ηυ   as *ee* in eel, plus *f*, before voiceless consonants; as *ee* in eel, plus *v*, before vowels and voiced consonants

οι   as *ee* in eel; *y* in yet, when after a consonant and before a vowel

ου   as *ou* in group, same as *oo* in food

υι   as *ee* in eel

Note that ει, οι, and υι are pronounced the same as the simple vowels η, ι, υ, all like *ee* in eel.

Combinations of two consonant letters (digraphs)

γκ as *g* in go initially; *ng* in finger, rarely *nk* in sink, elsewhere
γγ as *g* in go initially; *ng* in finger, rarely *nk* in sink, elsewhere
μπ as *b* in bet initially; *mb* in ember, rarely *mp* in empty, elsewhere
ντ as *d* in did initially; *nd* in end, rarely *nt* in enter, elsewhere
τζ as *dz* in adz; *j* in judge in some foreign words
τσ as *ts* in hats; *ch* in chug in some foreign words

Consonantal units

For purposes of syllabification, any combination of consonants that may begin a Greek word is a unit. Hence, the following are consonantal units:

βδ, βλ, βρ
γλ, γν, γρ
δμ, δν, δρ
θλ, θν, θρ
κλ, κμ, κν, κρ
μν

πλ, πν, πρ, πτ
σβ, σθ, σκ, σμ, σπ, στ, στρ, σφ, σχ
τλ, τμ, τρ
φθ, φλ, φν, φρ
χθ, χλ, χν, χρ

Also, any group of three consonants, the first two and the last two of which are units, as listed above, are likewise regarded as consonantal units. Thus, χθρ is a unit, because χθ and θρ are units.

Rules for syllabification

1. Diphthongs, digraphs when they represent a single sound, and consonantal units may not be divided.
2. Division is made on a vowel or on a diphthong before a single consonant, digraph, or consonantal unit: πα-τέ-ρας, παι-διά, βί-βλος.
3. In a group of two or more consonants, the division is made before the last consonant, digraph, or consonantal unit: γλῶσ-σα, πορθ-μός, 'Αγ-γλία, ἄν-θραξ.
4. Division may be made between vowels not constituting a diphthong or between a diphthong and another vowel: εὐ-ειδής, θέ-ατρον, λα-ϊκός, οὔ-ϊα.
5. Certain adverbial prefixes are kept intact. These are: ἀν, δια, δισ, δυσ, εἰσ, ἐκ, ἐν, ἐξ, μισ, προς, συν, ὑπερ, and ὡσ: ἀν-αρχία, ἐξ-άδελφος, ὡσ-τε.
6. Compound words are divided according to their component parts (and each part according to rules 1 to 5): φιλ-άνθρωπος, τρισ-άθλιος.
7. Foreign words in Greek orthography are regarded as naturalized words and divided according to rules 1 to 5: 'Αγ-γλία, Βά-σιγ-κτων, 'Εδου-άρ-δος; but foreign compound words are divided according to their component parts: Τσεχο-σλοβακία.

Illustrative word divisions

[The numbers in parentheses refer to the syllabification rules]

ἀγνω-στι-κὸς	(2, 2)	με-λαγ-χο-λία	(2, 3, 2)
αἱ-μορ-ρο-ΐ-δες	(2, 3, 4, 2)	με-τα-βάλ-λον-ται	(2, 2, 3, 3)
αἰ-σθαν-τι-κὸς	(2, 3, 2)	μισ-αν-θρω-πία	(5, 3, 2)
'Αμε-ρι-κα-νὸς	(2, 2, 2)	μπαρ-μπέ-ρης	(3, 2)
ἀν-ω-δύ-νως	(5, 2, 2)	ναυ-αρ-χεῖ-ον	(6, 3, 4)
ἀπο-στρα-τεύ-ο-μαι	(2, 2, 4, 2)	νε-ο-ελ-λη-νι-κὸς	(4, 6, 3, 2, 2)
βα-σί-λει-ον	(2, 2, 4)	Οὐά-σιγ-κτων	(2, 3)
γλαύ-κω-μα	(2, 2)	πο-λι-τεῖ-αι	(2, 2, 4)
δι-ά-γνω-σις	(4, 5, 2)	πλη-ρε-ξού-σι-οι	(2, 2, 2, 4)
δισ-ε-κα-τομ-μύ-ρι-ον	(5, 2, 2, 3, 2, 4)	προσ-ἐγ-γι-σις	(5, 3, 2)
δύσ-καμ-πτος	(5, 3)	συμ-βαλ-λό-με-νοι	(3, 3, 2, 2)
εἰσ-έρ-χο-μαι	(5, 3, 2)	συν-οι-κέ-σι-ον	(5, 2, 2, 4)
ἐκ-λαμ-πρό-της	(5, 3, 2)	συν-ο-μο-λο-γῶ	(5, 2, 2, 2)
'Ελ-λά-δος	(3, 2)	συ-στη-μα-τι-κὸς	(2, 2, 2, 2)
'Εξ-ο-χό-τη-τα	(5, 2, 2, 2)	σχο-λαρ-χεῖ-ον	(2, 3, 4)
'Εξ-ω-τε-ρι-κὸς	(5, 2, 2, 2)	σω-μα-τεμ-πο-ρία	(2, 2, 3, 2)
εὐ-ερ-γέ-της	(6, 3, 2)	σω-φρο-νι-στή-ρι-ον	(2, 2, 2, 2, 4)
Εὐ-ρω-πα-ϊ-κὸς	(2, 2, 4, 2)	τε-λει-ο-ποί-η-σις	(2, 4, 2, 4, 2)
Ζω-άρ-κεια	(4, 3)	τη-λέ-γραμ-μα	(2, 2, 3)
'Ηλεκ-τρο-σκό-πι-ον	(2, 2, 2, 4)	τμη-μα-τάρ-χης	(2, 2, 3)
'Ηνω-μέ-ναι	(2, 2)	τρισ-ά-γι-ος	(6, 2, 4)
θε-ο-κρα-τι-κὸς	(4, 6, 2, 2)	τρισ-χί-λι-οι	(6, 2, 4)
ἰδι-ο-συγ-κρα-σία	(4, 6, 3, 2)	ὑπερ-ά-γα-θος	(5, 2, 2)
κα-τά-θλι-ψις	(2, 2, 2)	ὑπερ-άν-θρω-πος	(5, 3, 2)
κα-ταρ-τι-σμὸς	(2, 3, 2)	ὑπέρ-λαμ-προς	(5, 3)
Κων-σταν-τῖ-νος	(3, 3, 2)	φιλ-ά-δελ-φος	(6, 2, 3)
λε-ξι-κο-γρά-φος	(2, 2, 6, 2)	χα-λύ-βδι-νος	(2, 2, 2)
μα-γνη-τι-σμὸς	(2, 2, 2)	ψευ-δο-μάρ-τυς	(2, 2, 3)
μαι-ευ-τι-κή	(4, 2, 2)	ὠρύ-ο-μαι	(4, 2)
με-γα-λει-ό-της	(2, 2, 4, 2)	ὠφε-λι-μό-της	(2, 2, 2)

Accents and diacritics

The three accent marks used in Greek now all represent the same thing—loud stress, although in Classical Greek they are supposed to have represented different pitch accents:

1. The acute (´), which may occur on the vowel, or on the second vowel of a diphthong, in any one of the last three syllables of a word.

2. The circumflex (˜, ^), which may occur on the vowel, or on the second vowel of a diphthong, in either of the last two syllables of a word. The circumflex never appears over ε or ο.

3. The grave (`), which may occur only on the vowel, or on the second vowel of a diphthong, in the last syllable of a word; such a word must be followed directly by another word, not a period or comma.

Greek orthography also employs two "breathing" marks:

1. The rough breathing, or spiritus asper ('), which occurs on an initial vowel, or on the second vowel of an initial diphthong. It has no phonetic value, although in Classical Greek it represented an *h* sound before the vowel or diphthong; in transliteration, it may be represented by *h*.

2. The smooth breathing, or spiritus lenis ('), which occurs on an initial vowel, or second vowel of an initial diphthong. It has no phonetic value, and in Classical Greek represented a lack of *h* sound before the vowel.

In text, these breathings and the grave and acute accent marks are placed above and to the left of capital vowel letters, rather than directly above.

Some words, called enclitics, may appear with no written accent at all; the word preceding an enclitic, however (unless it too is an enclitic), will always have at least one accent mark and may have two; e.g., τοιαῦτά ἐστι.

Another diacritical mark is the diaeresis (trema) (¨), which occurs on the second of two vowels to indicate that they do not form a diphthong, which otherwise they would form: καΰμένος (pronounced *kaeeménos* instead of *kavménos*).

These diacritical marks may form combinations, as follows:

῎ lenis acute	῞ asper grave	῍ dieresis acute
῍ lenis grave	῏ circumflex lenis	῎ dieresis grave
῞ asper acute	῟ circumflex asper	

An iota is often placed beneath the vowel α, η, or ω, mainly to indicate a declensional or conjugational inflection: ῇ, the nominative plural of ἡ; τιμᾷ, third person singular of τιμῶ. This iota is called iota subscript.

Capitalization

Capitalization is practically the same as in English. The pronoun of address is usually capitalized. (This does not apply to Classical Greek.) Capital letters do not take diacritical marks. If a lowercase accented vowel is capitalized, the accent mark is dropped. (In Classical Greek this is quite true but this statement should perhaps be modified to the effect that it applies to whole words spelled out in capitals, not to those beginning with capitals; the example illustrates the case well.) An initial capital vowel, however, carries the accent mark before it. The iota subscript may be placed either beneath the vowel or changed into a regular iota and placed right after the vowel. Thus the words ἅγιος, ᾅδης, and ἀπό, if capitalized, are set ῞ΑΓΙΟΣ, ῞ΑΔΗΣ, and ᾽ΑΠΟ. ῞Αδης may also be set ῞Αιδης. In Classical Greek iota subscript cannot stand under capital; if the letter under which it stands is capitalized then iota subscript becomes iota adscript; e.g., ΤΗΙ ΩΙΔΗΙ—τῇ ᾠδῇ or ᾽Ιλιδῇ.

Punctuation

The comma, the period, and the exclamation point are the same as in English and are used similarly. The semicolon and the colon are represented by a point above the line. The question mark resembles the English semicolon. The scheme for quotation marks is the same as in the western languages.

Abbreviations

Α. Ε.	Αὐτοῦ᾽Εξοχότης, His Excellency		Ν. Δ.	Νέα Διαθήκη, New Testament; Νομοθετικὸν Διάταγμα, Legislative Ordinance
Α. Μ.	Αὐτοῦ Μεγαλειότης, His Majesty			
Β. Δ.	Βασιλικὸν Διάταγμα, Royal Decree		ν. ἡμ.	νέον ἡμερολόγιον, New Calendar
βλ.	βλέπε, see		Ο′	᾽Εβδομήκοντα, Septuagint
δηλ.	δηλαδή, that is, namely, to wit		Π. Δ.	παλαιὰ Διαθήκη, Old Testament; Προεδρικὸν Διάταγμα, Presidential Order
δρ.	δραχμή, drachma			
δράμ.	δράμιον, dram		πλ.	πληθυντικός, plural
Δ. Φ.	Διδάκτωρ Φιλοσοφίας, Ph. D.		π. μ.	πρὸ μεσημβρίας, a.m.
Δ. Ν.	Διδάκτωρ Νομικῆς, LL. D.		πρβλ.	παράβαλε, compare, cf.
ἔ. ἀ.	ἔνθα ἀνωτέρω, loc. cit.		π. Χ.	πρὸ Χριστοῦ, B.C.
ἰδ.	ἰδέ, see		π. χ.	παραδείγματος χάριν, for example, e.g.
Ι. Χ.	᾽Ιησοῦς Χριστός, Jesus Christ			
Καθ.	Καθηγητής, Prof.		σεβ.	σεβαστός, Hon.
Κος	Κύριος, Mr.		σελ.	σελίς, page
Κα	Κυρία, Mrs.		στήλ.	στήλη, column
κτλ.	καὶ τὰ λοιπά, etc.		σύγκρ.	σύγκρινε, compare, cf.
κ. τ. ὅ.	καὶ τά ὅμοια, and the like		τ. ἔ.	τοῦτ᾽ ἔστιν, that is, i.e.
κφλ.	κεφάλαιον, chapter		τόμ.	τόμος, volume
λπτ.	λεπτά, lepta		Τ. Σ.	τόπος σφραγῖδος, L.S., locosigilli
μέρ.	μέρος, part		τρ. ἔτ.	τρέχοντος ἔτους, current year
μ. μ.	μετὰ μεσημβρίαν, p.m.		φ.	φύλλον, folio
μ. Χ.	μετὰ Χριστόν, A.D.		χιλ.	χιλιόμετρον, kilometer

Cardinal numbers

εἷς (ἕνας), μία, ἕν(α)	one	εἴκοσι ἕνα (m. and n.), εἴκοσι μία (f.)	twenty-one
δύο	two		
τρεῖς, τρία	three	εἴκοσι δύο, etc.	twenty-two, etc.
τέσσαρες, -α	four	τριά(κο)ντα	thirty
πέντε	five	σαράντα	forty
ἑξ(ι)	six	πενῆντα	fifty
ἑπτά (ἐφτά)	seven	ἑξῆντα	sixty
ὀκτώ	eight	ἐβδομῆντα	seventy
ἐννέα	nine	ὀγδῶντα	eighty
δέκα	ten	ἐνενῆντα	ninety
ἕνδεκα	eleven	ἑκατόν	one hundred
δώδεκα	twelve	ἑκατὸν ἕνας, etc.	one hundred and one, etc.
δεκατρεῖς (m. and f.), δεκατρία (n.)	thirteen	διακόσια	two hundred
		τριακόσια	three hundred
δεκατέσσαρες (m. and f.), δεκατέσσαρα (n.)	fourteen	τετρακόσια, etc.	four hundred, etc.
		χίλια	thousand
δεκαπέντε, etc.	fifteen, etc.	δύο χιλιάδες, etc.	two thousand, etc.
εἴκοσι	twenty	ἕν ἑκατομμύριον	one million

NOTE.—Modern Greek uses the Arabic figures for ordinary number work. Where western languages use Roman numerals, the Modern Greek uses the same scheme of letters as used in Classical Greek. (See p. 420.)

Ordinal numbers

πρῶτος	first	εἰκοστός	twentieth
δεύτερος	second	εἰκοστὸς πρῶτος,	twenty-first, etc.
τρίτος	third	etc.	
τέταρτος	fourth	τριακοστός	thirtieth
πέμπτος	fifth	τεσσαρακοστός	fortieth
ἕκτος	sixth	πεντηκοστός	fiftieth
ἕβδομος	seventh	ἑξηκοστός	sixtieth
ὄγδοος	eighth	ἑβδομηκοστός	seventieth
ἔννατος	ninth	ὀγδοηκοστός	eightieth
δέκατος	tenth	ἐνενηκοστός, etc.	ninetieth, etc.
ἐνδέκατος	eleventh	ἑκατοστός	hundredth
δωδέκατος	twelfth	χιλιοστός	thousandth
δέκατος τρίτος, etc.	thirteenth, etc.	ἑκατομμυριοστός	millionth

Months

Ἰανουάριος	January	Ἰούλιος	July
Φεβρουάριος	February	Αὔγουστος	August
Μάρτιος	March	Σεπτέμβριος	September
Ἀπρίλιος	April	Ὀκτώβριος	October
Μάιος	May	Νοέμβριος	November
Ἰούνιος	June	Δεκέμβριος	December

Days

Κυριακή	Sunday	Πέμπτη	Thursday
Δευτέρα	Monday	Παρασκευή	Friday
Τρίτη	Tuesday	Σάββατο(ν)	Saturday
Τετάρτη	Wednesday		

Seasons

ἄνοιξις	spring	φθινόπωρον	autumn
καλοκαῖρι	summer	χειμών (χειμῶνας)	winter

Time

ὥρα	hour	μήνας	month
ἡμέρα	day	ἔτος	year
ἑβδομάς	week		

REFERENCES.—K. Petraris and W. H. D. Rouse, A Handbook of the Modern Greek Spoken Language (1941); A. Thumb and J. Kalitsunakis, Grammatik der neugriechischen Volkssprache (1928); Hubert Pernot, Grammaire de grec moderne (1930); I. Kykkotis, English-Greek and Greek-English Dictionary (1942); H. and R. Kahane, Ralph L. Ward, Spoken Greek (1945); J. T. Pring, comp., The Oxford Dictionary of Modern Greek (Greek-English) (1965); D. C. E. Swanson and S. P. Djaferis, Vocabulary of Modern Spoken Greek (English-Greek and Greek-English) (1959); F. W. Householder, K. Kazazis, and A. Koutsoudas, Reference Grammar of Literary Dhimotiki (1964); O. Mavrophidou, A Handbook of the Greek Stylized (Katharevusa) Language (1953); A. Thumb, A Handbook of the Modern Greek Language (1964).

HEBREW

בְּרֵאשִׁית בָּרָא אֱלֹהִים אֵת הַשָּׁמַיִם וְאֵת הָאָרֶץ: וְהָאָרֶץ הָיְתָה תֹהוּ
וָבֹהוּ וְחֹשֶׁךְ עַל־פְּנֵי תְהוֹם וְרוּחַ אֱלֹהִים מְרַחֶפֶת עַל־פְּנֵי הַמָּיִם: וַיֹּאמֶר
אֱלֹהִים יְהִי אוֹר וַיְהִי־אוֹר: וַיַּרְא אֱלֹהִים אֶת־הָאוֹר כִּי־טוֹב וַיַּבְדֵּל
אֱלֹהִים בֵּין הָאוֹר וּבֵין הַחֹשֶׁךְ: וַיִּקְרָא אֱלֹהִים ׀ לָאוֹר יוֹם וְלַחֹשֶׁךְ קָרָא
לָיְלָה וַיְהִי־עֶרֶב וַיְהִי־בֹקֶר יוֹם אֶחָד: Genesis 1: 1–5—

Alphabet, transliteration, and pronunciation

		Name	Transliteration	Phonetic value	Numeral value
א		'Alef	' or omit	originally a glottal stop; now silent	1
ב		Bēth	b, v	b, v	2
ג		Gīmel	g	g in go	3
ד		Daleth	d	d	4
ה		Hē	h	h; silent at end of word	5
ו		Wāw	w	originally w; now v	6
ז		Zayin	z	z	7
ח		Ḥēth	ḥ	a strong h	8
ט		Ṭēth	ṭ	originally emphatic t; now t	9
י		Yōd	y	y in yes	10
כ	ך	Kaf	k, kh	k, kh as German ch	20
ל		Lamed	l	l	30
מ	ם	Mēm	m	m	40
נ	ן	Nūn	n	n	50
ס		Samekh	s	s in so	60
ע		'Ayin	'	originally a laryngal voiced spirant; now silent	70
פ	ף	Pē	p, f	p, f	80
צ	ץ	Ṣadē	ṣ	originally emphatic s; now ts in pets	90

[Concluded on following page]

	Name	Transliteration	Phonetic value	Numeral value
ק	Qōf	q	originally velar *k;* now *k*	100
ר	Rēsh	r	*r,* as in French uvular or Italian trilled	200
שׂ	Śīn, Shīn	ś, sh	ś; originally palatal; now *s* in so; *sh* as in shoe	300
ת	Tāw	t	*t;* originally also like *th* in thin	400

Hebrew uses no capitals at beginning of words, such as proper names.

Hebrew follows English and American usage with regard to quotation marks and italics.

In transliteration, especially of names, the macrons over vowels and the dots under consonants, as well as ' and ', are often omitted; ' is also printed as '. For *f*, *ph* is often used. For *ś*, an ordinary *s* is often found, and then samekh is sometimes represented by *ś*. For *sh*, *š* is sometimes used, especially in scholarly works. There are other special transliteration practices to be found in scholarly works.

Hebrew is read from right to left. Its alphabet consists of 22 letters, all consonants; the vowels are represented by vowel signs or points, as explained under Vowels below.

Special characters

Five of the letters (*kaf, mēm, nūn, pē,* and *ṣadē*) have a so-called final form, shown immediately to the right of its respective regular form. This final form is used as the final letter of a word.

Eight of the letters represent two sounds each, distinguished by means of a dot, as follows:

ב as *b* or *v*   בּ as *b* or *bb*
ג as *g;* also like Dutch *g*   גּ as *g* in big, *gg*
ד as *d;* and like *th* in then   דּ as *d, dd*
ה as *h* or silent   הּ as *hh* (stronger aspiration)
כ as *k* or German *ch*   כּ as *k, kk*
פ as *p* or *f*   פּ as *p, pp*
שׁ as *sh*   שׂ as *s* in sin
ת as *t* or *th*   תּ as *t, tt*

Some of the letters seem to be more or less similar. These are grouped, for the convenience of identification, within brackets below:

[Bēth ב   Kaf כ]   [Daleth ד   Kaf (final) ך   Rēsh ר]   [Mēm (final) ם   Śamekh ס]

[Gimel ג   Nūn נ]   [Teth ט   Mēm מ]   ['Ayin ע   Ṣadē צ]   [Ḥeth ח   Hē ה   Tāw ת]

[Wāw ו   Zayin ז   Yōd י   Nūn (final) ן]

Vowels

The vowels are represented by marks called vowel points. These are placed above or below the consonant and, with the exception of the furtive pataḥ, have the effect of a vowel following the consonant; e.g., בַּ (*ba*), בֵּ (*bē*). The forms, names, and sounds of the vowels are as follows:

Long Vowels		Short Vowels	
ָ Qameṣ *ā*	*a* as in palm	ַ Pataḥ *a*	*a* as in part (short)
ֵ Ṣere *ē*	*ei* as in vein	ֶ Segol *e*	*e* as in bed
ִי Hirik gadol *ī*	*i* as in machine	ִ Hirik katon *i*	*i* as in big
ֹ Holam *ō*	*o* as in no	ָ Qameṣ katon *o*	*o* as in soft
וּ Shuruk *ū*	*oo* as in moon	ֻ Kubbuts *u*	*u* as in full

The furtive pataḥ

All vowels are pronounced as if they follow the consonant to which they are ascribed, with the exception of final ח, which is pronounced not *ḥa,* but *ah.* This pataḥ is termed "furtive pataḥ."

The shwa

Sometimes shwa represents the sound of the first *e* in believe; e.g., שְׁמַע (shema); it may be transliterated ᵉ. At other times it is not pronounced, as in אַבְרָם (avrom), so that a consonant cluster results. Also, shwa is written, according to certain rules for writing Hebrew, before the points for *a*, *e*, and *o* to represent a very short vowel; e.g., חֲלִי, אֱמֶת, אֲנִי. These vowel point combinations, ⁓, ⁓, and ⁓ are transliterated *ă*, *ĕ*, and *ŏ*, respectively.

Punctuation and accentuation

Although the principles and marks of punctuation in modern Hebrew are, in the main, as in English, Scriptural Hebrew employs, in addition to the vowel points, 21 accent marks, which are placed either singly or in various combinations above or below the consonantal characters they modify. These have a threefold object: (*a*) to indicate stress; (*b*) to direct cantillation—the chanting in which the Scriptures are intoned; and (*c*) to indicate distinctions in the meanings of words, e.g., בְּנֵי, they build, but בָּנוּ, in us.

As marks of cantillation, accent marks are divided into two classes: disjunctives and conjunctives, the former corresponding to marks of separation in English— the period, semicolon, comma, etc., the latter indicating that the word bearing them is connected in sense with that which follows. The table presents the forms, names, and classifications of these accents:

Disjunctives

Form	EMPERORS (קֵסָרִים)	Name		Form	PRINCES (מִשְׁנִים)	Name
בְ	Silluq	סָלּוּק		ב֡	Zarqā'	זַרְקָא
בָ	'Ethnāh	אֶתְנָח		ב֠	Paštā'	פַּשְׁטָא
				ב֢	Yᵉthīv	יְתִיב
				ב֖	Tᵉvīr	תְּבִיר
	KINGS (מְלָכִים)			ב֤	'Azlā'	אַזְלָא
				בֵ	Gērēš	גֵּרֵשׁ
בֺ	Sᵉgōltā'	סְגוֹלְתָּא		ב֞	Gēršayim	גֵּרְשַׁיִם
ב֔	Zāqēf Qāṭōn	זָקֵף קָטֹן	ז		COUNTS (שְׁלִישִׁים)	
ב֕	Zāqēf Gādōl	זָקֵף גָּדוֹל		ב֗	Pāzēr	פָּזֵר
ב֖	Ṭippᵉhā'	טִפְּחָא		ב֟	Qarnēy Fārāh	קַרְנֵי פָרָה
בֿ	Rᵉvīa'	רְבִיע		ב֪	Tᵉlīšāh Gᵉdōlāh	תְּלִישָׁה גְדוֹלָה
ב֙	Šalšeleth	שַׁלְשֶׁלֶת		ב֩	Tᵉlīšāh Qᵉṭannāh	תְּלִישָׁה קְטַנָּה
				ב׀	Pᵉsīq	פְּסִיק

Conjunctives

Form	Name			Form	Name	
בֽ	Mūnah	מוּנַח		ב֧	Dargā'	דַּרְגָּא
בֽ	Mahpakh	מַהְפָּךְ		ב֨	Merkā'	מֵרְכָא
בֽ	Qadmā'	קַדְמָא		ב֥	Merkā' Kᵉfūlāh	מֵרְכָא כְפוּלָה

There are also three supplementary marks of interpunction: The *soph-pasuk* (:), terminal mark of a verse; the *pesik* (|), for a pause within the verse; and *makkeph* (-), the elevated hyphen between words.

Syllabification

Words in modern Hebrew may be divided between syllables of three or more letters.

The calendar

The Hebrew calendar was given its present fixed form by Hillel II about A.D. 360. It is based on a year of 12 months, alternating 30 and 29 days, with an intercalary month of 29 days in leap year. These months, with their corresponding periods in the Gregorian calendar, are as follows:

Tishri	תשרי	September–October
Heshvan	חשן	October–November
Kislev	כסלו	November–December
Tevet	טבת	December–January
Shevat	שבט	January–February
Adar	אדר	February–March
Veadar	ואדר	Intercalary month
Nisan	ניסן	March–April
Iyar	איר	April–May
Sivan	סין	May–June
Tammuz	תמז	June–July
Av	אב	July–August
Elul	אלול	August–September

The year begins on the first day of the month of Tishri, which is the day of the Molad, or appearance of the new moon, nearest the autumnal equinox. The actual date is, however, sometimes shifted 1 or 2 days, according to specific regulations; thus, New Year may not fall on either a Friday or a Sunday, since that would conflict with the observance of the Sabbath; nor, for a like reason, may it come on a Wednesday, since that would cause Atonement Day to come on a Friday.

To convert a given year (anno Domini) into its corresponding Hebrew year (anno mundi), add 3,760 to the former, bearing in mind, however, that the year begins in September. As the Hebrew calendar omits the thousands, the year 5705, corresponding to the Christian year 1945, is represented in Hebrew characters by תשה, 705, these characters, as already explained, denoting 400, 300, and 5, respectively.

The days of the week are referred to as first day, second day, etc., the seventh being called Sabbath (שבת). The holidays, festivals, and fasts, with their dates, are as follows:

Rosh Hashana (New Year, Tishri 1)	ראש השנה
Tsom Gedaliah (Fast of Gedaliah, Tishri 3)	צום גדליה
Yom Kippur (Day of Atonement, Tishri 10)	יום כפור
Sukkoth (Feast of Tabernacles, Tishri 15–22)	סכות
Simhath Torah (Rejoicing Over the Law, Tishri 23)	שמחת תורה
Hanukkah (Feast of Dedication, Kislev 25)	חנכה
Asarah be-Tevet (Fast of Tevet, Tevet 10)	עשרה בטבת
Purim (Feast of Lots, Adar 14)	פורים
Pesah (Passover, Nisan 15–21)	פסח
Shabuoth (Feast of Weeks, Sivan 6)	שבעות
Tishah be-Av (Fast of Av, Av 9)	תשעה באב

Abbreviations

In Hebrew, abbreviations are set as follows: If of one letter, one prime mark (') is used after the letter; if of more than one letter, a double prime ('') is used

just before the last letter. Vowel points are always omitted. The abbreviations most frequently used are as follows:

Sir, Master, Mr.; thousand	א', אדון, אלף
Aleph Beth (the alphabet)	א"ב, אלף בית
Said our learned ones of blessed memory	אחז"ל, אמרו חכמינו זכרונם לברכה
The Land of Israel (Palestine)	א"י, ארץ ישראל
God willing	איה, אם ירצה השם
Synagogue	בהכ"נ, בית הכנסת
Sons of Israel, the Jews	ב"י, בני ישראל
In these words, viz.	בזה"ל, בזה הלשון
The author	בע"מ, בעל מחבר
Gaon (title of Jewish princes in the Babylonian exile), His Highness, His Majesty.	ג', גאון
The laws of Israel	ד"י, דיני ישראל
The Holy One, Blessed be He (the Lord)	הקב"ה, הקדוש ברוך הוא
Destruction of the First Temple	חב"ר, חרבן בית ראשן
Destruction of the Second Temple	חב"ש, חרבן בית שני
Exodus from Egypt	יצ"מ, יציאת מצרים
As it was said; as it was written	כמ"ש, כמו שנאמר; כמו שכתב
A.M. (anno mundi)	לב"ע, לבריאת עולם
The Holy Language (Hebrew)	לה"ק, לשון הקדש
Good luck; I congratulate you	מז"ט, מזל טוב
The Sacred Books	סה"ק, ספרים הקדושים
The Holy Scroll	ס"ת, ספר תורה
May he rest in peace	ע"ה, עליו השלום
In the Hereafter	עוה"ב, עולם הבא
New Year's Eve	ער"ה, ערב ראש השנה
Sabbath Eve	ע"ש, ערב שבת
Verse; chapter	פ', פסוק; פרק
The judgment of the court	פב"ד, פסק בית דין
Saint (St.); Zion	צ', צדיק; ציון
Recognition of God's justice	צה"ד, צדוק הדין
The reading of the Holy Scroll	קה"ת, קריאת התורה
First of all	קכ"ד, קדם כל דבר
Our Rabbis of Blessed Memory	רז"ל, רבותינו זכרונם לברכה
Rabbi Moses, son of Maimon (Maimonides)	רמב"ם, ר' משה בן מימן
Catalog	רש"ס, רשימת ספרים
Year; line; hour	ש', שנה; שורה; שעה
Sabbath days and holidays	שו"ט, שבתות וימים טובים
As stated	שנ', שנאמר
Babylonian Talmud	ת"ב, תלמוד בבלי
The Books of the Law, the Prophets, and Hagiographa (Old Testament)	תנ"ך, תורה, נביאים, כתובים

Cardinal numbers

one	אחד, אחת	twenty	עשרים
two	שנים, שתים	thirty	שלשים
three	שלשה, שלש	forty	ארבעים
four	ארבעה, ארבע	fifty	חמשים
five	חמשה, חמש	sixty	ששים
six	ששה, שש	seventy	שבעים
seven	שבעה, שבע	eighty	שמנים
eight	שמנה	ninety	תשעים
nine	תשעה, תשע	hundred	מאה
ten	עשרה, עשר	thousand	אלף

In forming the numbers from 11 to 19, the terms עשרה in the feminine and עשר in the masculine are used, preceded by the proper unit number; for 21 and upward, the term corresponding to the proper tenth digit is followed by the proper unit term preceded by the conjunction ו, and; e.g., twelve שנים עשר, twenty-four עשרים וארבע, etc.

Ordinal numbers

first	ראשן	sixth	ששי
second	שני	seventh	שביעי
third	שלישי	eighth	שמיני
fourth	רביעי	ninth	תשיעי
fifth	חמישי	tenth	עשירי

After 10 the ordinals are similar in form to the cardinals with the addition of the definite article ה; e.g., העשרים, the twentieth.

Seasons

spring	אביב	autumn	סתיו
summer	קיץ	winter	חרף

Time

hour	שעה	month	חדש
day	יום	season	מעד
week	שבוע	year	שנה

REFERENCES.—J. Philips and A. Hyman, Complete Instructor in Hebrew (1919); J. Weingreen, A Practical Grammar for Classical Hebrew (1939); A. S. Waldstein, English Hebrew and Hebrew English Dictionary (1936); P. Arnold-Kellner and M. D. Gross, Complete Hebrew-English Dictionary (1923).

HUNGARIAN

Az ótátrafüredi vendéglőben már nem muzsikált a cigány és a vendégek nagy része is elutazott már haza. Akik még ott maradtak, az a pár ember, elfért a vacsoránál három-négy asztal körül. Pedig most járt a leggyönyörűbb idő, az esős nyarat tiszta, napsütéses ősz váltotta föl.—K. Csathó, 'A varjú a toronyórán'.

Alphabet and pronunciation

A	a	*aw* in law, but shorter
Á	á	*a* in father; in family names sometimes written *aa, aá*
B	b	*b*
C	c	*ts*
Cs	cs	*ch* in church
D	d	*d*
Dz	dz	as *d* followed by *z*
Dzs	dzs	as *j* in judge
E	e	*e* in met
É	é	somewhat like *ei* in eight
F	f	*f*
G	g	*g* in go
Gy	gy	somewhat like *dy* in did you, said rapidly
H	h	*h*
I	i	*i* in hit; at the end of historic family names sometimes written *y*
Í	í	*ee* in meet
J	j	*y* in yes
K	k	*k*
L	l	*l*
Ly	ly	*y* in yes
M	m	*m*
N	n	*n;* before *g*, as *ng* in finger; before *k*, as in sink
Ny	ny	somewhat like *ny* in canyon
O	o	*o* in November (short)
Ó	ó	*o* in no; in family names sometimes written *oo, oó*
Ö	ö	like short German *ö* or French *eu;* in family names sometimes written *eö, ew*
Ő	ő	like long German *ö* or French *eu;* in family names sometimes written *eő*
P	p	*p*
Q	q	
R	r	trilled *r*
S	s	*sh* in shoe
Sz	sz	*s* in so
T	t	*t*
Ty	ty	somewhat like *ty* in tune
U	u	somewhat like *oo* in good
Ú	ú	*oo* in food

[Concluded on following page]

Ŭ	ü	like short German *ü* or French *u*
Ű	ű	like long German *ü* or French *u*
V	v	*v;* in historic family names sometimes written *w*
W	w	
X	x	
Y	y	
Z	z	*z* in zone
Zs	zs	*s* in pleasure

Special characters

Hungarian uses the Latin alphabet with the addition of the following special characters: *Á á, É é, Í í, Ó ó, Ö ö, Ő ő, Ú ú, Ü ü,* and *Ű ű.*

Vowels and consonants

The vowels are *a, á, e, é, i, í, o, ó, ö, ő, u, ú, ü,* and *ű;* the remaining letters of the alphabet are consonants.

The vowels *á, é, í, ó, ő, ú,* and *ű* are long; the other vowels are short. Double consonants are pronounced long, somewhat in the manner of $n(k)n$ in penknife. When doubled, *cs, gy, ly, ny, sz, ty,* and *zs* are written *ccs, ggy, lly, nny, ssz, tty,* and *zzs.*

The combination *qu* is pronounced *kv; w* is usually pronounced *v; x* is pronounced as though written *ksz.* The letter *y* in many family names is pronounced as though written *i.*

Diphthongs

Standard Hungarian has no diphthongs. Each vowel is fully articulated.

Compound letters

The compound letters and their sounds are:

ch as *ch* in church (old spelling and foreign words as *technika, mechánika*)

cs (see Alphabet and pronunciation)

cz now written *c,* like *ts*

dz as *d* followed by *z* (see Alphabet and pronunciation)

dzs as *j* in judge (see Alphabet and pronunciation)

gh as *g* in go (old spelling)

gy (see Alphabet and pronunciation)

ly (see Alphabet and pronunciation)

ny (see Alphabet and pronunciation)

ph as *f* (in foreign words)

rh as though written *r* (old spelling and foreign words)

sz (see Alphabet and pronunciation)

th as *t* (old spelling and foreign words)

ty (see Alphabet and pronunciation)

zs (see Alphabet and pronunciation)

Main rules for syllabification

1. Every word consists of as many syllables as the number of vowels in it. Consonants alone do not constitute syllables: *fi-a-i, ro-ko-na-ink, a-me-ri-ka-i, ma-gyar, ki-ált.*

2. Vowels which constitute syllables in themselves may be left at the end of the line or transferred to the next line: *dia-dal* or *di-adal, fia-tal* or *fi-atal, hiá-ba* or *hi-ába.* The same rule applies to the division of derivative forms: *árui-ból* or *áru-iból, könyvei-tek* or *könyve-itek.*

3. However, it is not customary to leave one letter at the end of the line or to bring one over to the next: *aka-rat* (not *a-karat*), *ha-zai* (not *haza-i*).

4. If there is only one consonant between two vowels it is attached to the second syllable: *a-dok, pa-pír, ko-sár.*

5. Double letters indicative of long consonants between two vowels are divided: *fil-lér, ket-tő; em-ber-rel, víz-zel, szeb-bé, job-bat, hit-tem, tol-las, sok-kal.*

6. Compound letters may not be divided; they are treated as single (short) consonants: *asz-tal, mor-zsa, tarisz-nya, ar-chívum; kin-cses, má-zsás, almana-chot.*

7. Divided double compound letters representing long consonants (such as *ccs, ggy, lly, nny, ssz, tty* for *cscs, gygy, lyly, nyny, szsz, tyty*) are repeated in full forms: *hosz-szú* (from: *hosszú*), *fagy-gyú* (from: *faggyú*), *haty-tyú* (from: *hattyú*).

8. The compound consonants *dz* and *dzs* are separated as follows: (a) when a consonant appears before them: *brin-dza* (from: *brindza*), *lán-dzsa* (from: *lándzsa*); (b) when a vowel appears before them: *mad-zag* (from: *madzag*), *maharad-zsa* (from: *maharadzsa*).

9. In a group of two or more consonants, division is made before the last consonant (including compound letters): *ab-rak, al-szik; temp-lom, lajst-rom; nyolc-kor, part-ra, rend-ben; sakk-ban, rossz-ra; kard-dal, kulcs-csal, rongy-gyá.*

10. Compound words are divided according to their formative elements: *vas-út, kert-ajtó, rend-őr, csak-is; egyszer-egy, kis-asszony, tölgy-erdő, rozs-szalma.* The same applies to derivatives of compound words: *vas-útas, rend-őri, kis-asszonynak.*

11. The same rule applies to certain nominal and adverbial prefixes (originally separate words) which are kept intact, such as: *al, alá, át, el, elé, elől, fel, fenn (fent), hátra, ki, kinn (kint), leg, meg, össze, szét, túl, viszont,* in words like *al-elnök, át-adás, fel-adat, ki-esés, leg-első, meg-ette, össze-írás.*

12. Frequently used foreign words are divided as the original stock of the Hungarian vocabulary: *ar-zén, elekt-romos, gra-fikon.* The same applies to compound foreign words of wide acceptance in which the etymological boundaries between the components may not be apparent for the general Hungarian speaker: *de-magóg, demok-rácia, inf-luenza, inst-ruktor, mo-narchia, prog-ram, ref-lex.* But: *extra-profit, kilo-gramm, melo-dráma.*

13. Last syllables of the Hungarian derivatives of foreign words are divided according to the rules of Hungarian syllabification: *eminen-sek, helikopte-ren, extrapofi-tért, heliocentriku-san, refle-xek.*

14. Infrequently used foreign words and components of foreign words are divided according to their respective conventions: *dia-fragma, bif-sztek, champi-gnon.*

15. Not compound forms of Hungarian and foreign proper names, including family names, are divided according to the rules of Hungarian syllabification: *Köl-csey, Mó-ricz; Schil-ler, Tolsz-toj; Bor-sod, Moszk-va; Sziny-nyei* (from: *Szinnyei*), *Berety-tyó* (from: *Berettyó*), *Megy-gyes* (from: *Meggyes*). The same applies to derivatives of proper names: *Balo-ghot* (but *Ba-logh*), *Gorki-jig* (but *Gor-kij*), *Budapes-ti* or *budapes-ti* (but *Buda-pest*), *Regensbur-gig* (but *Regensburg*); *Kovács-csal* (from: *Kováccsal*), *Wass-sal* (from: *Wassal*), *Végh-gel* (from: *Végghel*), *György-gyel* (from: *Györggyel*), *Grimm-mel* (from: *Grimmel*).

16. Since *ch* and *x* are regarded as symbols for short (single) consonants, they are treated in syllabification of foreign words as single letters: *Mün-chen, Ri-chard, Me-xikó, Xer-xes.* The same applies to syllables in derivatives beginning with these letters: *Züri-chig, Féli-xet;* but *Félix-szel* (from: *Félixszel*).

Illustrative word divisions

[The numbers in parentheses refer to the syllabification rules]

aka-dá-lyoz	(1, 3, 6)	is-me-re-tes	(9, 1, 4)
akasz-ta-ni	(1, 3, 4, 6)	jog-el-le-nes	(10, 5, 4)
Ál-la-mok	(5, 4)	ki-kvár-té-lyoz	(11, 14, 9, 6)
al-or-vos	(11, 9)	ki-pró-bál-ni	(11, 4, 9)
alu-szé-kony	(1, 6, 4)	kis-is-ko-la	(10, 9, 4)
ame-ri-kai	(1, 4)	kom-pro-mit-tál-ni	(14, 14, 5, 9)
an-tro-po-ló-gia	(14, 4, 4, 4)	kon-gresz-szus	(14, 15)
át-ál-lít	(11, 5)	leg-drá-gább	(11, 4)
azo-no-sí-tás	(1, 3, 4)	leg-e-rő-sebb	(11, 1, 3, 4)
ba-rá-ti-as	(4, 1)	le-gön-gyöl	(11, 6)
bo-lyon-ga-ni	(6, 9, 1, 4)	ma-gya-ros-ság	(6, 5)
ci-ga-ret-ta	(1, 4, 5)	meg-a-la-kit	(11, 1, 3, 4)
cí-mez-ni	(1, 4, 4)	mik-rosz-kóp	(12, 6)
Cseh-szlo-vá-kia	(10, 14, 1, 3)	Né-met-or-szág	(2, 10, 6)
cse-le-ked-ni	(4, 4, 9)	né-me-tül	(2, 3)
csil-lag-év	(5, 10)	nép-ok-ta-tás	(10, 9, 3)
cu-kor-nád	(4, 10)	név-a-lá-í-rás	(10, 1, 11, 1, 3)
de-ka-gramm	(12)	or-vo-si	(9, 4)
el-ad-ni	(11, 9)	or-vos-sá-gos	(9, 5, 4)
elő-a-dás	(11, 1, 4)	oszt-ha-tat-lan	(4, 4, 9)
elő-ze-tes	(11, 4)	ön-ál-lót-lan	(10, 5, 9)
em-be-rek	(1, 4)	őr-ál-lás	(10, 5)
em-ber-is-me-ret	(9, 10, 9, 4)	ős-e-lem	(10, 1, 4)
fel-ál-lí-tás	(11, 5, 3, 4)	szét-osz-tás	(11, 9)
fél-esz-ten-dő	(10, 6, 9)	Szov-jet-o-rosz-or-szág	(15, 1, 4, 10, 6)
fent-em-lí-tett	(11, 9, 1, 4)	túl-é-rő	(11, 1, 3)
fe-nye-ge-tés	(1, 6, 4)	út-le-vél	(10, 4)
gőz-ha-jó	(10, 4)	vi-szont-ha-tás	(6, 11, 4)
gyó-gyá-szat	(6, 6, 6)	vi-szo-nos-ság	(6, 3, 5)
gyó-gyít-ha-tó	(6, 9, 4)	za-var-gás	(4, 9)
hi-á-nyos	(1, 6)	zűr-za-var	(10, 4)
iga-zít-ha-tó	(1, 4, 4)	zsar-nok-ság	(4, 4)
írás-hi-ba	(10, 1, 4)		

Stress and diacritics

Without exception, stress is on the first syllable. Diacritical marks (see Special characters) are used to denote vowel modifications.

Capitalization

1. Forms of address in letters, etc., and titles are capitalized: *Felséges Uram* (Your Majesty); *Méltóságod* (Your Lordship); *Tisztelt Uram* (Dear Sir).

2. Proper names and those referring to God are capitalized.

3. Adjectives formed from proper names and names of months are lowercased: *budapesti* (of Budapest); *január, március, szeptember* (January, March, September).

4. Titles of newspapers and periodicals (with the exception of definite and indefinite articles and the conjunction if they appear beyond the first word in such a title) are capitalized: *Acta Linguistica, Élet és Tudomány, Magyar Nemzet, Orvosi Hetilap, Történelmi Szemle.*

5. Titles of scientific handbooks, dictionaries, encyclopedias, linguistic monuments or other unique publications are capitalized: *Magyar Szófejtő Szótár, Révai Nagy Lexikona, Halotti Beszéd, Jókai Kódex, Toldi Szerelme.*

But titles of poems, books, and monographic series are capitalized generally only by capitalization of the first letter of the title: *Nemzeti dal, A magyar vers ritmusa, Ember és világ.*

6. Personal pronouns (second and third persons singular and plural and their declinative forms) are capitalized in correspondence and public addresses: *Te, Ön; Ti, Önök; Téged, Önt; Titeket, Önöket.*

7. Names of nations, ethnic groups, ethnolinguistic, and religious units are lowercased: *amerikai* (American); *észt* (Estonian); *magyar* (Hungarian); *olasz* (Italian); *szász* (Saxonian); *székely* (Székely, Siculian); *indián* (Indian); *néger* (Negro); *germán* (Germanic); *román* (Romance, also Rumanian); *szláv* (Slavic); *buddhista* (Buddhist); *római katolikus* (Roman Catholic); *református* (Reformed); *zsidó* (Jewish).

Punctuation

The most important differences are as follows:

1. Period is used in dates after numbers, indicating the year, the month, and the day (in that order): *1848. III. 15;* the same date may be written as follows: *1848. március 15.* or *1848. márc. 15.*

2. Period is used generally after the ordinal numbers when indicating a position of somebody or something in a set or line: *12. törvénycikk* (Law Article XII); *1956. évi* (of the year of 1956); *IX. kerület* (IXth district).

3. Period is used after the number of pages in a source referred to when the absence of a period could become the source of confusion: *Petőfi összes művei V. k. 24* (Petőfi's All Works, volume V, [page] 24); but *Petőfi összes művei V. k. 24.* (Petőfi's All Works, volume V, page 24; i.e., 24th page), because the number 24 without a period would mean that volume 5 contains only 24 pages.

4. Period is used after most of the abbreviations *(see Abbreviations).*

5. In compound and complex sentences each sentence is separated by a comma; accordingly, the conjunction *hogy* (that), *de* (but), *hanem* (but), and the relative pronouns, when linking a subordinate clause, are preceded by a comma.

6. Hungarian equivalents of inserted words such as *however, indeed, too, therefore,* are not placed between commas (as is the case in English) unless there is another reason for doing so.

7. Speech is not separated by a comma but by a dash.

8. In correspondence, salutation is not separated by a comma but by an exclamation mark.

9. The colon is used in the front of a quotation which is preceded by a quoting sentence or reference.

10. The colon is used in the front of the title of a work when listed after the author's name: *Arany: Toldi; Vörösmarty: Csongor és Tünde.* In the context of a sentence, however, the colon is omitted: *Arany Toldijának ítélték a díjat.* (The prize was given to the "Toldi" by Arany). *Mikszáth "Különös házasság" című regényéből filmet készítettek.* (A motion picture was made from the novel "A Peculiar Marriage" by Mikszáth.)

11. The colon introduces an enumeration: *Hárman ültek a kocsiban: az apa, az anya és a fiú.* (There were three sitting in the car, the father, the mother, and the son.)

12. In works of *belles lettres* (novels, short stories, etc.) the dialog is written in alternating lines with a dash in the front of each sentence:
—*Maguk hova mennek?* (Where are you going?)
—*Budapestre.* (To Budapest)
—*Mikor indulnak?* (When are you leaving?)
—*Amikor akarja.* (Any time you wish)

13. A sentence, interjected in the context of another, is separated by the dash: "*Nem hagyta cselédit—ezért öli bú—vele halni meg, ócska ruhába'!*" ("He could not suffer, that was his deep concern, to let his servants die with him in worn-out clothes!")

14. Words or phrases which appear (as explanations to certain elements in the sentence) within the context of the sentence are put in parentheses: *A szófajoknak (beszédrészeknek) többféle csoportosítása lehetséges.* (There are more possibilities for the grouping of the types of words; i.e., the parts of speech.)

15. If the parenthesized words or phrases appear at the end of that part of a compound or complex sentence which is separated from the rest by a comma, the comma is used after the closing half of the parenthesis: *Vannak olyan szavaink (pl. fagy, les, nyom stb.), amelyek igék is, névszók is.* (We have words like frost, watch, print, etc., which are used as verbs as well as nouns.)

16. In Hungarian, the initial half of the quotation mark appears on the lower level, the conclusive half on the upper level of a line: „ . . . . . . "
The quotation within a quotation is indicated by the so-called 'inner quotation mark' which is: >>. . . . . .<<

Word order

1. Surname is given first, followed by Christian name: *Nagy János* (John Nagy).
The same applies to statements regarding authorship, etc.: *Szerkesztette: Nagy János* (Edited by John Nagy). *Írták: Kovács Pál és Szabó József* (By Paul Kovács and Joseph Szabó).

2. Words denoting profession or used in addressing a person (with full name) follow the Christian name: *Nagy János tanár* (Prof. John Nagy), or the last name (when the Christian name is not indicated): *Kovács művész úr* (The artist Mr. Kovács).

3. The word order in a date is the reverse of that in English; first comes the year, then the month, and at the end the day: *1848. március tizenötödike* (March 15 of 1848); *január elseje* (the first of January).

Abbreviations

a.	alatt, under	jegyz.	jegyzet, note, footnote
áll.	állami, state-connected	K	kelet, east
ált.	általános, general		kötet, volume
Bp.	Budapest	kb.	körülbelül, circa
bp.-i	budapesti, of Budapest	ker.	kerület, district
c.	címû, entitled	ker.	keresztény, Christian
D	dél, south	köv.	következő, following, next
db.	darab, piece	krt.	körút, avenue
de.	délelőtt, a.m.	l.	lap, page
DK	délkelet, southeast	l.	lásd!, see!
DNy	délnyugat, southwest	m	méter, meter
Dr. or dr.	doktor, doctor (degree)	m.	magyar, Hungarian
du.	délután, p.m.	min.	miniszter, minister (in the Cabinet)
É	észak, north		
ÉK	északkelet, northeast	ny.	nyugalmazott, retired
ÉNy	északnyugat, northwest	Ny	nyugat, west
érk.	érkezik, arrives	ó	óra (o-clock), hour
évf.	évfolyam, year (of publication)	p	perc, minute
		pl.	például, for example, e.g.
f	fillér, penny	pu.	pályaudvar, railway station
f.é.	folyó évi, of the current year		
		s.k.	saját kezével, signed
fej.	fejezet, chapter	stb.	s a többi, etc.
ford.	fordította, translated by	szerk.	szerkesztette, edited by
Ft	forint, florin	tc.	törvénycikk, law article
gimn.	gimnázium, high school	t.i.	tudniillik, i.e.
hiv.	hivatalos, official	u.	utca, street
i.e.	időszámításunk előtti, B.C.	ua.	ugyanaz, same as
i.sz.	időszámításunk szerinti, A.D.	vm.	vármegye, county

Cardinal numbers

egy	one	harminc	thirty
két (kettő)[1]	two	harmincegy, etc.	thirty-one,
három	three		etc.
négy	four	negyven	forty
öt	five	ötven	fifty
hat	six	hatvan	sixty
hét	seven	hetven	seventy
nyolc	eight	nyolcvan	eighty
kilenc	nine	kilencven	ninety
tíz	ten	száz	hundred
tizenegy	eleven	százegy, etc.	one hundred
tizenkét (tizenkettő)	twelve		and one,
tizenhárom, etc.	thirteen, etc.		etc.
húsz	twenty	kétszáz, etc.	two hun-
huszonegy	twenty-one		dred, etc.
huszonkét (huszon-	twenty-two,	ezer	thousand
kettő),[1] etc.	etc.		

Ordinal numbers

első	first	tizenharmadik, etc.	thirteenth,
második	second		etc.
harmadik	third	huszadik	twentieth
negyedik	fourth	huszonegyedik	twenty-first
ötödik	fifth	huszonkettedik, etc.	twenty-sec-
hatodik	sixth		ond, etc.
hetedik	seventh	harmincadik, etc.	thirtieth,
nyolcadik	eighth		etc.
kilencedik	ninth	harmincegyedik	thirty-first
tizedik	tenth	harminckettedik, etc.	thirty-sec-
tizenegyedik	eleventh		ond, etc.
tizenkettedik	twelfth	századik	hundredth
		ezredik	thousandth

Months

január (jan.)	January	julius (jul.)	July
február (feb.)	February	augusztus (aug.)	August
március (márc.)	March	szeptember (szept.)	September
április (ápr.)	April	október (okt.)	October
május (máj.)	May	november (nov.)	November
junius (jun.)	June	december (dec.)	December

Days

vasárnap	Sunday	csütörtök	Thursday
hétfő	Monday	péntek	Friday
kedd	Tuesday	szombat	Saturday
szerda	Wednesday		

Seasons

tavasz	spring	ősz	autumn
nyár	summer	tél	winter

Time

óra	hour	hó, hónap	month
nap	day	év, esztendő	year
hét	week		

REFERENCES.—Zoltán Bánhidi, A Textbook of the Hungarian Language (1966); Ferenc Kiefer, On Emphasis and Word Order in Hungarian (1967); Augustus A. Koski and Ilona Mihalyfy, Hungarian Basic Course (1963–64); John Lotz, Hungarian Reader (1962); László Országh, Hungarian-English and English-Hungarian Dictionary (1967); Ferenc Papp, Reverse-Alphabetized Dictionary of the Hungarian Language (1969); U.S. Library of Congress, Reference Department, Slavic and Central European Division, Hungarian Abbreviations; a Selective List, compiled by Elemer Bako (1961); János Zsilka, The System of Hungarian Sentence Patterns (1967).

[1] The ordinal két is used when followed by a noun; otherwise kettő.

ITALIAN

Un tratto importante, che caratterizza il grande movimento della civiltà italiana risorgente e che risulta, non pure dalla poesia e filosofia di quel tempo, ma anche dall'opera dei politici e degli stessi guerrieri, è quell'impronta diffusa di umanità, in cui si avvolge come in una rosea nube il loro pensiero e la loro vita, pur diretti come sono ad un unico ideale: il risorgimento della Patria.—Giovanni Vidari, Le civiltà d'Italia (1934), as quoted by Young and Cantarella, Corso d'Italiano (1942), p. 320.

Alphabet and pronunciation

A	a	*a* in far
B	b	*b;* all consonant letters may be doubled, and then pronounced long, as *n(k)n* in penknife, etc.
C	c	*c* in scan (=*k*) before *a, o, u,* and consonants; before *e* or *i,* similar to *ch* in chant; *cia, cie, cio,* and *ciu* pronounced as *cha* in chart, *che* in check or *cha* in chafe, *cho* in chortle, and *chu* in Manchu, respectively; *ccia,* etc., sound like *tch,* etc.; *scia, scie, scio,* and *sciu* pronounced as *sha* in sharp, *she* in shepherd, *sho* in show, and *sho* in shoe, respectively
D	d	*d*
E	e	*a* in grate; *e* in bell
F	f	*f*
G	g	*g* in gay before *a, o, u,* and consonants; before *e* or *i* like *j; gia, gie, gio,* and *giu* pronounced as *ja* in jar, *je* in jet, between *ja* in jaw and *jo* in joke, and *ju* in jury, respectively; *ggia,* etc., sound like *d* plus *ja,* etc.
H	h	silent, but makes a preceding *c* or *g* hard
I	i	*e* in me; *i* preceded by *c, sc,* or *g* and followed by *a, o,* or *u* is silent unless stressed; before or after more highly stressed vowel, *i* is similar to *y* in yes and in boy, respectively
J	j	*y* in yes; now obsolete and replaced by *i*
K	k	*k;* only in foreign words
L	l	*l* in million
M	m	*m*
N	n	*n*
O	o	*o* in note; *aw* in saw
P	p	*p* in spin
Q	q	always with following *u; qu* pronounced as in quick
R	r	*r* in three
S	s	*s;* usually *z* between two vowels; *scia, scie, scio,* and *sciu* are pronounced *sha, she, sho,* and *shu,* respectively
T	t	*t* in step

[Concluded on following page]

U u *oo* in coo; before or after more highly stressed vowel, *u* is
 similar to *w* in wet and how, respectively
V v *v*
W w }only in foreign words
X x }
Y y *i;* only in foreign words
Z z *ts* in quarts or *ds* in adz

Special characters

Italian uses the Latin alphabet. It has no special characters; accents are
employed only to a limited extent.

Vowels and consonants

The vowels are *a, e, i, o, u,* and *y;* the other letters of the alphabet are
consonants.

Diphthongs

The combination of an *i* or *u* with another, more highly stressed, vowel may
be regarded as diphthongal.

Digraphs

The digraphs and their sounds are:

ch as *c* in cat only before *e, i*   *gn* as in cognac (=*ny* in canyon)
gh as *g* in go only before *e, i*   *qu* as in squalor
gl as *ll* in million [1]   *sc* as *sh* in shall (before *e* or *i*)

Consonantal units

For the purpose of syllabification, a mute consonant followed by a liquid consonant is a consonantal unit. Hence, the following are consonantal units:

bl, br   *dr,*   *gl, gr*   *tl, tr*
chr, cl, cr   *fl, fr*   *pl, pr*   *vl, vr*

Also the combination of the letter *s* with any other following consonant, digraph,
or consonantal unit is a unit for purposes of syllabification.

Rules for syllabification

1. Digraphs and consonantal units may not be divided.
2. Division is made on a vowel before a single consonant, digraph, or consonantal unit: *ami-co, ba-gno, ca-pra, giu-sto, ma-schera, ro-stro.*
3. In a group of two or more consonants, division is made before the last
consonant, digraph, or consonantal unit: *sab-bia, ac-qua, ist-mo, an-che, com-pro.*
4. Division may be made between vowels only if they are strong, that is, *a, e, o.*
Hence, only the following vowel groups may be divided: *aa, ae, ao; ea, ee, eo;
oa, oe, oo: be-ato, co-atto, po-eta,* etc.
5. Prefixes are kept intact only if this conforms to rules 2 to 4: *con-stare* (rule
3), *pro-emio* (rule 4), *pro-getto* (rule 2), *sub-marino* (rule 3); but *co-nestabile* (rule
2), *proi-bire* (rule 2), *su-bordinare* (rule 2).[2]
6. Compound words are divided according to their component parts (and each
part according to rules 1 to 5): *gentil-uomo, cento-uno.*
If a compound is formed with an apostrophe, division may not be made on
the apostrophe; thus *dell'albero, un'arte, dovrebb'essere* may be divided only
del-l'al-be-ro, un'ar-te, do-vreb-b'es-se-re, respectively. A compound may be divided
also by making use of the full article or word: *dello albero, dovrebbe essere.*
7. Foreign words and components of foreign words (not naturalized) follow
the conventions of the language of origin: *Wash-ington, Haps-burg, Hamp-shire,
reichs-bank, Wag-ner.*

---

[1] In a few words *gl* is not a digraph and is pronounced as *gl* in angle; for example: *Ganglio, glicerina,
geroglifico, glifo, gloria, negligere,* etc.
[2] Usage varies as to this rule; some orthographers still prefer dividing on the prefix. The rule given in
the text above follows the recommendation of Leone Donati, Corso Pràtico di Lingua Italiana, 207, 1934,
Orell Füssli Editori, Zurigo e Lipsia. It is followed by most dictionaries as well as general works extant.

Illustrative word divisions

[The numbers in parentheses refer to the syllabification rules]

ab-bo-na-men-to	(3, 2, 2, 3)	fo-to-e-lio-gra-fia	(2, 6, 2, 2, 2)
ac-quie-sce-re	(3, 2, 2)	Fre-de-ris-bur-go	(2, 2, 7, 3)
ae-re-o-li-to	(2, 4, 2, 2)	gen-til-uo-mo	(3, 6, 2)
af-fli-to	(3, 2)	ge-o-gno-sti-co	(4, 2, 2, 2)
ame-ri-ca-no	(2, 2, 2)	in-du-stria-le	(3, 2, 2)
bi-gliet-taio	(2, 3)	ine-scu-sa-bi-le	(2, 2, 2, 2)
bis-a-vo-lo	(6, 2, 2)	ine-spli-ca-bi-le	(2, 2, 2, 2)
bi-so-gni-no	(2, 2, 2)	in-fi-schio	(3, 2)
Bre-ta-gna	(2, 2)	inin-tel-li-gen-te	(3, 3. 2, 3)
Buck-ing-ham	(7, 7)	inor-ga-ni-co	(3, 2, 2)
co-o-pe-ra-zio-ne	(4, 2, 2, 2, 2)	in-scrit-to-re	(3, 3, 2)
co-stret-to	(2, 3)	in-te-res-se	(3, 2, 3)
cre-sce-re	(2, 2)	iscri-zio-ne	(2, 2)
de-mo-cra-ti-co	(2, 2, 2, 2)	ist-mi-co	(3, 2)
dia-gno-sti-co	(2, 2, 2)	isto-lo-gi-co	(2, 2, 2)
di-scor-so	(2, 3)	istru-men-to	(2, 3)
di-sgra-zia	(2, 2)	ita-lia-no	(2, 2)
di-sor-di-ne	(2, 3, 2, 2)	Kam-tsciat-ka	(7, 3)
di-spo-si-zio-ne	(2, 2, 2, 2)	l'al-tr'ie-ri	(3, 2)
di-stin-ti-vo	(2, 3, 2)	ma-gne-ti-co	(2, 2, 2)
emi-sfe-ro	(2, 2)	ma-gni-fi-cen-te	(2, 2, 2, 3)
Epi-sco-pa-to	(2, 2, 2)	me-sme-ri-smo	(2, 2, 2)
esa-e-dro	(4, 2)	me-te-o-ri-te	(2, 4, 2, 2)
espa-tria-zio-ne	(2, 2, 2)	mil-li-gram-mo	(3, 2, 3)
espe-rien-za	(2, 3)	mi-san-tro-po	(2, 3, 2)
estra-di-zio-ne	(2, 2, 2)	mi-scre-den-te	(2, 2, 3)
exe-qua-tur	(2, 2)	neu-tra-liz-za-re	(2, 2, 3, 2)
fan-ta-sma-go-ria	(3, 2, 2, 2)	tra-sfor-ma-zio-ne	(2, 3, 2, 2)
fa-sci-smo	(2, 2)	tra-spor-ta-re	(2, 3, 2)
fi-lan-tro-pi-smo	(2, 3, 2, 2)	ve-sci-chet-ta	(2, 2, 3)
fo-sfo-re-scen-za	(2, 2, 2, 3)	zo-o-sper-ma	(4, 2, 3)

Stress and diacritics

No simple rules can be formulated for word stress in Italian. The majority of words receive their stress on the penultimate (next to the last) syllable: *aMIco*, *comPLEto;* fewer words are stressed on the antepenultimate (third from the last) syllable: *FABrico*, *gramMAtica;* only a limited number are stressed on the ultimate (last) syllable, but in this case the vowel carries the grave accent: *cittÀ fabbriCO.*

☆ Accent marks are used only to a limited degree—chiefly to indicate a final stressed syllable. Generally a grave (`) is used when the final vowel is open and an acute (´) is used when that vowel is closed. Word types illustrating these usages are:

(a) Nouns ending in *ta* or *tu* having the singular and plural alike: *libertà, virtú* (from the Latin *libertade, virtude,* etc.).

(b) Verbs in the third person singular past absolute and first and third persons singular future: *comprò* (he bought), *comprerò* (I shall buy), *comprerà* (he will buy); similarly in the second and third conjugations: *vendé, venderò, venderà; finí, finirò, finirà.*

(c) Homonyms. The most common of these homonyms are:

ché, because	*che,* that	*né,* neither, nor	*ne,* of it, of them
colà, there	*cola,* strainer	*piè,* foot	*pie,* pious
costà, there	*costa,* shore	*però,* therefore	*pero,* pear tree
dà, gives	*da,* by, from, to	*sè,* himself	*se,* if
dí, day	*di,* of	*sì,* yes	*si,* himself, one
è, is	*e,* and	*tè,* tea	*te,* thee
là, there	*la,* the, her	*testè,* just now	*teste,* heads
lì, there	*li,* the, them		

(d) Monosyllables terminating in two vowels, to indicate that the preceding vowel is shortened: *ciò, già, giú, piú, può, quà.*

(e) Terminations *ia* and *io* in which the *i* is to be stressed: *magìa, desìo.*

The acute is used by some editors to distinguish words differently stressed,

where otherwise a misunderstanding might arise: *malvágia* (wicked), *malvagía* (malmsey, a wine). This use is rare.

The circumflex is used to indicate contraction: *cacciâr* (for *cacciarono*), *ginnast* (for *ginnasii*). This use is rare.

The dieresis (trema) is used in poetry over the *i* to indicate that it is to be sounded separately from a following vowel: *armonïoso* (pronounced *armoni-oso*, instead of *armonio-so*). This use is rare.

Capitalization

Capitalization in Italian is similar to that in English, with a few exceptions:

(*a*) Proper adjectives are lowercased: *la lingua italiana*, the Italian language, but *gl'Italiani*, the Italians (proper noun).

(*b*) The names of days and months are lowercased.

(*c*) Titles followed by name are lowercased: *il signor Donati*, Mr. Donati; *il principe Umberto*, Prince Umberto.

(*d*) The pronoun *io*, *I*, is lowercased, but the pronouns of formal address, *Ella*, *Lei*, *Loro*, all meaning *you*, are sometimes capitalized. These pronouns, however, in modern Italian usage, and *Lei* in particular, are *not* capitalized in a written text except for that of a letter, and a formal one at that. *Ella* is often capitalized in poetry.

(*e*) In poetry, the first word of each line is usually lowercased.

Punctuation

Punctuation is similar to that of English. The comma is used to point off all clauses, restrictive as well as descriptive. Commas are not used, however, with the conjunction *e* in a series of several words. The apostrophe is used to indicate vowel elision only: *un'opera d'arte* (for *una opera di arte*), *sopra 'l letto* (for *sopra il letto*). The space after the apostrophe is no longer required.

Quotation marks:

Used less often than in English.

In the text of a dialog they are often substituted by a new paragraph for each speech, sometimes preceded by a long dash.

Titles of books, poems, and articles are usually entered in quotation marks in a text. Titles of books are sometimes entered in italic, and periodicals, more often than books, are also entered in italic in a text.

[No authority specifically stating this found. However, the use of quotation marks as stated above can be seen in Hall's text. In any Italian text or newspaper the above use of italic can also be observed.]

Abbreviations

a/c.	a conto, account	es.	esempio, example
a.c.	anno corrente, current year	fasc.	fascicolo, number, part
		f(err).	ferrovia, railroad
a.D.	anno Domini, in the year of our Lord	f.co	franco, post free
		F.lli	Fratelli, brothers
a.m., ant.	antimeridiano, a. m.	Giun.	Giuniore, junior
a.p.	anno passato, last year	I. Cl.	prima classe, first class
c.m.	corrente mese, instant	Ill.mo	Illustrissimo, most illustrious
C.ª	Compagnia, company		
d.C.	dopo Cristo, after Christ	lit., £	lire
Dep. prov.	Deputato provinciale, member of the provincial parliament	LL. MM.	Loro Maestà, Their Majesties
		N.ⁱ	Numeri, numbers
disp.	dispensa, number, part	N.º	Numero, number
ecc.	eccetera, etc.	On.	Onorevole, Honorable
Ed.	Edizione, edition; Editore, editor	p.m., pom.	pomeridiane, p.m.

Cardinal numbers

uno	one	sei	six
due	two	sette	seven
tre	three	otto	eight
quattro	four	nove	nine
cinque	five	dieci	ten

Cardinal numbers—Continued

undici	eleven	trenta	thirty
dodici	twelve	quaranta	forty
tredici	thirteen	cinquanta	fifty
quattordici	fourteen	sessanta	sixty
quindici	fifteen	settanta	seventy
sedici	sixteen	ottanta	eighty
diciassette⎱ diciasette⎰	seventeen	novanta	ninety
		novantuno, etc.	ninety-one, etc.
diciotto	eighteen		
diciannove⎱ dicianove⎰	nineteen	cento	hundred
		cent(o)uno, etc.	one hundred and one, etc.
venti	twenty		
ventuno	twenty-one		
ventidue	twenty-two	duecento, etc.	two hundred, etc.
ventitrè, etc.	twenty-three, etc.		
		mille, mila	thousand
ventotto, etc.	twenty-eight, etc.	duemila, etc.	two thousand, etc.

Ordinal numbers

primo, -a	first	ventesimo	twentieth
secondo	second	ventunesimo	⎱twenty-first,
terzo	third	ventesimo primo, etc.	⎰ etc.
quarto	fourth	trentesimo	thirtieth
quinto	fifth	quarantesimo	fortieth
sesto	sixth	cinquantesimo	fiftieth
settimo	seventh	sessantesimo, etc.	sixtieth, etc.
ottavo	eighth	centesimo	hundredth
nono	ninth	centesimo primo, etc.	one hundred and first, etc.
decimo	tenth		
decimo primo⎱ undicesimo⎰	eleventh	duecentesimo	two hundredth
dodicesimo	twelfth		
tredicesimo	thirteenth	trecentesimo, etc.	three hundredth, etc.
quattordicesimo⎱ decimo quarto,⎰ etc.	fourteenth, etc.	millesimo	thousandth

Months

gennaio (genn.)	January	luglio	July
febbraio (febb.)	February	agosto	August
marzo	March	settembre (sett.)	September
aprile	April	ottobre (ott.)	October
maggio (magg.)	May	novembre (nov.)	November
giugno	June	dicembre (dic.)	December

Days

domenica	Sunday	giovedì	Thursday
lunedì	Monday	venerdì	Friday
martedì	Tuesday	sabato	Saturday
mercoledì	Wednesday		

Seasons

primavera	spring	autunno	autumn
estate	summer	inverno	winter

Time

ora	hour	mese	month
giorno	day	anno	year
settimana	week		

REFERENCES.—Mario Hazon, Ed., Garzanti Comprehensive Italian-English, English-Italian Dictionary, New York, McGraw-Hill, 1963; Robert A. Hall, Jr., Italian for Modern Living, New York, Chilton Co., 1961.

LATIN

Gallia est omnis divisa in partes tres, quarum unam incolunt Belgae, aliam Aquitani, tertiam qui ipsorum lingua Celtae nostra Galli appellantur. Hi omnes lingua institutis legibus inter se differunt.—Caesar, De Bello Gallico I. 1.

Alphabet and pronunciation

A	a	long: *ah;* short: *o* in hot	O	o	long: *o* in note; short: *o* in fort
B	b	*b*			
C	c	*k*	P	p	*p*
D	d	*d*	Q	q	*k*
E	e	long: *e* in there; short: *e* in met	R	r	*r*
			S	s	*s*
			T	t	*t*
F	f	*f*	U	u	long: *oo* in food; short: *oo* in good; like *w* after *q,* and usually after other consonants before another vowel
G	g	*g* in go			
H	h	*h*			
I	i	long: *ee;* short: *i* in sit			
J	j	*y* in yet			
K	k	*k*	V	v	*w*
L	l	*l*	X	x	*ks*
M	m	*m*	Y	y	*ee; i* as for *i*
N	n	*n*	Z	z	*z*

Consonants

Formerly *u* and *v* were written with *v,* and *i* and *j* with *i.* Modern texts customarily distinguish both pairs. Thus: *uva, visu, janua, Jove.*

K, z, and *y* are rather rare, occurring mostly in loanwords. *Q* is used only in the combination *qu,* pronounced *kw.*

The digraphs *ch, ph,* and *th* are pronounced as *k, f,* and *t,* respectively.

Vowels

Each of the five vowels is either long or short in each occurrence, and an accurate pronunciation will reflect this difference. Elementary texts usually mark the long vowels with a macron; thus: $\bar{a}, \bar{e}, \bar{i}, \bar{o}, \bar{u}.$

Diphthongs

Two short vowels may occur together in the same syllable, in which case the second of the two is a semivowel; i.e., *u* as the second element of a diphthong is pronounced like *w,* and *i* or *e* in this position is pronounced like *y.* The commonest diphthongs are *ae* and *au,* pronounced to rhyme with high and how. Less common are *ei* (as in vein), *eu, oe* (as *oi* in oil), and *ui.*

Consonantal units [1]

The following combinations are referred to as consonant clusters in the rules given below for syllabification: *bl, br, cl, cr, dr, fl, fr, gl, gr, pl, pr, tl, tr, scr, str, spl, spr.*

The digraphs *ch, ph,* and *th* are treated just like *c, f,* and *t* in consonant clusters.

---

[1] Some Latin lexicographers still use the classic method of determining consonantal units; namely, any group of consonants which can begin a word constitutes a consonantal unit and may begin a syllable. This method is still in use in Greek syllabification; but in present-day Latin orthography it has been largely replaced by the Romance-language method, given in the text and recommended by Allen and Greenough. (See References.)

Rules for syllabification

1. Diphthongs, digraphs, and consonant clusters may not be divided.
2. Division is made on a vowel or on a diphthong before a single consonant, a digraph, or a consonant cluster: *ca-sus, si-pho, pa-tres, cae-lum*.
3. In a group of two or more consonants, division is made before the last consonant, digraph, or consonant cluster: *vit-ta, mag-nus, punc-tus, bac-chor, am-plus*.
4. Division may be made between vowels not constituting a diphthong: *pu-er, di-es, fili-us, Tro-ius*.
5. Certain adverbial prefixes are kept intact. These are: *ab, ante, circum, cis, con, de, ex, extra, in, inter, intro, ob, per, prae, praeter, per, post, pro(d), propter, re(d), sub, super, supra,* and *trans: ab-eo, con-scriptum, inter-esse*.
6. Compound words are divided according to their component parts (and each part according to rules 1 to 5): *quot-annis, et-enim, sic-ut*.
7. The letter *x* is retained with the preceding syllable: *dix-it*.

NOTE.—The above rules do not apply to anglicized Latin scientific names used in English works. Their syllabification follows the English practice.

Illustrative word divisions

[The numbers in parentheses refer to the syllabification rules]

ab-a-li-e-no	(5, 2, 4, 2)	prod-es-se	(5, 3)
ab-scin-do	(5, 3)	proe-li-um	(2, 4)
ac-cli-na-tus	(3, 2, 2)	pro-stra-tum	(5, 2)
ad-ae-qua-tus	(5, 2, 2)	pro-sub-ac-tum	(5, 5, 3)
ad-emp-tus	(5, 3)	pu-bli-ca-tus	(2, 2, 2)
am-plex-us	(3, 7)	quam-ob-rem	(6, 6)
cir-cum-ac-tus	(3, 5, 3)	quem-ad-mo-dum	(6, 6, 2)
Cis-al-pi-nus	(5, 3, 2)	re-cru-des-co	(5, 2, 3)
con-sue-tus	(5, 2)	red-ac-tus	(5, 3)
de-spon-sum	(5, 3)	re-duc-tus	(5, 3)
et-e-nim	(6, 2)	re-frac-tum	(5, 3)
ex-em-plum	(7, 3)	re-spec-tus	(5, 3)
in-a-nis	(5, 2)	res-pu-bli-ca	(6, 2, 2)
in-ep-ti	(5, 3)	ses-cen-ti	(6, 3)
in-ter-ea	(3, 5)	sua-de-re	(2, 2)
ne-sci-tus	(6, 2)	sub-ac-tio	(5, 2)
ob-la-tus	(5, 2)	su-pra-scan-do	(2, 5, 3)
per-ac-tus	(5, 3)	trans-ab-i-tum	(5, 5, 2)
per-e-git	(5, 2)	trans-ad-ac-tum	(5, 5, 3)
pe-ri-cli-ta-tio	(2, 2, 2, 2)	tran-su-tum	(3, 2)
post-ea-quam	(5, 6)	tri-um-pho	(4, 3)
post-hu-mus	(5, 2)	tu-mul-tu-o-sus	(2, 3, 4, 2)
post-sce-ni-um	(5, 2, 4)	una-ni-mus	(2, 2)
pos-tu-la-tus	(3, 2, 2)	usus-fruc-tus	(6, 3)
prae-scrip-tus	(5, 3)	va-li-dus	(2, 2)
prae-ter-i-tum	(2, 5, 2)	Xe-no-phon	(2, 2)

Stress

Words of two syllables are always stressed on the first syllable: *ROma, LIber.*
In words of more than two syllables, the stress is on the next to the last syllable if that syllable ends in a consonant, a long vowel, or a diphthong. Otherwise the stress is on the third from the last syllable. Thus: ho-NO-ris, CON-su-lis.

Capitalization and punctuation

American editors usually follow the English conventions in capitalization and punctuation.

Abbreviations

a., annus, year; ante, before
A.A.C., anno ante Christum, in the year before Christ
A.A.S., Academiae Americanae Socius, Fellow of the American Academy [Academy of Arts and Sciences]

A.B., artium baccalaureus, bachelor of arts
ab init., ab initio, from the beginning
abs. re., absente reo, the defendant being absent
A.C., ante Christum, before Christ

Abbreviations—Continued

A.D., anno Domini, in the year of our Lord

a.d., ante diem, before the day

ad fin., ad finem, at the end, to one end

ad h.l., ad hunc locum, to this place, on this passage

ad inf., ad infinitum, to infinity

ad init., ad initium, at the beginning

ad int., ad interim, in the meantime

ad lib., ad libitum, at pleasure

ad loc., ad locum, at the place

ad val., ad valorem, according to value

A.I., anno inventionis, in the year of the discovery

al., alia, alii, other things, other persons

A.M., anno mundi, in the year of the world; Annus mirabilis, the wonderful year [1666]; **a.m.**, ante meridiem, before noon

an., anno, in the year; ante, before

ann., annales, annals; anni, years

A.R.S.S., Antiquariorum Regiae Societatis Socius, Fellow of the Royal Society of Antiquaries

A.U.C., anno urbis conditae, ab urbe conolita, in [the year from] the building of the City [Rome], 753 B.C.

B.A., baccalaureus artium, bachelor of arts

B. Sc., baccalaureus scientiae, bachelor of science

C., centum, a hundred; condemno, I condemn, find guilty

c., circa, about

cent., centum, a hundred

cf., confer, compare

C.M., chirurgiae magister, master of surgery

coch., cochlear, a spoon, spoonful

coch. amp., cochlear amplum, a tablespoonful

coch. mag., cochlear magnum, a large spoonful

coch. med., cochlear medium, a dessert spoonful

coch. parv., cochlear parvum, a teaspoonful

con., contra, against; conjunx, wife

C.P.S., custos privati sigilli, keeper of the privy seal

C.S., custos sigilli, keeper of the seal

cwt., c. for centum, wt. for weight, hundredweight

D., Deus, God; Dominus, Lord; **d.**, decretum, a decree; denarius, a penny; da, give

D.D., divinitatis doctor, doctor of divinity

D.G., Dei gratia, by the grace of God; Deo gratias, thanks to God

D.N., Dominus noster, our Lord

D. Sc., doctor scientiae, doctor of science

d.s.p., decessit sine prole, died without issue

D.V., Deo volente, God willing

dwt., d. for denarius, wt. for weight pennyweight

e.g., exempli gratia, for example

et al., et alibi, and elsewhere; et alii, or aliae, and others

etc., et cetera, and others, and so forth

et seq., et sequentes, and those that follow

et ux., et uxor, and wife

F., filius, son

f., fiat, let it be made; forte, strong

fac., factum similis, facsimile, an exact copy

fasc., fasciculus, a bundle

fl., flores, flowers; floruit, flourished; fluidus, fluid

f.r., folio recto, right-hand page

F.R.S., Fraternitatis Regiae Socius, Fellow of the Royal Society

f.v., folio verso, on the back of the leaf

guttat., guttatim, by drops

H., hora, hour

h.a., hoc anno, in this year; hujus anni, this year's

hab. corp., habeas corpus, have the body—a writ

h.e., hic est, this is; hoc est, that is

h.m., hoc mense, in this month; huius mensis, this month's

h.q., hoc quaere, look for this

H.R.I.P., hic requiescat in pace, here rests in peace

H.S., hic sepultus, here is buried; hic situs, here lies; **h. s.**, hoc sensu, in this sense

H.S.S., Historiae Societatis Socius, Fellow of the Historical Society

h.t., hoc tempore, at this time; hoc titulo, in or under this title

I, Idus, the Ides; **i.**, id, that; immortalis, immortal

ib. or **ibid.**, ibidem, in the same place

id., idem, the same

i.e., id est, that is

imp., imprimatur, sanction, let it be printed

I.N.D., in nomine Dei, in the name of God

in f., in fine, at the end

inf., infra, below

init., initio, in the beginning

in lim., in limine, on the threshold, at the outset

in loc., in loco, in its place

in loc. cit., in loco citato, in the place cited

in pr., in principio, in the beginning

in trans., in transitu, on the way

i.q., idem quod, the same as

i.q.e.d., id quod erat demonstrandum, what was to be proved

J., judex, judge

J.C.D., juris civilis doctor, doctor of civil law

J.D., jurum doctor, doctor of laws

J.U.D., juris utriusque doctor, doctor of both civil and canon law

Abbreviations—Continued

L., liber, a book; locus, a place

£, libra, pound; placed before figures, thus £10; if l., to be placed after, as 40 l.

L.A.M., liberalium artium magister, master of the liberal arts

L.B., baccalaureus literarum, bachelor of letters

lb., libra, pound (singular and plural)

L.H.D., literarum humaniorum doctor, doctor of the more humane letters

Litt. D., literarum doctor, doctor of letters

LL.B., legum baccalaureus, bachelor of laws

LL.D., legum doctor, doctor of laws

LL.M., legum magister, master of laws

loc. cit., loco citato, in the place cited

loq., loquitur, he, or she, speaks

L.S., locus sigilli, the place of the seal

l.s.c., loco supra citato, in the place above cited

£ s. d., librae, solidi, denarii, pounds, shillings, pence

M., magister, master; manipulus, handful; medicinae, of medicine; m., meridies, noon

M.A., magister artium, master of arts

M.B., medicinae baccalaureus, bachelor of medicine

M. Ch., magister chirurgiae, master of surgery

M.D., medicinae doctor, doctor of medicine

m.m., mutatis mutandis, with the necessary changes

m.n., mutato nomine, the name being changed

MS., manuscriptum, manuscript; MSS., manuscripta, manuscripts

Mus. B., musicae baccalaureus, bachelor of music

Mus. D., musicae doctor, doctor of music

Mus. M., musicae magister, master of music

N., Nepos, grandson; nomen, name; nomina, names; noster, our; n., natus, born; nocte, at night

N.B., nota bene, mark well

ni. pri., nisi prius, unless before

nob., nobis, for (or on) our part

nol. pros., nolle prosequi, will not prosecute

non cul., non culpabilis, not guilty

n.l., non licet, it is not permitted; non liquet, it is not clear; non longe, not far

non obs., non obstante, notwithstanding

non pros., non prosequitur, he does not prosecute

non seq., non sequitur, it does not follow logically

O., octarius, a pint

ob., obiit, he, or she, died; obiter, incidentally

ob. s.p., obiit sine prole, died without issue

o.c., opere citato, in the work cited

op., opus, work; opera, works

op. cit., opere citato, in the work cited

P., papa, pope; pater, father; pontifex, bishop; populus, people; p., partim, in part; per, by, for; pius, holy; pondere, by weight; post, after; primus, first; pro, for

p.a., or per ann., per annum, yearly; pro anno, for the year

p. ae., partes aequales, equal parts

pass., passim, everywhere

percent., per centum, by the hundred

pil., pilula, pill

Ph. B., philosophiae baccalaureus, bachelor of philosophy

P.M., post mortem, after death

p.m., post meridiem, afternoon

pro tem., pro tempore, for the time being

prox., proximo, in or of the next [month]

P.S., postscriptum, postscript; P.SS., postscripta, postscripts

q.d., quasi dicat, as if one should say; quasi dictum, as if said; quasi dixisset, as if he had said

q.e., quod est, which is

Q.E.D., quod erat demonstrandum, which was to be demonstrated

Q.E.F., quod erat faciendum, which was to be done

Q.E.I., quod erat inveniendum, which was to be found out

q.l., quantum libet, as much as you please

q. pl., quantum placet, as much as seems good

q.s., quantum sufficit, sufficient quantity

q.v., quantum vis, as much as you will; quem, quam, quod vide, which see; qq. v., quos, quas, or quae vide, which see (plural)

R., regina, queen; recto, right-hand page; respublica, commonwealth

℞, recipe, take

R.I.P., requiescat, or requiescant, in pace, may he, she, or they, rest in peace

R.P.D., rerum politicarum doctor, doctor of political science

rr., rarissime, very rarely

R.S.S., Regiae Societatis Sodalis, Fellow of the Royal Society

S., sepultus, buried; situs, lies; societas, society; socius or sodalis, fellow; s., semi, half; solidus, shilling

s.a., sine anno, without date; secundum artem, according to art

S.A.S., Societatis Antiquariorum Socius, Fellow of the Society of Antiquaries

sc., scilicet, namely; sculpsit, he, or she, carved or engraved it

Abbreviations—Continued

Sc. B., scientiae baccalaureus, bachelor of science

Sc. D., scientiae doctor, doctor of science

S.D., salutem dicit, sends greetings

s.d., sine die, indefinitely

sec., secundum, according to

sec. leg., secundum legem, according to law

sec. nat., secundum naturam, according to nature, or naturally

sec. reg., secundum regulam, according to rule

seq., sequens, sequentes, sequentia, the following

S.H.S., Societatis Historiae Socius, Fellow of the Historical Society

s.h.v., sub hac voce or sub hoc verbo, under this word

s.l.a.n., sine loco, anno, vel nomine, without place, date, or name

s.l.p., sine legitima prole, without lawful issue

s.m.p., sine mascula prole, without male issue

s.n., sine nomine, without name

s.p., sine prole, without issue

S.P.A.S., Societatis Philosophiae Americanae Socius, Fellow of the American Philosophical Society

s.p.s., sine prole superstite, without surviving issue

S.R.S., Societatis Regiae Socius or Sodalis, Fellow of the Royal Society

ss, scilicet, namely (in law)

S.S.C., Societas Sanctae Crucis, Society of the Holy Cross

stat., statim, immediately

S.T.B., sacrae theologiae baccalaureus, bachelor of sacred theology

S.T.D., sacrae theologiae doctor, doctor of sacred theology

S.T.P., sacrae theologiae professor, professor of sacred theology

sub., subaudi, understand, supply

sup., supra, above

t. or temp., tempore, in the time of

tal. qual., talis qualis, just as they come; average quality

U.J.D., utriusque juris doctor, doctor of both civil and canon law

ult., ultimo, last month (may be abbreviated in writing but should be spelled out in printing)

ung., unguentum, ointment

u.s., ubi supra, in the place above mentioned

ut dict., ut dictum, as directed

ut sup., ut supra, as above

ux., uxor, wife

v., versus, against; vide, see; voce, voice, word

v. —— a., vixit —— annos, lived [so many] years

verb. sap., verbum [satis] sapienti, a word to the wise suffices

v.g., verbi gratia, for example

viz, videlicet, namely

v.s., vide supra, see above

Cardinal numbers

unus, una, unum	one	duodetriginta	twenty-eight
duo, duae, duo	two	undetriginta	twenty-nine
tres, tria	three	triginta	thirty
quattuor	four	quadraginta	forty
quinque	five	quinquaginta	fifty
sex	six	sexaginta	sixty
septem	seven	septuaginta	seventy
octo	eight	octoginta	eighty
novem	nine	nonaginta	ninety
decem	ten	centum	hundred
undecim	eleven	centum et unus, etc.	hundred and one, etc.
duodecim	twelve		
tredecim	thirteen	ducenti, -ae, -a	two hundred
quattuordecim	fourteen	trecenti	three hundred
quindecim	fifteen	quadringenti	four hundred
sedecim	sixteen	quingenti	five hundred
septendecim	seventeen	sescenti	six hundred
duodeviginti	eighteen	septingenti	seven hundred
undeviginti	nineteen	octingenti	eight hundred
viginti	twenty	nongenti	nine hundred
viginti unus, etc.	twenty-one, etc.	mille	thousand

Ordinal numbers

primus	first	duodecimus	twelfth
secundus	second	tertius decimus,	thirteenth,
tertius	third	etc.	etc.
quartus	fourth	duodevicesimus	eighteenth
quintus	fifth	undevicesimus	nineteenth
sextus	sixth	vicesimus, vigesi-	twentieth
septimus	seventh	mus	
octavus	eighth	vicesimus primus,	twenty-first,
nonus	ninth	etc.	etc.
decimus	tenth	centesimus	hundredth
undecimus	eleventh	millesimus	thousandth

Months

Januarius	January	Julius	July
Februarius	February	Augustus	August
Martius	March	September	September
Aprilis	April	October	October
Maius	May	November	November
Junius	June	December	December

Days

dies solis } dies dominica }	Sunday	dies Mercurii	Wednesday
		dies Iovis	Thursday
dies lunae	Monday	dies Veneris	Friday
dies Martis	Tuesday	dies Saturni	Saturday

Seasons

ver	spring	autumnus	autumn
aestas	summer	hiems	winter

Time

hora	hour	mensis	month
dies	day	annus	year
hebdomas	week	saeculum	century

REFERENCES.—Allen and Greenough, A New Latin Grammar (1920); J. R. V. Marchant and Joseph F. Charles, Cassell's Latin-English and English-Latin Dictionary (1909); Edgar H. Sturtevant, The Pronunciation of Greek and Latin (1940).

NORWEGIAN

Fra De forente Stater kom bare 6,9 pst. av importen, først og fremst hvete. Norge innførte også hvete fra Argentina, Kanada og Sovjet-Russland, og bare en femtedel av de norske bilene kom direkte fra Amerika. Norges største eksportvare var papir og cellulose (19,2 pst.), så kom som nummer to fiskeprodukter og hermetikk (15,3), som nummer tre metaller (13 pst.).—Einar Haugen, Spoken Norwegian, p. 505.

Alphabet and pronunciation

A	a	in stressed syllables followed by one consonant or none, like *a* in father, but tending toward *aw* in law, in stressed syllables followed by two or more consonants and in unstressed syllables, like *a* in father, but very short, resembling more *u* in but
B	b	*b;* formerly often written for sound *p*
C	c	*s* in so before *e, i, y;* like *k* before *a, o, u,* or consonant; occurs only in foreign words; now practically obsolete, being written *k* or *s;* combination *ch,* like *ch* in chorus; in French words, like *sh*
D	d	*d;* often silent after *l, n, r,* and at end of words
E	e	in stressed syllables followed by one consonant or none, like *i* in pit, but longer; before *r,* like *a* in man; in stressed syllables followed by a consonant other than *r* plus another consonant, like *e* in let, but tending toward *i* in pit; in stressed syllables followed by *r* plus another consonant, like *a* in hat; in the words *De* and *de,* like *ee* in meet, but shorter; in unstressed syllables, like *a* in sofa
F	f	*f*
G	g	*g* in go; before *i, y, ei,* or *øy,* almost always like *y* in yes; after *e* at end of a few words (*jeg, meg, deg, seg*), like *y* in say; silent before *j,* in the word *og,* in suffix *-ig,* and in a few other words; in French words, often like *sh*
H	h	*h;* silent before *j* or *v*
I	i	in stressed syllables followed by one consonant or none, like *ee* in meet; in stressed syllables followed by two or more consonants and in unstressed syllables, like *ee* in meet, but shorter
J	j	*y* in yes; in French words, like *sh*
K	k	*k;* before *i, y, j, ei,* or *øy,* like strong *h* in hue—i.e., like German *ch* in ich
L	l	*ll* in million, sometimes silent before *j*
M	m	*m*
N	n	*n;* combination *ng,* like *ng* in singer; combination *nk,* like *nk* in sink; in French words, *en* and *an* often pronounced as through written *ang*
O	o	in stressed syllables followed by one consonant or none, like *o* in go, but with lips pursed, resembling more *oo* in food; in stressed syllables followed by two or more consonants and in unstressed syllables, like *u* in put

[Concluded on following page]

P	p	*p*
Q	q	always followed by *v* (or *u*), combination being pronounced and now written *kv;* occurs only in foreign words
R	r	before vowel, like *r*, but slightly trilled, with tip of tongue against gums just above upper teeth; resembles Scotch burr or Italian *r;* before *d, l, n, t,* the *r* loses its trill and sounds somewhat like American *r;* always combines with following *s* to produce sound *sh;* in French words, often silent when final after *e*
S	s	*s* in sing; before *j* like *sh;* combination *sk* before *i, y, j, ei,* or *øy* almost always like *sh;* always combines with preceding *r* to produce sound *sh;* in foreign words, combination *sc* like *s,* or in a few words like *sk; sch* like *sh,* or in a few words like *sk; si* followed by vowel (now written *sj*) like *sh*
T	t	*t;* combination *tj* sometimes pronounced as though written *kj;* silent in word *det* and in *-et,* definite article suffixed to all neuter nouns; in Latin words when followed by *i* and another vowel, like *ts;* ending *tion* (now written *sjon*) pronounced as though written *sjon*
U	u	in stressed syllables followed by one consonant or none, like *oo* in food; in stressed syllables followed by two or more consonants and in unstressed syllables, like *oo* in food, but shorter
V	v	*v;* silent in word *av* and after *l*
W	w	*v;* occurs in foreign words
X	x	*ks;* at beginning of words, like *s*
Y	y	in stressed syllables followed by one consonant or none, like *ee* in meet, with lips rounded as in pronouncing *oo* in food, being similar to long German *ü* or French *u;* in stressed syllables followed by two or more consonants and in unstressed syllables, like *ee* in meet, but shorter, with lips rounded as in pronouncing *u* in put, being similar to short German *ü* or French *u*
Z	z	*s* in sing; occurs only in foreign words
Æ	æ	formerly sometimes written *Ä, ä;* many words formerly written with *æ* now written with *e;* in stressed syllables followed by one consonant or none, like *a* in care; in stressed syllables followed by two or more consonants and in unstressed syllables, like *a* in hat, this sound occurring only before *r*
Ø	ø	formerly often written *Ö, ö;* in stressed syllables followed by one consonant or none, like *i* in pit, but longer, with lips rounded as in pronouncing *oo* in food, being similar to long German *ö* or French *eu;* in stressed syllables followed by two or more consonants and in unstressed syllables, like *e* in pet, with lips rounded as in pronouncing *u* in pull, being similar to short German *ö* or French *eu*
A	å	formerly written *Aa, aa;* in stressed syllables followed by one consonant or none, like *aw* in law; in stressed syllables followed by two or more consonants and in unstressed syllables, like *aw* in law, but shorter

Norway has two official languages, bokmål and nynorsk. The designations for these languages derive from an act of legislation of 1929. Before that time the languages were known as riksmål and landsmål, respectively. The term riksmål is still used unofficially in Norway today. Bokmål, also known in the past as Dano-Norwegian, was originally a written language acquired from Denmark during the centuries the two nations were united (1397 to 1814). It differed in many ways from the speech of the Norwegian people, and in its written form was almost identical with Danish until 1907. Since then there have been a number of language reforms—including major ones in 1907, 1918, 1938, and 1959—promulgated by the Storting, the Norwegian Parliament, for the purpose of making the orthography correspond more closely with the spoken language. These changes were binding only for government officials and schoolbooks. Private individuals and publishers have been free to use the new systems or not, as they have seen fit. As a consequence there exists a variety of styles in the literature of the 20th century.

The other official language, nynorsk, is a synthetic language based on rural Norwegian dialects and originating in the 1850's. Since that time, it has also undergone a number of official reforms as well as changes in name. While its official status is equal to that of bokmål, nynorsk enjoys less popularity and is used with less frequency than bokmål. Approximately 85 percent of the works published in Norway are in bokmål, and the percentage of the population using nynorsk has been estimated at approximately 22 percent.

The two languages, and their dialects, are in any event very similar, and in their struggle for supremacy are constantly influencing each other. The result may in the end be a single "compromise" language.

However that may be, the linguistic situation in Norway, both in its written and spoken aspects, is very much in a state of flux, and it is particularly difficult to make clear-cut statements about it.

Special characters

Norwegian uses the Latin alphabet with the addition of three special characters—the last three shown in the alphabet.

The letters *c*, *q*, *w*, *x*, and *z* are now used only in foreign words and proper names. Even in popular words of foreign origin they are preferably avoided by substituting *k* or *s* for *c*, *kv* for *qu*, *v* for *w*, *ks* for *x*, and *s* for *z*.

Fraktur type (German text) was abolished officially in 1907, and is now scarcely in use anywhere.

Vowels and consonants

The vowels are *a*, *e*, *i*, *o*, *u*, *y*, *æ*, *ø*, and *å;* the so-called back vowels being *a*, *o*, *u*, and *å;* the front vowels *e*, *i*, *y*, *æ*, and *ø*. The other letters of the alphabet are all consonants.

Combinations of vowel letters (diphthongs)

The diphthongs and their sounds are as follows:

ai as *ai* in aisle
au as *ou* in our
ei as *ei* in weigh
oi (in foreign words), as *oi* in boil
øy (formerly written *øi*), like Norwegian *ø* followed by slight sound of Norwegian *y*, the two being sounded as one syllable

eu (in foreign words), like Norwegian *æ* followed by slight sound of Norwegian *u*, the two being sounded as one syllable
ou (in foreign words), like Norwegian *u*

Combinations of consonantal letters (digraphs)

The digraphs and their sounds are:

ch (in foreign words), as *sh* in shall or *ch* in chorus
gj as *y* in yes
hj
hv
kj
lj
ng
ph (in foreign words; obsolete)
ps (in foreign words)
qv (also written *qu*; in foreign words, obsolete)

sc (in foreign words)
sch (in foreign words)
sh (in foreign words)
sj (also formerly written *si*, *ti* in foreign words), as *sh* in shall
sk as *sh* in shall (before front vowels)
th (usually in foreign words), as *t*
tj
wh (in foreign words)

Consonantal units

For purposes of syllabification, consonant combinations are treated as units. In addition to the digraphs, the following are also consonantal units: *kv, skj, sp, spr, st, str.*

Rules for syllabification

1. Diphthongs, digraphs, and consonantal units may not be divided.
2. Division is made on a vowel or on a diphthong before a single consonant, a digraph, or a consonantal unit: *ale-ne, hvi-ske, hu-stru, bei-ning.*
3. In a group of two or more consonants, division is made before the last consonant, digraph, or consonantal unit: *af-ten, dan-ske, sek-sten, tjenst-lig, blom-ster.*
4. Division may be made between two vowels not constituting a diphthong or between a diphthong and another vowel: *fri-er, lei-er.*
5. Certain adverbial prefixes are kept intact. These are: *ad, an, av, bak, be, bi, bort, efter, er, for, fra, frem, ge, in, inn* (formerly *ind*), *med, mis, ned, om, opp* (formerly *op*), *over, på* (formerly *paa*), *til, under, unn* (formerly *und*), *ut, ute,* and *ved: ad-splitte, an-bringe, av-klipp, bak-slag,* etc.
6. Certain suffixes are kept intact. These are: *aktig (agtig), artet, asje, het (hed), inne (inde)*: *barn-agtig, god-artet, lekk-asje, matt-het, vert-inne.*
7. Compound words are divided according to their component parts (and each part according to rules 1 to 6), the compounding *s*, if used, going with the preceding component: *aften-avis, aften-blad, aftens-tid.*
8. Foreign words and components of foreign words (not naturalized) follow the conventions of the language of origin: *pa-triot, anti-kvar, inter-esse, mid-shipman.* Under this rule are also included scientific and technical words, which editors prefer to treat etymologically: *me-trisk, hemi-tropi, dia-gnose.*

Illustrative word divisions

[The numbers in parentheses refer to the syllabification rules]

ame-ri-kan-ske	(2, 2, 3)	re-gje-ring	(2, 2)
ar-ke-o-lo-gi	(3, 4, 2, 2)	re-pre-sen-ta-sjon	(8, 2, 3, 2)
av-brek-ke	(5, 3)	re-pu-blikk	(2, 8)
be-skjef-ti-gel-se	(5, 3, 2, 3)	re-pu-bli-kan-ske	(2, 8, 2, 3)
der-et-ter	(7, 3)	sam-men-brin-ge	(3, 7, 3)
egen-ar-tet	(6, 3)	selv-an-kla-ge	(7, 5, 2)
eks-al-te-re	(8, 3, 2)	ska-des-er-stat-ning	(2, 7, 5, 3)
en-gel-ske	(3, 3)	stats-for-fat-ning	(7, 5, 3)
eng-len-der	(3, 3)	sy-ste-ma-tisk	(2, 2, 2)
er-ind-ring	(5, 3)	tids-reg-ning	(7, 3)
eu-ro-pei-ske	(2, 2, 2)	til-gren-sen-de	(5, 3, 3)
for-en-te	(5, 3)	tre-å-rig	(7, 2)
gjen-gjel-de	(3, 3)	ty-de-lig	(2, 2)
halv-å-rig	(7, 2)	un-der-of-fi-ser	(3, 5, 3, 2)
inn-plan-te	(5, 3)	un-der-skri-ve	(3, 5, 2)
in-ter-es-sant	(3, 8, 3)	unn-dra	(5, 2)
kjens-gjer-ning	(3, 3)	unn-skyld-ning	(5, 3)
ned-sla-ge-ne	(5, 2, 2)	uor-dent-lig	(3, 3)
om-ar-bei-de	(5, 3, 2)	urett-mes-sig	(7, 3)
over-ens-komst	(5, 3)	ut-ar-bei-de	(5, 3, 2)
pa-ra-graf	(2, 8)	ute-stå-en-de	(5, 4, 3)
pa-tri-ot	(8, 4)	uvil-kår-lig	(3, 3)
pa-tri-o-ti-ske	(8, 4, 2, 2)	vå-pen-ø-vel-se	(2, 7, 2, 3)
post-skrip-tum	(8, 3)	yt-rings-fri-het	(3, 7, 6)
på-dra	(5, 2)	æt-ling-arv	(3, 7)
på-gjel-den-de	(5, 3, 3)	øn-ske-lig	(3, 2)

Stress and diacritics

Most words are stressed on the first syllable, except when they begin with a prefix such as *be-, er-, for-, ge-,* in which case the syllable following the prefix is stressed. Words borrowed from French are usually stressed on the last or next to last syllable. In compound words, the first component receives the primary stress, the second receives secondary stress.

In stressed syllables, vowels are long before one consonant or none, but short before two consonants or more. However, the letter *m* is never doubled at the end of a word, even though it nearly always follows a short vowel. Some words which usually occur unstressed in the sentence are written with only one consonant following the short vowel. The addition of an ending beginning with a consonant usually, but not always, makes the vowel short. Under such conditions, a long vowel may stand before two or more consonants.

Norwegian words of one syllable when pronounced in isolation or in accented positions in a sentence, and is one of the syllables of longer words, are spoken with a stress or loudness accompanied by pitch. The pitch is raised in monosyllables and in many longer words. Other words of more than one syllable have a pitch on the accented syllable that falls and then rises again on the next syllable. It is not possible to tell from the spelling which pitch-stress combination is to be used.

Consonants when written double are always pronounced long; compare with the long *d* in English midday.

With the exception of *d* (sometimes replaced by *aa*), *á* (variant for *æ*), *ó* (variant for *ø*), diacritics are used only in foreign loanwords and in certain proper names.

Capitalization

Capitalization is now as in English, except that the polite personal pronouns *De, Dem,* and *Deres* are capitalized, but proper adjectives and the names of the months and the days of the week are lowercased. A capital is not required to begin a new line of poetry, and only the first word of titles is capitalized.

Previously, Norwegian followed the German custom of capitalizing all words that functioned as nouns.

Punctuation

Punctuation is very much like that of English. Norwegian used to punctuate like German, with commas before every clause, but the tendency is away from that now. A comma is not used before the word *og* in an enumeration (A, B, C og D), but is often used where English would have a semicolon or a period. Sometimes commas are used instead of periods for decimals: 10,6. Commas are not used between thousands: 1 000 000.

Abbreviations

adr.	adresse, address	H.K.H.	Hans Kongelige Høj-hed, His Royal Highness
ang.	angående, concerning, re		
A/S	Aksjeselskap, joint-stock company	H.M.	Hans Majestet, His Majesty
avd.	avdøde, deceased	Hr.	Herr, Mr., Sir
bl.a.	blant annet, among others	ifl.	ifølge, according to
		kap.	kapitel, chapter
d.å.	dette år, this year	m.a.o.	med andre ord, in other words
d.e.	det er, this is, i.e.		
d.v.s.	det vil si, that is	m.fl.	med flere, et al.
e.K.	etter Kristi, after Christ, A.D.	m.h.t.	med hensyn til, as regards to
el.	eller, or	m.m.	med mere, etc.
f.	født, born, née; for, for; før, before	nl.	nemlig, namely
		o.a.	og annet, and others
f.eks.	for eksempel, for example, e.g.	o.fl.	og flere, etc.
		o.s.v. (osv)	og så videre, and so forth
f.K.	før Kristus, before Christ	p.ct. (pct)	prosent, percent
f.o m.	fra og med, from and with (including)	s.	side, page; søndre, south
Frk.	Frøken, Miss	u.	under, under
Hds. Maj.	Hennes Majestet, Her Majesty	yr.	den yngre, junior
		ø.	øre, half farthing

Cardinal numbers

en, et(t) *ein, ei	one	atten	eighteen
to eit(t)	two	nitten	nineteen
tre, tri	three	tjue (tyve)	twenty
fire	four	tjueen (en og tyve,	twenty-one, etc.
fem	five	etc.)	
seks	six	tretti (tredve)	thirty
sju (syv)	seven	førti	forty
otte	eight	femti	fifty
ni	nine	seksti	sixty
ti	ten	sytti	seventy
elleve	eleven	åtti	eighty
tolv	twelve	nitti	ninety
tretten	thirteen	hundrede	hundred
fjorten	fourteen	hundrede og en, etc.	one hundred and
femten	fifteen		one, etc.
seksten	sixteen	to hundrede, etc.	two hundred, etc.
sytten	seventeen	tusen	thousand

Ordinal numbers

første	first	ellevte	eleventh
annen (annet)	second	tolvte	twelfth
tredje	third	trettende, etc.	thirteenth, etc.
fjerde	fourth	tjuende (tyvende)	twentieth
femte	fifth	tjueførste	twenty-first, etc.
sjette	sixth	(enogtyvende)	
sjuende (syvende)	seventh	trettiende (tredevte)	thirtieth
åttende	eighth	førtiende, etc.	fortieth, etc.
niende	ninth	hundrede	hundredth
tiende	tenth	hundrede og første	one hundred and
			first

Months

januar (jan.)	January	juli	July
februar (feb.)	February	august (aug.)	August
mars	March	september (sept.)	September
april (apr.)	April	oktober (okt.)	October
mai	May	november (nov.)	November
juni	June	desember (des.)	December

Days

søndag, *sundag	Sunday	torsdag	Thursday
mandag, *måndag	Monday	fredag	Friday
tirsdag, *tysdag	Tuesday	lørdag, *laurdag	Saturday
onsdag	Wednesday		

Seasons

vår	spring	høst, *haust	autumn
sommer	summer	vinter	winter

Time

time	hour	måned, månad	month
dag	day	år	year
uke	week		

REFERENCES.—P. Groth, A Norwegian Grammar (1924); Jakob Sverdrup og Marius Sandvei, Norsk Rettskrivningsordbook (1940); J. Brynildsen, Norsk-Engelsk Ordbook (1927); Einar Haugen, Beginning Norwegian (1937); H. Scavenius. Norsk-English Ordbok (1943); Einar Haugen, Spoken Norwegian (1944); Einar Haugen, Norwegian English Dictionary (1965); Finn-Erik Vinje, Norsk språk (1972).

NOTES.—Words appearing in parentheses represent unofficial forms which are still widely used. Words preceded by asterisks are nynorsk forms.

POLISH

Życie i dzieje tych odłamów narodu polskiego, które już od paru pokoleń przeniosły się na daleki kontynent zachodni i tam, w ramach państwowych Stanów Zjednoczonych Ameryki Północnej, kształtują swój los, są nam bardzo mało znane.—W. Doroszewski, Język polski w Stanach Zjednoczonych A. P., Warsaw, 1938, p. 1.

Alphabet and pronunciation

A	a	*a* in father	Ó	ó	like Polish *u*
Ą	ą	like in French *bon*	P	p	*p*
B	b	*b*	Q	q	used only in quoting foreign words
C	c	*ts* in hats			
Ch	ch	like Scottish *loch*, strong *h*	R	r	*r* trilled *r*
			Rz	rz	*z* in azure
Cz	cz	*ch* in chin	S	s	*s* in so
Ć	ć	between *ts* and *ch* in chin	Sz	sz	*sh* in shoe
			Szcz	szcz	*sh* plus *ch*, somewhat like *sti* in question
D	d	*d*			
Dz	dz	*dz* in adz	Ś	ś	between *s* and *sh*
Dź	dź	between *dz* and *j* in judge	Ść	ść	*ś* plus *ć*
			T	t	*t*
Dż	dż	*j* in judge	U	u	*u* in rule
E	e	*e* in set	V	v	used only in quoting foreign words
Ę	ę	somewhat like *an* in man, or like French *in*			
			W	w	*v*
			X	x	is rendered *Ks;* is used in foreign words and names; examples: Aquae Sextiae, Huxley, and in some Old Polish names and words; examples: Jaxa, Kxięstwo.
F	f	*f*			
G	g	*g* in go			
H	h	like *h* in hook			
I	i	*i* as in machine			
J	j	*y* in yard, boy			
K	k	*k*			
L	l	*l* in million			
Ł	ł	*l* in bell	Y	y	*y* in rhythm
M	m	*m*	Z	z	*z* in zone
N	n	*n*	Ź	ź	between *z* in zone and *s* in pleasure
Ń	ń	*ny* in canyon			
O	o	*o* in port	Ż	ż	*s* in pleasure

Special characters

Polish uses the Latin alphabet with the addition of the following special characters: Ą ą, Ć ć, Ę ę, Ł ł, Ń ń, Ó ó, Ś ś, Ź ź, and Ż ż. Note also the following somewhat similar characters frequently confused: Ź Ż, ź ż, and ł l.

Vowels and consonants

The vowel letters are *a, ą, e, ę, i, o, ó, u,* and *y.* The remaining letters of the alphabet are consonant letters.

Diphthongs

The sequences of *i* or *j* followed by one of the vowel letters may be called diphthongs, as are the sequences of a vowel followed by *j: ia, ja, ią, ją, ie, je, ię, ję, ji, io, jo, ió, jó, iu, ju, aj, ej, ij, oj, ój, uj.* The sequences beginning with *i* are not found initially or after a vowel.

Digraphs

The digraphs are: *ch, cz, dz, dź, dż, rz, sz, szcz* and *ść.* Their sounds are shown in the alphabet table.

Consonantal units

The following groups of consonants are for purposes of syllabification treated as units:

bl, bł, br, brz
chl, chł, chr, chrz, chw
dl, dł, dr, drz, dw
fl, fr
gl, gł, gr, grz, gw
kl, kł, kr, krz, kw

pl, pł, pr, prz
sc, sk, skr, skrz, śm, sp, spr, sprz, st,
str, strz, stw
tl, tł, tr, trz, tw
wl, wl, wr, wrz

Rules for syllabification [1]

1. Diphthongs, digraphs, consonantal units, and one-syllable words may not be divided.

2. Division is made on a vowel or on a diphthong before a single consonant, a digraph, or a consonantal unit: *uli-ca, mię-so, ko-chać, je-szcze, do-bry, do-brze, bli-sko, ko-me-dia, wę-grzyn.*

3. In a group of two or more consonants the division is made before the last consonant, digraph, or consonantal unit: *leś-ny, lek-ko, lep-szy, pań-stwo, maj-ster, pierw-szy.*

4. Division may be made between vowels not constituting a diphthong or between a diphthong and another vowel: *po-ić, po-ema, oce-an, ma-jor.*

5. Certain adverbial prefixes are kept intact. These are: *bez, do, na, nad(e), naj, ni, nie, o, ob(e), od(e), po, pod(e), poza, prze, przed(e), przy, roz(e), społ, u, wy, za,* and *ze: bez-interesowny, do-słać, na-słać, nad-inspektor, nade-słać, ni-gdzie, nie-krwawy,* etc.

6. Compound words are divided according to their component parts (and each part according to rules 1 to 5): *kraj-obraz, krótko-trwały.*

7. Foreign words and components of foreign words (not naturalized) follow the conventions of the language of origin: *golf-sztrom, foks-trot, kop-sztyk, super-arbiter.* This rule applies also to technical and scientific terms, which editors prefer to divide etymologically: *san-gwinik, dia-gnostyka, strato-sfera, hiper-mnezja.*

Illustrative word divisions

[The numbers in parentheses refer to the syllabification rules]

ame-ry-kań-ski	(2, 2, 3)	ge-o-me-tria	(4, 2, 2)
an-ty-kwa-riusz	(3, 7, 2)	Hisz-pa-nia	(3, 2)
atlan-tyc-ki	(3, 3)	ide-o-lo-gia	(4, 2, 2)
au-tor-stwo	(2, 3)	in-kwi-zy-cja	(7, 2, 2)
bez-in-te-re-sow-ny	(5, 3, 2, 2, 3)	in-stru-ment	(3, 2)
bez-względ-ny	(5, 3)	jak gdy-by	(6, 2)
bi-blij-ny	(2, 3)	kom-pa-nion	(3. 2)
człeko-kształt-ny	(6, 3)	ludo-znaw-stwo	(6, 3)
di-e-lek-trycz-ny	(7, 2, 3, 3)	la-go-dzić	(2, 2)
dia-gno-sty-ka	(7, 2, 2)	mek-sy-kań-ski	(3, 2, 3)
do-słow-ny	(5, 3)	mi-mo-środ-ko-wy	(2, 6, 3, 2)
do-zna-wać	(5, 2)	na-de-rwać	(2, 5)
dwu-znacz-ność	(6, 3)	nad-gni-ły	(5, 2)
elo-kwen-cja	(7, 3)	na-gmin-ny	(5, 3)
en-cy-klo-pe-dia	(3, 2, 2, 2)	naj-mniej-szy	(5, 3)
eu-ro-pej-ski	(2, 2, 3)	nie-słusz-ny	(5, 3)
fe-u-da-lizm	(4, 2, 2)	obe-gna-li-śmy	(5, 2, 2)
foto-gra-wiu-ra	(2, 2, 2, 2)	ob-ra-do-wać	(5, 2, 2)
fre-kwen-cja	(7, 3)	ob-słu-ga	(5, 2)

[1] Syllabification usage varies considerably among Polish printers, especially as regards the division of consonantal groups. Editors usually permit printers to divide such groups optionally, provided the division does not override phonetics and etymology. The rules given here, being designed for consultants who might not be fully familiar with Polish, are somewhat restrictive, but they insure invariably correct and consistent word division.

Illustrative word divisions—Continued

ode-rwa-nie	(5, 2)	rzecz-po-spo-li-ta	(6, 2, 2, 2)
od-wzo-ro-wa-nie	(5, 2, 2, 2)	samo-wznie-ca-nie	(2, 6, 2, 2)
od-zna-cze-nie	(5, 2, 2)	samo-zwa-niec	(2, 6, 2)
po-de-słać	(2, 5)	san-gwi-nicz-ny	(7, 2, 3)
pod-in-spek-tor	(5, 3, 3)	spół-ob-wi-nio-ny	(5, 5, 2, 2)
po-gnie-wać	(5, 2)	stro-i-ciel	(4, 2)
poza-służ-bo-wy	(2, 5, 3, 2)	super-ar-bi-ter	(2, 7, 3, 2)
przede-wszyst-kiem	(5, 3)	śmier-tel-nie	(3, 3)
przed-szkol-ny	(5, 3)	War-sza-wa	(3, 2)
prze-wra-cać	(5, 2)	wy-sło-wie-nie	(5, 2, 2)
przy-gnę-biać	(5, 2)	wy-słu-chać	(5, 2)
prze-zna-cze-nie	(5, 2, 2)	za-słab-nię-cie	(5, 3, 2)
pu-blicz-ność	(2, 3)	ze-wnętrz-ność	(5, 3)
re-pu-bli-ka	(2, 2, 2)	zjed-no-czo-ne	(3, 2, 2)
ro-ze-gnać	(2, 5)	zwie-rze-nie	(2, 2)
roz-mna-żać	(5, 2)	żyw-no-ścio-wy	(3, 2, 2)

Stress and diacritics

Stress is usually on the penultimate (next to the last) syllable: *MAT-ka*, *głę-BO-ki, spo-wo-DO-wać.* In verbs of the first and second person plural past tense and in words of Latin and Greek origin the stress is on the antepenultimate (second from the last) syllable: *BY-li-śmy* (we were), *BY-li-ście* (you were), *a-ryt-ME-ty-ka, MU-zy-ka, re-TO-ry-ka.*

The diacritical marks used are the inverted cedilla ($_c$), to indicate the nasal sounds *ą* and *ę;* the acute ('), to indicate the palatalization of a consonant; the stroke (/), to indicate the hard *ł;* and the superior dot (·), to indicate the post-palatal *ż.*

Capitalization

Capitalization is practically the same as in English, except that proper adjectives are lowercased and names of days and months are lowercased. Initial caps are used in titles of periodicals.

Punctuation

Punctuation is practically the same as in English, except that the comma is used to mark off restrictive as well as nonrestrictive clauses.

Alphabetization

The letters *ą, ć, ę, ł, ó, ś, ź,* and *ż* are regarded as separate characters and are so alphabetized. The complete alphabetic order is: *a, ą, b, c, ć, d, e, ę, f, g, h, i, j, k, l, ł, m, n, ń, o, ó, p, r, s, ś, t, u, w, y, z, ź, ż.*

Abbreviations

a.	albo, or, or else	r.b.	roku bieżącego, current year
im.	imienia, named for	s-ka	spółka, company, association
i t. d.	i tak dalej, et cetera	str.	stronica, page
itp.	i tym podobne, and the like	sz.	szanowny, honorable
jw.	jak wyżej, as above	ś. p.	świętej pamięci, deceased
N. or Nr	numer, number	św.	święty, Saint
np.	na przykład, for instance	t.j.	to jest, that is
p.	pan, pani, Mr., Mrs.	tzn.	to znaczy, that is
por.	porównaj, compare with, cf.	tzw.	tak zwany, so-called
r.	rok, year	w.	wiek, century

Cardinal numbers

jeden, jedna, jedno	one	dwanaście	twelve
dwa, dwaj, dwie, dwoje	two	trzynaście	thirteen
trzy, trzej, troje	three	czternaście	fourteen
cztery, czterej, czworo	four	piętnaście	fifteen
pięć	five	szesnaście	sixteen
sześć	six	siedemnaście	seventeen
siedem	seven	osiemnaście	eighteen
osiem	eight	dziewiętnaście	nineteen
dziewięć	nine	dwadzieścia	twenty
dziesięć	ten	dwadzieścia jeden, etc.	twenty-one, etc.
jedenaście	eleven		

Cardinal numbers—Continued

trzydzieści	thirty	pięćset	five hundred
czterdzieści	forty	sześćset	six hundred
pięćdziesiąt	fifty	siedemset	seven hundred
sześćdziesiąt	sixty	osiemset	eight hundred
siedemdziesiąt	seventy	dziewięćset	nine hundred
osiemdziesiąt	eighty	tysiąc	thousand
dziewięćdziesiąt	ninety	dwa tysiące	two thousand
sto	hundred	trzy tysiące, etc.	three thousand, etc.
sto jeden, etc.	one hundred and one, etc.		
dwieście	two hundred	pięć tysięcy, etc.	five thousand, etc.
trzysta	three hundred	sto tysięcy	hundred thousand
czterysta	four hundred	milion	million

Ordinal numbers

pierwszy, -sza, -sze	first	trzydziesty	thirtieth
drugi, -ga, -gie	second	czterdziesty	fortieth
trzeci	third	pięćdziesiąty	fiftieth
czwarty	fourth	sześćdziesiąty	sixtieth
piąty	fifth	siedemdziesiąty	seventieth
szósty	sixth	osiemdziesiąty	eightieth
siódmy	seventh	dziewięćdziesiąty	ninetieth
ósmy	eighth	setny	hundredth
dziewiąty	ninth	sto pierwszy, etc.	one hundred and first, etc.
dziesiąty	tenth		
jedenasty	eleventh	dwusetny	two hundredth
dwunasty	twelfth	trzechsetny or	three hundredth
trzynasty	thirteenth	dwóchsetny	
czternasty	fourteenth	czterechsetny	four hundredth
piętnasty	fifteenth	pięćsetny	five hundredth
szesnasty	sixteenth	sześćsetny	six hundredth
siedemnasty	seventeenth	siedemsetny	seven hundredth
osiemnasty	eighteenth	osiemsetny	eight hundredth
dziewiętnasty	nineteenth	dziewięćsetny	nine hundredth
dwudziesty	twentieth	tysiączny	one thousandth
dwudziesty pierwszy, etc.	twenty-first, etc.	dwutysięczny	two thousandth
		milionowy	millionth

Months

styczeń (stycz.)	January	lipiec (lip.)	July
luty	February	sierpień (sierp.)	August
marzec (mar.)	March	wrzesień (wrzes.)	September
kwiecień (kwiec.)	April	październik (paźdz.)	October
maj	May	listopad (listop.)	November
czerwiec (czerw.)	June	grudzień (grudz.)	December

Days

niedziela	Sunday	czwartek	Thursday
poniedziałek	Monday	piątek	Friday
wtorek	Tuesday	sobota	Saturday
środa	Wednesday		

Seasons

wiosna	spring	jesień	autumn
lato	summer	zima	winter

Time

godzina	hour	miesiąc	month
dzień	day	rok	year
tydzień	week	wiek	century

REFERENCES.—The Kościuszko Foundation Dictionary: English-Polish, Polish-English. New York, 1960–62. 2 v. (Poland's millenium series of the Kościuszko Foundation).
Contents.—v. 1. English-Polish, by K. Bulas and F. J. Whitfield. v. 2. Polish-English, by K. Bulas, L. L. Thomas, and F. J. Whitfield.

Polska Akademia Nauk.
Słownik języka polskiego. Redaktor naczelny Witold Doroszewski. Warszawa, Wiedza Powszechna, 1958–1968. 10 v. 1-volume supplement 1969.
It is projected in 10 volumes; to date (1965) seven volumes, covering the letters A to R appeared.
Słownik wyrazów obcych. [Komitet redakcyjny: Zygmunt Rysiewicz et al. Wyd. 5., fotooffsetowe. Warszawa] Państwowy Instytut Wydawniczy [1959] 720 p.

Teslar, Józef Andrzej.
A new Polish grammar by Joseph Andrew Teslar in collaboration with Jadwiga Teslar. 8th ed., rev., with key to the exercises. Edinburgh, Oliver and Boyd, 1962. xxiv, 469 p.

Szober, Stanisław.
Słownik poprawnej polszczyzny. Wyd. 4., uzup. [Warszawa] Państwowy Instytut Wydawniczy, 1963. 857 p.
First ed. published in 1937 under title: *Słownik ortoepiczny.*

Jodłowski, Stanisław.
Zasady pisowni polskiej i interpunkcji, ze słownikiem ortograficznym. Wyd. 15. dostosowane do uchwał Komitetu Językoznawczego Polskiej Akademii Nauk z 20 stycz. 1956. Wrocław, Zakład Narodowy im. Ossolińskich, 1964. 348 p.

Jodłowski, Stanisław.
Słownik ortograficzny i prawidła pisowni polskiej. Wyd. 5., zmienione według uchwał Komitetu Językoznawczego Polskiej Akademii Nauk z r. 1956. Wrocław, Zakład Narodowy im. Ossolińskich, 1958. 728 p.

Polska Akademia Nauk.
Pisownia polska; przepisy, słowniczek. Wyd. 12. oprac. na podstawie wyd. 11. według uchwały Komitetu Językoznawczego Polskiej Akademii Nauk z 20 stycz. 1956. Wrocław, Zakład im. Ossolińskich, 1957. 167 p.

Klemensiewicz, Zenon.
Prawidła poprawnej wymowy polskiej. Wyd. 4. Wrocław, Zakład Narodowy im. Ossolińskich, 1964. 30 p. (Biblioteczka Towarzystwa Miłośników Języka Polskiego, nr. 10)

PORTUGUESE

Concluindo êste ponto: há o fato da língua brasileira, que percebemos nos atritos com as diferenças, especialmente as diferenças portuguêsas, que estão mais próximas de nós. Fora dêsses atritos, nós não nos damos conta dela: vivêmo-la. E há o conflito entre ela e a formação literogramatical que recebemos na escola e no livro de erudição. É o chamado problema da língua brasileira, em que a consciência da nacionalidade, o patriotismo político e o espírito objetivo das ciências positivas se debatem contra a rotina, a filologia, a gramática, e o diletantismo tais como se radicaram em algumas cidades brasileiras.—Herbert Parentes Fortes, A Questão da Língua Brasileira (1962?), p. 10.

Alphabet and pronunciation [1]

A	a	stressed: *a* in m*a*ma; unstressed: *a* in sof*a*
B	b	*b*
C	c	*s* in so; before *e* or *i;* elsewhere like *k*
D	d	*d*
E	e	stressed: like *e* in Hey! (close, written *ê*), or *e* in get (open, written *é*); unstressed: *ee* in see
F	f	*f*
G	g	*su* in measure, before *e* or *i;* elsewhere like *g* in go
H	h	silent
I	i	*e*
J	j	*su* sound in measure
K	k	*k;* used only in foreign words
L	l	*l* in lay everywhere, except in final position, like *ll* in hill
M	m	*m* before vowel; after vowel, nasalizes vowel and is itself weakened in closure; final unstressed *am* like Portuguese, *ão*
N	n	*n* initially and intervocalically; before consonants, drops nasalizing preceding vowel
O	o	stressed: somewhat like *o* in sow (close, sometimes written *ô*), or like *aw* in saw (open, sometimes written *ó*); unstressed: *o* in obey, or *ou* in bayou when final
P	p	*p*
Q	q	always followed by *u* (see Digraphs)
R	r	*r* initially, and *rr* medially, like Parisian *r;* single *r* (between vowels or before and after consonants), like the sound of *tt* in butter (colloquial American English pronunciation)

[Concluded on following page]

---

[1] The pronunciation shown is that of Brazilian Portuguese; in Portugal unstressed vowels are more slurred, and certain consonants have slightly different sounds.

S	s	*s* initially or before and after consonants; between vowels or when the next letter of the following word is a vowel, *z*
T	t	*t*
U	u	*u* in Ruth
V	v	*v*
W	w	*w* or *v*, only in foreign words
X	x	*sh* in shoe initially, and often elsewhere; otherwise as *x* in box (=*ks*), or as *s* or *z*
Y	y	*y;* used only in archaic Portuguese
Z	z	*z* in gaze; final often like *z* in azure

Special characters

Portuguese uses the Latin alphabet, with the addition of the following special characters: the acute (ˊ), the circumflex (ˆ), the grave (ˋ), and the dieresis (¨).

The Portuguese system of writing vowels makes use of diacritical marks to indicate all of the vowel distinctions operant in the Portuguese language. Thus, *i, é, ê, a, ó, ô*, and *u* for the nonnasalized vowels; *ĩ, ễ, ã, õ*, and *ũ* for the nasalized vowels. The dieresis is used over the letter *u* to indicate that the *ü* has the value of *w*, as in wet. The cedilla is used with the letter *ç* to indicate the value of *s* before *a, o*, and *u*.

Vowels and consonants

The vowels are *a, e*, i, o**, and *u*, all of which have nasalized variants. The letter *y*, which occurs only in foreign words, is treated as a vowel before a consonant, otherwise as a consonant. The other letters of the alphabet are all consonants.

Diphthongs and triphthongs

A diphthong is a combination of two vowels. This is pronounced as one syllable, the first vowel receiving the predominant sound: p*ai* (pronounced p*Ai*). If the second vowel, however, carries an accent mark, the two vowels do not constitute a diphthong and are pronounced separately: p*aís* (pronounced pa-*Is*).

A diphthong may also be a combination of two weak vowels. In such case the first vowel receives the predominant sound and the second one is slurred over: fl*uido* (pronounced fl*Uido*), part*iu* (pronounced part*Iu*). If the second vowel, however, carries the acute mark, the two vowels do not constitute a diphthong: r*uído* (pronounced r*u-I*do), mi*úido* (pronounced mi-*U*do).

In diphthongs in which the first element is stressed, the final *i* and *e* have the value of *y* in boy; the final *o* and *u* have the value of *w* in cow. In diphthongs where the second element is stressed, the initial *i* and *u* have the value of *ee* in fee, and *u* in Ruth; other vowels retain their normal values.

A triphthong is a combination of three vowels, the middle one of which is stressed, the others weak, and is pronounced as a single syllable, the stressed vowel receiving the predominant sound: ig*uais* (pronounced ig*uAis*). If one of the weak vowels, however, carries an accent mark, the vowels do not constitute a triphthong: part*ieis* (pronounced part*I-eis*).

Digraphs

The digraphs and their sounds are:

ch as *sh* in ship; in archaic forms, like *k* in kite (archaic refers to works written before the orthographic reforms of 1942)

gu as *g* in go, only before *e, i; gü* before *e, i* to indicate the sound of *gw*

lh as *li* in million

nh as *ny* in canyon

ph as *f* (in the older orthography only)

qu as *k* before *e, i;* before *a* and sometimes before *o* as *qu* in quality (=*kw*); *qü* is used before *e, i* to indicate the sound of *kw*

th as *t* (in the older orthography only)

*Open and close forms.

Consonantal units

For the purpose of syllabification, the following are consonantal units:

bl, br	*dl, dr*	*gl, gr*	*tl, tr*
chl, chr, cl, cr	*fl, fr*	*pl, pr*	*vl, vr*

Rules for syllabification

1. Diphthongs, triphthongs, digraphs, and consonantal units may not be divided.
2. Division is made on a vowel or on a diphthong before a single consonant, a digraph, or a consonantal unit: *ba-lão, ba-nhar, ma-dre, flui-do*.
3. In a group of two or more consonants, division is made before the last consonant, digraph, or consonantal unit: *par-te, guer-ra, sump-to, per-cha, sem-pre*.
4. Division between vowels is avoided. In narrow measure, however, division is admissible between two strong vowels.· Hence, in the interest of good spacing, the following vowels may be divided: *aa, ae, ao; ea, ee, eo; oa, oe, oo* (but not the nasal vowels *ãe, ão,* and *õe,* etc.): *do-ente, le-oa, po-ema*.
5. According to the new orthography, only the prefix *ex* is kept intact, but division may be made on the other prefixes if such division conforms to rules 2 to 4: *con-sócio* (rule 3), *in-justo* (rule 3), *pro-mover* (rule 2), *re-organizar* (rule 4); but *cons-tar* (rule 3), *ins-pirar* (rule 3), *pros-crever* (rule 3), *reū-nião* (rule 2).
6. Compound words (hyphened) are divided preferably on the hyphen (and each part, according to rules 1 to 5): *além-atlántico, sub-rogar*.
7. Foreign words and components of foreign words (not naturalized) follow the conventions of the language of origin: *Wash-ington, co-gnac, cre-scendo, Reichs-amt*. Technical and scientific terms are regarded as naturalized words and are divided according to rules 1 to 6.

Illustrative word divisions

[The numbers in parentheses refer to the syllabification rules]

aban-do-nar	(3, 2)	maio-ri-da-de	(2, 2, 2)
abas-te-cer	(3, 2)	má-xi-mo	(2, 2)
aba-ti-men-to	(2, 2, 3)	mi-san-tró-pi-co	(2, 3, 2, 2)
ab-so-lu-to	(3, 2, 2)	mis-ce-lâ-nea	(3, 2, 2)
abs-tra-to	(3, 2)	ne-ces-si-da-de	(2, 3, 2, 2)
an-ti-a-é-reo	(3, 3, 4, 2)	ne-cro-ló-gi-co	(2, 2, 2, 2)
bem-es-tar	(6, 3)	ˈneu-tra-li-zar	(2, 2, 2)
bi-blio-te-ca	(2, 2, 2)	no-ro-es-te	(2, 4, 3)
bi-ci-cle-ta	(2, 2, 2)	no-va-ior-ki-no	(2, 6, 3, 2)
Bra-si-lei-ro	(2, 2, 2)	nú-me-ro	(2, 2)
com-pre-en-de	(3, 4, 3)	ob-je-to	(3, 2)
con-so-an-te	(3, 4, 3)	obli-quân-gu-lo	(2, 3, 2)
co-ra-ções	(2, 2)	obs-cu-ran-te	(3, 2, 3)
dei-xan-do	(2, 3)	obs-tru-ção	(3, 2)
de-se-qui-lí-brio	(2, 2, 2, 2)	oce-â-ni-co	(4, 2, 2)
elip-sói-de	(3, 2)	oxi-gê-nio	(2, 2)
em-bai-xa-dor	(3, 2, 2)	pa-le-ó-gra-fo	(2, 4, 2, 2)
es-ta-du-ni-den-se	(3, 2, 2, 2, 3)	pa-lha-bo-te	(2, 2, 2)
ex-er-ci-do	(5, 3, 2)	Pa-na-me-ri-ca-no	(2, 2, 2, 2, 2)
fer-rô-lho	(3, 2)	pa-râ-me-tro	(2, 2, 2)
go-niô-me-tro	(2, 2, 2)	pa-trió-ti-co	(2, 2, 2)
he-mis-fé-rio	(2, 3, 2)	pe-ga-nhen-to	(2, 2, 3)
hi-gros-có-pio	(2, 3, 2)	pei-xei-ra	(2, 2)
inad-mis-sí-vel	(3, 3, 2)	por-tu-guê-sa	(3, 2, 2)
in-com-pre-en-sí-vel	(3, 3, 4, 3, 2)	pro-ble-ma	(2, 2)
ine-ren-tes	(2, 3)	pù-bli-ca-men-te	(2, 2, 2, 3)
in-ex-is-ten-te	(5, 5, 3, 3)	re-pre-sen-tan-tes	(2, 2, 3, 3)
ins-ta-la-ções	(3, 2, 2)	re-pú-bli-ca	(2, 2, 2)
in-te-res-sa-dos	(3, 2, 3, 2)	se-mi-o-fi-cial	(2, 2, 2, 2)
inu-ti-li-zar	(2, 2, 2)	se-nho-res	(2, 2)
ju-rí-di-co	(2, 2, 2)	su-bal-ter-nos	(2, 3, 3)
lin-güís-ti-co	(3, 3, 2)	subs-cre-ver	(3, 2)
lu-xu-rian-te	(2, 2, 3)	trans-pi-rar	(3, 2)

Stress and diacritics

Stress in Portuguese words normally falls on the next-to-last syllable: *filosofIa, punIa, punIam, louvarIas, continUo, continUe;* otherwise on the last syllable: *continUa.* Words ending in *l, r,* and diphthongs followed or not by *s: canAl entendEr, varÃo, varÕes, sarAu, arrAis.*

Words contrary to the above rule have their stress marked either with an acute or a circumflex: The use of the acute indicates that the stressed vowel is open; the circumflex indicates that the stressed vowel is closed. Besides indicating that the vowel receives prominent sound, therefore, stress can also mark the opening or closing of a vowel; in either of these cases, the meaning of a word can change radically: e.g., *trôco* (small change), *troco* (I change); *sábia* (wise woman), *sabia* (he/she knew), *sabiá* (Brazilian bird), etc.[3]

Accent marks are used as mere diacritics for other purposes, as follows:

(a) The acute mark is used over the *e* or *o* in the stressed diphthongs *ei, eu, oi,* to indicate that the *e* or *o* is open; otherwise, the *e* or *o* is closed: *réis,* plural of *real* (but *reis,* plural of *rei*), *batéis,* plural of *batel* (but *bateis,* second person plural of *bater*), *sóis,* plural of *sol* or second person singular of *soer* (but *sois,* second person plural of *ser*); also *véu(s), chapéu(s), herói(s), jóia, gibóia,* etc.

(b) The acute is used over the *i* or *u* to indicate that the diphthong does not adhere to the normal penultimate (next-to-last) stress and that the prominent sound should be shifted to the marked vowel: *puniríamos, país, saída, saúde, baú,* etc.

(c) The circumflex is used over stressed *e* or *o* to close the vowel and to indicate that there are other words spelled like them with the stressed *e* or *o* open: *rêgo* (furrow), *rego* (first person singular of *regar*); *rôgo* (request), *rogo* (first person singular of *rogar*); *dêmos* (present subjunctive of *dar*), *demos* (present indicative of *dar*), *côrte* (court), *corte* (cut, edge), etc.

(d) The acute and circumflex are used as in (c) on monosyllables ending in *a, as, e, es, o, os: pá(s), sé(s), vê(s), mês, pó(s), pôs* (from *pôr*), etc.

(e) The acute and circumflex are used on certain words carrying sentence emphasis to distinguish them from words spelled like them but not receiving sentence emphasis: *quê* (interrogative), *que* (relative); *porquê* (interrogative), *porque* (conjunction); *pôr* (verb), *por* (preposition); *pára* (verb), *para* (preposition); *péla* (noun), *pela* (preposition), etc.

(f) The grave and circumflex are used to indicate primary stress in adverbs ending in *mente: ràpidamente, sòmente, cortêsmente* (from *rápido, só, cortês*).

(g) The dieresis (¨) is used over the *u* in *gu, qu* before *e* or *i* to indicate that the *u* is to be pronounced but not stressed. In other cases the *u* in *gu* and *qu* before *e* or *i* is silent: *conseqüência,* but *arguir, arguí* (first person preterite), and *argui* (third person present).

(h) The grave is used as a marker of contractions (the preposition *a* + a following pronoun or article): *à* (to the), *a* (the); *aquêle* (that one), *àquele* (to that one), etc.

(i) The tilde (˜) is used to indicate a nasal vowel. It is also used at times to indicate a contraction: *Roiz̃* (=*Rodriguez*), *q̃* (=*que*), *sñça* (=*sentença*).

Capitalization

Capital letters are used as in English with the exception that names of months, days of the week, and proper adjectives are lowercased.

Punctuation and hyphenation

Punctuation marks are used as in English.

The apostrophe as a sign of contraction between prepositions and pronouns has practically disappeared: *neste* (instead of, formerly, *n'este, 'neste,* or *n-este*), in this; *dêsse* (instead of *d'êsse*), of that; *daquém* (instead of *d'aquém*), on this side; *dêle* (instead of *d'êle*), of him, his; etc. The apostrophe is still retained, however, in proper nouns and a few compounds: *Sant' Ana, Nun' Alvares.* (Note also compounds in paragraph following.)

The hyphen is employed, aside from its use in syllabification, to indicate compounds whose elements retain their phonetic independence: *mãe-d'água,* reservoir; *mão-d'obra,* workmanship; *contra-almirante,* rear admiral; *pára-raios,* lightning conductor. It is also used to set off suffixed and infixed pronouns in verb forms: *dê-me,* give me; *dizem-no-lo,* they say it to us; *fá-lo-ia,* I would do it; also after the monosyllabic forms of *haver* when followed by *de* and an infinitive: *hei-de ler,* I must read, but *havíamos de ler,* we had to read.

---

[3] On the whole, the rules here recommended follow those now valid in Brazil.

Abbreviations

cm	centímetro, centimeter	pp.	páginas, pages
D.	Dom, Sir; Dona, Lady	S. Excia.	Sua Excel(l)ência, His Excellency
Dr.	doutor, doctor		
Dra.	doutora, doctress	S.	São (contraction of santo), Saint
EE. UU. da A., E.U.A.	Estados Unidos da América, United States of America	Snr., Sr.	senhor, Mr.; also Lord
		Snra., Sra.	senhora, Mrs.
Exmo.	Excel(l)entíssimo, Excellency	Snrta., Srta.	senhorita, Miss
hect.	hectare, hectare	Sta.	Santa, Saint
Il(l)mo.	Il(l)ustríssimo, Illustrious	V. E., V. Exa.	Vossa Excel(l)ência, Your Excellency
l.	litro, liter	Vmcê., V. M.	Vossa Mercê, Your Grace
m.	metro, meter		
p.	página, page		

Cardinal numbers

um, uma	one	trinta	thirty
dois, duas	two	quarenta	forty
três	three	cincoenta, cinqüenta	fifty
quatro	four		
cinco	five	sessenta	sixty
seis	six	setenta	seventy
sete	seven	oitenta	eighty
oito	eight	noventa	ninety
nove	nine	cem, cento	hundred
dez	ten	cento e um(a), etc.	one hundred and one, etc.
onze	eleven		
doze	twelve	duzentos, -as	two hundred
treze	thirteen	trezentos, -as, etc.	three hundred, etc.
catorze	fourteen		
quinze	fifteen	mil	thousand
dezasseis, dezaseis	sixteen	mil e um(a), etc.	one thousand and one, etc.
dezassete, dezasete	seventeen		
dezoito	eighteen	dois mil, etc.	two thousand, etc.
dezanove	nineteen		
vinte	twenty	um milhão	million
vinte e um, etc.	twenty-one, etc.		

Round millions used adjectively are followed by *de: Um milhão de contos*, or *1,000,000 de contos*.

Ordinal numbers

primeiro	first	quadragésimo, quarentésimo	fortieth
segundo	second		
terceiro	third	quinquagésimo	fiftieth
quarto	fourth	sexagésimo	sixtieth
quinto	fifth	septuagésimo	seventieth
sexto	sixth	octogésimo	eightieth
sétimo	seventh	nonagésimo	ninetieth
oitavo	eighth	centésimo	hundredth
nono	ninth	centésimoprimeiro, etc.	one hundred and first, etc.
décimo	tenth		
undécimo décimo primeiro }	eleventh	ducentésimo	two hundredth
		tricentésimo	three hundredth
duodécimo, décimo segundo	twelfth	quadringentésimo	four hundredth
		quingentésimo	five hundredth
décimo terceiro, etc.	thirteenth, etc.	sexcentésimo	six hundredth
vigésimo	twentieth	septingentésimo	seven hundredth
vigésimo primeiro, etc.	twenty-first, etc.	octingentésimo	eight hundredth
		noningentésimo	nine hundredth
trigésimo	thirtieth	milésimo	thousandth

Months

janeiro (jan.)	January	julho (jul.)	July
fevereiro (fev.)	February	agôsto (agto.)	August
março (mço.)	March	setembro (set.)	September
abril (abr.)	April	outubro (obro.)	October
maio	May	novembro (nov.)	November
junho (jun.)	June	dezembro (dez.)	December

Days

domingo	Sunday	quinta-feira	Thursday
segunda-feira	Monday	sexta-feira	Friday
têrça-feira	Tuesday	sábado	Saturday
quarta-feira	Wednesday		

Seasons

primavera	spring	outono	autumn
verão	summer	inverno	winter

Time

hora	hour	mês (mez)	month
dia	day	ano	year
semana	week		

REFERENCES.—Aurélio Buarque de Hollanda, Pequeno Dicionário Brasileiro da Língua Portuguêsa (1963); Frederick B. Agard, Hélio Lobo, and Raymond S. Willis, Jr., Brazilian Portuguese (1944); Alvaro Franco, Dicionário Inglês-Português [e] Português-Inglês (1941).

RUSSIAN

Тамань—маленький городок на берегу моря. * * * Во всём городе только один каменный дом, у самого въезда в город. В нём почта и военное начальство.—M. Yu. Lermontov, Taman', D. C. Heath & Co. edition, p. 1.

Alphabet, transliteration,[1] and pronunciation

А	а	a	*a* in far [2]
Б	б	b	*b*
В	в	v	*v*
Г	г	g	*g* in go [3]
Д	д	d	*d*
Е	е	ye, e [4]	*ye* in yell, *e* in fell [5]
Ё	ё	yë, ë [6]	*yo* in yore, *o* in order [7]
Ж	ж	zh	*z* in azure
З	з	z	*z* in zeal
И	и	i	*i* in machine [8]
Й	й	y	*y* in boy
К	к	k	*k*
Л	л	l	*l*
М	м	m	*m*
Н	н	n	*n*
О	о	o	*o* in order [9]
П	п	p	*p*
Р	р	r	*r*
С	с	s	*s* in so
Т	т	t	*t*
У	у	u	*u* like the *oo* in Moon.
Ф	ф	f	*f*
Х	х	kh	*h* in how, but stronger, or *ch* in Scottish loch
Ц	ц	ts	*ts* in hats
Ч	ч	ch	*ch* in church
Ш	ш	sh	*sh* in shoe
Щ	щ	shch	*sh* plus *ch*, somewhat like *sti* in question
Ъ	ъ	" [10]	([11])
Ы	ы	y [12]	*y* in rhythm
Ь	ь	' [12]	([13])
Э	э	e	*e* in elder
Ю	ю	yu	*u* in union
Я	я	ya	*ya* in yard

[1] U. S. Board on Geographic Names transliteration, 1944. (See p. 526 for Slavic transliteration as a whole.)
[2] When stressed; when unstressed, like *a* in sofa.
[3] Also pronounced as *v* in the genitive ending -го; often used for original *h* in non-Russian words, but is pronounced as *g* by Russians.
[4] *Ye* initially, after vowels, and after ъ, ь.
[5] Pronounced as *i* in habit, or the same sound with preceding *y*, when unstressed.
[6] *Yë* as for *ye*. The sign ё is not considered a separate letter of the alphabet, and the ¨ is often omitted. Transliterate as ё, *yë* when printed in Russian as ё; otherwise use *e*, *ye*.
[7] Only stressed.
[8] Like *i* in habit when unstressed; like *yie* in yield after a vowel and after ь.
[9] Like *o* in abbot when unstressed.
[10] The symbol '' (double apostrophe), not a repetition of the line above.
[11] No sound; used only after certain prefixes before the vowel letters е, ё, я, ю. Formerly used also at the end of all words now ending in a consonant letter. See Note on Old Spelling, p. 473.
[12] ' (apostrophe).
[13] Palatalizes a preceding consonant, giving a sound resembling the consonant plus *y*, somewhat as in English meet you, did you.

436

Special characters

Russian uses the Cyrillic alphabet. Many of the characters are the same as in Latin, with the following special ones: Б б, Г г, Д д, Ж ж, Й й, Л л, П п, Ф ф, Ц ц, Ш ш, Щ щ, Ъ ъ, Ы ы, Э э, Ю ю, and Я я. Note the following somewhat similar characters: З Э, Л П, У Ч, Ш Щ, э э, л п, ш щ. The Ы is a separate character and not a combination of Ь and I.

Transliteration

This is a mechanical process of substituting the transliteration letter or combination of letters for each Russian letter: Москва = *Moskva*, Киев = *Kiyev*, Русский = *Russkiy*, etc.

Vowels and consonants

The vowel letters are а, е, ё, и, о, у, ы, э, ю, and я, represented, respectively, by *a, e* or *ye, ё* or *yё, i, o, u, y, e, yu, ya*. The letters й, ъ, and ь are not called either vowels or consonants. All other letters are consonants.

Diphthongs

The sequences of a vowel followed by й are often called diphthongs. Their sounds are:

ай (*ay*) *ai* in aisle
ей (*ey, yey*) *ey* in they, or as *yea* (=yes)
ий (*iy*) like prolonged English *ee*
ой (*oy*) *oy*
уй (*uy*) *uoy* in buoy as pronounced by some (*ōo* plus *y*)

ый (*yy*) *y* in rhythm plus *y* in yield
эй (*ey*) *ey* in they
юй (*yuy*) *you* plus *y* in yield
яй (*yay*) *ya* in yard plus *y* in yield

Digraphs

The transliterations *ye, zh, kh, ts, ch, sh, shch, yu, ya* represent single Russian letters and should not be divided in syllabification.

Consonantal units

The following combinations of consonants should be treated, for syllabification purposes, as indivisible units:

бл, бр (*bl, br*)
вл, вр (*vl, vr*)
гл, гр (*gl, gr*)
дв, др (*dv, dr*)
жд (*zhd*)
кл, кр (*kl, kr*)

мл (*ml*)
пл, пр (*pl, pr*)
ск, скв, скр, ст, ств, стр (*sk, skv, skr, st, stv, str*)
тв, тр (*tv, tr*)
фл, фр (*fl, fr*)

These simplified rules have been followed for the past 2 years by the Library of Congress Card Division. (Based on practice in Bol'shaîa sovetskaîa entsiklopedîa, v. 36.)

General:

1. A single letter is not separated from the rest of the word.
2. A soft or hard sign is not separated from the preceding consonant.
3. Division is made at the end of the prefix (a fill-vowel is considered part of the prefix): со-глас-но воз-дух по-треб-ле-ние объ-ем пре-до-ста-вить.
4. In compound words, letters are not separated from the component parts of the word, and a fill-vowel goes with the preceding syllable:

сов-хоз зем-ле-вла-де-лец

Two vowels together:

1. Division is made between the vowels: сто-ит (*but:* рос-сий-ский).

One consonant between two vowels:

1. The consonant goes with the following vowel:

ма-не-ры по-вы-ше-ни-ем ста-тья-ми.

Two consonants between two vowels:

1. Division is made between the consonants. (*Exception:* ст goes with the following vowel): топ-ли-во управ-ле-ние ре-ак-тив-ный биб-ли-о-те-ка Поль-ша (*but:* пу-скает ча-сти).

Three or more consonants between two vowels:

1. If a consonant is doubled, division is made between the two:

искус-ство диф-фрак-ция.

2. ст is never separated.
3. Division is not made before the first nor after the last consonant. (*Exception:*

When ст begins the consonant group, it may be separated from the preceding vowel): мест-ность *or* ме-стность

4. Otherwise, division is optional: элек-три-че-ство *or* элект-ри-че-ство. Ан-глия *or* Анг-лия   цент-раль-ный *or* цен-траль-ный

Exception: The following are consistently divided as shown: марк-сизм Мо-сква

Rules for syllabification [1]

1. Diphthongs, digraphs, and consonantal units may not be divided.

2. Division is made on a vowel or on a diphthong before a single consonant, a digraph, or a consonantal unit: ба-гаж (*ba-gazh*), Бай-кал (*Bay-kal*), му-ха (*mu-kha*), рё-бра (*rë-bra*), каче-ство (*kache-stvo*), свой-ство (*svoy-stvo*).

3. In a group of two or more consonants, division is made before the last consonant, digraph, or consonantal unit: мас-ло (*mas-lo*), мас-са (*mas-sa*), мар-шал (*mar-shal*), точ-ка (*toch-ka*), долж-ность (*dolzh-nost'*), сред-ство (*sred-stvo*).

4. Division may be made between vowels not constituting a diphthong or between a diphthong and another vowel: оке-ан (*oke-an*), ма-як (*ma-yak*).

5. Certain adverbial prefixes are kept intact, except before ы. These are: без (бес), во, воз (вос), вы, до, за, из (ис), на, над, не, ни, низ (нис), о, об обо, от, ото, пере, по, под, пред(и), пред(о), при, про, раз (рас), с(о), and у. In transliteration these prefixes are respectively *bez* (*bes*), *vo*, *voz* (*vos*), *vy*, *do*, *za*, *iz* (*is*), *na*, *nad*, *ne*, *ni*, *niz* (*nis*), *o*, *ob*, *obo*, *ot*, *oto*, *pere*, *po*, *pod*, *pred*(*i*), *pred*(*o*), *pri*, *pro*, *raz* (*ras*), *s*(*o*), and *u:* без-вкусный (*bez-vkusnyy*), бес-связь (*bes-svyaz'*), во-круг (*vo-krug*), but раз-ыскать (*ra-zyskat'*), etc.

6. Compound words are divided according to their component parts (and each part according to rules 1 to 5): радио-связь (*radio-svyaz'*), фото-снимка (*foto-snimka*).

7. It is to be noted that the й (ĭ) always terminates a syllable: бой-кий (*boy-kiy*), рай-он (*ray-on*); the ъ ('') terminates a syllable except in words beginning with въ (*v''*), взъ (*vz''*), and съ (*s''*): отъ-ехать (*ot''-yekhat*) but съём-ка (*c''yëm-ka*), съест-ной (*s''yest-noy*); the ь (') terminates a syllable except before the soft vowels е (*e*), и (*i*), ю (*yu*), and я (*ya*): маль-чик (*mal'-chik*), but соло-вьев (*solo-v'yev*), бри-льянт (*bri-l'yant*), се-мья (*se-m'ya*).

8. Foreign words and components of foreign words (not naturalized) follow the conventions of the language of origin: Шек-спир (*Shek-spir*), мас-штаб (*mas-shtab*), Лоа-ра (*Loa-ra*) [not Ло-ара (*Lo-ara*) (from the French *Loire*)], се-ньор (*se-n'or*).

Illustrative word divisions

[The numbers in parentheses refer to the syllabification rules]

аме-ри-кан-ский *ame-ri-kan-skiy* }	(2, 2, 3)	вы-со-ко-нрав-ство *vy-so-ko-nrav-stvo* }	(2, 2, 6, 3)
ан-глий-ская *an-gliy-skaya* }	(3, 2)	го-су-дар-ствен-ный *go-su-dar-stven-nyy* }	(2, 2, 3, 3)
без-ал-ко-голь-ный *bez-al-ko-gol'-nyy* }	(5, 3, 2, 7)	до-школь-ное *do-shkol'-noe* }	(5, 7)
бес-сроч-ный *bes-sroch-nyy* }	(5, 3)	зав-траш-ний *zav-trash-niy* }	(3, 3)
ва-ку-ум *va-ku-um* }	(2, 4)	изъ-яс-не-ние *iz''-yas-ne-niye* }	(7, 3, 2)
во-гну-тость *vo-gnu-tost'* }	(5, 2)	ис-сле-до-ва-тель-ский *is-sle-do-va-tel'-skiy* }	(5, 2, 2, 2, 7)
во-до-вме-сти-ли-ще *vo-do-vme-sti-li-shche* }	(2, 6, 2, 2, 2)	Крон-штадт-ский *Kron-shtadt-skiy* }	(8, 3)
воз-зре-ние *voz-zre-niye* }	(5, 2)	на-всег-да *na-vseg-da* }	(5, 3)
вос-хва-ле-ние *vos-khva-le-niye* }	(5, 2, 2)	на-дви-га-ю-щий-ся *na-dvi-ga-yu-shchiy-sya* }	(5, 2, 4, 2, 7)
вы-здо-ро-веть *vy-zdo-ro-vet'* }	(5, 2, 2)	над-вя-зать *nad-vya-zat'* }	(5, 2)

Illustrative word divisions—Continued

не-сго-ра-е-мый *ne-sgo-ra-e-myy*	(5, 2, 4, 2)	под-жи-да-ние *pod-zhi-da-niye*	(5, 2, 2)
неф-те-хра-ни-ли-ще *nef-te-khra-ni-li-shche*	(3, 6, 2, 2, 2)	пред-ва-ри-тель-ный *pred-va-ri-tel'-nyy*	(5, 2, 2, 7)
ни-сколь-ко *ni-skol'-ko*	(5, 7)	пре-ди-сло-вие *pre-di-slo-viye*	(2, 5, 2)
об-ло-же-ние *ob-lo-zhe-niye*	(5, 2, 2)	пре-до-хра-нять *pre-do-khra-nyat'*	(2, 5, 2)
обо-зна-че-ние *obo-zna-che-niye*	(5, 2, 2)	при-вхо-дя-щий *pri-vkho-dya-shchiy*	(5, 2, 2)
объ-яс-ни-тель-ный *ob"-yas-ni-tel'-nyy*	(7, 3, 2, 7)	про-све-ще-ние *pro-sve-shche-niye*	(5, 2, 2)
од-но-звуч-ный *od-no-zvuch-nyy*	(3, 6, 3)	про-те-стант-ство *pro-te-stant-stvo*	(2, 2, 3)
от-зву-чать *ot-zvu-chat'*	(5, 2)	про-хва-тить *pro-khva-tit'*	(5, 2)
ото-зва-ние *oto-zva-niye*	(5, 2)	раз-вью-чи-вать *raz-v'yu-chi-vat'*	(5, 2, 2)
отъ-ез-жа-ю-щий *ot"-yez-zha-yu-shchiy*	(7, 3, 4, 2)	раз-мно-жать *raz-mno-zhat'*	(5, 2)
Па-ра-гвай *Pa-ra-gvay*	(2, 8)	рас-ска-зы-вать *ras-ska-zy-vat'*	(5, 2, 2)
пе-ре-гнать *pe-re-gnat'*	(2, 5)	соб-ствен-ный *sob-stven-nyy*	(3, 3)
пер-спек-ти-ва *per-spek-ti-va*	(8, 3, 2)	со-дей-ство-вать *so-dey-stvo-vat'*	(5, 7, 2)
пи-о-нер-ский *pi-o-ner-skiy*	(4, 2, 3)	со-е-ди-нён-ные *so-ye-di-nën-nyye*	(5, 2, 2, 3)
по-глуб-же *po-glub-zhe*	(5, 3)	сол-неч-ный *sol-nech-nyy*	(3, 3)
по-гля-ды-вать *po-glya-dy-vat'*	(5, 2, 2)	солн-це-сто-я-ние *soln-tse-sto-ya-niye*	(3, 6, 4, 2)
по-да-вать-ся *po-da-vat'-sya*	(5, 2, 7)	удоб-ней-ше *udob-ney-she*	(3, 7)

Stress and diacritics

No simple set of rules for syllabic stress can be formulated. The only dependable guide is a native, or a dictionary in the case of basic forms and a grammar for their inflectional shiftings.

The only diacritics are the dieresis and the breve. These do not indicate stress but modification of sound. Note alphabet.

Capitalization

Capitalization is practically as in English, except that proper adjectives, names of the months (except when abbreviated), and days of the week are lowercased.

Punctuation

Punctuation is very similar to that of English, but the comma is used for restrictive as well as nonrestrictive clauses. The dash is used between a subject and a complement when there is no verb *is* or *are*, and sometimes before a clause where the equivalent of the conjunction *that* has been omitted. Dialog is usually shown by dashes rather than quotation marks. Cited material is enclosed in quotation marks, which are usually in the French form—« », though sometimes in the German form—,, ", and rarely as in English.

Abbreviations

амер.	американский, American	г.	год, year; город, city; господин, Mr.
АН	Академия наук, Academy of Sciences	г-жа	госпожа, Mrs.
б.г.	без года, no date	гл.	глава, chapter
б.м.	без места, no place	гр.	гражданин, citizen; гражданка, citizen (female)
ВКП (б)	Всесоюзная Коммунистическая Партия (большевиков) All-Union Communist Party (Bolshevik)	до н. э.	до нашей эры, B.C.
		ж. д.	железная дорога, railroad
		и т. д.	и так далее etc.

Abbreviations—Continued

км.	километр, kilometer	СССР	Союз Советских Социали-
КПСС	Коммунистическая		стических Республик,
	партия Советского,		Union of Soviet Socialist
	Союза, Communist Party		Republics
	of the Soviet Union	с. ст.	старый стиль, old style
м.	метр, meter	США	Соединенные Штаты
мм.	миллиметр, millimeter		Америки, United States
н. ст.	новый стиль, new style		of America
н. э.	нашей эры, A.D.	ст.	статья, article; столбец,
обл.	область, oblast		column
отд.	отделение, section	стр.	страница, page
по Р. X.	по Рождестве Христове,	т.	том, volume; товарищ,
	anno Domini		comrade
см.	сантиметр, centimeter;	т.е.	то есть, that is
	смотри, see, cf.	ЦК	Центральный Комитет,
			Central Committee
		ч.	часть, part

Cardinal numbers

один, одна, одно m., f., n.	one	семнадцать	seventeen
два, две m. & n., f.	two	восемнадцать	eighteen
три	three	девятнадцать	nineteen
четыре	four	двадцать	twenty
пять	five	двадцать один, etc.	twenty-one, etc.
шесть	six	тридцать	thirty
семь	seven	сорок	forty
восемь	eight	пятьдесят, etc.	fifty, etc.
девять	nine	девяносто	ninety
десять	ten	сто	hundred
одиннадцать	eleven	сто один, etc.	one hundred and one, etc.
двенадцать	twelve	двести	two hundred
тринадцать	thirteen	триста, etc.	three hundred, etc.
четырнадцать	fourteen		
пятнадцать	fifteen	пятьсот, etc.	five hundred, etc.
шестнадцать	sixteen	тысяча	thousand

Ordinal numbers [2]

первый	first	шестнадцатый	sixteenth
второй	second	семнадцатый	seventeenth
третий	third	восемнадцатый	eighteenth
четвёртый	fourth	девятнадцатый	nineteenth
пятый	fifth	двадцатый	twentieth
шестой	sixth	двадцать первый	twenty-first
седьмой	seventh	сотый	hundredth
восьмой	eighth	сто первый, etc.	one hundred and first, etc.
девятый	ninth		
десятый	tenth	двухсотый	two hundredth
одиннадцатый	eleventh	трехсотый	three hundredth
двенадцатый	twelfth	четырехсотый	four hundredth
тринадцатый	thirteenth	пятьсотый, etc.	five hundredth, etc.
четырнадцатый	fourteenth		
пятнадцатый	fifteenth	тысячный	thousandth

Months

январь (Янв.)	January	июль	July
февраль (Февр.)	February	август (Авг.)	August
март	March	сентябрь (Сент.)	September
апрель (Апр.)	April	октябрь (Окт.)	October
май	May	ноябрь	November
июнь	June	декабрь (Дек.)	December

[2] The ordinal numbers here given are of the masculine gender. To convert them to feminine or neuter, it is only necessary to effect the proper gender changes: For the feminine, change ый to ая, ий to ья, ой to ая. For the neuter, change ый to ое, ий to ье, and ой to ое.

Days

воскресенье	Sunday	четверг	Thursday
понедельник	Monday	пятница	Friday
вторник	Tuesday	суббота	Saturday
среда	Wednesday		

Seasons

весна	spring	осень	autumn
лето	summer	зима	winter

Time

час	hour	месяц	month
день	day	год	year
неделя	week		

NOTE ON OLD SPELLING

On October 10, 1918, the Council of People's Commissars decreed the introduction of a spelling reform that had been proposed many years before but never adopted. The spelling used from that time in all official publications, except those of the Academy of Sciences (Akademiya Nauk), was this new spelling. The academy adopted the new spelling in 1924. All Russian publications, except for a few printed outside the Soviet Union, have used the new spelling since the institution of the reform.

The old spelling, found in books printed before the dates mentioned, differed in the following ways:

1. There were used the additional *i* (in the alphabet, after и and before к, as й was not considered a separate letter), ѣ (after ь), ѳ (after я), and ѵ (after е).

2. *I* was used only before another vowel letter and in the word міръ, world. It is now replaced by и (міръ became мир).

3. ѣ occurred in certain words and in some grammatical endings. It represented the same sound as *e* and is now replaced by *e* everywhere. In a few cases ѣ was pronounced like *ë*, and where *e* is now printed with dieresis (¨), the replacement of ѣ is, of course, *ë*.

4. Ѳ was used in words of Greek origin, for Greek θ (th). It was pronounced *f*, and is now replaced by *f*.

5. Ѵ was used in a few ecclesiastical words, for Greek υ (*u*, *y*). It was pronounced like и, and is replaced by that letter.

6. Ъ was used at the end of all words after a consonant not followed by ь. In this position ъ has simply been omitted since the reform. For some years after 1918, some publishers omitted ъ altogether, using an apostrophe for it after prefixes, but the use of the apostrophe is now discouraged, and ъ is used.

7. The prefixes из, воз, вз, раз, низ, без, чрез, через were written with final з everywhere, whereas now they are written ис, вос, etc., before к, п, с, т, х, ц, ч, ш, ѳ, щ.

8. Some adjective endings in the genitive singular were written -аго, -яго; these were replaced by -ого, -его.

9. The plural nominative of adjectives agreeing with feminine and neuter nouns was written -ыя, -ія; these endings were replaced by -ые, -ие, which had formerly been used only for adjectives agreeing with masculine nouns.

10. The pronoun "they" in referring to the feminine gender was written онѣ; this was replaced by они, previously used only for masculine reference.

11. Similarly, однѣ, однѣх, однѣми were replaced by одни, одних, одними.

12. The genitive pronoun "her" was written ея; this was replaced by её, formerly used only as accusative.

13. Ё was printed only in schoolbooks.

REFERENCES.—R. I. Avanesov and V. N. Simonov, Ocherk Grammatiki Russkogo Literaturnogo Yazyka (1945); S. C. Boyanus, A Manual of Russian Pronunciation (1935); V. K. Müller, Russian-English and English-Russian Dictionary (1944); Pravila russkoi orfografii i punktuatsii (1957); A. B. Shapiro, Russkoe pravopisanie (1961).

SPANISH

No hay que decir que la consideración que reclama el aspecto fonológico del lenguaje no viene a disminuir el interés del estudio fonético, indispensable, por su parte, para seguir la transformación de los vocablos, para conocer las tendencias que dominan en la evolución del idioma, para la comparación de los dialectos y para la determinación de las zonas y áreas de la geografía lingüistica.— Tomás Navarro, Estudios de fonología española, p. 10.

Alphabet and pronunciation

A	a	*a* in watt; *ai* as in aisle
B	b	*b*, at beginning of words and after *m*; more like *v* everywhere else
C	c	*c* in car, before *a, o, u*, and consonants; before *e, i* pronounced as *s* in so, in Spanish America; as *th* in thin, in Spain
Ch	ch	*ch* in chart
D	d	*d*
E	e	*e* in met; *ei* as in vein
F	f	*f*
G	g	*g* in go, before *a, o, u*, and consonants; like strong *h* before *e* and *i; gu* like *gw* before *a, o; gü* like gw before *e, i*
H	h	not pronounced
I	i	*i* in machine; *y* in yet, before and after vowels
J	j	*h*, but with more friction (same as *g* before *e, i*)
K	k	*k;* only in foreign words
L	l	*l* in lily
LL	ll	*y* in yet, in most of Spanish America; *lli* in million, in Spain, Colombia, and Ecuador
M	m	*m*
N	n	*n; nv* like *mb* in lumber
Ñ	ñ	*ny* in canyon
O	o	*o* in obey; *oi* as in oil
P	p	*p*
Q	q	always followed by silent *u, qu* being pronounced *k*
R	r	*r*, like tongue-tap *r* in British pronunciation of very
Rr	rr	*r* trilled, as in Scotch English or Italian
S	s	*s* in so, before most consonants and between vowels; *z* in zeal, before voiced consonants (*b, d, g, l, m, n, r, y*)
T	t	*t*
U	u	*u* in rule (=*oo* as in coo); *w* in wet, before vowels; silent in *gue, gui, qu*
V	v	*b* at beginning of words; more like *v* everywhere else
W	w	*w, v;* only in foreign words

[Concluded on following page]

442

X   x   *x* in ax (=*ks*), between vowels; *s* before consonants
Y   y   *y* in yet, initially and between vowels; *ay* as *ai* in aisle;
          ey as in they; *oy* as in boy
Z   z   *s* in so, in Spanish America; *th* in thin, in Spain

Special characters

Spanish uses the Latin alphabet with the addition of the characters Ñ ñ. Note that *ch*, *ll*, and *rr* are regarded as separate units; i.e., words beginning with *ch* will be entered in the dictionary after words beginning with *cz*, not between the groups of words beginning with *ce* and *ci*. The acute accent appears very frequently over one of the vowel letters in a word. The dieresis appears occasionally over *u* following *g*; its occurrence elsewhere is so rare as to be negligible.

Vowels and consonants

The vowels are *a*, *e*, *i*, *o*, *u*, and sometimes *y*. The other letters are consonants. The letter *y* is a consonant at the beginning of a word (before a vowel) and between two vowels.

Combinations of vowel letters (diphthongs and triphthongs)

The vowel *i* or *u* preceding *a*, *e*, *i*, *o*, *u*, or following *a*, *e*, *o*, is pronounced as a single syllable with the preceding or following vowel; if the diphthong occurs in a syllable which needs an accent mark (see Stress and diacritics), the acute accent is placed over the vowel other than *i* or *u*. The diphthongs are:

ai	ei	oi			ái	éi	ói	
au	eu	ou			áu	éu	óu	
ia	ie	io	iu		iá	ié	ió	iú
ua	ue	uo	ui		uá	ué	uó	uí

At the end of a word and in one-syllable words, *ay*, *ey*, *oy* replace the diphthongs ending in *i*.

Sequences of vowel letters which are not diphthongs, and which may be divided, are those in which *í* or *ú* precedes or follows another vowel: *aí*, *eí*, *oí*, *aú*, *eú*, *oú*, *ía*, *íe*, *ío*, *íu*, *úa*, *úe*, *úo*, *úi*.

Spanish also has triphthongs. A triphthong is a combination of three vowels, the middle one of which is stressed, the others unstressed; the combination is pronounced as a single syllable. The triphthongs are:

iai	iei	ioi	iui		uai	uei	uoi	
iau	ieu	iou			uau	ueu	uou	uiu

If the *i* or *u* at the beginning or the end of a sequence of three vowel letters has an acute accent, it is not part of a triphthong, and division may be made accordingly; e. g., *í-ai*, *ua-ú*, *ú-oi*.

Combinations of consonant letters (digraphs)

The digraphs are *ch*, *ll*, and *rr*.

Consonantal units

In Spanish certain consonants followed by *l* or *r* are pronounced in the same syllable with the following vowel. These consonant groups are: *bl*, *br*; *cl*, *cr*; *dr*; *fl*, *fr*; *gl*, *gr*; *pl*, *pr*; *tr*.

Rules for syllabification

1. Diphthongs, triphthongs, digraphs, and consonantal units may not be divided.

2. Division is made on a vowel or on a diphthong before a single consonant, a digraph, or a consonantal unit: *ca-sa*, *bue-no*, *re-yes*, *mu-cho*, *po-llo*, *co-rrer*, *ha-blar*, *li-bro*.

3. In a group of two or more consonants, division is made before the last consonant, digraph, or consonantal unit: *ac-ta*, *ac-ción*, *ist-mo*, *mar-cha*, *cen-tro*.

4. Division may be made between vowels not constituting a diphthong or triphthong or between a diphthong and another vowel: *ca-er*, *le-er*, *ba-úl*, *flu-ido*, *temi-ais*.

5. Certain adverbial prefixes are kept intact. These are: *anti, bis, circum, cis, des, inter, mal, pan, sub, super, trans,* and *tras: anti-artístico, bis-anuo* (never *bi-sanuo*), *circum-ambiente* (never *circu-mambiente*), *des-unión* (never *de-sunión*). Other prefixes are also divisible from the stem, provided the division conforms to rules 2 to 4: *contra-parte* (rule 2), *ab-negación* (rule 3), *ex-traer* (rule 3), *co-existir* (rule 4). Otherwise division on prefixes should be avoided, except in cases of exigency, such as very narrow measure: *ab-usar* (better *abu-sar*), *re-unir* (better *reu-nir*), *ex-ánime* (better *exá-nime*), *in-afectado* (better *ina-fectado*), *co-incidencia* (better *coin-cidencia*). In no case may division on a prefix be made, however, before an *s* followed by another consonant: *cons-titución* (never *cons-titución*), *pers-pectivo* (never *per-spectivo*), *subs-tancia* (never *sub-stancia*).[1]

6. Compound words are divided according to their component parts (and each part according to rules 1 to 5): *estado-unidense* (rather than *estadou-nidense*), *bien-estar* (There are not many compound words in Spanish the correct division of which does not coincide with rules 1 to 5.)

7. Foreign words and components of foreign words (not naturalized) follow the conventions of the language of origin: *Wásh-ington, Groen-landia* (never *Gro-enlandia*), *Gegen-stand, Frei-schütz, Ingol-stadt, Ste-phenson.* Scientific and technical words derived from Latin and Greek are treated as naturalized Spanish words and are divided according to rules 1 to 6: *diag-nóstico, hemis-ferio, anas-tomosis.*

Illustrative word divisions

[The numbers in parentheses refer to the syllabification rules]

Amé-ri-ca	(2, 2)	in-clu-yen-do	(3, 2, 3)
anas-to-mo-sis	(3, 2, 2)	in-ter-a-me-ri-ca-no	(3, 5, 2, 2, 2, 2)
an-te-o-jos	(3, 6, 2)	in-te-re-ses	(3, 2, 2)
an-ti-es-pas-mó-di-co	(3, 5, 3, 3, 2, 2)	in-te-rro-ga-ción	(3, 2, 2, 2)
an-ti-psó-ri-co	(3, 5, 2, 2)	íst-mi-co	(3, 2)
apro-xi-ma-ción	(2, 2, 2)	lla-me-an-te	(2, 4, 3)
au-to-ex-ci-tan-te	(2, 4, 3, 2, 3)	lu-ga-ri-llo	(2, 2, 2)
au-xi-liar	(2, 2)	ma-la-men-te	(2, 2, 3)
ba-le-á-ri-co	(2, 4, 2, 2)	mal-in-ten-cio-na-do	(5, 3, 3, 2, 2)
bis-a-nuo	(5, 2)	ma-yo-ría	(2, 2)
bri-llan-te	(2, 3)	me-tró-po-li	(2, 2, 2)
cas-te-lla-no	(3, 2, 2)	me-xi-ca-no	(2, 2, 2)
chan-chu-lle-ro	(3, 2, 2)	mid-ship-man	(7, 3)
cir-cum-am-bien-te	(3, 5, 3, 3)	mi-llo-na-rio	(2, 2, 2)
cir-cuns-tan-cia	(3, 3, 3)	mi-nis-tro	(2, 3)
cis-al-pi-no	(5, 3, 2)	mo-nos-per-mas	(2, 3, 3)
co-ne-xión	(2, 2)	ne-o-im-pre-sio-nis-mo	(4, 7, 3, 2, 2, 3)
con-se-cuen-cia	(3, 2, 3)	ne-o-yor-qui-no	(4, 2, 3, 2)
cons-ti-tu-cio-nal	(3, 2, 2, 2)	nos-o-tros	(6, 2)
cons-truc-ción	(3, 3)	obs-truir-se	(3, 3)
co-rres-pon-den-cia	(2, 3, 3, 3)	pa-í-ses	(4, 2)
cre-í-an	(4, 4)	pan-a-me-ri-ca-nis-mo	(5, 2, 2, 2, 2, 3)
cre-yen-do	(2, 3)	pa-ra-gua-yo	(2, 2, 2)
cual-quie-ra	(6, 2)	pe-re-gri-no	(2, 2, 2)
des-a-rro-llar-se	(5, 2, 2, 3)	pe-rió-di-co	(2, 2, 2)
des-em-ba-rrar	(5, 3, 2)	pe-rí-o-do	(2, 4, 2)
de-se-o-so	(2, 4, 2)	pe-ris-có-pi-co	(2, 3, 2, 2)
des-u-nir	(5, 2)	post-is-lá-mi-co	(7, 3, 2, 2)
diag-nós-ti-co	(3, 3, 2)	pro-rro-gar	(2, 2)
elip-soi-dal	(3, 2)	pú-bli-co	(2, 2)
en-te-rrar	(3, 2)	re-pú-bli-ca	(2, 2, 2)
es-o-tro	(6, 2)	san-güe-sa	(3, 2)
es-pa-ño-les	(3, 2, 2)	si-guien-tes	(2, 3)
es-ta-do-uni-den-se	(3, 2, 6, 2, 3)	sub-al-ter-nar	(5, 3, 3)
exac-ta-men-te	(3, 2, 3)	su-per-e-mi-nen-te	(2, 5, 2, 2, 3)
exa-mi-nar	(2, 2)	trans-al-pi-no	(5, 3, 2)
exe-quá-tur	(2, 2)	tras-an-te-a-yer	(5, 3, 3, 6, 2)
ex-hi-bi-ción	(3, 2, 2)	vos-o-tros	(6, 2)
fre-cuen-te-men-te	(2, 3, 2, 3)	Wal-len-stein	(7, 7)
ge-o-grá-fi-co	(4, 2, 2, 2)	Wásh-ing-ton	(7, 3)
he-mis-fé-ri-co	(2, 3, 2, 2)	Welt-an-schau-ung	(7, 7, 4)
ina-pli-ca-ble	(2, 2, 2)		

[1] This rule of the *s* is rigidly adhered to, because no Spanish word and hence no syllable can begin with a group of consonants the first of which is *s*.

Stress and diacritics

The tilde, the dieresis, and the acute accent are the diacritical marks used in Spanish. The tilde is used only over the *n*, and *ñ* is a special character representing a separate phoneme, the palatal *n*. The dieresis mark (¨) called *diéresis* or *crema* in Spanish, is to be found in a limited number of words, such as *vergüenza*, and *argüir*, to indicate that the vowel *u* must be pronounced.

The acute accent is used over a vowel to indicate that it is stressed; it is also used to distinguish homonyms. If there is no accent mark, a word ending in a consonant (including *y*, except *n* and *s*) is stressed on the last syllable; a word ending in a vowel, *n*, or *s* is stressed on the next-to-last syllable. Specifically, the acute accent is used as follows:

1. To indicate that the vowel is stressed.
2. To indicate vowels not forming a diphthong (see Diphthongs).
3. To distinguish words of the same spelling but of different meanings: *aún*, still, yet, *aun*, even; *dé*, give, *de*, of; *él*, he, him, *el*, the (but *el que, el cual*, he who, him who); *há*, ago, *ha*, has; *hé*, behold, *he*, I have; *mí*, me, *mi*, my; *más*, more, *mas*, but; *sé*, I know, be thou, *se*, oneself; *sí*, yes, oneself, *si*, if; *sólo*, only, *solo*, alone, single; *té*, tea, *te*, thee; *tú*, thou, *tu*, thy; *vé*, go, *ve*, sees.
4. To distinguish interrogative or exclamatory use from relative or declarative: *adónde*, where? *adonde*, where; *cómo*, how? *como*, as; *cuán*, how! *cuan*, how; *cuándo*, when? *cuando*, when; *cuánto*, how much? *cuanto*, as much; *cúyo*, whose? *cuyo*, whose; *dónde*, where? *donde*, where; *qué*, what? *que*, which; *quién*, who(m)? *quien*, who(m).
5. To distinguish pronouns from adjectives: *éste*, this one, *este*, this; *ése*, that one, *ese*, that; *aquél*, that one yonder, *aquel*, that.
6. Arbitrarily on monosyllabic aorists: *di*, I gave; *fui*, I was; *fué*, he was; *rió*, he laughed; *vi*, I saw; *vió*, he saw.
7. To avoid confusing the word *o* (or) with the zero: *2 ó 3*, but *dos o tres*, two or three.

Capitalization

The English style of capitalization is followed with few exceptions.

Adjectives derived from proper nouns are lowercased, as in *música colombiana* (Colombian music) and *teatro español* (Spanish theater).

Days of the week and months begin with a lowercase letter.

In titles of books, the general practice is to capitalize only the initial word and the proper nouns, as in *El ingenioso hidalgo don Quijote de la Mancha* (The ingenuous gentleman Don Quixote de la Mancha) and *Con los indios cuna de Panamá* (With the Cuna Indians of Panama). In the case of short titles there is a tendency to capitalize adjectives and common nouns, as in *Ortografía Castellana* (Castilian orthography) and *Enciclopedia de la Cocina* (Encyclopedia of cooking).

Punctuation and hyphenation

Punctuation is practically the same as in English. One conspicuous exception is the use of inverted interrogation and exclamation marks, which are placed at the exact beginning of the question or exclamation: *¿Habla usted español?* (Do you speak Spanish?) *Si quiere visitar el Brasil, ¿por qué no estudia portugués?* (If you want to visit Brazil, why don't you study Portuguese?) *¡Viva el astronauta!* (Long live the astronaut!) *No recibí invitación, ¡y no comprendo por qué!* (I did not receive an invitation, and I cannot understand why!)

Quotation marks are used to reproduce a statement, text, etc., but not a dialog as developed in prose fiction. In the latter case, preference is given in Spanish to em dashes at the beginning of each interlocutor's paragraph. Example:

—*Yo soy Juan de Aguirre, el marino, el hermano de su madre de usted, el que desapareció.*
—*¡Usted es Juan de Aguirre!*
—*Sí.*
—*¿Mi tío?*
—*El mismo.*
—*¡Y por qué no habérmelo dicho antes!*

(Pío Baroja, *Las inquietudes de Shanti Andía*)

The hyphen, as a rule, is used only in syllabification. The apostrophe is not employed in modern Spanish.

Abbreviations

a. de J. C.	antes de Jesucristo	no.	número
a.m.	ante meridiano	N.S.	Nuestro Señor, Nuestra
C.A.	Centro América		Señora
Cía.	Compañía	núm.	número
cm.	centímetro	O.	Oeste
d. de J. C.	después de Jesucristo	pág., págs.	página, páginas
D.	Don	Pbro.	Presbítero
D.F.	Distrito Federal	P.D.	Post Data
Dr., Dra.	Doctor, Doctora	P.ej.	Por ejemplo
E.	Este	p.m.	pasado meridiano
EE.UU.	Estados Unidos	Prov.	Provincia
E.U.A.	Estados Unidos de	Q.E.P.D.	Que en paz descanse
	América	R.P.	Reverendo Padre
Excmo.,	Excelentísimo,	S.	Sur
Excma.	Excelentísima	S.A.	Sociedad Anónima
Gral.	General	S.A.R.	Su Alteza Real
Hnos.	Hermanos	S.E.	Su Excelencia
Ilmo.,	Ilustrísimo, Ilustrísima	S.E. u O.	Salvo error u omisión
Ilma.		S.M.	Su Majestad
kg.	kilógramo	Sr., Sres.	Señor, Señores
km.	kilómetro	Sra., Sras.	Señora, Señoras
Lic.	Licenciado	S.R.L.	Sociedad de
m.	metro, metros		Responsabilidad
m/n	moneda nacional		Limitada
Mons.	Monseñor	Srta.	Señorita
M.S.	Manuscrito	S.S.	Su Santidad
M.S.S.	Manuscritos	S.S.S.	Su seguro servidor, Su
N.	Norte		segura servidora
N.B.	Nota bene	Sta., Sto.	Santa, Santo
N. de la	Nota de la Redacción	T.	Tomo
R.		Ud., Uds.	Usted, Ustedes
N. del A.	Nota del Autor	V.º B.º	Visto bueno
N. del T.	Nota del Traductor		

Cardinal numbers

uno, una	one	veinte y dos, veinti-	twenty-two, etc.
dos	two	dós, etc.	
tres	three	treinta	thirty
cuatro	four	cuarenta	forty
cinco	five	cincuenta	fifty
seis	six	sesenta	sixty
siete	seven	setenta	seventy
ocho	eight	ochenta	eighty
nueve	nine	noventa	ninety
diez	ten	ciento, cien	hundred
once	eleven	ciento uno, etc.	one hundred and
doce	twelve		one, etc.
trece	thirteen	doscientos, -as, etc.	two hundred,
catorce	fourteen		etc.
quince	fifteen	quinientos, -as	five hundred
diez y seis, dieciséis	sixteen	seiscientos, -as	six hundred
diez y siete, diecisiete, etc.	seventeen, etc.	setecientos, -as	seven hundred
		ochocientos, -as	eight hundred
veinte	twenty	novecientos, -as	nine hundred
veinte y uno (vein-tiuno)	twenty-one	mil	thousand

Round millions preceding units of quantity are followed by the preposition *de: tres millones de pesos, 3,000,000 de pesos.*

Ordinal numbers

prim(er)o, -a (1º)	first	sexto	sixth
segundo, -a (2º)	second	sé(p)timo	seventh
tercero, tercer	third	octavo	eighth
cuarto	fourth	noveno, nono	ninth
quinto	fifth	décimo	tentb

Ordinal numbers—Continued

undécimo	eleventh	nonagésimo	ninetieth
duodécimo	twelfth	centésimo	hundredth
décimotercio	thirteenth	centésimo primo, etc.	one hundred and first, etc.
décimocuarto, etc.	fourteenth, etc.		
vigésimo	twentieth	ducentésimo	two hundredth
vigésimo primero, etc.	twenty-first, etc.	tricentésimo	three hundredth
		cuadringentésimo	four hundredth
trigésimo	thirtieth	quingentésimo	five hundredth
cuadragésimo	fortieth	sexcentésimo	six hundredth
quincuagésimo	fiftieth	septingentésimo	seven hundredth
sexagésimo	sixtieth	octingentésimo	eight hundredth
septuagésimo	seventieth	noningentésimo	nine hundredth
octogésimo	eightieth	milésimo	thousandth

Months

enero	January	julio	July
febrero	February	agosto	August
marzo	March	se(p)tiembre	September
abril	April	octubre	October
mayo	May	noviembre	November
junio	June	diciembre	December

Days

domingo	Sunday	jueves	Thursday
lunes	Monday	viernes	Friday
martes	Tuesday	sábado	Saturday
miércoles	Wednesday		

Seasons

primavera	spring	otoño	autumn
verano	summer	invierno	winter

Time

hora	hour	mes	month
día	day	año	year
semana	week	siglo	century

REFERENCES.—Real Academia Española, Gramática de la Lengua Castellana (1931); Arturo Cuyás, Appleton's New Spanish-English and English-Spanish Dictionary (1940); Tomás Navarro, Estudios de fonología española (1949).

SWEDISH

Den germanska bosättningen i Skandinavien och Finland talade ett språk, ur vilket nutidens svenska, norska, danska, isländska och färöiska har utvecklat sig. Språket var, såvitt vi vet, väsentligen enhetligt över hela området. Det kallas urnordiska. Carl-Eric Thors, Svenskan förr och nu [1970] p. 18.

Alphabet and pronunciation

A	a	a in father	M	m	m
B	b	b	N	n	n
C	c	s in sent, before e, i, y; elsewhere k	O	o	o in often; oo in goose
			P	p	p
D	d	d; silent before j	Q	q	q
E	e	e in felt, prey	R	r	r trilled
F	f	f [1]	S	s	s; never z
G	g	y in yet, before stressed e, i, y, ä, ö, and after l and r in the same syllable; otherwise g in go, but silent before j	T	t	t [2]
			U	u	u in fuse; also roughly equivalent to unstressed ue in value
H	h	h; silent before j	V	v	v
I	i	i in sit; ee in tree	W	w	v
J	j	y in yet; in some foreign words pronounced sh	X	x	x
			Y	y	like German ü or French u
K	k	k; approximately ch in chair, before stressed i, e, y, ä, ö; a few exceptions in loan-words	Z	z	s; never z
			Å	å [3]	o in go; aw in saw ä
			Ä	ä	like e in felt; a in glaze
			Ö	ö	like German ö or French eu
L	l	l; silent before j			

[1] In the orthography employed prior to 1906, the v sound was represented in absolutely final position by f; medially by fv. Since 1906, v has represented f and fv, except in some proper names.

[2] In words of Latin origin, the combination ti in the suffix tion is pronounced as in English if preceded by any consonant except r (aktion, pronounced akshon), otherwise like ch in chair (nation, pronounced nachon; portion, pronounced porchon); in the combinations tia and tie like ts (profetia, pronounced profetsia; aktie, pronounced aktsie).

[3] In typesetting, if the character ä is not available, it is replaced by aa.

Special characters

Swedish uses the Latin alphabet with the addition of three special characters—the last three in the alphabet.

Vowels and consonants

The vowels are a, e, i, o, u, y, ä, å, and ö; the so-called back vowels being a, o, u, and å; the front vowels e, i, y, ä, and ö. The other letters of the alphabet are all consonants.

Diphthongs

The diphthongs in Swedish are au, pronounced like ou in house; eu, pronounced somewhat like e(ph)ew in nephew; oj as in boy; aj, pronounced like igh in high.

Digraphs

The digraphs and their sounds are:

ch as *sh*; rarely as *k* (och)
kj as *ch* in chair
ph as *f* (in foreign words)
sch as *sh* in shall
sj as *sh* in shall
sk as *sh* in shall (it is not a digraph
   if pronounced like *sk* in basket) [1]

skj as *sh* in shall
stj as *sh* in shall
th as *t* (in foreign words)
qu as *kv*

Nasals

The combination *ng* is pronounced like *ng* in sing-er (not fin-ger) and is termed a nasal: *ingen* (pronounced *ing-en*), *hängar* (pronounced *häng-ar*), *engelsk* (pronounced *eng-elsk*), *finger* (pronounced *fing-er*). The velar nasal *ng* must be distinguished, however, from the incidental collocation of the two letters resulting from compounding or affixing, in which case the *ng* is not a nasal: *angelägen* (from *an* plus *gelägen*), *ingripa* (from *in* plus *gripa*); nor is *ng* a velar nasal in words of foreign origin, such as *singular*, *evangelium*.

The letter *g* is also a velar nasal when it follows a short vowel and precedes the letter *n*: *lugn* (pronounced *lung'n*), *lugna* (pronounced *lung'na*), *vagnar* (pronounced *vang'nar*), *ugnar* (pronounced *ung'nar*).

Consonantal units

The combinations *kv* (the substitute for the Romance language *qu*), *sk*, *sp*, *st*, and *str* are treated for purposes of syllabification as units.

Rules for syllabification

1. Diphthongs, digraphs, and consonantal units may not be divided.
2. Division is made on a vowel or on a diphthong before a single consonant, a digraph, or a consonantal unit: *ta-la*, *re-gel*, *hu-set*, *ma-skin*, *pa-scha*, *be-kväm*, *reu-matisk*.
3. In a group of two or more consonants, division is made before the last consonant, digraph, or consonantal unit: *al-la*, *myc-ket*, *häs-sja*, *al-stra*, *hög-ste*, *fladd-ra*, *kan-ske*, *mar-schera*, *forsk-ning*.
4. Division may be made between vowels not constituting a diphthong or between a diphthong and another vowel: *se-ende*, *gå-ende*.
5. Certain adverbial prefixes are kept intact. These are: *an*, *av*, *bak*, *be*, *bi*, *bort*, *efter*, *en*, *ent*, *er*, *fort*, *fram*, *från*, *för*, *före*, *gen*, *genom*, *hop*, *in*, *med*, *miss*, *mot*, *ned*, *o*, *om*, *på*, *samman*, *sönder*, *till*, *under*, *upp*, *ur*, *ut*, *ute*, *veder*, *vid*, *åt*, *åter*, and *över*: *an-draga*, *av-tryck*, *bak-slag*, *be-kläda*, etc.
6. Certain suffixes are kept intact. These are: *aktig*, *artad*, *het*, *ska*, *skap(s)*, and *ske*: *del-aktig*, *ull-artad*, *envis-het*, *amerikan-ska*, *grann-skap*, *hand-ske*.
7. Compound words are divided according to their component parts (and each part according to rules 1 to 6): *där-emot*, *dess-utom*, *bank-aktie*, *blom-stjälk*, *bok-tryck*. The compounding *s*, if used, is kept with the preceding component: *dags-ljus*, *gevärs-exercis*, *guds-man*.
8. Foreign words and components of foreign words (not naturalized) follow the conventions of the language of origin: *por-trätt*, *atmo-sfär*, *manu-skript*. Under this rule are also included technical and scientific words, which editors prefer to treat etymologically: *tele-skop*, *dia-fragma*, *des-infektion*.
9. The letter *x* and the nasal *ng* are properly kept with the preceding syllable: *byx-or*, *lax-en*, *gung-an*, *konung-en*.[2]
10. When division is made on a syllable from which a letter was elided, the letter is restored to render the syllable integral: *till-lika* (from *tillika*). It is important to bear in mind that words divided under this rule, if subsequently reset and run over, must have their original spelling restored.

---

[1] The letters *sk* are a digraph and pronounced soft, like *sh*, when they occur before a soft vowel in a stressed syllable: *skära* (pronounced *sha'ra*), *skynda* (pronounced *shin'da*), *maskin* (pronounced *mashin'*); otherwise they are pronounced hard ,like the English *sk* (*skada*, *skriva*, *fisk*, *rusk*, *handske*, *fisket*, *ruskig*).
There are a few exceptions. Contrary to the rule, *sk* is soft in *människa* (pronounced *männi-sha*), *marskalk* (pronounced *marshalk*), *kanske* (pronounced *kanshe*). On the other hand, *sk* is hard, contrary to the rule, in *skiss*, *konfiskera*, *riskera*, *skelett*, *skeptisk*, and in a few other words of foreign origin.

[2] The practice varies, however, and many editors allow *x* to be brought over to the next syllable and *ng* to be divided, according to the convenience of the compositor; hence: *by-xor*, *la-xen*, *gun-gan*, *konun-gen* (cf. Axel Johan Uppvall and Gösta Robert Stene, Swedish Grammar and Reader, 1938, p. 3, Syllabification).

Illustrative word divisions

[The numbers in parentheses refer to the syllabification rules]

ame-ri-kan-ska	(2, 2, 6)	kor-re-spon-dent	(3, 8, 3)
an-slags-frå-ga	(5, 7, 2)	ma-je-stä-ter	(2, 2, 2)
at-mo-sfär	(3, 8)	ma-nu-skript	(2, 8)
av-prov-ning	(5, 3)	med-ar-be-ter-ska	(5, 3, 2, 6)
bak-grun-der	(5, 3)	me-del-ål-der	(2, 7, 3)
be-grep-pet	(5, 3)	miss-hand-ling	(5, 3)
bel-le-tri-stisk	(3, 8, 2)	mot-stå-en-de	(5, 4, 3)
bi-bli-o-tek	(8, 4, 2)	ned-tryckt-het	(5, 6)
bi-dra-gan-de	(5, 2, 3)	o-be-kväm-lig [3]	(5, 2, 3)
blom-nings-tid	(3, 7)	o-möj-lig [3]	(5, 3)
bort-slu-ta	(5, 2)	om-stjälp-ning	(5, 3)
bo-stä-der-na	(2, 2, 3)	på-se-en-de	(5, 4, 3)
des-in-fek-tion	(8, 3, 3)	sam-man-svärj-ning	(3, 5, 3)
ef-ter-skri-va	(3, 5, 2)	sta-ter-na	(2, 3)
en-skild-het	(7, 6)	sön-der-skju-ten	(3, 5, 2)
ent-le-di-ga	(5, 2, 2)	till-freds-stäl-lel-se	(5, 7, 3, 3)
en-trä-gen-het	(5, 2, 6)	un-der-hålls-kost-nad	(3, 5, 7, 3)
er-bju-dan-de	(5, 2, 3)	upp-hjäl-pan-de	(5, 3, 3)
ex-er-cis	(8, 3)	upp-rätt-hål-la-re	(5, 7, 3, 2)
fort-skri-da	(5, 2)	ur-sprung-lig-het	(5, 3, 6)
fram-al-stra	(5, 3)	ut-ar-ren-de-ra	(5, 3, 3, 2)
främ-jan-de	(3, 3)	ute-slut-ning	(5, 3)
från-trä-da	(5, 2)	ve-ten-skaps-man	(2, 6, 7)
för-en-ta	(5, 3)	vid-stå-en-de	(5, 4, 3)
fö-re-språ-ker-ska	(2, 5, 2, 6)	åter-av-trä-da	(5, 5, 2)
gen-klan-gen	(5, 3)	åt-skil-jan-de	(5, 3, 3)
ge-nom-ar-be-ta	(2, 5, 3, 2)	än-del-se	(3, 3)
ge-o-gra-fi-ska	(4, 8, 2, 6)	änd-sta-tio-nen	(7, 2, 2)
hi-sto-ria	(2, 2)	önsk-nin-gar	(3, 3)
hop-spa-ra	(5, 2)	öst-eu-ro-pe-isk	(7, 2, 2, 4)
in-bjud-ning	(5, 3)	över-ar-bet-ning	(5, 3, 3)
kom-pan-jo-ner	(3, 3, 2)	över-tax-e-ra	(5, 9, 2)

Diacritics and stress

With the exception of *å*, *ä*, and *ö*, diacritics are used only in foreign loan-words (*résumé*) and in certain proper names (*Tegnér*).

Syllabic stress falls on the root syllable in all simple native words and on the main, usually the first, component of compound words.

Capitalization

Capitalization is similar to that in English, except that proper adjectives, days of the week, months, and holidays are lowercased. In compound names, only the first word is usually capitalized (*Förenta staterna*, United States; *Karl den store*, Charles the Great), and the second-person pronouns *Ni*, *Eder*, *Er* are capitalized in correspondence.

Punctuation

The rules of punctuation are essentially the same as in English, although Swedish punctuation is perhaps somewhat closer, the comma, especially, being used more freely. The apostrophe is not used to indicate possession, except in foreign names and those terminating in the letter *s:* *Shakespeare's dramer* (Shakespeare's dramas), *Valerius' visor* (the ballads of Valerius).

Abbreviations

Where the last letter of the abbreviation is the last letter of the complete word, the period is not used.

a.-b.	aktiebolag, joint-stock company	b., bd	band, volume, volumes
adr.	adress, address, c/o	bl. a.	bland annat, bland andra, among other things, or among others
ang.	angående, concerning		
anm.	anmärkning, remark, observation	d.	död, dead
		d:o	dito, ditto

---

[3] The division on the prefix *o-* (meaning un- or non-) should be avoided except in very narrow measure to avoid bad spacing.

Abbreviations—Continued

dr, d:r	doktor, doctor
d.v.s.	det vill säga, that is, that is to say
d.y.	den yngre, junior
d:ä.	den äldre, senior; det är, that is
ell.	eller, or
etc.	et cetera, and so forth
ex.	exempel, example (illustration), e.g.
f.	född, born
f.d.	för detta, before this, formerly
frk.	fröken, Miss
f.ö.	för övrigt, besides
förf.	författare, author; författarinna, authoress
H.M.	Hans Majestät, His Majesty
hr	herr, Sir, Mr.
i st. f.	i stället för, in place of
jfr	jämför, compare, cf.
kap.	kapitel, chapter
kl.	klockan, o'clock
kr.	krona, crown; kronor, crowns (coin)
kungl.	kunglig, royal
m.a.o.	med andra ord, in other words
m. fl.	med flera, with others, and others
m.m.	med mera, etc., and so forth
n.b.	nota bene, mark (notice) well
nr, n:o	nummer, numro, number
näml.	nämligen, namely, viz, to wit
obs.	observera, observe
o.d.	och dylikt (dylika), and the like
o.s.a.	om svar anhålles, an answer is requested
o.s.v.	och så vidare, and so forth
p.s.	postskriptum, postscript
red.	redaktör, editor
s., sid.	sida, page; sidor, pages
s.d.	samma dag, the same day
s.k.	så kallad, so called
t. ex.	till exempel, for instance
t.o.m.	till och med, even
und.	undantag, exception

Cardinal numbers

en, ett	one	aderton	eighteen
två	two	nitton	nineteen
tre	three	tjugu (tjugo)	twenty
fyra	four	tjuguen (tjuguett)	twenty-one
fem	five	tjugutvå, etc.	twenty-two, etc.
sex	six	tretti(o)	thirty
sju	seven	fyrtio	forty
åtta	eight	femtio	fifty
nio	nine	sextio	sixty
tio	ten	sjuttio	seventy
elva	eleven	åttio	eighty
tolv	twelve	nittio	ninety
tretton	thirteen	hundra	hundred
fjorton	fourteen	hundra ett, etc.	one hundred and one, etc.
femton	fifteen		
sexton	sixteen	två hundra, etc.	two hundred, etc.
sjutton	seventeen	tusen	thousand

Ordinal numbers

(den) första (-e)	first	nittonde	nineteenth
andra (-e)	second	tjugonde	twentieth
tredje	third	tjuguförsta	twenty-first
fjärde	fourth	tjuguandra, etc.	twenty-second, etc.
femte	fifth		
sjätte	sixth	trettionde	thirtieth
sjunde	seventh	fyrtionde	fortieth
åttonde	eighth	femtionde	fiftieth
nionde	ninth	sextionde	sixtieth
tionde	tenth	sjuttionde	seventieth
elfte (elvte)	eleventh	åttionde	eightieth
tolfte (tolvte)	twelfth	nittionde	ninetieth
trettonde	thirteenth	hundrade	hundredth
fjortonde	fourteenth	hundra första	one hundred and first, etc.
femtonde	fifteenth		
sextonde	sixteenth	två hundrade, etc.	two hundredth
sjuttonde	seventeenth	tusende	thousandth
adertonde	eighteenth		

Months

januari (jan.)	January	juli	July
februari (feb.)	February	augusti (aug.)	August
mars	March	september (sept.)	September
april (apr.)	April	oktober (okt.)	October
maj	May	november (nov.)	November
juni	June	december (dec.)	December

Days

söndag	Sunday	torsdag	Thursday
måndag	Monday	fredag	Friday
tisdag	Tuesday	lördag	Saturday
onsdag	Wednesday		

Seasons

vår	spring	höst	autumn
sommar	summer	vinter	winter

Time

timme	hour	månad	month
dag	day	år	year
vecka	week		

REFERENCES.—Axel Johan Uppvall and Gösta Robert Stene, Swedish Grammar and Reader (1938); Edwin J. Vickner, Simplified Swedish Grammar (1946); Walter E. Harlock, Svensk-Engelsk Ordbok (1947); Axel Johan Uppvall, Swedish Phonology (1938); D. Milanova, Svensk-Rysk Ordbok (1962).

TURKISH

Ey, Türk Gençliği, birinci vazifen Türk istiklâlini, Türk Cümhuriyetini ilelebet muhafaza ve müdafaa etmektir. Birgün İstiklâl ve Cümhuriyeti müdafaa mecburiyetine düşersen, vazifeye atılmak için içinde bulunacağın vaziyetin imkân ve şeraitini düşünmeyeceksin. Mevcudiyetinin ve istikbâlinin yegâne temeli budur. Bu temel senin en kıymetli hazinendir.[1]—K. Atatürk.

Alphabet and pronunciation

A	a	*a* in father	L	l	*l* in link
Â	â	see Special characters	M	m	*m* in man
B	b	*b* in bed	N	n	*n* in no
C	c	*j* in judge	O	o	*o* in or
Ç	ç	*ch* in church	Ö	ö	like German *ö* or French *eu*
D	d	*d* in do			
E	e	*e* in red	P	p	*p* in pin
F	f	*f* in far	R	r	*r* in red, somewhat more trilled than in English
G	g	*g* in go			
Ğ	ğ	*y* in yet, between front vowels (*i, e, ü, ö*); silent or voiced spirant between back vowels (*ı, a, u, o*); after a vowel, final or before a consonant, prolongs the vowel	S	s	*s* in sun
			Ş	ş	*sh* in shall
			T	t	*t* in tin
			U	u	*u* in push
			Û	û	see Special characters
			Ü	ü	like German *ü* or French *u*
H	h	*h* in hat	V	v	*v* in van, sometimes more like *w*
I	ı	*i* in till	Y	y	*y* in yet or boy
İ	i	*i* in machine	Z	z	*z* in zeal
J	j	*z* in azure	'		like glottal catch "uh-oh"
K	k	*k* in kit			

Special characters

Turkish uses the Latin alphabet with the addition of the following special characters: Â â, Ç ç, Ğ ğ, İ, ı, Ö ö, S ş, Û û, and Ü ü. The characters Ğ ğ occur also as Ġ ġ. Note the characters İ I, i ı. The circumflex accent (ˆ) is frequently used over vowels *a* and *u*. It sometimes indicates prolongation of the vowel, sometimes palatal (*y*-like) pronunciation of neighboring *k, g,* or *l*. Turkish orthography uses no digraphs. Since ı and i are two different letters, the ligature fi should not be used; *f* and ı or i should be separate letters.

Vowels and consonants

The vowel letters are *a, e, i, ı, o, ö, u, and ü*. The remaining letters of the alphabet are consonants. The apostrophe ('), which indicates hiatus or slight glottal catch, counts as a consonant.

[1] [TRANSLATION:] O, Turkish Youth, your first duty is to look after and eternally to protect the Turkish Independence. If one day you are called upon to defend the Republic and the Independence, you will take over your duty neither flinching nor being deterred by any circumstances or situations in which you may find yourselves. This is the only foundation to your existence and future. This foundation is your most valuable treasure.

Consonantal units

For the purposes of syllabification, there are no consonantal units in Turkish, although in foreign words deference is shown to consonantal units according to the language of origin.

Rules for syllabification

1. Turkish, not having diphthongs, digraphs, or consonantal units, has no groups of vowels or consonants which may not be divided, provided division conforms to rules 2 to 8 below.

2. Division is made on a vowel before a single consonant: *ha-va, zi-ya, sa-kin*.

3. In a group of two or more consonants. division is made before the last consonant: *bil-mek, bil-lûr, ört-mek, sat-hî, sal-ya*.

4. In words of Arabic root, vowels may be divided: *ma-ani, mu-af, cema-at, gayri-tabiî*.

5. Turkish has no prefixes in the conventionally accepted sense. The negative particle *gayri*, however, acts as a prefix and is kept intact: *gayri-matbu*.

6. Compound words are divided according to their component parts (and each part according to rules 1 to 5): *göz-ağrısı, hanım-eli, açık-göz*.

7. Foreign words and components of foreign words (not naturalized) follow the conventions of the language of origin: *fa-brika, am-plifikatör, ka-blo, tel-graf, boy-skavt*. In this rule are also included scientific and technical words, which editors prefer to treat etymologically: *pan-kreas, proto-plasma*.

8. Division may be made on the apostrophe indicating hiatus: *mes'-ul*.

Illustrative word divisions

[The numbers in parentheses refer to the syllabification rules]

A ce-mis-tan	(2, 3)	İs-tan-bul	(3, 3)
a-kort-la-mak	(3, 2)	i-yi-leş-mek	(2, 3)
Al-man-ya	(2, 3)	ır-ga-la-mak	(3, 2, 2)
alt-mış-al-tı	(3, 6, 3)	kü-tüp-ha-ne	(2, 3, 2)
A-me-ri-kan	(2, 2)	lâ-a-let-ta-yin	(4, 2, 3, 2)
an'-a-nan	(8, 2)	li-to-ğra-fi	(2, 7, 2)
an-fi-te-atr	(3, 2, 4)	ma-no-me-tre	(2, 2, 7)
An-gli-kan	(7, 2)	man-ye-zi-um	(3, 2, 4)
An-ka-ra	(3, 2)	ma-te-ri-ya-list	(2, 2, 2, 2)
an-si-klo-pe-di	(3, 7, 2, 2)	me-bus-luk	(8, 3)
as-ri-leş-tir-mek	(3, 2, 3, 3)	met-he-dil-mek	(3, 2, 3)
baş-ağ-rı-sı	(6, 3, 2)	me-tro-po-lit	(7, 2, 2)
baş-lı-ba-şı-na	(3, 2, 2, 2)	met-ruk	(3, 3)
be-ra-et	(2, 4)	mev-su-ki-yet	(3, 2, 2)
bey-yi-ne	(3, 2)	mo-no-plân	(2, 7)
bil-kül-li-ye	(3, 3, 2)	mu-sah-hah	(2, 3)
bi-na-en-a-leyh	(2, 4, 6, 2)	mü-el-lef	(4, 3)
bi-pa-yan	(2, 2)	nes-het-mek	(3, 3)
bir-le-şik	(3, 2)	or-to-ğraf	(3, 7)
bi-ta-raf-lık	(2, 2, 3)	pro-to-plas-ma	(2, 7, 3)
can-a-cı-sı	(6, 2, 2)	ri-a-ye-ten	(4, 2, 2)
cum-huri-yet	(3, 2, 2, 2)	ser-best-çe	(3, 3)
çağ-rıl-mak	(3, 3)	tak-si-me-tre	(3, 2, 7)
dağ-a-la-sı	(6, 2, 2)	tay-va-re-ci-lik	(3, 2, 2, 2)
dev-let-ler	(3, 3)	Türk-çe-si	(3, 2)
ec-ne-bi-lik	(3, 2, 2)	Türk-çü-lük	(3, 2)
el-al-tın-dan	(6, 3, 3)	us-ta-lık-lı	(3, 2, 3)
en-ter-nas-yo-nal	(3, 3, 3, 2)	uz-laş-tır-mak	(3, 3, 3)
fa-bri-ka-tör	(7, 2, 2)	ü-leş-tir-mek	(3, 3)
gayri-ka-bil	(3, 5, 2, 2)	ül-tra-vi-yo-le	(7, 2, 2, 2)
ha-yır-lı	(2, 3)	va-kit-siz	(2, 3)
hay-si-yet	(3, 2)	Vaş-ing-ton	(7, 3)
hü-kû-met	(2, 2)	ya-ra-şık-sız	(2, 2, 3)
ih-ba-ri-ye	(3, 2, 2)	ye-tiş-mek	(2, 3)

Stress and diacritics

Stress is not marked in Turkish orthography. The only diacritics are the dieresis, cedilla, and circumflex, all of which are explained under Special characters.

Capitalization

Capitalization is practically as in English.

If name of any particular law, *Türk eşya kanunu*, only first word of law is capitalized.

Türkiye Büyük Millet Meclisi, Tanrı, Allah Kızılay Kurumu İstanbul, Varlik Yaymevi.

Punctuation

Punctuation is similar to that in English, but the comma and dash are used somewhat more frequently than in English. Quotation symbols: « ».

Examples: Kutlu, Şemsettin. Eski Türk hayatı; fıkralar, olaylar.

Abbreviations

A. Ş.	Anonim Şirket, anonymous firm; Inc.	Ml.	Matmazel, Miss
a y n.	aynı müellif, the same author; idem	Mm.	Madam, Mrs.
mll.		msl.	meselâ, for example, e.g.
B.	Bey (Bay), Sir, Mr.	no.	Nümero, number
B. D.	Birleşik Devletler, United States	Pş.	Paşa, Pasha
		s.	sahife, page
Bl.	Bölük, Company, Co.	sk.	sokak, street
Bn.	Bayan, Miss or Mrs.	sm.	santimetre, centimeter
Gn.	Genel, General	Ssi.	Sürekası, Company, Co.
Hz.	Hazretleri, His Excellency, His Majesty	T. C.	Türkiye Cumhuriyeti, The Republic of Turkey
ilv.	ilâve, supplement	T. L.	Türk Lirası, Turkish pound
km.	kilometre, kilometer	v. b.	ve başkalar, and others, et al
M.	Mösyö, Monsieur, Mr.	v. s.	ve saire, etc.

Cardinal numbers

bir	one	otuz	thirty
iki	two	kırk	forty
üç	three	elli	fifty
dört	four	altmış	sixty
beş	five	yetmiş	seventy
altı	six	seksen	eighty
yedi	seven	doksan	ninety
sekiz	eight	yüz	hundred
dokuz	nine	yüz bir, etc.	one hundred and one, etc.
on	ten		
on bir	eleven		
on iki	twelve	iki yüz, etc.	two hundred, etc.
on üç, etc.	thirteen, etc.	bin	thousand
yirmi	twenty		
yirmi bir, etc.	twenty-one, etc.		

Ordinal numbers [2]

birinci	first	on birinci	eleventh
ikinci	second	on ikinci	twelfth
üçüncü	third	on üçüncü, etc.	thirteenth, etc.
dördüncü	fourth		
beşinci	fifth	yirminci	twentieth
altıncı	sixth	yüzüncü, etc.	hundredth, etc.
yedinci	seventh		
sekizinci	eighth	bininci, etc.	thousandth, etc.
dokuzuncu	ninth		
onuncu	tenth		

Months

Ocak (Kânunusani)	January	Temmuz	July
Şubat	February	Ağustos	August
Mart	March	Eylül or Eylûl	September
Nisan	April	Ekim (Teşrinievel)	October
Mayıs	May	Kasım (Teşrinisani)	November
Haziran	June	Aralık (Kânunuevel)	December

[2] The ordinals are formed regularly from the cardinals by the addition of -inci, -uncu, or -üncü, in accordance with the principle of vowel harmony.

Days

Pazar	Sunday	Perşembe	Thursday
Pazartesi	Monday	Cuma	Friday
Salı	Tuesday	Cumartesi	Saturday
Çarşamba	Wednesday		

Seasons

ilkbahar	spring	sonbahar	autumn
yaz	summer	kış	winter

Time

saat	hour	ay	month
gün	day	yıl, sene	year
hafta	week		

REFERENCES.—N. A. McQuown and Sadi Koylan, Spoken Turkish (1944); A. Vahid Moran, Türkçe-İngilizce sözlük (1945); James W. Redhouse, İngilizce-Türkçe lûgatı (1950); F. Heuser und İ. Şevket, Türkisch-Deutsches Wörterbuch (Istanbul, 1942).

SLAVIC LANGUAGES AND THEIR ALPHABETS

The Slavic languages are usually divided into three groups:

(a) West Slavic, which includes Polish, Sorb or Wendish (also called I usatian), Czech, and Slovak; Polabian, now extinct, also belongs to this group, as do Kashubian (almost extinct) and Slovinzian (extinct). Polish is the language of Poland. Sorb or Wendish is spoken along the river Spree in both Upper and Lower Lusatia. Czech and Slovak are two separate, though very similar, languages; Czech is spoken in western and central Czechoslovakia (Bohemia and Moravia), and Slovak in the eastern part of the country (Slovakia). Polabian was spoken in the regions adjacent to the Elbe River. Kashubian and Slovinzian were found in the region around Danzig in Pomerania.

(b) East Slavic, which comprises Russian, Ukrainian, and White Russian. Russian is spoken throughout the Soviet Union, but was originally native only to central and northern European Russia. White Russian is spoken in the White Russian Soviet Socialist Republic. Ukrainian is found in most of the Ukrainian Soviet Socialist Republic; the variety of Ukrainian spoken in what was formerly sub-Carpathian Russia in Czechoslovakia was often referred to as Ruthenian. Ukrainian was formerly called Little Russian, and Russian proper was then designated as Great Russian.

(c) South Slavic, which includes Slovene, Serbo-Croatian, Macedonian, and Bulgarian. Serbo-Croatian is a single literary language, the Serbian areas writing it in the Cyrillic alphabet, while the Croatian areas use the Latin alphabet (in the form given as transliteration for Serbian Cyrillic). Serbo-Croatian is the language of all Yugoslavia, but Slovene is used in Slovenia (northwest Yugoslavia) and Macedonian in Macedonia (southeast Yugoslavia). Correspondence between Serbian and Croatian alphabets insures correct spelling of the Serbo-Croatian language in Roman alphabet. Bulgarian is spoken in Bulgaria.

The West Slavic languages and Slovene and Croatian have always been written in the Latin alphabet. The other Slavic languages use modern forms of Cyrillic. Cyrillic was devised in the 10th century, being based on the Greek alphabet. It was created for the purpose of writing Old Macedonian, which is usually called Old Church Slavic, and the old form of the alphabet, not given below, is now found only in printed ecclesiastical materials. Old Church Slavic is sometimes called Old Church Slavonic.

Slavic (Cyrillic) alphabets

Russian: А а, Б б, В в, Г г, Д д, Е е, Ё ё, Ж ж, З з, И и, Й й, К к, Л л, М м, Н н, О о, П п, Р р, С с, Т т, У у, Ф ф, Х х, Ц ц, Ч ч, Ш ш, Щ щ, Ъ ъ, Ы ы, Ь ь, Э э, Ю ю, Я я; used now only outside of the U.S.S.R.: I i, Ѣ ѣ, Ѳ ѳ, Ѵ ѵ

Ukrainian: А а, Б б, В в, Г г, Д д, Е е, Є є, Ж ж, З з, И и, І і, Ї ї Й й, К к, Л л, М м, Н н, О о, П п, Р р, С с, Т т, У у, Ф ф, Х х, Ц ц, Ч ч, Ш ш, Щ щ, Ь ь, Ю ю, Я я, '; used now only outside of the U.S.S.R.: Ґ ґ

White Russian: А а, Б б, В в, Г г, Д д, Е е, Ё ё, Ж ж, З з, І і, Й й, К к, Л л, М м, Н н, О о, П п, Р р, С с, Т т, У у, Ў ў, Ф ф, Х х, Ц ц, Ч ч, Ш ш, Щ щ, Ы ы, Ь ь, Э э, Ю ю, Я я; used now only outside of the U.S.S.R.: Ґ ґ

[Concluded on following page]

457

Bulgarian: А а, Б б, В в, Г г, Д д, Е е, З з, Ж ж, И и, Й й, К к, Л л, М м, Н н, О о, П п, Р р, С с, Т т, У у, Ф ф, Х х, Ц ц, Ч ч, Ш ш, Щ щ, Ъ ъ, Ь ь, Ю ю, Я я; formerly also used: Ѣ ѣ, Ж̱ ж̱, I-Ж̱ ı-ж̱

Macedonian: А а, Б б, В в, Г г, Ѓ ѓ, Д д, Е е, Ж ж, З з, Ѕ ѕ, И и, Ј ј, К к, Ќ ќ, Л л, Љ љ, М м, Н н, Њ њ, О о, П п, Р р, С с, Т т, У у, Ф ф, Х х, Ц ц, Ч ч, Џ џ, Ш ш, '

Serbian: А а, Б б, В в, Г г, Д д, Ђ ђ, Е е, Ж ж, З з, И и, Ј ј, К к, Л л, Љ љ, М м, Н н, Њ њ, О о, П п, Р р, С с, Т т, Ћ ћ, У у, Ф ф, Х х, Ц ц, Ч ч, Џ џ, Ш ш

The Cyrillic alphabet has been adopted recently in the Union of Soviet Socialist Republics for use with various non-Slavic languages, such as Moldavian, Kirghiz, Tajik, Mongolian, and others. Usually the Russian form is used as a base, with special letters added as needed.

Transliteration of Cyrillic alphabets

The transliteration given first place here is that of the United States Board on Geographic Names, adopted in 1944. It is identical with that used by the (British) Permanent Committee on Geographical Names, adopted about the same time. The Board on Geographic Names transliteration has been officially adopted only for Russian, Bulgarian, and Serbian; for the other languages here given it is applied by extending the same principles and supplying new symbols or digraphs as needed. Certain additions to avoid possible ambiguity are also given.

The Library of Congress uses a transliteration that differs at certain points from that of the Board on Geographic Names. These differences are indicated.

In works on Slavic in the fields of linguistics and philology, still other transliterations are used. These are also indicated, the word "linguistics" being used to mean linguistics and philology.

In the list below, the transliterated symbol holds for all six languages when it s not marked. Where different uses are recommended for different languages, or where a letter is used only in some of the languages, these facts are stated.

Alphabets, pronunciation, and transliteration

А	а	*a*
Б	б	*b*
В	в	*v*
Г	г	*g* in Russian, Bulgarian, Macedonian, and Serbian; *h* in White Russian and Ukrainian; linguistics, always *g*
Ѓ	ѓ	*g* in White Russian and Ukrainian only; no longer used in the Soviet-Union; linguistics, *g*
Ѓ	ѓ	*g'* in Macedonian only; linguistics, *ǵ*
Д	д	*d*
Ђ	ђ	*đ* or *dj* in Serbian only; Library of Congress and linguistics, *đ*
Е	е	*ye* in Russian initially and after a vowel or ъ or ь, *e* elsewhere; in White Russian, always *ye*; in the other languages, always *e*; Library of Congress and linguistics, always *e*
Ё	ё	*yë* and *ë* in Russian, as for *ye* and *e*; in White Russian, $\widehat{o}$; not used elsewhere; Library of Congress always uses *ë* in Russian; linguistics, *ė* or *ë*
Є	є	*ye* in Ukrainian only; Library of Congress, *ie*; linguistics, *ē* or *je*

[Continued on following page]

Ж ж   *zh;* linguistics, *ž* in Serbian

З з   *z;* *z͡h;* Library of Congress in Ukrainian

Ѕ ѕ   *dz* in Macedonian only; linguistics, *ʒ́* or *dz*

И и   *i,* except in Ukrainian, where it is *y;* linguistics, always *i*

Й й   *y;* not used in Macedonian and Serbian; Library of Congress, *ĭ;* linguistics, *ĭ* and *j*

І і   *ī* in Ukrainian and Russian; *i* in White Russian; not used elsewhere; no longer used in U.S.S.R.; Library of Congress and linguistics, *ī*

Ї ї   *yi* in Ukrainian; Library of Congress, *ï;* linguistics, *ï* and *ji*

Ј ј   *j* in Macedonian and Serbian only

К к   *k*

Ќ ќ   *k* in Macedonian only; linguistics, *ḱ*

Л л   *l*

Љ љ   *ļ* or *lj* in Macedonian and Serbian only; linguistics, *ļ*

М м   *m*

Н н   *n*

Њ њ   *ń* or *nj* in Macedonian and Serbian only; Library of Congress, *nj;* linguistics, *ń*

О о   *o*

П п   *p*

Р р   *r*

С с   *s*

Т т   *t*

Ћ ћ   *ć* in Serbian only

У у   *u*

Ў ў   *w* in White Russian only; Library of Congress, *ŭ;* linguistics, *u̯*

Ф ф   *f*

Х х   *kh;* Library of Congress uses *h* for Serbian; linguistics, *x* and *ch*

Ц ц   *ts;* Library of Congress, *t͡s* for Russian, *c* for Serbian and Macedonian; linguistics, *c;* to avoid ambiguity, Cyrillic *ТС* may be transliterated as *t.s,* or the Library of Congress symbol for ц may be used

Ч ч   *ch,* except *č* in Macedonian and Serbian; linguistics, *č*

Џ џ   *dž* in Macedonian and Serbian only; linguistics, *ǰ*

Ш ш   *sh,* except *š* in Macedonian and Serbian; linguistics, *š;* Library of Congress uses *s͡h* in Ukrainian to avoid ambiguity with cr=*sh*

Щ щ   *shch* in Russian, White Russian, and Ukrainian; *sht* in Bulgarian; not used in Macedonian and Serbian; linguistics, *š* and *šč* (or *št* for Bulgarian)

Ъ ъ   double apostrophe (") no longer used at end of a word in Russian and Bulgarian; not used elsewhere. Library of Congress uses *ŭ* in the middle of word in Bulgarian; linguistics, *ŭ*

Ы ы   *y* in Russian and White Russian only

Ь ь   single apostrophe ('); not used in Macedonian and Serbian; Library of Congress, *';* linguistics, *ĭ*

Ѣ ѣ   *yě* and *ě* in Russian, no longer used; *ye* in Bulgarian, no longer used; not used elsewhere; Library of Congress, *i͡e;* linguistics, *ě*

[Concluded on following page]

Э э   *e* in Russian (or *ê* to avoid ambiguity); *è* in White Russian; not used elsewhere; Library of Congress, *ė*; linguistics, *è*

Ю ю   *yu*; not used in Macedonian and Serbian; Library of Congress, *i͡u*; linguistics, *ü* and *ju*

Я я   *ya*; not used in Macedonian and Serbian; Library of Congress, *i͡a*; linguistics, *ä* and *ya*

Ѳ ѳ   *f* in Russian only; no longer used

Ѵ ѵ   *ý* in Russian only; no longer used

Ж ж   *d* in Bulgarian only; no longer used; Library of Congress, *ŭ* no longer used in Bulgaria; linguistics, *ǫ*

I-Ж I-ж   *yd* in Bulgarian only; no longer used; linguistics, *ę̄* or *j ̨*

'   Ukrainian and Macedonian only, instead of older ъ; transliterate by double apostrophe ("), single apostrophe (') is used for ь in Ukrainian; linguistics, '

The old form of Cyrillic used for Old Church Slavic had letters similar in shape to а, б, в, г, д, е, ж, з, s, и, i, к, л, м, н, о, п, р, с, т, у, ф, х, ц, ч, ш, щ, ъ, ы, ь, ѣ, ю, ж, i-ж, ѳ, and ѵ. In addition there were ω (Greek)=*ō*, іа (equal to modern я), і-е (equal to Ukrainian е), А=*ę* (nasal *e*), ІА=*ę̄* (*yę* or *ję*), ξ (Greek)= *ks* (*x*); ψ (Greek)=*ps*; ы appeared as ъı or ьı, and also as ъи (*ŭĭ. ĭĭ. ŭi*). A still older form of this alphabet, the Glagolitic, has letter shapes that are very different from those of the original Greek or modern Cyrillic; this alphabet lacked the letters ω, ы, і-а, і-е, ξ, ψ, but had a letter corresponding to Serbian ђ.

INDEX

[Numbers in parentheses refer to rules; italic indicates exact terminology]

[For lists of capitalization, spelling, compounding, and abbreviations, see Guide to Capitalization, p. 35; Spelling, p. 63; Guide to Compounding, p. 81; Abbreviations, p. 135]

461